D0309166

THE
NEW GREEK COMEDY

303
12.7.1921

THE LOEB CLASSICAL LIBRARY

Edited by E. CAPPS, Ph.D., LL.D.; T. E. PAGE, Litt.D.;
and W. H. D. ROUSE, Litt.D.

Each Vol. fcap. 8vo. 400–600 pp., clear type. Cloth, 5s. net; Leather, 6s. 6d. net.

A series of Greek and Latin Texts with English Translations on the opposite page. The Series is to contain all that is best in Greek and Latin Literature from the time of Homer to the Fall of Constantinople.

VOLUMES ALREADY PUBLISHED.

LATIN AUTHORS.

APULEIUS: THE GOLDEN ASS. (Metamorphoses.) Trans. by W. ADDLINGTON (1566). Revised by S. GASELEE.

CAESAR: CIVIL WARS. Trans. by A. G. PESKETT.

CATULLUS. Trans. by F. W. CORNISH. TIBULLUS. Trans. by J. P. POSTGATE. PERVIGILIUM VENERIS. Trans. by J. W. MACKAIL.

CICERO: DE FINIBUS. Trans. by H. RACKHAM.

CICERO: DE OFFICIIS. Trans. by WALTER MILLER.

CICERO: LETTERS TO ATTICUS. Trans. by E. O. WINSTEDT. 3 Vols. Vols. I. and II.

CONFESSIONS OF ST. AUGUSTINE. Trans. by W. WATTS (1631). 2 Vols.

HORACE: ODES AND EPODES. Trans. by C. E. BENNETT.

OVID: HEROIDES AND AMORES. Trans. by GRANT SHOWERMAN. 2 Vols.

OVID: METAMORPHOSES. Trans. by F. J. MILLER. 2 Vols.

PETRONIUS. Trans. by M. HESELTINE. SENECA: APOCOLOCYNTOSIS. Trans. by W. H. D. ROUSE. [2nd Impression

PLAUTUS. Trans. by PAUL NIXON. 5 Vols. Vol. I.

PLINY: LETTERS. MELMOTH'S Translation revised by W. M. L. HUTCHINSON. 2 Vols.

PROPERTIUS. Trans. by H. E. BUTLER. [2nd Impression

SUETONIUS. Trans. by J. C. ROLFE. 2 Vols.

TACITUS: DIALOGUS. Trans. by Sir WILLIAM PETERSON. AGRICOLA AND GERMANIA. Trans. by MAURICE HUTTON.

TERENCE. Trans. by JOHN SARGEAUNT. 2 Vols. [2nd Impression

VIRGIL. Trans. by H. R. FAIRCLOUGH. 2 Vols. Vol. I.

GREEK AUTHORS.

APPOLLONIUS RHODIUS. Trans. by R. C. SEATON.

THE APOSTOLIC FATHERS. Trans. by KIRSOPP LAKE. 2 Vols. [2nd Impression

GREEK AUTHORS (continued).

APPIAN'S ROMAN HISTORY. Trans. by HORACE WHITE. 4 Vols.

DAPHNIS AND CHLOE. THORNLEY'S Translation revised by J M. EDMONDS; and PARTHENIUS. Trans. by S. GASELEE.

DIO CASSIUS: ROMAN HISTORY. Trans. by E. CARY. 9 Vols. Vols. I., II., III., and IV.

EURIPIDES. Trans. by A. S. WAY. 4 Vols. [2nd Impression

GALEN: ON THE NATURAL FACULTIES. Trans. by A. J. BROCK.

THE GREEK ANTHOLOGY. Trans. by W. R. PATON. 5 Vols. Vol. I.

THE GREEK BUCOLIC POETS (THEOCRITUS, BION, MOSCHUS). Trans. by J. M. EDMONDS. [2nd Impression

HESIOD AND THE HOMERIC HYMNS. Trans. by H. G. EVELYN-WHITE.

JULIAN. Trans. by WILMER CAVE WRIGHT. 3 Vols. Vols. I. and II.

LUCIAN. Trans. by A. M. HARMON. 7 Vols. Vols. I. and II.

MARCUS AURELIUS. Trans. by C. R. HAINES.

PHILOSTRATUS: THE LIFE OF APPOLLONIUS OF TYANA. Trans. by F. C. CONYBEARE. 2 Vols.

PINDAR. Trans. by Sir J. E. SANDYS.

PLATO: EUTHYPHRO, APOLOGY, CRITO, PHAEDO, PHAEDRUS. Trans. by H. M. FOWLER.

PLUTARCH: THE PARALLEL LIVES. Trans. by B. PERRIN. 11 Vols. Vols. I., II., III., and IV.

PROCOPIUS: HISTORY OF THE WARS. Trans. by H. B. DEWING. 7 Vols. Vols. I. and II.

QUINTUS SMYRNAEUS. Trans. by A. S. WAY.

SOPHOCLES. Trans. by F. STORR. 2 Vols. [2nd Impression

ST. JOHN DAMASCENE: BARLAAM AND IOASAPH. Trans. by the Rev. G. R. WOODWARD and HAROLD MATTINGLY.

THEOPHRASTUS: ENQUIRY INTO PLANTS. Trans. by Sir ARTHUR HORT, Bart. 2 Vols.

XENOPHON: CYROPAEDIA. Trans. by WALTER MILLER. 2 Vols.

DESCRIPTIVE PROSPECTUS ON APPLICATION.

LONDON: WILLIAM HEINEMANN.
NEW YORK: G. P. PUTNAM'S SONS.

THE
NEW GREEK COMEDY

Κωμῳδία Νέα

BY

PH. E. LEGRAND

PROFESSOR IN THE FACULTÉ DES LETTRES OF THE
UNIVERSITY OF LYONS

TRANSLATED BY

JAMES LOEB, A.B.

WITH AN INTRODUCTION BY

JOHN WILLIAMS WHITE, Ph.D., LL.D.

Original published by the Annales de l'Université de Lyon

LONDON : WILLIAM HEINEMANN
NEW YORK : G. P. PUTNAM'S SONS
1917

566029 1838

CANCELLED
KING'S COLLEGE
LIBRARY

BIBL.
COLL. REGAL.
CANT.

London : William Heinemann. 1917.

TO

MY DEAR COLLEAGUES

FERNAND ALLÈGRE

PROFESSOR OF GREEK LANGUAGE AND LITERATURE

AND

PHILIPPE FABIA

PROFESSOR OF CLASSICAL PHILOLOGY

A TOKEN OF MY ESTEEM AND FRIENDSHIP

THE TRANSLATOR'S PREFACE

ACQUAINTANCE with the Comedies of Aristophanes very naturally makes the student of Greek literature eager to learn something about the plays of the comic writers who succeeded the great master of this style of composition. I had the privilege of making Professor Maurice Croiset's admirable book, *Aristophane et les partis à Athénes*,[1] accessible to American and English readers who are not sufficiently conversant with French to derive full benefit from the original. When I cast about for a work that would afford a luminous and comprehensive view of the later Comedy, it was again a book by a learned Frenchman that seemed best fitted for Anglo-Saxon needs. Professor Philippe E. Legrand's *Daos, Tableau de la comédie grecque pendant la période dite nouvelle—Κωμῳδία Νέα*, which here appears in an English version, is, in the French original, a much bigger book, containing much detailed information intended specially for scholars. My purpose, however, was to offer his learned but graphic account of this interesting period of Greek literature to general readers in America and England, rather than to specialists, and I ventured to suggest to him the omission of these details. With native courtesy he accepted my suggestion and readily undertook the difficult and, I fear, ungracious task of adapting his book to the particular purpose I had in mind. Its size has thus been reduced by almost one-third, but I am convinced that the force of the argument has not been lessened nor the effect of the narrative in any way marred. I beg to express my grateful appreciation of the obliging courtesy with which Professor Legrand assented to my request.

I have also ventured to alter the title of his work to one which I feel is better adapted to a translation.

---

[1] Maurice Croiset, *Aristophanes and the Political Parties at Athens*, translated by James Loeb. Macmillan & Co., Ltd., London, 1909.

vii

In the comedies of Menander and of his successors we miss the wild flights of fancy, the rollicking humour, the biting sarcasm, the personal vituperation and, above all, the political satire that make the plays of Aristophanes so racy and refreshing. As compensation we get, in the plays of the Middle and New Comedy, a valuable and interesting picture of the domestic life of Athens, of the quarrels and intrigues of lovers, of the motley throng of virtuous or immoral, bartering, bantering men and women, who fill the streets, market-places and houses of the city on which our imagination still loves to dwell.

The limits Professor Legrand set himself in his book prevented him from including a consideration of the influence that these later Greek comedies and the Latin plays, which were so directly inspired by them, have had upon French, Italian, Spanish and English comedy. Such an investigation would have led him too far afield. The attentive reader of these modern plays will often be reminded of incidents and scenes which are conscious or accidental imitations of ancient models, and I can conceive of no more interesting piece of work than a comprehensive study of these influences would afford.

If this book yields its readers as much profit and pleasure as I found in translating it, my pleasant labour will have been amply repaid.

I am under great obligations to Dr. T. E. Page for the trouble he has taken in subjecting my manuscript to a critical reading; to Professor John Williams White for the delightful and scholarly Introduction with which he has enriched the book; and to Professor Edward Capps for kindly supervising the compilation of the detailed Index, which I hope will greatly add to the value of the book.

JAMES LOEB, A.B.

INTRODUCTION TO THE
ENGLISH VERSION

THE Greek world suffered greater changes in the generation that followed the battle of Chaeronea than in any preceding century of its history. Sparta yielded leadership to Thebes at Leuctra, as Athens had surrendered to Sparta at the disastrous close of the Peloponnesian War, but by the issue at Chaeronea the city-states of all Greece were forced to submit to the absolute monarch of a land that they had regarded with scorn as barbarian. Portentous event followed event with bewildering rapidity, and it was soon apparent that Macedonia had become the mistress not alone of Hellas but of the whole world. Only eight years after Chaeronea, but when the youthful Alexander had already penetrated even to the heart of Asia, the orator Aeschines vividly portrayed the universal disaster. "What manner of strange and unexpected event," he asked, "has not befallen in our time? We have not lived the lives of ordinary men—nay, we were born to be a tale of wonder to those who shall come after us. Is not the king of Persia, he who dug the canal through Athos, who bridged the Hellespont, who demanded earth and water from the Greeks, who dared to write to us, 'I am the Lord of all, from the rising to the setting of the sun,' is not he now fighting, not for lordship, but for his own life? And see the fate of Greece! Thebes, our neighbour Thebes, has been snatched from our midst in the space of a single day. The wretched Lacedaemonians, who once aspired to leadership, are at this moment on their way to Alexander in Asia with hostages, the living proofs of their disastrous fortunes, there to submit themselves and their country to his will and beg for mercy from their incensed master. And we, men of Athens, citizens of a great state that once was the common refuge and saviour of the Greeks, whither their embassies came in confident hope of succour, we, alas ! are now no longer striving for leadership but are contending for the very soil of our native land."

Imperial Athens had fallen, never to be restored, whatever vain hopes may have been cherished by Demosthenes and Lycurgus. Shorn of all power of resistance, she sullenly but contemptuously accepted the deification of Alexander, but her very contempt is evidence that she failed to understand the deep political significance of Alexander's mandate to all Greece. On his death, the event for which her citizens had hardly dared to hope, she led the revolt against Macedonian suzerainty, but with fatal results : a Macedonian garrison was settled in the Piraeus and her democratic constitution was modified by a restriction of the franchise that established an oligarchy. This garrison maintained for many a year the rule of Demetrius of Phalerum, whom Cassander had appointed governor and whom his fellow-citizens regarded as a tyrant. The democracy was restored by force of arms towards the end of the century by another Macedonian baron, Demetrius the Besieger, but the spirit of true democracy was dead. The Athenians gave the youthful Demetrius and his father the title of king, created two new tribes and named them after them, deified the father and son and paid them divine honours. Demetrius was ill fitted for the part : he took up his quarters in the Parthenon, the shrine of the Maiden Goddess, and turned it into a brothel.

During this momentous generation Athens lay in the backwater of current events, undisturbed except for two brief periods, just after Chaeronea and just after Alexander's death, by the swift onward rush of the world's doings. This time of enforced peace was for her an interval of great material prosperity. During the twelve years of the financial administration of the state by Lycurgus, commerce again flourished in the city that once had been the centre of trade of the ancient world, the silver mines of Laurium were reopened, industries prospered, private fortunes accumulated, and the revenues of the state were trebled. The Panathenaic stadium and the gymnasium in the Lyceum were built, and the great theatre was reconstructed and completed. Nor did Athens lack even then statesmen who steadfastly cherished the hope of her restoration to power and prepared her in these years of peace for war, loyal men whose very patriotism obscured their vision. The fortifications of the Piraeus were strengthened, new docks were built, the navy was increased, the war department reconstructed, and the principle was then first adopted of universal military training of citizens for obligatory service at the call of the state.

The ten years of the regency of Demetrius of Phalerum, the pupil of Theophrastus and the intimate friend of Menander, were also in the main years of peace and material prosperity. The public revenues were maintained at the amount realised in the administration of Lycurgus. Commerce suffered little decrease, although new centres of trade had been gradually establishing themselves in the East under the impulse of Alexander's conquests, and probably the private wealth of the country was greater when the régime of Demetrius came to an end in 307 than it had been at any previous period in this century. But the military power of Athens was now but the shadow of what it had been in the preceding decade. She had lost her fleet off Amorgos in the year following the death of Alexander, and her native forces had been greatly diminished, since only citizens possessed of the franchise were subject to conscription for military service, and the constitutional changes introduced in the same year had reduced the number of voters to less than one half of the entire citizen population. The circle of her influence had been gradually contracted, she withdrew more and more within herself, wealth bred luxurious habits of life, and morals became loose. The best evidence of her moral decadence is found in the sumptuary laws promulgated by Demetrius and enforced by a board of special magistrates invested with inquisitorial powers. This legislation was intended to check ostentation, extravagance, and debauchery.

Such in brief were the political and social conditions under which the New Greek Comedy developed and attained its highest expression in the plays of Menander, who brought out his first comedy in the year in which Cassander's Macedonian troops garrisoned the Piraeus, and died in the first decade of the following century.

The New Comedy is the final manifestation of genuine creative power in Attic literature. Poets were still writing tragedy at Athens in the time of Menander, and the public flocked to the theatre to hear their plays, but their art had degenerated into mere imitation of great originals, and lacked vitality. The themes of these later tragedies, notwithstanding Aristotle's warning, were still drawn from ancient legend, and had been treated again and again. With lifeless conventionality, even the form of the earlier tragedy was maintained. The public thronged to the theatre to hear these new plays, one would think, chiefly from curiosity to learn what possible variations on a trite theme the aspiring poet had been able to invent, and, as if to facilitate comparison, a play of one of the early tragedians was reproduced at the same festival. Aeschylus, Sophocles, and Euripides were still supreme. The legislation of Lycurgus protecting the text of their tragedies is evidence of the reverent esteem in which these old masters of the tragic art were still held.

The relation of the New Comedy to the Old was altogether different. No poet of the Old Comedy had the honour of reproduction intact in the period of the New. That this would have been impossible—unless the audience had been furnished with a copiously annotated libretto— marks the contrast between the two styles. Comedy is a humorous reflection of the life of the men and women of its day; it may be extravagant, but must ring true to experience. Now the conditions of life and the outlook upon life were as different as possible in the times respectively of Aristophanes and Menander. The New

Comedy was a development from the Old through the mediating period of the Middle Comedy, as it has been called, and although the remaining fragments of some fourteen hundred Greek comedies known to us by name are scanty, we can still trace the great stages of its evolution with fair confidence; but a new comedy had come in the course of a hundred years and more to be as unlike a play of Cratinus as Athens in the regency of Demetrius was unlike the Athens of Pericles. Even the form had changed: parabasis, parode, and debate, the primitive parts of comedy, had all disappeared; in Aristophanes the structural elements of the play, although clearly differentiated, are so skilfully linked that connection of part with part is never obtrusive, but a new comedy was divided into acts and the mechanism was apparent; the chorus of twenty-four of the old play, whose songs composed in many rhythms are an inherent part of it and whose leaders participate intimately in the dialogue, had declined in the new into a company of revellers or the like that came upon the scene in the *entr'acte* as if by chance and then disappeared,—an inartistic although possibly an amusing stopgap.

Eleven plays of Aristophanes happily are still extant and all the world may learn the nature and contents of an old Greek Comedy. We are not so fortunate in the case of the New Comedy; no complete play of Menander or of any of his immediate fellow-craftsmen has been preserved in the original. Students of literature, therefore, are especially indebted to Professor Legrand for the comprehensive and authoritative work of which Mr. Loeb has made so engaging a translation. Here we find all available sources of information analysed with scientific precision and with the sympathetic appreciation of a man of letters. The ordered results of this detailed investigation are most instructive.

One striking characteristic of the New Comedy emerges conspicuously, the extreme narrowness of its range— " c'est toujours la même chose ! "

"Fabula iucundi nulla est sine amore Menandri."

What old comedy has a love intrigue as the basis of its plot? We are surprised at this apparent lack of invention in the poets of the New Comedy. The eastern world in Menander's time was seething with unrest. Men were fighting everywhere; political relations were constantly shifting; colonists racially unconnected were uniting in founding scores of new cities; life was in commotion and confusion and full of adventure. Here, we should think, an imaginative poet might have found themes in plenty. But these stirring events lay apart, and Attic comedy in all its periods was local, so local that its conventional scene was Athens. Tales of these great happenings abroad did reach Athens and were humorously referred to in the theatre by foreigners and gasconading mercenaries, introduced as persons of the play. When Athens herself was drawn as an active and independent factor within the circle of events, as just after Alexander's death, the situation precluded a comedy composed on the model of the old political plays. Aristophanes wrote at least three comedies in which he ridiculed the party bent on continuing the long and fratricidal war with Sparta, but a Peace play in tacit support of the policy of Phocion and Demades in the spring of 322, when Greece, on the pan-Hellenic call of Athens, was at grips with Antipater, would have been hooted from the theatre. Even Phocion patriotically took the field when the fighting began.

At other times during the entire period of the New Comedy political comedy was precluded by fear of the strong arm of the Macedonian rulers. What comic poet would have dared publicly to ridicule Cassander, Demetrius Poliorcetes, or Antigonus Gonatas? Even mere references to persons of political importance are extremely rare— there are a bare dozen in the Greek fragments—and nearly all of them are casual and refer gibingly to personal habits. The only serious case is the attack in 301 of Philippides on Stratocles, the notorious demagogue who openly imitated Cleon. The poet assailed him for bringing the gods into

contempt, for altering the calendar, for turning the Parthenon into a brothel, all obvious references to proposals
made by Stratocles in honour of Demetrius Poliorcetes;
but the latter was at this time in Asia, engaged in a fatal
struggle with enemies far more dangerous than a comic
poet, and Philippides, who was by profession a politician
as well as poet, left Athens immediately after the play—
in fear of the vengeance of Stratocles. We need only
recall the freedom with which poet after poet of the Old
Comedy had attacked Pericles and Cleon to realise how
comedy had changed. There are other traces of the criticising spirit in the New Comedy, reprehension of luxury and
lawlessness, of corruption in the courts, of the arrogance of
philosophers, but the censorial element, which constitutes
so considerable a part of the Old Comedy, is here so in-
considerable as hardly to be noticeable. The prevailing
theme of these new comedies is love, but generally love
of a stereotyped form. The girl is the victim of untoward
happenings; the lover is one of the *jeunesse dorée* of Athens;
at the end of the play we witness a recognition and a
reconciliation or marriage. Grant the difference between
ancient and modern social conditions, and Menander's
comedies are nearer akin to the modern novel than to the
plays of the Old Comedy.

Yet these comedies were not monotonous, witness their
vogue in ancient and modern times. This was due to
the art of half a dozen poets of distinction, who developed
their common theme with infinite variety of detail, subtly
conceived, but true to life, in language that was simple
but finely expressive of the most delicate shades of meaning.
The audience was highly cultivated. Athens had lost her
military and political significance, but was still the literary
and intellectual centre of the world, the gathering-place
of men of letters and students of art, philosophy, and
science. Alexander and his successors in Asia had dealt
gently with her. When the elder Antigonus was urged
to hold her under firm control, he magnanimously replied
that he was content with her good will. " For Athens,"

he said, " is the beacon-tower of the world, and will quickly flash the glory of my deed abroad to all mankind."

The Athenians in the audience were chiefly of the propertied classes, for the free admission of poor citizens to the theatre was withdrawn during at least a part of this period—men of wit and refinement, cultivated but luxurious, aristocrats in feeling but indulgent to the outer world, maintaining, if I may venture a parallel, the Brahminical attitude of good Bostonians about the middle of the nineteenth century, who entertained no doubt whatever that Boston was then the centre of culture in America, and, confident of their own superiority, accepted as of right the wondering admiration of those beyond the pale. The comedies that pleased this great audience were a simple but faithful picture of one phase of contemporary life in Athens, in the period of its decay, if you will, although still resplendent—but they were more than that. Strip them of the conventions of time and place and circumstance and they portray sentiments, emotions, passions as old— and as young—as the race of men, and are of universal appeal. So it is that they have become through Plautus and Terence an inherent and permanent part of the literature of Europe, and as Molière's *Amphitryon* and *L'Avare* and Shakespeare's *Comedy of Errors* and plays of many other poets testify—still amuse and charm on the modern stage the men and women of our own day.

JOHN WILLIAMS WHITE.

Harvard University,
September 1, 1916.

CONTENTS

INTRODUCTION

PART I
THE SUBJECT MATTER OF NEW COMEDY

CHAPTER I

CHAPTER II

CHAPTER III

CHAPTER IV

CHAPTER V

xvii

PART II

THE STRUCTURE OF THE PLAYS OF NEW COMEDY

PART III

PURPOSE OF NEW COMEDY AND THE CAUSES OF ITS SUCCESS

CONTENTS

CHAPTER II

CHAPTER III

THE NEW GREEK COMEDY

INTRODUCTION

PLAN AND SCOPE OF THIS WORK

THERE already exist several comprehensive works on
Menander and New Comedy (κωμῳδία νέα)—for
instance, C. Benoit's *Essai historique et littéraire
sur la Comédie de Ménandre* (1854), and Guillaume Guizot's
*Ménandre, étude historique et littéraire sur la Comédie et la
Société grecques* (1855), several chapters of Denis' *Histoire de
la Comédie grecque* (1886, Vol. II., Ch. XIX–XXI), a chapter
of Maurice Croiset's *Histoire de la Littérature grecque* (1899,
Vol. III., Ch. XIII)—and had I not, in composing this
volume, made use of other material than my predecessors,
my labour would no doubt have been in vain. But thanks
to recent discoveries and to the constant progress of philo-
logical research, possibly also as a result of a somewhat
reckless disposition, I have been able—or have thought
myself able—to place reliance on a larger amount of
documentary evidence. I intend to make my description
of New Comedy fuller and more complete than the earlier
descriptions, and I earnestly hope that authorities on the
subject will not think it any the less accurate.

Two kinds of documents enable us to form an idea of
what the νέα was: first, the original fragments, taken in
connection with certain items of criticism and information by ancient authors; and then, more or less faithful
imitations and derivative works, both Greek and Latin.

Our store of original fragments has recently been considerably enlarged.[1] Especially during the past ten years
important bits of several of Menander's plays have been
published, as well as remnants of other comedies by
unknown authors, which are much more extensive and

---

[1] For the older known fragments I shall quote the collection made by
Th. Kock, *Comicorum atticorum fragmenta*, three vols., 1880–1888.

B

more interesting from a dramatic point of view than the meagre scraps in Kock's collection.[1]

None the less, the documents of the second kind still constitute our chief material. The authors whose names I have mentioned have been rather too sparing in their use of them. I, on the contrary, draw generously from them. I have, however, practically only made use of writings whose derivation from the New Comedy is not

[1] I shall not attempt to enumerate all these finds and much less to cite all the literature concerning them. The following are the most important—

I. Fragments of Menander : fragments published by Jernstedt in 1891 (*Fragments de comédies attiques de Porphyre Uspensky*, in Russian), one of which must belong to the Ἐπιτρέποντες and another to the Φάσμα (the latter has been discussed by Kock in the *Rheinisches Museum*, 1893, pp. 225 et seq., and by Körte in the *Berliner Philologische Wochenschrift*, 1907, pp. 649–650); fragments of the Γεωργός published by Nicole from a papyrus at Geneva (*Le Laboureur de Ménandre*, Bâle and Geneva, 1898), and again by Grenfell and Hunt (*Menander's Γεωργός, A Revised Text of the Geneva Fragment, Oxford*, 1898); fragments of the Περικειρομένη and of the Κόλαξ, in the *Oxyrhyncus Papyri*, Vol. II. (1899), No. 211, and Vol. III. (1903), No. 409; long passages of the Ἥρως, the Ἐπιτρέποντες, the Περικειρομένη, the Σαμία, published by Lefebvre (*Fragments d'un manuscrit de Ménandre*, Cairo, 1907), revised by Körte (*Berichte der k. sächsischen Gesellschaft der Wissenschaften*, LX., 1908, p. 87 et seq.); a fragment of the Περικειρομένη published by Körte (*ibid.*, p. 145 et seq.); a fragment which seems to belong to the Περινθία (*Oxyrhynchus Papyri*, Vol. VI. (1908), No. 855; regarding its being a part of the Περινθία see Körte, *Hermes*, XLIV., 1909, p. 309 et seq.).

In quoting from the Ἥρως, the Ἐπιτρέποντες, the Περικειρομένη and the Σαμία, I shall follow the numbers given by van Leeuwen, second edition (*Menandri quatuor fabularum fragmenta*, iterum edidit van Leeuwen, Leyden, 1908); in quoting from the Γεωργός and the Κόλαξ, those given by Kretschmar, who, in a dissertation (*De Menandri reliquiis nuper repertis*, Leipzig, 1906) has collected the fragments of Menander discovered between 1886 and 1906 (with the exception of four short and unimportant fragments, edited from a manuscript at Athens in the *Göttinger Nachrichten*, 1896, p. 315 and 317–318, which have been omitted).

II. Fragments of unknown authors : fragment of a prologue, edited by Kaibel from a papyrus at Strassburg (*Göttinger Nachrichten*, 1899, p. 549 et seq.); fragments numbered 10 and 11 in the *Oxyrhynchus Papyri*, Vol. I. (1898); fragments numbered 5 and 6 in the *Hibeh Papyri*, Vol. I. (1906); fragments edited by Jouguet from the papyri of Ghorân (*Bull. de Corr. hellén.*, XXX., 1906, p. 124 et seq.); cf. Körte, *Hermes*, XLIII., 1908, p. 38 et seq.); two fragments, one of which possibly belongs to the Κιθαριστής by Menander, published as number 19 in Vol. V. of the *Berliner Klassikertexte* (2nd part, 1907).

doubted by any one, such as the *palliatae*,[1] Lucian's *Dialogue of the Courtesans*, and the " amorous " and " parasitic " *Epistles* of Alciphron.[2] To determine how Plautus and Terence, how Alciphron and Lucian, imitated the comic writers of the fourth and third centuries, is a complex and delicate task, to which many scholars have for years devoted themselves. This is not the place to record the results of their investigations or to deal with the question as a whole. Were I to do so, I should, by entering upon a discussion of sources, anticipate the substance of a considerable part of this book. As we proceed, I shall show, either at the beginning of each chapter or in the course of the discussion itself, why I have thought it proper to include certain features borrowed from such and such derivative work. Too often—I admit it in advance—I rely solely upon my personal views. The reader must not take umbrage at this apparent presumption. I think that when a man has devoted several years of close study to a group of writings he may be excused for imagining that he *feels* certain qualities, characters and relations for whose existence he can adduce no proof. If I make mistakes, they are made in good faith and are not due to carelessness.

It may be that, when expanded as I propose to expand it, the study of the New Comedy will appear to overlap other studies, particularly that of the *palliata*. The only new feature of my work may perhaps be thought to consist in repeating, under the heading of Philemon, Menander, Diphilus or Apollodorus, what has often been said under the heading of Terence or Plautus, Lucian or Alciphron. Nor is there any denying that such a criticism would not be entirely wide of the mark, but I cannot admit its justice without making certain reservations. If

[1] I shall quote the comedies of Plautus according to Leo's edition (1895–1896); those of Terence, according to Dziazko's edition (1884); the fragments of the Latin comedy-writers according to Ribbeck's edition (*Comicorum romanorum fragmenta*, 3rd edition, 1898).

[2] *Alciphronis Epistulae*, ed. Schepers, 1905.

I were dealing with Plautus or with Terence I should make an effort to describe all the resources, all the methods, of their art; I should endeavour to point out their peculiar qualities and their peculiar faults. But as I am dealing with the *véa*, I shall proceed in a different way. The Latin comedies and their authors will only interest me from a special point of view : in so far as they are copies and interpreters of lost originals. Far from insisting on the features which give them a particular character and a kind of originality, I shall disregard this side of the question as much as possible. Further, I shall not pay attention to all the plays, nor to all the *Dialogues of the Courtesans*, nor to all the amorous or parasitic *Epistles*. From these various works I shall select, rightly or wrongly, certain elements which will help me to reconstruct the *véa*, while I shall exclude others. Moreover, I am fully aware that my book is, to a very large extent, a work of repetition and compilation. But compilations are not always useless. Indeed, it is necessary for the convenience of students that, from time to time, such a compilation covering each important subject should be made. Though the book I am about to publish may bring me no glory, it may be of service to others, and I ask from it nothing more.

I have repeatedly used the term *New Comedy*. I must define exactly what I mean by it. It has long since been generally accepted, on the testimony of ancient documents, that the history of Greek comedy must be divided into three periods : *ancient* comedy (ἀρχαία), during the fifth century; *middle* comedy (μέση), during the first two-thirds of the fourth century; *new* comedy (νέα), beginning with the time of Alexander—say, for the sake of establishing a date, from about 330—up to the time when this style of composition ceases to exist. In our days the correctness of this division has been called in question. Fielitz has maintained that it was made in comparatively recent times — in Hadrian's reign — and without sufficient reason, by some pedantic or careless grammarian.[1]

Others have thought that the person who first used the term κωμῳδία μέση did not use it in a chronological sense, and that middle comedy was *middle*, not in the order of time, but from the point of view of quality;[2] and this statement calls for a short examination.[3]

The passages which support the view that κωμῳδία μέση is equivalent to κωμῳδία μικτή, without any reference to time, are very few in number. An anonymous treatise Περὶ κωμῳδίας mentions the μέση in the third place, after the νέα: Γεγόνασι δέ μεταβολαὶ κωμῳδίας τρεῖς · καὶ ἡ μὲν ἀρχαία, ἡ δὲ νέα, ἡ δὲ μέση.[4] Perhaps, however, this arrangement can be explained on the ground that the division into three periods was subsequently introduced into a statement which originally recognised but two, or perhaps the redactor, owing to considerations of logic, did not wish to mention the *middle* before the two extremes by which it was determined. However that may be, the word μεταβολαί proves that he was thinking of periods of time.[5] Furthermore, in the list of poets who illustrated each of the three kinds of comedy, the representatives of the μέση are mentioned between the representatives of the ἀρχαία and those of the νέα (§ 12 et seq.); the only one whose name has survived—Antiphanes—is more recent than the former and earlier than the latter. Middle comedy is likewise mentioned in the third place in a sentence of a *proeme* by Tzetzes : καὶ πάλιν καθ' ἑτέραν διαίρεσιν τῆς κωμῳδίας τὸ μέν ἐστιν ἀρχαῖον, τὸ δὲ νέον, τὸ δὲ μέσον;[6] but nothing in what follows corresponds

---

[1] Fielitz, *De Atticorum comoedia bipartita* (Diss. Bonn, 1866), pp. 70–71.

[2] Cf. Von Wilamowitz, *Euripides' Herakles*, I. p. 134, n. 21; *De tribus carminibus latinis* (Ind. Schol. Göttingen, 1893–1894), p. 24.

[3] I shall quote the ancient texts concerning the history of comedy as they appear in Dübner's edition (*Scholia graeca in Aristophanem, cum prolegomenis grammaticorum*, Didot, 1855) and Kaibel's *Comicorum graecorum fragmenta*, I., 1899.   [4] An. III. Dübner, p. 14 = Kaibel, p. 7 (§ 2).

[5] Cf. Arist. *Poet.*, p. 1449a : αἱ μὲν οὖν τῆς τραγῳδίας μεταβάσεις καὶ δι' ὧν ἐγένοντο οὐ λελήθασι κτλ.

[6] Anon. V. Dübner and IXa, p. xviii, 67 et seq. = Kaibel, p. 17.

to the words τὸ δὲ μέσον, and these words were probably introduced where they are found by an interpolator. We have, finally, to consider a unique notice, the last sentence in the " Coislin Treatise ": τῆς κωμῳδίας παλαιά, ἡ πλεονάζουσα τῷ γελοίῳ · νέα, ἡ τοῦτο μὲν προιεμένη, πρὸς δὲ τὸ σεμνὸν ῥέπουσα · μέση, ἡ ἀπ' ἀμφοῖν μεμιγμένη.[1] Here there can be no question but that the μέση is described as a mixed class. Are we obliged to assume that the Coislin Treatise is the only one that contains the true doctrine, and that so many other passages in which μέση is, without a doubt, used in a chronological sense, simply repeat a misinterpretation? I maintain that this supposed misinterpretation would have been a most natural one. Μέσος, which is frequently enough used to designate the third item in a list of three things when the third item is midway between the other two and shares the nature of each, is also used, and not less generally, to designate a middle term chronologically speaking (for example : μέση ἡλικία); and associated with ἀρχαία and with νέα, μέση, in the expression κωμῳδία μέση, could not fail to be understood in this latter way. But just because this misunderstanding was practically unavoidable, and because it ought to have been easy to foresee it, we have a right to think that the inventor of the term would not have exposed the public to it; had he wished to designate a *mixed* class, he would no doubt have preferred some other epithet to the adjective μέση, one that was as much used in similar cases and which did not lend itself to ambiguity —μικτή. Rather than see a misinterpretation in all the ancient texts where " *middle* comedy " means comedy that flourished between the ἀρχαία and the νέα, I prefer to regard the interpretation contained in the Coislin Treatise as an exceptional one.

We have seen, then, that in ancient times the history of Greek comedy was thought to be susceptible of a division into three periods, one of which begins with the time of Alexander. Now let us see whether it is probable

[1] Kaibel, p. 53.

that this view arose as late as Fielitz maintains.   It seems
to me that he makes improper use of the argument *ex
silentio*, in order to prove his thesis.   Velleius Paterculus
expresses surprise somewhere in his writings at the fact
that the most illustrious representatives of a branch of
literature were often found united by fate within a very
limited period of time, and among the writers of ancient
comedy (*prisca illa et vetus comoedia*) he mentions Cratinus,
Aristophanes and Eupolis; among writers of New Comedy
(*nova comoedia*), Menander, Philemon and Diphilus; he
makes no mention of Middle Comedy.[1] Does it follow that
he does not admit its existence?   I do not think this conclusion inevitable, and I believe that the inferior quality
of the representatives of the μέση may well be sufficient
explanation of his silence regarding them.   The passages
in Plutarch,[2] Dion [3] and Quintilian [4] (following Dionysius
of Halicarnassus), in which likewise only two kinds of
comedy are mentioned, the old and the new, are not
any more convincing.   They express the opinions of
rhetoricians or moralists who looked at the matter from
special points of view, regarded from which the division
into three periods would have had no interest for them;
they are not writing chapters of literary history.   Fielitz
was again led into error by his too ready belief that the
evidence which was unfavourable to his view came solely
from the authors—or the compilers—in whose works he
found it, while, in point of fact, it is in part derived from
a far earlier source.   When, for example, Athenaeus, in
discussing the comic writer Sotades, describes him in the
following terms : οὐχὶ ὁ τῶν ἰωνικῶν ᾀσμάτων ποιητὴς ὁ
Μαρωνείτης, ἀλλ᾿ ὁ τῆς μέσης κωμῳδίας ποιητής,[5] this learned
remark is, without a doubt, not from the pen of Athenaeus
himself; he took it, we know not whence, but most probably from some book that was already old in his day.
The title of a work by a certain Antiochus of Alexandria,

---

[1] Vell. Paterc., I. 16, 2.   [2] Plut., *Quaest. Sympos.*, VII. 8, 3, 4–10.
[3] Dion Chrys., XVIII. (Περὶ λόγου ἀσκήσεως), p. 477 R.
[4] Quint., X. 1, 66 et seq.   [5] Ath., p. 293 A.

preserved by the same Athenaeus—Περὶ τῶν ἐν τῇ μέσῃ κωμῳδίᾳ κωμῳδουμένων ποιητῶν—suggests similar reflections. Fielitz exerted himself to prove that the abovementioned work may have been written a short time before the *Deipnosophists*; but that is not very plausible. The minute erudition which the title implies, the great number of texts and commentaries that were necessary to fulfil what it promised, were not to be found together anywhere in all probability, except at Alexandria during the best period of Hellenistic philology. It was in those surroundings that the expression κωμῳδία μέση which Antiochus uses, and the division into three periods to which that expression refers, must have originated.

Moreover, it is only a matter of minor interest to determine when the term " middle comedy " was first used; the most important thing is the question of the competence of those who first used it. The fact cannot be disguised that in none of the documents in which a threefold division appears are the μέση and the νέα seriously differentiated. In most of them it is stated that ancient comedy made fun of people openly (φανερῶς, ἀπαρακαλύπτως, προδήλως), middle comedy in a disguised fashion (αἰνιγματωδῶς, συμβολικῶς, ἐσχηματισμένως), and that New Comedy no longer attacked any one except foreigners, slaves and beggars. Now foreigners and beggars appear to have played a very small part in the νέα; slaves held a larger place, but still not so large a one as this classification would have it appear. Indeed, the difference indicated between the μέση and the νέα is really artificial and futile. But too much importance must not be attached to these statements. The various passages in question probably belong to a very ancient work, earlier than the most flourishing period of what we call the νέα; and in it, consequently, only two periods were distinguished : the ἀρχαία and, under the name of *new comedy* (νέα, νεωτέρα), that which we call the μέση. The grammarians who took note of this work—and before them, the original author, perhaps a contemporary of Menander or of his immediate successors—knowing of the existence of three periods and

wishing to corroborate it, thought that in differentiating
the two latter they could rely upon the same criterion
which had previously served to differentiate the first : the
Aristotelian criterion—the difference between λοιδορία,
αἰσχρολογία (open scurrility) and ὑπονοία or ἔμφασις (innu-
endo). This accounts for the combination which I have
criticised. This combination is, apparently, not the
original statement of the theory of the three periods; it
presupposes the existence of that theory and tries to
bring it into agreement with other, still older, theories ; [1]
it does not discover the true principle. It is, therefore,
still possible that this principle was sound. We must not
forget that the division into three periods, even if it did not
arise before the time of Hadrian, was the work of scholars
who knew Greek comedy infinitely better than we do;
Athenaeus says that he had read eight hundred plays of
the middle period.[2] To reject, in our dense ignorance, the
judgment of people who were so well informed would be
singularly audacious; I shall certainly not do so *a priori*.

Moreover, quite apart from considerations of tradition, another very practical reason obliges me to disregard comedy prior to 330 : for we have hardly any
records of it.[3] In Kock's collection the fragments which
can properly be dated as belonging to the middle period
occupy relatively little space; they are collected in the
second volume—the smallest of the three—before the
fragments of Philemon. Furthermore, not everything
that comes before them need be taken into account.
Certain poets whom Kock regarded as representatives of
the μέση now appear to us, thanks to inscriptions which
have been better elucidated, as poets of the new period;
for example, Simylus, of whom really nothing but his

---

[1] *i. e.* theories based upon the bipartite division, Old and New.
[2] Ath., p. 336 D.
[3] For the chronology of the Greek comedy-writers, see particularly
Wagner, *Symbolarum ad comicorum graecorum historiam criticam*, Capita IV.
(Leipzig, 1905); Wilhelm, *Urkunden dramatischer Aufführungen in Athen,*
(Vienna, 1908); Capps, articles in the *American Journal of Philology*
(1900 and 1907).

name has survived, and Diodorus, the brother and contemporary of Diphilus. Of the fragments attributed to
the celebrated Antiphanes, who was born between 408
and 405, and died between 334 and 331, one must set
aside those which belong to Antiphanes the younger, the
son of Panaetius, who lived a generation later. The
scraps which appear under the names of Nicostratus and
Epigenes should, in each instance, be divided between
two men of the same name, one of whom lived in the
time of the *νέα*. Some notable authors, who, in the collection, precede Philemon and Diphilus, were as a matter of
fact still writing when the latter were flourishing; this
must have been the case with Dionysius and Timocles,
and possibly also with Amphis and some others. Above
all it is the case with Alexis. If fragment 244 is by him,
this poet, whose first victories are possibly not earlier
than 355 and may have been youthful victories, must
have lived until after the marriage of Ptolemy Philadelphus
with his sister Arsinoë and until the time of the Chremoni-
dean war; the greater portion of this interminable career
would therefore coincide with the so-called new period. No
doubt some authors, whose style was already fixed about
the year 330, may subsequently, for a decade or more, have
remained true to their original style of writing. For this
reason we still include writers like Amphis and Timocles in
the *μέση*. It is less admissible that Alexis should, during a
period of time which exceeded half a century, have obstinately disregarded any new phase in the development of
comedy. Notwithstanding the fact that he is generally represented as one of the leaders of the middle period, we may,
I believe, occasionally borrow certain features from him.

Thus, in recent years, critical study tends to rob the
μέση of a portion of what for a long time appeared to
belong to its domain. Must we, by a contrary process,
restore certain texts to it which are commonly attributed
to the *νέα*? A new fragment of Philemon [1] has led to

---

[1] Fragment of the Λιθογλύφος, preserved by Didymus, in his *Commentary
to Demosthenes*, X. 70.

the plausible conjecture that this poet, who was born between 365 and 360, was writing as early as the year 342. But his successes are of much later date; at the great festival of Dionysus he first gained a prize in 327; at the Lenaea, probably not before 320. In the course of a life which was almost twice as long as that of Menander, Philemon did not write as many comedies as his rival, and yet he does not appear to have ceased writing in his old age, so that we are justified in surmising that his youthful writings were few in number. As a matter of fact, apart from the new fragment, nothing of what remains of his writings seems to be earlier than 330. In spite of the time of his birth and of his first productions, Philemon should properly be regarded as an author of the new period. I should be more inclined to claim for the μέση several poets of inferior rank, to whom Kock gives a later date : for instance, Dioxippus, about whose date we have no exact knowledge; Strato, placed by Suidas in the middle period; and Sosipatrus, who mentions a certain cook Chariades as among the living, of whom Euphron later speaks as though he were dead. As to Stephanus, the son of Antiphanes, and author of a play called Φιλολάκων, it is very difficult to make up one's mind; according as one identifies the Θουρία, of which he speaks, with the Messenian city or with the country of Thurii, the βασιλεύς, whom he introduces, with a king of Sparta, with Alexander of Molossus or with Pyrrhus, Stephanus will belong more probably to the one or the other period; I incline to placing him in the νέα. With the exception of these three or four poets, Meineke's classification, which Kock generally retained, should, I think, be followed.

On the other hand, modern discoveries almost exclusively concern the New Comedy, comedy after 330. Only a few endings of lines from the Ἀνθρωπογονία by Antiphanes [1] and two fragments of the Ἥρωες and of the Ἰκάριοι by Timocles, of the same date as the new fragment of

---

[1] *Oxyrh. Pap.*, III. No. 427.

Philemon,[1] can with certainty be attributed to the middle
period. A few of the fragments from Ghorân are, according to Blass, written in a style which is not that of the
νέα. They are the shorter and more mutilated ones. The
others, if they are not by Menander (as the first editors
were inclined to think), or even if they do not belong
to the best period of the New Comedy, are the work
of an imitator and not of a forerunner. As to the fragment published in Volume VI of the *Oxyrhynchus Papyri*,
Körte's investigations seem to establish that it is not
earlier than the time of Menander, as was formerly thought,
but that it belongs to a work of the master of the νέα
himself—to the Περινθία. The fragments in Volume II,
the Strassburg prologue, and the long Berlin fragment (if
it is not a bit of Menander's Κιθαριστής), are of a doubtful
period. The fragment in the Hibeh Papyri belongs to a
play the scene of which was laid in Egypt and must have
been written at a time when Egypt had been Hellenised.

So much for the original documents. I shall now turn
to the imitations; the closest and most numerous of
which—the Latin comedies—have nearly all been dated
approximately.[2]

Without entering into the details of the argument I
shall point out what, in each case, warrants our considering
them the product of the νέα. Now it is the name of the
author, now some feature or features from which we can
reach a *terminus post quem*. We know on unimpeachable
authority that the *Heauton Timoroumenos* is a copy of
the play of the same name by Menander, and that the
Stichus—or rather, as we shall see later on, the beginning
of the *Stichus*—is a copy of his Ἀδελφοὶ ά; that the *Andria*,
the *Eunuchus*, the *Adelphi* were chiefly based on three
of the same poet's comedies—the Ἀνδρία, the Εὐνοῦχος
and the Ἀδελφοὶ β'—and, secondarily, on the Περινθία

---

[1] Didymus' *Commentary to Demosthenes*, X. 70.

[2] See especially for the prototypes of Plautus: Hüffner, *De Plauti
comoediarum exemplis atticis quaestiones maxime chronologicae*, Diss.
Göttingen, 1894; Schanz, *Gesch. der römischen Litteratur*, I. (4th ed.),
pp. 72 et seq.

and the *Κόλαξ*, also by Menander, and the *Συναποθνῄσκοντες*
by Diphilus; that the *Mercator* and the *Trinummus*
are imitations of works of Philemon—the *Ἔμπορος* and
the *Θησαυρός*; and the *Casina* and *Rudens* imitations of
works by Diphilus—the *Κληρούμενοι*, and a play whose
title is unknown; that the *Hecyra* and *Phormio* are imitations of works of Apollodorus of Carystus—the *Ἑκύρα* and
the *Ἐπιδικαζόμενος*. A comparison of the Menander fragments 125 and 126 with verses 816–817, 308–309 of the
Bacchides proves that this comedy is an imitation of
the *Δὶς ἐξαπατῶν*. The *Cistellaria*, in which another fragment of Menander—No. 558—is translated almost word
for word (89–93) must have been an imitation of the play
of which this fragment is a part. In the *Aulularia*, one
of the forms of stinginess attributed to Euclio (300–301)
closely recalls a similar trait which Menander attributed
to the *φιλάργυρος* Smicrines. This gives us some warrant
for the belief that Menander furnished the model for the
Aulularia. At any rate, this model, which apparently
made mention of the *γυναικονόμοι*,[1] was not earlier than
the government of Demetrius of Phalerum. The prototype of the *Mostellaria* was written during the lifetime of
Philemon and of Diphilus,[2] after the death of Alexander
and of Agathocles (289);[3] there is every likelihood that
it was the *Φάσμα* by Philemon. The *Ὀναγός*, the prototype
of the *Asinaria*, was the work of a certain Demophilus,
of whom we know nothing. In modern times it has been
thought that lines 712–713 made fun of the divine honours
and of the epithet *Σωτήρ* granted to several of the
Diadochi; that lines 68 et seq. alluded to the plot of some
earlier comedy, possibly the *Ναύκληρος* by Menander.
Nor are these surmises without plausibility, but as Demophilus had no great reputation, Plautus would, certainly,
not have dreamt of imitating him, if, at the time when
he wrote, the plays of the Greek poet were already anti-
quated. In the *Amphitryon* there is an indication of its

---

[1] *Aul.*, 504.
[2] *Most.*, 1149: *Si amicus Diphilo aut Philemoni es. . .*   [3] *Ibid.*, 775.

date in a few lines of Sosia's speech, describing the military
manœuvres of the time of the Diadochi.[1] Its Greek prototype was not, therefore, as has been sometimes maintained, a comedy of the middle period, and it has been
suggested that it may have been a play by Philemon, the
Νύξ, of which the actual title was probably Νὺξ μακρά.
The original of the *Curculio*, to judge by lines 394–395,
was later than a siege of Sicyon, which was either the
siege of 303 or one that took place ten years earlier. The
original of the *Epidicus*, performed immediately after a
campaign of the Athenians against Thebes, probably dates
from the year 292 or 289. In the *Miles*, the name Seleucus,
and in the *Truculentus*, the reference to a " Babylonian "
soldier who conquered Syria and carried on war in Phrygia,
Arabia and the Pontus, takes us back to the time of
Alexander's successors. Lines 411–412 of the *Menaechmi*,
which it would be a mistake to regard as an addition by
Plautus, point to a period subsequent to the accession of
Hiero (275 or 270). The chief model for the *Pseudolus*,
in view of line 533, must have been contemporaneous
with the most brilliant successes of Agathocles (309–308
or 302). The Καρχηδόνιος, from which the *Poenulus* got its
name, was written after the death of Apelles (line 1271);
on the other hand, lines 663–665 of the Latin play appear
to me to contain an allusion, obscured and mutilated by
Plautus, to the events subsequent to the battle of Sellasia
(221).[2] As for the *Captivi*, the very fact that the scene is
laid in Aetolia obliges us to place the original in a time
when the people of Aetolia played an important part in
the affairs of Greece, which was only the case from the
time of Alexander. The date of the war between Aetolia
and Elis which forms the basis of the plot, cannot, I
believe, be definitely fixed, and I should be inclined to
place it in the third century, preferably in the second half.
Which, then, of the works of Plautus and of Terence
belong to the middle period? Of entire plays, there is
none but the *Persa*. In this comedy the Persians are

---

[1] *Amph.*, 242 et seq.　　　[2] Cf. *Rev. Ét. Gr.*, XVI. (1903), pp. 365–366.

spoken of as being still an independent people (line 506); the Greek original was therefore written before the conquests of Alexander. On the other hand, it is possible that in the " contaminated " plays, certain parts, to which the preceding remarks do not extend, were copies of originals older than other parts of the context. For example, the middle and the end of the *Stichus*, a few scattered scenes of the *Pseudolus* and of the *Truculentus*, and that part of the *Miles* where Sceledrus is made sport of. But we have no means of dating the secondary models upon which these parts were based; at least an attempt to do so would be subject to grave doubts and can be made only on the strength of literary considerations.

The sources of the Latin fragments are naturally less clear than those of complete or almost complete comedies. Still, we are in a position to note some facts about them. The greater part of them is derived from about one hundred and thirty *palliatae* of which the titles are preserved. Of these titles, sixty repeat the known titles of Greek comedies. Furthermore, more than fifty of them have equivalents in the repertory of the *véa* or in that of Alexis, a poet of the period of transition, and many of them have no equivalent elsewhere. As regards the comedies for whose titles equivalents are found only in the repertory of the *μέση*, we can name barely more than four or five. These statistics are not without an interest of their own, and on a number of points where they afford somewhat vague evidence, more precise testimony can be adduced. Terence, Cicero and Aulus Gellius expressly say that Plautus' *Commorientes* was an imitation of Diphilus'[1] *Συναποθνῄσκοντες*; that the *Phasma* by Luscius Lanuvinus, the *Plocium* and the *Synephebi* by Caecilius, were imitations of plays with similar titles by Menander.[2] The prologue of the *Eunuchus* seems to show that two comedies of Menander supplied the models for the *Colax* by Naevius, the

---

[1] *Ad.*, prol. 6–7.
[2] *Eun.*, prol. 9; Cic., *De finibus*, I. 2, 4; *De opt. gen. or.*, 18; Gell., II. 23; III. 16, 3.

Colax by Plautus and the *Thensaurus* by Luscius.[1] The
juxtaposition of the names of Menander and Turpilius in
a sentence of Servius regarding Phaon, proves that the
Leucadia of Turpilius was a copy of a play by Menander.[2]
Turpilius' *Epiclerus*, like Menander's, brought upon the
stage a person who, through lack of sleep, becomes garrulous, and a son who is chosen as arbiter by his father
and mother;[3] here again Turpilius imitated Menander.
He also, as I believe, imitated him in the *Paedion*; fragments 372 and 373 of Menander's Παιδίον are the best
possible comment to fragment VIII of the Latin play;
moreover, in both plays there is question of a marriage.
The *Titthe* by Caecilius contains the story of the substitution of a child, just as Menander's play does.[4] In
his *Karine*, jewels are mentioned as in Menander's play.[5]
In the *Synaristosae*, he praises the power of love, just as
Menander praises it in a fragment of the Συναριστῶσαι.[6]
This leads me to infer that he copied him in each of these
three instances. The *Gladiolus*, by Livius Andronicus,
appears to have contained a swaggering soldier;[7] this is
probably also true of Philemon's[8] Ἐγχειρίδιον, and this
resemblance is doubtless not accidental. Nor is it an
accident that a fragment of Turpilius, belonging to his
Demetrius, translates a sentence of Alexis' Δημήτριος;[9]
nor that a line of Naevius, author of the *Ariolus*, repeats
a line of Philemon, author of the Ἀγύρτης;[10] nor that the
fragments of Naevius' *Glaucoma* and of Alexis' Ἀπεγλαυκωμένος both deal with a cook.[11]

Thus we have a certain number of points of contact

[1] *Eun.*, prol. 25 and 30, 10.   [2] (Servius) *ad Aeneid.*, III. 279.
[3] Turpilius, *Epiclerus*, fr. I. and Men., fr. 164; Turpilius, fr. III. and
Rhetor. anon. Spengel, I. p. 432, 17.
[4] Caecilius, *Titthe*, fr. I., IV. and Men., fr. 461; Caecilius, inc. fab. fr.
XXIII. and Men., fr. 460.
[5] Caecilius, *Karine*, fr. I., II. and Men., fr. 258.
[6] Caecilius, inc. fab. fr. XV. and Men., fr. 449.
[7] See the only extant fragment.   [8] Philem., fr. 21.
[9] Turpilius, *Demetrius*, fr. V. and Alexis, fr. 46.
[10] Naevius, inc. fab. fr. I. and Philemon, fr. 133 (cf. fr. 2–3).
[11] Naevius, *Glaucoma*, fr. I. and Alexis, fr. 15.

which force themselves upon us, or which can be established, between the fragments of the *palliatae* and those of the new period. Were we to attempt to establish similar relations in respect of the μέση, we should not be able to do so — a still further reason to believe that the Latin comedy-writers strove particularly and almost exclusively to imitate the νέα.

As regards Alciphron and Lucian, it is very difficult to fix even an approximate date for the comedies from which they drew their inspiration, for they did not, like the Latin poets, in each case follow a definite comedy. The *Dialogues* and *Epistles* are clever variations executed on themes of the repertory, rather than imitations in the strict sense of the word, and the reminiscences in which they abound may be derived from works varying widely from one another. Doubtless Lucian was acquainted with at least some authors of the middle period; he quotes Alexis [1] and alludes to the Μαλθάκη by Antiphanes.[2] Possibly he borrowed from Antiphanes the setting and several ideas of the *Timon*. In Dialogue II, a detail— the mention of the ναυτοδίκαι—takes us back to a time earlier than the beginnings of the νέα; but other features point—though not precisely—to the time of Alexander's successors. A scholiast maintains that Lucian borrowed the entire subject matter of his *Dialogues* from the comic repertory, and *particularly from the plays of Menander*.[3] It would appear as though the more general statement were correct, or nearly so,[4] and this leads me to believe that the more specific statement is also correct. This affirmation by the scholiast is, moreover, not in any way surprising; the renown of Menander, the prince of comedy and the creator of the immortal Thais, render him naturally enough an object of Lucian's especial interest.

For similar reasons one is tempted to admit *a priori* that Alciphron harked back to the comic writers of the

---

[1] *De lapsu in salut.*, 6.   [2] *Rhetor. praec.*, 12.
[3] *Scholia in Lucianum* (ed. Rabe, 1906), p. 275.
[4] Cf. *Rev. Ét. Gr.*, XXI. (1908), p. 75.

C

new period rather than to their less distinguished predecessors. Like the *Dialogues* of Lucian, various details
of his *Epistles* fit into the νέα. Several of the courtesans
with whom he deals (Lamia, Leontion) are historical
characters of that epoch. He wrote two letters in the
name of Menander's *Glycera* (IV, 2 and 19), another in
Menander's own name (IV, 18), and gave the lover of
one of his heroines the name Diphilus (IV, 10). But, on
the other hand, Phryne and Hyperides—the latter died
in 322—take up considerable space in the amorous corre-
spondence (IV, 3, 4, and 5) and Praxiteles also plays a
part therein (IV, 1). As to the writers of the parasitic
epistles and the persons to whom they are addressed, they
represent a type which, as we may now affirm, was at
least as much in favour at the time of the μέση as later
on. In the writings of Alciphron, chronological evidence
is therefore less exact and, above all, less unequivocal than
it was in Lucian's writings. Such evidence as he furnishes
can only be applied with a great deal of care in a special
study of New Comedy.

In any case, however, it is clear that between the μέση
and the νέα, defined, as I have done, chronologically, the
documentary material is very unevenly divided, and as
I shall limit my investigations to the latter period, I have
the greater part of it at my disposal. Moreover, I need
hardly say that I have by no means a preconceived intention
of discovering only differences and contrasts between the
comedy before 330 and that of a later date. I shall quite
as gladly point out the features which the νέα took over
from earlier comedy, as those which are peculiar to itself,
or which seem to me to be so. Wherever there is evidence
of the continuity of comedy, I shall not fail to give it
consideration.

* * *

The original of the *Captivi*, as has already been pointed
out, was probably written in the second half of the third
century; that of the *Poenulus* at the time of the battle
of Sellasia, that is to say, in 221. After this date we have

no remnants of Greek comedy save a few names of authors and a few titles of plays. Still, the study upon which we are embarking will cover the space of a whole century of comedy. During this lapse of time several generations of poets succeeded one another, and many comic writers, all of whom may not have had the same tastes or practised the same art, lived and wrote contemporaneously or followed one another in quick succession. Is it not a futile and unreasonable undertaking to bring together into a single picture features scattered among the writings of so many authors, in so many works of different dates? It does not seem so to me. Notwithstanding the growth of our knowledge, the time has not yet come, if indeed it will ever come, when the various poets of the *véa* can appear before us as distinct literary individualities. The monographs which have been devoted to some of them have as yet yielded rather meagre results in the way of differentiating between them—results to which I shall call attention when occasion offers. In regarding Menander, his contemporaries and successors during the entire third century, generally speaking, as representatives of one and the same style of literary composition, I believe that I am alive to the demands and limitations of the present state of our knowledge.

PART I
THE SUBJECT MATTER OF NEW COMEDY

CHAPTER I

WHAT NEW COMEDY REJECTED

IN the first part of my study, I wish to point out what constituted the subject matter of comedy during the new period. This first part will be essentially an inventory. But before passing in review those elements of which the presence in the repertory can be established, or at least suspected, I must call attention to a few elements which the *véa* rejected, though they were regarded with favour when it began its career.

§ 1.

PERSONAL INVECTIVE

First among these, if we may trust the ancient critics, is personal abuse. We are told that New Comedy no longer vilified men of wealth or of station; it refrained from making even a veiled attack on any individuals except foreigners, slaves and beggars.[1] This is not absolutely correct. The writers of the *véa*, Meineke rightly remarks,[2] did not always refrain from having their say about public affairs. A comic character congratulates Demetrius of Phalerum on having driven out the philosophers.[3] Others speak, not without irony, of a new law limiting the number of guests who are allowed to assemble at a banquet.[4] Another character empties his cup in honour of King Ptolemy, of the sister-queen Arsinoë, of peace re-established among the Greeks.[5] Another drinks to the health of Antigonus, of young Demetrius and his wife Phile, and rejoices at their recent victory.[6] Criticism is levelled at Lamia, the mistress of Poliorcetes, who levies a regular war-tax at Athens in order to give her lover a banquet.[7]

---

[1] Schol. Dionys. Thrac., p. 15, Kaibel; Treatise IV. Dübn., περὶ κωμῳδίας (Kaibel, p. 13). Cf. J. Tzetzes, p. 21, 28, 37, Kaibel.
[2] *Historia critica*, pp. 436 et seq.   [3] Alexis, fr. 94.
[4] Timocles, fr. 32; Men., fr. 272.   [5] Alexis, fr. 24.
[6] Alexis, fr. 111.   [7] Cf. Plut., *Dem.*, 27 (= fr. adesp., 303).

Fun is made of the mystery that surrounds the treaty concluded by Antigonus and Pyrrhus.[1] And it is not only foreign princes, like Magas of Cyrene, Dionysius of Heraclea, and Seleucus Nicator, who are roughly handled or ridiculed.[2] In order to be agreeable to Antipater, Archedicus attacks Demochares, nephew of Demosthenes and one of the leaders of the nationalist party, with a degree of virulence such as is not found in any of the fragments of the middle period.[3] Philippides had a better inspiration when he raised his voice against Stratocles, a favourite of Poliorcetes, " who has turned the Acropolis into an evil resort and has introduced prostitutes into the temple of the Maiden Goddess. It is owing to him that the frost has bitten our vines, it is because of his godlessness that the sacred peplus is torn in two, because he rendered divine honours to men. This is what undermines the commonwealth, not comedy." [4] $T α \tilde{v} τ α$ $κ α τ α λ \acute{v} ε ι$ $δ \tilde{η} μ ο ν$, $ο \dot{v}$ $κ ω μ \omega δ \acute{ι} α$. Note this last expression. It seems to indicate that at the time when Philippides wrote, at the very end of the fourth century, comedy had not renounced politics.

Perhaps the difference between the $μ \acute{ε} σ η$ and the $ν \acute{ε} α$ lay not so much in the kind of people it attacked as in the greater or lesser frequency of its attacks. In the fragments of Menander, of his contemporaries or of his successors, the shafts of satire hurled at living persons— of course, I take no account of mere inoffensive remarks— are certainly rarer than in the earlier fragments. In Alciphron, Glycera writes to her friend Bacchis, " I would give a great deal not to lose the love of Menander. If we had any tiff or any quarrel, I should have to undergo the bitter insults of a Chremes or of a Pheidylus in the theatre." [5] As far as we know, there is no good reason for Glycera's fears. It is in the writers of the middle

---

[1] Phoenicides, fr. 1.
[2] Philem., fr. 144; Men., fr. 21–23; fr. adesp., 450 (Dionysius).
[3] Archedicus, fr. 4.   [4] Philippides, fr. 25.
[5] Alc., IV. 2. Similarly, if we are to believe Machon, Gnathaena feared that Diphilus might make her pay for her infidelity by reproducing it upon the stage (Ath., p. 579 E).

period — Antiphanes, Philetaerus, Amphis, Anaxilas, Epicrates, Alexis, Timocles and Theophilus—that we hear railing at famous courtesans, denunciation of their covetousness, their shamelessness and their bad behaviour, spiteful tales of their intrigues, criticism of their physical imperfections, disclosures about their advancing years, and pitiless mockery at their old age. Neither Menander nor the other poets of the νέα appear to have followed such examples. Archedicus gives a fantastic explanation of the nickname Σκοτοδίνη of a certain Nicostrata : ὅτι δῖνόν ποτ᾽ ἦρεν ἀργυροῦν ἐν τῷ σκότῳ.[1] Philippides tells a rather naughty story about Gnathaena : how, when swallowing some ὄρχεις, she said that they were a dainty dish.[2] These two attacks were not very malicious, and they are the liveliest bits in the fragments of the new period that refer to fashionable favourites. Menander does indeed mention some such women, but he neither insults them nor makes fun of them. It appears that into one of his comedies he introduced his mistress Glycera.[3] But if we may trust Alciphron, to whom we owe this bit of information, he did it without malice, for Glycera insists upon the play being performed before the King of Egypt, so that, in taking it to Alexandria, Menander should carry with him the portrait of his beloved. Surely she would not have been so insistent had the portrait been a repulsive one.

Nor were the courtesans of the day abused in Philemon's comedies; as far as we know, the only time that this poet speaks of one of them, he does so in order to sing her praises ![4]

The men about town and the parasites had to suffer rather more. Philemon, Euphron and Menander levelled some shafts against Callimedon-Carabus, a great amateur of fish, as also against his son Agyrrhius.[5] Menander and Apollodorus of Gela made sport of Chaerephon, a rare spunger.[6] Other spungers appear now and again : Philo-

---

[1] Arched., fr. 1.   [2] Philipp., fr. 5.   [3] Alc., IV. 19, 20.
[4] Philem., fr. 215.   [5] Philem., fr. 42 ; Euphr., fr. 9 ; Men., fr. 319.
[6] Men., fr. 56, 277, 320, 364 ; Σαμία, 258–259 ; Apollod., fr. 24, 26.

xenus-Pternocopis and the infinitely slim Philippides in
Menander; [1] Phoenicides, Corydus, Neilus, Phyromachus,
in Euphron; [2] Chaerippus, in Phoenicides; [3] "Lightning"
Damippus, in Anaxippus. [4] Both Diphilus and Menander
branded the prodigality of Ctesippus, son of Chabrias, who
went so far as to sell the stones of his father's monument. [5]

Note that the majority of these persons were notorious
before 330 and that they had already called forth the wit
of other comic writers. Philippides is repeatedly mentioned by Aristophon and by Alexis. Callimedon-Carabus
was a contemporary of Demosthenes; and Antiphanes,
Eubulus, Alexis and Timocles had a great deal of fun at
his expense. Chaerephon served as a butt for several
authors of the μέση, such as Antiphanes, Nicostratus,
Alexis, Timotheus and Timocles; he was one of the friends
of Cyrebion, the brother-in-law of the orator Aeschines.
Corydus is ridiculed by Cratinus the younger, who may
possibly have begun to write in the last years of the fifth
century. In Alexis he appears in connection with Carabus
and Cyrebion, who have already been mentioned, and with
the wealthy Blepaeus, of whom Demosthenes speaks;
he also appears in Timocles. Phoenicides is mentioned by
Antiphanes together with a certain Taureas, whom Philetaerus, the son of Aristophanes, also ridiculed. Phyromachus appears in Alexis in connection with the courtesan
Nannion, who was already notorious about 345–340.
Neilos, to whom Timocles refers, must belong to the same
period. Ctesippus, at the time when Menander and
Diphilus attacked him, was not less than fifty, and I
imagine that his behaviour had for a long time been a
source of scandal. In a word, at the beginning of the new
period, the men about town and the spungers of whom
we have just spoken had established a certain rank, so
to speak, in the *personnel* of comedy, and they were not
suddenly dismissed. But their places were not taken by
others.

---

[1] Men., fr. 276, 365.   [2] Euphr., fr. 8.   [3] Phoenic., fr. 3.
[4] Anaxippus, fr. 3.   [5] Diph., fr. 38; Men., fr. 363.

But matters stood otherwise with another class of men whom the μέση often brought on the boards—the philosophers. Several of them who did not flourish until after 330—Stilpo, Crates, Monimus, Epicurus, Cleanthes, Zeno— are named or clearly aimed at in a certain number of fragments. But the fragments rarely tell us about the individual peculiarities of these wise men or about the details of their lives. Generally it is only of their ideas that they speak. Fun is made of Zeno's " new philosophy," which teaches one how to be hungry;[1] the wisdom of Epicurus is belauded for making good consist in pleasure;[2] ironical commendation is bestowed upon the metaphysics of Monimus, for whom everything was smoke;[3] the arguments of an interlocutor are compared with the " stoppers " which Stilpo puts in the mouth of his adversaries.[4] References of this kind are no longer what can properly be called personalities.

Hitherto my search has not been very successful. If I add a joke of Menander's about Androcles, who refuses to grow old[5]—a character that appears to have been bequeathed by the middle comedy[6]—and the passage from Epinicus in which fun is made of Mnesiptolemus, an absurd author,[7] I shall, I believe, have enumerated about all the satirical attacks on individuals which the fragments afford after the year 330. As we see, their number is small.

Apart from the fragments, certain titles of comedies furnish some hints—titles consisting of the name of a man or of a woman ; for it is natural to suppose that the person from whom a comedy was named ordinarily played a con-

---

[1] Philem., fr. 85.   Cf. Posid., fr. 15.

[2] Baton, fr. 3, 5; Damoxenus, fr. 2; Hegesippus, fr. 2.   Cf. fr. adesp., 127, 305.

[3] Men., fr. 249.   [4] Diph., fr. 23.   [5] Men., Σαμία, 261–263.

[6] I believe that it is the same character from whom a play of Sophilus derived its title, the wealthy man for whom were written, about 340–345, the speech of the pseudo-Demosthenes against Lacritus (cf. Men., *l.c.* : πολὺ πράττεται).   He was very old when Menander spoke of him.

[7] Epinicus, fr. 1.

siderable part in it. The repertory of the μέση abounds in titles of this sort.[1] Doubtless many of them are the names of fictitious persons, created by the poet's fancy; others must designate real persons—contemporaries who were made fun of on the stage. As, however, we have no detailed knowledge of Athenian events of that period, we are not able to distinguish between the two categories with any degree of certainty, and it will be prudent not to include a name in the second category unless we have some reason to believe that, at the time when the play was written, it was borne by a man of a kind to interest the comic writers, or if the name is too commonplace. For instance, I am not prepared to admit that Eubulus' Πάμφιλος took its title from the name of a contemporary. Philotis is a name suitable for a courtesan, but we know of no famous courtesan of the fourth century who bore it. I am, therefore, not willing to believe without further proof that Antiphanes' Φιλῶτις introduced some notorious woman. This applies to many such titles, so that there is great uncertainty about them. We are, however, justified in considering some of them as names of contemporary characters. Foremost among these are the names of courtesans: Anteia, Bacchis, Clepsydra, [Anti]-laïs, Lampas, Nannion, Neaera, Neottis, Opora, Plangon, Philyra, Chrysis; then the name Polyeuctus, borne by a politician; that of the philosopher Plato; that of the cook Nereus, who supplied two plays with their titles; that of the parasite Moschion; of the flute-player Batalus; of Androcles, the banker or usurer; and that of Autocleides, the paederast. To these we may add the names of two foreign princes, Philip of Macedon and Dionysius, tyrant of Syracuse. That makes nearly thirty comedies in which satirical attacks on an individual must have played a large part. Still others, whose titles are realistically descriptive names or such as

---

[1] More than sixty titles, some of which are common to several plays. A careful examination of these titles has recently been made by Breitenbach in a dissertation, *De genere quodam titulorum comoediae atticae* (Bâle, 1908).

never occurred among the names in common use in the
theatre, might, without too great rashness, be added to
the list : thus the *Φιλίσκος* by Antiphanes, the *Φιλωνίδης*
by Aristophon, the *Δωρίδης* by Alexis, the plays entitled
Ἀμφικράτης, Ἀρχιστράτη, Εὐθύδικος, Καλλωνίδης, Κλεοφάνης,
Λεωνίδης, Μίδων, Σώσιππος, Κάλλαισχρος, Δεξιδημίδης,
Νεοπτόλεμος; or the diminutives, which possibly betray
a satirical purpose : Ἄντυλλος, Λεπτινίσκος, Λυκίσκος,
Παρμενίσκος.

What material does the new period afford us for a similar
enumeration?   At most ten or eleven titles, three or four
of which designate foreigners : Philemon's *Πύρρος*, unless
indeed this word simply means " the red-headed man ";[1]
Diphilus' Ἄμαστρις, the name of a niece of Darius who was
successively the wife of Craterus, of Dionysius of Heraclea,
and of king Lysimachus; *Συνωρίς*, the name of a courtesan;
possibly *Τελεσίας*, which is supposed to be the name of a
parasite.   In Menander we find *Θαΐς* and *Φανίον*, names of
courtesans; in Hipparchus *Θαΐς*; in Anaxippus, *Κεραυνός*,
surname of a spunger; in Strato, if it be at all permissible
to quote him here, *Φοινικίδης*, the name of a famous
gourmet; in Posidippus, Ἀρσινόη, probably the name of a
Lagid or a Seleucid princess; in Epinicus, *Μνησιπτόλεμος*,
the name of the writer of the history of Antiochus the
Great.   It may be that even this list is too long.   It is
particularly open to question whether Athenaeus was not
mistaken in recognising an historical personage in Menander's Thais.   The real Thais followed Alexander to Asia
and was subsequently the mistress of Ptolemy Soter :
so she was not the favourite of all Athens at the time
Menander wrote.[2]

In a word, it is not improbable that between the middle
period and the new period the importance of the satirical

---

[1] Breitenbach suggests that in Stobaeus we should read—instead of
Φιλήμονος ἐκ Πύρρου—Φιλήμονος ἐκ Πυρ<φό>ρου. As a matter of fact, the
quotation which follows is taken from the Πυρφόρος.

[2] Menander's Θαΐς was apparently imitated by Afranius; but that
does not imply that it contains any very pointed satire of a particular
person.

element, which had already become much slighter in
Aristotle's [1] time, continued to diminish. Such examples
of this style as we have in the works of the principal poets
of the νέα are generally derived from their earliest comedies.
It was quite at the beginning of his career, more than ten
years before 330, that Philemon branded Aristomedes the
thief; it must have been before 318 that he tormented
Carabus; it may have been after 308 onwards that he
spoke ill of Magas. The plays of Menander from which
I have taken most of the examples are, almost all of them,
youthful works; the Ὀργή, written, at the very latest, in
316, and possibly as early as 321; the Ἀνδρόγυνος, which
must have been written shortly after the Lamian War;
the Κεκρύφαλος, in which the gynaeconomoi are spoken
of as officials recently created; [2] the Μέθη, earlier than the
disappearance of Carabus in 318; the Σαμία, which the
name Androcles prevents us from dating too late; the
Ἁλιεῖς, written, I believe, before the death of Dionysius
of Heraclea—that is to say, before 305—and not necessarily towards the end of his life, at a time when the royal
treasury at Cyinda was still well filled. Diphilus'
Ἐναγίζοντες, in which Ctesippus is abused, is likewise
early in the list of that author's writings, and must be
contemporaneous with the Ὀργή. The Ἄμαστρις was
possibly contemporaneous with the Ἁλιεῖς. Thus the taste
for personalities was not from the start foreign to the
great comic writers of the third period. Their predecessors of the earliest periods had left it to them as an
heritage, but they gave it up more or less completely, and
it never revived. It would appear that Menander in
particular abandoned the old traditions. Athenaeus says
of him: ἥκιστά γ᾽ ὢν λοίδορος.[3] No doubt Aristotle's
theory, which distinguished between comedy and iambic

---

[1] Arist., *Poet.*, IX. 3, p. 1451 B, 11 et seq. *Eth. Nic.*, IV. 14, p. 1128 A,
20 et seq.

[2] The creation of the gynaeconomoi probably dates from the first years
of the reign of Demetrius of Phalerum (cf. Gilbert, *Griechische Staatsalterth.*,
I², p. 178, *n.* 2).

[3] Ath., p. 549 C.

poetry,[1] a theory which the poet, a pupil of Theophrastus, must have known, had something to do with this.[2]

§ 2.
MYTHICAL ELEMENTS, THE SUPERNATURAL

Personal invective is not the only kind of resource which the *νέα* renounced. As early as the fifth century comic writers had occasionally brought the adventures of gods and heroes upon the stage; in the fourth century this kind of travesty became the rage. The comedy of the middle period, says Platonius, " made a business of ridiculing the stories told by the poets." [3] We are still in a position to judge of the correctness of this assertion : Meineke fills more than a page and a half of his *Historia Comicorum* [4] with extant titles of mythological plays written between 400 and 330. In the repertory of the *νέα*, on the contrary, mythological subjects apparently played a small part. The *Amphitryon* is an example of this type, but a unique example among extant comedies; and as far as one can judge from the titles and fragments of the lost plays, the proportion of mythological plays among them was likewise very insignificant.

It is only in Diphilus' comedies that titles which indicate, or seem to indicate, a legendary character, are rather frequent : Ἀνάγυρος, Δαναΐδες, Ἑκάτη, Ἡρακλῆς, Ἥρως, Θησεύς, Λήμνιαι (Turpilius : *Lemniae*), Πελιάδες and Σαπφώ. On the other hand, I find but three among Philemon's titles : Ἥρωες, Μυρμιδόνες and Παλαμήδης. Menander supplies four : Δάρδανος (Caecilius : *Dardanus*), Ἥρως, Τροφώνιος, Ψευδηρακλῆς. Among the less known writers of the new period we find less than ten such titles : Κένταυρος (Lynceus, Theognetus), Σίσυφος and Ψευδαίας (Apollodorus of Gela), Ἀμφιάρεως (Apollodorus of Carystus, Philippides), Ἑρμαφρόδιτος and Μύρμηξ [5] (Posidippus), Θεῶν ἀγορά and

---

[1] Arist., *Poet.*, V. 3, p. 1449 B, 8; IX. 3, p. 1451, 14.
[2] Diog. Laert., V. 2.   [3] Περὶ διαφορᾶς κωμφδιῶν, § 11 (Kaibel, p. 5).
[4] pp. 283–284.
[5] Myrmex was the name of an Attic hero; cf. Roscher's *Lexikon*.

Μοῦσαι (Euphron), *Πάν* (Timostratus). I may add, at random, eight titles supplied by comic writers *aetatis incertae* and one of a *palliata*: *Σαμόθρακες* (Athenion), *Διόννσος* and *Ἑλένη* (Alexandrus), *Ἀχελῷος* (Demonicus), *Μανέκτωρ* and possibly *Ἑρμίονη* (Menecrates), *Κέκρωπες* (Menippus), *Εἰλείθνια* (Nicomachus), *Aethrio*[1] (Caecilius). We thus get a list of about thirty titles, more than half of which had already been employed. It is not much.

Moreover, it must be admitted that not all the comedies which bore these titles were mythological plays. The plot of one of Menander's comedies, now known to be the *Ἥρως*, has survived; there was nothing legendary about this comedy, which merely took its title from the character who recited the prologue—*Ἥρως θεός*. Possibly this was also the case with other works whose title was the name of a god. Sometimes the god's name may have implied that the play contained references to his worship, or to some occurrences, some episodes of daily life, over which that god presided. I am quite ready to believe that in the comedies that went by the name of *Ἀμφιάρεως* the scene was placed at Oropus, near the Amphiaraeum, and that they contained ridicule of the practices of that famous sanctuary. Similarly, under the title *Τροφώνιος* comedy-writers may have criticised the superstition which supported the oracle at Lebadeia. Hecate was the patroness of sorcerers. Pan overcame men with " panic " terror; Eileithyia watched over women's confinements; the Muses inspired artists; the fact that these names served as titles does not supply exact information as to the nature of the subject matter. Other names, we may assume, had a sort of metaphorical value : a clever man was called Palamedes; a funny rogue, Cercops; Sisyphus was famous for his rascality; the Centaurs for their wantonness; Menander's pseudo-Heracles was perhaps not a person who tried to pass himself off for Heracles, but an absurd braggart. In a word, several titles which at first sight appear to have something to do with mythology are susceptible of a different inter-

[1] If the king of the gods, *aetherius Juppiter*, *αἴθριος Ζεύς*, is meant.

pretation. Who was the hermaphrodite who lent his name to a play by Posidippus? Was he the legendary son of Aphrodite and Hermes, or rather some person who was reputed to have the attributes of both sexes? Who were the Lemnian women after whom one of Diphilus' comedies was named? Were they the renowned followers of Hypsipyle, who murdered their husbands and loved the Argonauts, or were they women of Lemnos without fame or history? Who was the Dardanus of Menander's play? Was he Dardanus, son of Zeus, or was he a barbarian from the region of Illyria, one of those whom the Greeks generally called Δαρδανεῖς or Δαρδάνιοι, the Romans *Dardani*, and who were apparently made fun of in antiquity? Or was he a slave known by the name of his race, like so many Daoses and Getas and Syruses? According to Meineke, the *Aethrio* by Caecilius was simply an Ἀισχρίων whose name was changed. As to the Myrmex by Posidippus—if the word does not mean " an ant "—there is nothing to show he was not a mere mortal.

Thus, more than one of the comedies I have just enumerated ought probably to be left out of consideration. Similarly, other plays, which do not bear especially suggestive titles, have sometimes been regarded as comedies dealing with a legendary subject. But no convincing argument has been forthcoming for any of them. For example, it is still very doubtful whether Philemon's comedy called Νύξ dealt with the story of *Amphitryon*; Νύξ is not Νὺξ μακρά. In connection with the title Ἀνδρόγυνος ἤ Κρής, the name of a comedy by Menander, a Cretan legend told by Antoninus Liberalis has been cited.[1] I should be more inclined to think of a braggart, as several fragments make it seem probable that a person of this kind appeared in the play, and the appellation ἀνδρόγυνος, " a man with a woman's heart," which was commonly used as an insult, may very well have been appropriate to him. Moreover, it would not be at all surprising if the poet represented this braggart as a Cretan, because at the time

---

[1] *Metam.*, 17; cf. Ov., *Metam.*, XII. 172 et seq.

D

of the New Comedy Crete supplied a great many mercenaries. As regards the Λευκαδία, I have stated elsewhere why I do not believe that it brought the famous Phaon on the stage.[1] The action of the Λευκαδία, which takes place in Leucadia, could only have presented entirely fictitious characters supposed to be contemporaries of the poet.

Apart from plays with legendary subjects, the fantastic and the supernatural frequently appeared in the repertory of the old comedy. Here the actors were not only men; they were also gods, symbolical beings or personified abstractions—the Just and the Unjust, Clouds, Islands, Cities, and so forth. Or they were animals that spoke and acted like human beings—birds, frogs, fish, and so forth. The scene of action was not confined to terrestrial surroundings. Trygaeus ascended to Olympus, Xanthias and Dionysus went down to Hades, Peisthetaerus and Euelpides constructed the fanciful Cloud-Cuckooville 'twixt heaven and earth. How much of this compound of the real and the unreal, of the possible and the impossible, remained in the μέση? It is not easy to be sure; but we may assert that the νέα retained hardly any of it. In Plautus and Terence, gods and supernatural beings appear only in the prologue; after explaining the plot of the play they do not reappear; and this was probably also the case in almost all the plays of the new period. As for the stage setting, it never appears to have been placed elsewhere than in this everyday world of ours. In a general way, the New Comedy must have had a regard for physical probability. Here we meet with no miracles, with no metamorphoses; the miraculous return to youth which the titles Ἀνανεουμένη and Ἀνανεοῦσα would seem to proclaim, was possibly nothing more than a decoy, or a false promise of a sorceress, or else it took place only in the imagination of some crazy old woman. The *Menaechmi* is the only Latin play besides the *Amphitryon* in which, to a certain extent, we are called upon to admit the inadmissible. For, however much one may

[1] *Rev. Ét. Gr.*, XVII. (1904), pp. 310 et seq.

imagine the twins as resembling one another, one can hardly
believe that both of them—the one a bourgeois living in
his good town, the other just back from a long voyage
at sea—should wear identical clothes, shoes and hats,
have their hair dressed in an identical manner, and be
so much alike that the people among whom they move
most intimately insist on taking one for the other.   I
repeat that this case occurs but once in Plautus and
Terence; all the other material that remains at our
disposal for the reconstruction of the νέα does not admit
of our citing a single other instance of this sort.

CHAPTER II

THE SOURCES OF OUR KNOWLEDGE
OF THE SUBJECT MATTER OF NEW COMEDY—
EXAMINATION OF THE CHIEF SOURCES

I BEGAN my definition of the comedies of the new period by pointing out what they did not contain. I shall now take up the most important part of my task : the description of what they did contain. Like all dramatic works, they brought upon the stage persons who are involved in *adventures*. Among these persons, it is natural to seek *a priori* representatives of certain *social classes*, various *types of passion* and more or less defined *characters*. The chief divisions of the inquiry are imposed by the very nature of the subject.

As for the available material, the fragments of the original plays supply an appreciable amount of it. But we shall derive even more from the Latin plays. The time has therefore now come to explain both why and to what extent the constituent elements of Plautus' and Terence's comedies can be traced to their prototypes.

These comedies, at least those of Plautus, contain a certain number of details which have a clearly Roman colouring. Let us begin by examining the details of this character, which are of a kind to arouse our distrust, and let us, as far as may be, determine their import.

Many of them concern only the form in which the adventures are presented, and have nothing to do with their nature, or with the essential characteristics of the actors. For instance, expressions borrowed from official language, like the following, among many others—

> Si de damnosis aut si de amatoribus
> *dictator* fiat nunc Athenis Atticis.
> (*Pseud.*, 415–416.)

> Ibo intro, ubi de capite meo sunt *comitia*.
> (*Aul.*, 700.)

Si *centuriati* bene sunt *maniplares* mei.

(*Miles*, 815.)

Quin ruri es in *praefectura* tua?

(*Cas.*, 99.)

Ubi tu es, qui me *convadatu's* Veneris *vadimoniis*?
Sisto ego tibi me et mihi contra itidem <tu te> ut
sistas suadeo.

(*Curc.*, 162–163.)

Me sibi habeto, ego me *mancupio* dabo.

(*Miles*, 23.)

Omnes ordine sub signis ducam *legiones* meas
avi sinistra, *auspicio liquido*.

(*Pseud.*, 761–762.)

or geographical or topographical details applying specially
to Italy, like the description of the Forum, like the mention of the Porta Trigemina, the Capitol, the Velabrum,
and the *vicus Tuscus*, or that of the slopes of Mount
Massicus, or of Campanian carpets and Campanian slaves.
Further instances are appeals to Latin gods, expressions
borrowed from Latin mythology and religious rites, allusions to events in Roman history (wars against Carthage,
victories gained over enemies, the Lex Praetoria *de cir-
cumscriptione adulescentium*, etc.); reference to certain
Romans (the poet Naevius, the comedian Pellio, the *gens
Papiria*, etc.); reference to foreign contemporaries of
Plautus with whom Rome had relations (Attalus I of
Pergamon, Antiochus the Great, etc.); or pleasantries
like the following—

. . . plusculum annum

fui praeferratus apud molas *tribunus* vapularis.

(*Persa*, 21–22.)

Quid si aliquo ad ludos me *pro manduco* locem?

(*Rud.*, 535.)

Ex unoquoque eorum exciam crepitum *polentarium*.

(*Curc.*, 295.)

Quid, *Sarsinatis* ecqua est, si *Umbram* non habes ?
(*Most.*, 770.)

. . . At nunc Siculus non est; *Boius* est, *Boiam* terit.
(*Capt.*, 888.)

The addition of such details as these certainly makes it harder to appraise the Greek originals in matters of *form*; but it has not changed their *substance*.

Other details are more important, whether regarded from the point of view of psychology or from that of the plot. When the *advocati* of the *Poenulus* rebel against Agorastocles' too sharp admonitions, they declare that they do not mean to be abused, though they are poor and *plebeians*.[1] In the *Menaechmi*, the hero is kept in the forum for an interminable time by the lawsuit of a worthless *client*,[2] who is brought before the *aediles*.[3] In the opening scene of the *Aulularia*, Euclio makes up his mind to go out of his house in order to receive his share of a distribution of money which the *magister curiae*[4] is about to make to the *curiales*. Later on, Pythodicus relates that the old miser came in tears to the *praetor* because a kite had stolen a piece of meat, and that he wished to summon the bird to court (*vadarier*[5]). Still further on, Euclio threatens a cook that he will denounce him to the *triumvirs* because he has a knife in his hand.[6] In the *Asinaria*, Diabolus addresses the same threat to Cleareta and to Philaenium under the pretext that they are corrupting the young men.[7] In the *Truculentus*, Diniarchus rails at Phronesium, whom he regards as a poisoner (*venefica*), and plans a *manus injectio*.[8] Lycus, the pander in the *Poenulus*, who has unwittingly harboured a slave of Agorastocles, the bearer of a sum of money, but has denied having him in his house, fears that he may be brought to court *optorto collo*;[9] being

---

[1] *Poen.*, 515.
[2] *Men.*, 574, 576, 579, 588; cf. 581, 585 (*patronus*).
[3] *Ibid.*, 587, 590.   [4] *Aul.*, 107, 179.   [5] *Ibid.*, 317–318.
[6] *Ibid.*, 416.   [7] *As.*, 131.
[8] *Truc.*, 762.   [9] *Poen.*, 727, 790.

unable to repay twice the amount he has unwittingly embezzled,[1] he sees himself handed over to his enemy (*addictus*).[2] In his fright he begs the young man to compromise without having recourse to the *praetor* [3] and to be satisfied with the *simplum*.[4] Dordalus, another pander in the *Persa*, is in a most distressing situation because he had bought a pretended captive girl who has not been *mancupata*; [5] when her father, who is a citizen, appears and claims his daughter (*adserit manu*),[6] Dordalus has no one to fall back upon and is obliged to take the full responsibility for having kept a free girl in confincment. The same legal procedure to which Saturio, in the *Persa*, resorts—*adserere liberali causa*—is proposed by Agorastocles in the *Poenulus*, and then by Hanno,[7] and may be fraught with *supplicia multa* [8] for Lycus. Dordalus, in the *Persa*, calls upon the *praetor* [9] to free Lemniselenis. In the *Aulularia*, the *Curculio*, the *Poenulus* and the *Trinummus*, a father or a brother, when giving away a daughter or a sister in marriage, exchanges with the future husband the *certa verba* of a Roman betrothal : *Spondesne?—Spondeo*.[10]

The plot of the *Aulularia* is explained by the *Lar familiaris* of the house of Euclio; it is owing to that god, Roman in namc and charactcr, that Euclio has found the treasure; it is at his behest that, at the end of the play, Megadorus decides to ask for the hand of Phaedrium. In the *Mercator*, Charinus is preparing to go into voluntary exile, and bids farewell to the *penates* of his fathers, to the *Lar pater* of his family, and commends his parents to them.[11] Euclio deposits his treasure in the sanctuary of *Fides*; subsequently he takes it from there to a grove sacred to *Silvanus*.[12] A boasting soldier,

---

[1] *Poen.*, 183–184, 563–564, 1351.   [2] *Ibid.*, 185–186, 564, 1341, 1361.
[3] *Ibid.*, 1361.   [4] *Ibid.*, 1362.
[5] *Persa*, 525, 532, 589.   [6] *Ibid.*, 163, 716–717.
[7] *Poen.*, 905–906, 965, 1102, 1348, 1392.
[8] *Ibid.*, 1352.   [9] *Persa*, 487.
[10] *Aul.*, 256; *Curc.*, 674; *Poen.*, 1157; *Trin.*, 502, 573, 1161–1163.
[11] *Merc.*, 834–835.   [12] *Aul.*, 582 et seq., 674 et seq.

on arriving at the house of his mistress, pretends to be the god *Mars* visiting *Neriene*.[1] And so forth.

It would be easy to add further instances, but it would be a mistake on that account to credit the Latin imitator with too great a degree of originality. One can readily believe that, if it was possible, without changing the main lines of the original, here and there to add a Roman detail or to substitute a national equivalent for a foreign detail, Plautus took pleasure in doing so. And conversely, wherever we find an episode or a characteristic in connection with which, after eliminating the Roman details, we can with ease mentally supply a Greek equivalent, there is nothing to prevent our attributing the episode or characteristic in question to the original model.

Let us return to some of the examples quoted above. Upon what does the plot of the *Persa* depend in its essential features? It is only necessary that the pander should be worried on account of the purchase he has made in good faith, and that he should be exposed to serious disaster in consequence. Now, the former condition would be realised, in the light of Greek law, from the very fact that the imaginary Persian had sold his captive ἄνευ βεβαιώσεως;[2] the latter condition would be realised at the same time, as whoever lost a γραφὴ ἀνδραποδισμοῦ was liable to the death penalty.[3] Greek law can also afford sufficient ground for Lycus' plight. As he has deprived freeborn girls of their liberty and is unable to prove that he has purchased them in good faith, he may run the risk of having them taken away without receiving any compensation by an ἀφαίρεσις εἰς ἐλευθερίαν, which anybody can institute against him.[4] In any event he runs the much more serious risk of being dealt with as an ἀνδραποδιστής. For having harboured his neighbour's

---

[1] *Truc.*, 515.

[2] Cf. Meier-Schömann, *Der attische Prozess* (revised by Lipsius, 1883–1887), p. 719.

[3] *Ibid.*, p. 458; Beauchet, *Histoire du droit privé de la république athénienne*, Vol. II. pp. 412, 524–525.

[4] *Der att. Prozess*, p. 663.

slave, the bearer of a sum of money, and for having
denied that he had taken him into his house, he is
liable to a δίκη κλοπῆς.[1] The danger of being fined twice
as much, which seems to be a constant source of worry
to experts in Roman law,[2] is therefore quite natural.[3] It
is of little consequence that in a Greek country he does
not incur any annoyance comparable to the *addictio*; if
he is not in a position to pay the fine imposed, he must
compromise with his enemy and give up Adelphasium;
nor, doubtless, would Milphio and Agorastocles like anything better. In the original of the *Aulularia*, the miser
may have conceived the idea of having recourse to " the
Eleven " to arrest his thief; this would have been a
humorous application of the legal procedure known as
ἐφήγησις. The offences imputed to Congrio, Cleareta and
Phronesium were liable to legal prosecution at Athens just
as they were at Rome, at Athens by means of δίκη αἰκίας,
γραφὴ φαρμάκων, conducted before the astynomoi, whose
business it was to keep an eye on the courtesans.[4] Of
course, grumblers or dismissed lovers could also indulge in
their anger without having recourse to the courts. The
adventure of Menaechmus, in its essential features, might
have taken place in a Greek city—and in a performance
of the *véa*. In place of *clients*, in the Roman sense of the
word, well-to-do citizens in Greece had dependents and
were their official patrons. I believe that this is what
Xenophon alludes to in the *Oeconomicus* (II, 6), when he
mentions προστατεῖαι as among the duties of the rich.
One of Menaechmus' dependents has committed some
crime in the agora and is obliged to appear before the
agoranomoi. Menaechmus, in self-defence, acts as his
συνήγορος. Distributions of money such as that in which
Euclio indulges were, apparently, unknown in Plautus'

---

[1] Cf. Glotz, *Dictionnaire des Antiquités*, s. v. Klopé, pp. 827–828.

[2] Cf. Pernard, *Droit romain et droit grec dans le théâtre de Plaute*, pp. 177
et seq.

[3] Cf. *Der att. Prozess*, p. 453; Glotz, *loc. cit.*, p. 829, col. 1.

[4] The words " *apud magistratus faxo erit nomen tuom* " (*Truc.*, 761),
remind one of the Athenian procedure ἔνδειξις.

time. The magistrate who has to preside over them bears a strange name, which possibly the Romans did not know and by which, in any event, they only designated some obscure subordinate officials; and it is most likely that this name—*magister curiae*—originated in an attempt to translate the Greek word δήμαρχος, *curiales* being the Latin for δημόται, and that in the original work there was a distribution of "spectacle money" (θεωρικόν). The irascibility of the *advocati* in the *Poenulus*—their Greek name is συνήγοροι—can be accounted for, without attributing it to a social distinction between them and Agorastocles, simply on the ground of inequality of fortune. The repeated references in Latin comedy to the ordinary methods of enfranchisement are of no importance from the point of view of the plot. In the original of the *Persa*, the pander, instead of taking his slave to the "praetor," may have taken her to court in order to proclaim that thenceforth she was to be free.[1] One can imagine the formula of the *sponsalia* left out of the scenes where it occurs, without calling for any change in the course of events. Probably it often took the place of the quasi-ritual words that were exchanged, at the time of the ἐγγύησις, between the future husband and the κύριος of the bride. In the original plays the θεοὶ πατρῷοι or ἐφέστιοι may have been mentioned instead of the *Lar* and the *Penates*. The part allotted to the *Lar familiaris*, at the opening of the *Aulularia*, would be just as suitable for a god, or for some hero, for whom the miser's family entertained a traditional devotion; it would suit Hermes, the god of lucky finds, if a statue of Hermes embellished the πρόθυρον of Euclio, as it did so many πρόθυρα of Athenian houses. *Fides* was, I believe, substituted for Pistis; *Silvanus* for Pan; *Neriene* may have been substituted for Aphrodite.

In very many passages it is an easy matter to find equivalents such as I have just pointed out, and where occasion offers I shall call attention to them. Upon the

---

[1] Beauchet, *Droit privé de la rép. ath.*, Vol. II. p. 473.

whole, I do not believe that a single essential element of a plot, a single important feature of a character in the plays of Plautus, is fundamentally, necessarily, undeniably Roman.

Without wishing to dress up their actors and plots in the fashion of their own country, the Latin transcribers may well have omitted details which might have been without interest for their audience or might even have offended them.

Occasionally we can place our finger directly on such an omission. In Menander's Ἑαυτὸν τιμωρούμενος the passage has been discovered which corresponds to the following words in Terence—

> . . . agrum his regionibus
> meliorem neque preti maioris nemo habet.
> (*Heaut.*, 63–64.)

for—

> . . . καὶ τῶν Ἁλῆσι χωρίων
> κεκτημένος, κάλλιστον εἶ, νὴ τὸν Δία,
> ἐν τοῖς τρισί <ν> γε καί, τὸ μακαριώτατον,
> ἄστικτον.

How colourless the Latin translation is compared with these lines! It suppresses all indication of locality, Ἁλῆσι; it makes no mention of the " three domains," which were probably famous in that region; it suppresses a legal custom, ἄστικτον. In the commentary to the first scene of the *Phormio*, Donatus declares that in Apollodorus it was the barber himself who told the two cousins about the despair of the young orphan girl; he had witnessed it when he had gone to cut her hair as a sign of mourning; and Donatus adds this remark : *quod scilicet mutasse Terentium, ne externis moribus spectatorem Romanum offenderet.*[1] Likewise in the opening scene of the *Phormio*, when Davus enumerates all the family events in honour of which slaves give presents to their master, he mentions the initiation of children.[2] This is conveyed

---

[1] Commentary to line 91.   [2] *Phorm.*, 49.

by one word, without any more precise statement—*ubi initiabunt*. But in Apollodorus the initiation into the mysteries of Samothrace is expressly mentioned. Here again Terence has eliminated a distinctly Hellenic detail. In these three cases the omissions are of little consequence. There are instances of more serious ones. At the end of the *Epidicus*, it becomes clear that the pretty captive Telestis is the step-sister of Stratippocles, the young man who loves her. Upset by this discovery, he exclaims : " You have ruined me by discovering me, my sister ! " And his slave consoles him : " You are a fool; keep quiet. You have in your house a mistress awaiting you, the lyre-player whom I procured for you." But this con- solation is likely to be unavailing. In the first place, because Stratippocles no longer loves the lyre-player, and then, because the father of the family, who had been induced to purchase her by the representation that she was his lost child, would lose no time in re-selling the maiden, once he was undeceived. It is very probable that the outcome was different in the Greek comedy and that, as the Athenian law permitted marriages between brothers and step-sisters, Stratippocles married Telestis. Plautus was obliged to reject a solution which was inadmissible in the eyes of Romans.

I believe that what we have found to be the case in a few instances occurred frequently.

Still, many things in Plautus and in Terence have re- tained a decidedly Greek character. The scene of action is always in some Greek country. The places from which the actors come and whither they go are towns in the Greek or Greco-oriental world. When Charinus, in the *Mercator*, seeks for a spot to which he may go as an exile, on his imaginary journey, he mentions only Hellenic places.[1] Nearly all the persons who move in these Greek surround- ings have Greek names; sometimes these names are muti- lated, but they are always meant to sound Greek. These

[1] *Merc.*, 645 et seq., 932 et seq.

persons live at the end of the fourth or during the third
century—that is to say, at the time of Menander, Apollodorus and Posidippus, and they do not hesitate to allude
to men and to occurrences of that period : to Demetrius
and Clinias, or unknown persons, or the dancers Hegias
and Diodorus, the musician Stratonicus, the painter
Apelles, and even the comedy-writers Philemon and
Diphilus, King Agathocles, the siege of Sicyon, the downfall of Cleomenes, and so forth. They are thoroughly
conversant with Greek mythology and with the great
men of Greece, and talk glibly about Phrixus and
Bellerophon, Parthaon and Calchas, Linus, Phoenix,
Geryon, Autolycus, Cycnus, Tithonus, Ganymede (whom
they call Catamitus), Alcmaeon (whom they call Alcumeus),
Nestor and Ajax, Lycurgus and Orestes, Solon and
Thales of Miletus. They know the story of Hecuba
and that of the sons of Heracles. They are familiar
with the favourite sports of Greece—boxing and the
five parts of the pentathlon. They boast of possessing
Attic grace, and make fun of Sicilian wit. The festivals they celebrate are Greek festivals : the Aphrodisia,
the Dionysia, the Eleutheria; they have attended the
Olympic and Nemean Games and seen the Panathenaic
procession, which conveys the beautiful cloak of Athena
to the Acropolis. They drink Greek wines, and, like the
Athenian contemporaries of Hyperides and Lynceus of
Samos, they are partial to fish. They take part in banquets ἀπὸ συμβολῶν. They reckon in drachmae and oboli.
They use Spartan keys and dwell in houses that are ornamented with paintings after the fashion of Hellenistic
times. At their doors they address Apollo Agyieus.
They are ephebi, quartered at the Piraeus. They have
on the tip of their tongue such official titles as agoranomoi, generals, demarchs, comarchs, tyrants, satraps.
They recognise the privilege of sanctuary for guilty or
ill-treated slaves. They purify their children five days
after they are born. Their family relations vary in
many particulars from those which obtained among the

fellow-countrymen of Cato. As for the life of pleasure which many of them lead, Plautus was the very first to designate it by the words *congraecare, pergraecari*. Indeed, the scandals and the gallant exploits which are frequent occurrences in that life of pleasure, the courtesans, procurers, parasites, culinary artists, who ordinarily play a part in it, must have been almost unknown at Rome during the first decades of the second century before Christ. The same applies to the bragging soldier and to the flattering slave whom some ancient Latin commentators criticise in Terence as a fantastic creation. Even a most cursory reading of the *palliatae* makes clear the existence of manifestly exotic features at every turn. This is so often the case that the poets themselves occasionally seek to explain it and to apologise for it. At the beginning of the *Phormio*, Terence lets Geta explain a point of Attic law : "There exists a law which permits any orphan girl to marry her nearest relative, and which also insists that the nearest relative should marry her." [1] "Do not be surprised," says Stichus in the play that bears his name, " if poor slaves amuse themselves with drink, make love, and invite one another to supper; at Athens we are permitted to do so ! " [2]

Granted the facts which I have established in the preceding paragraphs—Plautus' indifference to local colour, Terence's timidity regarding certain details that are too manifestly foreign—there can hardly be any doubt as to the source of those elements which bear the Hellenic stamp. With very rare exceptions they must come directly from the models which the Latins copied. They belong, therefore, to our inquiry just as much as if we had found them in the original works, and it is not only, as one might think at first sight, the chapters that have to do with habits and adventures which they will help us to enrich. In order, however, to distinguish in the works of the comic writers between their portrayal of society and that which reflects emotions and character, some effort of analysis

[1] *Phorm.*, 125–126. [2] *Stich.*, 446–448. Cf. *Cas.*, prol. 67 et seq.

is required. As a matter of fact, the same sentences, the same words that make clear a given stage setting, that refer to a local custom, a passing fashion, a peculiarity of the social or political organism, frequently also possess an interest from the point of view of psychology. In one play a man who goes *to the Piraeus* to learn whether any ship has arrived *from Ephesus*, is a father on whom time hangs heavy in the absence of his child.[1] Another man who boasts of having gone *to Asia* in his youth and of having made his fortune *as a mercenary*, refers to his exploits in order to humiliate his idle son.[2] A slave, standing *before the façade of a Greek house*, invites his old master to admire its painted decorations, thereby showing how impertinent he is, as these decorations do not exist.[3] A youth goes up *to Athens from the Piraeus, where he is in garrison ;* we see him rush in, furious, because a friend of his family, the worthy *Archidemides*, has detained him on the way, and has made him lose sight of a young woman whom he had been following. The fact is that our hero is of a particularly inflammable disposition and that he has been " struck all of a heap." [4] Another person declares, as though he were an Athenian familiar with the tragic plays, that he is torn asunder *like Pentheus rent in twain by the Bacchantes*—he is a lover who wishes by these words to convey an idea of the pangs of his love.[5] There is no need of giving further examples. At every turn we find Hellenic features combined, as we have seen, with remarks of a more general import. They guarantee the origin of the latter.

But this is not all. In addition to the fact that the abundance of exotic detail in Plautus and in Terence gives promise of an ample collection of trustworthy material, it justifies us in believing that these authors did not, as a rule, make any alterations in their models. If, in portraying their characters, they respected traits that might possibly disconcert their audience, there was even more

---

[1] *Bacch.*, 285 et seq.   [2] *Heaut.*, 110 et seq.   [3] *Most.*, 832 et seq.
[4] *Eun.*, 289 et seq.   [5] *Merc.*, 469.

reason why they should allow that to stand which partook of the nature of a lasting and universal truth and which had an interest that was not only Greek, but also human.

And yet we must here differentiate between the two poets. It would seem that Plautus, much like the Roman public of his day, had little taste for psychological refinements and for outbursts of sentiment. He himself informs us that in the *Casina* he left out the rôle of the youthful lover;[1] while in the *Asinaria*, the *Aulularia* and possibly other plays as well, he must have cut down his part. " Contamination "—that is to say, the combining in one and the same work passages borrowed from several originals—was practised by him with all the brutality of an author whose one desire was to lend variety and life to the performance. The *Stichus* is an example of this method. The opening scenes give promise of a charming character comedy; but Plautus soon got tired of a subject that was no doubt too calm for him. He neglects Pinacium and Panegyris, who have both wit and heart, and introduces Gelasimus, who is merely full of spirit. Then he neglects Gelasimus and introduces merry slaves who drink and bawl and cut capers. Elsewhere also his characters play the buffoon at the most solemn moments and in a most unnatural way. Or else, conflicts of emotion which alone can account for the behaviour of an actor are merely hinted at. It would be surprising if an author who so often scorned to portray passion and character had, at other times, of his own accord taken pains to do so. If Plautus ever did anything beyond inventing the language of his plays, it would be to conceive some comical or fantastic episode; his inventions were certainly not in the domain of psychology. We shall not go far astray if we trace back to Greek works all the pathetic passages, the ingenious observations and delicate analyses that occur in his plays.

As for Terence, the question is quite different. He likewise practised " contamination," but with great

[1] *Cas.*, prol. 64–68.

skill, and apparently without omitting anything that in his model was devoted either to psychological description or to the portrayal of sentiment. Varro praised him for this : *in ethesin poscit palmam*.[1] Moreover, we know from the commentary of Donatus that he occasionally retouched Menander's or Apollodorus' characters with a view to making them more perfect. Thus, it appears that in the *Phormio* he cut out a wish that was too ingenuously selfish.[2] In another place he gave more space to the parasite's profession of faith than Apollodorus had given it.[3] When Geta interprets Demipho's thoughts for him, in order the more readily to allay his distrust, the poet attributes a remark to him which, in the original, was made by Demipho himself.[4] In the *Andria* he transforms a cold and didactic speech addressed by Davus to Mysis into a question which meant the same thing, but conveyed a greater sense of urgency.[5] When the father of the family thinks that he is being deceived by his son, Terence represents him as being more unhappy than he is in Menander's play.[6] In the *Adelphi* Demea does not even answer the greeting of Micio when he comes upon the stage. Donatus declares that this is a bit of rudeness which was not to be found in the original.[7] Further on, it is said that if Ctesipho had not been allowed to have his music girl, he would have gone into exile; in the Ἀδελφοί he contemplated suicide.[8] When, towards the end of the play, an attempt is made to induce Micio to marry the aged Sostrata, Micio rebels, as he naturally would; in Menander's play he apparently bore his fate willingly, or at least did not offer so much resistance.[9] Did Terence, then, invent so much, add or suppress so much in the process of drawing

---

[1] *Nonius Marcellus*, p. 374 M.; Menipp., 399 Büch.
[2] Or was it an inconsiderate wish ? Donatus' note to line 482 can be interpreted either way.
[3] Donat., note to line 339.
[4] *Ibid.*, note to line 647.
[5] *Ibid.*, note to line 791.
[6] *Ibid.*, note to line 891.
[7] *Ibid.*, note to line 81.
[8] *Ibid.*, note to line 275.
[9] *Ibid.*, note to line 938.

E

his characters that we need have constant scruples when we quote him? The changes indicated by Donatus are not of great consequence, and it is hard to understand why they should have been thought worthy of special mention if many others of greater importance had existed. Donatus—or the authors upon whom he relied—must have pointed out only such of them as constituted something exceptional in the works of Terence. As for Varro's remark, it does not necessarily allude to a gift of independent observation and creation. What it meant to convey is, no doubt, that Terence, when compared with Plautus, Caecilius and the other writers of the *palliata*, reproduced the subtlety of the Hellenic models with greater fidelity.

In a word, we may make use of almost all the Latin plays in studying the *subject matter* of the New Comedy.

The same remark applies to the *Dialogues of the Courtesans*, if we can trust the following remark of a scholiast : Ἰστέον ὡς αὗται πᾶσαι αἱ ἑταῖραι κεκωμῴδηνται καὶ πᾶσι μὲν τοῖς κωμῳδιοποιοῖς, μάλιστα δὲ Μενάνδρῳ, ἀφ᾽ οὗ καὶ πᾶσα αὕτη ἡ ὕλη Λουκιανῷ τῷ προκειμένῳ εὐπόρηται. Elsewhere I have attempted to establish by analysis and detailed comparison how much truth there is in what the scholiast says.[1] It will suffice here to state the conclusion reached in that preliminary study. Very many elements of the *Dialogues*—such as personal characteristics of the persons referred to, details of their adventures —can be traced with more or less certainty to extant comedies. On the other hand, those which, for some distinct reason, appear to run counter to the taste of the comic writers are very rare. Thus statistics are favourable to the scholiast, and incline us to the belief that he was not guilty of much exaggeration; and when we come to elements of which the source is uncertain and whose relations to comedy are in no wise determinable, and yet

[1] *Les Dialogues des Courtisanes comparés avec la Comédie*, in the *Rev. Êt. Gr.*, XX. (1907), pp. 176–231; XXI. (1908), pp. 39–79.

cannot be positively disproved, these statistics lead to the belief that they are borrowed from the νέα. Although this evidence, considered in relation to each specific case, lacks definiteness, and although it does not force us to any logical conclusion, it none the less deserves to be collected.

As for the *Epistles* of Alciphron, their dependence upon comedy was doubtless neither as constant nor as close as was that of the *Dialogues of the Courtesans*. No one claims that their entire contents were borrowed from the comic stage. As a matter of fact, they contain only a few details whose equivalents in the comic poets are known to us on good authority, and several of these may have found their way there *via* Lucian.[1] An examination of the whole of them results in complete, or almost complete, uncertainty as to the source of the component parts, and it is necessary to conjecture the probabilities for each of these component parts separately.

Enough has been said to explain—and I hope also to justify—my attitude toward our chief sources of information. My reasons for occasionally making use of some documents borrowed from other writers will be made clear when occasion offers.

---

[1] *Rev. Ét. Gr.*, XX. (1907), pp. 177–181.

CHAPTER III

THE DRAMATIS PERSONAE

THE *dramatis personae* of the comic stage first claim our attention, and in the chapter which I devote to them we shall pass from their superficial and general features to their most intimate and special ones.

§ 1.

FOREIGNERS—RUSTICS

During the period of New Comedy—as in the preceding one—the titles of many plays were taken from a race (*'Ανδρία, Βοιωτίς*, etc.). Furthermore, in the works of which the Latin comedy has preserved a copy, foreigners appear quite frequently on the stage : a pander recently come from abroad, a merchant summoned by his affairs, a soldier on leave, a bourgeois on a business trip, a person in search of a relative, etc. Or else the scene itself is placed in a foreign country. Thus the comic writers had ample opportunity to introduce national characteristics. Let us examine to what extent they did so.

This examination will occasion us some disappointment. In the first place, we shall discover that the plots whose scene is laid in foreign parts are not as frequent as is generally supposed. It is a mistake to claim for Attica alone all the notable works of the *νέα* or even all the works of the principal comic writers. The originals of the *Captivi* and the *Poenulus*, whose plots are placed in Aetolia, were perhaps performed at Pleuron or at Calydon; that of the *Cistellaria*, in which Sicyon is the place of action, at Sicyon itself; the original of the *Curculio*, which has the sanctuary of Epidaurus as its setting, may have been performed in the famous theatre of Polycleitus; and so on. Consequently the Aetolians, Sicyonians, or Epidaurians of these various plays were by no means strangers to the audience, and the poet—if he was not himself from Aetolia, Sicyon, or Epidaurus—would have wasted his efforts had he brought into relief their national peculiarities.

Let us now turn to the comedies the plots of which really were laid elsewhere than in the town in which they were performed. As far as we know, it appears that the choice of a foreign setting was often forced upon the poets, or at least that it often appeared advisable to them, for reasons that had nothing to do with a desire to depict an exotic society. This is clearly the case in the plays which dealt with a legendary subject, where the place of action was in each instance fixed by tradition. Furthermore, in plays of pure imagination a foreign setting appears to be the necessary corollary of certain features of the story. It has been maintained that such and such a plot is placed outside Athens in order to humour Athenian respectability, because among the characters is found the harbourer of a stolen child, and that the Athenian public would not permit so vile a person to remain at Athens. This hypothesis seems somewhat risky. The following are simpler and safer examples of dependence on the nature of the story which I desire to point out. In the *Miles*, where a lover goes in pursuit of his mistress who has been taken away from him, the scene cannot be laid at Athens because the young lover is an Athenian. Similarly, when the play contains a person who has been stolen in his infancy and who at the close of the play is to be the object of an *anagnorisis*, it is quite natural that the action should take place far away from the country of his birth, and if this person is represented as being a fellow-countryman of the audience, the scene of the action would be placed in what was for them a foreign country, as is the case in the *Rudens*. It is clear that under such circumstances, though the poets chose some country other than their own for the scene of their dramas, they had no intention of tying themselves down to a study of local colour.

It may be that one or the other of the plays of which the title was the name of a race in the plural, carried the audience into the land of that race, on the track of some traveller, and that it entertained them by the portrayal of foreign customs. None the less, the fragments which strictly conform to such an hypothesis are very few in number, and they are fragments of Antiphanes, Timocles, Clearchus and Xenarchus—that is to say, poets of the μέση. It is also in the works of the representatives of the μέση that we occasionally find reminiscences of travel, chiefly gastronomic reminiscences, and it is possibly from these that Alciphron drew his inspiration when he wrote *Epistles* III, 15, and III, 24, in which parasites, back from Corinth, tell of their misadventures. Among the fragments that certainly belong to the νέα a fragment of Diphilus— fragment 32 of the Ἔμπορος—is about the only one of this kind that I can cite, and here, too, the scene is at Corinth. A Corinthian explains to a stranger who is passing through the town—in all probability to the ἔμπορος—how in his country they watch the epicures who spend too much money, and investigate whence they get their income.

In a word, the extant plays of the νέα contain very few descriptions of exotic surroundings, and it is upon individual types of foreigners that we are obliged to fall back.

Here, again, the hopes that one entertains at first are not fully realised. Terence's *Andria*, an imitation of Menander's Ἀνδρία, is a striking example of the fact that race titles do not of themselves afford any sure information; for the " Andrian woman " does not even appear in it. In the Σαμία, the Samian woman Chrysis does appear and she plays an important part; but her behaviour, her attitude, her words, are exactly the same as though she were a native of Attica. Many characters of the repertory who were represented as foreigners must have been portrayed as such simply for reasons of dramatic fitness or from an excess of national pride. To the former category belong the parents in search of a child that has disappeared, like Hanno in the *Poenulus*, and the young girls whom worthy citizens are to recognise as their daughters after

long years of separation—like Phanium in the *Phormio*,
or the woman who is supposed to have come from Andros;
or the persons who appear towards the end of a play in
order to bring about a recognition. Had Hanno and his
daughters, Phanium and her father Crito, or Glycerium
and Chremes always lived in the same town, their meeting
and *anagnorisis* might very readily have taken place
sooner, and the initial situation would have been devoid
of probability. Similarly, if the donkey-seller in the
Asinaria had been an Athenian, there would be less
chance of his not knowing Saurea; so he, too, comes
from foreign parts, from the land of the horse-dealers,
Thessaly. Had Dordalus in the *Persa*, or Lycus in the
Poenulus, for a long time been neighbours of Toxilus and
Agorastocles, they would no doubt have known Sagaristio,
the intimate of Toxilus, and Collybius, Agorastocles'
bailiff. So Dordalus is supposed to have come recently
from Megara to Athens, and Lycus from Anactorium to
Calydon. On the other hand, it is disagreeable for an
audience composed of self-respecting men to recognise
pimps, procuresses, and courtesans, or even concubines
and blustering soldiers, as their fellow-countrymen. That
difficulty is easily overcome : blustering soldiers, concubines, courtesans, procuresses and pimps are labelled
" foreigners."

However, there can have been nothing foreign about
most of the various characters I have just enumerated, beyond the label. Hanno of the *Poenulus*, and
the pretended Persians of the *Persa*, are the only ones
among the *dramatis personae* of Plautus and Terence
upon whose nationality the poets laid stress. And even
here they do not put themselves to any great psychological strain. What serves to make Sagaristio and his
companion funny is merely their oriental dress and the
high-sounding burlesque names with which Sagaristio
beplumes himself. What is meant to characterise Hanno
is, in the first place, his general appearance, the colour
of his skin and his costume, and then the jargon which

he uses. The Greek poets appear to have been quite familiar with the use of these two devices. Some of the extant fragments mention either physical defects that were said to be common among certain races,[1] or articles of raiment, peculiarities of dress that were characteristic of one country or another.[2] It is probable that both the former and the latter were displayed to the audience. In two lines of Menander's Σικυώνιος one of the actors admits that the σχῆμα of a foreigner—by this I think he means his attire—exposes a man to unpleasant remarks;[3] and in all likelihood something of the sort happened to him in the course of the play. Other fragments—especially those of the middle period—give us glimpses of actors who speak a dialect.[4] Or else some one uses words or idioms that are not Attic and the persons to whom he speaks reprove him for them;[5] thereupon the foreigner offers an explanation or sometimes gets angry. In one of Posidippus' plays a Thessalian protests against the Athenians for claiming that they alone speak true Greek.[6] In the " Coislin Treatise," in which a few bits of Aristotle's theories appear to be preserved, we read that the writer of comedies ought to make his actors speak his own language—δεῖ τὸν κωμῳδοποιὸν τὴν πάτριον αὐτοῦ γλῶσσαν τοῖς προσώποις περιτιθέναι; and then come the words τὴν δὲ ἐπιχώριον αὐτῷ ἐκείνῳ, which should probably be emended to αὐτῷ τῷ ξένῳ, or to ἑκάστου τῷ ξένῳ. The exception thus made would lead us to believe that in Aristotle's time it was not uncommon for actors to use a dialect. But the νέα did not attain its full development in Aristotle's time.

In addition to their dress and speech, what comedy

[1] Apollod. *Car.*; fr. 12; fr. adesp., 866.
[2] Antiph., fr. 91. The τρίβωνες of the Lacedaemonians and their huge beards appear for a long time to have amused the audience; cf. Meineke, *Historia critica*, p. 486.
[3] Men., fr. 439.
[4] Eubulus, fr. 12; Alexis, fr. 142; Euphron, fr. 3; fr. adesp., 283, 677.
[5] Alexis, fr. 143; Xenarchus, fr. 11; Diphilus, fr. 47.
[6] Posid., fr. 28.

appears most frequently to have noticed in foreigners was their ignorance of good manners, and in particular of good manners at table, of the refinements of cooking and of the usages of polite society. The fragments of the middle period are full of allusions to the gluttony and dullness of the Boeotians, to excesses of every kind committed by Sicilians, Thessalians and Corinthians, and to the exaggerated frugality of the Spartans. The same themes continued, from time to time, to inspire the authors of the subsequent period.[1] Menander himself was not above sneering at the Boeotian " asses' jaw-bones." [2]

According to one of Diphilus' actors, the Rhodians prefer wine in which a shad has been cooked to perfumed wine; the inhabitants of Byzantium insist upon having all their food salted and seasoned with garlic or sprinkled with wormwood.[3] Elsewhere some one or other, possibly a courtesan, initiates a barbarian in the art of drinking.[4] In a fragment by Lynceus, a native of Perinthus, who has been invited to Athens by a Rhodian, forbids the cook, in his own name and in that of his host, to serve a whole lot of little dishes, after the Athenian fashion. He wishes to have good big portions of food to which every one can help himself after his own fashion.[5] In Phoenicides, a Samian sneers at Attic dainties, such as myrtle berries, honey and figs, and declares that all these things are not worth a partridge such as he gets at home.

We might glean still more malicious remarks about one race or another from the comic fragments, but all of them, as is the case in the Latin comedy writers, were, I believe, merely cursory remarks; sometimes, indeed, they were mere figures of speech. It must have been very rarely that an actor by his behaviour on the stage proved the correctness of what people said about his compatriots.

* * *

Next to the true foreigners we must place those other persons who, to the eyes of the poets and to those of a

---

[1] Philem., fr. 76; Diph., fr. 22, 96, 119; Men., fr. 462; Eudoxus, fr. 2.
[2] Men., fr. 011.   [3] Diph., fr. 17.   [4] *Ibid.*, fr. 20.   [5] Lync., fr. 1.

good part of their audience, must have appeared as semi-
foreigners—the rustics. In the fourth and third centuries, the towns of Greece had not yet become big cities,
but several of them, and above all others, Athens, had
developed a city life which was distinctly different from
life in the country. Indeed, many of the middle-class
folk who appeared on the stage were landed proprietors
and lived alternately in the country and in the city,
so that there was no reason why they should not feel at
home in both places. But others, like the good Cleaenetus
of the Γεωργός, or like Demea of the *Adelphi*, lived in the
country only. The same applies in an even stricter
sense to the slaves who were engaged in the various
branches of agriculture. The titles of several lost comedies—most of them of the middle period—apparently
foreshadow a portrayal of these true rustics; especially
the title Ἄγροικος (or Ἄγροικοι), which occurs several
times, beginning with the age of Antiphanes; then other
titles, such as Ἀμπελουργός, Κηπουρός, Αἰπόλοι, Προβατεύς,
Γεωργός; or titles that are names of demes : Θορίκιοι,
Φρεάρριοι, Ἐπιτροπεύς, Ἁλαιεῖς. I shall endeavour to trace
the characteristics of these rustic figures.

Nearly everything that is to be known about the rustics
of comedy can be found in Ribbeck's book *Agroikos*,[1]
but we must use it with discrimination. For Ribbeck
does not confine his researches to the characters in comedy,
much less to those of the νέα only. Moreover, the type
which he studies does not coincide exactly with that of
the peasant. The ἄγροικοι of former times did not all
lead a *rural* life any more than those we now call *rustic*
or boorish. Accordingly, by no means all the evidence
of which Ribbeck made use is within the scope of my
investigations. If I merely retain such part of it as belongs to my subject, what may be said is as follows.

The comic writers primarily noticed, and by preference
pointed out, the quite superficial shortcomings of the

[1] *Agroikos, eine ethnologische Studie* in the *Abhandlungen der k. sächsischen
Gesellschaft der Wissenschaften*, Vol. X. (1885).

peasant, just as they did those of the foreigner : slovenly
dress, vulgar speech, ignorance of polite conventions and
of the sights of the city, lack of appreciation of the elegan-
cies of life. The country folk came upon the stage dressed
in goatskins.[1] Grumio, in the *Mostellaria*, and the young
man who treats Mousarion with scorn, in Lucian's seventh
dialogue, smell ill.[2] Stratylax, in the *Truculentus*, turns
up his nose at Astaphium's neat and dainty attire, her
rouge and her perfumes, and declares that he would rather
sleep with his oxen than with her;[3] his speech is careless
and he mangles his words;[4] he is a noisy and abusive
fellow;[5] his young master Strabax, the youth "with the
iron teeth,"[6] ill-kempt and dirty,[7] himself confesses that
he is a *stultus*.[8] Tired of waiting for his lady-love in a
bed in which he grows numb, he goes to fetch her without
ceremony, and, indifferent to her pretty ways, he does not
even try to hide his impatience to be doing something
more decisive.[9] Several of Alciphron's *Rustic Epistles*
are written by men who have never seen anything;[10]
and possibly the author derived this idea from comedy.
But one thing must be said: among the extant comic
fragments, those which it is most worth while to quote
here belong to the middle period. In the Ἀγροικοι by
Anaxandrides, one of the *dramatis personae* admits his
astonishment at sight of a well-set table.[11] Other peasants
in Antiphanes, clinging to their own ways, refuse to eat
of a big fish because they say that big fish are all man-
eaters.[12] In the works of the new period we do not meet
with rustics who display such simplicity. In the *Casina*,
Olympio is competent to go to market, to hire a cook,
to buy a fish. Syriscus, in the Ἐπιτρέποντες, is quite
accustomed to go to town.

---

[1] Varro, *De re rust.*, II. 11, 11. Cf. Ἐπιτρ., 12–13; Alc., III. 34.
[2] *Most.*, 39–41; Luc., *Dial. Mer.*, VII. 3.
[3] *Truc.*, 270 et seq., 276–279, 289 et seq. Cf. Alc., II. 8.
[4] *Ibid.*, 683, 688; cf. 262.
[5] *Ibid.*, 256 et seq., 268, 269, 286 et seq., etc.
[6] *Ibid.*, 943.   [7] *Ibid.*, 933.   [8] *Ibid.*, 922.   [9] *Ibid.*, 914 et seq.
[10] Alc., II. 17, 28, 37.   [11] Anax., fr. 2.   [12] Antiph., fr. 68, 129.

The rustic, as he appears in comedy, is not only rude, an ill-mannered table-companion and a scorner of refinements. As a rule his sensibility is blunted, he is dull-witted, lazy and narrow-minded. The range of pleasures that appeal to him is extremely limited,[1] and very few things affect him. Politics do not interest him.[2] To his mind glory is a mere castle in the air.[3] As for intellect and culture, he regards them as frivolous luxuries; philosophers appear to him as good-for-nothings, engaged in idle discussions.[4] Boutalio, the type of the ἄγροικος in a play by Antiphanes, was at the same time a model of stupidity.[5] In the *Casina*, Olympio has difficulty in replying to the slave Chalinus during their dispute; he allows himself to be interrupted, loses his head, and forthwith indulges in the most terrible threats.[6] His dull imagination laboriously invents complicated torments which he takes satisfaction in enumerating;[7] he has no sense of the ridiculous, and although he knows the special circumstances under which his marriage is to take place he struts about boastfully, dressed in white and with a wreath on his head.[8] Ctesipho, in the *Adelphi*, lacks initiative, courage and cleverness. The excellent Cleaenetus, of the Γεωργός, who, when occasion offers, gives wise counsels, accompanies them with this touching admission:[9] "I am a peasant, I cannot deny it, and I have not much experience in city affairs."

A characteristic which the writers of comedy appear to have taken pleasure in pointing out is the difficulty the rustics had in expressing their thoughts, and their ignorance of the refinements of speech. "I am a peasant," says one of the actors, "and I call things by their name."[10] In the Ἐπιτρέποντες, Daos does not trust his ears when he discovers that the charcoal-burner Syriscus is a good talker. He himself can place but a very meagre eloquence

---

[1] Arist., *Eth. Eudem.*, p. 1230 B. Cf. *Eth. Nicom.*, p. 1104 A.
[2] Fr. adesp., 347.   [3] Alc., II. 13.
[4] Philem., fr. 71; cf. Alc., II. 11, 38.   [5] Schol., Aristoph., *Frogs*, 990.
[6] *Cas.*, 389–391.   [7] *Ibid.*, 120 et seq.   [8] *Ibid.*, 767–768.
[9] Men. fr. 97.   [10] Fr. adesp., 227.

at the service of his rascality; nervous before the beginning of the discussion, upset after its conclusion, he stupidly repeats over and over again the same useless complaints.[1] When Alciphron insinuates that a rustic who is eloquent and can understand a joke is a very rare curiosity, he shares the view of the comic writers.[2]

Often twitted about his clumsiness and his dullness of wit, the man from the country occasionally pretends to disdain the skill which he does not possess; as Grumio does, when he reproaches the citizen Tranio for his cleverness and voluble speech. At other times the recognition of his own inferiority makes him sensitive and irritable. "Impudent woman," Stratylax cries out to Astaphium, " in order to make fun of a man from the country you invite him to a debauch."[3] Indeed, distrust in all its manifestations and the fear of being cheated seem to be peculiar to the rustic; witness Olympio's attitude in the scene of the drawing of lots,[4] or that of Chremes in the *Eunuchus*, towards the advances of Thais and the civilities of Pythias,[5] or that of Strabax who will not part with his bag.[6]

In connection with this distrust I may mention two other characteristics which Ribbeck points out in his *Agroikos* : superstition—that is to say, fear of the supernatural—and stinginess, which is often fear with regard to the future. We have no proof that the comic writers portrayed the peasant as being especially superstitious. On the other hand, original fragments and imitations repeatedly denounce the excessive stinginess of the rustic. In Antiphanes, a peasant, when asked to choose the meat of which he is to partake, at once excludes that of animals which produce something, such as

---

[1] 'Επιτρ., 19; 5 and 20; 141, 144 and 155.
[2] Alc., II. 26; III. 34.   [3] *Truc.*, 263.
[4] *Cas.*, 384–385, 387, 395. The suspicion expressed in lines 379–380, which Leo's edition attributes to Chalinus, would, it seems to me, be more naturally expressed by Olympio, for it is Chalinus who had gone to fetch the *sitella* and everything that was required for drawing lots.
[5] *Eun.*, 507 et seq.; 532 et seq.   [6] *Truc.*, 956, 960.

wool or cheese.[1] Strabax's father, who is a peasant, has accumulated his wealth through saving and privations (*parsimonia duritiaque*),[2] Demea, in the *Adelphi*, lives in the country *parce ac duriter*.[3] In a fragment of Titinius we read : " The man of the fields is exactly like an ant." [4]

The characteristics which we have thus far noted do not make a very sympathetic person of the peasant in comedy, but his shortcomings and his absurdities are not without their compensation. Generally speaking, it seems as though there were more honesty in the country than elsewhere. This is above all noticeable among the slaves, and especially so when a rustic slave is compared with a city slave. The crabbed Stratylax is very much attached to his old master, and is very careful of the household property. So is Grumio, who is full of wrath at the scandalous conduct of Tranio—a wrath which even succeeds in loosening his tongue. Even the absurd Olympio has a real sense of duty,[5] and he speaks of a *fugitivus*, of a *litteratus*, with all the signs of a virtuous indignation.[6] This same Olympio, in line 418—if indeed he is serious in what he says—manifests an ingenuous confidence in the justice of fate.[7]

A similar sentiment is repeatedly expressed by Grumio,[8] and it contrasts with the scepticism of the person with whom he is talking.[9] Syriscus, in the Ἐπιτρέποντες— side by side with him, however, Daos stands for rustic rascality—declares that it is every one's duty to secure, as far as he is able, the triumph of justice; he is charitable and unselfish. From the slaves, shall we pass to the free men ? Like Grumio, Cleaenetus relies on distributive justice,[10] and personally he practises it under the guise of gratitude. He is, besides, a sensible man and has a gentle heart. This character alone would suffice to prove that comedy was not obstinately unjust to the

---

[1] Antiph., fr. 20. [2] *Truc.*, 310–311. [3] *Ad.*, 45; cf. 866; Men., fr. 10.
[4] *Fullonia*, fr. XIII. [5] *Cas.*, 104–105. [6] *Ibid.*, 397, 401.
[7] *Most.*, 18–19, 55–57, 59, 70. [8] *Ibid.*, 18–19, 55–57, 59, 70.
[9] *Ibid.*, 58. [10] Men., fr. 94.

ἄγροικοι. Without indulging in the illusions of the idyll
or of the pastoral romance, it recognised their good qualities and gave them praise more frequently than one would
think at first sight. It is undeniable that the poets did
not intend to condemn everything in the hard, rough life
led by Demea and the grandfather of Charinus [1]—that
life for which the country affords, so to speak, the
necessary setting.

Indeed, comedy did not fail now and again to point
out some eccentricity or vice of the townspeople. Stratylax, after his conversion (which I believe was only feigned),
ironically sums up under two heads what he has learned
in the city : to enjoy himself with a courtesan [2] and to
humbug.[3] Other characters besides the " grumblers "
found fault with the lack of vigour, the τρυφή, of the
city; and among them were some who, to judge by their
attitude, seem to have played the part of " wise men " :
Parmeno, of the Πλόκιον,[4] and some actor in the Ὑδρία.[5]
It is in the city that comedy places the idlers, the in-
defatigable talkers, the newsmongers, who are sharply
dealt with at the beginning of the Trinummus, the indiscreet fellows who interfere with other people's business.[6]
It is the city that generally supplies the pettifoggers and
intriguers, the men who will do anything for a bit of money,
the flatterers and parasites. When Alciphron contrasts
the people—evidently city people—who earn a dishonest
livelihood in the agora and in the courts,[7] with the
honest peasant (γεωργὸς ἀπράγμων καὶ ἐργάτης), he must
be following the example of comedy.

§ 2.

POOR AND RICH—SYCOPHANTS AND PARASITES

Notwithstanding the reforms which Antipater and
Demetrius had introduced in the constitution of Athens,

---

[1] Men., 61 et seq.   [2] Truc., 678.   [3] Ibid., 683.
[4] Men., fr. 405.   [5] Ibid., fr. 466.
[6] Trin., 202.   [7] Alc., III. 34.

the society in which the majority of the writers of the *νέα* lived was a democratic society. We must, therefore, not expect to find among their *dramatis personae* differences of caste for which the actual surroundings did not afford a pattern. Nevertheless, a few fragments protest against the pride of birth.[1] Several others, especially in the middle period, allude to the arrogance of certain high officials, particularly the generals, and to the deference the common people showed them.[2] It may be that this arrogance and this abject deference were represented on the stage. But this is not the case in the extant parts of the plays. The only social difference which is there expressed and references to which are worth studying is that between the poor and the rich.

It is to be noted that the rich people who appear on the stage have, as a rule, no especial marks to distinguish them as such. And there is good reason for this. In the first place, most of them are not really rich. If one pays attention to the sums that are mentioned, to the positive statements, one will find that many a good bourgeois whose wealth is supposed to be inexhaustible—according to the statement of his son or his slave—has barely more than is required for a comfortable existence. Chremes, in the *Heauton Timoroumenos*, calculates that he ought to have two talents[3] as dower;[4] and the whole estate of his godfather does not amount to more than fifteen talents.[5] Pataecus, in the *Περικειρομένη*, gives Glycera a dower of three talents.[6] Demipho, in the *Phormio*, regards the loss of a talent as an insupportable disaster.[7] In the estate of his brother, the best part of the fortune of his dowered wife Nausistrata consists apparently of her properties in Lemnos; but these properties, at the time when they were best administered, yielded two talents

---

[1] Men., fr. 290, 533.
[2] Amphis, fr. 30; Alexis, fr. 16, 25, 116, 303; *Oxyrh. Pap.*, Vol. I. No. 11.
[3] An Attic talent was worth about $1000.—(Tr.).
[4] *Heaut.*, 940.   [5] *Ibid.*, 145.   [6] Περικ., 354.   [7] *Phorm.*, 644.

at the very most; [1] and even this statement is not above suspicion, for it is Nausistrata herself who makes it. The plutocrat, the πλούταξ, the man who rolls in wealth, is a character to whom occasional reference is made in Latin plays and in the original fragments : for instance, the Ionian plutocrat (Ἰωνικὸς πλούταξ) whom a cook, in Menander, names among the chief types of banqueters; [2] Theotimus of Miletus, and the Elian Thensaurochrysoni-cochrysides—both of them fictitious persons—of whom Chrysalus (in the *Bacchides*) and Philocrates (in the *Captivi*) relate marvellous things.[3] But these plutocrats remain behind the scenes. If others of the same kind came upon the stage to speak and act before the audience, we know absolutely nothing about the part they played.

Nor are we much better informed about another kind of rich man who is one of the most entertaining varieties —the newly rich. That he did not escape the attention of the comic writers is attested clearly enough by a number of fragments. One of Philippides' characters makes fun of the rascals (μαστιγίαι) who, after making a fortune, have the coarse food for which they retain a preference served on costly platters.[4] In a passage of the Κόλαξ, some one reminds a *parvenu* of his former—quite recent— poverty: "Man, last year you were a beggar, a corpse; to-day you are rich." [5] Elsewhere a certain Stratophanes is apostrophised, who formerly possessed naught but a wretched cloak and a single slave.[6] The remarks contained in fragments 252, 323, 587, and 665 of Menander, and in the fragment *adespoton* 487, must have been about νεόπλουτοι. Latin comedy does not supply any detailed descriptions to supplement this meagre information. Several characters in Plautus and in Terence, like Menedemus in the *Heauton Timoroumenos* and Demipho in the *Mercator*, have made their own fortunes, but long

---

[1] *Phorm.*, 789.
[2] Men., fr. 462.
[3] *Bacch.*, 332; *Capt.*, 277 et seq.
[4] Philippides, fr. 9.
[5] Men., fr. 731 = Κολ., 49–50. Cf. fr. 294 = Κολ., 42–44.
[6] *Ibid.*, fr. 442.

F

enough ago to allow of their having become accustomed to their estate; and they show no signs of being *parvenus*.

The exclusion of the πλούταξ and of the νεόπλουτος deprives us of those varieties of rich men whose portrayal would have been most interesting, for it is in them that vanity and the love of display are most apparent. In their absence, representation of this type is rare in the extant remains of the νέα. To the fragments already quoted from Menander and Philippides we can add but a very few other passages, in which the rich man referred to is some braggart soldier.[1]

The display of wealth is merely ridiculous. But now and again, in the fragments and imitations, more serious shortcomings are laid at the door of the rich. They are said to be haughty, tyrannical, hard and unjust towards the poor; they think of nothing but money, and money is the only criterion by which they judge men and things. Did the poets themselves share this view? We have no means of knowing, but we can affirm that nothing or nearly nothing in the words and behaviour of the " bourgeois " who appear in the plays warrants so severe a judgment.

Doubtless Demipho, in the *Phormio*, and Aeschinus, in the *Adelphi*, believe that in paying—the former, the price of the woman he carries off, and the latter, the dower for the daughter-in-law whom he intends dismissing— they are doing all that can reasonably be expected of them, and that a few coins handed over with a bad grace ought to suffice to silence their opponents.[2] But in justice to them we must consider who their opponents are. Aeschinus is opposed by Sannio, a pander; Demipho by Phormio, the sycophant, and the old man thinks that Phanium is the latter's intriguing accomplice—a mistake which cleverer people than he might have made. " Humble " folk of this sort surely do not deserve more gentle treatment and consideration than the fawning

---

[1] *Miles*, 1063–1064; *Eun.*, 468, 471.
[2] *Phorm.*, 407 et seq.; *Ad.*, 191 et seq.

sycophants who, in comedy, often afford diversion to the capricious and idle rich; to ill-treat them is a venial offence. But there is another grievance. Philto, in the *Trinummus*, speaks of the poor with a hard-heartedness which will, no doubt, be regarded as revolting : " To give drink and food to a beggar is to do him a bad service. What one gives him is lost and one merely prolongs his life in misery." [1] But, very probably, Philto exaggerates in order to warn his son Lysiteles against an excess of sensibility; and in practice he takes care not to push this theory to extremes. Indeed, in one of the following scenes, in the absence of Lysiteles, he speaks about the rich and the poor in quite a different manner and without a trace of hard-heartedness. So we ought not to blame Philto too severely for a few unfortunate words. It would also be unfair to blame Agorastocles, in the *Poenulus*, too much for the excesses of speech in which he indulges in addressing the *advocati*.[2] It is the impatience of a lover and not the arrogance of a rich man that inspires his too sharp reproaches. In a fragment of Menander's Κυβερνῆται a poor man harshly reproaches a youth for despising the poor; [3] but we have no means of knowing the occasion for this reprimand. The lovers in the Γεωργός and in the Πλόκιον, whatever else one may think of them,[4] never thought of insulting defenceless poverty as exemplified in their mistresses.

In the extant remains of comedy the only characters who manifest a certain insolence toward those who are not favoured by fortune are, not rich men, but the servants of rich men. Trachalio, in the *Rudens*, addresses the fishermen who are going to work in rather ungracious terms.[5] In the *Poenulus*, Milphio treats the witnesses who are hired by Agorastocles with great haughtiness,[6] and how that rascal Geta, in the new fragments of the Γεωργός, talks to poor Myrrhina![7] We must not hold

---

[1] *Trin.*, 339–340.   [2] *Poen.*, 504 et seq., 529 et seq.
[3] Men., fr. 301.   [4] *Ibid.*, fr. 94; Caecilius, *Plocium*, fr. XVIII.
[5] *Rud.*, 310–334.   [6] *Poen.*, 583 et seq.   [7] Γεωργ., 42 et seq., 59, 77 et seq.

the masters responsible for the impertinence of such knaves, for they themselves are much less spoiled by their superior advantages, and some of them are not devoid of kindness of heart. Micio, in the *Adelphi*, gives without much urging. A young man in the *Δύσκολος* declares to his father that it is the duty of the rich to make people happy.[1] A character in the *Ἁλιεῖς* affirms that the possession of wealth may make one kind to others.[2] It is only in matrimonial matters that the rich generally show a great fondness for money. Not that young suitors hesitate, whatever their fortunes or their prospects may be, to sue for the hand of a poor girl. But a father who knows that his own purse is well filled does not give a very cordial welcome to a dowerless daughter-in-law. To resign himself to such a contingency he would have to possess the easy temper of a Micio, or the generosity of Philto, one of the wise old men of the *Trinummus*. As a rule, fathers, in comedy, regard their sons' marrying women without dowers as one of the greatest calamities. Davus, in the *Andria*, knows their views on this subject, and the assurance he gives Pamphilus regarding the plans of the aged Simo is most significant : *inveniet inopem potius quam te corrumpi sinat.*[3]

All these instances show the effects of wealth on social relations. Did the writers of comedy pursue the study of these effects still further? Did they portray the rich man as effeminate, languishing, knowing nothing of the sad realities of life, and incapable of facing them, exhausted by his very good fortune? It is not to the point to state that, throughout comedy, the *bons vivants*, young and old alike, are nearly always men in comfortable circumstances; it goes without saying that poor devils have other things to do than to seek pleasure, and that other more sordid hardships preserve them from heartache. One must live first before leading an evil life.

Occasionally the relation of wealth to loose habits is pointed out in explicit terms : witness lines 109 and

[1] Men., fr. 128.   [2] *Ibid.*, fr. 19.   [3] *Andr.*, 396.

following of the *Heauton Timoroumenos* (*Nulla adeo ex re istuc fit nisi ex nimio otio . . .*). Similarly Philolaches, in the *Mostellaria*, when examining his conscience and telling of the degeneration of his morals, begins by confessing his indolence : *venit ignavia*.[1] As for more telling remarks, I find little that is worth gleaning. Young Pheidias, who is lectured in fragment 530 of Menander, is a sort of hypochondriac or *malade imaginaire*—we should call him a " neurasthenic "—whose energy has been dissipated by an uninterrupted course of good living.

Comedy shows us a number of people who are suddenly brought face to face with poverty. One of them, Clitipho of the *Heauton Timoroumenos*, seems greatly disturbed thereat. Others take it good-naturedly. Clinia and Charinus, whose allowances have been cut off by their fathers, courageously take up the trying life of commerce or of husbandry. The spendthrift Lesbonicus calmly faces the fact that he is obliged to enlist as a mercenary and sacrifices what remains of his fortune in order to give his sister as large a dower as possible. The young lover in the *Vidularia* who has been saved from a shipwreck and is cast penniless on the shores of Attica, declares that he is ready to undertake the hardest work, and says that notwithstanding his delicate appearance, his soft hands and white skin, he will cultivate the soil, as he has no choice.[2]

Such, then, are the rich men of New Comedy, as far as we have any information about them. As we have seen, they are portrayed discreetly and without much malice. Despite the proverbs which proclaim that opulence covers many faults and much disgrace, that the lustre of wealth hides faults of birth, lowness of character and other short-comings,[3] the wicked rich man is not a type in comedy.

In the works of the comic writers the poor have more marked features than the rich and appear under more

---

[1] *Most.*, 137.   [2] *Vidul.*, 31 et seq.

[3] Men., fr. 90, 404, 485; Caecilius, *Plocium*, fr. VIII.; Turpilius, *Demiurgus*, fr. II.

diverse guises. Some of them are philosophers and are
reconciled to their lot; [1] but I imagine that the poor of
this kind were few in number in comedy, just as they
are in real life. A few fragments depreciate wealth and
praise poverty—or rather a gilded competency, [2] but
probably not all of them were spoken by poor men.
Indeed, one of them appears to me to be ironical. For
most unfortunate people, poverty was " an untractable
wild beast." [3] The obligation to work which it imposes
on its victims is cursed in more than one passage. [4] Wealth,
on the contrary, is generally regarded as the supreme
blessing. [5] Full of illusions, erroneously regarding wealth
as happiness, the poor in comedy eagerly hope to become
rich. Awake or asleep, [6] they delight in dreams in which
their faith in the omnipotence of money and their inex-
perience in handling it are manifested with equal ingenuousness. Merely because he has picked up a travelling-
bag on the beach, whose contents are as yet unknown,
Gripus, in the *Rudens*, already sees himself in imagination
a clever merchant, an influential person, and the founder
of a city. [7]

It is in their relation to the wealthy that the poor best
reveal the feelings peculiar to their estate and that they
differ most from one another. There are some who, like
Hegio in the *Adelphi*, are able to remain dignified and just,
and, notwithstanding the inequality of fortune, to deal
with every one as man to man, on an equal footing. [8]
There are even some who, upon unexpectedly discovering
the hidden sorrows that afflict a rich neighbour, find words
of brotherly compassion for him. [9] But it must be admitted
that such noble sentiments appear only exceptionally.
Feeling hurt when they see that they are so little esteemed

[1] Cf. Philem., fr. 92.

[2] Men., fr. 588, 612, 624, 666; Diph., fr. 69, 104.

[3] Fr. adesp., 183; Men., Γεωργ., 78.

[4] Men., fr. 597; cf. 14, 404, 405–406, 633; Diph., fr. 105; fr. adesp.,
115, 273.

[5] Cf. Philem., fr. 96; Men., fr. 281. [6] Cf. Alc., II. 2.

[7] *Rud.*, 930 et seq. [8] *Ad.*, 462 et seq.

[9] Men., fr. 281; Philem., fr. 96.

and that people do not trust their word,[1] the poor are generally suspicious and sensitive. Hegio, who is so wise and so self-contained, proves this when he speaks of his relatives,[2] and several characters in comedy confirm the correctness of his words by their behaviour. Euclio, in the *Aulularia*, when Megadorus politely addresses him, is sure that the affability of his rich neighbour is a cover for some evil design.[3] After Megadorus has declared his intention to marry his daughter, Euclio is promptly offended because he thinks he is being derided.[4] The *advocati* in the *Poenulus*, although they are a pretty sorry lot, are not less suspicious : " However destitute and wretched we may be," they say to Agorastocles, " we have enough to eat. Do not crush us with your contempt. What little we possess belongs to us, and not to you; we ask nothing of any one, and nobody asks anything of us. Not one of us will burst his spleen to please you." [5] Phormio himself affects the pride of a " poor but honest " citizen. After receiving the thirty minae for which he has declared himself willing to marry Phanium, he goes in search of his dupes, Demipho and Chremes, and meets them as they are on the way to his house. On seeing them he exclaims : " Why were you coming to my house ? Do you think that I do not live up to my promises, once I have made them ? Go to ! Poor as I am, up to this day I have never cared for anything but to be worthy of confidence." [6]

The charge of avarice which this rascal denies with so much scorn was repeatedly made against the rich by the poor. " He has got wind of my gold," Euclio thinks, as soon as he sees Megadorus coming to him.[7] Phormio pretends that he believes that the reason for Demipho's disowning his young cousin is that the relationship is not of any advantage to him.[8] If a rich man is a day behind-

---

[1] Men., fr. 93, 856; Philem., fr. 102; fr. adesp., 230.
[2] *Ad.*, 605 et seq.   [3] *Aul.*, 184.   [4] *Ibid.*, 221–222.
[5] *Poen.*, 536 et seq.   [6] *Phorm.*, 902 et seq.   [7] *Aul.*, 185, 216.
[8] *Phorm.*, 357–358, 393 et seq.

hand in paying a salary, if he makes any remarks, he is suspected of stinginess and theft.[1] " That's just like our rich people ! " cries one of the *advocati*, who is cross because Agorastocles did not invite him to dinner. " If one does them a service their gratitude does not weigh as much as a feather." [2] In a fragment of Menander, a more serious-minded person, whose name is not known, complains that he is working merely so that some one else—evidently a rich man—shall come and enjoy the fruit of his labour.[3]

Behind all these complaints there lurks, among the poor, an undeniable envy, which the comic writers have remarked.[4] Did this envy go so far as to make those who felt it hope for social reform and a fairer distribution of property? I can discover no trustworthy indication that this was the case. But this envy, at any rate, led them freely to accuse the rich of setting the laws at naught, of laying claim to special privileges, of hating democracy; and, when they acted as judges, it led them even more freely to welcome such imputations against the rich. Phormio is well aware of this when frigidly and with an ironical threat he declares to the aged Demipho, who is furious at the marriage of his son : " You are a clever man. Go find the magistrates, in order that they may give another verdict—in your favour—in this matter, since you alone are king,[5] and you alone can secure two verdicts in the same case ! " [6] The rich know this too, and that is why, with far more reason than they are charged with arrogance or accused of bribing judges and witnesses, they dread calumny. That is what troubles Demeas in the midst of his anger, and the fear of being slandered before a popular tribunal, which is jealous of the rich and tender towards the poor, makes him disposed to compromise.

Owing to this class hatred there flourishes a type of rascal who has apparently been more than once intro-

---

[1] Men., fr. 303.   [2] *Poen.*, 811–812.   [3] Men., fr. 597.
[4] Cf. Philem., fr. 92; *Aul.*, 481–482; *Capt.*, 583.
[5] Cf. *Ad.*, 175.   [6] *Phorm.*, 403–406.

duced in New Comedy.[1] and with whom one of the extant plays permits us to become acquainted—the sycophant. Phormio, in his cynical confessions, reveals the secret of his strength : " A man's weak spot is where one can grab something from him. As for myself, people know that I have nothing." [2] As he has nothing, he risks nothing, and as neither care for his honour nor scruples of conscience stand in his way, he rushes head foremost into the most questionable intrigues. As a professional scandal-monger, he has in course of time acquired a mastery of that art, of which he is proud and which guarantees him impunity. The whole gamut of the law, the tricks of sharp practice, the art of swaying public opinion, all these have no mystery for him. Insults do not affect him—nay, he sometimes even welcomes them with the idea of converting them into weapons. In the midst of an uproar he never loses his coolness, and in the anger and excitement of his adversaries he recognises the symptoms of the fear he inspires. Alternately violent, sly, conciliatory or cordial, he gradually gets people at his mercy.

The sycophants terrorise the rich. Another class of poor people—and they are legion in comedy—choose quite a different way of living at their expense : they fawn and cringe. They are the parasites.[3] The aspect under which they represent poverty is anything but flattering. Their ideals are very low. Their dreams are not even of all the pleasures of a comfortable and indolent life—a parasite in love, a parasite who has a mistress, is almost unknown—but almost exclusively of the grossest pleasures of all, the pleasures of the stomach. With one accord, Terence, Horace and Apuleius call them *parasiti edaces*.[4] The gluttony of this sort of people is insatiable, indomitable; everywhere and always, at the most trying and

---

[1] Cf. Alexis, fr. 182; Men., fr. 93, 223, 688; Philippides, fr. 29; Alciphron, III. 34; *Heaut.*, prol. 38, etc. [2] *Phorm.*, 334–335.

[3] Ribbeck, Kolax (in the *Abhandlungen der k. sächsischen Ges. der Wiss.*, IX 1884)

[4] Ter., *Heaut.*, prol. 38; Hor., *Ep.*, II. i, 173; Ap., *Flor.*, XVI.

pathetic moments, they think of but one thing : eating, eating well; above all, eating a great deal. And, doubtless, this constant thought of food is not exclusively due to a long experience of hunger, because we find among the parasites not only beggars born, but also people who were formerly rich and have dissipated their fortunes.[1] But in most cases we may regard it as a sign of destitution.

The parasites of comedy have various ways of earning the food with which they gorge themselves. Alciphron shows us poor devils who are veritable scapegoats. Their ears are boxed, they are flogged, cups are smashed in their faces, gravy, blood, boiling water are poured over them, they are tormented and humiliated in a thousand ways, they are treated like low buffoons, like dogs.[2] There is no doubt that Alciphron got the idea for these dreary pictures from the comic poets. As a matter of fact, the fragments which prove this belong to the middle period—fragments of Antiphanes, Aristophon and Axionicus.[3] But in the *Eunuchus*, Gnatho—who is taken from Menander's Κόλαξ — still sees the custom of initiating neophytes at its height;[4] the head of his colleague Ergasilus only too often makes the acquaintance of the plates and fists of the other guests.[5] Curculio loses an eye at a feast.[6] Long after the period of the μέση the masks of parasites continued to have crushed ears, a permanent allusion to the melancholy advantages of the profession.[7]

One can understand that, in order to escape these calamities, the parasites make every effort to be useful or agreeable. They are not dainty in their choice of means, nor always very happy. In Alciphron, several of them think it right to open the eyes of a too confiding husband and inform him of his wife's misconduct.[8] Useless display of zeal! With the help of

---

[1] *Eun.*, 234 et seq.; Alc., III. 25.

[2] Alc., III. 3, 4, 7, 9, 12, 13, 15, 25, 32, 34, 35.

[3] Antiph., fr. 155; Axion., fr. 6; Aristophon, fr. 4. Cf. *Persa*, 60; also Nicolaos, fr. 1, 29.

[4] *Eun.*, 244–245. Cf. Harpocration, s. v. αὐτοληκύθοι(= Men., fr. 464).

[5] *Capt.*, 88–89, 472.   [6] *Curc.*, 397–398.

[7] Pollux, IV. 148.   [8] Alc., III. 26, 27, 33.

a false oath the accused wife gets out of the scrape, and
the denouncer is confounded. More frequently the parasite helps along his patron's adventures, and particularly
his amorous adventures. For him he comes to blows,
breaks down doors, intrudes into houses, murders, strangles,
kidnaps,[1] makes purchases in the market, bargains with
panders.[2] He goes on diplomatic missions to a cold or
irritated lady,[3] endures her rebuffs [4] or the threats of a
successful rival,[5] offers her—with a word about their
value—the gifts which are to render her more compliant; [6]
he gives advice to a clumsy and inexperienced lover,[7] and
makes more or less honourable [8] compromises in his name;
for jealous patrons he prepares the text of a contract
which is to enable them to lock up their mistress and
tyrannise over her.[9] For those who are in love and short
of money, for sons who are afraid of their fathers, he
rivals a rascally slave in wickedness; he steals, forges,
adopts false names, false rank, he quotes imaginary
genealogies and invents relationships wholesale.[10] His
compliance may go even further. The parasite of the
Persa involves his daughter, against her will, in an
impudent hoax; he lends her to the man who feeds
him—a slave!—has her disguised as a captive, examined
as a chattel that is for sale, purchased by a pander
and for a short time associated with courtesans. Two
fragments of Menander (254 and 723) suggest similar
adventures. In the Σικυώνιος, a parasite marries; [11] was
the marriage upon which he enters of the same kind as
that of Olympio, the rustic of the *Casina*? The idea is,
perhaps, worth a moment's consideration. In the *Phormio*,
at any rate, when Phormio insists on marrying Phanium,
Demipho immediately suspects the existence of some

---

[1] Alc., III. 5. Cf. Antiphanes, fr. 195.   [2] *Capt.*, 474–475.
[3] Lucian, *Dial. Mer.*, XIII.   [4] Alc., III. 2.
[5] *Bacch.*, 592 et seq.   [6] *Eun.*, 228 et seq.   [7] *Ibid.*, 435 et seq.
[8] *Ibid.*, 1054 et seq.   [9] *As.*, 746 et seq.
[10] *Curculio, Phormio*. In the *Parasitus Medicus* a parasite, I believe,
disguises himself as a physician for the better success of some intrigue.
[11] Men., fr. 444.

disgracéful intrigue,[1] and in Alciphron a parasite upon
whom a fair lady heaps her favours, calmly watches her
giving herself to rich friends as well as to himself.[2]

The spectacle of such baseness inclines us to be indulgent
towards the wretched people who merely play the buffoon
and the jester in order to gain their bread. The talent
of provoking laughter is one of the most useful assets of
the parasite. When Gelasimus, in the *Stichus*, holds the
amusing auction sale of his belongings, he makes apt
reference to *logi ridiculi* [3] and *cavillationes*.[4] Like Saturio,
in the *Persa*, he has a collection of clever sayings, which
he repeats to himself as he sits down to table.[5] In the
Captivi, Ergasilus declares that in luckier days some of
his jokes secured him free meals for a whole month. In
several of Alciphron's *Epistles* parasites boast of their
cleverness at merry-making, and of their songs, jokes, and
gift of conversation.[6] But the best way to please is, after
all, to flatter, and so the poor devil who lives at the expense
of the rich man is often a shameless flatterer. There is a
famous passage in the *Eunuchus*, copied from the Κόλαξ,
in which Gnatho explains his methods—

" There are some men who wish to be first in everything,
but who are not. To these men I attach myself. I do not
come to them in order to make them laugh, but I laugh
with them of my own accord, and at the same time I
admire their cleverness. Whatever they say, I praise it;
if they say just the opposite, I also praise it; if they say
no, I say no; if they say yes, I say yes. In a word, I
have made it a rule to praise everything. This is by far
the most profitable business, nowadays." [7] With more or
less spirit, many spungers in comedy practised this system.
Those whom we know best—Gnatho-Strouthias, Artotrogus,
and Chenidas in Lucian—do not take the trouble to invent
subtle flattery, as they have to do with fools. They lavish
the most absurd compliments upon their patrons and give

---

[1] *Phorm.*, 932–934.   [2] *Alc.*, III. 28.   [3] *Stich.*, 221.
[4] *Ibid.*, 228.   [5] *Ibid.*, 454. Cf. *Persa*, 392.
[6] *Alc.*, III. 7, 8, 13, 14.   [7] *Eun.*, 248 et seq.

them most extravagant assurances of their admiration. To judge by certain fragments we may suppose that some of their colleagues even outdid them in vulgarity.[1] Moreover, as we see in the *Eunuchus*, they indemnified themselves by making fun of their silly patrons, not only when they were by themselves and out of sight, but even to their very faces, in terms that were barely disguised.

There are, as we have seen, different degrees and a sort of hierarchy among the parasites. But in all the degrees of this hierarchy their position is humiliating. Gnatho himself, who is so full of scorn for the scapegoats and buffoons, has to suffer the indignity of having a slave, the servant of his master's rival, treat him with insulting familiarity, mock him and insult him.[2] How do the parasites in the works of the comic poets put up with such ill-treatment? It is not to be expected that they should openly resent these outrages, for by doing so they would run the risk of being discharged. An irascible parasite, like the one Diphilus portrays, who protested against a too outspoken insult,[3] was, no doubt, an exception and a rare exception. It is in the absence of their master that the most sensitive of them are indignant and lament their lot. Moreover, it is not injury to their self-respect that generally forms the subject of their complaints, but the meagreness of the food supply, or extreme ill-usage, or excessive tedium.[4] There is but one parasite—in Alciphron—whose pride is hurt;[5] sprung from a rich and noble family he must necessarily be doubly sensitive to the gross insults of a parvenu. Professional, born parasites find it easier to be resigned. Now and again one of them in ambiguous words makes a weak apology for his subserviency or for his equivocal conduct, and lays the blame on necessity.[6] The majority of them are completely at ease in their humiliation. As long as they have something to eat, it matters little to them that they are always relegated to

[1] Cf. Diodorus, fr. 2, 35–40.   [2] *Eun.*, 489–491.
[3] Diph., fr. 74–75.   [4] Men., fr. 563; Alexis, fr. 195.
[5] Alc., III. 25.   [6] Alexis, fr. 212; *Trin.*, 847 et seq.

the lowest end of the table, and are given no more room to lie down than a dog.[1] If need be, they are content to get remnants only and food of an inferior quality.[2] As for gibes, insults, and injurious nicknames, they care little for such things.[3] Nay, they even eagerly laud the advantages, the excellence—even the glory !—of the profession of the parasite.[4]

Finally, the parasites never have any real affection for their patron, or any real gratitude. Occasionally they do wish him a long life, health and prosperity,[5] but in doing so they think only of themselves, and of continuing a relationship that is to their advantage.[6] When occasion offers they do not hesitate to commit theft in the house in which they live.[7] If the man who supports them is a vain fool, like the soldier to whom Gnatho has attached himself, they eagerly join his enemies in plucking him. When their protector has aroused their spite they do not hesitate to exploit such secrets as a long intimacy has revealed to them : witness Peniculus, who informs Menaechmus' wife of the escapades of her husband.

§ 3

TYPES OF PROFESSIONAL PEOPLE

A good many of the characters whom I have sketched had a profession : the agriculturalists had an honest and respectable one, the sycophants and parasites a disreputable one. But it was not, strictly speaking, their customary occupations that gave to each of them a distinctive character; in the one case it was their dwelling-place and in

---

[1] *Stich.*, 488–489, 493, 620; *Capt.*, 471.

[2] Alc., III. 37. Cf. Axionicus, fr. 6, 14–15.

[3] *Menaech.*, 77 et seq.; *Capt.*, 69 et seq. Cf. Alexis, fr. 178; Antiphanes, fr. 195, 10 et seq.; Nicolaus, fr. 1, 31–32.

[4] Men., fr. 937; *Eun.*, 232 et seq.; Diodorus, fr. 2. Cf. Antiphanes, fr. 144; Timocles, fr. 8.

[5] *Capt.*, 139 et seq.; Alexis, fr. 202; Luc., *Dial. Mer.*, XIII. 2.

[6] *Ibid.*, 139 et seq.; Alexis, fr. 202; Luc., *Dial. Mer.*, XIII. 2.

[7] Alc., III. 10, 11, 17. The κόλακες in Eupolis already did the same (fr. 155, 168).

the other their destitution. But in the case of others, whom I am about to describe to the reader, their temper is more closely connected with their avocations.

Among the second group there are many who, like the parasite, live at the expense of the rich. I shall first consider them, and first and foremost among them the courtesans.

By a curious chance these persons, to whom so many fragments of the middle period refer, hardly appear in the subsequent period. Still, we have a few lines giving a characterisation of the morals of Menander's Θαΐς, who was regarded as an embodiment of the perfect type of courtesan.[1] Possibly I ought to add all or a part of what Propertius says in a passage in which that illustrious lady —*Thais pretiosa Menandri*—is held up as a model to a young débutante.[2] But Latin comedy, Lucian's *Dialogues*, and Alciphron's *Epistles*, are safer guides to the lost originals; and as the master's description of his Thais has not come down to us, a character drawn by one of his imitators—Phronesium, in the *Truculentus*—no doubt deserves to be regarded as a good example of the genus.

Absolute heartlessness, unscrupulousness and impudent greed are the most striking characteristics of the courtesans in the third, as well as in the fourth, century. They value a man merely according to what he is able to give them. At the beginning of the *Truculentus*, Diniarchus, more than two-thirds ruined, returns from a voyage, and knocks at the door of his former mistress. He is received by the servant Astaphium, and she, as a worthy mouthpiece of Phronesium, tells him that, in her eyes and in those of her mistress alike, a man without money no longer counts for anything. It is only after hearing the unhappy Diniarchus speak of a house and property that he still owns, that Astaphium suddenly softens and declares that, after all, his former love cannot regard him as a stranger and that she invites him to

[1] Men., fr. 217. [2] Prop., IV. 5, 43 et seq.

come in.[1] Cleareta in the *Asinaria*, Mousarion's mother
in the seventh *Dialogue* of Lucian, Myrtale in the fifteenth,
Petale and Philoumene in Alciphron (IV, 9, 15) counsel
or themselves practise the same shameless greed.[2]

Menander's Thais "was always asking for something";[3]
Lysiteles, in the *Trinummus*, and Diniarchus, in the
Truculentus, well know that lovers of a pretty woman
must expect constant demands to be made upon them.
Moreover, his mistress is not the only one to pluck an
incautious lover; she has at her heels a whole band
of allies, servants and maids. In his effort to entertain
all these people, the lover ruins himself. As for pretexts for asking for something, they are never lacking.
Diniarchus lays down the following as a rule among
courtesans : " If you have not yet made a present, a
hundred requests are already prepared. It is either a
lost jewel, a torn cloak, a slave girl that has just been
bought, a bronze or silver vase or a chased one, or a Greek
clothes-press, or some other object that the lover is
obliged to present to his girl."

Several scenes in the *Truculentus* serve as illustrations
of these general observations. In them we see Phronesium
busily engaged in " plucking " her lovers. One request
follows close on the heels of another, and those who make
the presents are lucky if they get more than a smile and
a " thank you " in return for them. Diniarchus' rival,
the soldier Stratophanes, presents Phronesium with two
Syrian slaves whom he has brought with him for her from
his conquests—two deposed princesses, he calls them.
The gift meets with a very bad reception.[4] A mantilla
does not please her any better. Incense from Arabia,
perfumes brought from Pontus, she does not even deign
worthy of a look, or of a word of thanks.[5] Later on

---

[1] *Truc.*, 164 et seq.
[2] See also Naevius, fr. inc. fab. IX.; Trabea, fr. I.; Turpilius, *Lindia*,
fr. VI.
[3] Men., fr. 217 : αἰτοῦσαν πυκνά.   [4] *Truc.*, 50 et seq.
[5] *Ibid.*, 533–534, 537, 539–541.

Stratophanes appears again, purse in hand. He gives and gives again, and each time his gift elicits the same monotonous refrain from the lips of his fair one : *parum est*.[1] Even when the gifts are for the moment well received, the lover must not expect gratitude to last long. Diniarchus has sent the supplies for a superb supper and five minae of silver. Presently he arrives in person and wishes to enter Phronesium's house, but the servant stops him and explains that Phronesium is engaged in dismissing another admirer.[2] As soon as the money given by Stratophanes has been put in a safe place, Phronesium turns her back on the unfortunate soldier and listens to the entreaties of the young rustic, Strabax. Stratophanes and Strabax engage in an absurd contest of extravagance, and the woman for whom they are competing ironically watches them vie with each other in ruining themselves.[3]

To complete the picture, I must add that Phronesium—like the Thais of whom Propertius tells us—appears to be absolutely indifferent to the physical advantages or shortcomings of her various suitors. She just as readily permits the ill-favoured and dirty Strabax to embrace her as Stratophanes or Diniarchus.[4] Similarly Myrtale, in Lucian, gives herself to her frightful Bithynian without showing any sign of disgust.[5] Only beginners, like Philinna in the third *Dialogue*, and Mousarion in the seventh, feel an aversion to ugly men. An experienced woman well knows that, in order to offset their ugliness, they pay more than good-looking young fellows do ;[6] and that is the only thing that interests her.

How does the unfeeling, cold and rapacious courtesan secure her victims? Chiefly by awakening their sensuous desire. This is the main purpose of the endless care she takes of her person and of the artifices of her toilet which some poets of the μέση have maliciously revealed, of the ointments and perfumes which she uses so freely, and of

[1] *Truc.*, 910.   [2] *Ibid.*, 739 et seq.
[3] *Ibid.*, 949–950.   [4] *Ibid.*, 934.
[5] *Dial. Mer.*, XIV. 4.   [6] *Ibid.*, VI. 4.   Cf. Ovid, *Am.*, I. 8, 67.

G

the elegance of her appointments.[1] This is the purpose
of her skilful dancing and playing; for music, says Menander, provokes love,[2] and dancing affords a chance to show
a pretty leg and to display the suppleness of a fresh,
young, vigorous body. This is the purpose of her pro-
vocative and coquettish ways. Of course, a well-behaved
courtesan does not throw herself into men's arms, but
she does not hesitate to brush up against them, or to
let them do as much to her. Under pretext of showing
her ring or of looking at some one else's, she places her
hand[3] in a man's hand, or else she does so when stepping
upon the banqueting couch or getting down from it.[4]
With her foot she presses the foot of her neighbours at
table,[5] and if they indiscreetly slip a hand under her
dress, she does not raise the slightest objection.[6] When
she drinks she rather likes to have the lips of her male
companions placed upon the traces her own lips have left
on the rim of the cup.[7] When she coughs she makes a
point of extending her rosy tongue a little more than she
properly should.[8] Languorous glances, covert promises,
are her stock in trade.[9] Menander's Thais is skilled in
the art of persuasion, the more so because she is beautiful.[10]
Naevius' Tarentilla, a copy of a Greek model, understands
how to attract several aspirants at a time.[11] To awaken
the desire of a young gallant, and then to hold aloof and
put him off, is sometimes a good way to make his passion
more ardent, and this is probably what the woman did
after whom a play of Menander's is named : Ἀνατιθεμένη.

In addition to her sensual allurements the courtesan
has yet other baits. She flatters men's vanity either by

---

[1] Cf. *Poen.*, 210 et seq.; *Most.*, 157 et seq., 272 et seq.; *Truc.*, 322
et seq., etc.
[2] Men., fr. 237.
[3] *As.*, 778; Naevius, *Tarentilla*, fr. II.; Tibullus, I. 6, 25–26.
[4] *Ibid.*, 776–777.
[5] *Ibid.*, 775; Naevius, *Tarent.*, fr. II.; Ovid, *Am.*, I. 4, 44.
[6] *Heaut.*, 562–563; *Bacch.*, 482.   Cf. *Miles*, 652.
[7] Cf. *As.*, 772.   [8] *As.*, 794 et seq.
[9] *Ibid.*, 784; Naevius, *Tarent.*, fr. II.; Luc., *Dial. Mer.*, I. 2; VI. 3.
[10] Men., fr. 217.   [11] *Tarent.*, fr. II.

feigning a love for them which she does not feel,[1] or by pretending that she discovers and admires the highest manly qualities in them—courage, strength, pride. We may recall the extravagant praise, the comedy of amorous transports, by which Acroteleutium and her maid Milphidippa, in the *Miles Gloriosus*, awaken the desire of Pyrgopolinices. True, it is no special credit to them, as Pyrgopolinices is a fool, suffering from excessive lust.

One and the same play by Plautus—a copy of Menander—affords us two seduction scenes of a livelier interest, in which the fine Attic spirit of the original may be clearly discerned. At the beginning of the *Bacchides*, Pistoclerus is a very well-behaved young man. In order to do an absent friend, Mnesilochus, a service, he enters into relations with two courtesans, the sisters Bacchis, one of whom, the Samian Bacchis, had met Mnesilochus at Ephesus, and is loved by him. She has just arrived at the house of her sister, Bacchis the Athenian, and there awaits her lover. But before giving herself to him she is obliged to pay a forfeit to a ferocious soldier to whom she had plighted herself for a year. The soldier demands immediate payment, on pain of returning and taking back his mistress, by force if need be. Bacchis the Athenian very cleverly uses this situation to get Pistoclerus into her toils—

" My sister begs me to find somebody who will protect her against this soldier. . . . I implore you, be her protector." [2] Of course, Pistoclerus does not dare to refuse ; he would look like a coward. But he seems to be inclined to waylay the soldier as he goes by, without compromising himself in the society of the two women. That does not suit Bacchis—

" It is better for this matter to be settled in our house. You can wait here without any risk until he comes. At the same time you can have something to drink, and when you have drunk I shall give you a kiss." [3] Pistoclerus objects and gives vent to his fears—

---

[1] Men., fr. 217.   [2] *Bacch.*, 42 et seq.   [3] *Ibid.*, 47 et seq.

" Your caresses are nothing but a bait. What you suggest to me, woman, is, I think, not good for me. I fear your enticements—you are a cunning creature." [1] And the worthy Bacchis says by way of reassuring him—
" If you suddenly wish to take liberties with me, I shall stop you myself." [2]   She thereupon promptly resorts to an appeal to the young man's courage, to the devotion he owes to his friend. Pistoclerus begins to lose control over himself. He still makes some virtuous remarks, and tries to call himself back to the right path by picturing to himself the effeminate life one leads with women like Bacchis. But it is clear that the picture he paints inspires him with more desire than abhorrence. Bacchis follows up her advantage. She now freely enlarges upon what she had casually said : " The soldier will believe that I am your mistress."

B. " Pretend that you love me." P. " Shall I pretend just for fun or in good earnest? " B. " Come, come. Let us get to business, that is better. When the soldier comes you must embrace me." P. " Why must I do that? " B. " He must see you doing so. I know what I am about." [3]   The poor youth promptly loses his balance and a voluptuous vision dazzles him.

" If, by chance," he asks Bacchis, " there were to be a lunch, a drinking bout or a dinner such as you are accustomed to have at your social gatherings, where should I be seated? " [4]

Bacchis thinks the time has come to show all her cards—
" Next to me, my love, so that a handsome boy may be seated next to a handsome girl. In our house this seat is always vacant for you, even if you come unexpectedly." [5]

Once more Pistoclerus holds back; he refuses to take the fair enchantress by the hand and to follow her into the house. But this is the last effort of his will, and Bacchis soon overcomes it.[6]

[1] *Bacch.*, 50 et seq.   [2] *Ibid.*, 57.   [3] *Ibid.*, 75 et seq.
[4] *Ibid.*, 79 et seq.   [5] *Ibid.*, 81 et seq.   [6] *Ibid.*, 89 et seq.

At the close of the play there is another scene of seduc-tion.[1] This time the victims are two old men—Philo-xenus, Pistoclerus' father, and Nicobulus, father of Mnesilochus. They come in great anger to make an uproar at the door of the courtesans, in order to get their sons out of the house. The two sisters appear on the balcony. At first they make fun of the old men and treat them like superannuated bucks. But presently, in the midst of their raillery, a few remarks make plain their project and prepare the way for the success of their plot. Thus, one of them with subtle flattery says to the other with the air of an expert—"These bucks were good in their day;" and shortly afterwards she insinuates that they are now old and good for nothing. This retrospective praise awakens tempting memories of his former pranks in one of these worthies, Philoxenus. Their scorn annoys him and provokes him to prove that, notwithstanding his white hair, he is still good for something. When the two Bacchides talk in a whisper and look towards him out of the corner of their eyes, he is quickly stirred and inflamed. His companion Nicobulus holds out longer, but the bad example affects him. Thereupon the Athenian Bacchis increases her alluring promises, which include an offer to return to the old man one-half of the money that has been extracted from him. To these promises she adds remonstrances and philosophical remarks on the shortness of life. When Nicobulus weakens and expresses his fear of giving his son and his slave too great an advantage over him, Bacchis, who has her own notions about family hierarchy, reassures him by means of this fine declaration—

"Tell me, honey of my heart, even if that happens, he is your son. Where do you suppose that he could get the money, if you do not give it to him?" In due course Nicobulus also is won over.

Once they have captured their lovers, they must keep them and divert them. Hence the occasional coolness

[1] *Bacch.*, 1120 et seq.

with which an experienced woman meets hot desire, and
the niggardliness—as Turpilius calls it [1]—with which she
surrenders herself. A true courtesan cannot allow her
lover to regard himself as her lord and master, or, in the
belief that he is sure to find her docile, to grow slack in
his attentions.[2] She constantly invents some new trick
to keep him at her mercy without worrying about the
annoyance or the sorrow she occasions him. The heroine
of the *Truculentus* pretends to have had a son by Stratophanes while he was away campaigning, and says she was
in danger of losing her life when she gave him birth. She
counts on this son to enable her to pluck the officer, and
she—or her servant—calls attention to his resemblance
to his pretended father. She pleads for the support of
the child by recalling the suffering it has caused her, and
by growing tender over her motherhood and her fidelity.[3]
Later on she indulges in other tactics. In order to annoy
and worry Stratophanes, she graciously receives, in his
presence, gifts sent by Diniarchus.[4] When he sees this,
the soldier cries out : " What, you dared to say that you
loved another ? " " It suited me to do so," Phronesium
coolly replies. Indeed, to provoke jealousy appears to
have been a common trick of the courtesans in comedy.[5]
Bacchis, in the *Heauton Timoroumenos*, hopes to increase
the passion of one of her suitors, a soldier, by refusing to
listen to his entreaties and by going to Clitipho ; [6] subsequently, when the money promised by Clitipho is too
slow in coming, she harps upon the soldier.[7]

These tricks are, if I may use the phrase, tricks of
attack. For her defence, the courtesan employs other
tricks. If she wishes to evade the entreaties of a youth
whom she does not care for, an opportune headache
suffices,[8] or else some vow which demands temporary

---

[1] Turpilius, *Demiurgus*, fr. 1.

[2] Luc., *Dial. Mer.*, VIII. 2; XII. 2. Cf. Ov., *Am.*, I. 8, 95–96; *Ars
Am.*, III. 580 et seq.

[3] *Truc.*, 518 et seq. [4] *Ibid.*, 582 et seq.

[5] Cf. *Dial. Mer.*, VIII.; Alc., III. 14. [6] *Heaut.*, 366 et seq.

[7] *Ibid.*, 730 et seq. [8] *Truc.*, 632.

chastity offers a convenient pretext.[1] If there is need of
disarming the suspicions of a jealous lover or of concealing
the breaking of a contract, she is never at a loss for lies
or clever precautions. For example, she will wipe her
hands after having touched money so that the metal
may not leave an incriminating odour on the skin; or a
lover who has been surreptitiously admitted will, if need
arises, be introduced as the lover of a friend.[2] But it
is chiefly for the purpose of gaining pardon for their
infidelity that the fair ones use diplomacy. When Thais,
in the *Eunuchus*, wishes to induce Phaedria to leave the
seat next to her vacant for the soldier Thraso, she counts
on the young man's kind heart, makes him pity the fate
of Pamphila, and stirs his sympathy for her own loneliness
as a stranger in Athens, who has so much need to make
friends by rendering a service.[3]

Phronesium, in the *Truculentus*, does not ask Diniarchus
for permission to prefer his rival; indeed, she does not
seek to disguise the fact that the soldier Stratophanes is,
for the time being, her acknowledged lover. Far from
doing so, by making a confidant of him and by pretending
that she is concealing nothing from him, she endeavours
to keep the young man under her thrall—and succeeds.
She frankly tells him of the deceit she is practising upon
Stratophanes, as though he were too clear-sighted to
allow himself to be duped, and too delicate to betray a
secret. She gives him to understand what she thinks of
the vulgar veteran and how superior he, Diniarchus, is to
such a dullard. In a word, she treats him as a dear and
absolutely devoted friend, but with a shade of pity, as
though she regretted that he is no longer rich enough to
remain her chief victim.[4]

Grasping, coquettish, mendacious and profligate in her
relations with men, such is the woman who has made love
her profession. It is quite likely that the comic writers
portrayed her as full of spite against respectable women,

---

[1] *As.*, 806–807.   [2] *Most.*, 267 et seq.
[3] *Eun.*, 144 et seq.   [4] *Truc.*, 387 et seq.

full of slander and jealousy against other courtesans, her
competitors. As a matter of fact, both original fragments and Latin imitations are practically silent on this
topic. But in Lucian and in Alciphron the courtesans
are much less reserved. Myrtion in the former, Leaena
in the latter, roundly abuse the young women who are
obliged to marry their lovers; [1] Tryphaena eloquently
curses Philemation " the Sepulchre "; [2] the Thais of the
first *Dialogue* delights in enumerating the shortcomings of
Gorgona. But they do still worse : Thais and Pyrallis join
Diphilus and Lysias in injuring Philinna, in making Ioessa [3]
disconsolate ; Glycera has taken Habrotonon's lover away
from her, and Gorgona subsequently takes him away from
Glycera ; [4] Thais' relations to Megara are strained on
account of Strato, and Euxippe tells her malicious tales
about a lover who has deserted her, and so on. I believe
that these spiteful actions and these quarrels reflect, on
the comic stage, the rivalries which existed among the
courtesans. Two comedies, one by Antiphanes and the
other by Nicostratus—perhaps the younger Antiphanes
and the second Nicostratus—were entitled Ἀντερῶσα,
which can mean *The Rival*; and this rival, if there was
a rival, doubtless belonged to the same social class as
Lucian's heroines.

The writers of the νέα made, then, quite a detailed
study of the faults of the courtesan. To one point, however, it appears that they shut their eyes—or rather their
ears. If we are to judge by the anecdotes which Athenaeus
has preserved for us, such women in Menander's time were
occasionally very free in their speech. They were prone
to use offensive language, and such jokes as they made
were more indecent than witty. But of such free speech
what remains to us of comic literature affords but few
examples. Two fragments only attribute gross or vul-
garly obscene remarks to women.[5] Habrotonon, in the

---

[1] Luc., *Dial. Mer.*, II. i; Alc., IV. 12.   [2] *Ibid.*, XI. 3.
[3] *Ibid.*, III. 2; XII. 1.   [4] *Ibid.*, I. 1.
[5] Diphilus, fr. 50; Philippides, fr. 5.

'Ἐπιτρέποντες, discloses to the audience—and possibly to Onesimus—the secrets of her bedchamber,[1] but she does so without any evil purpose and with an ingenuous simplicity which shows close observation of character on the part of the poet. It is by no means certain that Alciphron found the models for his sprightly tales, like those in *Epistles*, IV, 13 and 14, in the comic writers. In the Latin plays, even in those of Plautus, the courtesans usually observe the decencies of language.

Moreover, all of them are not equally wicked. Athenaeus tells us that Philemon, in one of his comedies, applies the epithet χρηστή to a courtesan.[2] He adds that Menander strongly protested, ὡς οὐδεμιᾶς οὔσης χρηστῆς. But this was a sally, the expression of a passing resentment on the part of the poet who was the disgruntled lover of Glycera; and subsequently he takes a less severe view of the matter. The comedies of Plautus and of Terence prove that the Greek comic writers did see and did portray more or less respectable courtesans.

We may leave out of consideration the young girls, daughters of good families, who have been abandoned or stolen during their infancy and whom chance has put into the hands of a procuress or of a pander, and who are against their will brought up to the profession of a courtesan but have not as yet practised it. Such girls are, in point of fact, not real courtesans. But apart from these, we occasionally meet with a few more or less sympathetic types of women. Gymnasium, in the *Cistellaria*, who has no pangs whatsoever about the baseness of her life, nevertheless has a kind heart. She appears to be honestly grieved by seeing Selenium overwhelmed by sorrow. When she discovers that this sorrow is occasioned by love, she makes an effort to cure it, though her arguments are such as one might expect from a prostitute. Unskilled in the art of consoling, she at least commiserates with Selenium and agrees to do her the service for which she asks. Philotis, too, at the beginning of the *Hecyra*,

---

[1] 'Ἐπιτρ., 221 et seq.   [2] Ath., p. 594 D = Philem., fr. 215.

is deeply moved by the " persecution " of which Bacchis has been the victim. In a fragment of Phoenicides an ill-starred courtesan confides in a certain Pythias who, I believe, is her friend.[1]

The kindness which these women display is towards their comrades. Others give evidence of it towards persons who are utter strangers to their guild : Bacchis, in the *Heauton Timoroumenos*, towards young Antiphila, whose scrupulous fidelity she admires; Habrotonon, in the Ἐπιτρέποντες, towards a poor abandoned baby, whose attractiveness has moved her; Thais, in the *Eunuchus*, towards an Athenian family, strangers to her, who had previously lost a child; Bacchis, in the *Hecyra*, towards the parents and parents-in-law of her former lovers. The behaviour of the last three is not really disinterested. By making an effort to find the parents of the abandoned child, Habrotonon hopes to secure her own enfranchisement.[2] Thais confesses that by obliging a family of good position she hopes to find protectors.[3] The worthy Laches obliges Bacchis to choose between war and peace.[4] But in each of these three cases personal profit is only a secondary motive. Habrotonon does not wait until she recognises that her interest and that of the infant may be identical before displaying her good will. Bacchis, even before Laches has named his terms, appears to be moved by the best feeling—so much so, indeed, that her decent and dignified attitude impresses him, and when her visit to Philumena has cleared up the mystery and reconciled the young couple, she is thoroughly delighted. One may even find that, carried away by his desire for novelty, Apollodorus went too far, for the Bacchis who (in lines 833 and following) indulges in such noble expressions can hardly be the same woman whose wiles and coquettishness Parmeno had described shortly before.[5] The author of the *Eunuchus* did not go to such extremes nor indulge in such contradictions. His Thais, likewise, is anxious to

---

[1] Phoenic., fr. 1.   [2] Ἐπιτρ., 321 et seq.   [3] *Eun.*, 147 et seq.
[4] *Hec.*, 764 et seq.   [5] *Ibid.*, 158–159.

be thought better than her kind; she wishes to have the regard of Phaedria, for whom she feels affection, if not love. It pains her to think that he could doubt her word and suspect her of imposture. But these fine sentiments are only touched upon cursorily;[1] the poet does not insist upon them.

Moreover, the *véa* recognised that a true passion might sometimes exist in the demi-monde. Several Latin comedies—the *Mostellaria*, the *Asinaria*, the *Pseudolus*—bring upon the stage courtesans who are really in love. Of course, I realise that not all of these enamoured women are worthy of a like confidence. One may suspect some degree of self-interest in Phoenicium, in the *Pseudolus*, for this young woman is the slave of a pander, and her love is closely connected with her enfranchisement. But Philematium, in the *Mostellaria*, has already been freed, and Philaenium, in the *Asinaria*, has always been free. In the case of both of these women, their love, very far from being of any advantage to them, can only be a hindrance and an obstacle to the success of their careers. Both of them are assailed by evil thoughts and resist them. They must, therefore, be regarded as honourable exceptions among a class of women who are generally heartless. In Lucian's *Dialogues* and in Alciphron's *Epistles*, the type of courtesans who are in love is quite freely represented : Bacchis in the latter,[2] and Myrtion, Mousarion and Ioessa in the former,[3] are touching examples.

Around the courtesan there assemble various other persons on whom the stamp—I may say the blight—of their profession is deeply impressed : the maid, the procuress and the pander.

The first of these, as we see her in the *Truculentus*, in the *Miles*, in the ninth *Dialogue* of Lucian, is, as it were, a reflection of her mistress, the profligate courtesan, whose sayings she repeats, whose vices she shares and whose evil designs she subserves.

---

[1] *Eun.*, 197 et seq.   [2] Alc., IV. 11.   [3] Lucian, *Dial. Mer.*, II.; VII., XII.

The procuress has a more distinctly marked personality. As a rule, in the *véa* she is not—as in the first mimiamb of Herondas—an agent for debauch, who, at the request of a gallant, tries to suborn such and such a woman. At least, all that tends to make us see her in this light is summed up in a title that is common to a play by Apollodorus of Carystus and to one by Nicostratus—*Διάβολος* (which may mean *Temptress*), and in fragment 878 of Menander. Most frequently she is represented either as an attendant of a courtesan, or as her real [1] or supposed [2] mother. In each case she is herself a superannuated courtesan, a courtesan *emerita*. We also hear her expound the theory of her trade with the greatest force and skill. The procuress in the *Cistellaria* says that one must only pretend to love,[3] for as soon as one really loves one puts one's lover above one's own interests. If a woman wishes to retain her lovers for a long time, adds the procuress in the *Demiurgus*, she must always be niggardly of her favours.[4] Above all, she must beware of remaining true to a single man. Scapha, in the *Mostellaria*, found out how foolish it was to do so.[5] The right thing to do is not to let your heart speak, not to hesitate to swear a false oath, and to exploit every one you meet. This is the advice Syra gives Philotis at the beginning of the *Hecyra*.[6] In the *Asinaria*, Cleareta goes still further, and declares that this method must be pursued with vivacity.[7] All these fine precepts, the procuress, when she is a servant, a friend, or even a kindly disposed mother, is content to preach. When she is a high-handed mother who proposes to live on her daughter's earnings, she may try to insist on their being put into practice. Of this we have an example in the *Asinaria*.

The pander appears to have played quite a considerable part in the comedies of the new period. Menander himself, Philemon, Diphilus, Apollodorus of Carystus, Posi-

---

[1] *As.*, *Cist.*; Lucian, *Dial. Mer.*, III., VI., VII., XII.
[2] *Cist.*   [3] *Ibid.*, 95 et seq.   [4] Turpilius, *Demiurgus*, fr. 1.
[5] Cf. *Most.*, 200 et seq.   [6] *Hec.*, 63 et seq.   [7] *As.*, 178 et seq.

dippus and several of the writers whom Plautus imitated have in turn brought him upon the stage. Like the procuress he is an enemy, a hindrance, to lovers; but he does not waste time in discussions. There is no instance where the women under his charge seek to soften him or thwart him with their preferences or antipathies. For them, as for all of his slaves, he is the master, a relentless master who is always ready with a threat, if he does not actually hold the whip in his hand.[1] The luxury with which he surrounds the women whom he exploits, the careful education he gives some of them, are certainly no proof of his being well disposed towards them; they are the devices of the speculator, and represent investments that bring a heavy return. Towards amorous young men he behaves like a merchant who wishes to sell his wares at the highest price. To increase the price, he heightens the passion of his client, either by letting him get accustomed to the society of the woman he loves, or by keeping him in doubt, or by making him compete with another would-be purchaser. If the young man is short of money, the pander has no further use for him. He meets the most pathetic appeals with silence, or else he answers them sarcastically;[2] "no money, no woman," such, in a word, is the rule he follows. This is natural enough, because he is in business. But he does not only lack kindness of heart; his passion for money is so great that it kills even his honesty as a business man. With a light heart he breaks his most solemn promises if he sees the slightest advantage in doing so. To promise a courtesan to one of her lovers at an agreed price payable on a certain day, and then to sell her to another who appears sooner and with a fuller purse—that is one of his daily performances. In the *Phormio*, Dorio expresses himself very clearly on this subject.[3] Everybody regards the pander as an object of hatred and contempt. Something exceptional must happen before a respectable man who has

[1] Cf. *Pseud.*, 178, 199–201, 214–224, 228–229.
[2] *Pseud.*, 308 et seq.; *Poen.*, 751 et seq.; *Phorm.*, 486 et seq.
[3] *Phorm.*, 525–526.

passed the age of wild pranks receives him at his table,
as Daemones does in the *Rudens*. And no doubt few
solid married citizens and fathers of a family would agree
to associate with him, as Simo does in the *Pseudolus*,
and to ask a service or to render him one, if need be.
Respectable people turn their backs upon him in disgust.
Fools are obliged to win his favour, though they make up
for that constraint as soon as they can, by heaping
insults upon him, or even by thrashing him. But he remains indifferent to disgrace. He calmly accepts the most
offensive epithets; [1] he even saves his enemies the trouble
of hurling them at him, and calmly applies them to himself in advance.[2] He consoles himself for all insults by
fingering his money, and if he occasionally threatens to
bring a suit against those who insult him,[3] it is not with
the object of vindicating his honour, but with a view to
securing satisfaction in money.

Courtesan, procuress and pander constitute a group of
professional types in whose character the odious side
predominates. In the soldier we reach a second group
of persons who are primarily comic.

In his *Alazon*, Ribbeck has made a list of the Greek
and Latin plays in which a soldier appears.[4] It is a long
list, and in it the works belonging to the new period, and
especially those of Menander, abound.

Life in camp gave the soldier whom the comic writers
portray a vulgarity that makes him very disagreeable.
" There can be no such thing as a well-behaved ($\varkappa o\mu\psi\acute{o}\varsigma$)
soldier," says Menander, " even if a god were to mould
him." [5] At the beginning of the *Hecyra*, Philotis cannot
get over her joy at having broken off relations with her
soldier, *milite inhumanissimo*.[6] The soldier in the *Eunuchus*
is distinguished by his lack of tact.[7] In Lucian's thirteenth

---

[1] *Pseud.*, 357 et seq.   [2] *Ad.*, 188–189.   [3] *Ibid.*, 163 et seq.
[4] *Alazon, ein Beitrag zur Antiken Ethologie* (Leipzig, 1882), pp. 80–81.
See also Plautus, *Cornicula* (fr. II.).
[5] Men., fr. 732.   [6] *Hec.*, 85 et seq.   [7] *Eun.*, 456–457.

Dialogue, Leontichus thinks he can overcome Hymnis' repugnance by promising her double pay. Besides being clumsy of speech, the soldier is brutal and readily grows aggressive. In the Περιχειρομένη, Polemo, in a fit of jealousy, ill-treats Glycera and cuts off her hair; subsequently he wishes to make an assault upon the house in which she has taken refuge. Thraso, in the *Eunuchus*, throws Chremes bodily out of the house;[1] in a scene copied from the Κόλαξ, he comes at the head of a mob to attack Thais' house.[2] In the *Bacchides*, Cleomachus threatens to carry off his mistress, if she refuses to accompany him or to pay him a forfeit.[3] Stratophanes, in the *Truculentus*, draws his sword against Diniarchus' emissary, the peaceable Cyamus.[4]

A further striking characteristic of the stage soldier is his stupidity, his lack of initiative. The writers of comedy had well observed how much of his individuality a man loses through the constraint of military discipline and the habit of unreasoning obedience. One of Philemon's characters says that the soldier does not deserve the name of man, and calls him a victim fattened for slaughter when the proper time comes.[5] In a fragment of Apollodorus the words στρατιώτης and ἐλεύθερος are used to convey opposite meanings.[6] More skilled in fighting than in thinking, the soldier allows himself to be led like a child, often into a trap, by any of his companions. Thraso cannot undertake anything without the help of his parasite. Pyrgopolinices eagerly and gratefully accepts the perfidious advice of his slave.

But above all else, the soldier is a braggart. *Miles gloriosus*—this title of one of Plautus' plays conveys the essence of the type. Moreover, his boasting takes very many different forms. First and foremost he loves to tell extraordinary tales of the distant lands which he claims

---

[1] *Eun.*, 737.

[2] *Ibid.*, 771 et seq. In the Κόλαξ, Bias probably assaulted the house of his rival Pheidias.

[3] *Bacch.*, 42 et seq., 603, 842 et seq.   [4] *Truc.*, 613 et seq.

[5] *Philem.*, fr. 155.   [6] *Apoll.*, fr. 10.

to have traversed. Antamoenides, in the *Poenulus*, pretends that he has seen flying men.[1] Any traveller can indulge in such lies, but the soldier is not satisfied with them. As we might expect, he is, above all, anxious to have people admire his courage and his strength, and so he tells endless tales of pretended prowess. He enumerates the generals under whom he has served,[2] displays his wounds and recalls where he got them;[3] he either tells or gets one of his comrades to tell how many of the enemy he has massacred, how many tribes he has subjugated.[4] These soldier tales, sometimes embellished with most preposterous conceits, must have been very frequent, at a certain period,[5] in the works of the *νέα*, and it is probable that Plautus follows his Greek models in two passages,[6] in which he points out and condemns their too frequent occurrence. But the soldier is not satisfied with strictly military bluster. A doughty warrior, rival of the gods in battle, he also claims to be a valiant boon companion. In the *Κόλαξ*, Bias boasts that, in Cappadocia, he thrice emptied a vessel containing ten measures of wine, and is delighted when his parasite declares : " You are a mightier toper than Alexander." [7] Next to bodily prowess comes wealth. Rare are the soldiers who, like a person in Menander's *Παρακαταθήκη*, admit that they have not made a fortune.[8] The majority, if we may trust their words, have come home from their campaigns and their journeys into strange lands, laden with gold. In the *Σικυώνιος*, a soldier who shows off his newly gained wealth gets a pretty lively rebuff.[9] Polemo, in Lucian, like Pyrgopolinices,[10] measures his gold by the bushel, he walks about in purple clothes, and his slave Parmeno

---

[1] *Poen.*, 470 et seq.   [2] Men., fr. 340; fr. adesp. 129.
[3] *Ibid.*, fr. 562; Phoenicides, fr. 4.
[4] *Poen.*, 473; *Miles*, 42 et seq.; *Curc.*, 442 et seq.
[5] Cf. Men., fr. 76, 77, 78, 286, 563; Phoenicides, fr. 4.
[6] *Truc.*, 482 et seq.; *Epid.*, 431 et seq.
[7] Men., fr. 293.   Cf. Epinicus, fr. 2; Damoxenus, fr. 2.
[8] *Ibid.*, fr. 382.   [9] *Ibid.*, fr. 442.
[10] *Miles*, 1063 et seq.

wears a ring glistening with precious stones.[1] In Phile-mon's Βαβυλώνιος another of these heroes promises his girl that he will make her as rich as Pythonice, the mistress of Harpalus.[2] In fact, when the soldier really has money, he is generous, as is shown by the attitude of Pyrgopolinices toward Philocomasium at the moment when he dismisses her.[3] But very often the soldier's wealth is as unreal as his exploits.[4]

The soldiers appear to have indulged in yet another form of vainglory : they bragged of their social standing. According to Thraso, the king could not get along without his society;[5] whilst Pyrgopolinices gives us to understand that he is one of Scleucus' intimates.[6] And finally, the soldier wishes to be successful with women, or at least to be thought so. A sure way to please Bias is to name the most notorious courtesans of the day as among his conquests.[7] Stratophanes, in the *Truculentus*, is indig-nant at the mere thought that a woman might prefer " a curly-headed youngster who lives in safety and beats the tambourine,"[8] to himself, the man of arms. As for Pyrgopolinices, he does not doubt for a moment that every woman dotes on him.[9] This fatuous desire to appear a Lothario is the last professional characteristic feature of the soldier which deserves our attention, although Menander has endowed his Bias (Thraso in the *Eunuchus*) with one further absurd trait : the claim to being a wit.[10] But this absurdity is only casually associated with the military profession.

After the soldier come several characters which, though they belong to quite a different social class, have, in common with him, a decided tendency to be boastful : the cook, the physician, the philosopher, the soothsayer or sorcerer, and the begging priest.

---

[1] *Dial. Mer.*, IX. 1–2. [2] Philem., fr. 16. [3] *Miles*, 983, 1204–1205.
[4] Phoenic., fr. 40; cf. Nicostratus, fr. 7; Hipparchus, fr. 1.
[5] *Eun.*, 397 et seq. [6] *Miles*, 75 et seq., 947 et seq.
[7] Men., fr. 295. [8] *Truc.*, 609–610. [9] *Miles*, 58 et seq., 1040 et seq.
[10] Men., fr. 297; *Eun.*, 414 et seq., 422 et seq.

H

The cook does not play much of a part in Latin comedy. In Terence he does not appear at all, and in only one play by Plautus, the *Pseudolus*, is any lengthy development given to his rôle. Elsewhere, in the *Aulularia*, the *Casina*, the *Curculio*, the *Menaechmi* and the *Mercator*, he comes on the stage only casually. And yet it would seem that in the νέα, taken as a whole, his appearance was far from rare, and the greatest of the comic writers—excepting, perhaps, Apollodorus of Carystus — took a delight in introducing him into their plays. A rhetorician mentions the μάγειροι among the customary characters of Menander,[1] and we know that cooks do appear in more than half-a-dozen of that poet's works. Their presence in Philemon, Diphilus, Posidippus is proved by a relatively large number of fragments. And finally, in the fragments of many of the minor poets, which Kock has assembled in Volume III of the *Fragmenta*, passages belonging to the rôle of cooks are quite frequent.

Ἀλαζονικόν ἐστι πᾶν τὸ τῶν μαγείρων φῦλον, says Athenaeus.[2] The vanity of the culinary artist affords the comic writers an inexhaustible theme. Sometimes it is the vanity of a simple *cordon bleu*.[3] Elsewhere the cook, who, no doubt, in the long run feels the need of making a greater impression, has pretensions of a loftier kind. His horizon expands, he gets away from his oven, and instead of singing the praises of his dishes, shows an ever growing inclination to philosophise about cooking. He gives himself the airs of a subtle psychologist, boasting that he knows how to adapt his dishes to the age, to the nationality, to the social standing and even to the sentiments of his clients;[4] or else he claims that the culinary art is a compendium of all human knowledge.[5] In vain do those

---

[1] Hermog., p. 352, 17 Sp. = Men., fr. 942.   [2] Ath., p. 290 B.

[3] Philem., fr. 60, 79; Alexis, fr. 110; Dionysius, fr. 1; Nicostratus, fr. 8; Hegesippus, fr. 1; Euphron, fr. 11; Archedicus, fr. 2.

[4] Men., fr. 462; Diph., fr. 17, 18; Dionysius, fr. 2; Anaxippus, fr. 1; Posid., fr. 26; Naevius, *Ariolus*, fr. II.

[5] Sosipatrus, fr. 1; Nicomachus, fr. 1; Posid., fr. 27; Damoxenus, fr. 2; Demetrius, fr. 1; Euphron, fr. 11; Athenion, fr. 1.

whom he wearies with his dissertations seek to silence
him; once started, he talks and talks and talks, and
nothing in the world can stop him. It is a sight to see
the solemn airs with which he comes upon the scene of
his activities ! [1] It is amusing to hear him inquiring in
language which is occasionally interlarded with poetic
terms, about the number of guests, the plates to be set,
and the arrangement of the places,[2] and complaining that
he has not all the facilities that he requires.[3] Above all,
it is amusing to hear him give his instructions : the brevity
of his commands to his scullions is that of a true *chef*; [4]
no priest could be more solemn than he when offering a
sacrifice.[5] Is he not himself somewhat of a priest ? Our
friend, the cook, would like to have people think so, and
he concludes that this similarity of function ought to make
his person inviolable.[6]

Charlatanism is the dominant characteristic of the cook
on the stage. But we have still to complete his picture.
Provider of fine entertainments which are frequently given
in secret, witness of forbidden love-episodes, the cook
generally displays an insolent familiarity towards the
gallants who engage him, and if he occasionally sees them
caught in the act, he is greatly amused at their plight.[7]
His profession opens many doors to him, and he delights
in gossiping with the servants,[8] seeks to discover family
secrets,[9] and, when occasion offers, lays pilfering hands on
everything that he finds. In Plautus, people are always
on their guard against his thieving ways, and not without
good cause. In a fragment of Euphron a cook boasts
that, following the example of the seven great masters
who are, as it were, the seven wise men of the kitchen,

---

[1] Posid., fr. 26.
[2] Alexis, fr. 173; Men., Σαμία, 71 et seq.; fr. 518; Strato, fr. 1.
[3] Alexis, fr. 174.
[4] Men., fr. 292; Damoxenus, fr. 2; Anaxippus, fr. 6.
[5] Men., fr. 292.   [6] Athenion, fr. 1; Men., fr. 130.
[7] *Merc.*, 753 et seq.   [8] *Aul.*, 294 et seq.
[9] For instance, at the beginning of the Ἐπιτρέποντες. Cf. Themistius,
Orat., XXI. p. 262 C (= fr. adesp., 112).

he too has invented something—he has invented the art
of stealing.[1] In another fragment of the same poet's
works a cook teaches his pupil the principles of that art;
he even gives evidence of a comparative delicacy of feeling—he says one must not steal from those who pay well,
but only from those who are stingy.[2]

The physician is dealt with in a few fragments.[3] The
comic writers insinuate that the credulity of his patients
constitutes about the whole of his science. Do they not
imagine that they are relieved as soon as they see him?[4]
Does not the simplest medicine, if given under a high-
sounding or especially under an exotic name, appear to
them to be something wonderful?[5] The physician profits
by this state of mind. In order to increase his importance
he exaggerates the seriousness of every evil that he is
called upon to cure; of a trivial illness he says, "This is
serious"; of a serious sickness, "This is terrible."[6]
Following the example of several poets of the μέση, Philemon wrote a play called Ἰατρός; what remains of it is
not interesting. This is also true of the Ἀσκληπιοκλείδης
by Alexis, in which the hero must have been a physician,
or else a man who was infatuated with medical science;
and of Plautus' Parasitus medicus, in which a parasite
doubtless played the part of an Aesculapius and travestied
his prototypes. Apart from the Menaechmi we only hear
a physician speak in two very short fragments, one by
Alexis and the other by Diphilus. In Diphilus he promises
the prompt recovery—or the death!—of his patient.[7] In
Alexis he boasts of the difficulty of a cure that he has
undertaken.[8] These fragments give us glimpses of men
of the same type as their colleagues in the Menaechmi—
that is to say, perfect charlatans.[9]

Like the physicians, the philosophers were reproached

[1] Euphron, fr. 1.   [2] Ibid., fr. 10.
[3] Philem., fr. 75, 134; Philem. the younger, fr. 2–3; fr. adesp. 455.
[4] Philem., fr. 108.   [5] Alexis, fr. 142.
[6] Men., fr. 497.   [7] Diph., fr. 98.
[8] Alexis, fr. 112 (from the Κρατεια, also called the Φαρμακοπώλης.)
[9] Menaech., 882 et seq.

by the New Comedy for their theatrical manners and their
pompous talk.   They raise their eyebrows,[1] and wear long
beards; [2] they do not dress like ordinary mortals; [3] they
discourse endlessly about the supreme good; [4] they affect
austerity, contempt for wealth and every pleasure, and
pretend that they devote themselves exclusively to searching for wisdom; [5] all of which does not keep them from
drinking hard or from being quick to recognise the best
bits at dinner.[6]   Their wisdom is limited to their talk.[7]
In a fragment of Anaxippus a cook denounces their
gluttony.[8]   One of Baton's characters, who makes a very
vigorous attack on so-called Platonic love,[9] may possibly
have accused them of yet other vices.   I do not think
it improbable that in certain comedies—as is the case in
the tenth *Dialogue* of Lucian and in several of Alciphron's
Epistles [10]—there were represented philosophers who gave
young men wrong ideas and corrupted their morals.   One
of Alexis' *dramatis personae* enthusiastically praises a
famous decree of Sophocles which expelled philosophers
from Attica.   This enemy of philosophy is, I believe, a
father of a family who has had some sad experience
similar to that of Strepsiades.   At all events there is no
room for doubt that the audience occasionally saw philosophers upon the stage.   One of Philemon's plays bore
the title *Φιλόσοφοι*.   Fragment 1 of Theognetus is aimed
directly at a disciple of the Portico.   We possess a fragment of a play by Posidippus, entitled *Μεταφερόμενοι*,
which reads as follows : " So much so that in ten days
time he will wear a more sober air than Zeno." [11]   *Μεταφερόμενοι* may mean—*Those who change their opinion* or
their manner of living.   I can readily conceive that

[1] Baton, fr. 5.   [2] Phoenicides, fr. 4.
[3] *Ibid.*, fr. 4; Philemon, fr. 146.
[4] Philemon, fr. 71; Theognetus, fr. 1; Damoxenus, fr. 1; Baton,
fr. I. 5, 6.
[5] Philemon, fr. 85; Baton, fr. 2; Phoenicides, fr. 4; Theognetus, fr. 1;
Turpilius, *Lindia*, fr. IV.
[6] Baton, fr. 5.   [7] Anaxippus, fr. 4.   [8] *Ibid.*, fr. 1, 38–40.
[9] Baton, fr. 7.   [10] Alc., II. 11, 38; III. 28.   [11] Posid., fr. 15.

Posidippus introduced a Stoic teacher who boasted, like Aristaenetus in the tenth *Dialogue*, that he was bringing a young voluptuary back to the path of virtue.

Of the soothsayers, sorcerers, and mendicant priests of either sex we know next to nothing. They supplied several comedies with titles : [1] the Ἀγύρτης by Philemon, the Μηναγύρτης and the Ἱέρεια by Menander—and to these I may add the Θεοφορουμένη. They are mentioned in two other plays by Menander, the Ἡνίοχος and the Παιδίον. They were seen at work in the Θετταλή, the comedy by Diphilus to which fragment 126 belongs. Some fragments of the middle period represent them as practising medicine [2] and, above all, as indulging in boasting.[3] I presume that they remained unchanged in the νέα.

A third group of characters—and a far more homogeneous one in point of their professions—are the men of affairs: bankers, usurers and merchants. Possibly these persons occurred quite frequently in the comedies taken as a whole.[4] To-day a few scenes in Plautus are our only means of becoming acquainted with them, and they do not suggest a minute study of character. The usurer in the *Epidicus* hardly opens his mouth.[5] The usurer in the *Mostellaria* and the banker Lyco, in the *Curculio*, both complain about hard times,[6] but this is always and everywhere a pet habit of business men. The banker is careful and formal about the execution of a contract, and the usurer is obstinate in his claims. These two figures are only sketched very summarily. The character of the donkey-seller in the *Asinaria* is, to my mind, more carefully drawn.[7] He too is obstinate and suspicious, but in addition to these characteristics he possesses a third which

---

[1] One of Alexis' plays, of uncertain date, was entitled Μάντεις, another Θεοφόρητος.

[2] Antiphanes, fr. 154.   [3] Anaxandrides, fr. 49.

[4] Philemon and Diphilus each wrote an Ἔμπορος; Menander and Eudoxus each wrote a Ναύκληρος; and Alexis a Τοκιστής.

[5] *Epid.*, 631 et seq.   [6] *Curc.*, 371 et seq ; *Most.*, 532 et seq.

[7] *As.*, 392 et seq.

is no less proper for a merchant and which is brought
out in an amusing way—imperturbability. Not that our
donkey-seller remains indifferent to the impertinence of the
two slaves who are addressing him—he seems to be more
surprised at them than offended—but the verbose arguments with which they try to confound him, the assurances of good faith, the appeals to his sense of fairness,
all fail to move him. Without saying a word he waits
until the babblers cease talking, or else, as a matter of
courtesy, he replies in a few words that do not commit
him—a *fortasse*, a sceptical and indifferent *haud negassim*.
He shows himself a man who is accustomed to the haggling
of trade and does not attach any importance to it.

After this third group of professional persons little
remains to be pointed out. Lydus, in the *Bacchides*, is
an amusing pedagogue. The ferule is his passion; he
regrets the good old times when, as he says, men remained
subject to the tyranny of an usher until they were well
advanced in years. That his pupil has grown up, that
he is becoming emancipated, that he simply calls him
" Lydus " and no longer " pedagogue," is more than his
small routine brain can understand and tolerate. Accustomed to lecture boys, he cannot make up his mind to
drop the tone of reprimand, even when he speaks to
Philoxenus. He loves to be emphatic and, like many
other slaves in comedy who held the same office, he em-
bellishes his dissertations with allusions to mythology.

At the beginning of the *Curculio* there appears a duenna
who is a drunkard. An equally bibulous midwife comes
casually upon the scene in the *Andria*—where, by the
way, she behaves very properly. Her counterpart in the
Περινθία must have been freer in her conduct.[1] Among
the characters in Menander's Ψευδηρακλῆς there was a
nurse who was also addicted to wine;[2] among those of
the Ἀρρηφόρος there was possibly another nurse whose
tongue never stopped wagging;[3] a retired nurse who is

---

[1] Men., fr. 397.   [2] *Ibid.*, fr. 521.   [3] *Ibid.*, fr. 66.

garrulous and fond of drink appears in the Σαμία.[1]   In
the *Rudens* there were fishermen; and fishermen also
played a part in the Ἁλιεῖς, the Καρχηδόνιος, and elsewhere in Menander.[2]   They do not appear to have had
any special characteristics.

Finally, a certain number of comedies, besides those
with which I have already dealt, bore as their title the
name of a profession; but we cannot draw any more
trustworthy conclusions from titles of this kind than we
could from those which were based on the name of a race.
Both these kinds of titles were, by the way, less frequent
in the age of New Comedy than they had been previously.

§ 4

SLAVES

The comic writers of the new period brought a whole
host of slaves upon the stage.   First, there are pedagogues,
active or retired, trustworthy men to whom the master
confides the duty of looking after his son, of helping him
in his travels or his business, and of keeping him on the
narrow path of virtue when he himself is away from home.
Then there are the old servants acquainted with the secrets
and the worries of the family, old serving-maids who
have brought up their mistress; and, not to mention the
courtesans who are slaves, there are the abigails and
the duennas and the major-domos or heads of the household.   These constitute the aristocracy of the slaves, as
it were.   By their side we find lackeys who accompany
the young men on their amorous exploits and wait for
them as they come from their festive gatherings; military
servants, farmers and field labourers, servants engaged in
various kinds of household work, little urchins who run
on errands, or guards who at a signal from their master
lay hands on a guilty comrade, bind him and drag him
off to prison, etc.   We have already met with some of

---

[1] Σαμ., 21 et seq., 87–88.　　　[2] Men., fr. 260, 717, 863.

these persons whose occupation stamps them with the
characteristic mark of their profession, but the majority
have not been included in my analyses hitherto, and even
those who were included have merely been touched upon
casually. We must, therefore, examine how the New
Comedy depicted the mentality of the slave as a whole.
This is a good opportunity to do so, between the study
of the characters who represent various social classes and
that of the family types.

One of the most common characteristics of the slaves
in comedy, and the one that strikes us at once, is their
cunning, their rascality. In this respect the Getas and
the Davuses enjoyed a well-established reputation.[1]
Fathers of families, their usual victims, mistrust them at
every turn, and the young men think themselves sure of
success as soon as they appeal to the slave's slyness.
Indeed, Daos—or by whatever other name he is known—
is never at a loss for a device. A few minutes for reflection, a few tosses of the head, a few frowns, and a plan
worked out in all its details springs from his brain. If
need be, he improvises. He takes in a situation at a
glance. If some unforeseen incident arises which may
increase his chances of success, like the arrival of Harpa
in the *Pseudolus* or that of the donkey-seller in the *Asinaria*,
he immediately turns it to account. Occasionally his
quickness and presence of mind enable him to profit by
what would have been an awkward *contretemps* for a
less crafty tactician—for example, the sudden appearance
of the soldier towards the middle of the *Bacchides*, or that
of Chremes at the conclusion of the *Andria*. A single
effort does not exhaust his inventive faculty: Stratippocles,
in the *Epidicus*, is able to reiterate his demands; Demea,
in the *Adelphi*, knows how to repeat his ill-timed reappear-
ances; Theopropides, in the *Mostellaria*, understands how
to renew his attacks; a slave is bound to show a bold
front to the end, and it is not only when fortune favours

---

[1] Cf. Gal., *De nat. facult.*, I. 17 (= Men., fr. 946); Prop., IV. 5 (Roth-
stein), 44; Ovid, *Am.*, I. 15, 17; Apul., *Flor.*, XVI.

him that he is fertile and daring, but even failure leaves him in possession of his resources and full of self-confidence. So too, when one of his projects falls through, or threatens to do so, our friend the slave does not lose courage, but retreats in good order and renews the attack at some other point; witness the *Andria* and the *Heauton Timoroumenos*; nay, more than that, out of a failure which ought to discredit him for a long time, he manages with extra-ordinary audacity to extract the elements of an immediate and startling revenge. It seems that the comic writers hardly ever made fun of a dull slave. Sceledrus, in the *Miles*, is the only specimen of the kind in Plautus and in Terence, and there is no reason to believe that the writers of comedy introduced the type of a stupid slave, brutalised by his wretched position. On the other hand, we find among the slaves a number of fine talkers whose duty it is to amuse the audience, and of them the Romans said: *philosophantur, delicias faciunt.* Daos is not only crafty, he is also witty.

In the matter of morals the slaves of the New Comedy leave much to be desired, and the list of shortcomings with which they are charged is a long one.

The slightest, though not the least surprising, of these shortcomings is lack of reverence for everybody, including their masters. As a matter of fact, it is in the works of Plautus that this lack of reverence is shown in its most brutal aspect, and possibly the Roman poet is, in more than one case, solely responsible for the excesses of language in which his actors indulge. But let us disregard the gross language. Assuredly Plautus, who is so anxious to excuse anything foreign in the behaviour of his slave characters— in the *Stichus*, for instance, and in the prologue to the *Casina*—would not, of his own accord, have represented them in a disrespectful attitude for which Roman society in the second century could not afford him an example. Besides, this attitude is also found in Terence and in Menander himself. In the *Heauton Timoroumenos* Syrus compliments Chremes on his sharpness, sings the praises of the pretty Bacchis, and in his presence finds fault with his neighbour Menedemus, as though he were chatting with one of his own class.[1] The Syrus of the *Adelphi* parodies Demea's moral teachings to his face.[2] Onesimus, in the *Ἐπιτρέποντες*, greets his master's father-in-law with airy *persiflage*, makes fun of his calculating nature, gives him a lecture on philosophy and as a final shot pays him such compliments as the following : " See, you yourself were nothing but a dull beast, for all your wise airs." [3] If the slaves show so little respect for the men upon whom they depend when the latter remain dignified and severe, it is even more natural that they should become too familiar when the master, especially a young master, confides his troubles and his weaknesses to them and asks them for help. Sceparnio's remarks about young Plesidippus in the *Rudens*, or those of the two rascals in the *Asinaria* about the merchant, serve to give us an idea of the liberties that a slave in the *νέα* allowed himself with free men who were neither his masters nor friends of his masters.

But I repeat that this lack of respect is only a slight fault when compared with a great many others. As a rule, slaves are indiscreet, inquisitive, and given to slander. In the *Hecyra*, Parmeno, without much urging, reveals to Philotis the secrets of Pamphilus' life. In the *Ἐπιτρέποντες* Onesimus listens at the keyhole,[4] and in the *Phormio* Geta does the same.[5] In the *Aulularia* Pythodicus tells the cooks about the stingy disposition, true or imagined, of neighbour Euclio. In the *Poenulus* Syncerastus confides things to Tom, Dick and Harry which might ruin his master.

Gossip, as such, has a great charm for slaves, for they are lazy and only seek ways of wasting their time. In comedy they are cursed at for their indolence, their slowness, their lack of good-will and for the carelessness with which they perform their duties. Ballio's diatribe is

---

[1] *Heaut.*, 518 et seq.   [2] *Ad.*, 422 et seq.   [3] *Ἐπιτρ.*, 480 et seq.
[4] *Ibid.*, 404 et seq.   [5] *Phorm.*, 866 et seq.

well known,[1] and without searching elsewhere than in the fragments of Philemon and of Menander, we find enough to justify it. A slave, sent to market, comes back with something quite different from what he had been told to fetch; another,[2] who has been told to carry a load, sets it down before the door and gapes in the air; [3] in another passage a woman employed in a mill chatters more than she works.[4] Everything that calls for increased energy or action is detested by the slave. Geta, in the Μισούμενος, says that he is exhausted by his master's nocturnal excursions, on which he is obliged to accompany him;[5] Palinurus, in the Curculio, says the same thing.[6] The servant Polemo, in the Περικειρομένη, and Parmeno, in the Hecyra, think that they are obliged to walk a great deal too much.[7] Stasimus, in the Trinummus, thinks with terror of the hardships of military life which he is afraid he will have to share with Lesbonicus.[8] In the eyes of city servants, being sent to the country, where one must run about and sweat in the sun, is the worst of all punishments.[9]

To the slave's mind a good part of happiness consists in lounging about or dozing in a corner. Another element of enjoyment is the gratification of sensual appetites. Slaves delight in being rakes, and truth compels the admission that herein they do not differ from free men. But above all they are drunkards and gluttons. The " Daos in a lively mood," whom Dio Chrysostomus cites among the characters in comedy,[10] no doubt belongs to the νέα, and fragment 229 of Menander must belong to a scene similar to one of the closing scenes of the Pseudolus. In the Ἥρως, Geta's ideal is to fill his belly well;[11] Daos, in the Περικειρομένη, is capable of forgetting his duty if he is within reach of a good meal.[12] In Latin comedy

---

[1] Pseud., 133 et seq.   [2] Philem., fr. 145.   [3] Men., fr. 420.
[4] Ibid., fr. 943.   [5] Ibid., fr. 341.   [6] Curc., 181 et seq.
[7] Περικ., 164 et seq.; Hec., 814–815.
[8] Trin., 595 et seq., 721 et seq.   [9] Cf. As., 342; Most., 19.
[10] Dio Chrys., XXXII. p. 699 R = fr. adesp. 306.
[11] Men., fr. 345; Ἥρ., 16–17.   [12] Περικ., 281–283.

his comrades in service, even the most distinguished of them, like Syrus of the *Adelphi*, take a very lively interest in free dinners.[1]

In order to gratify this taste for good food, and also to increase their savings, which some day are to enable them to purchase their liberty, slaves do not hesitate to steal. In a fragment of a play by Posidippus a slave-cook mentions stealing meat as a peccadillo of daily occurrence.[2] Strobilus, in the *Aulularia*, coolly appropriates a pot full of gold belonging to Euclio. Stasimus, in the *Trinummus*, who looks after the finances of a young spendthrift, abstracts a very comfortable sum for his own use.[3] Apparently he shares the opinion of one of Menander's characters : " When the master himself squanders his whole fortune, if you take nothing for yourself, you injure yourself without helping him." [4]

And finally, slaves are liars, impudent and imperturbable liars; they lie in order to deceive their foes, they lie in order to gain the respect of their masters, they lie in order to hide their escapades, they lie in order to disguise the fact that they have lied ! In their eyes perjury is not reprehensible; nay, it is even one of the things in which they glory.[5] Mysis, in the *Andria*, is quite surprised at seeing the precautions—they are purely formal precautions—that Davus takes to avoid swearing a false oath.[6] On the other hand, Davus cannot understand why Pamphilus hesitates to lie in order to get out of a scrape,[7] and another knave of the same species, Syrus, in the *Heauton Timoroumenos*, appears to think the scruples of Chremes rather silly when the latter refuses to pretend that he is giving his daughter to Clinia.[8]

Such being the characteristics of the majority of slaves, one cannot expect them to be restrained by conscientious scruples or by a sense of honour. Dread of punishment is the beginning, and often also the end, of their good

---

[1] *Ad.*, 763–764. [2] Posid., fr. 2. [3] *Trin.*, 413. Cf. Philemon, fr. 32.
[4] Men., fr. 580. [5] *As.*, 562. [6] *Andr.*, 726–730.
[7] *Ibid.*, 383 et seq. [8] *Heaut.*, 780 et seq.

behaviour. Of this we can form an idea from those remarks of Phaniscus in the *Mostellaria*, of Strobilus in the *Aulularia*, and of Messenio in the *Menaechmi*, which, in substance, are all derived from Greek originals.[1] In many a case, however, this dread is no longer effective. Backs become callous from too frequent beating, and the skin becomes hardened by blows and tires the arms of the flogger. The slaves in Latin comedy scorn floggings, chains and the various punishments that await them,[2] and notwithstanding the silence of the original fragments, we may assume that this indifference was also found in the characters of the new period. This is a further illustration of their degraded state.

As we have seen, the slave in the *véa* is often a despicable creature, but take it all in all, and considering the conditions of his life, he might have been represented in a much more repulsive light. We must not forget that we are dealing with a period in which theorists define him as " a living tool,"[3] and even in comedy, in the midst of buffoonery and laughter, the frightfulness of his condition strikes us harshly. Upon what do the tortures which are so often mentioned and which may make his flesh turn pale, his blood flow and his bones break—upon what do they depend? On the caprice of his master. Defenceless and exposed to injustice, to the moods and the brutality of others, the slave in real life must have been filled with hatred; but it is not so on the stage. Antiphanes, in a passage where he enumerates the dangers of life, speaks of slaves who kill their masters;[4] our Davuses and Getas are certainly not the kind of men who contemplate such a crime. As a rule, their worst crime is cheating. In all comedy there is but a single slave—Stalagmus of the *Captivi*—who is a real criminal. When he runs away he kidnaps his master's son, but this

---

[1] *Most.*, 857 et seq.; *Aul.*, 587 et seq.; *Menaech.*, 966 et seq.
[2] *As.*, 318 et seq.; 548 et seq., 574–575, et seq.; *Bacch.*, 365; *Capt.*, 650; etc.
[3] Arist., *Polit.*, I, 2, 4 (p. 1253 B, 31–32).
[4] Antiphanes, fr. 204.

black villain does not appear until the end of the play—
just in time to get his punishment.

What forces drive the slave to do wrong? Frequently
it is compulsion. A young man commands his servant
to procure money or a woman for him, or to hide an
escapade, or to thwart a disagreeable plan; promptly,
and despite himself, the slave is engaged in some lying
or thieving business. Occasionally he protests, tries to
talk sense to his master, and makes clear to the young
fool the risks that he, poor devil, runs in serving him.[1]
But the youth cares not for advice nor for complaints,
and if he is not obeyed, he threatens with the lash or
the treadmill. And what is the slave to do, standing as
he does between two dangers? Pseudolus makes it clear
to the aged Simo;[2] by obeying he averts the nearer
danger, and trusts to luck or to his own shrewdness to
avoid the more distant one when the time comes. However, we must not exaggerate the part played by compulsion. Sometimes it is purely and simply the slave
himself who takes the initiative and embarks on dangerous ventures for his master's sake; witness Syrus, in the
Heauton Timoroumenos. Generally the slave lies and steals
without any special repugnance. Besides, even when he
lies or steals for some one else he may profit by doing
so, because he is generally given a share of the spoils.
Chrysalus, Pseudolus, Libanus, Leonides and Tranio take
part in their master's orgies—a pleasant prospect which
ought to suffice to fill them with zeal! Another advantage
that arises from this association is that the slave who is
the organiser-in-chief of all knavery, acquires the right
of speaking frankly to free men, of ordering them about
and of lecturing them.[3] Besides, something like the pride
of the specialist prompts him to hatch the most complicated plots, and he delights in knowing that he is the
author and the centre of so many schemes.[4] The thought

[1] Philem., fr. 18; *Epid.*, 146–147; *Eun.*, 381.   [2] *Pseud.*, 502–503.
[3] *Miles*, 782 et seq., 902 et seq., 1175 et seq.; *Andr.*, 705 et seq.; *Pseud.*,
235, 387 et seq., 720 et seq.; etc.
[4] Men., fr. 946; *Miles*, 813; *Pseud.*, 574 et seq.

that he may eclipse his rivals and establish a record for
shrewdness fills him with joy in advance.[1] He scornfully
despises victories won over a dull rival,[2] but as soon as
he finds himself face to face with crafty adversaries who
are on the defensive, he gets excited and thinks of nothing
but the end that is to be gained. When he does succeed,
he sings veritable songs of triumph and self-glorification,
with which certain of Plautus' imitations—thoroughly
Greek in spirit—acquaint us,[3] and of which fragment 924
of Menander appears to me to be an original bit. Such
behaviour reveals more vanity than real malice. When
all is said and done, the desire to do harm is rarely the
motive that actuates slaves.

On the contrary, it is not unusual in comedy to find a
slave who is capable of affection, sympathy and devotion
for the family which he serves or for one of its members.
The most mischievous knaves in all comedy are occasionally imbued with these feelings. In the *Phormio* Geta
declares that if he were thinking of himself only, he would
run away as soon as Demipho returned; if he remains and
exposes himself to the wrath of the father of the family
it is from compassion for the son—so he says in a soliloquy.[4]
In the *Andria* Davus finds the following reason for dis-
obeying Simo and helping Pamphilus: "If I were to for-
sake Pamphilus I should have to fear for his life." [5] Besides compulsion, personal interest and vainglory, we must
frequently include among the motives of the rascally
slave a real affection for his young master, his τρόφιμος.
The latter, moreover, is well aware of this, and when he
makes peace with the paternal powers, he always stipu-
lates for the impunity of his faithful ally.[6] We may even
say that in the soul of certain knaves there is sometimes
found a curious loyalty towards the very man whom they

[1] Men., fr. 751; *Oxyrh. Pap.*, Vol. I, No. 11; *Bacch.*, 649 et seq.,
Turpilius, *Thrasyleon*, fr. VI.
[2] Men., fr. 393.
[3] For example, Chrysalus' *canticum* in the *Bacchides*, 925 et seq.
[4] *Phorm.*, 188.   [5] *Andr.*, 210.
[6] *Bacch.*, 521 et seq., 689-691; *Most.*, 1168 et seq.; *Andr.*, 955.

rob and abuse. In the *Trinummus*, Stasimus, during the absence of Charmides, is not ashamed to profit by the thriftlessness of the latter's son, but when Charmides returns in time to straighten out his affairs, Stasimus welcomes him with a joy that is apparently not feigned.

Elsewhere, affection for the master is still more unqualified. It is so, for instance, among a number of women servants, old nurses and others, who console, help, and, if occasion offers, protect some unfortunate woman when she is in a scrape—witness Philinna, in the Γεωργός; Canthara, in the *Adelphi*; Syra, in the *Mercator*; Doris, in the Περικειρομένη; Mysis, in the *Andria*; Staphyla, in the *Aulularia*; Sophrona, in the Ἐπιτρέποντες, and Sophrona, in the *Phormio*. Irreproachable loyalty is also found among the male slaves, and they are lauded in fragment 644 of Menander. Such a one is Grumio or Stratylax, before his " change of heart," or Lampadio, or Geta, in the *Adelphi*, or Parmeno, in the Πλόκιον, whom Aulus Gellius[1] calls " *servus bonae frugi* "; and such were, in all probability, the characters who give their names as titles for a number of comedies of the decadent period called Φιλοδέσποτος. Polemon's servant, in the Περικειρομένη, takes an interest in his master's love affairs.[2] In the Ἐπιτρέποντες Onesimus has watched the wife of Charisius during the latter's absence and informed him—with more zeal than tact—of the unpleasant things that he has observed. In the *Miles* Palaestrio on his own initiative starts in pursuit of the ravisher who had carried off Pleusicles' sweetheart. Messenio protects Menaechmus' purse against Menaechmus himself, and unhesitatingly comes to blows for him. Now and again we hear a slave say that he is contented and protesting that he is loyal.[3] Daos, in the Ἥρως, apparently sings the praises of Laches;[4] with a trustfulness that does honour to them both, he confides to him his fondness for Plangon and begs him to

[1] Aul. Gell., II. 23, 15.   [2] Περικ., 68–70, 166 et seq.
[3] Men., fr. 1093 = Philem., fr. 227.
[4] Ἥρ., 48 (Robert's emendation).

I

intercede for him with Gorgias, the brother and *kyrios* of the young woman. Elsewhere, master and slave converse in a cordial manner—the former counsels and the latter consoles.[1] And it is not only in the houses of the poor, who are hardly less wretched than their slaves, that such sympathy may exist. The poor man in Philemon,[2] who is surprised at the troubles of the rich and has pity for them, addresses his remarks to a certain Sosia. Now that is the name of a slave, and the Sosia in question was, no doubt, the slave of some rich man. He laments over the unhappiness of which he is a witness and by means of his wailing moves the poor man to pity. The heroic example of Tyndarus in the *Captivi* shows us how far the affection of a slave for his master can go; he does not hesitate to risk his life in order to free Philocrates from captivity.

The slaves in comedy hardly take an interest in anybody except their master. Towards their comrades in service they are, as a rule, indifferent or even evilly disposed; each of them laughs at the misfortunes of his neighbours, spitefully figures out the punishments that await them, is jealous of them and, if he has any authority over them, lets them feel it to their sorrow.[3] As for foreigners, the slave, for the most part, regards them as nothing more than interlopers or dupes. Still, there are some honourable exceptions to this egotism. Syriscus, in the ᾽Επιτρέποντες, is a slave. Doubtless he is a privileged person, a χωρὶς οἰκῶν, who has a wife and household, and plies his trade at home in return for paying his master a rental; still he is a slave. Now Syriscus has a compassionate soul; he wishes, if possible, to spare his temporary ward the evil—slavery—from which he suffers, and without any selfish interest he eagerly and passionately demands the child's

---

[1] Philem., fr. 73, 90, 133; Men., fr. 155, 407, 481, 649; Philippides, fr. adesp., 115.

[2] Philem., fr. 96.

[3] [Men.], fr. 698. See the attitude of the pseudo-Saurea toward Libanus, of Thesprio toward Epidicus, and the exchange of amenities between Pinacium and Phaniscus (*Most.*), etc.

γνωρίσματα. Another person in the same play, Habrotonon, also a slave and desirous of liberty, is disturbed at the thought that the little boy, son of a citizen, runs the risk of growing up in bondage, and she reproaches Onesimus for not taking active steps on his behalf.[1]

On the other hand, it is fair to say that the diligence with which some slaves fulfil their tasks redounds to their credit. We have already found this virtue in several rustics, Grumio, Stratylax and Olympio. Lydus, in the *Bacchides*, is the type of a zealous pedagogue, whose zeal, by the way, meets with a poor reward, while he himself is repudiated by his master. No doubt it was also a pedagogue who addressed to a youth some moral lecture which is preserved in the fragments,[2] and who indulged in commendable remarks about his duties which are interpolated in lines 592 et seq. of the *Aulularia*. Traces of this professional pride are found even in the most ticklish situations; witness the reasoning with which Parmeno, in the *Eunuchus*, consoles himself for having introduced Chaerea, against that young man's wish, to Thais.[3]

Finally, we meet with slaves who manage to retain a certain dignity in their abasement. I do not, of course, refer to the absurd pride of a Geta who is proud of his birth,[4] nor of a Thracian who, if we are to believe his words, was a prince among his people;[5] but to true moral dignity, to the consciousness of being a human being. In a fragment of Philemon we read : " Even if a man be a slave, O master, he is none the less a man, if he is a man; "[6] and in another fragment of the same author a slave says that every man in this world, in no less or greater degree than himself, is the slave of some person or of some thing.[7] Though he does not indulge in such fine aphorisms, Syriscus' attitude, in the Ἐπιτρέποντες, gives evidence of similar levelling instincts. When he begs Smicrines to be arbiter

---

[1] Ἐπιτρ., 251–253.   [2] Men., fr. 530, 531.   [3] *Eun.*, 930 et seq.
[4] Men., fr. 547.   [5] *Ibid.*, fr. 828.
[6] Philem., fr. 22 : ἄνθρωπος οὗτός ἐστιν, ἂν ἄνθρωπος ᾖ.
[7] *Ibid.*, fr. 31.

between himself and Daos, he addresses him politely, but
without obsequiousness and more freely than a poor man
of the lower classes would to-day address a gentleman.
The latter at first testily gives him a rebuff, but he is not
disconcerted and insists in the name of justice and the
public interest. He is not afraid to reprimand a man who
is far above him in station, and finally gains his point.[1]

§ 5

THE FAMILY

We are now ready to take up the study of the family.
I shall begin by seeing what sort of a picture our poets
painted of marriage and of married life.

New Comedy is misogynous. Diphilus says : " It is difficult to find a good woman." [2] When, in the *Aulularia*,
which is probably an imitation of Menander, Megadorus
addresses his sister with the words : *optima femina*, she,
being doubtless used to other appellations, is greatly
surprised. " There is no such thing as an excellent
woman," she declares with a curious humility; " each one
is worse than the other." To which Megadorus condes-
cendingly replies, " That is my opinion too." [3] Stupidity,
a natural propensity to take the wrong side and to cling
to it obstinately, an irascible and untractable temper, a
spirit of contradiction, vanity, garrulousness, greediness,
jealousy, lack of modesty, faithlessness, heartlessness, ingratitude, hypocrisy, lying—all these are charged against
women in general. Wherever women are, there all evils
are found. They are the most wicked animals in the world,[4]
and Prometheus, who created them, well deserved his
punishment.[5]

As the νέα professed so unfavourable an opinion of the
fair sex, we cannot expect it to extol marriage. In two
fragments—both by Menander—we hear a defence of the
institution of marriage, or rather a plea of extenuating

---

[1] 'Επιτρ., 13 et seq.   [2] Diph., fr. 115.   [3] *Aul.*, 135 et seq.
[4] Men., fr. 488.   [5] *Ibid.*, fr. 535.

circumstances in its favour.[1] Marriage is an evil, a necessary evil, if you will, but undeniably an evil [2]—a thing
that one wishes one's enemies.[3] Even the fathers of marriageable daughters say so.[4] Alexis declares that it is
better to be disfranchised than to be married.[5] Another
poet, perhaps Philemon, says that it is better to bury a
wife than to marry her.[6] In a fragment of Menander we
read that he who marries ought to esteem himself happy
if he is not thoroughly unhappy,[7] and in another still more
pessimistic fragment marriage is compared to a sea of
trouble, not to a Libyan or Aegean Sea, in which only three
out of every thirty ships are wrecked, but to a sea on which
there is no hope of safety.[8] Eubulus, a poet of the middle
period, wrote : " May the second man who took a wife
die a terrible death. Of the first one who did so I shall
not speak ill because he, no doubt, had no experience of
this plague; but the second man knew how great a calamity
a woman is." [9] Menander goes still further : " May he die
a wretched death who was the first to get married, and
then the second, then the third, then the fourth and so
on." [10] One must be young and inexperienced to have
a desire to marry. A man who has been a bachelor up
to a mature age does not usually dream of changing his
state; he congratulates himself upon being free and wife-
less.[11] He regards proposals of marriage as he would a
shower of stones,[12] and if he succumbs, it is under pressure from his family, like Micio, in the *Adelphi*, or like
Megadorus, through the influence of some god.

Such scenes of married life as New Comedy portrayed
were generally sufficient warrant for these sarcastic remarks
and for such apprehensions. There are only three Latin
plays—the *Amphitryon*, the *Stichus* and the *Hecyra*—in

---

[1] Men., fr. 325, 647.
[2] Philem., fr. 196, 198; Men., fr. 651, fr. adesp., 132.
[3] Fr. adesp. 296–297.   [4] Men., fr. 532.   [5] Alexis, fr. 262.
[6] [Philem.], fr. 236.   [7] Men., fr. 648, cf. 532.   [8] *Ibid.*, fr. 65.
[9] Eub., fr. 116.   [10] Men., fr. 154, cf. fr. adesp. 110.
[11] Philem., fr. 239, Men., fr. 1 (= *Ad.*, 43–44); Philippides, fr. 6.
[12] *Aul.*, 151–152.

which we see contented homes; and in each of them harmony reigns under quite special conditions; for Amphitryon,
Pamphilus, and the two husbands in the *Stichus*, come home
after a long absence. As regards the last two, I must
add that while their young wives awaited them with an
affectionate loyalty, they themselves appear to be not less
impatient or less delighted to see them once more. As
for Pamphilus, he is on his honeymoon; legally married
for less than a year, the union of his heart is still more
recent.

Apart from the Latin comedies, a few passages admit
of the supposition that an edifying married life was
represented in the *νέα*. Pamphilia and Charisius, in the
'*Επιτρέποντες*, lived in tender accord before the birth of
the supposed bastard. When the complication which had
separated them for a time is straightened out, they become
reconciled and doubly devoted to one another. At the
beginning of the *Περινθία* it was, as we know, to his wife
—and not to his enfranchised slave, as in the *Andria*—
that the father confided his anxieties and his plans. In
fragment 160 of Menander, a person whom I believe to be
a woman, a married woman, gives a man good advice. In
fragment 827 homage is paid to the excellent discretion
of a wife. In fragment 848 some one exclaims : *ὦ Ζεῦ
πολυτίμηθ᾿, ὡς καλαὶ νῷν αἱ γυναί (sic)*; if *καλαί* here refers
to moral qualities, it is possible that this line comes from
'*Αδελφοὶ ά*, the model which Plautus followed in the *Stichus*.
Finally, in fragment 608, some unknown person angrily
defends his wife's reputation. That is all; and it is, as
we see, very little.

As compared with these rare evidences of mutual esteem
and of satisfaction, quarrels and recriminations are of very
frequent occurrence, and comedies, as is natural, since they
were written by men, make a special point of the grievances of husbands. To judge by the way in which a friend
tries to console him,[1] the *misogynist* in Menander blames
his wife for having an immoderate love of luxury, for

[1] Men., fr. 325, 7.

senseless extravagance in dress, in furniture and perfumes.[1] In the *Hecyra* Laches declares that, in order to offset the extravagances of Sostrata, he is obliged to live in the country.[2] In the *Miles* Periplecomenus mentions the dread of being incessantly bombarded with demands for money as one of the reasons that keeps him from getting married.[3] Megadorus, in the *Aulularia*, is inexhaustible on that subject.[4] Moreover, it is not only on account of the cost that the luxury of their wives and the artifices of their toilets annoy the husbands so much. Sometimes it is also because they think such things improper. "Leave the house," says a husband in Menander; "a respectable woman ought not to dye her hair golden." [5]

Besides these sumptuary expenses, the *misogynist* must have found fault with the expenses due to an exaggerated piety. At any rate, he very much disliked to see his wife constantly engaged in offering sacrifices.[6] "It is us, the married men," says one of his companions in misery, "whom the gods ruin by preference; for us there is always some festival to be celebrated." [7] Superstition is a feminine weakness of which husbands in comedy appear to have complained more than once. In his satire on married life, Periplecomenus speaks of matrons who are anxious to satisfy a whole tribe of female charlatans.[8]

Yet another grievance : women talk too much, and have a mania for being effusive to excess. Daemones, in the *Rudens*, on coming home, expects his wife to weary his brain with her chatter.[9] Subsequently, when she has found her daughter again, he reproaches her because she will not stop embracing her.[10] Under analogous conditions Chremes, in the *Heauton Timoroumenos*, overwhelms his wife with sarcastic remarks.[11] It must be admitted that Daemones and Chremes are unreasonably grumpy; the happy event at which their wives rejoice may well excuse a few superfluous words.

[1] Men., fr. 332, 333, 334 (?); Philem., fr. 81. [2] Hec., 224 et seq.
[3] Miles, 690 et seq. [4] Aul., 483 et seq. [5] Men., fr. 610.
[6] Ibid., fr. 326. [7] Ibid., fr. 601. [8] Miles, 693–694.
[9] Rud., 905. [10] Ibid., 1203–1205. [11] Heaut., 879 et seq.

But now we come to something more serious : at every opportunity the wives pick a quarrel with their husbands and oppose them. Laches, in the *Hecyra*, and a character in one of Naevius' plays are melancholy over the recognition of this fact;[1] Chremes, in the *Heauton Timoroumenos*, groans over it.[2] As a matter of fact, neither the Sostrata in the *Heauton Timoroumenos* nor the Sostrata in the *Hecyra* gives any evidence of so cantankerous a disposition. But other matrons on the comic stage made themselves liable to this reproach. In the *Mercator*, Dorippa, the wife of Lysimachus, who was to have waited for him in the country, goes to town in order to follow him, and she boasts of this escapade.[3]

Often the quarrelsome disposition of a woman degenerates into tyranny. The unfortunate Menaechmus has to submit to a close cross-examination every time he goes out or comes home : " Where are you going? What are you doing? What are you after? What are you going to fetch? What are you taking away with you? What did you do out of doors? " so that Menaechmus declares : " I have married a customs officer who obliges me to declare everything that I have done and everything that I am doing."[4] In one of Philemon's comedies a tyrannical wife is brought back to her senses.[5] In Menander's ʿΥποβολιμαῖος the extremes to which another " masterful woman " goes call forth similar remarks from some one.[6] The household in which the husband trembles in the presence of his imperious better half is a commonplace of the comic poets. Hardly has such a husband, whom the world deems happy and who, when away from home, puts on airs—hardly has he crossed the threshold of his house than he falls under the dominion of his wife.[7] And what is at the bottom of this dominion? Most frequently, money. Men cringe before their wives because their wives are richer than they. The New Comedy is full of

---

[1] *Hec.*, 202; Naevius, *Agitatoria*, fr. 11.   [2] *Heaut.*, 1006–1007.
[3] *Merc.*, 667–669.   [4] *Menaech.*, 114 et seq. ; 117–118.
[5] *Philem.*, fr. 132.   [6] *Men.*, fr. 484.   [7] *Ibid.*, fr. 302.

curses against a dowered wife and of lamentations by husbands, who, as one of them says, have sold their freedom for a dower.[1] A passage of the Πλόκιον, preserved by Aulus Gellius, especially deserves to be quoted here. The speaker is a husband whose wife Crobyle has just forced him to sell a little slave girl, a good and clever servant, at whom she had taken umbrage : " She will sleep on both ears now, the pretty heiress ! She has just performed a great and glorious feat of prowess. . . . Alas, that I should have taken this Crobyle with her sixteen talents and her cubit-long nose. And what conceit ! Can I possibly stand her ? No, by the Olympian Zeus and by Athene, no ! . . . I have married a Lamia who had a dower. Didn't I tell you so ? Yes, didn't I tell you so ? She is mistress of my house, of my estates, of absolutely everything; I have a mistress, by Apollo, and the most untractable of the untractable." [2] More than one husband, in Latin comedy, is of the same opinion as the husband of Crobyle. More than one wife proudly boasts of the number of talents she brought as dower, haughtily finds fault with the business management of the head of the family, or even takes the administration of her dower out of his hands, and entrusts it to one of her slaves.

The wife's sharp temper frequently enough takes the most unpleasant form of all—that of jealousy. It must be admitted that the husbands, in comedy, are not all free from reproach. Hardly any one of them prides himself on his conjugal affection. There are some, like Simo in the *Mostellaria*, who are satisfied if they can escape a tête-à-tête and avoid the advances that are made to them.[3] There are others who go a step farther and who, having grown old by the side of spouses of whom they are tired, seek amorous adventures. This is what Demaenetus in the *Asinaria* does, and Lysidamus in the *Casina*, and Menaechmus in the play of the same name, and Chremes in the *Phormio*. All these worthies appear to have a quiet conscience, and if they think of their legitimate spouses

---

[1] Alexis, fr. 146.   [2] Men., fr. 402–403.   [3] *Most.*, 692 et seq.

at all, it is merely in order to make comparisons—not very flattering ones—between them and their rivals. But if they happen to be found out, their infidelities, which the law tolerates, expose them to redoubtable outbursts of passion at home. Injured in her feelings and, above all, wounded in her pride and her interests, the wife storms, scolds, threatens, sends for her father in order that he may secure her a divorce, or else—and this is the supreme humiliation—makes her son the arbiter between herself and her husband. And the husband, abashed, anxious, above all else, to disarm such wrath, has recourse to the poorest excuses, to the most absurd wheedling. Thus we see that wives have their reasons for not confiding blindly in their husbands, but occasionally they go to the opposite extreme and see wrongs which do not exist—or, let us say, which do not as yet exist. This is the case in the *Mercator*, as far as Lysimachus is concerned, who, it is true, has all the appearances of wrongdoing against him; this was the case in the *Πλόκιον*,[1] and is the case in the *Rudens*, in which Daemones abstains from harbouring Palaestra and Ampelisca, because his wife would regard them as his mistresses.

Did the husbands have a monopoly of adultery in the household as portrayed in comedy? Both the fragments and the Latin plays make several allusions to the infidelity of married women as a matter of common occurrence.[2] But it is one thing to call attention to the corruption of morals and another thing to bring it upon the stage. As far as their morals are concerned, the matrons in Terence always deserve the epithet he gives them — *matronae bonae*.[3] In Plautus, Pyrgopolinices is led to believe that his neighbour, who is supposed to be the legitimate wife of a man who lives at Ephesus, is smitten with him and is ready to be his mistress;[4] the aged Nicobulus is told that

---

[1] Aul. Gell., II. 23, 8 et seq.
[2] Cf. Men., fr. 261, 366, 535, 657; Euphron, fr. 12; Baton, fr. 3; fr. adesp., 225, 272; *Andr.*, 315 et seq.
[3] *Eun.*, prol. 37.   [4] *Miles*, 964 et seq.

his son has the wife of a soldier as his mistress;[1] but in both cases these statements are downright lies. The mention of a γραφὴ μοιχείας in Menander's Χαλκίς,[2] and that of the degrading punishment which was at that time inflicted on adulterers in the Ἀποκληρομένη by Posidippus,[3] are evidently very weak clues that do not permit one to make any conjecture about the contents of the two plays. One of Philemon's comedies was called Μοιχός; in the Ἁλιεῖς by Menander, reference is made to a μοιχός who had made his escape;[4] in the Διάβολος by Apollodorus, the statement is made that no door is closed tightly enough to keep out the μοιχοί and the cats.[5] At first sight these details appear very suggestive. But what is the meaning of the word μοιχός? Simply a seducer; but he may be the seducer of a concubine, of a mistress, or of a wife. Nor can we get any evidence against the virtue of matrons out of the title Ἀπολείπουσα, for this word has nothing to do with the desertion of bed and board, but refers to the legal procedure by which an offended wife asks the archon to dissolve her marriage. Nevertheless, in Apollodorus' Ἀπολείπουσα it appears that a woman escaped from her house by means of a rope-ladder;[6] probably she wished to escape from her husband's ill usage. Finally, there remain some passages in the epistolographers, and in them we do find several examples of unfaithful married women;[7] but we have no warrant for saying that they are taken from comedy.

In what survives of the νέα opinions are much more divided about the joys and sorrows of paternity than they are on the question of marriage.[8] Paternity is, moreover, regarded in very different lights, according as it has to deal with a son or with a daughter. A son, we read in Menander, constitutes the happiness of his parents, if

---

[1] *Bacch.*, 851 et seq.   [2] Men., fr. 512.   [3] Posid., fr. 4.
[4] Men., fr. 16.   [5] Apoll. Car., fr. 6.   [6] *Ibid.*, fr. 1.
[7] Alc., III. 26, 33; Arist., II. 22.
[8] Cf. Men., fr. 166, 418, 649, 656; 603, 655.

he is gifted; but a daughter is an encumbrance.[1] Posidippus says that even a poor man brings up his son; even a rich man abandons his daughter.[2] As a matter of fact we know how frequent the exposing of daughters is in New Comedy; we hardly know of an instance of the exposing of a son. Daughters—I speak of legitimate daughters —were generally exposed for reasons of economy. One father wishes to avoid the cost of their maintenance and education,[3] another wishes to escape the necessity of giving them a dower.[4] If they were brought up it was usual to regret the money they cost, or to complain of the difficulty of getting them married. " A daughter is a burden and hard to settle," says a character in the ʽΑλιεῖς,[5] and another, in the Δακτύλιος, philosophises as follows on the experience of Danaus in antiquity : " Who was ever so forsaken by the gods as not to be willing joyfully to give up his daughters, especially when he had fifty of them ? " [6]

However this may have been, parents in comedy as a general rule love their children. The most unfair attitude that they take is possibly that of a father in one or two of Menander's comedies—the ʽΥποβολιμαῖος and the Ναύκληρος—in which he treats one of his sons with every tenderness and the other with indifference. As for the recriminations which either the stupidity or the bad behaviour of his offspring calls forth from the head of the family—recriminations in which the Latin poets abound and which are also found in a few original fragments [7]— they do not preclude affection.

This affection especially manifests itself when a father or a mother is in danger of losing a child. In the *Heauton Timoroumenos* Menedemus becomes deeply despondent after Clinia has gone to serve in a foreign land, and, as the account which he gives his neighbour Chremes shows,[8] there is a large share of remorse in his unhappiness. In

---

[1] Men., fr. 60. [2] Posid., fr. 11. [3] *Heaut.*, 835 et seq.
[4] *Phorm.*, 646–647, with Donatus' note (= Apoll. Car., fr. 22).
[5] Men., fr. 18. [6] *Ibid.*, fr. 102.
[7] Alexis, fr. 108; Baton, fr. 5. [8] *Heaut.*, 121 et seq.

the *Captivi* it is paternal affection alone that animates Hegio. In order to free his son, who is a captive at Elis, he recklessly spends his money and takes up a far from respectable profession, and one that is repugnant to his character—that of a slave-dealer; and as long as Philopolemus is separated from him, joy finds no place in his soul. Nicobulus, in the *Bacchides*, who has sent Mnesilochus to Ephesus, is consumed by anxiety because he does not return. In the *Epidicus* the unhappy Philippa, whose daughter is a captive of the Athenians, follows the army that bears her away, searches for her, alone and unaided, in a strange town, is greatly cheered when she thinks her daughter has been found, and is dissolved in tears when her hopes are deceived. Time does not always cure the sorrow caused by separation. More than ten years after the kidnapping of his daughters, Hanno, in the *Poenulus*, seeks for them throughout the world. Daemones, in the *Rudens*, cannot look at Palaestra without thinking of the daughter he has lost.[1] Affection remains alive in the hearts of parents even for a child whom they have barely seen. In the *Epidicus* Periphanes employs a trusty slave to bring presents to Telestis, whom Philippa had borne him in secret. As soon as she can do so without disgracing herself, Phanostrata, in the *Cistellaria*, goes in search of the daughter whom she had borne before her first marriage and whom she had exposed. The reappearance of a child that had disappeared is generally welcomed by its parents as a blessing. It is true that their joy—at any rate in the Latin copyists—is often rather hinted at than expressed, unless, indeed, its further expression, which would be a stale theme to the audience, is left to be imagined as occurring behind the scenes. But that does not prevent their joy from being sincere; without lengthy effusions, a phrase, a word, proves it to be so and shows its intensity.

The test of absence is one of the severest and most

---

[1] *Rud.*, 742 et seq.

frequent tests to which the affection of parents is subjected in the *véa*. But there is no lack of other opportunities for them to manifest their solicitude. A mother
is anxious about her daughter's confinement,[1] or because
she has been deserted by a faithless suitor,[2] or threatened
with disgrace.[3] Or a father, even though he be brutal
or avaricious, is indignant at the outrage to which his
child has been subjected,[4] or deplores her unfortunate
marriage,[5] or trembles for his son, whose morals are, as
he thinks, endangered.[6] " If I had had children," says
Periplecomenus, " by Pollux, what distress they would
have given me ! I should have been in constant anxiety.
Had one of them had a fever, I should have thought that
I was dead. Had he fallen when he was drunk, or been
thrown from his horse, I should have been afraid that he
had broken his leg or his neck ! " [7] Even when there is
no serious reason for fear, parents create bugbears and
grow tender over the most worthless scamp, as though he
were a defenceless innocent. Witness the worthy Micio
in the *Adelphi*.[8]

Notwithstanding all this love, the majority of parents in
comedy are at odds with their children, though rarely
with their daughters. Moreover, speaking generally,
daughters who are under the tutelage of their parents do
not play much of a part on the stage. In the *Asinaria*
we meet with one—a courtesan who contends with a
mother in order to be allowed to follow her own bent
and to love the man of her choice. In the *Cistellaria*
Gymnasium plies without repugnance the trade her
mother has forced upon her. Selenium owes it to her
mother's kindness that she is able to belong only to
Alcesimarchus. It will be recalled after how many remonstrances—they are always respectful—and with how much
bitterness Saturio's daughter, in the *Persa*, obeys her
father, who lends her to Toxilus so that she may take part

---

[1] *Adelphi.*   [2] Γεωργός, *Adelphi.*   [3] *Hecyra.*
[4] *Aulularia.*   [5] Ἐπιτρέποντες.   [6] *Bacchides, Eunuchus.*
[7] *Miles,* 718 et seq.   [8] *Ad.,* 28 et seq.

in a degrading comedy. All the young women whom we
have mentioned belong to the lower social classes, a sort
of contraband world. But young women of the middle
class play a still more unimportant part. Nowhere,
either in Plautus or in Terence, do they appear upon the
scene, and there is hardly a Greek or a Latin fragment
that we could think of allotting to them. At any rate
there is no proof that the comic writers ever represented
respectable young girls championing their love against
the ill-will or the adverse plans of their parents. On
several occasions, in the Latin imitations, we hear that
the marriage of a daughter of good family is decided
upon,[1] and certainly those among whom she lives are not
indifferent to that which may jeopardise or assure her
happiness; but they make no effort to. find out whether
she has any predilection of her own. The only extant
plays in which daughters of a good family are in conflict
with paternal authority are the 'Επιτρέποντες and the
Stichus. In both of these plays it is a question of married
daughters.

Thus, as far as children are concerned, interest centres
almost entirely in the sons. As regards parents, the
mother is hardly taken into consideration. However, an
exception must be made in the case of the mothers of
courtesans of whom we have just spoken. Besides, the
courtesans, as a general rule, never have a father, or no
longer have one. In regular and complete families the
mother is relegated to the background. A compassionate
and gentle nature is generally her distinguishing feature.
" Mater indulgens," says Apuleius, when he enumerates
the types found in Philemon.[2] In lines 991–993 of the
Heauton Timoroumenos Terence follows Menander in
declaring that " all mothers come to the aid of their sons'
follies and usually protect them against their fathers'
injustice." As a matter of fact, in the Casina, the mother
helps along her son's plans regarding the young slave girl.

[1] In the Trinummus, the Andria and the Aululuria.
[2] Ap., Flor., XVI.

At the end of the *Phormio*, Phaedria's mother, Nausistrata, gets Chremes to permit the young man to keep his
mistress and to let him have the thirty minae extorted by
Phormio, so that he may acquire an undisputed right to
Pamphila. At the close of the *Heauton Timoroumenos*
Clitipho's mother intercedes for him when his father is
about to disinherit him. The usual indulgence of mothers
in comedy does not, however, prevent their being match-
makers. "You are all like that," says Laches to his
wife, in lines 240–241 of the *Hecyra*; "you want your
sons to get married." At the opening of the *Heauton
Timoroumenos* Sostrata offers her son Clitipho a whole
band of maidens from among whom to choose a bride.
In Lucian's second *Dialogue* it is Pamphilus' mother who,
when a neighbour gets married, reproaches her son for
remaining a bachelor too long. In the seventh *Dialogue*
it is the mother of Chaereas, and her skill at discovering a
good match, that worries the old courtesan. Indulgent
even towards misconduct and, by virtue of their sex,
more susceptible in matters of a sentimental sort than
their husbands, the mothers, it seems, must have been
the allies of their sons when the latter became enamoured
of a poor girl or thought of marrying below their station.
In two instances, however, the fragments appear to attribute to them an exactly opposite attitude. "Trust your
mother Crobyle, and marry your cousin," we read in
fragment 929 of Menander. It is likely enough that the
Crobyle who spoke these words was the Crobyle of the
Πλόκιον, the detestable dowered wife who is so proud of
her wealth. It may be that after her husband had, in an
access of energy, sanctioned his son's marriage with a poor
neighbour, she, tyrannical as she was, and full of contempt for people without means, objected to this plan
and suggested a wealthy heiress. Elsewhere it is again a
mother who wearies her son by constantly insisting on the
advantages of being "well born";[1] we can assume that
she did this in the course of a discussion on the subject

[1] Men., fr. 533.

of matrimony. Notwithstanding these few instances of disagreement, one may say that, in comedy, mothers and sons get on well together. Several fragments afford touching and decided evidence of maternal tenderness or of the filial affection by which mothers are rewarded.¹ In the *Hecyra*, in particular, we find these two feelings carried to a high degree of nobility.

I have still to deal with the sons and fathers. The point on which they generally disagree is that the fathers try to force them to break off some attachment or clandestine marriage and to oblige them to marry a wife of their choosing. But the feelings which inspire the fathers vary according to circumstances.

Sometimes it is egotism, the wish to arrange their affairs according to their own convenience without regard for the inclinations of the young men. In the Γεωργός the father, for reasons unknown to us, wished his son to marry his half-sister.² In the *Phormio* Antipho is sacrificed by his tyrannical father in order to pacify an uncle: Demipho wishes him to marry Phanium, a daughter of the bigamist Chremes, so that strangers may not make inquiries into the origin of that young woman, and that Nausistrata, Chremes' wife, may remain ignorant of that worthy's infidelity.³

More frequently, fathers get into conflict with their sons for pecuniary reasons. Nearly all of them are fond of money and are by no means delighted at becoming the fathers-in-law of poor girls. Above all, they cannot bear to have their fortunes jeopardised by foolish adventures, and used to pay for courtesans. Theopropides, in the *Mostellaria*, thinks that the worst misdeeds—if not all the misdeeds—of young Philolaches consist in his extravagance. He is visibly relieved when Callidamates, Philolaches' friend, guarantees that he will not have to pay for his son's pranks.⁴ Luckily for the honour of fathers,

¹ Men., fr. 763; Philem., fr. 156; Alexis, fr. 267.
² Γεωργ., 9–12.   ³ *Phorm.,* 601 et seq.   ⁴ *Most.,* 1162 et seq.
K

there are but few in comedy who, like Theopropides, attach importance to money only. Nevertheless, pecuniary considerations are almost always mentioned among the reasons for their severity. Sometimes they fear that they are going to be ruined themselves;[1] sometimes, while resigned as far as they themselves are concerned, or sure that they will not suffer need during the few years of life that remain to them, they become indignant at the thought that after their death their fortunes will be squandered and their children will be beggars.[2]

Sometimes the horror of extravagance which is usual in the fathers in comedy is increased when they compare the happy and indolent life of their sons with their own hardworking and penurious youth. Such comparison engenders, if I may say so, a certain envy of the young men whom their labour has made rich. This feeling is very evident in a father in one of Philemon's comedies—Demipho of the *Mercator*—and in Menedemus, in Menander's *Heauton Timoroumenos*. The former, so his son tells us, kept on repeating " how he, on growing to manhood, had not given himself up, as I had, to love, idleness and sloth, and that he would not have been in position to do so, as his father kept him strictly,"[3] and so forth. " At your age," says another father, " I did not think of making love. I was poor, and I left this country to go to Asia, where I found glory and profit in the profession of a soldier."[4]

The motives we have enumerated are not of a very lofty order. Some fathers have nobler ones. When they insist on a marriage, it is sometimes because they see—or because they sincerely believe that they see—a promise of happiness for the young man concerned. When they attempt to break off a youth's illicit attachment or to prevent his leading a dissipated life, it is often from a desire to guard his reputation and his virtue. In the *Trinummus* Philto gives his son Lysiteles admirable

[1] *Heaut.*, 930–931.   [2] *Ibid.*, 969; fr. inc. XXXVIII. 5.
[3] *Merc.*, 61 et seq.   [4] *Heaut.*, 110 et seq.

advice—advice which is, by the way, superfluous, as Lysitcles is an exemplary son.[1] In the *Heauton Timoroumenos* Chremes gives Clitipho his explanation of the source of the apparent severity of fathers : " Their objections are nearly always the same. They do not wish to have their sons run after women too much, nor to be constantly merry-making. They give only as much money as is absolutely necessary. But all this is for their sons' good. Once the heart is caught in the meshes of an evil passion, it is inevitable, Clitipho, that a man's behaviour should harmonise with it." [2] Though they do not speak in so doctrinaire a way, other fathers are inspired by the same principles. They feel that they are the keepers of a soul, and they perform the duties of teachers and educators conscientiously, if not skilfully. The money that is lost through their sons' fault does not disturb them so much as the prospect of an entirely spoiled life and of a good name jeopardised. They dread scandal, and upbraid the delinquent for his weakness, for his neglect of the proprieties and for his contempt for the law, and threaten him with disgrace. A young man who misbehaves is, in their eyes, a subject for the doctor, an unfortunate creature who is ruining himself, and he appears to them as having plunged into an abyss of misfortunes from which it is their business to rescue him.

However frequent the manifestations of paternal severity may be in the writers of comedy, they did not absolutely assign to the fathers the rôle of kill-joy. A father who, like Demea in the *Adelphi*, is indignant about all of his son's escapades, appears to have been a rare type, and with severity there goes in most cases—at least in Menander and his imitators—a certain admixture of indulgence.

This indulgence is generally the outcome of resignation. Many a father shuts his eyes, or did shut his eyes for a time, to the faults of his offspring, because he knows in advance that any attempt to correct these faults would

[1] *Trin.*, 305 et seq.   [2] *Heaut.*, 204 et seq.

be vain and void. His motto is that you cannot put old heads on young shoulders. All that one has a right to expect and to demand of young men during certain years is that they do not go to the extremes of scandalous conduct, that they keep their honour unblemished, and that they do not seriously imperil their patrimony. But it would be vexatious if, in later years, when the time shall have come to think of settling down, they were not ready to drop their former habits. But time and satiety can be relied upon to lead them to do so. Thus reasons Philoxenus, in the *Bacchides*, when the recollection of his last year's sins no longer troubles him. Thus reasons Simo in the *Andria*, and Laches and Phidippus in the *Hecyra*.[1] It even happens that a father is gratified at discovering proof of a good disposition in a young man's behaviour towards his woman friend or mistress. Simo, in the *Andria*, goes to the funeral of Chrysis, the pretty courtesan with whom his son had had relations, and the eagerness with which Pamphilus takes charge of the funeral, his mournful air and his tears, evoke his friendly sympathy.[2] Phidippus is ready to forgive his son-in-law for having occasionally visited his former mistress. He says : " Were he able to break off an attachment that had lasted so many years, I should believe that he was neither a man nor a sufficiently faithful husband to my daughter." [3]

Occasionally thoughts of their own past lead fathers in comedy to be indulgent. Not all of them have had a toilsome youth, like Demipho and Menedemus, and some of them were, in their day, sons of rich families, and had profited by their opportunities. As a matter of fact, they do not always remember their past of their own accord. Witness the worthy Simo, in the *Pseudolus*, to whom his old friend Callipho addresses a retrospective

---

[1] *Andr.*, 151 et seq.; *Hec.*, 118–119, 541 et seq.; 683 et seq. Similarly the father who appears in a Berlin fragment (*Berliner Klassikertexte*, Vol. II, p. 118).

[2] *Andr.*, 109 et seq.   [3] *Hec.*, 554 et seq.

harangue,[1] and Chremes, in the *Heauton Timoroumenos*, whose admonitions call forth ironical remarks from his son.[2] Other fathers, however, like Periphanes in the *Epidicus*, of their own accord recall the indulgences they allowed themselves in bygone days,[3] but they are not any the more easy to deal with, for all that. And finally, still others find in their own memories a justification for the behaviour of the young men : Philoxenus, for example, in the *Bacchides*, and Moschio's father, in a Berlin fragment.[4] The latter comes back from the country, quite surprised at being summoned by his son, for, up to that time, the young man had made it a rule to avoid his father's society, from fear of being scolded. However, that worthy scolds without anger. " For," says he, " I myself was one of those who was said to know how to squander a fortune. This time, at least, my wife has not deceived me. Moschio is certainly my son; he is good for nothing." [5] In the *Bacchides* the pedagogue Lydus has just called Philoxenus' attention to the behaviour of his son Pistoclerus, who has taken one of the Bacchis sisters as his mistress. Philoxenus receives the news in a phlegmatic manner : " Well, Lydus, it is the wisest course to be moderate in one's severity. It is less surprising for my son to commit a folly at his age than for him not to do so. I did just the same in my youth." [6] And, rather than interfere himself, he empowers a young man, Mnesilochus, Pistoclerus' friend, to do so ! In the *Adelphi* Micio shares Philoxenus' views ; in his younger days he had behaved himself through force of circumstances, as he had no money,[7] but he is very sure that, had he possessed the means, he would have led a jovial life ; and this conviction suffices to absolve Aeschinus.[8] As for Demaenetus, in the *Asinaria*, how could he do otherwise than regard Argyrippus' love affair with favour, since his own father had, in times gone by, done him the same service ?

[1] *Pseud.*, 436 et seq.   [2] *Heaut.*, 213 et seq.   [3] *Epid.*, 382 et seq.
[4] *Berliner Klassikertexte*, Vol. II. pp. 117–118.   [5] *Bacch.*, 59–62.
[6] *Ibid.*, 408 et seq.   [7] *Ad.*, 104.   [8] *Ibid.*, 103–107.

But this sort of leniency has its dangers. As far as the sons are concerned this is clear; but it also has its dangers for the fathers. By dint of harking back to the past too much, one easily conceives the desire of prolonging it and of living it over once more in the present. When Philoxenus comes to the Bacchis sisters to draw his son out of their clutches, he himself yields to the allurements of these pretty women. At the close of the play we see him in turn entering the halls of perdition in order to dine in loose company with Pistoclerus and to share in his debauchery. In the *Asinaria* Demaenetus abets his son and proposes to have a share in his fun. He gets an invitation to a good dinner, in the course of which he embraces Philaenium, and, had his plan not been thwarted, he would have spent the night with the fair lady.

Lastly, a father's indulgence may have reason and method in it. The infamous Demaenetus prides himself on not being like the majority of fathers—" All fathers who will follow my advice will be easy-going, so that their sons may love them better and be more kindly disposed towards them. That is what I try to do. . . . My son Argyrippus has to-day begged me to get him some money for his girl; I am most anxious to satisfy him. . . . My son has thought me worthy of his entire confidence; it is right that I should appreciate this disposition of his." [1] These words of Demaenetus are like a parody of the views of certain other fathers in comic literature. Chremes, in the *Heauton Timoroumenos*, blames Menedemus for his excessive severity, which was only a feigned severity. According to him, fathers and sons should show themselves to one another as they are. The son ought to confide in his father as he would in a friend, and the father ought to receive these confidences without pretending to be more displeased at them than he actually is, and without fear of showing that his kindness disposes him to forgive.[2] In still clearer terms

---

[1] *As.*, 64 et seq.

[2] *Heaut.*, 155 et seq.; cf. 925 et seq.

Micio advocates tolerance and reciprocal trust,[1] and pretends that, in doing so, he is moved by lofty educational considerations.[2] As a matter of fact, weakness, and the unavowed desire to avoid taking active measures, have a great deal to do with his fine leniency. Can Micio seriously believe that he will improve Aeschinus' morals by always forgiving, by paying for all that young man's follies without a word, by even praising his pranks and by offering him the premium of encouragement? No doubt he has a right to expect that nothing will be hidden from him; but even this hope is not to be fulfilled, for Aeschinus keeps him in the dark about the main thing—his intimacy with the girl who lives next door. Yet at least he can hope that Aeschinus will never lie in order to get out of a scrape. But is mendacity the only vice against which Micio desires to guard his son? He will gain his affection, it is true, by more respectable means than Demaenetus employs; but does he, in all conscience, believe that to gain a son's affection constitutes the whole task of a good educator?

With such diversity existing among fathers, it goes without saying that the attitude of sons is not uniform, either. It does not, however, vary in different cases as much as one might suppose, and, as a rule, it is more or less correct. Argyrippus, who beholds his father Demaenetus in a state of the lowest degradation, remains deferential towards him. Did other sons who joined in their fathers' debauches indulge in greater freedom, and take advantage of a scandalous good fellowship to treat the authors of their being cavalierly? We have no proof whatsoever that this was the case. Though fathers and sons were almost always at loggerheads, it appears that the conflict was never a brutal one. In the majority of Latin comedies there is not a single scene, at least not before the close, in which they are found face to face; and

---

[1] *Ad.*, 49 et seq.   [2] *Ibid.*, 55–56; 76 et seq.

when they do meet, it is without violent words and without any shocking violation of filial respect. A few Greek fragments apparently depict family differences.[1] In these fragments, as in the Latin plays, the young man's language remains proper and courteous. Generally speaking, sons, in comedy, appear to be thoroughly imbued with the maxim that has been attributed to Menander : to insult one's father is to blaspheme the gods.[2]

Nay, we may even say that sons hardly ever cross their fathers openly or light-heartedly. In one of Menander's plays a man brings a suit against his parents. He is reprimanded vigorously, and his conduct is regarded as evidence of insanity.[3] When Pamphilus, in the *Andria*, is forced by Simo to marry the very same day, and finds no way of refusing, he finally declares that he is ready to obey. At their fathers' command, Charinus, in the *Mercator*, Clinia, in the *Heauton Timoroumenos*, and Pamphilus, in the *Hecyra*, break off, or at least interrupt, their illicit relations. Clitipho, Clinia's friend, does as much. Of the young men who deceive their fathers or make a levy on their purses, few act for themselves, as Strabax does in the *Truculentus*; most of them let their slaves act and, at best, give them meagre support. Charinus deems it criminal to lie to the aged Demipho;[4] Calidorus, in the *Pseudolus*, declares that filial piety prevents him stealing from Simo.[5] If a son has secretly got into a position to displease his father, he is always greatly disturbed on being found out. Antipho hides when Demipho comes back; Clinia, after his return to his beloved Antiphila, does not dare to appear before Menedemus; Aeschinus, in the *Adelphi*, and the young lover in the *Γεωργός*, only confess the engagements they have contracted when driven to the last extremity.

If we inquire to what feelings this docility and anxiety

---

[1] Men., fr. 128, 247–248, 283, 554, 629; Apoll., fr. 16; fr. adesp. 281.
[2] [Men.], fr. 715.   [3] Men., fr. 806.
[4] *Merc.*, 209.   [5] *Pseud.*, 291.

are due, we find that in many cases fear undeniably plays a large part in them. Sharp reprimands and humiliating admonitions were, in themselves, very real punishments for proud and sensitive young men. And then the head of the family might assign a too flighty son some task well fitted to mortify him—set him to work in the fields, or send him abroad to trade or settle some business transaction. But, above all, he might cut off his allowance and drive him from home without a penny. In the *Phormio* and in the *Andria*, the threat of some such retaliation evidently haunts Antipho and Pamphilus; in a more imminent form this threat has much to do with sobering Clitipho, in the *Heauton Timoroumenos*. Nevertheless, fear does not account for everything. Side by side with it in the souls of the young men we discover a true respect for their father, the conviction that he is acting for their best interests, trust in his greater good sense, and appreciation of his care and kindness. Before leaving Attica, Clinia probably indulged in the reflections which Menedemus attributes to him : he said to himself that age and affection made Menedemus more competent than he was to judge of what he ought to do,[1] and when he thinks that he has been betrayed by Antiphila, his father's admonitions, which taught him to mistrust women, come back to his mind.[2] Antipho recognises that his father only desires what is best for him, and suffers at the thought that he fears the latter's return.[3] Charinus cannot bear to lose the respect of Demipho, " whom it is his duty to please." [4] Aeschinus is in despair at having pained Micio, and, when he meets him, is ashamed of his behaviour.[5]

Nowhere do we hear a son say anything seriously disagreeable about his father. Hardly ever does he wish him ill.[6] As a rule, it is the courtesans who speculate on

---

[1] *Heaut.*, 115–116.   [2] *Ibid.*, 260 et seq.   [3] *Phorm.*, 153 et seq.
[4] *Merc.*, 79–82.   [5] *Ad.*, 681 et seq.; cf. Men., fr. 586.
[6] I do not think that Philolaches' exclamation in lines 233–234 of the *Mostellaria* should be taken seriously, any more than that of an actor in Naevius' *Tribacelus*, or Strabax's brutal expression in lines 660–661 of the *Truculentus*.

the death of the head of the family, and the cynical slaves and facetious friends who hope for it, or pretend to hope for it.[1] The sons do not willingly contemplate that eventuality; witness the pious reticence of Chaereas, of which the old courtesan makes fun, in the seventh *Dialogue* of Lucian : ἐὰν ὁ πατὴρ, . . . καὶ κύριος γένωμαι τῶν πατρῴων, καὶ πάντα σά. The kind of misfortunes the sons in comedy, or at least the sons in Menander's comedies, invoke from the bottom of their hearts upon a father who interferes with their fun is doubtless shown in lines 519–520 of the *Adelphi*, spoken by young Ctesipho : " Would to heaven that, without doing himself very great harm (*quod cum salute eius fiat*), my father might so fatigue himself that for three days he could not stir from his bed." In a word, New Comedy does not appear to have brought a bad son upon the stage.

On the other hand, we must not expect to find great demonstrations of filial affection in the comic writers. As the majority of their plots represent conflicts between fathers and sons, they do not afford occasion for it. The title Φιλοπάτωρ, borne by several comedies, proves nothing. In a fragment of Menander's Ξενόλογος reference is made to a son who, after having been carefully brought up by an impecunious father, deeply appreciates the sacrifices made for his education, and relieves his father's poverty.[2] These few lines must belong to a prologue, and we have no means of knowing whether the " good son " had an active part in the play itself.

In real life, husband and wife, parents and children, are the chief persons in the life of the family, and they are nearly the only ones whom New Comedy attempted to portray.

Mothers-in-law—especially the mothers-in-law of young women—certainly had a very bad reputation in the days

---

[1] *Ad.*, 521, and Donatus' note; Turpilius, *Philopator*, fr. XI.; *Bacch.*, 732; cf. *As.*, 528–529.

[2] *Men.*, fr. 354.

of Apollodorus, as various passages of the *Hecyra* bear
witness.[1] But this reputation is not confirmed anywhere
in the writers of comedy. The only mothers-in-law that
we know in all comic literature—Sostrata and Myrrhina,
in the *Hecyra*—are free from reproach. Indeed, the former
is full of affection and devotion for her daughter-in-law.
As for the father-in-law—the father-in-law of the husband
—his habitual rôle consists in interfering in the young
household when his daughter thinks she has cause for
complaint.[2] He does so, however, with a bad grace, and
fellow feeling for the male sex counts for more with him
than family sentiment. He is quick to find his daughter
in the wrong, accuses her of an inclination to tyrannise,
and preaches submission. The only things—or nearly the
only things—that the father-in-law in comedy resents are
extravagance on the part of the young husband, bad
management of his affairs, and the attempt to get control
of his wife's property. The father-in-law of Menaechmus,
who is so ready to forgive his infidelity, does not forgive
him for stealing a mantle. Antipho, in the *Stichus*, has
a disagreement with his two sons-in-law about money.
What most worries Smicrines, in the Ἐπιτρέποντες, is the
extravagance of Charisius.[3]

The stepmother, who appears in so disagreeable a light
in tragedy, is hardly found in the fragments of the νέα.
A comic writer praises the law of Charondas which censured fathers of a family who, having become widowers,
marry a second time;[4] but, apparently, he did so more
from horror of marriage than from solicitude for the
children of the first marriage. In the Σαμία, Chrysis,
Demeas' concubine, is full of kindness towards his son,
whose love affair she encourages. A παλλακή in the
Ψευδηρακλῆς brought up the two daughters of her
deceased mistress, whose place she has taken with the

[1] *Hec.*, 240 et seq.; 276 et seq.; 532 et seq.
[2] *Menaechmi. Mercator.*
[3] Ἐπιτρ., 467 et seq., 484; Men., fr. 177; fr. adesp. 105 (attributed
by Capps to the Ἐπιτρέποντες, *Berliner philol. Woch.*, 1908, p. 1198).
[4] Fr. adesp. 110.

widower,[1] and there is nothing to show that she did so without affection.

Among the characters in Philemon's plays Apuleius mentions the " scolding uncle " (*patruus objurgator*),[2] but neither in the Latin plays for which Philemon furnished the model nor in what remains of the νέα does the " scolding uncle " appear. In this passage of Apuleius there is evidently an attempt at symmetry. The characters mentioned are grouped three by three, and the epithets given to each group all have a similar ending. Perhaps the *patruus objurgator* was mentioned alongside of *miles proeliator* and the *sodalis opitulator* chiefly with a view to completing a trio, and did not owe this distinction to his real importance.

Brothers and sisters appear in a few Latin plays.[3] In the *Eunuchus* Phaedria and Chaerea hardly meet, and they take little interest in one another. Pamphilippus and Epignomus, in the *Stichus*, take still less. On the other hand, in the *Adelphi*, Aeschinus does not hesitate to compromise himself in order to help Ctesipho, and when his good nature has placed him in a most cruel predicament, he refuses to get out of it by betraying his brother;[4] Ctesipho in return displays very great gratitude[5] towards Aeschinus. In the *Phormio* Demipho is devoted to Chremes' interests, and strives to spare him painful domestic scenes. In Menander's Ἀδελφοί the character who corresponds to Hegio, the brother of Sostrata,[6] eagerly undertakes the defence of his sister and of his niece. In the *Aulularia* Eunomia is full of solicitude for Megadorus, to whom she recommends marriage. The friendly disposition displayed by Aeschinus, Demipho, Hegio and Eunomia was probably very common among the brothers and sisters in comedy. Several lost plays were called Φιλάδελφοι; perhaps one of them portrayed

---

[1] Men., fr. 520.   [2] Ap., *Flor.*, XVI.

[3] In addition to two of Menander's plays, comedies by Alexis, Euphron, Philemon, Diphilus and Apollodorus bore the title Ἀδελφοί.

[4] *Ad.*, 623 et seq.   [5] *Ibid.*, 256 et seq.

[6] Donatus, Commentary to line 351.

fraternal affection. At the same time, I must remark
that very often a brother is of less consequence than a
friend, especially a friend of the same age, a *synephebos*.
"*Sodalis opitulator*," says Apuleius.[1] In fully half a
dozen Latin comedies we meet with two young men, for
the most part of the same age (*aequales*), who, without
being brothers or relatives, mutually help one another with
money and good offices.[2] This was probably also the case
in the plays by Philemon, Menander, Apollodorus and
Euphron, called Συνέφηβος or Συνέφηβοι.

If, now, we examine the relations between the elders,
the majority of the old men who, here and there, espouse
the cause of the father of a family with the greatest zeal
are in no way related to him. In a word, New Comedy did
not give good brothers much prominence. We may add
that hostile brothers were perhaps not unknown. One
of Menander's plays, the Ναύκληρος, appears to have
brought them upon the stage,[3] and fragment 809, which
sings the praises of cordial relations between brothers,
may just as well be an exhortation as a mere statement.

At this point I shall end my study of the characters
drawn from the family circle. In addition, no doubt, to
the characters of whom we have spoken above, there are
still many others who are related to one another by ties of
blood or marriage. Their number is, however, too small,
and the degree of their consanguinity too distant, to
warrant a special study.

As for maxims relating to the family in general, they
have but a secondary interest.[4] The following picture of
a family dinner, found in a fragment of Menander, is more
entertaining—

"What an experience, to drop into a family dining-
room! The father, cup in hand, is the first to speak,
gives advice and drinks a draught. Then the mother

---

[1] Ap., *Flor.*, XVI.

[2] *Bacchides, Epidicus, Mercator, Mostellaria, Pseudolus, Heauton Timoroumenos.*

[3] Men., fr. 350.

[4] *e. g.*, Men., fr. 4; Diph., fr. 102.

follows. Then an aunt chatters; after her an old gentleman with a deep voice, the aunt's papa; after him an old lady who calls you ' dear child.' The ' dear child ' says ' yes ' to every one." [1]

We can guess what provokes all this wearisome moral discourse addressed to the patient listener, and we shall not be much mistaken in supposing that it is some amorous escapade.

§ 6

LOVERS

Many characters in the *véa* are represented as being in love, and among them men are in the majority. Naturally the young men predominate, and, among these, the unmarried ones. Except for Amphitryon,[2] the list of husbands who dote on their wives includes, as far as we know, only Charisius in the *'Επιτρέποντες*, and Pamphilus in the *Hecyra*. The list of faithless young husbands is limited to Menaechmus, for, in Charisius' case, it was much against his will and under quite special conditions that he deserted Pamphila. On the other hand, almost all the amorous greybeards are fathers of a family, who are tired of their old and ugly spouses and seek amusement outside their homes. As far as the women are concerned, we know that those who seek amorous adventures are not usually found among the young girls of good family. The wife who deceives her husband does not occur—or hardly occurs—in comedy. The wife who is in love either remains behind the scenes, or else, if she appears on the stage, does not give free rein to her feelings. Alcmena is a single exception, and Alcmena belongs to the region of fable. As for jealous matrons, their jealousy is not due to love but to pride, or to a horror of vice, or else, purely

---

[1] Men., fr. 923.

[2] In Plautus, Amphitryon is called *senex* (1072; cf. 1032). But there is nothing in his part that fits in with this attribute. Alcmena's husband, the Theban general, can, at most, be a middle-aged man. I may incidentally remark that " middle age " is not represented among the characters of New Comedy, or at least not among the prominent characters.

and simply, to a spirit of contradiction. The *νέα* recruits its amorous women elsewhere than in polite society. Some of them are courtesans, others are the slaves of their lovers. The majority of them belong by birth to respectable families, but have left the paternal roof very early and have grown up in the homes of poor and more or less respectable people who pass them off as their daughters, or in the house of a pander who waits for an opportunity to sell them to good advantage.

As a rule, it is the men who take the first step in an amorous adventure. The courtesans who tempt, like Bacchis the Athenian, act from design, not from passion. Acroteleutium, in the *Miles*, wishes to make fun of Pyrgopolinices when she pretends to offer herself to him unasked. In the *'Αποκληομένη* by Posidippus, it appears that a woman made tender advances and was rebuffed, but there is nothing to show that this woman was still in the preliminary stages of a liaison. In a word, I do not believe that the woman who offers her love, like Simaetha in Theocritus, was portrayed in comedy.

Why does one fall in love? One of Menander's characters asks himself this question and finds great difficulty in answering it.[1] As a matter of fact, it is often nothing else than the woman's beauty that stirs the lovers in comedy, and what they desire is nothing but sensuous pleasure. Especially when old men meddle with love, they seek merely to tickle their senses; the only thing that moves them is the spirit of lechery. Like Trygaeus and Philocleon, they are merely hot with desire. Senile love, it is true, is intentionally painted in repulsive and ridiculous colours by the writers of comedy, but young people also, young lovers, with whom the poet sympathises, are more than once influenced merely by fleshly desire. The mere charm of a beautiful face or of a fine figure sufficed to determine the conduct of Lyconides, in the *Aulularia*, of Aeschinus in the *Adelphi*, and of ever so

[1] Men., fr. 541.

many other youths whose relations with their mistresses began by their ravishing them. Similarly, mere beauty can occasion the " thunder-strokes " (love at first sight) which are so frequent in comedy. How should Chaerea and Moschio have noticed anything but the agreeable appearance of Pamphila as she crossed the street, or of Glycera as she stood at her threshold? When Calidorus, in the *Pseudolus*, is bereft of his mistress, he apparently mourns only the loss of purely sensual pleasures.[1] The intoxication of the senses is described at length by an enthusiastic lover, in fragment 536 of Menander. A detail which serves to disclose what the love of certain persons in comedy is worth, is the way they behave in the presence of rivals, avowed or merely imagined. In several Latin plays we meet with lovers who agree to strange bargains and bear a separation without much grief. I shall not dwell upon the adventure of Argyrippus, in the *Asinaria*, for it is with distinct chagrin and dislike that he temporarily gives up his mistress Philaenium to his father. But at the close of the *Eunuchus*—and I believe the scene is an imitation of what occurred in Menander's Κόλαξ [2]— Phaedria resigns himself to sharing Thais' favours with Thraso, and, in the *Truculentus*, Diniarchus does not even dream of demanding sole possession of Phronesium. Love that comes from the heart does not admit of such compromises, nor of such leniency, for which there is but one explanation—that those who indulge in them are above all else seeking for sensuous pleasures.

Thus the lovers in the νέα are much inclined to physical passion; and yet it would be a slander to think that they are always ruled by their senses. In the ῞Ηρως, Daos, a slave, loves Plangon, who, he thinks, is a simple servant and the daughter of a freedman. Of course, he has no lack of opportunity for paying the young woman most urgent

---

[1] *Pseud.*, 63 et seq.

[2] It is proper to add that Pheidias' love in the Κόλαξ was not concerned with a woman like Thais and was not of the same kind as that of Phaedria in Terence's *Eunuchus*.

court, but he has no designs against Plangon's virtue and asks her most properly to marry him.[1] Among the young lovers there are some who, like the *misoumenos* Thrasonides, are smitten with a woman whom they have in their power, and yet respect her, because they desire that she should give herself to them willingly.[2] There are some who, like Clinia in the *Heauton Timoroumenos*, cannot bear the thought that any one else has a share in the favours of their well-beloved, and repeatedly we can discover in the soul of this or that character a more lofty motive for love than mere admiration for a good figure.

In the first place, it is the pleasure which a polite and distinguished bearing affords them. To behave properly in society, and especially at table, is one of the duties which people versed in the art of love—or rather of making one's self beloved—point out to their pupils, the young courtesans. In the sixth *Dialogue* of Lucian the aged Crobyle calls the attention of her daughter Corinna to it. In the *Eunuchus* Parmeno, who is likewise an experienced person, hopes that the sight of courtesans *en négligé* in their homes will cure Chaerea of his liking for them : " To see the untidiness, the filth, the poverty of these creatures, to see how badly they behave and how greedy they are as soon as they are at home alone, how they devour black bread dipped in yesterday's soup—to know all this is the salvation of a young man." [3]

It is qualities of mind and heart that lovers, or at least some of them, value in their mistresses, even more than good manners. Toxilus, in the *Persa*, is sure that the supposed captive girl, a fine talker and clever at repartee, will have a brilliant career as a courtesan owing to these accomplishments.[4] In the *Poenulus*, Agorastocles almost dies with laughter when he hears the sanctimonious moralisings of Adelphasium.[5] In the *Mostellaria* Philolaches

---

[1] ῟Ηρ., 41 et seq.
[2] *Men.*, fr. 336.   Cf. Diog. Laert., VII. 130.
[3] *Eun.*, 934 et seq.   [4] *Persa*, 563 et seq.
[5] *Poen.*, 289 et seq., 308 et seq.

L

feels his love growing when, hidden from Philematium's view, he hears her express her gratitude, her affection and her fidelity.[1] Plangon, in the Ἥρως, enchants Daos by her good behaviour and correct bearing.[2] Above all, in Terence we repeatedly see mention made of motives that are anything but sensuous mentioned as accounting for a love affair. In the *Heauton Timoroumenos* it is the respectability of Antiphila to which Clitipho and Bacchis render homage;[3] it is the great tenderness with which she requites Clinia—that tenderness which causes her to faint when she hears of his return[4] and when she finds herself face to face with him;[5] it is the mutual regard existing between the two lovers;[6] in a word, to go to the root of the matter, it is the similarity of their inclinations.[7] Motives of the same kind are more or less explicitly alleged in the *Phormio* and in the *Andria*. Phanium, in the *Phormio*, is, according to the testimony of disinterested persons, an entirely proper young woman; *ingenua*, *liberalis*, says Antipho's young cousin;[8] *perliberalis*, insists Nausistrata, a matron, from whom one might have expected a preconceived severity.[9] Glycerium, in the *Andria*, has been brought up on principles of honour and virtue,[10] she has given Pamphilus her heart and her life,[11] and her character harmonises with that of her lover.[12]

I must add that in the last two plays the young men's love is strengthened by a sense of duty. The mistress of the one and the clandestine wife of the other have trusted themselves to their honour, and they feel their responsibility towards them. This feeling, which we may call chivalrous, is strongly marked in the rôle of Pamphilus. One need only recall the splendid tirade in lines 277–299. The same note is sounded in the *Phormio*, lines 468–470. In this instance profound pity is added to the feeling of responsibility in a more marked way than in the *Andria*.

---

[1] *Most.*, 205 et seq., 222 et seq.   [2] Ἥρ., 40.
[3] *Heaut.*, 226, 381 et seq.   [4] *Ibid.*, 304 et seq.
[5] *Ibid.*, 403 et seq.   [6] *Ibid.*, 394.   [7] *Ibid.*, 393.   [8] *Phorm.*, 168.
[9] *Ibid.*, 815.   [10] *Andr.*, 274.   [11] *Ibid.*, 272.   [12] *Ibid.*, 696.

It is under the influence of pity that love entered the heart of Antipho when he saw Phanium, poor and deserted, weeping over her mother's body. He has delivered her from the poverty into which she would have relapsed without his aid, and he loves her the more for this—with the complacent love that every man feels for his good deeds.

Just the opposite is the case with Pamphilus, in the *Hecyra*. He loves Philumena in order to make reparation for his behaviour towards her. He had married her without feeling affection for her. At first he treated her with contempt and continued to prefer his former mistress, the courtesan Bacchis. Then little by little, as Parmeno explains : " He got to know himself and to know Bacchis and the young wife he had at home. . . . His heart, both moved by pity for his wife and repelled by the exactions of Bacchis, freed itself from its trammels. He transferred his love to his home, where he had discovered a disposition that harmonised with his own." [1] Thus, for the third time, we find that love is accounted for by a similarity of taste and character, and there is no trace of the brutal desire which is sometimes indiscriminately attributed to all lovers in the *νέα*. Many of them are quite as sensitive and have quite as fine characters as the majority of modern lovers.

One thing that should, I believe, be noted, is the composure with which they see their liaisons or their amorous adventures end in marriage. Nothing would be more natural if the woman they courted had from the outset been known to them as a woman whom one could marry, and if they had been duly informed of her social position and her morals at the time when they entered into clandestine relations with her. Apart from all other feelings, a sense of honour must have prescribed their course under such conditions. But there are cases where the woman was at first regarded as a foreigner, as a slave, as a courtesan, and where the young man was not called upon to

[1] *Hec.*, 161 et seq.

make any reparation as far as she was concerned, and yet, notwithstanding all this, eagerly marries her when her real character is revealed.[1] It even happens that he passes her off for what she is not, in order to be able to marry her.[2] Of course, this attitude may show that marriage is often not taken seriously in comedy, but it would appear that, here and there, we may be justified in reaching a contrary conclusion—namely, that the young man's passion was not a mere passing fancy, and that he had been drawn to his mistress by something more than a mere amorous caprice—by a well-founded regard.

At all events, there is no reason to doubt the disinterestedness of young lovers. The writers of comedy, who so often portrayed a household in which a dowered wife is rampant, apparently did not introduce the fortune-hunter. If, now and again, a young man is charged with money-seeking—as in the *Cistellaria*,[3] or in the second *Dialogue* of Lucian—it is owing to some mistake that is quickly discovered. Rarely do pecuniary considerations keep a lover from following his inclination. This may have been the case in the original version of the *Poenulus*. In the *Aulularia* a few lines of the prologue might give rise to doubts regarding Lyconides' generosity,[4] and it seems that at the close of the play, in a scene that is lost, he fought with his father-in-law about the ownership of the precious pot. But the exceptional circumstances of the case must be taken into account. Lyconides has to deal with an old miser in whose hands money is useless. He is in possession of the treasure which his slave Strobilus has stolen, and his behaviour when he asks for the dowry is therefore not that of a skinflint. If he waited so long before declaring his love, it was from fear of enduring reproaches, rather than from a disinclination to marry a poor girl. As a rule, far from looking for a dowry, the young men treat it with indifference when people offer it

---

[1] Ἥρως, Περικειρομένη, *Casina, Curculio, Cistellaria, Epidicus, Poenulus, Rudens, Eunuchus, Heauton Timoroumenos.*

[2] *Phormio.*   [3] *Cist.,* 492 et seq.   [4] *Aul.,* 25 et seq.

of their own accord. We even meet with a young bridegroom—in the *Trinummus*—who obstinately refuses to accept the dowry that his wife is to receive.

Hitherto I have spoken only of young men who are in love. Girls who are honestly in love, if they appear at all, often do nothing beyond appearing. We find—or we suspect—that they have the same reasons for loving which move the young men, ranging from sensuality—ingenuously admitted by one of Lucian's courtesans,[1] and less ingenuously by Phoenicium, in the *Pseudolus*[2]—to real sympathy. There is, however, a kind of love which, in comedy, is peculiar to women and which must be classed by itself—the love that comes from gratitude. In the *Mostellaria* Philematium declares that she is for all time devoted to Philolaches because he freed her from slavery. Philaenium, in the *Asinaria*, and Selenium, in the *Cistellaria*, are grateful to Argyrippus and Alcesimarchus for the respect with which they have treated them and for their affectionate courtesy, notwithstanding they were courtesans or daughters of courtesans.[3] It may be that Philematium is mistaken about the nature of her feelings; the other two girls are, without a doubt, truly in love.

We now know *whence* love comes into the hearts of people on the comic stage. *How* it comes is a problem that comedy does not attempt to solve. As far as we know, Chaerea is the only one who falls in love in the course of a play, and it will be recalled how suddenly he is smitten. As a rule, the lovers are all afire and aflame at the very outset of the play, and the portrayal of the perturbation caused by their passion begins forthwith.

This perturbation is violent, for Eros is a very powerful god. It is a commonplace of comic writers to declare that love leads men to rave and makes them blind and mad. A lover no longer calls his soul his own, he is entirely possessed by his fancy, which makes him forget food

---

[1] Luc., *Dial. Mer.*, VII. 3.   [2] *Pseud.*, 66–68.
[3] *Most.*, 204–205, 214, 220–221; *As.*, 525; *Cist.*, 92–93.

and drink. The presence of the person he loves suffices to upset him; on seeing Thais, Phaedria is all of a shiver.[1] On seeing Clinia after a long absence, Antiphila almost faints away.[2] Pleusicles and Philocomasium swoon in one another's arms in the presence of the man whom they are deceiving.[3] The happiness of love is proclaimed to be the greatest happiness in the world, greater than that of riches or of kings.[4] Lovers compare themselves to the very gods.[5] When Clinia, in the *Heauton Timoroumenos*, knows that he can marry Antiphila, he declares that henceforward nothing can trouble him— he is so happy.[6] In the *Eunuchus*, Chaerea, after having possessed Pamphila, would gladly consent to die lest by continuing to live he might see his bliss poisoned by some sorrow.[7] The lover who reaches the goal of his desires and whose passion is requited and meets with no hindrance is, as it were, drunk with joy. He thinks of nothing but his happiness, speaks of nothing else, and does not wish others to speak of anything else. When he hears a bit of news that delights him, he never tires of hearing it repeated. He is anxious to make known the happy outcome of his love, and makes a confidant of Tom, Dick and Harry. Overflowing with contentment himself, he would like to have universal contentment prevail about him. He feels a wholly groundless gratitude towards everybody and everything. When Polemo begins to hope that Glycera will come back to him, he promises Doris that she shall be freed and calls her his very dear one.[8] Chaerea, who has been given permission to marry Pamphila, is full of affection for Parmeno, for Thais, for his brother and for the whole world.[9]

Happy he who can experience so delightful an ecstasy ! But, alas, all is not joy in love; the bitter is mixed with the sweet, and often predominates. Love, says Gymnasium,

---

[1] *Eun.*, 83–84.
[2] *Heaut.*, 403 et seq.
[3] *Miles*, 1334 et seq.
[4] *Curc.*, 178 et seq.
[5] *Andr.*, 959 et seq.; *Heaut.*, 693; *Curc.*, 167–168.
[6] *Heaut.*, 679–680.
[7] *Eun.*, 551–552.
[8] Περικ., 332–333, 339.
[9] *Eun.*, 1034 et seq., 1051 et seq.

doubtless lets us taste much sweetness, but it also abounds in bitterness, it overflows with it.[1] Those who submit to its laws have to endure a harder lot than that of a poor labourer.[2] Love is the prince of tormentors.[3] For every scene in which we see a lover exulting, there are ten in which other lovers lament and complain that they are being put upon the rack. It is chiefly the pangs of love that comedy portrays for us.

Manifold are their causes. Now, it is a third person who is evilly disposed, a severe father, a rival, a pander or a procuress that thwarts the two lovers; or again, the loved one remains indifferent, is unfaithful or pretends to be; or feelings hostile to his love struggle for the upper hand in the lover's heart. From these varied causes spring various pangs.

The simplest of them, and the most common, is the pang of privation : the lover suffers because he cannot possess the object of his desire, or because he has lost her. His suffering is all the greater because he is generally impatient—*fervidus amator*, says Apuleius [4]—and incapable of listening to reason. To live apart from Thais for two days appears to Phaedria, in the *Eunuchus*, to be almost unbearable. In order to endure it, he plans to go to the country, and to kill himself with work in order to forget his annoyance and to cure his sleeplessness. But this fine plan is not carried out; he only makes the two journeys —there and back; if he cannot possess his mistress he at least means to see her.[5] When Mnesilochus is away from Bacchis the Samian, he is like a body without a soul.[6] In the *Μισούμενος* the jilted lover is driven out of doors at night by his sad thoughts and awakens his slave Getas, who has nothing to do with the matter, to tell him of his mortification.[7] In the comic writers, as well as in the Alexandrian elegiac poets, sleeplessness appears to have been a regular consequence, as it were,

---

[1] *Cist.*, 67–70. [2] *Merc.*, 356. [3] *Cist.*, 203 et seq.
[4] Ap., *Flor.*, XVI. [5] *Eun.*, 629 et seq. [6] *Bacch.*, 193.
[7] Arr., *Diss. Epict.*, IV. 1, 9 Schw. ; Men., fr. 341.

of the worries of love. To it must be added the pallor
which overcomes Toxilus, in the *Persa*,[1] and his indifference
to the niceties of his toilet, and finally a sickly languor.[2]

Occasionally a thwarted lover grows whimsical, irritable,
and unjust. When Adelphasium, in the *Poenulus*, looks
crossly at Agorastocles, he vents his bad humour on the
back of the innocent Milphio.[3] In the *Mercator* Charinus
finds that the faithful Eutychus, who is so devoted to
him, is too slow and clumsy in serving him.[4] More
frequently still, the pangs of love make men sentimental.
Anticipating Acontius, the young lovers in comedy seem
to think that one can assuage one's sorrows by speaking
of them. They beset their friends and their trusted slaves
with their lamentations, or else they apostrophise heaven
and earth, and claim that the whole world should be concerned exclusively with themselves. Cicero has preserved
for us the most interesting passages of one of these extravagant tirades [5] in a few lines of Turpilius' *Leucadia*,
an imitation of one of Menander's plays. A lover proclaims his agony from the top of the Leucadian rock; he
calls the gods to witness, " if indeed," he adds with bitterness, " there be a god who cares for me." He invokes
the help of Apollo, of Neptune and the Winds, but is
severe on Venus, who has not listened to his prayers.
When carried to such a paroxysm, the lover's despair
borders upon insanity. Some distressed lovers exceed all
bounds and lose their heads entirely. Charinus, in the
Mercator, and Alcesimarchus, in the *Cistellaria*, suffer
from veritable attacks of insanity on the stage, and vie
with each other in their outpourings.

What can be done to escape this grievous obsession?
Charisius, in the 'Επιτρέποντες, and Polemo, in the
Περικειρομένη, stifle or try to stifle their troubles by
feasting with their friends. Elsewhere, the young men
leave the place where they had to suffer, in order to cheat

---

[1] *Persa*, 24. 　　　　　　　[2] Cf. *Cist.*, 113–115.
[3] *Poen.*, 135 et seq., 378–379. 　[4] *Merc.*, 595 et seq., 629 et seq.
[5] Cic., *Tusc.*, IV. 34, 72 (Turpilius, *Leucadia*, fr. XII.).

their grief. They go into exile or travel, as Charinus, in the *Mercator*, did, and still wishes to do. They enlist in an army, like Clinia of the *Heauton Timoroumenos*. For those whom this treatment does not cure or who are not willing to resort to it, there remains a last and radical resource—suicide. It is mentioned, more or less seriously, in the *Περικειρομένη*, the *Mercator*, the *Pseudolus*, the *Miles*, the *Epidicus* and the *Asinaria*, in which Argyrippus and Philaenium, filled with a like despair, dream of dying together and of being together carried to the grave.[1] It is also spoken of in Menander's *Ἀδελφοί*.[2] In the *Μισούμενος* it seems that the hero asks for his sword that he may kill himself with it.[3] In the *Cistellaria* Alcesimarchus holds his sword in his hand when Selenium interferes with his purpose.[4] Possibly the title of one of Crobylus' comedies—*Ἀπαγχόμενος*—and that of a play by Diphilus—*Συναποθνήσκοντες*—allude to suicide or to plans for suicide on account of love.

Occasionally yet other anxieties are added to the grief occasioned by an enforced separation, such I have just described. According to Parmeno, of the *Eunuchus*, " insults, suspicions, quarrels, reconciliations, war and a renewal of peace " follow in the train of love.[5] In the enumeration of the themes of comedy which is contained in one of Terence's prologues, *hating* and *suspecting* come immediately after *loving*.[6] Let us now examine what are the feelings of the jilted or betrayed lover and what attitude he takes towards the obdurate one or the betrayer.

Generally speaking, a rebuff, far from discouraging passion, results in exciting it to a still higher degree. Rivalry inflames the rivals. Every lover's quarrel is followed by a reawakening of love. Experienced courtesans are well aware of this, and we have already seen how skilfully they exploit these inconsistencies of the

---

[1] Περικ., 242, 325; *As.*, 607, 613–615; *Ep.*, 148; *Pseud.*, 89 et seq.; *Merc.*, 471–473; *Miles*, 1240–1241.

[2] Donatus, commentary to line 275 of the *Adelphi*.

[3] Arr., *Diss Epict.*, IV. 1, 19 Schw.; cf. Men., fr. 346.

[4] *Cist.*, 641.   [5] *Eun.*, 59–61.   [6] *Ibid.*, prol. 40.

human heart. As a rule, aspirants for the favour of one of these enticers entertain no illusions concerning her, and rightly despise her. But not infrequently they show no sign of their contempt, and never cease addressing her with tender words or even supplications. This is what Diniarchus, in the *Truculentus*, does, excepting in one scene where his wrath breaks forth; and doubtless more than one lover in comic literature, provided he was able to satisfy his passion, resigned himself to the knowledge that it was not requited.

Behaviour such as this merely required a certain amount of cowardice and callousness. But another class of lovers is more interesting—those who, after having been deserted by the object of their affection, still remain sufficiently in love to forgive everything, even desertion, or who even seek to find an excuse for the delinquent. To this class belong Selenium of the *Cistellaria*, and one of Philaenium's suitors in the *Asinaria*. Before he is quite sure whether Philaenium shares her mother's intention of ousting him, he reserves his curses for Cleaereta; at the most, in his first access of anger he makes a threat which includes the two women; but he quickly corrects himself : " You will see ! As for her, how could I be angry at her ? There is no reason for it, she in no way deserves it; it is you who made her act as she did, she obeys your orders. You are her mother, you are mistress here." [1] As for Selenium, she thinks she has positive knowledge of Alcesimarchus' infidelity; notwithstanding this, she makes the following touching recommendation to Gymnasium who is to look after her house : " If he comes while I am away, do not, I beseech you, receive him with severe reproaches. Notwithstanding all he has done to me, he is dear to me. Say nothing that might hurt him." [2]

It is rather curious that, in Plautus and Terence, there is an almost complete lack of scenes of reconciliation between lovers. When the behaviour of a faithless one is censured, it is generally by a third person, and most frequently not

[1] *Asin.*, 145–147.   [2] *Cist.*, 108–110.

in the presence of the culprit. If we except the *Truculentus*, in which Stratophanes' anger is due to his absurd vanity rather than to his injured love, there is only one instance—in the *Eunuchus*—where a lover reproaches his mistress for the favour she shows another man; and he does not persist in his recriminations. I can hardly believe that what is true of the few extant plays applied as well to all comedies. Without a doubt bitter reproaches, offensive insinuations, floods of cruel words were not unknown in the *véa*. In the fourth *Dialogue* of Lucian Melitta tells a friend how Charinus had harshly upbraided her for her supposed infidelity. In the twelfth *Dialogue* Lysias, in injurious terms, charges Ioessa with infidelity. Fragment 569 of Menander and a few verses of the *Leucadia* by Turpilius apparently belong to analogous scenes and to scenes of reconciliation.

The lovers' spite which embitters quarrels plays a considerable part in Lucian. Before giving Ioessa a chance to explain, Lysias humiliates her by publicly and in her presence paying court to one of her enemies, and by singing the praises of a worthless woman. Philinna and Diphilus, in the third *Dialogue*, make it their business to drive one another to distraction. Apparently Lysias, Philinna and Diphilus believe in the excellence of the method which Gnatho, in a scene of the *Eunuchus*, recommends to the soldier Thraso : " I tell you what. If Thais happens to speak of Phaedria, to sing his praises, in order to be disagreeable to you . . . there is but one way in which you can silence her. As soon as she says ' Phaedria,' you must answer ' Pamphila.' If she says ' Let us send for Phaedria for supper,'—' Let us have Pamphila come to sing.' If she praises the good looks of the one, you must, in return, praise the pretty face of the other. In a word, give her tit for tat, so as to annoy her also." [1] Thraso, as we know, in the course of the play puts this method into practice—with his characteristic awkwardness—and other heroes of comedy must have done

---

[1] *Eun.*, 437 et seq.

as much. For instance, the girl from Leucas thinks that
she has been offended by her lover and pretends to listen
to the advances of an old aspirant who rolls in wealth.[1]
Several of Lucian's characters go still further in the way
of retaliation. When Charmides, in the eleventh *Dialogue*,
is rebuffed by Philemation, he has Tryphaena to his
house—but gives her holiday all night. In the fourth
Dialogue, Charinus, who thinks he has cause to complain
of Melitta, ostentatiously shows himself in Simmiche's
company. Herein he behaves like certain lovers in
Menander—Charisius of the Ἐπιτρέποντες, and Polemo
of the Περικειρομένη. Partly to amuse themselves and
partly to take revenge, the one on his wife, the other on
his mistress, these two hire courtesans. They are, by the
way, no more polite to these unfortunate " substitutes "
than Charmides is to Tryphaena.

Occasionally a lover's spite takes brutal forms. It will
be recalled how insultingly Polemo, in the Περικειρομένη,
treats his mistress. In the *Eunuchus* Thais takes great
precautions when she sees that Thraso is angry : she entrusts her jewels to Dorias, who takes them home with her,
and she herself chooses the right moment to slip away.[2]
In the eighth *Dialogue* Chrysis and Ampelis have had
their clothes torn and their ears boxed by their jealous
lovers. The heroine of one of Menander's plays, the
Ῥαπιζομένη, must have been the victim of some similar
calamity. Here and there, unrequited lovers go so far
as to threaten death. In the *Truculentus* Stratophanes
wishes to cleave Phronesium and Strabax in two.[3] In the
Bacchides Cleomachus declares that if he finds the faithless Bacchis and Mnesilochus together, he will kill them
and have no mercy.[4] These are coarse soldiers; but in
the *Cistellaria* a young gentleman also speaks of murder-
ing a woman who rejects him, as well as her mother.[5]
We may, however, doubt the seriousness of his words.

[1] Cf. *Rev. Ét. Gr.*, XVII. (1904), p. 318.
[2] *Eun.*, 616, 627–628, 734.   [3] *Truc.*, 927.
[4] *Bacch.*, 859–860, 869.   [5] *Cist.*, 534.

In Lucian the woman resorts to the sorcerers when the man threatens and beats her.[1] Very probably this was also the case in comedy.[2] A fragment of Turpilius, a remark of Menander's,[3] a word in the *Truculentus*,[4] a line in the *Cistellaria*,[5] the titles of a play by Philemon and of one by Philippides,[6] all seem to me to show this. Above all, we know that in one of Menander's comedies, called the Θετταλή, magic played an important part.[7] Now, there was no comedy of Menander's that did not contain a love adventure, and therefore I do not think it rash to surmise that the magicians in the Θετταλή made their skill serve the same purpose as did the Syrian sorceress in the fourth *Dialogue*.

We have seen that the love of certain of the *dramatis personae* could, as Terence insinuates, change into hatred, or rather that the two emotions could exist at one and the same time, and rend the hearts of lovers. As for the torments of jealousy, it does not seem to me that the comic poets devoted much time to portraying them. In what remains to us of the νέα, the lovers who have been supplanted by a rival suffer because they have been superseded, but not especially because they see another person preferred to themselves. They are never haunted by the odious vision of caresses in which they have no share. Hardly ever do they make invidious comparisons, that might hurt their pride, between themselves and those who are preferred to them. Above all, I know of no character in comedy who worries without a cause and puts an evil construction on harmless occurrences—that characteristic habit of jealous people. All those who say they have been deceived, really are deceived, or else have some plausible reason for imagining that they are. Witness Polemo, in the Περικειρομένη. No doubt he is irritated too quickly and carries the expression of his wrath too far, but it must be admitted that his mistake was a most natural

---

[1] Luc., *Dial. Mer.*, I., IV., VIII.   [2] Turpilius, *Boethuntes*, fr. VI.
[3] Men., fr. 046.   [4] *Truc.*, 762.   [5] *Cist.*, 290.
[6] 'Ανανεουμένη, 'Ανανεοῦσα.   [7] Pliny, XXX. 6, 7.

one. He saw—saw with his own eyes—Moschio kissing
Glycera, and Glycera allowing herself to be kissed. How
could he guess what Moschio himself did not know—
that he saw before him a brother and sister exchanging
innocent caresses? Polemo is jealous just as every lover is
who sees his place in his mistress' affections taken by another
—that is to say, just as every man is liable to be jealous.

I have still to speak of the struggles lovers had with
themselves.

In the *Trinummus,* an imitation of one of Philemon's
plays, a young man, Lysiteles, makes an arraignment of
love, and finds fault with it in the name of social propriety.[1] It must be remarked that when Lysiteles makes
this wise speech he is not in love with any one. Another
one of Philemon's characters, who is deeply in love, Philolaches, mournfully declares, in one of the first scenes of
the *Mostellaria,* how far passion has degraded him.[2] But
this scene does not present the picture of a conflict, properly
speaking, for though Philolaches blushes for his fall, he
does nothing whatever to redeem himself and yields to
his fate. One of Menander's characters, Chairestratus in
the Εὐνοῦχος, must have been more dramatic. He does
not, like the former two, waste his time in speculation
that has no special point. It is vexation that makes him
speak, vexation at finding his mistress' door locked. The
beginning of Terence's play and a passage in one of Persius'
Satires have preserved for us a picture of his irresolution.[3]
He reproaches himself in a manner worthy of the most
austere mentor, but his access of pride is brief. The
prospect of making his fair one shed a tear, were it only
a feigned tear, suffices to upset him—

"Monstrous! Monstrous! Now I understand that
she is false and that I am unhappy. I am disgusted with
her, yet I am on fire with love. Knowing and realising it,
with eyes open and life in me, I go to destruction and
know not what to do." [4]

---

[1] *Trin.,* 267 et seq.   [2] *Most.,* 142 et seq.
[3] Ter., *Eun.,* 46 et seq.; Persius, *Sat.,* V. 161 et seq.
[4] *Eun.,* 70 et seq.

Diniarchus, in the *Truculentus*, displays the same clear-sightedness and the same resignation. He well knows that when a man is in love he runs the risk of being a dupe, and that he is inclined to be excessively credulous; [1] he takes Phronesium's protestations for what they are worth. For all that, he acts as though he believed they were sincere, and is quite clear that his desire for a rupture and for revenge will not hold out against a fond word from her. [2] There must have been very few persons in comedy who ceased to be in love because they were no longer able to respect the object of their affections. Pamphilus, in the *Hecyra*, to whom this happened with Bacchis, was, owing to his marriage, in an exceptional position, which enabled him to make instructive comparisons. Clinia, in the *Heauton Timoroumenos*, has a fine access of disgust and indignation when he imagines that, after an absence of a few months, his gentle Antiphila has been transformed into a luxurious courtesan. [3] But who can tell how long his anger would have lasted, and how he would have behaved, if what he dreads for a moment had been true?

In the *Hecyra* the struggle which the young lover undergoes in the course of the play is especially pathetic. Pamphilus used to love his wife. He discovers that she had been ravished before he married her. He thinks it impossible to retain her, but continues to love her. From the outset he is thoroughly convinced, as is Myrrhina, Philumena's mother (whose entreaties he eagerly recalls), that the unlucky woman had not really sinned and that she still deserves his respect. He is about to sacrifice his happiness to worldly consideration, and the sacrifice is all the harder because, in his desire to save Philumena's reputation, he is unwilling to declare its true motive. To those who urge him to renew his conjugal relations he is obliged to offer objections which he does not take seriously himself, and his love is displayed even in the midst of his refusal. [4] For a moment he appears to

[1] *Truc.*, 190 et seq.   [2] *Ibid.*, 700 et seq.
[3] *Heaut.*, 256 et seq.   [4] *Hec.*, 486 et seq.

waver.[1] The thought that if he takes back Philumena
he will be obliged to bring up the child of an unknown
father as his own son is the only thing that helps him
to persist in his first resolve.

A similar struggle must have been described in the
'Ἐπιτρέποντες by Menander. Charisius has made the
same discovery as Pamphilus and he too continues to love
his wife. But pride and a certain severity that reminds
one of the Stoics lead him at first to consider the unhappy
woman as a real culprit, unworthy of the affection of an
honest man.[2] Though he does not send her away, nor
proclaim her disgrace, he humiliates her and tries to forget
her. In vain. From the beginning of the play onwards
Charisius bitterly regrets that he has learned of her sad
mishap; in other words, he is on the point of forgiving
her. The poignant memory of a misdemeanour of his
own which the circumstances call up, the generosity of
Pamphila, who remains devoted to him notwithstanding
everything, hasten and complete his change of heart.
Even before he learns that his wife had never belonged to
any one else, Charisius is ready to keep her. In his case,
therefore, love gains a more complete victory over prejudice than in the case of Pamphilus. But it is helped
along by remorse, and as the inconvenient child has, so
to speak, disappeared, the victory is less difficult.

Many of the inward struggles which young lovers
undergo are due to the interference of a father. Of course,
all of them are not equally interesting from a moral point
of view. Sometimes the feelings that conflict with love
which are called forth by a father's interference are anything but heroic. When Clitipho, in the Heauton Timoroumenos, is on the point of being disinherited, he thinks
first and foremost of the poverty that awaits him;[3] if he
gives up Bacchis, it is not so much owing to sincere repent-
ance as to care for his own well-being. In the Phormio,
Antipho, who has made a better choice in his love, does
not even contemplate the possibility of championing it

<hr>

[1] Hec., 613, 615.   [2] 'Επιτρ., 433 et seq.   [3] Heaut., 880.

against his father's will. Let Demipho command, and Antipho will break off his relations with Phanium. Meanwhile, he is not ashamed to groan over his lost peace of mind, and regrets that there had been a possibility of his marrying the girl whom he had so greatly desired.[1] In a word, fear drives affection out of his heart and so far masters him as to make him disavow himself. Elsewhere love is really in conflict with obedience and filial respect. In the *Andria* the two feelings that fight for the upper hand in the heart of the young lover are clearly indicated in lines 261–262 : *amor . . . patris pudor.* Finally, the young man is beaten and offers to withdraw, but it cannot be said that his love is overcome by his respect for his father. I am inclined to believe that Pamphilus would, as he seems to imply in line 695, have been willing to lose Simo's love, together with his patrimony. But he cannot make up his mind to be taken for a rascal; his resolve is forced upon him by his feeling of honour.[2] A rupture which occurs under such circumstances does not imply a disavowal on the part of the lover, and is in no way humiliating for him, nor does it involve offence to the person with whom he breaks off relations. It is the act of a sensitive person who values his love and cannot consent to give it the appearance of an equivocal adventure.

Are considerations of honour, rightly or wrongly understood, and respect or dread of paternal authority the only feelings New Comedy portrayed in conflict with passion ?

Moschio, the young lover in the Σαμία, is annoyed at his father and thinks of punishing him by leaving the country and enlisting in a foreign army in a distant country. But his affection for Plangon keeps him from doing so : " For your sake, dear Plangon, I shall do none of the things which would be worthy of a man; it is impossible for me; Love, henceforward the master of my reason, does not allow me to." [3] This passage contains

---

[1] *Phorm.*, 157–160.   [2] *Andr.*, 897 et seq.   [3] Σαμ., 285–287.

M

an indication of a conflict : here love is shown at odds
with the sulky irritability of a spoiled child. But Moschio
promptly makes up his mind. He merely pretends to
go away in order to frighten Demeas—a puerile decision
which promptly satisfies both opposing feelings !

In the latter part of the thirteenth *Dialogue of the
Courtesans* we see love' and vanity at odds. The swaggering soldier Leontichus has just held forth, to young
Hymnis' wonderment, about the terrific courage to which
he lays claim. The fair one, frightened or feigning fright,
has fled, declaring that she could not live with a murderer,
a man dripping with blood, a hangman. Leontichus is
startled by this unforeseen outcome; he takes counsel
with his parasite Chenidas and finally says : " Go and tell
Hymnis that I lied, but not in everything that I said."
I do not believe that the thirteenth *Dialogue* is an accurate
paraphrase of a scene from comedy, but it is very possible
that some braggart in comedy found himself in the same
dilemma as Lucian's Leontichus.

Possibly other actors vacillated between greed and love.
The inconsistencies that could not fail to develop in the
conduct of an avaricious lover seem to have attracted the
attention of malicious comedy-writers; witness fragment
235 of Menander : " There is no man so stingy or so close-
fisted that he would not sacrifice some part of his wealth
to the god Eros." In the *Poenulus* Agorastocles does not
seem to be indifferent to money. Just as Euclio enjoyed
listening to Megadorus, so, too, Agorastocles takes the
keenest delight in hearing his well-beloved Adelphasium
inveigh against the excesses of luxury.[1] But it is hard to
understand why, as he is rich and free to do as he chooses,
he has not long ago purchased from the pander Lycus
the young woman of whom he is enamoured. I suspect
that in the original version a conflict of emotions was
portrayed, nearly all traces of which the Latin writer,
from lack of psychological insight, has effaced.

---

[1] *Poen.*, 289 et seq., 308 et seq.

§ 7
CHARACTERS AND INDIVIDUAL FIGURES

In one of Alciphron's *Epistles*, supposed to be addressed by Glycera to Menander, we read the following : " Egypt, the Nile, the promontory of Proteus, the tower of Pharus, all are now waiting, longing to see Menander and to hear *his misers* (φιλαργύρων), his lovers, *his superstitious people* (δεισιδαιμόνων), his *suspicious people* (ἀπίστων), and everything that he brings upon the stage." [1] Furthermore, the titles of several of his plays are derived from a moral attribute, and this would lead us to believe that New Comedy had made a special study of certain vices, shortcomings or absurdities; in other words, that it had sometimes risen to the dignity of character comedy. Unfortunately, little is left of what it produced of this kind.

In our study of professional types we have already met with a bad habit that, as it were, clings to some of them boastfulness. The boaster (ἀλαζών)—in Aristotle's opinion one of the types that is most capable of provoking laughter [2]—is defined in the *Ethica Magna* as follows : ὁ . . . ἀλαζών ἐστιν ὁ πλείω τῶν ὑπαρχόντων αὐτῷ προσποιούμενος εἶναι ἢ εἰδέναι ἃ μὴ οἶδεν.[3] Many ἀλαζόνες in comedy—soldiers, cooks, physicians, etc.—frankly carry out this programme, exalting their own virtues, and in explicit terms exaggerating the merits they possess or pretend to possess. Some of them, especially in Menander and his imitators, have a flatterer at hand who gives them the cue, enlarges upon their boasts, and, in case of need, comes to the aid of their exhausted imagination. In Lucian's thirteenth *Dialogue*, which is very

---

[1] Alc., IV. 19, 6.
[2] *Coislin Treatise*, § 7 (Kaibel, p. 52). Cf. Bernays, *Rh. Mus.*, VIII. (1853), p. 577 et seq.
[3] *Eth. Magn.*, I. p. 1193 A.

probably made up of reminiscences of the stage, the attitude of the braggart Leontichus towards his parasite Chenidas is very amusing. He begins by dictating the story he expects him to tell in such detail that there is nothing left for Chenidas to add to it. Then our hero unflinchingly develops a new theme, suggested by his acolyte. In the long run, however, he appears to feel the impropriety of singing his own praises—or is it that he fails to find praise that satisfies him? So he takes Chenidas to witness : " Tell me now, to whom does everybody compare me at this moment? " And Chenidas answers, " To whom else, by Zeus ! than to Achilles, the son of Thetis and Peleus? " Subsequently, when the descriptions of terrible slaughter have put Hymnis to flight, Leontichus, confounded, is ready to blame the too clever Chenidas for his failure, and grudgingly admits that he has gone too far. This dialogue, here and there, contains yet other cleverly observed features, which are possibly derived from a comic prototype. In the account Leontichus gives of his fight against the Galatians, he begins by declaring that the mere sight of him put the enemy to flight. Hence he is deprived of the opportunity to tell of his fine swordsmanship. To this he cannot make up his mind, and, without fear of the contradiction implied, he draws up a proper number of the fugitives in battle array so that he may slay them. We must also note the disparaging reference he makes to his comrades in arms : " And you, Chenidas, you came along shortly afterwards when the enemy had already fled," and the false retrospective modesty of the parenthesis : " I was only a chiliarchus at that time." The reader will recall the ingenuous words with which the conversation ends. Wavering between his love and his vanity, Leontichus does not care completely to sacrifice the latter to the former, and he instructs Chenidas to attempt a reconciliation by telling Hymnis that he had lied; " *but not about everything.*"

When the qualities to which they lay claim are put to

the test and are proved to be contrary to the facts, the
braggarts are in especial need of resourcefulness in order
to maintain their dignity. When Thraso attacks Thais'
lodgings, he prudently stays behind his men, out of the
reach of blows. But it must not be supposed that this
keeps him from representing himself as a very thunderbolt
of war. Pyrrhus, he declares, always used these tactics.[1]
One of the most amusing varieties of braggarts that diverted
the ancients is that of the πτωχαλαζόνες, the beggars who
wish to be thought rich. The *Rhetorica ad Herennium*
tells us of one who has to struggle against a thousand
obstacles.[2] The tribulations of the poor man are described
with much spirit, but it is impossible to determine whether
the author borrowed from the comic poets or not, although
a fragment of Alexis [3] shows that the πτωχαλαζών was not
unknown in comedy.

Side by side with the braggart, Aristotle recommends
the εἴρων as a type equally suitable for comedy. This
type is defined several times in Aristotelian treatises,
and has been made the subject of a monograph by Ribbeck.[4] In contrast with the ἀλαζών, who exaggerates his
station, his merits, and his possessions, the εἴρων is always
ready to depreciate all these things. He pretends to
recognise all sorts of superiority in others, so much so
indeed that, viewed superficially, his behaviour sometimes appears to be that of a vulgar flatterer. But his
purpose and the aim that he pursues distinguish him from
the κόλαξ. What he does is not done out of selfishness,
nor even from a desire to please. When he exalts others,
when he declares that he is their inferior, it is almost always
to sneer at them. At bottom, he has quite a good opinion
of himself, but his indolence or his cowardice, an inborn
tendency to mystify his fellows, or his irony, in the French

---

[1] *Eun.*, 783. *Idem hoc iam Pyrrhus factitavit.*

[2] *Rhet. Her.*, IV. 50 et seq. [3] Alexis, fr. 2.

[4] Ribbeck, *Ueber den Begriff des* εἴρων, in the *Rh. Mus.*, XXXI. (1876),
pp. 381 et seq.

sense of the word, generally leads him to assume an attitude of exaggerated modesty. The εἴρων is rarely met with in the extant portion of New Comedy. This may in part be due to the fact that in their adaptations the Romans could not appreciate a peculiarly Attic trait. It must also be due to the very nature of εἰρωνεία, which is not one of those loud characteristics that attract attention and readily adapt themselves to the laws of stage illusion. It is hard to conceive of a play in which an εἴρων is the chief person, and, as a matter of fact, such a play does not appear to have existed.

Among the characters that appeared on the comic stage, the grumblers, churls and misanthropists must have constituted an imposing group.[1]

One of Menander's comedies was called the Δύσκολος. A fragment of the prologue informs us that the scene was placed at Phyle, near the sanctuary of the Nymphs—that is to say, in a ravine of Mount Parnes, whither, no doubt, the hero went in search of solitude.[2] This hero, as we learn from an expression of the rhetor Choricius, was called Cnemon,[3] and it is very tempting to suppose that several of Aelian's epistles regarding a brutal fellow named Cnemon, who likewise lives at Phyle, contain reminders of his prowess.[4] One of Cnemon's neighbours, Callipides, writes to him complaining of his uncouth manners. Cnemon replies that he hates and abhors the entire human race and that he even detests himself. Callipides tries to calm his rage; he invites Cnemon to celebrate the festival of Pan with him and a few friends, in the hope that wine and the society of amiable women may cure him of his black thoughts. To this Cnemon replies more angrily than ever that he would like to have his neighbour before him so that he might kill him with his own hands, that he abhors all social gatherings, that he distrusts wine as much as an ambuscade, and that when he

---

[1] See the *Agroikos*, by Ribbeck.
[2] Men., fr. 127.
[3] *Revue de philologie*, 1877, p. 228.
[4] El., *Ep. Rust.*, 13–16.

honours the gods he offers them no sacrifices, in order to avoid making himself importunate to them.

Compared with such a misanthropist, the brutal characters who appear in extant comedy must, perforce, appear gentle. The most typical are Smicrines in the 'Ἐπιτρέποντες, Stratylax in the *Truculentus*, Demea in the *Adelphi*, and Euclio in the *Aulularia*. When Smicrines is politely addressed by Syriscus, who tells him that he has had a difference with his journeyman, he begins to snarl at the poor devil, and makes fun of the two strange litigants.[1] When Syriscus ventures to speak out of turn he threatens him with his stick.[2] After the verdict is given, he goes away, still sullen, without replying to the thanks Syriscus gives him.[3] In the last scene he tortures the unhappy Sophrona with insults and threats, and blames her for begging him not to take back her daughter by force.[4] Besides living in the country, Stratylax and Demea have this peculiarity in common that they place their brutality at the service of virtue. Their intentions are excellent, but they have very bad manners. As soon as Stratylax sees a woman loitering about his house he " shouts and drives her off as he would a goose stealing a bit of wheat." [5] He repels the graceful advances of the waiting-maid Astaphium, lavishes ill-sounding reproaches upon her and makes her fear his violence. As for Demea, we know from a note by Donatus that he was less discourteous in the original version than in the Latin transcription. In the former he acknowledged his brother's greeting, whereas, in the *Adelphi*, he ignores this demand of courtesy.[6] Other characteristics are probably copied from the Greek prototype : for instance, the triumphant eagerness with which Demea tells Micio of his adopted son's pranks and of the scandal they have created in the town, or his scornful laments over his brother's folly, and his threat against Syrus, whom he wishes to thrash.[7] As for Euclio, I do

---

[1] 'Ἐπιτρ., 11–13. [2] *Ibid.*, 31–32. [3] *Ibid.*, 153.
[4] *Ibid.*, 464 et seq. [5] *Truc.*, 251–252.
[6] *Ad.*, 81 and Donatus' note. [7] *Ibid.*, 782.

not think that the position in which he happens to find himself sufficiently explains the rage he displays when he beats Staphyla and threatens her with the most terrible punishment, and covers Congrio with blows, and lavishes insults upon Strobilus. If his strong-box did not afford him so much occasion to get angry, he would doubtless find it elsewhere. Whatever may have been the title of the play that Plautus imitated, Euclio is certainly a δύσκολος.

Next to the misanthropes and the δύσκολοι we may place the misers, since their characteristics are sometimes found combined in certain people. At least two comic writers of the new period—Philippides and Theognetus— wrote plays called Φιλάργυρος, in which, in all probability, men who are too fond of money played the leading part. Other misers—in the broad sense of the word—appear, as we know, in four or five of Menander's plays : the Δύσκολος, the Ὑδρία, the Ἐπιτρέποντες, the Θησαυρός, and probably in the Δακτύλιος. It is possible that the Aulularia is an imitation of the Ὑδρία.

Euclio, the hero of the Aulularia, certainly has very little resemblance to Harpagon, to whom he has often been compared. At first sight he reminds one rather of La Fontaine's cobbler who has unexpectedly grown rich and is much embarrassed by his wealth. His avarice, if it be avarice, is excusable on account of his poverty.[1] Before discovering the pot, he had lived for a long time, for better for worse, on the produce of a little field situated near the city; his poor house is void of everything but spiders' webs.[2] In his case the fear of privation is therefore explicable and, to a certain extent, pardonable; but he carries it too far. Of course, one must not take what Pythodicus [3] relates of him too literally; it is the slander of an impertinent servant, who is used to live in the houses of the rich, and yet it must be admitted that the general behaviour of our hero afforded some ground for such inventions. Moreover, the prologue seems to blame

<hr/>

[1] *Aul.*, 206.   [2] *Ibid.*, 13–14, 84.   [3] *Ibid.*, 298 et seq.

Phaedrium's father for having an excessively parsimonious nature. Euclio himself shows that, to a certain extent, both the prologue and Pythodicus are right, when he justifies himself and praises himself, as he does, for coming back from market without provisions,[1] and delights in listening to Megadorus' tirades against the extravagance of women,[2] and expresses his fear that the flute-playing girl who has been hired by his future son-in-law may drink too much wine,[3] and complains that the lamb he has just received—and received gratis—cannot bring him more profit.[4] In a word, if the hero of the *Aulularia* is not the typical miser, even if he is not a miser at all in the proper sense of the word, we may at any rate without unfairness say that he is remarkably close-fisted.

Generally speaking, the φιλάργυροι of New Comedy— always, or nearly always men of advanced years—were, as it seems, less anxious to make money than not to spend it. Like Euclio, the miser in the Δύσκολος and the miser in the Ὑδρία buried their money. Fragment 129 of the Δύσκολος criticises the custom of making sumptuous sacrifices in a rather amusing way, but evidently with a purpose. It declares that the brigands (τοιχωρύχοι) who offer them think less about the gods than about themselves; to the gods they offer the tail of the victim, the bile or uneatable bones, and with the rest they gorge themselves. Detestable custom! Incense, a cake that can be burnt on the altar and all of which goes up to the gods, that is what a pious man should offer. Fragment 175 of the Ἐπιτρέποντες contains the following maxim that is worthy of Harpagon : " A healthy, lazy man is worse than a fever-patient, for he eats double and with no results." And finally, we know from an expression of Choricius that Smicrines, an important character in one of the comedies cited above, feared—like Euclio—that the smoke might occasion him some loss by escaping from his house.[5]

---

[1] *Aul.*, 371 et seq.   [2] *Ibid.*, 496–497.   [3] *Ibid.*, 557 et seq.
[4] *Ibid.*, 561 et seq.   [5] *Revue de philologie*, 1877, p. 228.

In Euclio's case, the dread of being robbed is intensified by the fact that he has but recently come into possession of a treasure-trove. He loses his peace of mind and his good sense through watching his precious pot. He suspects everything, everything awakens his distrust, and he lives under the obsession of a fixed idea. And yet Euclio must not be regarded as a man in whom the love of money has crowded out all generous feelings. When allowance is made for the customs of the ancients, it cannot be said that he sacrifices Phaedrium by marrying her to an old husband without having consulted her. His ignorance of his daughter's misfortunes is shared by many fathers in comedy. When he hears of them he forgets his lost pot. At the end of the play he resigns himself to the loss of his treasure, and since he is, as I believe, secured against want, he even congratulates himself at being rid of a source of worry. In the 'Επιτρέποντες excessive fondness for money has left a deeper mark on Smicrines. A scholiast of Homer says of him that he cared more for his fortune than for his dearest affections,[1] and as a matter of fact, various passages in extant fragments show that he is more anxious to save Pamphila's dowry than to ensure her happiness. The true motive for his animosity toward Charisius is ingenuously displayed in his invectives against Sophrona : " Must I expect my daughter's fine husband to squander the dowry which belongs to me ? And must I have discussions about what is my own ? That is what your advice amounts to ! " [2] Onesimus knows quite well what is worrying the old man, and when Smicrines knocks at the door he greets him with these words : " Ah, old Close-fist, coming to fetch his dowry and his daughter (the dowry is mentioned first). . . . Very prudent : that's what I call the eagerness of a man who knows how to calculate (λογιστικοῦ ἀνδρός)." [3] And Smicrines quite agrees with him : it is against the *brigandage* of Charisius (ἅρπασμα) that he inveighs—that is to say, against his extravagance.

---

[1] Sch. Ambros., *Od.*, VII. 225.   [2] 'Επιτρ., 480 et seq.
[3] *Ibid.*, 467 et seq.

It is not impossible that the judgment of the scholiast of
Homer would have been applicable to other characters
in comedy besides the miser of the Ἐπιτρέποντες : a
fragment of the Δακτύλιος is apparently spoken by a father
of a family who is delighted to give his daughter in
marriage without providing her with a dowry;[1] though
in all probability a dowerless marriage was an unworthy
marriage.

Together with the φιλάργυροι Alciphron mentions the
ἄπιστοι. Suspicion was a secondary feature of the character of certain misers, or of certain ἄγροικοι. In one
instance, at least, in Menander's writings—in the play
called Ἄπιστος—suspicion must have been the predomi-
nant characteristic of the chief actor. It has been
assumed, though there are no convincing reasons for this
assumption, that the Ghorân fragments, discovered by
Jouguet, belong to this comedy. They are too incomplete to allow our forming a precise idea of the plot. All
we know is that a young man, a lover, probably on
his return from a journey, thinks that he has been betrayed
by all about him, and, among others, by a friend in whom
he had confided. His mistake and his utterances remind
one somewhat of Mnesilochus in the *Bacchides*. It may
be that his mistake, like that of Mnesilochus, was due more
to deceptive appearances than to an especially suspicious
temperament.

The third type cited by Alciphron is that of the superstitious man (δεισιδαίμων). One of Menander's comedies
was called Δεισιδαίμων. Superstitious men, and particularly superstitious women, probably appeared in several
other plays whose titles are sometimes significant : the
Μηναγύρτης, the Ἱέρεια, the Θεοφορουμένη, the Τροφώνιος,
and the Μισογύνης. And finally, a few interesting fragments have survived that bear no indication of their
origin. The most curious passage is fragment 109 of

[1] Men., fr. 103.

the Δεισιδαίμων, in which the hero tells a friend of a
terrible accident he has had : " May it turn out well for
me, revered gods ! In putting on my shoes I broke the
strap of my right shoe." A few sentences of fragment
534 and fragment *adespoton* 341 may be compared with this
passage. Fragments 530 and 544 of Menander ridicule
certain expiatory ceremonies. In fragment 601, from
the Μισογύνης, we hear of a woman who offers sacrifice in
her own house five times a day, while seven servants,
standing in a circle, beat cymbals and others utter piercing
shrieks. Fragment 245, from the ʿΙέρεια, concerns another
equally foolish devotee.

Such are the characters whose portrayal in comedy can
still be traced. As for others, like the insatiable man
(ἄπληστος), possibly a variety of the miser [1]—the ambitious
man (φίλαρχος), the discontented or melancholy man (αὐτὸν
πενθῶν),[2] the intriguing or indiscreet man, or the busy-
body (φιλοπράγμων, πολυπράγμων), the poltroon (ψοφοδεής),
the inconstant man (εὔριπος), of all these we know but one
thing—that New Comedy concerned itself with them.[3]

* * *

Although they do not, to any marked degree, give
evidence of a particular vice or shortcoming, a great many
characters in comedy have a psychological individuality.
There are some, no doubt, whose nature is but imper-
fectly indicated by their age, their social station, their
family or by their position as lovers. But in the case of
others, the very nature of their love, their conception of
filial duty, the manner in which they exercise paternal
authority, or live with their wives, depict characteristics
peculiar to them. In the foregoing chapters I have distinguished only the large categories—the dramatic rôle
characters. But such a classification must not mislead

---

[1] Unless, indeed, we have simply to deal with a parasite whom nothing
satisfies.
[2] Unless we ought to translate Αὐτὸν πενθῶν by " the man who grieves
about himself " and find in this title a reminiscence of some mystification.
[3] These adjectives have all served as titles.

us; it applies rather more to the costumes and the masks that the actors wore than to their real qualities. If we examine the most complete fragments of the Greek originals and the most careful Latin imitations, particularly those by Terence, we shall discover in them many a feature of which this classification took no account. The skill of the best poets of the νέα succeeded in creating the most diverse characters within the limits of each category. The essential elements remain the same in each case, but they appear in different combinations, according as one or the other of them predominates; and minor details of an infinite diversity combine with them to complete a distinct character in each instance.

Let me quote some examples—

It is an inadequate description of Simo, in the *Mostellaria*, to class him among the γέροντες, or among the discontented husbands, or among the εἴρωνες. His physiognomy is more complex. His cynical joy at having thwarted his wife's designs and at having thereby secured a good meal, the anxiety with which he observes the extravagance of his young neighbour, his indifference to his own home and to the decorum of his family, the irony of his replies to Theopropides when he comes home from the market-place—all these things fit together and combine, it is true, to make Simo a rather unsympathetic person; but he is lifelike, and his personality stands, as it were, in relief.

Demeas, in the Σαμία, is likewise a person whom one cannot, in fairness, place under a general heading. He has a character of his own, not very rare in quality, but nevertheless above the commonplace. Many another person would have cast aside all doubts after listening to the servants' gossip which he has overheard by chance: the child which he had regarded as his own must have sprung from the illicit relations of his son with his mistress. But Demeas does not, at first, admit this conclusion, because it disturbs him in his love of tranquillity, and because it would oblige him to proceed with vigour,

whereas he is a peace-loving person. He even shrinks
from formulating it, and, in order to counteract the suspicion which he feels, he affectionately recalls the fact
that Moschio was always the model of a respectful son.
Notwithstanding all the evidence, the matter does not
seem clear to him. He questions Parmeno, the factotum
of the house, who, next to himself, ought to know how
matters stand. Parmeno protests that he knows nothing.
And yet, now that he has given voice to his fears, Demeas
is sure that they are not imaginary. Without receiving
any new proof, he is suddenly convinced of what but
a moment ago appeared doubtful to him. Shall he
take vigorous measures against Moschio? No indeed!
Moschio is too dear to him, and he himself is too good-
natured. Chrysis, whom he loves less, suddenly appears
to him as the only culprit. That rogue of a Samian
woman must have inveigled the virtuous young man,
must have lain in wait for him, in order to make him forget
his duty at a time when he was drunk. She must be
punished, sent off; and in order to humiliate Moschio,
her innocent accomplice, she is to be sent off without
being told for what she is blamed. With the courage of
an excited coward, Demeas rushes into his house and
reappears almost immediately, followed by Chrysis, whom
he turns out of doors. The Samian woman, who has, no
doubt, ere this, witnessed similar explosions, does not
appear to be particularly disturbed. With more malice
than fitness she calls her friend's attention to the fact
that he is no longer sure of himself, and that one can
discern signs of relenting in his outbursts of anger. As a
matter of fact, Demeas is doing violence to his own feelings, and he is doubtless aware that his resolve would
weaken were he to listen to Chrysis; and so he keeps on
interrupting her. To force himself to feel disgusted with
her, he recalls the wretched state in which she was when
he took her in—barely clothed in a chemise; he pictures
to himself what will become of her—a haunter of feasts, a
drunkard, a woman who will sell herself for ten drachmae.

With the help of such precautions, he succeeds in returning home alone and leaving Chrysis in the street. But it is easy to divine that the rupture is not final. Even if events did not vindicate the Samian woman, Demeas would, we may be sure, find an excuse for calling her back. In the course of a few scenes our friend Demeas has shown of what stuff he is made. Henceforward he is more than a name, more than a character of the play, more than a type; he is an individual.

Let us take another example. Laches and Phidippus, in the *Hecyra*, are, as far as their social standing goes, two persons of the same class : two respectable citizens, two old husbands, two fathers of a family. Neither of them has a well-defined character. At first sight it would appear as though they shared the same colourless respectability that characterises all the other actors in the *Hecyra*. And yet, when we examine them more closely, how much one differs from the other ! From the very first scenes in which they appear, Phidippus, in contrast to Laches, shows himself to be a good, though a rather weak man, who avoids occasioning his family sorrow, and is not in the habit of making his wishes prevail. Later on, the different manner in which each of them greets Pamphilus —Laches' greeting consists of only a few words, that of Phidippus takes the form of a compliment—allows us to surmise that the one has more authority and the other more good nature. Everything else is in keeping. In his quarrels with Sostrata, Laches, without taking things in a tragic way, speaks firmly, like a man who has decided on a line of conduct from which he will not swerve, and who knows how to command. His wife's humility does not disarm him. When she declares that she wants to go off to the country, he tells her to go and pack her trunks. When Phidippus, on the other hand, learns of Philumena's clandestine confinement, he has a much greater cause for anger, and, as a matter of fact, he does get angry ; but his wrath is not by any means terrible, and it is not directed against his daughter, for whom he is eager to find excuse. In his conversation with his wife he soon gives up reproaching her, and undertakes the defence of Pamphilus, a task that is more to his taste. As soon as he finds an opportunity he will be most happy again to assure Myrrhina of his esteem. Like all weak characters, he indulges in quite ill-timed outbursts against Pamphilus and Bacchis—outbursts which, by the way, are not of long duration. Without good reason he accuses the former of losing his head about an inheritance, and of scorning an alliance with his family, and then becomes unduly conciliatory, and allows him and his father freely to follow their own inclinations, and almost apologises because he cannot answer for his wife's moods. He starts by declaring to Bacchis, in insulting terms, that such a person as she is not deserving of belief, but this does not prevent him from believing, the very next moment, everything she says. Laches is much more sober-minded and consistent. If he indulges in hard words about Pamphilus, it is because appearances are all against the youth and expose him to the suspicion of hypocrisy. To Bacchis, quietly and without ill-timed threats, he gives the choice between peace and war, and he does not, from prejudice, fail to recognise the sincerity in her answers. Such being the dispositions of the two fathers, it is not surprising to find that the initiative is generally taken by Laches. It is he who, before Pamphilus comes back, insists upon Philumena consenting to live with him again. Phidippus, caught between this impor- tunity and his daughter's obstinacy, has no other idea, poor man, than to get out of the way. After Pamphilus' return, it is again Laches who urges on his fellow-gossip, and whispers in his ear what he is to do. It is Laches who, at the height of the confusion, plainly tells the young man what Phidippus thinks, but has carefully kept hidden. It is Laches who comes to an understanding with Bacchis; Phidippus, who has thought of this under- standing—and this behaviour on his part is surprising— does not take the trouble to be present; to go and fetch a nurse on whom he lavishes pleasant words is certainly more in keeping with his methods.

But let us cut short the discussion with the consideration of the cases of two or three " severe fathers " who are the victims of troubles of the same kind : Simo in the *Andria*, Demipho in the *Phormio*, and Chremes in the *Heauton Timoroumenos*. All three have just discovered that their sons had disobeyed them and give vent to their displeasure, but each of them does so after his own fashion.

" There you have the respect of a son ! Aren't you sorry for me ? " says Simo to an old friend. " To think that one takes so much trouble for such a son ! " [1]

" You are quite right to make fun of me," says Chremes. " It is with myself that I am angry now. How many things would have made me guess it, had I not been so stupid ! Why did I not have my eyes open, unhappy man that I am ! " [2]

" And so," complains Demipho, " Antipho has married without my permission ! Neither my authority—but let us say nothing of my authority—nor even the fear of my displeasure could keep him from doing so. Not the slightest scruple ! What effrontery ! " [3]

In Simo's case it is his feelings that are hurt; with Chremes it is a case of wounded vanity, and with Demipho a blow at his tyrannical disposition. Their exclamations in the distress of the first moment show the great difference in their characters. An analysis of their several rôles would confirm this evidence.

Even more readily than among the old men we can point to distinct individualities among the young men, the lovers in comedy.

Compare Antipho of the *Phormio* with Pamphilus of the *Andria*. Each of them has affectionate relations with an excellent girl, and each of them is at loggerheads with his father. Throughout the play, Pamphilus hardly for a

[1] *Andr.*, 869–870.   [2] *Heaut.*, 915–917.   [3] *Phorm.*, 231–233.

N

moment appears to be in doubt as to his proper course. While he hopes that his interests can be safeguarded without his being obliged to push himself forward, he is frankly resolved to resist, if necessary; and, as a matter of fact, at the most critical moment he confesses his love to his vexed father : " Yes, I love Glycerium; I confess it, and if it is a fault, I admit my fault." [1] Antipho is not of the same calibre; he is timid and irresolute, and begins by losing his head. In place of the energetic declarations made by the lover in the *Andria*, he only makes lamentations and constantly renews the avowal of his insurmountable terror. Pamphilus reproaches himself for having relied too much on others.[2] Antipho sees that it is best for him to let his slave, his parasite or his cousin, act; and he passively awaits the outcome of their machinations, though he blushes at his own inactivity. He does not even possess the necessary energy to control and to criticise the actions of his allies. Pamphilus, when Davus has got him into a tight corner, overwhelms him with reproaches and threats; [3] under similar conditions Antipho does nothing but moan.[4]

Another lover of the most interesting sort, whose acquaintance we owe to recent discoveries, is the soldier Polemo, of the Περικειρομένη. As I have already pointed out, Polemo is not the typical jealous man. What places him above the commonplace is his impetuous nature, his spirit, which is at once impetuous and irresolute. At the beginning of the play he sulks, and tries to drown his sorrow by feasting with his comrades. He only succeeds in taking half-measures against Glycera; under a futile pretext he sends his servant to her to find out what she is doing. He would, no doubt, like to return himself, but cannot make up his mind to do so. Later on, when he plans to attack Myrrhina's house, we recognise the infuriated man who made havoc of his mistress' hair, and this fresh outburst of wrath, like the one that had pre-

---

[1] *Andr.*, 896.   Cf. Men., fr. 859.   [2] *Andr.*, 607–609.
[3] *Ibid.*, 610 et seq.   [4] *Phorm.*, 685 et seq.

ceded, is promptly followed by profound depression.
Confronted with the short and frigid remonstrances of
the prudent Pataecus, the soldier's anger is appeased in
the twinkling of an eye. The man who wanted to slaughter
everybody admits that he has no claim whatsoever on
Glycera, that she is free to bestow herself on whomsoever
she chooses, and that he can only regain her favour by
persuasion. Discouraged before he has made an effort,
he decides that there is nothing left for him to do but to
hang himself. Then, all of a sudden, he remembers that
Pataecus could easily, if he would, be of use to him, and
he refuses to let him go until he agrees to help him.
Thereupon he insists on displaying the fine gowns he had
once bought for Glycera as proofs of his love, and Pataecus
has perforce to admire the fine gowns without delay. The
same impatience, the same irresoluteness, the same tendency to exaggerate are displayed in one of the final
scenes. There Polemo learns from Doris, Glycera's
attendant, that the young woman has found her father;
he thereupon imagines that she is lost to him, declares
that he cannot live without her and threatens to kill
himself. Doris reassures him and sets out to return to
Glycera. As long as she remains in sight he overwhelms
her with advice, with protestations and with promises.
Left alone for a moment, he reproaches himself most
bitterly. When Doris returns, bringing good news and
words of forgiveness, he exults and is beside himself with
joy. From beginning to end the character is consistent.

Chaerea, in the *Eunuchus*, is neither an ordinary νεανίας
nor a commonplace lover. Whatever the situation, he is
ardent and resolute. As soon as he falls in love with
Pamphila he makes up his mind that she shall be his, and
the orders he gives his slave do not admit of a reply.[1]
The plan that is jokingly suggested to him—to enter
Thais' house disguised as a eunuch—pleases him at first
sight. He takes it up enthusiastically, and when Parmeno
is dumbfounded by so much audacity, and attempts to

---

[1] *Eun.*, 319–320.

withdraw, he imperiously silences him. He shows the
same resoluteness in carrying out his gallant exploit, and
the same exuberance when he has succeeded and tells the
audience of it. It turns out that Pamphila is a citizen.
That does not disturb Chaerea. He means to marry her,
and has no doubt that he will marry her, and that everybody will approve of the marriage. With fine confidence
he asks Thais, whom he had not even known a few
moments before, to champion his cause. He liberally
discounts his father's good will, and seems to think that
his resoluteness would even force the hands of the gods.

Similarly, among the slaves, whether they be honest
or knavish, we meet with some who are not merely
representatives of a particular class. Onesimus, in
the Ἐπιτρέποντες, talks too much; Messenio, in the
Menaechmi, is suspicious; Parmeno, in the Hecyra, is
indiscreet and inquisitive; his namesake in the Eunuchus
is a coward. Even in the exercise of the function that is
common to a good many of them—the art of deception—
some of them display an individual temperament. For
instance, Tranio, in the Mostellaria, is not content to
make the aged Theopropides believe whatever is necessary
in order to hide the sins of Philolaches, but derides him
to boot. When he accompanies him on a visit to a
neighbour, he makes a point of showing him, as though
it were in the vestibule, a painting that does not exist—
two buzzards of whom a crow is making fun, an image of
himself and the two old men whom he is taking for a
walk. Naturally enough, Theopropides sees nothing of
all this, and Tranio says : " Come, let's say no more about
it. I am not angry with you. Your age prevents your
seeing things clearly." [1] Here we find the same dare-
devil impudence that Tranio displayed in his first conversation with Grumio, or when he invented the story of
the purchased house, and which he again displays towards
the close of the play, when, as the saying is, he is about

[1] Most., 840.

to rush into the lion's jaws. The ways of a slave like Chrysalus, or like Davus in the *Andria*, are quite different.

Even purely episodic characters were sometimes—at least in Menander's comedies—carefully portrayed. For instance, the shepherd Daos, one of the litigants in the Ἐπιτρέποντες, appears in only one scene—that of the contest—and yet this suffices to give us the impression of a distinct personality. He is selfish, distrustful and dull, and at the same time sly. He is apparently as much astonished as he is annoyed at Syriscus' demands. What do people expect of him? He has generously surrendered one-half of what he has found—found unaided; has he not a right to keep the other half? He claims that he has, and I believe that he is sincere; and that explains why he is ready to abide by the decision of the first-comer. But as he listens to Syriscus, who has a glib tongue, he becomes anxious, and has recourse to all the cunning of a rustic. The account of the discovery and of the subsequent events which he gives in his speech is a masterpiece of assumed artlessness. Maliciously he relates how Syriscus insisted on getting the child; in a scornful way he incidentally underrates the value of the few things which he is asked to give up, the very things with which he is absolutely unwilling to part; and a few moments after having claimed that the child was a burden to him, he insinuates that in handing it over to some one else he has proved his generosity. His malice, by the way, is short lived. Once his suit has been dismissed he is nothing but a dullard, a numskull who whines pitifully and keeps repeating his absurd grievances with mechanical obstinacy.

Thus, as we have seen, there are a great many characters in extant comic literature that can supply material for a portrait, and their lively and characteristic outlines often appear all the more alive and characteristic because they are brought into relief through contrast. Such contrasts as I have pointed out between Pamphilus in the *Andria* and Antipho in the *Phormio*, between Simo, Chremes and

Demipho, are frequently found between the actors in a single play. Antipho has, as his counterpart, his cousin, who is audacious and so completely master of himself that he wins Geta's admiration; Chaerea has his brother, a timid man who is readily embarrassed by exaggerated scruples. Polemo, the brutal but sincere lover, easily discouraged, has as his rival a man-about-town, a young fop who thinks himself irresistible. In the *Phormio* we have the gentle and timid Chremes as a contrast to the domineering and harsh Demipho; in the *Heauton Timoroumenos* Menedemus, his own enemy, who sees the dark side of everything, as a contrast to Chremes, the optimist; in the *Andria* a third Chremes, who cannot refuse a request, as a contrast to Simo, who is so harsh in exacting what he wishes from his friends. Furthermore, we find Aeschinus side by side with Ctesipho in the *Adelphi*, Lysiteles side by side with Lesbonicus in the *Trinummus* —the one judicious beyond his years, the other a sympathetic " bad lot." In the *Heauton Timoroumenos* we have Clinia and Clitipho, in whom the difference which marks their father's natures is reflected; in the Γεωργός the violent Gorgias and the timid young lover; in the *Asinaria* the two aspirants whose parts Monsieur Havet has very aptly characterised : [1] Diabolus, determined and quick to resort to threats, Argyrippus, sentimental and humble. Among the old men we have, besides Laches and Phidippus, Micio and Demea in the *Adelphi*, Simo and Callipho in the *Pseudolus*, Philoxenus and Nicobulus in the *Bacchides*, each more uncompromising than the other. In the *Casina* we have Lysidamus and Alcesimus; in the *Mercator* Demipho and Lysimachus, more or less conscious of their years and of their duties. Among the female characters we have the two sisters in the *Stichus*, one of whom is obliged to encourage the fidelity of the other; the sisters in the *Poenulus*—Adelphasium, prouder and more sedate, and Anterastilis, the younger of the two, who is inclined to make fun of everything.

---

[1] *Revue de philologie*, XXIX. (1905), pp. 92 et seq.

Several lost comedies, one of which belonged to the new period, had the titles Ὅμοιοι, Ὅμοιαι; and it may be that they were plays in which the contrast between characters was all the more noticeable because the heroes were of the same age and of the same social standing, or because a very strong physical resemblance led them to be taken one for the other. Something of this kind occurs in the *Menaechmi* : Menaechmus Sosicles is much bolder, much more direct, if I may say so, than the kidnapped Menaechmus.

CHAPTER IV

ADVENTURES

SOME of the adventures in which the *dramatis personae* of New Comedy take part have already been mentioned, because it was impossible to avoid all reference to them in my review of the characters themselves. But in order to give a fairly complete idea of the *νέα* I must call attention to still others, and also co-ordinate what has been said of some of them by anticipation and incidentally. In this chapter I propose to fulfill this twofold task, and there will be found in it a review of the various incidents which the comic poets have, as far as we know, introduced into the composition of their plots.

Very few of these incidents can have been of a political nature. War, which is spoken of frequently enough, generally only supplies a subject of conversation—a pretext for bragging. Sometimes it explains the absence of a gallant soldier, who, after its close, reappears more or less unexpectedly, or else it is the cause of a family being dispersed. Rarely does a war have an immediate influence on the plot, and yet in the *Captivi* and the *Epidicus* its vicissitudes separate father and son, mother and daughter, and subsequently, contrary to all expectation, bring Hegio two children in place of the one of which they had deprived him, and supply Philippa with a second husband in addition to Telestis. As for military life, it may be that it was depicted in one of Diphilus' comedies, which is supposed to have been called the Ἐλαιὼν ἢ Φρουροῦντες, in the Φυλακή by Philemon, and in the Ψοφοδεής; but at best this is extremely doubtful.

From civic life and its duties the comic writers do not appear to have borrowed more than an occasional detail to adorn their plots. In the *Miles* and in the *Truculentus* the absence of the young lover is accounted for by a public service—an embassy to Naupactus, the duties of a magis-

tracy at Lemnos;[1] whilst in the *Aulularia*, Euclio leaves
his house to get his share of a distribution made to the
people.[2] But we meet with nothing else of this kind in
Latin comedy, and nothing is to be found in the Greek
fragments. Several comedies bore as their title either
the name of a public office—Ἀρεοπαγίτης, Ἄρχων, Δικασταί,
Νομοθέτης, Φύλαρχος—or that of a class of the population
—Δημόται, Ἔφηβος (Ἔφηβοι, Συνέφηβοι), Μέτοικος. But a
title of this sort, standing by itself, teaches us nothing
about the plot of the play.

Business life is represented in quite a number of
episodes in comedy.

Most of the journeys mentioned in Plautus and in
Terence are undertaken for the sake of profit. One
person goes on a long journey in order to rehabilitate his
fortune; another, in order to increase it or that of his
parents. In the *Bacchides*, Mnesilochus has gone to
Ephesus to collect a debt; in the *Hecyra*, Pamphilus has
been obliged to go to Imbros to take over an inheritance;
and in the *Andria*, Crito lands at Athens for the same
purpose. Business trips are mentioned in fragments of
Menander's Ἥρως, Γεωργός, Κόλαξ and Ναύκληρος, and
of the *Lindia*, by Turpilius, as well as in the anonymous
Strassburg prologue and elsewhere. Few incidents can
have been more commonly introduced by the writers of
New Comedy. Moreover, as a rule, these journeys end
in the course of the play, which amounts to saying that
the home-coming—either wished-for or feared—was a
favourite theme.

Though lawsuits, contracts, and the bargains and difficulties which may arise from them do not play so much of a
part as business journeys, they nevertheless occur quite frequently in comic plots. Several titles, such as Διαδικαζόμενοι, Ἐγκαλοῦντες, Ἐπιδικαζόμενοι, Ἐπίκληρος, Ἐπιτρέποντες,
Ἐπίτροπος, Ἐπαγγέλλοντες, Παρεκδιδομένη, Προεγκαλῶν,
Διαθῆκαι, Παρακαταθήκη, in themselves make more or less

---

[1] *Miles*, 102–103; *Truc.*, 91–92.   [2] *Aul.*, 107–108.

certain allusion to them. Latin imitations and other documents, here and there, give us further information. Quintilian praises the *judicia* contained in several of Menander's plays,[1] but the pleadings that took place before an audience were never, I imagine, attended by greater pomp and a more official character than was the debate in the Ἐπιτρέποντες; and probably these scenes represented arbitration. On the other hand, regular lawsuits sometimes took place behind the scenes. The *Phormio*, a translation of Apollodorus' Ἐπιδικαζόμενος, is an example, and shows the kind of litigation that a comedy with the title Ἐπίκληρος or Διαδικαζόμενοι may have contained. In the Μισογύνης, a γραφὴ κακώσεως appears to have been instituted,[2] and in the Χαλκίς there may have been a γραφὴ μοιχείας.[3] Twice in Plautus, in the *Casina* and in the *Menaechmi*, an actor comes back upon the stage and explains that his long absence was due to the importunity of some litigant, a relative or client, who had most inconveniently claimed his assistance in court.[4] Elsewhere actors account for their exits by saying that they are going to market or to a banker. In the *Mostellaria* we witness a discussion between a usurer and an insolvent debtor; subsequently we see a gentleman inspecting the house he thinks he has bought, and hear him criticising it and planning improvements. In the *Asinaria* landed proprietors either sell or give orders to buy cattle. In the *Mercator* and in the *Adelphi* the purchase of a slave girl takes place on the stage; in the *Curculio* and in the *Pseudolus* the sale has been agreed upon before the play begins, but the delivery is still to be made, and the entire interest centres upon it. In the *Vidularia*, as in the Γεωργός, an impecunious young man hires himself out to a private gentleman.[5] In the *Bacchides*, one of the sisters is bound to the soldier Cleomachus by a contract of hire similar in its essentials to the contract prepared by the parasite in the *Asinaria*,

---

[1] Quint., X. 1, 70.   [2] Men., fr. 327, 328.   [3] *Ibid.*, fr. 512.
[4] *Cas.*, 566 et seq.; *Menaech.*, 588 et seq.   [5] *Vid.*, 20 et seq.; Γεωργ., 46–47.

and is anxious to cancel it. In the Ἐπιτρέποντες, a χωρὶς
οἰκῶν, the charcoal-burner Syriscus, comes to pay his
master the ἀποφορά.[1] In the Ἥρως, Gorgias and Plangon
pay off by their labour the debt contracted by their
putative father, the freedman Tibeius.[2]

The life of pleasure appears to have supplied comedy
with favourite themes during the whole middle period,
and one phase of that life, above all others, seems to have
claimed the attention of the poets — the banquet. At
least that is what we gather from the words spoken by
Antiphanes one day when King Alexander showed little
pleasure in listening to his works : " O king, in order to
enjoy these things one must have frequently taken part
in banquets where every one pays his share, and one must
have fought more than once about a courtesan." [3] Traces
of this preference are also found during the period that
followed. There is not a single play by Plautus or by
Terence in which a banquet is not mentioned, if, indeed,
it is not spoken of at length or represented upon the stage.
The fragments of original works, Lucian's *Dialogues* and
the *Letters* of Alciphron, prove that this was generally the
case in the whole of comic literature. The players in
the νέα have banquets on the slightest provocation. At
the dinner-table they celebrate public festivals or happy
family events; at the dinner-table they seek solace for
their grief; a banquet is the means of purchasing or recom-
pensing the services of a parasite, a go-between, or a
duenna. As a rule, they hold banquets for no particular
reason, their only purpose being to pass the time in an
agreeable manner and in gay company, and about the
banquet are grouped various episodes. The host goes to
market or sends his servants there; the cook arrives with
the provisions; he is introduced and given advice, or
quarrelled with; he, being indiscreet and a thief, occasions
brawls and hubbubs, or, being puffed up with his own
importance, offers sacrifice to the gods, and superintends

---

[1] Ἐπιτρ., 161–163.   [2] Ἥρ., 36; cf. hypoth., 5.   [3] Ath., p. 555 A.

upon the stage the processes of his art. When they finish drinking, the guests are entertained by dances. Certainly it is about the festive board that the parasites exhibit most of their accomplishments, and there, too, does many a quarrel arise. When the feast is over, the servants come to fetch their masters as they go out of the banqueting hall; the guests scatter in a noisy *komos*, or else they stagger about and betake themselves to renewed orgies.

However great the importance of the banquet, it is not the only phase of the life of pleasure that is portrayed in the *νέα*. We hear of hunters—hunters who have come from town—in a fragment of the "Ἥρως.[1] The title of one of Philemon's comedies—'Εφεδρισταί or 'Εφεδρίζοντες—and a fragment of Diphilus[2] suggest scenes representing games. The *Mostellaria* contains a scene in the boudoir. In the *Poenulus*, two young women, in their finest array, start out for the Aphrodisia, and a young man declares his intention of doing so likewise. Menander wrote an 'Αφροδίσια, a Κανηφόρος, and an 'Αρρηφόρος; Philippides wrote an 'Αδωνιάζουσαι; Philemon wrote a Πανήγυρις; Baton wrote a Πανηγυρισταί; Alexis Hipparchus and Kallipos each wrote a Παννυχίς; Alexis a Χορηγίς; Paramonus a Χορηγῶν; Posidippus a Χορεύουσαι. It may be that in one or the other of these plays one saw or heard accounts of some part of a festival. On the other hand, some titles, like 'Αποβάτης, *Gumniasticus*, Παγκρατιαστής, Ἡνίοχος, and possibly Ναυμαχία, transfer us to the world of sport.

But it is to love adventures that the poets of the *νέα* chiefly devoted themselves. If we can trust Ovid, there was not a play of Menander's that did not contain one.[3] Plautus, probably following the Greek original, points out the absence of all love intrigues in the *Captivi* as a peculiarity.[4] Therefore this class of adventure above all others deserves to be studied in detail.

---

[1] Cf. Kretschmar, *De Menandri reliquiis nuper repertis*, p. 59.
[2] Diph., fr. 73.   [3] Ov., *Trist.*, II. 369.   [4] *Capt.*, 1030, 1032.

How does a love affair start? In very many cases the
comic poets do not explain this, and when the woman in
question is a courtesan who offers herself or is offered to
the desire of every comer, we can do without an explanation. In other cases the origin of a love affair is told in
various ways. The prologue of the *Mercator* informs us
that Pasicompsa was lent for one night and then sold to
Charinus by a host who treated his guests generously. In
the *Andria* Pamphilus is dragged to Chrysis' house by
his comrades, and though he resists the charms of the
mistress of the house, he falls in love with a young girl
whom she is bringing up. In the *Bacchides* Pistoclerus
has established relations with the sisters Bacchis in order
to oblige a friend. In the *Rudens* and in the *Phormio* a
girl who is being brought up to be a courtesan meets
and wins her lover on her way to her cithara teacher.[1]
In the *Eunuchus* it is mere chance that brings Pamphila
and Chaerea together. In the case of young girls who
live with their parents—whether real or putative—and
who seldom appear in public, it is often at a festival
that the first meeting takes place. Selenium, in the
Cistellaria, and Menander's heroine who speaks the words
contained in fragment 558 (she must be the prototype of
Selenium) have been noticed by their lovers at the Dionysiac procession.[2] The daughter of Phanias, in a Berlin
fragment, was noticed by Moschio as she was taking part
in a *deipnophoria*—that is to say, in a procession in honour
of Artemis at Ephesus.[3] Periphanes and Philippa, in the
Epidicus, met and became attached to one another at
Epidaurus, a place to which pilgrims resorted.[4] If it is
not in the course of a festival, it is, at any rate, in a temple
that a young lover in a play by Turpilius saw his mistress
for the first time, and was smitten by the bolt of
love.[5] I think the *Phormio* affords the only example of a
less commonplace meeting. Antipho hears people in the

---

[1] *Rud.*, 42–44; *Phorm.*, 80 et seq.   [2] *Cist.*, 89 et seq.
[3] *Berliner Klassikertexte*, V. 2, p. 119 (94 et seq.).
[4] *Epid.*, 540–541, 554.   [5] Turpilius, *Hetaera*, fr. I.–II.

barber's shop talking of the misfortune of a young foreign
girl who lives in the neighbourhood, the death of whose
mother has left her quite alone in the world. Curiosity
and pity lead him to go to see the unhappy girl, and he
falls in love with her as soon as he sets eyes on her.[1]

The first steps described above are honourable; but in
other instances the adventure starts in a more regrettable
way—by rape. The *Eunuchus* and a Latin fragment of
uncertain origin [2] afford instances of a premeditated rape,
but, as a rule, the crime is committed under the influence
of intoxication, generally at night, and often in the confusion of a nocturnal religious festival, while there are
instances where the culprit does not even know whom he
has violated. When they return to their senses, the brutal
lovers of the νέα pursue various courses. Aeschinus,
in the *Adelphi*, promptly goes in search of Pamphila's
mother, confesses to her, implores her forgiveness, promises
marriage, and meanwhile continues the relations he has
so cavalierly begun with the young woman. Such perfect
correctness is rare. Lyconides, in the *Aulularia*, has the
best intentions, but waits until circumstances shall force
him to carry them out. Diniarchus, in the *Truculentus*,
appears no longer to think of Callicles' daughter, though
she had been betrothed to him. In the *Cistellaria*,
Demipho, after violating Phanostrata at Sicyon, hurriedly
returns home without worrying about what is to become
of his victim. It is only after a long while that he offers
her reparation, and then it is merely owing to chance that
he does so. Pamphilus in the *Hecyra*, Laches in the
Ἥρως, and Charisius in the *Ἐπιτρέποντες*, have an equally
accommodating conscience.

In whatever manner they have started, love-affairs in
comedy are always on the eve of a crisis, and in order
to pass in review the manifold incidents involved, I shall
classify them according to the nature of the obstacles
that stand in the way of the lover's happiness.

The heartless women who keep their doors locked, or

---

[1] *Phorm.*, 91 et seq.   [2] Frag. inc. II. (p. 132).   Ribbeck.[2]

those whom a merciless master, a pander, a procuress or a
jealous lover keeps under lock and key, are the recipients
of nocturnal serenades, of clandestine visits, of the παρακλαυσίθυρα of which the opening of the *Curculio* has preserved an instance.   In the *Curculio* Phaedromus secures
an interview with Planesium at small expense : all he
needs to do is to give her duenna a jug of wine.   In the
Eunuchus Chaerea comes to Pamphila in the disguise to
which I have already referred.   In other cases the undertaking presents more difficulties.   In the *Miles Gloriosus*
the lovers only manage to come together by breaking
through a party wall, and when one of the soldier's servants
sees Philocomasium in Periplecomenes' courtyard, it is
necessary to invent a long story in order to allay his
suspicions and to pretend that a twin sister of the young
woman's, who has come to find her, lives in the adjoining
house, and then to arrange that Philocomasium should
appear, turn and turn about, first in the house of her
lover and then in that of her master, in the former case
under her own name, in the latter under that of her pretended sister—a complicated piece of comedy that calls
for the skill of a clever inventor of tricks.   The *Miles* is
the only Latin play which deals with the theme of a useless
surveillance, but I suspect that this theme was more than
once exploited in Greek comedy.   We know Apollodorus'
saying that no door is so well closed that a weasel and
an adulterer cannot find a way to open it.[1]   Xenarchus, a
poet of the middle period, enumerates the feats to which
every man who courts another man's wife must get accustomed : secretly to climb a ladder, to enter a house through
a hole in the roof, to be carried into a house in a bundle
of straw.[2]   Possibly certain gallants on the comic stage
performed some such feat in the course of a play, and
perhaps I ought here to mention the title of one of
Anaxippus' comedies, " The Man who Envelops Himself "
—'Εγκαλυπτόμενος.   However, to judge from the texts
which we possess, lovers' struggles with jailers, spies and

[1] Apollod., fr. 6.   [2] Xenarchus, fr. 4, 10–12.

duennas cannot have played a very important part in the *νέα*.

The same remark applies to the abductions effected without the woman's connivance, and to all the acts of violence to which an aspirant, tired of futile appeals, may have an idea of resorting. Again it is only in the *Miles* that such an episode is mentioned : Pyrgopolinices has carried off Philocomasium, and has taken her against her will from Athens to Ephesus.

A third category of episodes, which is likewise meagrely represented in the *νέα*, is based upon the competition between male or female rivals. To judge from a statement by Antiphanes, it appears that in his comedies and in the writings of his contemporaries, these competitions often took the form of a fight. In the period that followed, the rivals only resort to blows if one of them is a soldier. As a rule, the two aspirants compete in money and gifts, and no longer with fisticuffs. Moreover, it often happens that the play ends without their meeting, or that one of them does not appear at all, and in the majority of cases the subject of their rivalry is not enlarged upon; it is simply touched upon sufficiently to explain the anxiety of the lover or to make it appear more distressing. Only in a single instance—in the *Casina*—an amusing episode grows out of it : the two rivals—and, by the way, they are merely acting as proxies—draw lots to see who is to win the fair one.

In my study of the passion of love I have pointed out various incidents in which the jealousy and the spite of injured lovers are displayed—quarrels, ill-usage and recourse to a sorceress. I have still to explain how the disagreements arise. In Lucian, Charinus quarrels with Melitta because he has read the following two mendacious *graffiti*, written in charcoal in the Κεραμεικός : Μέλιττα φιλεῖ ῾Ερμότιμον, ῾Ο ναύκληρος ῾Ερμότιμος φιλεῖ Μέλιτταν.[1] Myrtio is cross with Pamphilus because she thinks that he is about to leave her in order to get married.[2] In

---

[1] Luc., *Dial. Mer.*, IV. 3.   [2] *Ibid.*, II. 3.

the twelfth *Dialogue*, Lysias enters his mistress' house
at night; he gropes his way to her bed and there, in the
darkness, hears two people breathing in their sleep. By
Ioessa's side he touches a soft and beardless chin, a closely
shaven head that smells of perfume, and quite naturally
he concludes that his mistress has deceived him. But he
is mistaken, for the person who shares Ioessa's couch, and
whom he took to be a handsome lad, is none other than a
girl friend Pythias, who owing to a sickness had been
obliged to shave off her hair and to wear a wig.[1] These
three stories of Lucian's are very largely made up of
details borrowed from comedy,[2] and yet I would not
venture to say that they had their prototypes in works of
the νέα. In fact, only a single comedy, the Περικειρομένη,
contains something of the kind : Polemo finds Glycera
and Moschio conversing in a suspicious manner, and
without any further information he thinks that he is
being deceived by Glycera.

Apparently the writers of comedy had a preference for
portraying the critical position of a lover who is the
victim of a pander, a procuress or a courtesan, and is
at the same time hampered by lack of money; they delighted in inventing countless expedients by which, with
the help of some expert rascal, he gets over these difficulties. Some of these expedients consist in a simple
abuse of confidence. In the *Truculentus* Strabax makes
unauthorised use of his father's name to secure the price
of a flock of sheep, and hastens to bring the money to
Phronesium. At the beginning of the *Bacchides* Chrysalus
displays greater shrewdness : he tells the aged Nicobulus
that he and his young master Mnesilochus, who had been
sent to Ephesus to collect a sum of money, had not been
able to bring back more than a small part of the sum
collected; the remainder, which he hides, is to be used
to ransom Bacchis. In other cases it is not a question
of withholding money that is forthcoming; the difficulty
is to lay hands on any. When efforts to borrow money

[1] *Ibid.*, XII. 3–4.   [2] Cf. *Rev. Ét. Gr.*, XI. (1908), pp. 48–52.

O

fail, it is, in most cases, obtained from the cashbox of the father, to which end the latter's affection and solicitude are frequently exploited in the most shameless fashion. In the second part of the *Bacchides* Chrysalus frightens Nicobulus by making him think that his son has been found guilty of adultery, and he extorts a whole fortune from the old man in order, as he says, to buy off the people who would otherwise molest Mnesilochus. In the *Epidicus* it is likewise under the pretext of freeing the daughter of Periphanes, who had become a slave, that Epidicus makes him give him the money needed to purchase the courtesan Acropolistis. Subsequently, when he is obliged by his young master, the fickle Stratippocles, once more to secure forty minae in order to pay for a new folly, he pretends to share the anxiety of the young man's father, who has had some vague intimation of his son's behaviour. He urges Periphanes to be severe and induces him forthwith to purchase Stratippocles' mistress, who is to disappear. Again Epidicus is instructed to close the bargain, and again he profits by the situation. In the *Phormio* the money that is extorted from Chremes, and which is to help along his son's love affair, is nominally destined to break off the marriage of his nephew Antipho. In the *Heauton Timoroumenos* there is another cock-and-bull story. Syrus cleverly takes advantage of the fact that Chremes has just found his daughter Antiphila, and assures him that the young woman had been turned over to Bacchis in settlement of a debt; if Chremes is honest he must redeem her; Chremes agrees, and artlessly pays the ten minae. In other cases the swindlers who manage the affair do not only count upon the credulity of an old man; they steal and commit forgeries. In the *Asinaria* Leonidas impersonates the steward Saurea, and in this capacity collects twenty minae from the donkey-seller. In the *Curculio* Curculio steals a ring and uses it to impersonate Platagidorus, the servant of Therapontigonus, and withdraws the money which the soldier had deposited with the banker Lyco.

All these intrigues have one point in common : their object is to satisfy with good hard cash the exactions of a woman, or of those who exploit her. In other cases, especially when lovers have to deal with a pander, the problem is solved in a different way by dispensing with payment altogether. In a scene of the *Adelphi* borrowed from Diphilus, Aeschinus shows us the simplest way of doing this—it is to carry off by main force that one of the pander's boarders whom one desires, thus placing oneself in a position to negotiate with him at a future time, to promise to pay later on, or to settle for half the price. In the *Pseudolus* the young lover's clever helpmate impersonates his rival's messenger and carries off the woman for whom the latter has already paid. In the *Poenulus* the pander is trapped by his own cupidity. Matters are so arranged that, against his wish and without his knowledge, he becomes the harbourer of a slave and of a sum of money belonging to the lover. In order to avoid still greater disaster he is obliged to give up possession of a courtesan without compensation.

Several of the adventures just mentioned call for a disguise, and I may say, by the way, that writers of comedy seem frequently to have resorted to this device. In the *Trinummus* we meet with a counterfeit traveller, in the *Miles* with a counterfeit sailor. In the *Casina* the slave Chalinus disguises himself as a young married woman in order to befool Lysidamus.

In addition to financial difficulties, and in many cases concurrently with them, a father's opposition produces a great variety of incidents in the course of a love affair. Quite frequently this opposition is not yet overt and actual, but is merely in prospect. The father knows nothing, and means must be devised to keep him from discovering how matters stand. In the *Mostellaria* and in the *Adelphi* the danger is imminent : Demea and Theopropides unexpectedly arrive just as their sons are making merry in company about whose character there can be no question. They must be got rid of at any cost,

and Syrus succeeds in doing so by sending Demea off to
the country or to the four corners of the town, and Tranio
by telling Theopropides that his house is haunted. In the
Heauton Timoroumenos, the *Mercator* and the *Phormio*, the
woman who causes the trouble is not hidden away, but
is introduced to the father of the family as being some one
else than she really is; for instance, the mistress of a
friend of his son's, a servant, or a poor relation. In the
Epidicus impudence is carried to the length of making
old Periphanes think that Acropolistis, the mistress of
Stratippocles, is his own daughter who has been brought
up far away from her father.

The father's attitude, however, is not always so passive.
When he knows what is going on he, in his turn, acts
with more or less energy and more or less openly. In the
Epidicus we have seen him endeavouring to remove the
woman who is debauching his son. If the woman is a
free woman and mistress of her acts, he sometimes, as in
the *Hecyra*, tries, by means of persuasion or intimidation,
to induce her to break off relations. Or else—as, for
example, in the *Andria*—he turns to the lover and his
adviser, threatens them and lectures them. But whether
the father knows what is going on or not, it is his determination to get his son married, and married according
to his (the father's) wishes, that most frequently interferes
with the smooth course of love; and, as a rule, he shows
this determination without giving any previous notice.
Some fine morning the young man hears that he is to be
married, and is invited to sign his death warrant the very
same day. Then his confusion is terrible, and, in order
to parry this unexpected blow, new devices are indispensable; above all, he must gain time. In the *Andria*
Pamphilus by chance discovers that the marriage with
which he is threatened is not proposed seriously. Strengthened by this knowledge, he disarms Simo by behaving in
a most docile manner. Subsequently, when the threat
grows serious, Davus betakes himself to the future father-
in-law and, by showing him how deeply Pamphilus is

committed elsewhere, persuades him not to take Glycerium's lover as his son-in-law. In the *Phormio* Antipho has anticipated matters without knowing anything about his father's matrimonial intentions. He takes advantage of the fact that he is left alone at Athens to marry an interesting orphan girl with the sanction of the court. Owing to this bold move he is in a much better position than the majority of sons. Phormio, his spokesman, is able to confront Demipho with the decision of the court and to exert a sort of legal pressure upon him.

Such, then, are the amorous adventures of young lovers in the extant remains of comic literature. When married men engage in illicit love affairs, their chief care is to keep their adventures from becoming known. The greybeard Demaenetus, in the *Asinaria*, succeeds in doing so for a short while only. He does manage to slip over to Philaenium's house unobserved, but his virago of a wife, who is informed of his escapade by a parasite, catches him *in flagrante delicto* and leads him home in a doleful mood. Demipho, in the *Mercator*, and Lysidamus, in the *Casina*, borrow the house of an obliging neighbour, in order to enjoy their freedom there. Lysidamus is in love with one of the maids and contrives to give her in marriage to his bailiff Olympio, who is not likely to make a jealous husband. Unfortunately for him his plan is discovered and the sly old fellow is baffled.

Along with love adventures, some of the above episodes touch upon family life, whilst others are more definitely taken from it. Quite frequently a young woman who has been seduced is confined on the very day that is pictured in the play. Those about her are worried and send for the midwife. Sometimes the confinement is to be kept secret, or at least withheld from the knowledge of certain people; and this gives rise to great confusion. In the Γεωργός Cleaenetus appeared unexpectedly, I believe, at Myrrhina's house, accompanied by the young girl's brother, and found her whom he had come to marry on the point of being confined. In the *Hecyra* the heroine is married, and married long enough to make her pregnancy appear perfectly legitimate in the eyes of the public. But the husband has some reason to think otherwise, and so Philumena is obliged to hide from him in order to prevent him from being enlightened by others, and from everybody else excepting her own mother, with whom, under some specious pretext, she takes refuge. As a rule, the mother of a child born out of wedlock, and those about her, let the child disappear as soon as it is born. In the *Σαμία* Plangon has the good fortune to keep her child quite close to her, in the very house of her lover Moschio, where it is looked upon as the son of the Samian woman, Chrysis, the concubine of Moschio's father. In the *Ἥρως* Myrrhina has entrusted her twins to a freedman of the family, who brings them up as though they were his own, and the time comes when, owing to curious circumstances, the young men live in their mother's house, along with the other servants, while circumstances keep her from declaring that she is their mother. In another comedy by Menander, of which we possess a partial synopsis,[1] we meet with a woman who, after an interval of many years, has to suffer from the consequences of a youthful mishap. She had given birth to a daughter before her marriage. After her marriage she had this daughter brought up secretly in the house adjoining the one in which she herself dwelt, and was in the habit of receiving her visits through an opening made in the wall which was decorated like a sort of oratory. One fine day her husband's son comes in unexpectedly and sees the young woman. At first he takes her for a goddess, and then, when he sees that she is merely a human being, falls in love with her. The two women's secret is, all at once, in danger, and the mother runs the risk of her past being exposed to her dishonour.

In the course of my study of the family, I said that more than one household among those brought upon the stage by the comic poets appeared to be on the point of

---

[1] The φάσμα, cf. Donatus' note to *Eunuchus*, prol. 9.

breaking up, either because the husband sought a divorce
or because the father of a married daughter wished to
take back his daughter, or because the wife thought of
going back to her parents. In no case does the rupture
take place. In all probability it did take place in the
plays called Ἀπολείπουσα or Ἀπολιποῦσα, and possibly
in others; but even there, I imagine, it did not last any
longer than the estrangement between Demeas and his
concubine, in the Σαμία.

Exposure, substitution and kidnapping of children were
frequent occurrences in New Comedy. Either the offspring
of illicit relations or the youngest child of a modest
household was exposed from dread of having the family
grow too large. As a rule, the child that had been exposed
was taken in by poor people and was regarded as their
offspring. By way of exception, the slave who had found
Casina gave her as a present to his mistress, and she
brought up the little girl almost with a mother's care.
Occasionally the unfortunate child was not exposed, but
given, either to a woman who wished to convey the impression that she had just been confined, or to people in
poor circumstances who hoped sooner or later to get some
profit out of it. Substitution, the popularity of which on
the stage is vouched for by a remark of Terence[1] and
by the titles Ὑποβολιμαῖος, Ψευδυποβολιμαῖος, which recur
several times, was practised not only by faithless courtesans, but also by women of good family, like Myrrhina
in the Περικειρομένη,[2] who desired to have a child.

Children were kidnapped in various ways; sometimes
pirates carried them off, sometimes an untrustworthy
pedagogue ran off with his pupil, and sometimes " stealers
of men," who carried on their operations in the midst of a
crowd and at festivals, did the kidnapping. After having
been carried off for the sake of gain or from a desire for
revenge, the child most frequently grew up in slavery,
and girls are generally discovered in the hands of a pander.
But it also happens that the victim of the kidnappers falls

[1] *Eun.*, prol., 39.   [2] Περικ., 1-3.

into good hands; witness Agorastocles in the *Poenulus*, who becomes the adopted son of the old man who had bought him. In the *Menaechmi* one of the twins was rescued, rather than kidnapped, and the man who found him in the street in Tarentum brought him up as his own child, and made him his heir.

Exposure, substitution, and kidnapping have generally taken place before the play begins. On the other hand, it is towards the end of the play that we meet with other episodes which also occur very commonly, and which, in the majority of cases, are correlated to the foregoing— namely, the "recognitions" (ἀναγνωρίσεις, or ἀναγνωρισμοί). There are many kinds of recognition, and, of these, chance recognitions constitute the greater part. Some are the crown and reward of years of travel and of patient search. A child may be recognised owing to its own recollection of the earliest days of its life; sometimes the testimony of those who have brought it up, exposed or rescued it, or who accompanied it into exile is given. More frequently the proof of a child's identity is furnished by a birthmark, or by some small trinket that it has always kept (γνώρισμα), a ring, a necklace, a bit of cloth, toys or amulets. Generally the ἀναγνώρισις results in the person concerned rising from a wretched or modest state to a better one; but there are exceptions to this rule. In Menander's Ὑποβολιμαῖος the supposed child of rich people, who had been brought up in their house, was apparently recognised as the son of a poor man who claimed him, and to whom he was himself preparing to return; but it goes without saying that in the end matters had to be so arranged as to spare him from making too painful a sacrifice.

In addition to children who have disappeared, other characters in comedy give rise to searches and recognitions. In the *Hecyra* a woman recognises her husband as her former seducer. The same episode occurs in the Ἐπιτρέποντες, in the Ἥρως, and probably also in the Φάσμα; and a similar occurrence has taken place before the

opening of the *Cistellaria*.[1] In the *Epidicus*, Periphanes
plans to go in scarch of his former mistress, with a view
to marrying her and assuring the future of his children.
This brings me to the discussion of a more normal act
of family life—marriage. A late act of reparation, such as
Periphanes contemplates, is not the only instance in which
a marriage is connected with a recognition. For instance,
there is the marriage project that drives a young lover to
despair, and which grows out of a father's solicitude for
an illegitimate daughter whom he wishes to see discreetly
settled.[2] But, above all, there is the ἀναγνώρισις, which
removes the obstacles that stand in the way of the regular
and definitive union of two lovers, by showing that a
passionately beloved mistress is a citizen, a girl of good
family—nay, even a rich heiress. Marriage of one kind or
another—whether a love match or a *mariage de raison*,
acquiesced in as a penance—is one of the most frequent
occurrences in the *véa*. It is the common *dénouement* and
the comic one *par excellence*.

Hitherto I have been able to make a more or less
satisfactory classification of the episodes that called for
our attention. Another set of comic episodes drawn from
daily life or having a more or less romantic character, do
not admit of such grouping. I shall simply enumerate them.
Among the most commonplace of these incidents I
must mention the comings and goings of certain characters
—troublesome fathers, jealous matrons—their journeys
from town to country and *vice versa*, visits to the market
and walks to the harbour. The titles of certain comedies (Alexis' Ἐισοικιζόμενος, Philemon's Ἐξοικιζόμενος,
Diophantus' Μετοικιζόμενος) apparently alluded to moving
or change of domicile, and fragments 830 and 853 of
Menander to quarrels between neighbours.
A few lines have survived belonging to a scene in which

---

[1] *Cist.*, 179.
[2] See the reconstruction of the Greek prototype of the *Epidicus* by
Dziatzko, *Rh. Mus.*, IV. (1900), pp. 108 et seq.

sleeplessness plays a part.[1] In the *Curculio* and in the
Γεωργός one of the characters is ill, or has been ill;
this must also have been the case in Menander's Ἀφρο-
δίσια,[2] in the play to which fragment 890 belongs, and
in the comedies in which a physician appears on the stage.
A man who is afflicted with blindness, or pretends to be
blind, no doubt played a part in the Ἀπεγλαυκωμένος
by Alexis, a man who has recovered his eyesight in the
Ἀναβλέπων by Posidippus, insane people, or people who
feigned insanity, in the works called Μαινόμενος, *Dementes*,
Ἑλλεβοριζόμενοι, and in a play imitated by Luscius.[3]
The *Casina*, the *Captivi*, the *Mercator* and the *Menaechmi*
also contain an account or a dramatic portrayal of
attacks of frenzy. Dreams are related in the *Curculio*—a
dream which one of Aesculapius' patients has sought
for and secured—in the *Mercator*, and in the *Rudens*.
Fragment 126 of Diphilus apparently belongs to a scene of
incantation. I need only mention the suggestive titles of a
play by Philemon and of one by Philippides—Ἀνανεουμένη,
Ἀνανεοῦσα; that of a play by Alexis—Μανδραγοριζομένη,
and Pliny's remark about Menander's Θετταλή: *complexa
ambages feminarum detrahentium lunam*. The belief in
divine apparitions gives rise to an interesting sudden
change of fortune in Menander's Φάσμα. Plautus' *Mostellaria* is an imitation of Philemon's Φάσμα, and contains
a ghost story. Another play with the title Φάσμα, a work
by Theognetus, probably contained a similar incident.

In the *Andria* and in the *Phormio* one of the characters
gives an account of a funeral, and there are various indications that the ceremonies connected with the cult of the
dead found a place in comic plots. Such indications are
found in the titles of two plays by Diphilus—Μνημάτιον,
Ἐναγίσματα or Ἐναγίζοντες—and in that of a play by
Menander, Καρίνη; and also in a fragment of the poet
Anaxippus,[4] and in the partial synopsis of the Θησαυρός,
preserved by Donatus. Elsewhere, we meet with episodes

---

[1] Men., fr. 164; Turpilius, *Epiclerus*, fr. 1; Apollodorus, fr. 3.
[2] Men., fr. 86.   [3] *Phorm.*, prol. 6–8.   [4] Anaxippus, fr. 8.

taken from life as it was commonly spent in a sanctuary.
I think this was the case in the comedies bearing the titles
Ἀμφιάρεως and Τροφώνιος, and possibly in Philemon's
Πυρφόρος. A sentence in the Πτωχή must have been connected with the sacrifice of a cake to Artemis; [1] two fragments of the Λευκαδία may be parts of a prayer or of a
religious song; [2] in this play, a ζακορή—that is to say, a
sort of female sacristan—was asked to light a fire; [3] in
the *Rudens* the priestess of Venus harbours Palaestra and
Ampelisca, sends one of them to fetch water from the
neighbouring farm, and tries to protect the suppliants
against the violence of Labrax. In the course of the
same play the two unhappy women take refuge at an
altar, and similar steps must have been taken more than
once in several cases by slaves who had been caught
wrongdoing.

Incidents occurring in the lives of slaves do not, by
the way, appear to have interested the writers of the νέα
as much as they had those of the foregoing period. Nevertheless I may cite a line from the Θετταλή in which a slave,
as I believe, tells of his escape; [4] and I may also recall
the theft committed by Strobilus in the *Aulularia*. A
fragment of the Ὑδρία reminds one of a very similar exploit,
which was possibly likewise performed by a slave.[5]

The treasure that Strobilus appropriates had been
buried, discovered, and buried a second time. This is
the kind of incident that apparently enjoyed favour in
comedy. With slight modifications it recurs in two of
the many plays called Θησαυρός—the Θησαυρός by Philemon, of which the *Trinummus* is an imitation, and in the
Θησαυρός by Menander. In the Ὑδρία and in the Δύσκολος [6]
we likewise hear of buried money. In the *Rudens* Gripus
brings up a bag filled with gold from the bottom of the
sea as though it were a fish.

Hiding in a corner in order to watch the acts and to
overhear the plans of others, listening at the door,

[1] Philemon, fr. 67.   [2] *Ibid.*, fr. 312, 313.   [3] *Ibid.*, fr. 311.
[4] *Ibid.*, fr. 232.   [5] *Ibid.*, fr. 468.   [6] *Ibid.*, fr. 128, 468.

indiscreet peeping between half-open doors, are devices of which comic actors, and especially those who play the part of slaves, made frequent use. Strobilus climbs up a tree to spy on Euclio; in the *Miles*, and in the *Synaristosae*,[1] inquisitive people watch from their roof what is going on in their neighbour's house. Elsewhere, a person who is asked to deliver a letter loses it or allows it to be taken from him.[2] In the Ἐπιτρέποντες, the *Cistellaria*, the *Vidularia* and the *Rudens*, tokens that lead to recognitions (γνωρίσματα) are lost for a time, and their disappearance baffles those concerned.

In the *Rudens*, and in the *Vidularia*, shipwrecked people are brought upon the stage. A storm has cast Pasibula, " the Andrian," and her father on the shore of Andros. The same sort of mishap is clearly indicated by the title Ναυαγός, with which we meet in each of the three periods of Greek comedy. Another accident to which travellers are exposed in comedy is the encountering of pirates. Pirates carried off Palaestrio on the high seas.[3] If we can believe Chrysalus, pirates were on the look-out for Mnesilochus at the entrance to the harbour of Ephesus,[4] and it seems that they played a part in Menander's Ἁλιεῖς [5] and in Turpilius' *Lemniae*.[6] Certain titles, such as Ἀνδροφόνος, Ἀκοντιζόμενος, Σφαττόμενος, Σφαττομένη, Ἀπαγχόμενος, Ἀποκαρτερῶν (the man who starves himself to death), Συναποθνῄσκοντες, Κωνειαζόμεναι, seem rather tragic for comedies, and it is probable that the murders or suicides to which they allude were not actually committed and possibly not seriously contemplated. In the Λευκαδία the heroine threw herself into the sea, but she was rescued by her lover. In the Αὑτὸν πενθῶν by Menander, a trickster made people think he was dead, and wore mourning for himself.

The title Ἀργυρίου ἀφανισμός, which is taken from the μέση if not from the ἀρχαία, recalls the familiar exploits of a Geta and a Davus. The title Ὅμοιοι, likewise taken

---

[1] Caecilius, *Synaristosae*, fr. 1.   [2] Turpilius, *Philopator*, fr. XIII.
[3] *Miles*, 117 et seq.   [4] *Bacch.*, 278 et seq.
[5] Men., fr. 15.   [6] Turpilius, *Lemniae*, fr. IV., V.

from the μέση, would fit such a comedy as the *Menaechmi*, in which two people who resemble one another are constantly confused. Other titles such as Ναυμαχία, Ὀργή, Εἰς τὸ φρέαρ, Ἀφανιζόμενος, Ἀγρυπνοῦντες, Συμπλέουσαι, Παρατηροῦσα, Νεμόμενοι, Προσκεδαννύμενος — rouse our curiosity without evoking the idea of any particular adventure; and the same way be said of many fragments. However entertaining the guessing game may be to which these documents invite us, I do not wish to indulge in it here.

CHAPTER V

RECAPITULATION
REALISM AND IMAGINATION IN NEW COMEDY
LITERARY SOURCES AND REPETITIONS

I HAVE pointed out and classified, as carefully as possible, such material of the *véa* as, notwithstanding the loss of nearly all the original works, can still be identified. I must now determine its quality and indicate its sources.

§ 1

CUSTOMS

Let us first give our attention to the matters that come within the domain of customs.

At the beginning of my survey I showed that the *véa* avoided the supernatural and that it almost always respected physical probability and, I may now add, the elementary social probabilities. Considered as a whole, its adventures and actors generally have a realistic character. In order to form a correct opinion of the talent for invention displayed by comic writers, I think it will be interesting, first of all, to emphasise my earlier statement and to inquire to what extent it can be verified in detail.

Such an inquiry is fraught with great difficulty. The descriptions that are commonly made of the state of Greek society at the close of the fourth and during the third century are, to a very large extent, based on fragments of comedies. This fact exposes us to the danger of constantly moving in a vicious circle, unless we are on our guard against doing so; and if we do avoid this danger, we shall only too often have to recognise that we lack any assured points of comparison.

However, they are not lacking everywhere; for in more than one instance, when we come to consider a person or an episode that at first may appear purely conventional, some document informs us of similar adventures or of similar persons that have an historical character.

For instance, the misdeeds of pirates, which are so common in comedy, must have been equally common in actual life. To be exact, such proof as we have for this assertion dates from a period subsequent to that in which the prototypes of Plautus' and Terence's comedies were written—from the latter part of the third century and from the second century. But, even long before that time, great insecurity prevailed at sea and along the coasts. Isocrates, Demosthenes and Hegesippus confirm this for the middle of the fourth century; at about this time Cleomis, tyrant of Methymna, is praised in an Attic decree for having ransomed certain citizens who had been prisoners of λῃσταί;[1] another decree, made at the instance of Moerocles, ordained "the clearing of the sea;"[2] by the treaty of 343–342 Philip bound himself to join with the Athenians in fighting piracy;[3] in 335–334 an Athenian fleet was equipped ἐπὶ τὴν φυλακὴν τῶν λῃστῶν;[4] and ten years later another fleet was sent to protect the commerce of the Adriatic against the Tyrrhenian pirates;[5] at Delos the accounts for the year 299 mention equipments εἰς τὴν φυλακὴν τῶν Τυρρηνῶν.[6] "Archpirates" appear in the wars between the Diadochi and the Epigoni of the first generation.[7] Theophrastus' coward, when he risks himself at sea, takes certain reefs for ἡμιολίαι—that is to say, for pirate ships;[8] and one of Leonidas' funeral epigrams is dedicated to a victim of Cretan λῃσταί, whose exploits are treated as something quite common.[9]

Speaking broadly, kidnapping cannot have been so exceptional and melodramatic a thing in a state of society where slavery existed as it is in our modern world. It was a commercial operation, criminal, but of common

---

[1] Dittenberger, *Syll².*, 135.
[2] [Demosthenes], *Adv. Theocr.*, § 53 et seq.
[3] Hegesippus; *De Halonn*; § 14.
[4] Dittenberger, *Syll².*, 530, line 280.
[5] *Ibid.*, 153, lines 226–227.
[6] Homolle, *Archives de l'intendance sacrée*, pp. 116–117.
[7] Diod., XX. 82, 4; Polyaenus, IV. 6, 18; Paus., I. 7; Dittenberger, *Syll².*, 213, lines 10 et seq.
[8] Theophr., *Char.*, XXV. (Δειλίας), 2.   [9] Leonidas, *Ep.*, 5, Geffcken.

occurrence. The γραφὴ ἀνδραποδισμοῦ, which could be brought not only against those who stole a slave, but also against any one who unlawfully reduced a free person to slavery, is mentioned quite frequently in literature. The word ἀνδραποδιστής is used by Hyperides—in the oration against Athenogenes, which is almost contemporary with the beginning of Menander's career—to designate a knave or any kind of rascal,[1] apparently because there was at the time frequent occasion to use the word in its proper sense.

As for criminal assaults and rape committed on the public highways, they were, no doubt, never of such common occurrence in actual life as they are in the comedies of the νέα; but it is equally certain that these incidents, which were so much favoured by the poets, cannot have shocked the audience on account of their great lack of probability. The streets of ancient Greek towns were, so to speak, not policed, or rather the functions of the police were limited to regulating traffic. Especially at night, when the streets were almost deserted, lonely wayfarers ran all kinds of risks, and the description of highwaymen robbing people who walk about at night is a commonplace of the portrayers of Athenian customs. In a famous scene of the *Ecclesiazousae* Blepyrus expresses his scepticism about the excellence of the new state of society which his wife proposes to introduce; she has just assured him that there will be no more thieves, and he exclaims : " What! People will not be robbed at night ? " At a period that is nearer to New Comedy, Alexis lets one of his actors say, as he sees a troupe of *comastai* approaching : " May I never meet you alone at night . . . ; I should not bring my cloak home with me, unless, indeed, I were to grow wings; "[2] and elsewhere the same poet says : " When a man buys abundant provisions, and, though otherwise a beggar, always has enough to do so—that fellow robs passers-by at night."[3] Such statements suggest the thought that where men ran the risk of losing their cloaks,

---

[1] Hyp., *Adv. Athen.*, § 12.   [2] Alexis, fr. 107.   [3] *Ibid.*, fr. 78.

women might run the risk of losing other things. If the objection were raised that the young men who, in comic literature, are guilty of rape are not infamous criminals, but gentlemen's sons, and that they cannot have been capable of such brutality, it would imply a too favourable opinion of the "refined" gentleman of the fourth and third centuries. Many an act of which we get knowledge from sources other than comedy, proves that the ways of the *jeunesse dorée* were at that period rather coarse. In the company of the most refined and most elegant courtesans young blades came to blows, like the lowest rabble,[1] and the courtesans themselves were occasionally exposed to discourtesy and violence. Gnathaena and her daughter were one day besieged in their dwelling[2] by a band of impatient lovers who loudly declared that they had brought axes and mattocks, and spoke of doing nothing less than tearing down the house, so that it is easy to imagine to what lengths they would have gone had they got the two women in some out-of-the-way spot. When violence was committed against a respectable young girl, it exposed its perpetrator to serious inconvenience—to a prosecution βιαίων, to the necessity of marrying his victim or of paying damages. But in the darkness of night, young fellows, in the hope of not being recognised and sometimes even not knowing with whom they had to deal, might fail to consider the consequences of their acts, and might behave towards any one as they would behave, if it so happened, towards women of loose morals, the only women—or practically the only ones—whose company they ordinarily sought. Moreover, it appears that the majority of delinquents acted under the influence of liquor. For these various reasons the crime charged against so many young men cannot have appeared to their contemporaries as something unheard of or monstrous; but, what might seem less credible, is that young girls should have ventured

---

[1] Demosth., *Adv. Con.*, § 14; Theophr., *Char.*, XXVII. ('Οψιμαθίας). 9; Ath., p. 551 A, 584 C.

[2] Ath., p. 585 A. Cf. Theophr., *op. cit.* (read ἑταίρας and θύραις).

P

out after nightfall. We must not forget, however, that
many of the heroines of comedy were ravished during a
festival (παννυχίς); for night festivals were quite frequent
in ancient times, and even if we had no formal evidence
like that of Cicero in the *De legibus*, we could easily surmise
to what perils they exposed feminine virtue.[1]

Next to rape, I may mention exposure of the children,
who were often its outcome. Mahaffy thinks that cases
of this sort were rare outside the theatre and, in support of his opinion, he points out that even in comedy
an abandonment is always relegated to the past incidents
of the plot, as though an effort had been made to with-
hold its odious and abnormal character from the criticism
of the audience.[2] This statement, however, is not strictly
correct; for in the *Hecyra* an abandonment is planned,
and planned by people whom the poet certainly did not
wish to render odious. Moreover, if the abandonment
of an infant usually takes place before the plot opens,
this is due to the very great popularity of other incidents
which necessarily took place many years later; for example, the recognition of a child that had been exposed—
most frequently a girl—and the marriage of that girl with
the young hero. Mahaffy's doubts do not, therefore,
appear to me to be well founded. As a matter of fact,
hardly anywhere in Greece did the law prohibit the
abandonment of infants,[3] and sometimes it even officially
authorised it. Plato prescribes it for the citizens of his
ideal republic, under certain conditions, and Aristotle
tolerates it. It was practised not only by girls who had
been seduced, by guilty wives, and by courtesans, but also
by respectable married people. Polybius points out that
the unwillingness of his contemporaries to bring up their
children, even when they are legitimate, was one of the
chief causes of the decrease in the population of Greece,[4]

---

[1] Cic., *De legibus*, II. 9, 2; 14, 35.

[2] Mahaffy, *Greek Life and Thought from the Age of Alexander to the
Roman Conquest*, p. 120.

[3] See the article *Expositio* in the *Dictionnaire des Antiquités* (Darem-
berg and Saglio).   [4] Polyb., XXXVII. 9, 7–10 (Hultsch).

and there is no convincing evidence that Greek parents
were more scrupulous a century and a half earlier.

Though substitution of children was, even in comedy,
less frequent than the abandonment of infants, it cannot
have given the impression of being a fanciful incident
in the fourth and third centuries.   As practised by courtesans who wish to retain their lovers, this form of deceit
is common to all periods.   In Greek society, and particularly at Athens, married women were perhaps tempted
to practise it on account of the unjust laws, which gave
the husband an unlimited right to repudiate his wife
whenever he chose.   Wives who had not presented their
husband with the heir he desired for the perpetuation of
the family, and those who were barren or had only
daughters, might well fear that their barrenness or the
chance that had given them only female issue might be
a cause for divorce, and so they sought a remedy in the
substitution of a child.   Mnesilochus, in Aristophanes'
Thesmophoriazousae, points out with great emphasis that
to feign a confinement is one of the tricks that women are
up to, and he reverts to the subject no less than four times.[1]
The orators likewise speak of the substitution of children.
Demosthenes charges Midias with being a supposititious
child, and proceeds to make a sarcastic comparison of his
two mothers, the real and the supposed one.[2]

What we have found to be the case in certain kinds
of especially important incidents might be established in
regard to many others.   Breaking through a party-wall
in order to set up a secret communication between two
houses, as is done in the Φάσμα and in the *Miles*, would at
first sight appear to be a stage device.   But it will appear
in a different light when we recall how fragile private
houses were in Greece during the classic period.   Athenian
thieves—τοιχωρύχοι, as they were called—passed through
the walls in order to enter a house.   The discovery of a
buried treasure is an extremely rare occurrence in our day,

---

[1] Aristoph., *Thesmoph.*, 340, 407–409, 502 516, 564–565.
[2] Demosth., *Adv. Mid.*, § 149.

but at a time when it was more difficult to invest money,
and when banking concerns were less known, and when,
furthermore, an insufficient police and frequent wars
caused great insecurity, the idea of burying his ready cash
might readily occur to many a hoarder, or even to many
an ordinarily economical and prudent person.[1] We know
the great detail with which Plato, in the eleventh book of
the *Laws*, prescribes what the finder of a hidden treasure
should do, and there is reason to believe that such happy
finds were quite common in his day, and that the hope of
making one engrossed many a mind.[2]

Comedy affords more than one instance of swindling
or cheating under cover of the law, and it may well be
asked whether all these frauds would have been possible
in actual life. As for some of them, there can be no doubt.
For instance, the plot of the *Phormio* has been closely
examined and studied step by step, with the help of
knowledge gained from other sources of the legal procedure and pettifogging of this period, and the conclusion
arrived at is that the comic poet adhered to the truth
from the beginning to the end of his play.[3] The fraud
concocted by Curculio, in the play which bears his name,
is of a kind that might be practised any day. That rascal
steals a token of recognition and by means of it withdraws the money which the soldier, Therapontigonus,
had deposited with a banker, and uses it to pay a pander.
But it is strictly in accordance with fact that the Greeks
received payments made through *trapezitae* or bankers with
whom they had an account,[4] and also that, in default
of witnesses, they used tokens or σύμβολα to establish
their identity, and that these tokens were frequently rings

---

[1] Plato, *Leg.*, pp. 913 A et seq.

[2] Cf. Aristoph., *Birds*, 599 et seq.; Xen., *Ages.*, X. 1. Need we recall
how the Phocians, during the Sacred War, dug in the soil of the temple
at Delphi, in the hope of finding marvellous treasures? (Diod., XVI.
56). Demosth., *Adv. Steph.*, I. § 81.

[3] Cf. Lallier, *Le Procès de Phormion*, in the *Annuaire de l'Association
des Études Grecques*, XII. (1878), pp. 49 et seq.

[4] [Demosth.], *Adv. Callipp.*, § 4.

or broken coins, the practice being especially referred to by Lysias, in his pleading on Aristophanes' inheritance.[1]

In the *Persa*, of which I think it permissible to speak, although it belongs to middle comedy, we find the same regard for the conditions of real life.[2] It is certainly not very probable that a man who is accustomed to business, and, moreover, to questionable business, should purchase a slave girl without any guarantee, especially when the seller appears to lay great weight on such a provision; but this is an improbability of a psychological kind which I shall not consider for the present. If we admit this, what follows affords no difficulty, and Dordalus—like his colleague Lycus, in the *Poenulus*—is really caught in the trap. He has no redress against those who have swindled him, although their bad faith is frankly admitted, for at Athens, just as in Rome, swindling did not lead to a charge of fraud. On the contrary, it is Dordalus who gets into hot water with the young girl's father : a γραφὴ ἀνδραποδισμοῦ is instituted against him. Hence it is easy to understand his fright and also that which several of his ilk manifest under similar circumstances; rather than appear in court, these honourable gentleman, who steal or harbour free girls, act wisely in compromising, even on onerous terms.

Apart from all fraud and chicanery, certain contracts of which comic writers speak would in our day be regarded as extraordinary. For instance, we repeatedly see a courtesan, a free courtesan, hiring herself out to a lover for a fixed period of time, and agreeing to pay a forfeit if she fails to carry out the terms of the contract.[3] This seems the dream of a crazy imagination, but it is nothing of the sort. Πορνεία κατὰ συγγραφήν was actually practised at Athens and in ancient Greece.[4] The orators have

---

[1] Lysias, *De bonis Aristoph.*, § 25.

[2] Cf. Dareste, *Le Persan de Plaute*, in the *Mélanges Weil* (1898), pp. 107 et seq.

[3] *Bacchides, Asinaria, Hecyra.*

[4] Cf. Schömann-Lipsius, *Der attische Prozess*, pp. 732–733; Beauchet, *Droit privé de la république athénienne*, Vol. IV. p. 42.

NEW GREEK COMEDY

even preserved for us the record of certain contracts—
they use the technical term συνθῆκαι to designate them—
which are even more scandalous than those found in
comedy; for, of the two parties to the contract, neither
is a woman.[1] But as a matter of fact, in addition to such
cases as these, where it is easy to establish the conformity
existing between the stage and real life, there are others
about which it is very difficult to form a sound judgment.
But it must be borne in mind that our knowledge of Greek
law, and even of Attic law, is very imperfect. The essential point is that, as far as we know, no writer of New
Comedy can anywhere be caught in a flagrant disregard
of facts, and that we can nowhere prove that in order to
meet the exigencies of his plot he invented a literary
jurisprudence or a fanciful method of dealing with things.

Nor does the νέα appear to have portrayed the family
differently from what the laws and the custom of the time
made it. In a curious passage of the first oration against
Aristogeiton (written when Menander was a boy) we
detect the motives of a Micio, a Laches, a Philoxenus and
of other lenient fathers in comedy : " Such and such a
house contains a father, grown-up sons and occasionally
even the children of these sons. It is inevitable that many
entirely divergent tastes should be manifested, for youth
and old age do not take pleasure either in the same talk
or in the same deeds. However, if the young people are
discreet they behave in a manner that enables them to
conceal their pranks, if possible; or if that be not possible,
in such a manner that one can easily see that they had the
intention of escaping notice. The old men, for their part,
if they see that the young people incline too much towards
extravagance, drink and love, see it without appearing
to see it. In this wise each follows his own bent and all
is well." [2]

Let us next consider the manifestations of paternal
authority. Has Chremes, in the *Heauton Timoroumenos*,

---

[1] Lysias, *Adv. Sim.*, § 22; Aeschines, *Adv. Tim.*, §§ 158, 160, 165.
[2] Demosth., *Adv. Aristog.*, I. § 88.

really the right to leave his son penniless, as he pretends
that he means to do, and to give everything to his daughter ?
It appears that at Athens a father could not disinherit his
son in his will; but he could during his lifetime disown
him and sever all existing ties, and exclude him from the
family and from his succession, by means of ἀποκήρυξις,[1]
and it is probably with ἀποκήρυξις that Chremes threatens
Clitipho. We have seen in how many instances a father
in comedy sets his heart on having the young hero marry,
or on keeping him from getting married. In real life,
however, Athenian fathers had no power to force their
sons to marry or to prohibit their doing so; but they could
not be compelled to give their rebellious sons the where-
withal to establish a household. Hence they were in a
position to make their sons pay severely for disobedience,
and could flatter themselves with the hope of gaining
their point by intimidation; and comedy does not claim
more than this. As far as daughters—and even married
daughters—are concerned, the father continued to be
their κύριος, and always had the right to take them back
from their husbands. This was done by Polyeuctus, with
whom a speech, attributed to Demosthenes, is concerned,
he was displeased with his son-in-law Leocrates, and took
his daughter from him to give her to Spoudias.[2] This
example proves that when the two young women in the
Stichus, who are so devoted to their absent husbands,
display such anxiety about their father's intentions, there
was good reason for their doing so. Nor is the tyranny
of the wife with a dowry an invention of the comic poets.
In the sixth book of the *Laws*, Plato says that there are
women whose dower makes them insolent, and husbands
who cringe before them,[3] and the danger appears to him
to be so great that in his ideal legislation he absolutely
prohibits dowries.[4] In the ᾿Ηθικὰ Νικομάχεια, Aristotle

---

[1] Schömann-Lipsius, *Der attische Prozess*, pp. 537–538; Beauchet, *Droit
privé de la républiquo ath.*, Vol. II pp. 128 et seq.

[2] Demosth., *C. Spud.*, § 4.   [3] Plat., *Legg.*, p. 774 C.

[4] *Op cit.*, p. 742 C.

also says that it is sometimes the women who command, when they inherit large fortunes.[1]

In some comedies we see unmarried sons of good family in the possession of property, borrowing, selling and buying. There is no question but that the majority of them had the right to act as they do; Athenian youths came of age very early—at the age of eighteen—and from that time onwards they were allowed to make contracts of every kind. In the *Mostellaria* Philolaches speculates, as it is said, with borrowed money, and it would have been in his power to do what Tranio says he did, even without the consent of Theopropides, since he did not involve his father in the transaction at all, while he would have the means to do so, as the property purchased would have served as surety for the loan. As a matter of fact, like so many young gentlemen in comedy, Tranio borrows simply to defray the cost of his dissipations, and the lender has absolutely no guarantee and no claim whatsoever on Theopropides. For all that, there is nothing improbable in his behaviour, nothing more improbable than there is in the behaviour of many a usurer of our day. He relies on the fear of scandal to make the old man yield, and if the worst comes to the worst, he is prepared to await his death and the opening of his will. People who buy anything from Lesbonicus, in the *Trinummus*, take greater risks, for, as the young man's father is still alive, he is selling what does not belong to him. But it must be borne in mind that Charmides is away, has been away a long time, and that the audience may think he is dead. Moreover, the only purchaser who is mentioned, Callicles, is a true friend of the family, who certainly does not propose to insist on the bargain when Charmides comes back.

The liberties taken by slaves on the comic stage, their familiarity, their insolence and also their slyness, were probably conventional characteristics. A Roman audience could not trust their eyes when they saw a race of

[1] Arist., *Eth. Nicom.*, VIII. 12, p. 1161 A; cf. *Polit.*, II. 6, 11 (p. 1270 A).

slaves drinking, making love and inviting one another
to supper; and, to make such a sight tolerable, Plautus
declares that such things did happen in Attica. As a
matter of fact, even in Greece the free ways of Athenian
slaves occasioned surprise and occasionally gave offence.
At Athens, says the Ἀθηναίων πολιτεία, which is supposed to have been written by Xenophon, a slave will
refuse to move out of your way.[1] Demosthenes says
the slaves at Athens enjoy liberty of speech and speak
their minds more freely than the citizens of many other
states.[2] On the other hand, it must be admitted that
the conditions under which slaves lived favoured the
development of shameless craftiness, of a great gift of
dissimulation and of complete unscrupulousness. By this
I do not mean to say that it was solely a strict adher-
ence to truth that led to the development and success of
the type of the *servus callidus*. I believe that we must
here make allowance for a certain Pharisaism on the
part of the poets and of the spectators, to whom it was
distasteful to represent or to see free men in positions
that were unworthy of them. In the *νέα* free men, as
a class, hate lies; at the close of the *Miles Gloriosus*
Pleusicles is embarrassed by his disguise as a sailor and
begs the audience to excuse this trick for the sake of
his love.[3] In the *Trinummus* Callicles apologises for
indulging in rascality, although his motive for doing so
is a good one.[4] When Pamphilus in the *Andria*, and
Chremes in the *Heauton Timoroumenos*, are requested to
take part in a trick, they at first bluntly refuse to do so.[5]
It is the business of slaves to spare people who are so
virtuous the annoyance of being compromised. In the
Persa Toxilus lies and steals on his own account; the
slaves under him lie and steal on behalf of their masters.

As for other characters known to comedy, there are
some whose close resemblance to living prototypes need

---

[1] [Xen.], Ἀθ. πολ., I. 10. [2] Demosth., *In Philipp.*, III. § 3.
[3] *Miles*, 1284 et seq. [4] *Trin.*, 787.
[5] *Andr.*, 383 et seq.; *Heaut.*, 782 et seq.

not be demonstrated at length; for example, that of the
courtesan. This literary type was developed in Attica,
and we need only glance through Book XIII of
Athenaeus or certain works of the orators to see that,
during the entire fourth century, there was no dearth of
living models, and to find material for numerous comparisons between the stage and actual life. The nicknames
of several such women—I need only mention that of
Clepsydra, who, we are told, was named thus ἐπειδὴ
πρὸς κλεψύδραν συνουσίαζεν ἕως κενωθῇ [1]—the anecdotes
that were current about some of them, such as the
story which tells of Gnathaena between two lovers, a
στρατιώτης and a μαστιγίας,[2] are sufficient proof that the
courtesans of real life quite equalled the heroines of the
comic stage in point of cynicism. Other surnames and
episodes were founded upon their greed : Phryne is
called Sestos, διὰ τὸ ἀποσήθειν καὶ ἀποδύειν τοὺς συνόντας
αὐτῇ.[3] Hippe " devours " a dealer in forage in order not
to give the lie to her name.[4] The speeches of Isaeus tell
us of young fools who allow themselves to be so capti-
vated by women of loose morals as to marry them;[5] of
old libertines who desert their wives in order to live with
prostitutes.[6] Lysias and Apollodorus denounce the great
indelicacy of lovers who are satisfied to share one
and the same mistress with a number of other men.[7]
In Hyperides, and in the speech against Neaera, we
meet with the superannuated courtesans Antigone and
Nicarete, who are still clever inveiglers, and have become
procuresses.[8] In the writings of Lynceus of Samos we
find Gnathaena—a competitor of Cleareta—grown old and
regulating the love affairs of her daughter, and seeing
to it that they are lucrative.[9] Again, in the speech

---

[1] Ath., p. 567 D.   [2] Ibid,. p. 585 A.   [3] Ibid., p. 591 C.
[4] Ibid., p. 583 AB.   [5] Isaeus, De Pyrrhii hered., § 17.
[6] Ibid., § 18 et seq.
[7] Lysias, De vulnere ex industria, § 10 and 16; Apollod., Adv. Neaer.,
§ 26 et seq., 29 et seq., 46 et seq., cf. Ath., p. 585 A.
[8] Apollod., Adv. Neaer., § 18 et seq.; Hyper., Adv. Athenog., § 2 et seq.
[9] Ath., p. 584 C.

against Neaera there is the ruffian Stephanus;[1] in the speech against Timocrates, a brother—more guilty than Saturio—who is accused of having sold his sister.[2] And finally, in a few lines of the *Life of Phocion*, we get a glimpse of a grasping pander who exploits the young men who are in love with his charges.[3] Examine historical documents even for a moment, and all the characters who on the stage lead a life of debauchery answer to their names.

This applies also to parasites and intriguers. Theopompus declares that Athens is full of flatterers, rascals, false witnesses and sycophants.[4] The speeches and orations of the period would seem to show that he is right. Here we see denunciators who grow rich through their calumnies, obsequious swindlers who become the body-servants of the rich, cut-throats who are ready for any scandal.[5] Here we hear it declared that it is always easy to find witnesses who will ensure the success of an imposture.[6] As for the poor devils who merely plied the trade of spungers, their tribe was very well represented. Among the plagues that were unknown at Pera, the ideal city of the cynics, Crates does not forget to mention " the voracious parasite " (μάργος παράσιτος).[7] A parasite who is an historical character appears as early as in Xenophon's Συμπόσιον—the buffoon Philippus.[8] Others who were celebrated at the time of middle comedy, or even at a still later period, and who are mentioned by Matron, Machon, and by Lynceus of Samos, appear to be very similar to the parasites in comedy : such are Corydus, Tithymallus, Philoxenus, Pternocopis, Archephron, Democles, surnamed Lagunio, and Chaerephon, the most

---

[1] Apollod., *Adv. Neaer.*, § 39 et seq., 64 et seq.
[2] Demosth., *Adv. Timocr.*, § 202.
[3] Plut., *Phoc.*, § 38.   [4] Ath., p. 254 B.
[5] Apollod., *Adv. Neaer.*, § 39, 68; Demosth., *Adv. Mid.*, § 138–139 (cf. 123–124); *Adv. Steph.*, I. § 66–67; *Adv. Con.*, § 34–35, 37, 39.
[6] Demosth., *Adv. Apat.*, § 37; cf. *Adv. Pataen.*, § 48.
[7] Crates, fr. 4, Wachsm., 3. In Theophrastus, 'Αηδίας, Chap. XX. § 10, the parasite appears as the usual adjunct of a well-to-do house.
[8] Xen., *Sympos.*, I. 11 et seq., II. 21 et seq.

famous of them all. Athenaeus recounts some acts and sayings of his which are sufficiently amusing. We see him hurrying quite a long way into the country to take part at a wedding dinner,[1] complaining to the carver about the portion that had been served to him, which contained too much bone.[2] Once when, as was his practice, he had come to a banquet without being invited and occupied the last seat, the *gynaeconomoi* came to count the guests. When they found one more than the allotted number and invited our friend to go away, he calmly replied, " Count once more, beginning with me." [3] These incidents and others of the same sort may have been derived from a comedy. But I need not add that the grossest flattery of the κόλακες on the comic stage had their equivalents in real life. It must suffice to recall one or two of the anecdotes preserved by Athenaeus and Lucian. When Alexander was devoured by flies, one of his courtiers exclaimed : " Oh, surely these flies will be much stronger than others, because they have tasted your blood." [4] One day when Poliorcetes coughed, his courtier Cynaethus exclaimed that he coughed musically.[5] But this had already been surpassed by the flatterers of the tyrant Dionysius. I quote Athenaeus' own words :
ἀποπτύοντος δὲ τοῦ Διονυσίου πολλάκις παρεῖχον τὰ πρόσωπα καταπτύεσθαι καὶ ἀπολείχοντες τὸν σίαλον, ἔτι δὲ τὸν ἔμετον αὐτοῦ, μέλιτος ἔλεγον εἶναι γλυκύτερον.[6] We see that Strouthias and Artotrogus may have been copied from nature.

The boastful soldier was likewise to be met with in real life in the age of New Comedy. It goes without saying that swaggerers existed at every period, in Greece as well as elsewhere, but from the fourth century onwards various circumstances co-operated to propagate this genus, and supplied increasingly rich material for malicious remarks on the part of the writers of comedy. In the first place, there was the growing importance of mercenaries. Their

---

[1] Ath., p. 243 E. [2] *Ibid.*, p. 243 F. [3] *Ibid.*, p. 245 A.
[4] *Ibid.*, p. 249 DE. [5] Lucian, *Pro imag.*, 20. [6] Ath., pp. 249–250.

livelihood depended on their courage and efficiency as soldiers, and they were naturally prone to exaggerate both of these qualities, and to strike martial attitudes that would impress the imagination. The Argive Nicostratus went to battle dressed like Heracles, with lion's skin and club.[1] Adaeus, a captain in the service of Macedonia, made such pompous reports that he was called " Philip's rooster." [2] Then came the campaigns of Alexander and the victories won by a handful of men over a horde of enemies, the capture of fabulous treasures, the triumphant exploration of very distant regions that were inhabited by people of another race and afforded a view of strange customs. And then followed the gigantic conflicts of the age of the Diadochi, the clash of immense armies, which were made even more formidable by the presence of barbarian troops and by the use of outlandish weapons, sieges in which both sides displayed a skill and employed resources hitherto unknown. It was an easy matter for the soldiers of this wonderful age to astound the inhabitants of the old Greek cities with their bluster. There is hardly a boast of a Bias or of a Pyrgopolinices for which a parallel and, to a certain extent, a justification cannot be found in the real life of the period. If they boast that they had cleft asunder whole clouds of adversaries, we can quote the incident of Alexander among the Oxydrachi, when, single-handed, he stormed the walls of a town he was besieging, and for quite a while alone withstood the attacks of its garrison.[3] If they claim to have killed a captain of the enemy in single combat before the arrayed armies, there is the case of Pyrrhus, who under similar conditions killed Pantauchus, a general of Demetrius' army, a Mamertine captain and the Spartiate Evalcus.[4] If the stage soldier gives us to understand that he is rolling in wealth, the veterans of the campaigns of Asia had actually been able to accumulate rich booty : witness those Argyraspides who, in 317, handed over

---

[1] Diod., XVI. 44.
[2] Ath., p. 532 E.
[3] Diod., XVII. 99.
[4] Plut., *Pyrrh.*, § 7, 24, 30.

their general Eumenes to Antigonus in order to get back
their baggage.[1] If he imagines that he is adored by
women, it is because he comes from a country where the
women, stooping under the yoke of slavery, throng round
their master in a submissive band, and are only too happy
to gain his favour.[2] If he lays claim to divine parentage,
did not Alexander, whom all the world imitates, have the
oracle proclaim that he was the very son of Ammon?
Were not some of his successors the object of a cult
during their lifetime? And do not people in Athens
itself say that Poliorcetes is the offspring of Poseidon and
Aphrodite?[3]

Of all the characters in the νέα, the cook is perhaps
the most conventional. In ancient times, Athens was
regarded as a city in which people ate moderately, and it
would seem as though the culinary artist was of little
consequence there. And yet, whatever we may think
and whatever may have been said about the sobriety of
the Athenians, it is undeniable that at Athens, as in the
entire Greek world, luxury in eating increased and became
more common in the course of the fourth century. Some
of Plato's utterances show this quite clearly.[4] Moreover,
we know of some Athenian gourmets, or at least of
some who lived at Athens;[5] and at about the same
period in which New Comedy flourished, Attica made its
contribution to culinary literature. It is an Athenian
banquet (ἀττικὸν δεῖπνον) that Matron of Pitane describes
in a poem that was no doubt written at Athens.[6] A
parasite, Chaerephon, of whom we have already spoken,
deals with a similar subject in a prose epistle addressed
to Cyrebion.[7] It is from Athens that Lynceus of Samos
sends his correspondent Hippolochus an account of three
great feasts in three ἐπιστολαὶ δειπνητικαί.[8] The same
Lynceus, in a fourth letter, compares the gastronomic

---

[1] Plut., *Eum.*, § 17.   [2] Cf. Diod., XVII. 77.   [3] Ath., p. 253, CE.
[4] Plato, *Gorgias*, pp. 462 D, 464 D, 500 B, 501 A, 518 B, 521 E.
[5] Hyperides, Callimedon, Cyrebion, etc.
[6] *Parodorum epicorum graecorum reliquiae*, ed. Brandt, pp. 53 et seq.
[7] Ath., p. 244 A.   [8] *Ibid.*, p. 128 AB, cf. 100 E, 101 E.

resources of Athens with those of Rhodes.[1] In a fifth epistle, written to the poet Poseidippus, he praises the figs of Attica.[2] In a community in which such things occupied people's minds a cook might well feel himself at home, and although the haughtiness which the comic poets attribute to him is rather surprising in a concocter of sauces, yet certain documents afford trustworthy proof of it. We detect, for instance, in the statement of Heracleides of Syracuse and of Glacus of Locris, who wrote the 'Οψαρτυτικά, towards the end of the fourth century, that the functions of a cook could not be exercised by slaves or even by the first comer among free men.[3] Sometimes the title of a treatise on cooking, such as the title of a work by Parmeno of Rhodes, who must have lived in the third century—Μαγειρικὴ διδασκαλία (and not 'Οψαρτυτικά)—implies an intention of placing cookery on a level with the rational and systematic sciences. The stage cook would gladly pass himself off as a physician.[4] Why should we be surprised at this, when physicians wrote books Περὶ ἐδεστῶν, Περὶ τροφῆς, entered into the details of the dishes that were suitable for this or that patient, and even brought out an 'Οψαρτυτικός, or gave an account of a συμπόσιον?[5] The cook poses as a wise man, as a benefactor of mankind;[6] is he not entitled to do so, when Epicurus declares that all happiness comes from the stomach, and when the masses, without any wish to follow the philosopher any further, gleefully adopt this formula? And, indeed, when the νέα was at its height, circumstances were very favourable for throwing a sort of halo around cooks, and we may be sure that they took fullest advantage of the fact.

In a word, the characters of comedy, like its adventures, corresponded in their day to actual, or at least to possible, people in real life. Their like was, I believe, to be met

---

[1] Ath., p. 109 D.   [2] Ibid., p. 652 C.   [3] Ibid., p. 661 E.
[4] Damoxenus, fr. 2, Nicomachus, fr. 1, lines 18, 30 et seq.
[5] Susemihl, *Geschichte der griechischen Litteratur in der Alexandrinerzeit*, I. p. 879.
[6] Athenion, fr. 1.

pretty nearly everywhere, if allowance be made for the justifiable exaggeration of comedy, and they themselves were no more the creatures of fancy than their names, the majority of which were borrowed from actual names of the period.[1]

But it does not follow that, as far as customs are concerned, the *νέα* always made its own observations. Before its time there existed literary works in which certain elements of which the *νέα* made use had, as it were, been selected and prepared in advance, and it could not fail to profit by them.

The cases must have been rare in which a comedy of the new period borrowed its plot or its *dramatis personae* from a written story. The almost complete absence of plays with legendary subjects puts epic poems and the ancient mythological tales out of question. Novels and short stories remain to be considered; but the existence of novels—novels of everyday life or novels of adventure— at the time of the *νέα* is an open question; and if the Greeks had short stories at so early a period, we know practically nothing about them. Still, one parallel must be pointed out. Several stories of quite different date and origin have a striking similarity with the plot of the *Miles*.[2] The resemblance is particularly marked between that comedy and a story coming from Cairo—the story of Kamaralsaman and the wife of the jeweller. In both cases the lovers come together through a secret passage which connects two adjoining houses; in both cases the woman plays a double part, and the person who entertains suspicions about her is reassured on finding her at home as often as he goes to seek her; in both cases the departure of the enamoured couple takes place before the eyes of the person who is being deceived, and meets with his complete approval; finally, in both cases, the fugitive

---

[1] See K. Schmidt, *Griechische Personennamen bei Plautus* in the *Hermes* for 1902.

[2] Cf. Zarncke, *Parallelen zur Entführungsgeschichte im Miles Gloriosus* (*Rhein. Mus.*, XXXIX. 1884, pp. 1 et seq.).

woman robs her dupe of a part of his belongings, and takes with her a servant who is her accomplice. The construction of the story is, by the way, more logical than that of the comedy. In the *Miles* the passage through the wall does not in any way serve to ensure the escape of Philocomasium; in the story it serves the manœuvres of the lovers and helps in the mystification of the husband to the very end. This fact seems to me to exclude the possibility that the Cairo story was copied, directly or indirectly, from Plautus' play or from its Greek prototype, if, indeed, there was only one prototype. If this is correct, an Ionic story may have been the source of both works, and in that case the author of the 'Αλαζών would have combined the episodes that were of a kind to bring out the character of his chief personage. If, however, we assume that the *Miles* is a "contaminated" play, the above arguments evidently lose all their force, for the concluding scenes, in which Philocomasium escapes without making use of the mysterious passage, do not then come from the same original as the scenes in which she plays her double part. But if we consider these scenes only, we find in them something less simple and less natural than in the Cairo story, as though the latter represented the original version and the first scenes of the *Miles* a variation upon it. In the story, it is to the person chiefly interested, to her husband, that his wife appears alternately under her own name and under that of another person; in the *Miles* it is to a subordinate personage—the vigilant Sceledrus. In the *Miles* it might occasion surprise that Sceledrus, who gives expression to his suspicion, does not demand that the two sisters should appear together; in the Cairo story the husband's failure to do so can readily be understood, for he does not openly express his uneasiness. Whatever opinion we may form of the composition of the *Miles*, it certainly seems that this play—or at all events its second act—affords an example of borrowing from a story, that is to say from a narrative work; but it is an isolated example.

Q

On the other hand, the dependence of the νέα on earlier drama, whether comic or tragic, is shown in many ways. Some of the plays may have been re-editings or διασκευαί of older comedies.[1] Partial re-editing and the borrowing of types and incidents are, at any rate, frequent and clearly recognisable.

The cook, for instance, is not an invention of the νέα, nor of Attic comedy in general. The Athenian writers of comedy took him over from the Dorian farce—in which, under the name of Μαίσων, he was the delight of the audience—and probably from the comic writings of Epicharmus. It is true the stupid and greedy Dorian Μαίσων had little resemblance to the infatuated artist with whom we have met in the νέα; but even at an earlier period, middle comedy, in which merry-making scenes were of frequent occurrence, and which, if I may say so, exhaled a constant odour of feasting, had afforded the cook excellent opportunities for the display of his talents and of his vainglorious disposition. As a matter of fact, fragments of Antiphanes and other specimens of the μέση, particularly fragments of Alexis, some of which probably antedate the beginning of the new period, show us the cook pretty much as he appears later on—self-important and loquacious.[2]

The swaggering soldier has ancestors in very old works of Hellenic literature. A fragment of Archilochus already contains a picture of him.[3] We know, too, how ready Attic comedy of the fifth century was to make fun of sword-danglers like the terrible Lamachus and, above all, of men like Peisander and Cleonymus, who pretend to be brave; and this tradition was preserved in the fourth century. Ephippus, Antiphanes and Heracleides make

---

[1] Ath., p. 127 B; Clem. Alex., *Strom.*, VI. 2, 26; cf. Euseb. *Praep. evang.*, X. 3, 13.

[2] Antiphanes, fr. 217, 222, 284, 300; Philetaerus, fr. 14–15; Cratinus the Younger, fr. 1; Ephippus, fr. 22; Anaxilas, fr. 19; Epicrates, fr. 6; Mnesimachus, fr. 4; Axionicus, fr. 8; Sotades, fr. 1; Alexis, fr. 48, 84, 124, 127, 129, 133, 149, 172, 173, 174, 175, 186, 187, 188, 189.

[3] Archilochus, fr. 58, Bergk, 3.

fun of certain notorious swaggerers of their day.[1] Alexis ridicules the way in which generals knit their eyebrows.[2] In a play called Φίλιππος, Mnesimachus introduced a warrior who claimed that he ate swords, torches and javelins, and used nothing but shields and cuirasses as cushions. Some other fragments of Antiphanes, of Alexis and of Ephippus contain boastful statements by travellers that leave nothing to be desired in their effrontery; for instance, that the King of Paphos had himself fanned by doves which were attracted by his perfumes;[3] or that people at a banquet were sprinkled with scent by birds that had just come out of an aromatic bath, instead of receiving it in flasks;[4] or that somewhere words froze in winter and thawed in summer;[5] or that the great king had to mobilise whole races of people for months at a time, in order to get a gigantic fish cooked.[6] The first of these marvellous tales was certainly told by a soldier, and the others may well have been invented by some forerunner of Pyrgopolinices and Antamoenides.

The courtesan had appeared upon the stage as early as the latter part of the fifth century. During the middle period she was installed as its queen. We know that more than one comedy of this period had the name of some real or imaginary woman of this class as its title— Chrysis, Neottis, Nannion, Clepsydra, Melitta, Malthake, Plangon, Neaera, and the like. Furthermore, many extant fragments denounce the greed of prostitutes, their duplicity, their impudence, their utter heartlessness, and their coquettish tricks.[7] Indeed, one may say that the works of Antiphanes, Aristophon, Amphis, Anaxilas, Epicrates and Timocles had established the type of the wicked courtesan in all its details, while the type of the " good courtesan " must have existed, at least in outline, if we may judge by fragment 212 of Antiphanes.

---

[1] Antiphanes, fr. 303; Ephippus, fr. 17; Herac., fr. 6.
[2] Alexis, fr. 16.   [3] Antiph., fr. 202.   [4] Alexis, fr. 62.
[5] Antiph., fr. 304.   [6] Ephippus, fr. 5.
[7] Antiph., fr. 2; Philetaerus, fr. 5, 8; Amphis, fr. 1; Ephippus, fr. 6; Anaxilas, fr. 22; Timocles, fr. 23; Xenarchus, fr. 4.

As for the pander, he plays quite an important part in the only play of the μέση that has survived—the *Persa*. A pander appeared in the Τοκιστής by Nicostratus, in the Συντρέχοντες by Sophilus, and possibly in the ῾Αρπαζομένη by Antiphanes. One of Eubulus' plays and one of Anaxilas' had the names of panders for their titles. Dordalus, in the *Persa*, who has insults heaped upon him, is really more ingenuous than wicked; but his fellow in the Πορνοβοσκός of Eubulus [1] is distinctly portrayed as a harsh man, a grasping rascal and a skinflint; and we may assume that he deserved his reputation.

The parasite, like the above-mentioned characters, had already had a long dramatic career when the νέα began to be written. The chorus of a play by Eupolis consisted of parasites who went by the name of κόλακες. One of Alexis' plays, written before the death of Plato, and one by Antiphanes, which probably belongs to the same period, had the title Παράσιτος, and, no doubt, had a parasite as their chief hero. From the beginning of the fourth century onwards, if not even earlier, the parasite is an acknowledged type in comic literature. The essential features of this type, in the shape in which we are acquainted with them, are already outlined in a fragment of Epicharmus; [2] they are reproduced, made more definite and repeated *ad nauseam*, in many fragments of the early period, and especially of the μέση.[3] It is among the remnants of the latter that we find most of the first-hand evidence of the shameless gluttony of the parasite, of his sufferings as a scapegoat, of his talents as a jester, and of his readiness to act as jack-of-all-trades. Saturio, in the *Persa*, is no less expert an entertainer than

---

[1] Eubulus, fr. 88.   [2] Epich., fr. 34–35, Kaibel.
[3] Eupolis, fr. 146, 148, 159, 162–163, 172, 178; Aristophanes, fr. 167, 272, 675; Phrynichus, fr. 57; Ameipsias, fr. 1, 19, 24; Theopompus, fr. 34; Sannyrion, fr. 10; Antiphanes, fr. 80, 82, 144, 159, 226–230, 243–244, 298; Anaxandrides, fr. 10; Eubulus, fr. 72, 115, 119; Amphis, fr. 10, 39; Aristophon, fr. 4; Alexis, fr. 116, 195, 201–202, 210, 212, 231, 256–257, 260; Antidotus, fr. 2; Axionicus, fr. 6; Epigenes, fr. 2; Sophilus, fr. 6; Timocles, fr. 8, 13.

Ergasilus, nor is the unnamed parasite of Antiphanes' Πρόγονοι a less desperate rascal than Phormio. In a word, with all due deference to Gnatho, " to please the man who foots the bill, to admire what the rich man says," is a rule that found a place on the programme of the professional parasite from the very start.[1] The only step in advance the parasite in the *véa* appears to have taken is to attach himself more particularly to the person of the boasting soldier, whose silly vanity swallows every compliment, and does not see that it is being laughed at.

The slave belongs to the first beginnings of Greek comedy. Among the superannuated characters whom Aristophanes claims—rightly or wrongly—to have ousted from the stage, he mentions that of the whining slave, who has fun poked at him by a fellow-slave after he has been flogged.[2] His Xanthiases and Carios, in more ways than one, herald the coming of the Syruses and Davuses of the *véa*. Like the latter, they are greedy, lewd, lazy, mendacious, rascally and indiscreet.[3] The only fault that they lack in order to be, even at this early period, the equals of their descendants, is craftiness,[4] but in the course of the middle period the slave in comedy perfected himself in that direction. Toxilus and Sagaristio, in the *Persa*, can stand comparison with their two colleagues in the *Pseudolus*—Pseudolus and Simia; and the waggish Paegnium can hold his own with Pinacium in the *Stichus*. Arguing and philosophising slaves are met with in Antiphanes and in Alexis,[5] while some expressions of these two poets and of Theophilus show that there was such a thing as an honest slave who was loyally devoted to his master.[6]

---

[1] Epich., fr. 35, 4; Eupolis, fr. 159, 9–10, 163, 178; Epilycus, fr. 2; Anaxandrides, fr. 42, 49; Anaxilas, fr. 33.

[2] *Peace*, 742 et seq.

[3] *Ibid.*, 90 et seq., 256; *Frogs*, opening scenes, 508 et seq., 738 et seq.; *Plutus*, 17 et seq., 190 et seq., 644 et seq.; etc.

[4] Still, it is worth noting the following significant words in a passage of the *Peace*: τοὺς δούλους τοὺς ἐξαπατῶντας (743).

[5] Antiphanes, fr. 86; Anaxandrides, fr. 4; Alexis, fr. 25.

[6] Antiphanes, fr. 265; Theophilus, fr. 1.

As for the portrayal of family customs, the course that the νέα pursued had been laid out much earlier. The μέση, the tragedies of Euripides, the comedies of Aristophanes, the Doric farce—to quote dramatic writings only—had vied with each other in having a hit at the fair sex. Women were, indeed, chiefly reproached for what New Comedy mentions least—greediness, drunkenness and incontinence. But occasionally they were scoffed at for their inquisitiveness, their silliness and garrulousness,[1] their indolence and fondness for spending money;[2] and their lack of loyalty, their indiscreetness,[3] their stubbornness, their sharp tongues and tyrannical dispositions[4] were stigmatised. The comic household in which the husband inveighs against his wife, but is humble in her presence, or in which the wife wishes to be master and teaches her husband his duty towards her, is not without its analogies in the heroic world as it was represented on the stage by the author of the *Medea*, the *Ion* and the *Iphigeneia*. In the *Clouds*, Strepsiades, who is so unluckily mated with the haughty Coesyra, foreshadows by a century the poor husband in the Πλόκιον and his numerous companions in misfortune. Some of the actors in the works of Antiphanes, of Anaxandrides and of Alexis curse the tyranny of the wife who has a dowry in as gloomy and fierce a fashion as do Menander's characters;[5] one of them complains of woman's inquisitiveness in almost the same terms that Menaechmus uses.[6] In fact, long before the beginning of the new period, comic writers

---

[1] Eur., *Iph. A.*, 231 et seq.; *Phoen.*, 194 et seq., 198; Aristoph., *Eccles.*, 120; Antiphanes, fr. 253; Alexis, fr. 92; Xenarchus, fr. 14.

[2] Eur., *El.*, 1068 et seq.; *Hec.*, 923 et seq.; *Hipp.*, 630 et seq.; *Med.*, 1156 et seq.; *Or.*, 1426 et seq.; fr. 324.

[3] Soph., fr. 742; Eur., *And.*, 85; *Hipp.*, 480–481; *Iph. T.*, 1032, 1298; *Or.*, 1103; fr. 323, 532, 673; Antiphanes, fr. 251; Xenarchus, fr. 6.

[4] Eur., fr. 504, 772, 801, 804; cf. *Andr.*, 213; *El.*, 931, 1052; *Suppl.*, 40; fr. 466, 549; Plato, fr. 98; Antiphanes, fr. 46; Amphis, fr. 1; Alexis, fr. 146, 5–6; Amphis and Alexis wrote plays called Γυναικοκρατία.

[5] Antiphanes (?), fr. 329; Anaxandrides, fr. 52; cf. Alexis, fr. 146; Euripides, fr. 504, 772.

[6] Alexis, fr. 262.

regarded marriage as a mistake, a calamity, a sort of
suicide.[1]

As for the types of parents and of children that I have
already analysed, their prototypes are less distinctly
recognisable in the extant parts of earlier comedy. And
yet such a passage from Antiphanes as, " Whoever at
this age still blushes in his parents' presence cannot be
bad," [2] reminds one of the attitude of Aeschinus.[3] It
may well be that fragment 156 of Alexis represents the
meeting of a strict father and a lenient father, a Demea
and a Micio, a Chremes and a Menedemus; and I suspect
that one or the other of the old fops, whom we meet
now and again,[4] was like Philoxenus or Demaenetus, the
sharer of his son's debauches.

When we come to consider adventures, we find that
such of them as serve as the framework for so many plays
in the new period were already old stage devices before
the time of Philemon and Menander; for example, rape,
the exposing or substituting of infants, and recognitions.
The stage history of all these episodes dates back to
tragedy in the fifth century, especially to the works of
Euripides. In his plays many young people—Creusa,
Auge, Canace, among others—had been ravished. Just
like Pamphila or the daughter of Euclio, Auge had been
ravished during a religious festival,[5] and just like Lyconides, her brutal lover, Heracles, apologises for his crime
on the ground that it was committed in the excitement
of drunkenness.[6] Ion, Telephus and Oedipus are the best
known of the many examples of heroes who had been
exposed immediately after birth. The substitution of a
child was one of the incidents of the *Melanippe Desmotis*;

---

[1] Antiphanes, fr. 221, 292; Anaxandrides, fr. 52; Eubulus, fr. 116;
Aristophon, fr. 5; Alexis, fr. 262.

[2] Antiphanes, fr. 261.   [3] *Ad.*, 643.

[4] Philetaerus, fr. 6; Amphis, fr. 19; Alexis, fr. 282; Xenarchus, fr. 4
(9–10); Theophilus, fr. 4; Nicostratus, fr. 19; Eubulus, fr. 112, 125;
Ephippus, fr. 21; Eriphus, fr. 1; Anaxandrides, fr. 1 (?).

[5] Cf. the fragment of the *Progymnasmata* by Moses of Chorene (line iii),
in which Wilamowitz has recognised an abstract of Euripides' *Auge*.

[6] Euripides, fr. 267.

Demosthenes' sarcastic remarks in paragraph 149 of his speech against Meidias show that it was not an unusual thing. As for recognitions, and particularly recognitions owing to a σημεῖον—a basket, a ring, a necklace, or some similar object—Aristotle vouches for the fact that the tragic writers whose works he had read made extensive use of them.[1] Beginning with the early part of the fourth century, comedy followed the practice of tragedy regarding these matters. Aristophanes himself, so one of his biographers tells us, had in one of his latest works, the Κώκαλος, introduced a rape, a recognition and other episodes that were taken up later by Menander.[2] Cratinus the younger wrote a Ψευδυποβολιμαῖος. Anaxandrides, as we know from a note by Suidas, made " the love and the misfortunes of virgins " familiar on the comic stage.[3]

However, it is not only in their openings and in their dénouements that certain plots of the νέα recall earlier plots. The only product of the μέση that we know in its entirety—the Persa—affords throughout material for comparison with other plays by Terence and by Plautus. The attitude of Toxilus, for instance, who enjoys himself to his heart's delight while his master is travelling, resembles that of Tranio in the Mostellaria or that of Stasimus in the Trinummus. The transfer of money effected by Sageristio has its more or less exact parallel in the Bacchides, the Phormio, the Asinaria and the Truculentus; the plot devised against the pander recurs in the Poenulus. Fragment 212 of Antiphanes speaks of the beginnings of a love affair in terms that would almost fit into the Andria, the Heauton Timoroumenos and the Phormio. Fragment 239 reproaches young men of the μέση with exploits, the tradition of which is piously preserved by the young men of the νέα—squandering their patrimony, enfranchising prostitutes, breaking open other people's doors. The disguises that are common in the νέα are already met with in tragedy : Odysseus disguises

---

[1] Aristotle, Poet., XI. 2–4; XVI.   [2] Vit. Aristoph., § 10.

[3] Suidas, s.v. ᾿Αναξανδρίδης.

himself as a beggar in order to enter Troy;[1] Telephus does likewise in order to appear among the Greeks; in order to spy upon the Bacchantes, Pentheus dresses as a woman; in Aristophanes, Mnesilochus, the father-in-law of Euripides, does the same, whereas the Ecclesiazusae usurp male attire. The lying messengers of comedy, Curculio, Simia, Trinummus, might quote Orestes as their authority, when he brings the false news of his own death to his mother and Aegistheus. At the close of Euripides' *Helena*, Menelaus plays a part very similar to that played by Pleusicles in the concluding scenes of the *Miles Gloriosus*; and Theoclymenus, like Pyrgopolinices, frankly favours the escape of the woman who had deceived him. The fathers who return home to their families after a long absence and find everything in disorder have their historic forbears in Aeschylus' Agamemnon, Euripdes' Heracles and Diomedes;[2] and several fragments of Eubulus, of Cratinus the younger and of Alexis give us a glimpse of them in middle comedy.[3] The prophetic dreams of Cappadox, of Daemones and of Demipho may be compared with certain episodes of the *Persae*, the *Choephoroe*, the *Elcctra*, the *Hecuba* and the *Iphigeneia in Tauris*. The scene in the *Curculio*, in which the cook expounds the pander's dream, may be compared with the scene in the *Wasps*, where Sosias interprets the dream of Xanthias. The attacks of frenzy—or of pseudo-frenzy—that befall Casina, Charinus and Menaechmus have their parallel in the ravings of Orestes or of Heracles. The scenes in which Palaestra and her companion seek an asylum at the altar of Venus, and the pander threatens to dislodge them by force from their place of refuge, or even to burn them, remind one of various passages in the *Heracleides*, the *Oedipus at Colonus*, the *Mad Heracles* and the *Andromache*. The episode that supplied the comedy of the Ἐπιτρέποντες with its title must have been copied from Euripides' *Alope*.[4]

[1] Cf. Eur., *Hec.*, 239 et seq.   [2] Diomedes in the *Oeneus*.
[3] Eubulus, fr. 133; Cratinus the younger, fr. 9; Alexis, fr. 297.
[4] Hyginus., *fab.* 187. Cf. *Revue de Philologie*, 1908, pp. 73–74.

Many more similar instances might be quoted, and in its portrayal of manners, in its choice of incidents for the construction of its plots, the *νέα* follows very frequently an old and beaten track. But the chief literary source from which the dramatists of this period draw their inspiration, or at least the source where we can best observe their borrowings, is the drama of their own contemporaries or of their immediate predecessors. New Comedy repeats itself; we have seen that it introduces certain types and certain incidents again and again. Coincidences of a more exact kind can be traced quite frequently. Let me point out a few of them.

In the *Hecyra*, the misfortunes of the young married couple are very nearly the same as in the *᾿Επιτρέποντες*. Pamphilus, like Charisius, has ravished a young girl whom he did not know and who subsequently becomes his wife; like Pamphila, Philumena is confined a few months after her marriage, and her husband is on the point of leaving her, although he continues to love her. In both plays the recognition takes place thanks to the same object—the ring which the young man has left in the possession of his victim—and owing to the intervention of a kindly courtesan who is, or had been, the mistress of the culprit. Here, it is true, we have only to deal with a similarity of setting. Elsewhere, there is a resemblance between two well-defined incidents, between two complex situations. In one of the early scenes of the *Pseudolus* a pander engages in a discussion with a young lover;[1] despite a formal promise, he has sold the young man's sweetheart to a soldier, and ought to hand her over to him on that very day. He turns a deaf ear to appeals, pretending he has urgent business that calls him away. Obliged, nevertheless, to stay and listen, he assumes a dogged indifference, is unmoved by all offers and incredulous towards all promises. He maintains that he has done no wrong in selling a slave who belonged to him, frankly acknowledges having broken his promise and cynically

[1] *Pseud.*, 250 et seq.

explains that he did so from selfish considerations. Finally,
half seriously, half ironically, he declares himself ready
to let the weeping lover have one last chance : if he gives
him an agreed sum before the soldier appears, the other
bargain is not to hold good, and the fair one is to belong
to the claimant who arrives first with full hands. Here
we have a scene that abounds in details; well, it is reproduced, feature by feature, in the third act of the *Phormio*.[1]

In the *Curculio* the lover's accomplice pretends to
be an emissary of his rival; disguised as an officer's
servant, and putting on the airs of a swaggering soldier,
he comes to claim the young woman whom his supposed
master has purchased. A letter sealed with the latter's
seal—the trophy secured by a previous act of rascality—
that prepares the way for his rascally act, serves to accredit
him, and allays all suspicion. Under the very nose of
the pander, and with his consent, he leads away the beautiful slave girl. Here, again, the episode is of a very special
kind, and yet it reappears, practically in the same form,
in another extant comedy—the *Pseudolus*. At the close of
the *Miles*, Pleusicles disguises himself as a pilot in order to
carry off his mistress;[2] a passage in the *Asinaria* mentions
the same disguise as being used at a similar juncture.[3]

When Polemo, in the Περικειρομένη, comes to attack
the house of Moschio, whither Glycera has betaken herself,
he reminds one of Thraso, in the *Eunuchus* (that is to say,
of Bias, in the Κόλαξ). The Φάσμα and the *Miles Gloriosus*
both contain the episode of the secret passage-way cut
through a party wall. The episode of the intercepted
transfer of money occurs both in the *Asinaria* and in the
Truculentus; in each case it is a question of the price of a
herd. There are many plays in which two young men
aid one another; in the *Adelphi* and in the *Heauton
Timoroumenos*, the mistress of the one is taken over by
the other on his behalf. Cleaenetus' offer of marriage,
in the Γεωργός, recalls, in more than one point, that of

---

[1] *Phorm.*, 485 et seq.   [2] *Miles*, 1176 et seq., 1296 et seq.
[3] *As.*, 68 et seq.

Megadorus, in the *Aulularia*; apparently both offers are made under similar conditions, and must have evoked emotions of the same kind in several actors of both plays. In the *Mercator* and in the *Phormio*, a son plays the part of arbiter and conciliator between his parents; the same thing took place in Menander's Ἐπίκληρος.[1] The *Mostellaria* and the *Asinaria* both introduce an interrupted banquet, the *Asinaria* and the *Menaechmi* a parasite who acts as an informer. We may add that Menaechmus takes the same liberties with his wife's belongings as Demaenetus proposes to take;[2] he steals one of her cloaks in order to give it to his mistress. The scene in the *Mercator* in which Lysimachus tries in vain to silence the cook, recalls the scene of the *Menaechmi* in which Peniculus does not allow either the signs that Menaechmus makes, or his entreaties, to interrupt him; and also that scene of the *Phormio* in which Phormio indefinitely prolongs the agony of poor Chremes. The *Vidularia* and the *Rudens* both interested the audience in a travelling-bag that had been lost in a shipwreck, recovered from the water by a fisherman, and claimed from the fisherman by some one who knew that it did not belong to him. This leads to arbitration and finally helps to bring about a recognition.

Thus we see how often, in that small part of comic literature which we know, analogous combinations and identical situations are repeated, sometimes even in two plays by the same author. How many repetitions should we not have to record if the whole of that literature had come down to us? Plautus and Terence repeatedly call especial attention to the novelty of an incident or of a variant.[3] Bacchis, in the *Hecyra*, and Thais, in the *Eunuchus*, themselves point out that their virtuous sentiments make them different from the mass of courtesans.[4] When the father, in the *Asinaria*, is indulgent

---

[1] Cf. Rhet. anon. Spengel, Vol. I, p. 432, 17.   [2] *As.*, 884–886.

[3] *Ibid.*, 256–257; *Pseud.*, 1239–1241; *Hec.*, 866–867; *Men.*, prol. 7 et seq.; *Truc.*, 482 et seq.; *Capt.*, 1029 et seq.

[4] *Hec.*, 776, 834; *Eun.*, 198.

towards the pranks of his son and the mother is less
obliging, Demaenetus points out the anomaly of the
situation.[1] In a scene of the *Eunuchus* which is borrowed
from the *Κόλαξ*, Gnatho, a refined courtier, does not wish
to be considered as one of the old-style parasites; he
poses—wrongly, by the way—as the founder of a school,
as an *εὑρετής* :[2] " In times gone by, a century ago, it was
thus that one earned a livelihood. We have a new method
and I am the inventor. . . ." Statements such as this,
which probably go back to Greek originals, are of the
greatest interest; they inform us of the current practice
of the comic writers, and prove that they were in the
habit of introducing things on the stage which had been
seen there before. There must even have been cases
where entire plays were repeated. Many titles of comedies
—some of which are not entirely commonplace—occur
several times in the works of contemporary poets. As
a matter of fact, the example of Philemon's *Φάσμα* and
of the *Φάσμα* by Menander, that of two plays by the same
authors which were both called *Θησαυρός*, and that of the
Ἀδελφοὶ ά and *Ἀδελφοὶ β'*, prove that like titles did not
necessarily imply like contents. Indeed, it may have
been considered smart, at intervals of several years or
of several months, to produce totally different plots under
the same title. Nevertheless, I imagine that, in many
cases, comedies which bore the same title had other things
in common besides their name. On the other hand, the
comic writers of the new period—like those of earlier days—
do not appear to have hesitated to repeat certain of their
own works with slight alterations. Witness what Terence
says in the prologue of his *Andria* about Menander's *Ἀνδρία*
and *Περινθία* : *Qui utramvis recte norit, ambas noverit ;
non ita sunt dissimili argumento*[3] . . . In all probability
this was not an isolated case.

Even in ancient times fault was found with the *νέα*
for its frequent repetitions of details and whole plots.
Aristophanes of Byzantium wrote a book called *Παράλληλοι*

---

[1] *As.*, 76 et seq. [2] *Eun.*, 246–247. [3] *Andr.*, prol. 10.

Μενάνδρου τε καὶ ἀφ' ὧν ἔκλεψεν ἐκλογαί;[1] and a certain
Latinus wrote a treatise in six books, *Περὶ τῶν οὐκ ἰδίων
Μενάνδρου*.[2] Nor, I suspect, were these works, and particularly the latter, free from malicious criticism of
Menander. Even an actual comic writer, Xenarchus,
who still belongs to the middle period, makes a tirade
against the incessant repetitions. " The poets," he says—
and he is thinking, I imagine, of his closest colleagues,
the comic poets—" the poets are mere babble (*λῆρος*);
they invent nothing new; none of them does anything
beyond furbishing up and re-arranging the same old
fooleries; fishmongers have more fertile imaginations. . . ."[3]
Under a playful form Xenarchus gives expression to a
very serious criticism.

No doubt, the circumstances under which the comic
writers of the fourth and third centuries wrote for the
stage make their course excusable to a certain extent.
Many of the plays that were written for a particular
competition were performed but once; those which were
repeated were not repeated often, nor in quick succession.
Hence, if an incident, a situation, or the construction of
a plot had met with favour, its author had a perfect right
to use it again in one of his subsequent works. Some
poets, too, were extremely productive; Menander wrote
more than a hundred plays in the course of thirty years.
If he had written only thirty plays, each of which had,
after the manner of our days, " held the boards " for weeks
and months, Latinus and Aristophanes of Byzantium
would have found fewer repetitions and plagiarisms to
point out in his works. At the time of the *νέα* there were
many festivals during which comedies were performed,
and in order to satisfy the demand novelties had to be
produced by the bulk. Is it surprising if many of them
were not as novel as might have been hoped? These
considerations should keep us from being too hasty or too
violent in throwing stones at the colleagues of Xenarchus;

---

[1] Porph. ap. Euseb., *Praep. evang.*, X. 3, 12, p. 465 D.
[2] *Ibid.*   [3] Xenarchus, fr. 7.

but, of course, they do not invalidate my earlier conclusions. Though an excuse has been found for their frequency the repetitions certainly do exist. There is no disguising the fact that in ancient Greece writers of comedy, and especially the latest of them—that is to say, the authors of the νέα— must often have worked according to a formula. If we still had all their works, and if we could compare them with earlier productions, many of them would perhaps appear to us, as the German comedies of eighty years ago appeared to Heine, as games of " patience " in which there is no element that had not already appeared in previous combinations.[1]

Certain features of extant plays seem to point to the plot or to the actors of other comedies that have disappeared. When Demaenetus praises the trick that his father plays on a pander, he may possibly be repeating the chief episode of Menander's Ναύκληρος; while it has been suggested that some words spoken by the slave in the *Pseudolus* recall occurrences in the Θησαυρός.[2] When Chrysalus, in the *Bacchides*, speaks with superb scorn of " the Parmenos and the Syruses who secure two or three minae "[3] for their masters, he is evidently thinking primarily of the rascally slaves of comedy. These details betray the fact that the poets had rather a tendency to regard the world of the stage as a separate world which lived and went its way outside the borders of real society; and for those of them who, from indolence or incapacity, gave in to this tendency, the work of studying manners and customs was singularly lightened and its value correspondingly diminished. They were merely called upon to exercise a sort of judicious control over the copies of copies and the variants of variants from which their new plays were to be constructed, and endeavour not entirely to lose contact with the real life that surrounded them. As a rule, they did exercise this control and maintain this contact. However, we

---

[1] *Letter to Lewald*, February 1838   [2] *Pseud.*, 412.
[3] *Bacch.*, 649–650.

occasionally meet with the older forms of an incident dressed up in a newer garb, with a corresponding loss of realism. The type of the " good courtesan " is less convincingly true than that of the heartless courtesan, with which it is intentionally contrasted. The philosophising cook, who pretends to have scientific attainments, must, if he existed at all, have been much rarer than the cook who was simply proud of his sauces. When Pseudolus openly defies Simo and tells him that he means to steal from him,[1] one would be inclined to think that he seeks to improve on the audacity of Chrysalus; but his impudence goes too far, and I think that a master, even though he were an Athenian master, would have replied to such impertinent talk with his whip. Similarly, when Simo warns Ballio that he had better be on his guard,[2] his attitude, which makes it harder for the slave to succeed, lends a new interest to a commonplace intrigue. Is it likely that a respectable citizen would thus ally himself with a man of evil repute, a pander? There are many other instances of the same kind, and it is not without its dangers for portrayers of manners, however skilful they may be, to restrict their sphere too closely, and allow the intervention of too many literary reminiscences between themselves and the society whose image they wish to present.

§ 2

Psychology

The psychology of the νέα suggests reflections similar to those I have just made about adventures and manners, but they can be presented in briefer terms.

This psychology, as we find it in the fragments and in the Latin imitations, is not flawless. Such traits of characters as vanity, boastfulness, cynicism, indifference to insults, servility, suspicion, brutality, greed and stinginess are manifestly exaggerated. Lovers are too quick to indulge in high-flown language about despair and death;

[1] *Pseud.*, 507 et seq.   [2] *Ibid.*, 896 et seq.

they lose their heads too easily; their curses are sometimes puerile, and deserve Cicero's mocking remarks. People like Hegio, in the *Captivi*, and Nicobulus, in the *Bacchides*, are quite too ingenuous, and their credulousness is excessive. Others, like Menaechmus and Sosicles, persist with a singular perseverance in not feeling the most natural suspicions and in failing to understand what is going on about them, and both in their narrations and elsewhere imprudently tell their business to the first comer. Others practise an exaggerated reserve; and there are some who, at a critical moment, and when hard pressed, take delight in misplaced pleasantries and waste time in talking. Finally, there are those who contradict themselves from one scene to another and are hardly recognisable as the same persons. I do not blame Demea or the "truculent" Stratilax for their conversion, which, I believe, is merely feigned. Nor do I blame Euclio for the way in which he consoles himself for having lost what he could not keep. I am quite willing to admit that the good Menedemus should for a moment yield to the pleasure of making fun of the man who gives him advice,[1] that misfortune should embitter the heart of Hegio, and make him more cruel than was his wont.[2] But I find it hard to admit that one and the same person—Chremes, in the *Eunuchus*—should within a space of a few minutes be so frightened and so resolute;[3] that a matron—Myrrhina at the opening of the *Casina*—who is capable of counselling one of her friends to be resigned to her married state, should almost immediately afterwards second this friend in her acts of retaliation; that Megadorus, an inveterate bachelor, should at once follow the advice given him to marry; that a sober and crabbed old man, like Nicobulus, should, even after holding back for a long time, or even for the purpose of recovering some of his money, allow himself to join his son in merrymaking. For such shortcomings the poets of the new period are, doubtless, not

---

[1] *Heaut.*, 910 et seq.   [2] *Capt.*, 659 et seq., 764–765.
[3] *Eun.*, 754 et seq., 797–803.

R

always responsible. Some of them must be the work of
their imitators, and may be due to the substitution of
one person for another, or to the fusion of two rôles into
one, as was probably the case in the *Eunuchus*. Or, again,
it may be that a trait which was merely sketched in outline, or a casual characterisation, was exaggerated and
clumsily accentuated when it was transferred from the
original to the copy. Nevertheless, considerations or
hypotheses of this kind do not suffice to exculpate the
Greek comic writers entirely. Yet it must be noted in their
defence that, in the *palliatae*, some inconsistency in psychology is often the price paid—and I believe freely accepted—
in order to gain advantages of another sort, and we shall
see this more clearly when we study the construction of the
plays, the springs of the action in them and the sources of
the comic element; for the present, I need only call attention to it. Now, to sacrifice the truth and naturalness of a
character for the sake of furthering the plot or the desire
to amuse the audience is certainly a mistake; this mistake does not, however, necessarily prove that those who
committed it lacked the capacity for close observation.

In short, if we except certain classes of rôles that are
a heritage from the μέση, and that were always more or
less sacrificed, the psychology of the νέα appears, as a rule,
to have been true. That is to say, it was true but superficial—and by this I mean that the observation of the
comic writers did not, as a rule, deal with the springs of
human activity and connections of thought and action
which were not absolutely obvious even to the least experienced observer. We have seen that people who have a
very clearly defined character, or who are marked examples
of a particular vice or a particular shortcoming, are rare
in comedy. This, in itself, is significant; for such people
are either not met with at all in actual life, or else it is
not easy to recognise them at first sight. Long and
patient observation is needed in order to assemble the
scattered elements of their personality. Now, the νέα

does not take so much trouble. Generally speaking, one may say that it concerns itself little with exceptional cases or with anything out of the commonplace.

Indeed, in that part of it which has come down to us, the characteristics whose psychological truthfulness—or falseness—cannot be seen at a glance so as to need no argument, are very rare. Among them we may quote the sudden decisions, the unexpected changes of attitude of several actors in the Σαμία. The reasoning, in fact, by which Demeas establishes Moschio's innocence is certainly unexpected—so much so, indeed, that the poet himself makes his actor say: παράβολος ὁ λόγος ἴσως ἐστ᾽, ἄνδρες, ἀλλ᾽ ἀληθινός.[1] Later on, Niceratus passes from extreme rage—he wishes to beat Demeas and to slay Chrysis—to a resigned gentleness;[2] and when Moschio discovers, rather late in the day, that his father has wronged him, he gives way to a singular caprice.[3] It requires a moment's reflection to show that these unexpected and sudden changes are not untrue to nature. We must remember that there are good-natured people who refuse to see the guilt of those whom they love or fear, and who, in perfect good faith, impute it to others; hot headed persons who get excited and become calm again in the twinkling of an eye; and capricious people whose habit of criticising makes them discover something to resent everywhere; and that Demeas, Niceratus and Moschio may each belong to one of these classes. The attitude taken by Mnesilochus, in the *Bacchides*, while he believes that he is being betrayed, has, it is true, something disconcerting about it. One would expect to see him in despair, but he delights in thinking how disappointed Bacchis will be when she sees him with empty hands.[4] In order to understand his thinking exclusively of revenge, one must remember one of the earlier scenes in which Mnesilochus appeared to be extremely anxious to acknowledge another man's good offices.[5] A spiteful disposition and a tendency to console

[1] Σαμ., 113–114. [2] *Ibid.*, 211 et seq. [3] *Ibid.*, 271 et seq.
[4] *Bacch.*, 512 et seq. [5] *Ibid.*, 394 et seq.

oneself for misfortunes by planning revenge, frequently, if I may say so, have gratitude as the reverse of the medal. Being what he is, Mnesilochus must feel as he does.

No doubt we might find in the extant plays or parts of plays yet other instances of stage psychology, and yet other situations, the possibility of which might be contested by a hasty observer. But I repeat that they are of rare occurrence. In a very great majority of cases the feelings entertained by the actors, the thoughts they express, and their line of conduct are what everybody might expect them to be, and what everybody regarded as inevitable. To recognise this fact is, in a certain sense, to praise the poets; for it amounts to saying that their portraits are true portraits of ordinary everyday folk; though this also implies that they never depict anything more rare, subtle, or profound. Regarded in this light, it is no longer praise.

As for the axioms that certain characters proclaim, very few of them can have been new to the audience. Easy success makes people vain; he who fails in all his undertakings becomes amenable to the suggestions of others; misfortunes are doubled by comparing them with the happiness of one's neighbours; one enjoys happiness more after having lived in misery; unhappy people seek the society of comrades in misfortune; the young are sorry for the young, the old are sorry for the old; it is easier to criticise or to advise than to act, to preach resignation and good behaviour than to practise them; we recognise our own faults much less readily than we do those of others; we are often better judges of a stranger's affairs than of our own; we only appreciate the seriousness of a mistake when it is too late; foolish people find fault with fortune; time is the great consoler; man is shaped by contact with his fellow men, he is corrupted by bad company; he who is not moved by insults is good for nothing; he who can blush is honest; wrath obscures judgment; the unexpected disconcerts; and so forth. None of the above statements betrays exceptional sagacity.

From the time of the *véa* onwards, the experience of Gnatho and of the worthy Chremes, their knowledge of love and of jealousy were no doubt commonplaces,[1] and I think there was more originality in the following remark by Charinus, which may come from the *Περινθία*: *Postquam me amare dixi complacitast tibi*.[2] But such remarks are rare.

Thus it is not so much by the keenness of their vision that the psychologists of New Comedy distinguished themselves, as by its quickness and accuracy. Their observation does not penetrate very far, and one cannot say that it " goes to the bottom of people's character," but it eagerly seizes upon even the slightest outward manifestations of various passions and moods. For example, it will not fail to make a note of the sophistries indulged in by an over-thrifty man who has not spent anything on his daughter's wedding,[3] or by a lover who, after having sworn that he would never again see the woman who had been his mistress for three days, comes back and hangs about her at the end of an hour,[4] or by a father who runs away at the very moment when he ought to assert his authority.[5] Nor will it fail to notice the artless selfishness of a Clitipho, when he advises his accomplice Syrus not to allow himself to be caught, as though Syrus were not the first person concerned in the matter;[6] or the surprise of a Simo, who is almost disappointed at not having to meet with unforeseen obstacles;[7] or the agitation of a Pamphilus, who, in order to get rid of an inconvenient person, sends his slave to the Acropolis, but forgets to tell him what he is to do there;[8] or the impetuous unfairness of a Phaedimus, who in good faith complains that people are " making a row with him " when it is he who is making it with others;[9] and so on. These are all delightful details, and though the invention

---

[1] *Heaut.*, 570 et seq.; *Eun.*, 439 et seq., 812–813.
[2] *Andr.*, 645.   [3] *Aul.*, 379 et seq.   [4] *Eun.*, 636 et seq.
[5] *Bacch.*, 408 et seq., 494 et seq.   [6] *Heaut.*, 352.
[7] *Andr.*, 421, 435–436.   [8] *Hec.*, 436.
[9] In the Ghôran Papyrus; cf. *Hermes*, XLIII (1908), p. 51 (lines 165–166).

of them may not have called for much effort or
required a very keen mind, they do show that the comic
poets had a happy faculty for seeing the spectacle of life
clearly—a gift that is not granted to every one—and,
what is even less common, for remembering what they
had seen.

Even though we lacked details of this kind which are
peculiarly fitted to attract attention, the sustained naturalness of so many scenes in which the most ordinary feelings
of the human heart are expressed, bear witness to the
presence of this capacity. We have seen how easy is
the flow of certain conversations in the *Bacchides*.[1] Read
in the same play—which abounds in excellent passages—
the scene beginning at line 640. Chrysalus comes on the
scene filled with pride at his recent exploit, and very well
satisfied with his rascality. The embarrassment displayed
by his two friends, Mnesilochus and Pistoclerus, begins to
cause him anxiety; word by word he draws out of Mnesilochus an account of what has taken place during his
absence. When the decisive sentence is spoken (*omne
aurum iratus reddidi meo patri*), his first thought, free from
all false shame, is of his own affairs and of the punishment
that awaits him. Mnesilochus reassures him, and, glad
to have been able to prove that he has by no means acted
like an ungrateful person, he uses the opportunity forthwith to make a new appeal for help. Chrysalus retorts
that for the moment he has run dry; and Mnesilochus,
whose memory of the outbursts of paternal wrath is quite
fresh, has no alternative but to acquiesce. But the remarks of Nicobulus, which Mnesilochus repeats to him,
rouse the energy of Chrysalus; the old man's challenge
goads him on and he promises all that is asked of him.
The young men, as often happens, mistake what they
desire for what they have a right to expect, and their
dejection changes to joy. In the space of a few lines the
most contradictory feelings possess the souls of the actors,

---

[1] Cf. above, p. 83 et seq.

following one another, perhaps, somewhat too quickly, but in a very natural progression.[1]

If we look for scenes containing less psychological variety, we shall find one in the Ἐπιτρέποντες. After Onesimus has told the charcoal-burner why he has not yet shown the ring that is to reveal the secret, Habrotonon, who had been present during their talk, approaches.[2] What she has just heard reminds her of something she had seen the year before, during the night of the Tauropolia, when Charisius lost his ring : a young girl who had become separated from her comrades had come back to them bathed in tears and with her garments torn. Even before he gives expression to the suspicion which this communication must have awakened, Onesimus asks who the young girl was. Habrotonon does not know, but it is easy for her to find out. She does, however, know that it was a pretty girl and that she was of good family. Onesimus is overjoyed at the thought that it might well have been Charisius' victim. Habrotonon, who agrees with him, urges him to inform the young man, but his recent experiences have made him discreet, and he wishes first of all to find the unknown girl of the Tauropolia. The courtesan, on the other hand, refuses to set out on her search there and then; how could she make public the misfortunes of a respectable girl, and so compromise her, before being quite sure that Charisius was the culprit and was disposed to make reparation for his crime ? Affecting to have the greatest deference for Onesimus' superior wisdom, she proposes the following plan : she is to enter the banqueting hall, wearing the ring so that it can be plainly seen. Charisius will see it and will ask Habrotonon where she got it; she will pretend that it was left in her hand during the night of the Tauropolia when an unknown man ravished her. Charisius—for he is already a bit intoxicated, and besides, what harm is there in having

---

[1] Similar, and no less natural, changes of front must have been portrayed in a passage of the Περικειρομένη, the text of which is unfortunately mutilated (77 et seq.).

[2] Ἐπιτρ., 247 et seq.

crumpled the dress of a prostitute in the dark?—will
unsuspectingly declare that he is the unknown man.
Then the child is to be brought to him, and Habrotonon
will say that she is its mother and he will not be in a
position to deny it; whereupon a search is to be made for
the real mother. Onesimus approves, but he has one fear :
he does not place much faith in Habrotonon's word. No
doubt she hopes that Charisius will enfranchise her while
he thinks that she is the mother of his son; but what if,
her object thus attained, she leaves him in the lurch and
takes no further interest in the matter? The courtesan
reassures him : does she look like a woman who wishes to
take on the burden of a child? Onesimus does not insist,
but, to make matters safer, he declares that he will find
a way to revenge himself if he is deceived. Habrotonon
is also suspicious and makes him repeat again and again
that he approves her plan; and the compact is made.
During this entire conversation both participants reason
quite correctly; their attitude accords entirely with their
respective positions, interests and characters.

At the beginning of the *Eunuchus*,[1] when Phaedria once
comes face to face with Thais, he is defeated at once, and
is well aware of it. For all that, he makes a show of
defence, the phases of which are very cleverly described.
He begins with a bitter allusion to the occurrences of the
previous day, to the brutal treatment of which he had been
the victim. Then, when Thais affects to treat the matter
as of no consequence, comes a protest which, on the part
of the unhappy lover, is at once a reproach addressed to
the heartless one and an admission of his own folly.
Thais tells the story of the young girl in whom she takes
so much interest, and Phaedria lets her do so, as he is most
anxious to believe in her sincerity and to find an excuse
for her. The mention of a hated rival irritates him for
a while, calls forth a cry of jealousy, and leads him to seek
for a confirmation of his suspicions even in Thais' story.
But in her reply the courtesan has only to pronounce a

---

[1] *Eun.*, 86 et seq.

few words that are honey to his ears, and he clings to them with the whole force of a reviving hope; " he yields, conquered by a single word," and eagerly grasps the chance to surrender. In the first scene of the *Cistellaria* [1] Selenium's repugnance to confessing her love, especially in the presence of vulgar women who are unable to understand it, can be read between the lines of the dialogue. In order to find courage to make her confidence, the love-lorn girl expatiates upon the affection she feels for Gymnasium and her mother, of their devotion and their readiness to serve her. But the cynical remarks of the old procuress frighten her; she shrinks back into herself and for a long while breaks the silence only by a distinctly disapproving sentence : *at satius fuerat eam viro dare nuptum potius.* Finally, the picture, so complacently outlined, of the life of shame that threatens her fills her with despair; without uttering a word she becomes confused and turns pale. Then it is Gymnasium who plies her with questions and from the rather vague replies gathers the truth : *amat haec mulier !* Elsewhere, in the *Menaechmi,* in the *Mercator,* and in the *Casina,* there is an amusingly truthful portrayal of the embarrassment of a person who has been caught red-handed and has no good excuse to offer and cannot invent a bad one.[2] In the *Eunuchus* there is the anxiety of a coward who would rather withdraw to seek support than stand his ground against the enemy;[3] in the *Σαμία* the indecision of a spoiled child who wavers between a wish to frighten his family by pretending to go abroad and the fear that he will be allowed to go.[4] In the *Ἐπιτρέποντες* we see the amazement of an angry man who, owing to impertinent harangues, forgets his wrath for a few moments;[5] in the *Heauton Timoroumenos* the ecstacy of a lover who is drunk with joy, who does not listen to what is said to

---

[1] *Cist.,* 1 et seq.
[2] *Menaech.,* 609 et seq.; *Merc.,* 719 et seq.; *Cas.,* 236 et seq.
[3] *Eun.,* 761 et seq.   [4] *Σαμ.,* 387 et seq.
[5] *Ἐπιτρ.,* 488 et seq.

him, and interrupts people who speak to him;[1] in the
Περικειρομένη the confusion of another lover who is at the
same time moved by remorse, by fear, and by hope.[2]
Elsewhere we meet with an irritated person who, without
any note of warning, opens the conversation with rebukes
and accusations;[3] or with an affectionate mother who at
once reveals her kindness of heart by the first words she
addresses to her son : *Gaudeo venisse salvum. Salvan
Philumenast?*[4] And so on.

In order to produce pictures that were at once as superficial and as minute as I think many of their pictures
were, the authors of the *véa* doubtless did not feel the
need, nor had they always the opportunity, of imitating
older works. The things they described could be seen
in real life quite as well as in some written description;
and in many cases they consisted of details which were
so fixed as not to permit of any variants. Still, though
they had no *models*, in the proper sense of the word, for
the psychology they depicted, they had literary *antecedents*,
and some mention must be made here of those which were
most important and most nearly contemporaneous.

Love, which these authors so often portrayed upon the
stage, had been the theme of many dramatic performances
before their time. While it had hardly found a place in
the tragedies of Aeschylus and Sophocles, it had, from the
time of Euripides onwards, gained a preponderating place
in tragedy, and had appeared under the most varied
aspects. Middle comedy, for its part, did not stop at
relating amorous adventures; some fragments discuss the
passion,[5] while others express its delights.[6] Furthermore,
when Menander appeared upon the scene, the stage already
possessed a poetic interpretation of love. For example,
it was recognised that people who are in love cannot hide

---

[1] *Heaut.*, 690 et seq.   [2] Περικ., 325 et seq.
[3] *Andr.*, 908 et seq.; *Phorm.*, 254 et seq.   [4] *Hec.*, 353–354.
[5] Aristophon, fr. II.; Anaxandrides, fr. 61; Amphis, fr. 15; Alexis,
fr. 20, 70, 234, 239, 245.
[6] Timocles, fr. 10; Theophilus, fr. 12; Eubulus, fr. 104.

their feelings any more than intoxicated people can : [1]
Toxilus, in the *Persa*, betrays his state of mind by a tired
look and by the customary pallor.[2] At a much earlier
period Phaedra had displayed the languor and the neg-
lected garb that are marks of Selenium's grief, and had
also set the example for the rambling talk in which Alcesimarchus and Charinus indulge. The soliloquies in which
the young lovers of the *νέα* make confession of their love
to the moon, possibly had their prototypes in Euripides'
tragedies. Were our opportunities for comparison not
so limited, we should, no doubt, be able to point out even
more exact parallels. Did not Andromeda, who declares
to her liberator : ἄγου δὲ μ’, ὦ ξέν’, εἴτε πρόσπολον θέλεις,
εἴτ’ ἄλοχον, εἴτε δμωΐδα,[3] serve as a model for women who
were in love and also grateful to the man they loved, for
slave girls who were picked out by their master and set
free, or for poor girls, like Pasicompsa, Philematium and
Antiphila, who were rescued from a life of poverty ? Was
not Laodamia, who implores the gods to restore to her
her well-beloved Protesilaus, and then follows him to the
grave,[4] the ancestress of affectionate courtesans such as
Philaenium, who complain to a cruel mother at being
separated from their lover, and respond to the latter's
declared intention of committing suicide by promising
not to survive him ? Did not Medea teach the Leucadian [5]
woman, or any of her imitators, the madness of jealousy ?
Did not the courtesans who go to consult a sorceress
have in mind tragic heroines like Medea or Deianeira,
who employed philtres to revenge themselves, or to make
themselves beloved. We know that Menander and other
poets of the *νέα* admired and imitated Euripides ; [6] and
there is every reason to believe that they imitated him
more particularly in the very thing that brought both
him and them so much fame—in that most intimate link
between tragedy and comedy—the portrayal of love.

---

[1] Antiphanes, fr. 235.   [2] *Persa*, 24.   [3] Eur., fr. 133.
[4] In the *Protesilaus* by Euripides.   [5] Λευκαδία of Menander.
[6] Philem., fr. 130 ; Diph. fr. 60 ; Quint., X. 1, 69.

The portrayal of moral types, as well as that of passion, had been essayed in drama before the time of New Comedy. The titles of several plays of the early and middle periods, some of which crop up again later on, denote faults of character,[1] and in addition to the evidence of these titles we have that of a few fragments. I have already said that the type of the flatterer, of the swaggerer and of the rustic became fixed very early. Phrynicus' μονότροπος was, according to the description he gives of himself, a worthy precursor of Cnemon : " I lead," he says, " the life of Timon, without a wife or a servant, full of anger (ὀξύθυμον), unapproachable, not knowing how to laugh, not talking with any one, with ideas of my own (ἰδιογνώμονα)." Timon,[2] to whom the μονότροπος compares himself, must have appeared in person in one of Antiphanes' comedies, that was named after him. Lucian's little work, called Τίμων, was perhaps inspired by this play—I believe it was certainly inspired by a comedy [3]—and gives us some idea of how the comic writers represented the hero.

Two other types of character for the portrayal of which the comic writers of the νέα may have drawn on the earlier literature are the miser and the superstitious man. At a very early date superstition had provoked the ridicule of Athenian wits. Cratinus, in his Τροφώνιος and in his Θρᾷτται, and Aristophanes in almost all his works, delighted in poking fun at it. In the fourth century Antiphanes [4] rails at the Metragyrtes,[5] and one of his comedies was called Μετραγύρτης, and another Οἰωνιστής. After Cratinus and before Menander, Cephisodorus and Alexis had each written a Τροφώνιος. Among the works of Alexis we also find quoted a Μάντεις and a Θεοφόρητος. These titles are, as it appears to me, suggestive, but they are merely titles; and of all the plays cited above, nothing of interest has survived.

[1] Ἄγροικος, Ἄγροικοι, Δύσκολος, Ἐπιχαιρέκακος, Μεμψίμοιρος, Μισοπόνηρος, Μονότροπος, Πολυπράγμων, Φιλάργυρος, Φιλάργυροι. See Kock's Index.
[2] Phrynichus, fr. 18.
[3] Cf. Revue des Études anciennes, XI (1907), pp. 132 et seq.
[4] Antiphanes, fr. 159.
[5] Priests of Cybele who went about begging.(—Tr.).

About the antecedents of the miser we are better informed. Apart from Philiscus' play, misers appeared, in the age of the μέση, in the Δύσκολος by Mnesimachus, in the Ὅμοιοι by Ephippus, possibly in the Τίμων by Antiphanes, in the same author's Νεοττίς and in Anaxilas' Ἄγροικος. Like their fellows in the νέα, the misers of the middle period appear chiefly to have been close-fisted men who dread being in want. One of Antiphanes' misers lives more penuriously than the followers of Pythagoras. Another, on his return from market, boasts that he has made magnificent purchases in preparation for a wedding, but to judge from the details he gives of them one may suppose that this magnificence is quite relative. In a play by Mnesimachus, an uncle who is rather a curmudgeon, but otherwise a good-natured man, explains to his nephew how he should set about making his demands less galling : "Use diminutives and put me on a wrong scent. Fish, for example—call them little fish (ἰχθύδια). If you speak of another dish, call it a little dish (ὀψάριον). Then I would ruin myself much more readily." In the Ὅμοιοι it is the miser who treats himself in this fashion; and these two passages give proof of keen insight.

In addition to dramatic works there is another kind of literary product whose relations to New Comedy must here claim our attention—the essays in moral philosophy that were so popular from the fourth century onwards.

Of the numerous works on love of whose existence there is a record we know very little. We know that the volume written by Clearchus of Soli, about which our ignorance is least absolute, contained a study of certain usages of gallantry then current, and inquired into their origin and discussed their symbolism. Apparently its author had more interest in the manifestations of love than taste for abstract analysis, and so it may be that he, and others like him, suggested to the comic poets the idea of certain dramatic situations, or even certain subjects for plots. But as we lack all documentary evidence we cannot state this positively.

We are better informed about the descriptions of

characters. Aristotle's works, pseudo-Aristotelian writings, and the work of Theophrastus contain some examples, and the very names of their authors—Aristotle, whose *Poetics* contains, in its second half, a theory of comedy; Theophrastus, who wrote a treatise *Περὶ κωμῳδίας* and who was Menander's teacher—invite us to make comparisons in this matter. As far as Aristotle's works are concerned, these comparisons are—it must be admitted— not very profitable. Many of the characters which the philosopher studied do not fit into comedy. Besides, the descriptions he gives of them are not of a kind to be appropriated by dramatic authors. Aristotle seeks the essence of things; he points out the mainsprings of man's actions in all kinds of circumstances, but does not quote individual examples. The perusal of his works may have developed the comic writers' taste for observing, and may have sharpened their sense of observation, but it cannot have supplied them with ready-made observations, and, under the circumstances, the extent of his influence cannot be accurately determined.

The case is different with Theophrastus. As a rule, he gives his attention to simple defects that are ridiculous rather than objectionable; he studies them from without, and illustrates them, if I may use that word, by a mass of small details, some of which doubtless are not suitable for reproduction on the stage, while many of them are. The points of contact between his collection and comic literature are clear; so much so, indeed, that it has been supposed that the *Characters* were, to a great extent, taken from the drama. Without entering into a comprehensive discussion of this view, I may merely recall the fact that two chapters—Chapter VIII (*Λογοποιίας*) and Chapter XXIII (*'Αλαζονείας*)—appear to contain allusions to certain events of the year 319,[1] and in all probability the entire work dates back to this period; in other words,

---

[1] See the essay by Cichorius, *Die Abfassungszeit von Theophrasts Charakteren*, at the beginning of the publication of the *Philologische Gesellschaft* of Leipzig (1897), pp. lvii–lxii.

it is just about contemporaneous with the beginnings of
the νέα, and earlier than nearly all of Menander's writings.
We may therefore treat it as a possible source, and, to
take it up in detail, several of the boastful remarks that
Theophrastus attributes to his ἀλαζών reappear, with
hardly any modifications, on the lips of soldiers in comedy.
For example, the following : ὡς μετ᾽ Ἀλεξάνδρου ἐστρα-
τεύσατο, καὶ ὅπως αὐτῷ εἶχε, καὶ ὅσα λιθοκόλλητα ποτήρια
ἐκόμισε,[1] or : γράμματα . . . ὡς πάρεστι παρὰ Ἀντιπάτρου
τριττὰ δὴ λέγοντα παραγίνεσθαι αὐτὸν εἰς Μακεδονίαν.[2] Gnatho's
behaviour, when he dies with laughter at hearing Thraso's
witticisms, is foreshadowed in the *Characters*.[3] Like the
truculentus, the ἄγροικος speaks very loudly,[4] and has a
contempt for perfumes.[5] A detail contained in Chapter X
(Μικρολογίας) — ὀψωνῶν μηδὲν πριάμενος εἰσελθεῖν (§ 12)—
is made use of in the *Aulularia*; [6] another—ἀπαγορεῦσαι τῇ
γυναικὶ μήτε ἅλας χρηννύειν μήτε ἐλλύχνιον μήτε κύμινον μήτε
ὀρίγανον μήτε ὀλὰς μήτε στέμματα μήτε θυηλήματα (§ 13)—
reminds one pretty closely of some of Euclio's injunctions.[7]
Several details in Chapter VI (Ἀπονοίας)—ὀμόσαι ταχύ,
κακῶς ἀκοῦσαι, λοιδορωθῆναι δυνάμενος (§ 2), δεινὸς δὲ καὶ
πανδοκεῦσαι και πορνοβοσκῆσαι (§ 5), ἀπάγεσθαι κλοπῆς (§ 6)—
make one think of the Ballios and Lycuses of comedy.
Instances of superstition that are quoted in Chapter XVI
(Δεισιδαιμονίας)—καὶ ἐὰν ἴδῃ ὄφιν ἐν τῇ οἰκίᾳ κτλ. (§ 4), καὶ
ἐὰν μῦς θύλακον ἀλφίτων διαφάγῃ κτλ. (§ 6), κἂν γλαῦκες
βαδίζοντος αὐτοῦ ἀνακράγωσιν κτλ. (§ 8), καὶ ὅταν ἐνύπνιον
ἴδῃ κτλ. (§ 11)—are also cited in fragments of the new
period. Cases, indeed, of similarity, whether close or
distant, between the *Characters* and the νέα, are by no
means lacking, but, as a rule, they are of a kind that
can be explained as the result of a coincidence. In the
majority of instances it is extremely improbable that
they were due to borrowing, whilst in no case was it very
probable.

---

[1] Theoph., *Char.*, XXIII. 3.   [2] *Ibid.*, 4.
[3] *Char.*, II. 4.   [4] *Ibid.*, IV. 5.   [5] *Ibid.*, 3.
[6] *Aul.*, 371 et seq.   [7] *Ibid.*, 91 et seq.

In a word, all that we can properly affirm is that the works of the philosophers must have encouraged the writers of comedy to study moral types. A certain number of comedies have the same titles as certain chapters of Theophrastus.[1] Possibly this shows that in some cases the attention of the comic writers was called to one or the other shortcoming by what the philosophers had said about it. To assume that there was any closer affinity between the two groups of authors would assuredly be hazardous.

§ 3

LANGUAGE

Hitherto I have dealt with the realistic treatment of manners, characters and emotions. In order to give a more complete idea of the excellence of observation shown in the *véa*, a few words must be added regarding the language spoken by the actors.

An ancient grammarian says of the poets of the middle period : " They did not attempt to use a poetic style, but, employing the language of ordinary life, they had the excellences of prose." [2] Another grammarian contrasts the strength and grandeur of ancient comedy with the lucidity of the new (τὸ σαφέστερον).[3] Plutarch, in his *Comparison of Aristophanes and Menander*, finds fault with the patchwork style of Aristophanes, in which are mingled " the tragic, the comic, the pretentious (τὸ σοβαρόν), the ultra-commonplace, the obscure and the simple, pompousness and loftiness (ὄγκος καὶ δίαρμα), gossip and futilities that turn one's stomach." [4] He adds that, in

---

[1] Κόλαξ, Ἄγροικος, Δεισιδαίμων, Ἄπιστος, Ἀλαζών, Ψοφοδέης (δειλία), Φιλάργυρος (μικρολογία), Φίλαρχος (ὀλιγαρχία).

[2] Anon. Didot III, περὶ κωμῳδίας (= Kaibel II.), § 12. (When applied to *middle* comedy, this remark calls for reservations). Compare Plutarch's words (*Quaest. conviv.*, VII. 8, 3, 7) : ἥ τε γὰρ λέξις ἡδεῖα καὶ πεζὴ κτλ.

[3] I. Tzetzes, περὶ κωμῳδίας, § 14 (Kaibel, pp. 17–18) = Didot IX. a, lines 73–75.

[4] Plut., *Compar. Aristoph. et Men.*, I. 5.

spite of so many incongruities, the author has not succeeded in allotting to each of his actors the language that
he ought to speak.[1] But he finds nothing of this sort
in Menander. " His style is so polished and so consistent
in its harmonious construction that, whatever passion
or whatever character it has to express (διὰ πολλῶν ἀγομένη
παθῶν καὶ ἠθῶν), and even where it adjusts itself to the
most diverse persons (παντοδαποῖς ἐφαρμόττουσα προσώποις),
it retains its unity (μία φαίνεται) and always remains the
same (τὴν ὁμοιότητα τηρεῖ), because it employs common
expressions that are familiar and in current use. Among
all the noted artisans that have ever existed, no one,
whether he was a cobbler, a tailor, or plied some other
trade, was able to make a boot, a mask or a cloak, that
would fit a man, a woman, a child, an old man, or a slave
equally well; but Menander's style is such that it suits
every character, every station and every age. . . ." [2]
We see that this critic has special praise for the unity of
Menander's style, but it is clear that he does not mean a
uniformity that would sin against dramatic truthfulness;
for, if he did, the antithesis he makes between the two
authors would be curiously imperfect. Unity and evenness do not mean uniformity; evenness of style excludes
incongruities, but it does not exclude delicate and discreet
shading. Though the clauses διὰ πολλων ἀγομένη παθων καὶ
ἠθῶν, παντοδαποῖς ἐφαρμόττουσα προσώποις in Plutarch's
statement are grammatically subordinate, they are quite
as important as the others. What is praised in Menander's
style is, roughly speaking, the appropriateness and
accuracy of his language.

Other ancient critics, the Atticists at the time of the
Antonines, who certainly have no intention of praising
Menander, give similar testimony. They examined the
text of Menander as minutely as professors of language
and grammar would examine a pupil's task; they
found fault with many details, and occasionally their
pedantic indignation is expressed with amusing vehemence.

[1] Plut., *Compar. Aristoph. et Men.*, I. 6.   [2] *Ibid.*, II. 1-2.

S

"By Heracles!" declares Phrynichus, one of the most
important of them, "I am surprised to see the most distinguished minds of Greece taking such a huge interest in
this maker of comedies . . . who used a lot of words of
base alloy (κίβδηλα ἀναρίθμητα ἀμαθῆ), thereby proving his
ignorance."[1] Elsewhere he exclaims : "Oh, Menander,
where did you collect all this mire of unclean words (ὀνομάτων
συρφετόν) with which you soil the language of your
fathers?"[2] He finds fault with the word αἰχμαλωτίζειν,
and says : "It is such base alloy that even Menander did
not make use of it."[3] There is the same severity, though
expressed with less peevish pedantry, in the *Onomasticon*
by Julius Pollux. There we read : "Menander is not an
author who writes good Greek, nor one whom one must
always follow; but when the proper word with which to
designate this or that is lacking, one may consult him; for
all categories, all things and all objects the names of which
do not appear in other authors, one may consider oneself
lucky to get them even out of Menander."[4] In another
passage, after having pointed out the use of the feminine
forms μεθύση, μεθύστρια, to designate a drunken woman,
Pollux scornfully adds : ὁ γὰρ μέθυσος ἐπὶ ἀνδρῶν Μενάνδρῳ
δεδόσθω.[5] These criticisms are well worth collecting, and
it is easy to convert them into praise. What fault, in
a word, did the Atticists find with Menander? That he
did not speak like Plato, like Aeschines the Socratic, or like
Demosthenes. But, in actual life, no one had ever spoken
thus, and, above all, no one spoke thus at the time when
Menander wrote. In course of time language was gradually
transformed; differences of dialect disappeared; even in
the streets of Athens a more cosmopolitan language, the
κοινή, little by little, took the place of pure Attic. When
Menander introduced new expressions, and words that a

[1] Rutherford, *The New Phrynichus*, p. 492, No. CCCXCIII.
[2] *Ibid.*, p. 497, No. CCCC. Cf. p. 492, No. CCCXCII; p. 499, No.
CCCCIV; p. 491, No. CCCXCI.
[3] *Ibid.*, p. 500, No. CCCCVII. Cf. p. 479, No. CCCLXVI; p. 500,
No. CCCVI.
[4] Pollux, *Onom.*, III. 29.   [5] *Ibid.*, VI. 25.   Cf. IV. 161.

person like Phrynichus considered incorrect, vulgar and semi-barbaric, he no doubt merely reproduced the usages of language which had been adopted by his contemporaries and the living prototypes of the characters whom he brought upon the stage. In other words, he was a realist.

Greater realism and a greater conformity with the language of current speech—or, rather, more consistent realism and more sustained conformity with the common idiom—these are, according to the testimony of the ancients, the features that marked the difference between the style of the νέα and that of the earlier periods. It is only within recent times that we have been able to judge for ourselves how far this realism went. Had the writers of Latin comedy thought it their business to make accurate translations—and this was not the case—they would merely have given us a vague idea of it, as all translations are but an approach to the original. In order to form a judgment of the nature of the language of New Comedy we must go back to the fragments. Now the fragments that were formerly known, and which are found in Kock's collection, offer little of interest in this regard. Most of them are too short. Many of them consist of maxims or of brief dissertations, which the philosophers who compiled them had culled either from the least dramatic parts of the comedies or from such parts as gave very little idea of the plays in their entirety. Occasionally one can observe in these fragments how certain poets had the gift of presenting philosophical reflections in a lively fashion and without pedantry, by either cutting up the argument into a sort of dialogue or into a discussion that the thinker maintains with himself,[1] or else, by putting the thought into the mouth of an assumed speaker.[2] One can also occasionally observe how certain poets temper the expression of serious thought and of deep feeling by employing familiar terms and pro- verbial sayings and by the use of an easy unconstrained

[1] Men., fr. 363, 460, 472, 533, 536, 537, 541; Philem., fr. 213.
[2] Ibid., fr. 223.

syntax.[1] But such testimony is rare and merely illustrates a certain kind of aptitude, and that not one of which comic writers had most commonly to give proof; whilst of other aptitudes which are more essential—for example, skill in handling dialogue—we only get a glimpse in one or two fragments that remain.[2] Fortunately, however, the discoveries of the last ten years, and chiefly those at Kôm Ishkaou, have furnished us with documents of a much greater importance. As far as Menander, at least, is concerned, we are now in a position to judge of the correctness of the statements made by the ancients.

I may at once say that the passages edited by Nicole and Lefebvre make a very favourable impression when they are read through with special attention to their stylistic qualities. In the ideas expressed in them, in the themes which they develop—in what, that is to say, Aristotle calls διάνοια—there is nothing, or almost nothing, out of keeping with the intellectual or moral qualities of the *dramatis personae*. This remark applies more especially to two kinds of elements : the maxims and the allusions to mythology. A *priori* one might fear that both of these would be out of place when spoken by simple folk, such as the greater part of the characters in comedy were. Several passages of the Σαμία and of the 'Επιτρέποντες are all that could be desired to dissipate such a fear. Let us listen to Demeas talking with Niceratus, and to Syriscus pleading before Smicrines.

" *Have you not heard tragedians* relate how Zeus changed himself into a shower of gold, and drifting through a roof, made love to a young girl who was shut up inside. . . .[3] *You have, I am sure, seen tragedies performed* ; well, then, you know of what I am thinking—of a certain Neleus, of Pelias. It was an old goat-herd who, like myself, was clad in the skin of a she-goat, who found those heroes." [4] Thus it is through tragedy that our actors know of the adventures

---

[1] Men., fr. 65, 302, 402, 403, 530, 532, 535.
[2] *Ibid.*, fr. 283, 348.   [3] Σαμ., 244 et seq.   [4] 'Επιτρ., 108 et seq.

of Danaë, of Pelias and of Neleus. Now, in Menander's day, tragedy was a popular form of entertainment; at the time of the Country Dionysia it found its way even to the most humble villages; it was owing to it that boorish rustics who wore skins of she-goats learned the story of legendary heroes, without having to leave their homes. That Sophrona should seriously threaten to recite to Smicrines an entire tirade from Euripides' *Auge*[1] is no doubt a bit of exaggeration, of poetic licence. But neither the knowledge of mythology displayed by Demeas or by Syriscus, nor the use they make of it, go beyond the bounds of probability, any more, it seems to me, than does the wisdom of this or that actor, or even his knowledge of philosophy. We knew beforehand, through Orion, this passage of the ʾΕπιτρέποντες : " Under all conditions justice must prevail everywhere. He who happens to be present by chance must make his best efforts to help accomplish this. It is the common interest of all men." [2] Left isolated and by itself, this passage appears rather sententious for a scene in comedy. But let us put it back into the context. It is the worthy Syriscus who pronounces it, when he begs Smicrines to act as arbiter between himself and Daos. In such a situation a maxim gains the weight of a detailed argument; moreover, it conveys the sentiments which animate the entire rôle of Syriscus, and one cannot deny its propriety without at the same time condemning the entire character. Another passage of the ʾΕπιτρέποντες, which belongs to the part of Onesimus, was known by David the Armenian and by Johannes Philoponus, who quoted it, the former in order to convey an idea of the atheism of the ancient Greeks, the other in order to illustrate one of Epicurus' theories : " Do you believe, Smicrines, that the gods have sufficient leisure to distribute good and evil to each of us every day ? " [3] These words and some that follow them certainly imply that Onesimus had a certain amount of philosophical

---

[1] ʾΕπιτρ., 527.   [2] Men., fr. 173 = ʾΕπιτρ., 15 et seq.
[3] *Ibid.*, fr. 174 = ʾΕπιτρ., 544 et seq.

training, a certain acquaintance with the systems that were then in vogue. But is there anything inadmissible in that? Charisius, Onesimus' young master, was well educated; he had taken lessons of the philosophers; from these lessons, from this education, the slave who was attached to his person may have gathered some scraps.

Let us now consider the " style "—the λέξις—in the exact sense of that word. The first thing that strikes us in the lengthier fragments of Menander is the fact that restrictions occasioned by the metre are hardly ever felt. Rarely, and at long intervals, a word—and most frequently a simple particle, such as δέ, δή, γάρ, and their like—is shifted from its natural position, in order to comply with metric or rhythmic laws. As a rule, however, the construction is just what logic requires or sense demands, and in point of suppleness and vivacity the versified speech of the Γεωργός, of the Σαμία, and of the Ἐπιτρέποντες has no need to envy prose.

Furthermore, the general tone, phrasing, and vocabulary of almost all the scenes are strikingly natural. Glance through the Lefebvre fragments. Twice or three times, at the very most—at the beginning of Charisius' soliloquy,[1] in the " imprecations " of Demeas,[2] and in an expression of Parmeno's [3] — one might point out an exaggerated dignity and some traces of pompousness. And, even then, in two or three instances the pompousness is intentional and is meant to amuse. On the other hand, a great many expressions appear to be borrowed from current speech, from the language that the gentle classes, or even the masses at that time, used in their conversation. This applies to some metaphors, like : ἀπέσκλη, he dried up, meaning " he died "; ἐντεθρίωκε, ἐσκεύακε, Moschio took Niceratus in, he fixed him in fine style; κατακόπτεις, you cut me up, meaning " you weary me "; βουκολεῖς, you deceive me, literally you lead me out to pasture (equivalent, I think, to you are leading me a pretty dance); εἰ μὴ καταπέπωκε, unless he swallowed something (this refers

---

[1] Ἐπιτρ., 429 et seq.   [2] Σαμ., 110–111.   [3] Ibid., 329.

to things that Daos is by law obliged to return); ποικίλον
ἄριστον, a *variegated*, haphazard breakfast; etc.

— to some expressions like τὸν μικρόν, *the little fellow*;
ἐν ἑαυτοῦ εἶναι, to *be quite at one's ease*; πρὶν πτύσαι,
quicker than you can spit, meaning " in the twinkling of
an eye "; τὸ πέρας, after all is said and done; τὸ δεῖνα,
" I mean " (" *thingamabob*," "*what-do-you-call-it ?* ");

— to interjections like πάξ, silence; παῦ (for παῦε),
stop it;

— to insults or insulting adjectives : λέμφος, ἀπόπληκτος,
παχύδερμος, σκατοφάγος, ἐργαστήριον, μαστίγιας, λαικάστρια,
ἱερόσυλος, θηρίον;

— to hyperbole that has become commonplace : θεῖον
μῖσος, κακὸν παμμέγεθες, πάνδεινα πράγματα;

— to threats and exaggerated curses : κατάξω τὴν
κεφαλὴν σου, ἀποκτενῶ σε, ἀποσφαγείην;

— to decidedly brutal expressions : εἰσφθείρεσθαι, ἀποφθεί-
ρεσθαι, to go to the devil; κεκραγέναι, to bawl;

— to familiar diminutives : παιδάριον, γύναιον, μειρακύλλια,
ἑταιρίδιον, πορνίδιον, οἰκίδιον;

— possibly to certain compound words, for example,
to words with the prefix συν-, like συναπαιτεῖν, συναρέσκειν,
συνευρίσκειν, συνεκκεῖσθαι;

— to nouns, verbs, and adjectives that are either rare
or are used in a special sense : κερμάτιον, a little sum,
change; λῆρος, a mere nothing; περίεργος, preoccupied;
ἡδύς, a good fellow; κακοήθης, a rogue; μέτριος, not bad;
μέλημα, the object of one's affections; διαφόρως, in a superior
way; χαριέντως, nicely; λαλεῖν, to say, to speak without
meaning anything, like gossiping; παράγειν, to go, to betake
oneself somewhere; συνάγειν, to sit down at table; χολᾶν,
to lose one's head; βλέπειν, to see nothing but;

— to abstract terms that are used in preference to other
forms of expression : δὸς τὴν χάριν; κατὰ τὴν δόσιν τῆς
μητρός; οὐχ εὕρεσις τοῦτ᾽ ἔστιν, ἀλλ᾽ ἀφαίρεσις; οὐκ ἔνεστιν
οὐδὲ εἷς παρ᾽ ἐμοὶ μερισμός; ἄν συναρέσῃ σοι τοὐμὸν ἐνθύμημι
ἄρα; καὶ καταλαμβάνεις διαλλαγὰς λύσεις τ ἐκείνων τῶν
κακῶν; νυνὶ δ᾽ ἀναγνωρισμὸς αὐτοῖς γέγονε; αὕτη ἐστὶν ἡ

σωτηρία τοῦ πράγματος; φορὰ γὰρ γέγονε τούτου νῦν καλή, etc.

Above all, the vocabulary of these fragments has one thing in common with that of ordinary conversation—the fact that there is but little variety in it. Words with general meanings that are inexact and colourless recur at every turn. For instance, such ultra-commonplace expressions as τὸ πρᾶγμα, τὸ γεγονός; " general utility " verbs like ἔχειν, λαμβάνειν, which could often be replaced to advantage by other verbs with a more definite meaning; the various forms of the perfect γεγονέναι; likewise λαλεῖν, which has already been mentioned in another connection; μανθάνειν and its composites; βαδίζειν, τηρεῖν; also βραχύ, θᾶττον, σφόδρα, ἐπιεικῶς, ἀκριβῶς, πυκνά, ἐκποδών; also τάλας and δύσμορος, very often used in exclamations; πονηρός, δεινός, ἕτοιμος, εὐπρεπής, κομψός, κόσμιος, ἀστεῖος, συνήθης, προπετής, εὐτρεπής, ἄτοπος; ταραχή and its derivatives; μέρος, meaning rôle; μαίνεσθαι, οἰμώζειν; μάχεσθαι, to pick a quarrel; ἀφανίζειν, to suppress, etc. Repetitions of words are especially frequent in Lefebvre's fragments. The same verb or composites of the same verb are often repeated in several successive lines.[1] One actor has no scruples about repeating—sometimes after a very short interval— a phrase that either he or some other actor has already used.[2]

As to word-form, perhaps the most noticeable thing is the frequent occurrence of pronouns or of adverbs in -ι, which the Athenians must have used regularly. There are no abnormal or faulty forms, and such forms as crabbed purists attacked and criticised with severity in Menander's comedies were, certainly, very few and far between. As a general rule, the poet did not allow his love of linguistic truthfulness to carry him to the point of admitting jargon and barbarisms into the speech of even his most humble characters. His use of case, time and mood is almost

---

[1] 'Επιτρ., 60–62, 274–277; Σαμ., 46–48, etc.
[2] Ibid., 45–46 and 118; 297–300 and 314–315; Περικ., 35–36 and 110–111, etc.

always in accord with the laws of classical grammar. At
the very most, we might find a few passages in which
the perfect, without any apparent reason, is used in
preference to the aorist, the present or the imperfect.

The phraseology is neither more correct nor more complex than one would expect in familiar conversation.
There are no long, learnedly constructed, articulated and
well-balanced sentences, such as orators use. If there is
an echo of a lawyer's eloquence in the talk of Daos and of
Syriscus, it is a distant and faint echo. Where Daos
attempts to point out what, in his opinion, is paradoxical
in the claims of his adversary, he expresses himself as
follows—

> εἰ καὶ βαδίζων εὗρεν ἅμ᾽ ἐμοὶ ταῦτα κ[αὶ
> ἦν κοινὸς Ἑρμῆς, τὸ μὲν ἂν οὗτος ἔλα[βε δὴ,
> τὸ δ᾽ ἐγώ. Μόνου δ᾽ εὑρόντος, οὐ παρὼν [σύ γε
> ἅπαντ᾽ ἔχειν οἴει σὲ δεῖν, ἐμὲ δ᾽ οὐδὲ ἕν; [1]

As Croiset remarks, his reasoning is really as follows :
Even had both of us made the find, I ought to have had
my part; I made it all by myself, how can I agree to have
nothing? But Daos, who is an indifferent logician, and
has no experience as an orator, cannot refrain from adding
extraneous ideas to the essential one, thereby obscuring
it. By heaping up the details of a picturesque story, he
runs the risk of his argument being lost sight of. As for
the symmetry of his words, it is by no means rigidly maintained. As soon as he states what he is asked to state,
he loses his coolness; up to this time he had spoken
of Syriscus in the third person; now he addresses him
directly. In Syriscus' speech, which is not bad, considering that he is a charcoal-burner, there is no sentence
that exceeds five or six lines. One of the longest of them
suggests an alternative—

> Νῦν γνωστέον,
> βέλτιστέ, σοι ταῦτ᾽ ἐστίν, ὡς ἐμοὶ δοκεῖ,

[1] Ἐπιτρ., 66 et seq.

τὰ χρυσί᾽ ἢ ταῦθ᾽ ὅ τι ποτ᾽ ἐστί πότερα δεῖ
κατὰ τὴν δόσιν τῆς μητρός, ἥτις ἦν ποτε,
τῷ παιδίῳ τηρεῖσθ᾽ ἕως ἂν ἐκτραφῇ,
ἢ τὸν λελωποδυτηκότ᾽ αὐτὸν ταῦτ᾽ ἔχειν,
εἰ πρῶτος εὗρε, τἀλλότρια.[1]

The development of the thought is clear and correct, but although somewhat lengthy, it lacks fullness, and needs somehow to be rounded off. Each line carries the expression of the thought a step further, as it were, and one might say that the speaker was not able at once to get a complete view of what he had to present, and that he discovered it bit by bit.

The author of the treatise Περὶ ἑρμηνείας mentions the frequent omission of the connecting particle as one of the characteristics of Menander's style.[2] And, indeed, this is perfectly true of the extant fragments. Daos' speeches alone supply many examples—

Ἀνειλόμην· ἀπῆλθον οἴκαδ᾽ αὖτ᾽ ἔχων·
τρέφειν ἔμελλον· ταῦτ᾽ ἔδοξέ μοι τότε.[3]

Τοιουτοσί τις ἦν. Ἐποίμαινον πάλιν
ἕωθεν. Ἦλθεν οὗτος. . . .[4]

Ὅλην τὴν ἡμέραν
κατέτριψε· λιπαροῦντι καὶ πείθοντί με
ὑπεσχόμην. Ἔδωκ᾽· ἀπῆλθεν, μυρία
εὐχόμενος ἀγαθά· λαμβάνων μου κατεφίλει
τὰς χεῖρας.[5]

I might quote similar passages by the dozen; and the omission of the connecting particle is not less frequent when the tone of a passage is impassioned. Let us listen to Smicrines storming when he comes to take back his daughter—

Ἂν μὴ κατάξω τὴν κεφαλὴν σου, Σωφρόνη,
κάκιστ᾽ ἀπολοίμην. Νουθετήσεις καὶ σύ με;

---

[1] Ἐπιτρ., 90 et seq. [2] Demetr., Περὶ ἑρμην., 193.
[3] Ἐπιτρ., 33–34. [4] Ibid., 39–40. [5] Ibid., 53 et seq.

Προπετῶς ἀπάγω τὴν θυγατέρ᾽, ἱερόσυλε γραῦ;
'Αλλὰ περιμείνω καταφαγεῖν τὴν προῖκά μου
τὸν χρηστὸν αὐτῆς ἄνδρα καὶ λόγους λέγω
περὶ τῶν ἐμαυτοῦ; ταῦτα συμπείθεις με σύ;
Οὐκ ὀξυλαβῆσαι κρεῖττόν; Οἰμώξει μακρά,
ἂν ἔτι λαλῇς τι. Κρίνομαι πρὸς Σωφρόνην;
"Μετάπεισον αὐτήν, ὅταν ἴδῃς." Οὕτω τί μοι
ἀγαθὸν γένοιτο, Σωφρόνη, κτλ. . . .[1]

With the mute text before us, it is really puzzling to
distinguish how much of this violent passage Smicrines
speaks in his own name and how much he attributes to
Sophrona, how much of it is to be taken literally and how
much is to be regarded as ironical. We certainly have
before us the jerky, breathless utterance of a man who is
choked with anger, an utterance which needs to be interpreted by the accents and the gestures of the speaker.
The asyndetic style—λέξις λελυμένη—was, so says the
treatise Περὶ ἑρμηνείας, entirely adapted to the stage,
ὑποκριτική, for in its very disconnectedness it resembled
the language that was actually spoken.

Besides these asyndeta, the parentheses, the bold
elisions and the careless or almost incorrect constructions
which distinguish Menander's style, in many instances,
co-operate in making it resemble everyday language.
῎Εστι δ᾽ἀνθρακεύς (I must tell you that he is a charcoal-
burner), Daos casually observes, when, in the course of
his speech, he first mentions Syriscus.[2] When speaking of
the matters in dispute, he says : Μικρὰ δὲ ἦν ταῦτα καὶ λῆρος
τις, οὐδέν (it was a small matter, a bagatelle, a nothing).[3]
Τὸ τέλμ᾽ εἶδες παριοῦσα; (Did you see the pond as you
passed by?), asks Smicrines, stopping in the middle of a
sentence in which he threatens Sophrona with a prolonged
immersion in cold water.[4]

When I begin to cite elliptical phrases, the choice
becomes embarrassing. Τίς οὖν; asks Daos;[5] he means
to say, " Who will act as judge between us?" Τί γάρ σοι

---

[1] 'Επιτρ., 464 et seq. [2] Ibid., 40. [3] Ibid., 59–60.
[4] Ibid., 474. [5] Ibid., 4.

μετεδίδουν; "Why did I give you a share *of what I found*?" [1]
Μικρόν γ᾽ ἄνωθεν, declares the same Daos a little further on,
at the beginning of his harangue; [2] he means to say :
" I shall recur to the matters referred to a little while
ago." Πρὶν εἰπεῖν, [3] μόνου δ᾽ εὑρόντος [4]—in both these cases
the personal pronoun—ἐμέ, ἐμοῦ—is omitted, and must be
inferred from the context : " Τί γάρ ; " ἐγώ· "περίεργός εἰμι." [5]
ἐγώ, standing by itself, means, "*said I*." Οὐκοῦν ἐγὼ μετὰ
ταῦτα [6]—one must mentally add λέξω. Ὅτῳ βούλεσθ᾽
ἐπιτρέπειν ἑνὶ λόγῳ ἕτοιμος [7]—the word εἰμί is lacking.
Κοινόν ἐστι τῷ βίῳ πάντων, [8] περὶ τούτων ἐστί, [9] οὐκ ἔστι
δίκαιον, [10] ἄραρε, [11] παιδίου ᾽στιν, οὐκ ἐμά, [12] νῦνι δ᾽ ὑπόνοιαν καὶ
ταραχὴν ἔχει, [13] οὐκοῦν συναρέσκει σοι, [14] καὶ γὰρ δίκαιον; [15]
in all these instances the subject must be supplied. Elsewhere the object or the attribute must be supplied. Σὺ
δ᾽ ἐπόησάς με δούς, [16] that is to say : σὺ δ᾽ ἐπόησάς με κύριον
τοῦ παιδίου δοὺς τὸ παιδίον. Κατιδών μ᾽ ἔχουσαν, [17] that is
τὸν δακτύλιον. Elsewhere, an adverb stands for a whole
sentence. Αὔριον δέ, [18] *until to-morrow, then*. Οὔπω γάρ, [19]
certainly not, *I did not know it* before. Elsewhere the
same is true of nouns. Βρυχηθμὸς ἔνδον, τιλμός, ἔκστασις
συχνή, [20] means : he roared, he tore his hair, he repeatedly
fell into fits. Occasionally words of the greatest importance
must be added to the text. Τί οὖν τότε, δτ᾽ ἐλάμβανον
τοῦτ᾽, οὐκ ἀπῄτουν ταῦτά σε, [21] but why, *you will say* . . . ?
Κοινὸς Ἑρμῆς, [22] a find by both of us, *you claim!* The
following are some colloquial instances of brachylogy :
Τραφεὶς ἐν ἐργάταις ὑπερόψεται ταῦτα [23]—here ταῦτα signifies
the life of the ἐργάται. Ἴδωμεν εἰ τοῦτ᾽ ἔστιν [24]—let us see
whether *what we surmise* is actually the case. Here is a
clumsily constructed phrase : Τοῦ διαμαρτεῖν μηδέ ἐν προτέρᾳ
λέγουσα; [25] word for word it means " in order to deceive

---

[1] Ἐπιτρ., 5.   [2] *Ibid.*, 23.   [3] *Ibid.*, 47.   [4] *Ibid.*, 68.
[5] *Ibid.*, 44–45.   [6] *Ibid.*, 77.   [7] *Ibid.*, 198–199.   [8] *Ibid.*, 18–19.
[9] *Ibid.*, 30.   [10] *Ibid.*, 131.   [11] *Ibid.*, 185.   [12] *Ibid.*, 186.
[13] *Ibid.*, 240.   [14] *Ibid.*, 333.   [15] *Ibid.*, 346.   [16] *Ibid.*, 90.
[17] *Ibid.*, 299.   [18] *Ibid.*, 197.   [19] *Ibid.*, 262.   [20] *Ibid.*, 414.
[21] *Ibid.*, 96–97.   [22] *Ibid.*, 100.   [23] *Ibid.*, 104–105.   [24] *Ibid.*, 336.
[25] *Ibid.*, 307–308.

me not even in one point by being the first to speak,"
instead of " saying nothing first, in order to deceive me."
And so on.

Yet another detail must be pointed out : comic actors
who give an account of some adventure very often introduce, in direct discourse, remarks which they themselves
have made or which they have heard. In the Ἐπιτρέποντες
Daos quotes the words of Syriscus, his own words, and
even what he has said to himself—always in direct discourse.[1] Onesimus frequently quotes the exclamations
and the laments of his master.[2] In the Περικειρομένη
Daos repeats verbatim the harangue with which he was
greeted in Myrrhina's house.[3] In the Σαμία Demeas
repeats the exclamations of the busy servants, the gossip
with the old nurse and her conversation with the little
maid ;[4] and Daos, in the Γεωργός, the despairing cries of
Cleanetus' servants ;[5] and so on. Need I say that this is
the usual procedure of popular rhetoric ?

I hesitate to continue this analysis. Realism in style
is something more easily felt than described. In order
to appreciate the language of Menander's actors, one must
read, in the original text, the soliloquies and the dialogues
which fortunate discoveries have recently restored to us.
We must compare the passages whose tone is the loftiest
and the most affecting—like the soliloquy of Charisius or
the lamentations of Polemo—with the most purely pathetic
passages in the tragedies of Euripides, or almost any
passage of dialogue with those conversations in Aristophanes' plays in which caricature is least in evidence, and
with the conversations of Herondas' characters; or the
narrations of a Daos or of Demeas with analogous passages
in the works of the best prose-writers—such as Lysias
or Hyperides, who were also past masters in the art
of portraying character (ἠθοποιία). The difference will,
assuredly, be perceived at once. More than any other

---

[1] Ἐπιτρ., 36–38, 44 et seq. [2] Ibid., 207–208, 409, 411–412, 415 et seq.
[3] Περικ., 129 et seq. [4] Σαμ., 12, 27 et seq., 37 et seq.
[5] Γεωργ., 57.

piece of Greek writing, certain passages of Menander give the reader the feeling that he is listening to live men expressing themselves in their own vernacular.

What is true of certain scenes of the Ἐπιτρέποντες, of the Σαμία, of the Περικειρομένη and of the Γεωργός was, no doubt, as a rule, not true of all the plays of the νέα. In some cases the comic poets, with a view to provoking laughter, deliberately imputed language to an actor that was not in harmony with his social standing or with the dramatic situation—a point to which I shall revert when I review the comic elements of the plays. Sometimes it was through negligence or incapacity that the poets were untrue to nature. In fragment 531 of Menander an old servant lectures his ward, and apologises for using an expression that is borrowed from tragedy. More than one actor in comedy must have been guilty of similar borrowings without apologising for them. Of this the scene from the Περικειρομένη, which Körte has recently published,[1] affords an interesting proof. Here we read sentences like the following—

> Κρήνην τιν᾽ [εἶπε] καὶ τόπον <γ᾽> ὑπόσκιον.　　(367)
> Τίς δ᾽ οὗτός ἐστιν; εἰ θέμις, κἀμοὶ φράσον.　　(369)
> Τί γίνεταί ποθ᾽ ; ὡς τρέμω, τάλαιν᾽ [ἐγώ].　　(375)
> Ἤκουσα τὴν ναῦν, ἢ παρεῖχ᾽ ἡμῖν τροφήν,
> [δειν]ὸν καλύψαι πέλαγος Αἰγαίας ἁλός.　　(378–379)
> Τάλαιν᾽ ἔγωγε, τῆς Τύχης ἐφόλκιον.　　(380)[2]

In this entire passage the speaker is changed only at the end of a line, often from line to line, after the manner of tragedy. Hence a certain formality, a certain stiffness, which is all the more noticeable because several half-lines—again after the manner of tragedy—are, to speak frankly, mere padding, and, as it stands, the passage might perfectly well occur in a tragedy. It deals with an ἀναγνωρισμός, and probably the author did not think it necessary to

---

[1] In the *Berichte der sächs. Ges. der Wissenschaften*, 1908, pp. 147 et seq.

[2] For the reader's greater convenience, the lines are numbered according to Körte's *Menandrea, Editio Minor* (Teubner, 1910).(—Tr.).

trouble himself about realism in treating a hackneyed theme. If we had the complete works of Menander we should, I believe, find more than one defect of this sort, especially in his earlier plays. It was not all at once— so Plutarch assures us—that the author of the Ἐπιτρέποντες acquired the mastery we have admired.[1]

As for his rivals and successors, there is reason to believe that they were inferior to him in style as well as in other respects. The author of the treatise Περὶ ἑρμηνείας says so quite clearly, as far as Philemon, the most famous of them, is concerned.[2] If we may believe him, the latter's style was of that periodic and closely connected kind (λέξις συνηρτημένη καὶ οἷον ἠσφαλισμένη τοῖς συνδέσμοις), which is better adapted for reading than for the stage; and, as a matter of fact, some of the extant fragments appear to justify this opinion. In fragment 94 we read : " The just man is not the man who commits no act of injustice, but the man who is in a position to commit them but does not wish to do so (οὐχ᾽ ὁ μὴ ἀδικῶν, ἀλλ᾽ ὅστις . . .); not the man who refrains from stealing little things, but he who has the strength not to steal big things when he might take them and keep them with impunity (οὐδ᾽ ὅς . . ., ἀλλ᾽ ὅς . . .); not he who merely observes these rules, but he who has an honest and sterling character, and desires to be just and not merely to seem to be so (for the third time : οὐδ᾽ ὅς . . ., ἀλλ᾽ ὅς . . .)." It must have been hard for the actor who had to speak this ponderous passage to avoid appearing pedantic. Elsewhere absurd conceits disfigure Philemon's style. For example, in fragment 23 : " nothing is more charming or more worthy of a well-brought-up man than to be able to exercise self-control when hurt. For if he who is hurt does not show it, he who hurts is hurt while hurting " (ὁ λοιδορῶν γάρ, ἂν ὁ λοιδορούμενος μὴ προσποιῆται, λοιδορεῖται λοιδορῶν).

Through the medium of Plautus' adaptations (in more than one passage of the *Trinummus*, the *Mercator*, or the

---

[1] Plut., *Compar. Aristoph. et Men.*, II. 3.   [2] Demetr., Περὶ ἑρμην., 193.

Mostellaria) we can still trace how the language of the Greek prototype was sometimes too pretentious and too formal, or how the development of the theme was too lofty for the comic stage. Nor are the plays translated from Philemon the only ones which, on examination, confirm this remark. In other plays translated from Diphilus, like the *Rudens* and the *Casina*, or from unknown authors, like the *Amphitryon* and the *Poenulus*, we occasionally find traces of affectation or of a loftiness of tone that ill accord with the bourgeois spirit. The inappropriate and unintentional imitation of tragic style which had been common at the time of the μέση—many fragments of Antiphanes and of other comic writers of the same period, as well as several passages from the *Persa*, give proof of this—cannot, when everything is taken into consideration, have been of rare occurrence in the comedies of the subsequent period.

We must not, therefore, be too optimistic in generalising from such conclusions as we have been led to by the perusal of a few pages of Menander. Even in the most flourishing period of New Comedy truth and naturalness of style was, beyond question, the distinctive merit of the greatest writers and a characteristic of their best works. But wherever it *was* found it contributed, I believe, in a very large measure to the success of the work and of its author. When Quintilian sings the praises of Menander, of whom he says that he knew how to picture to the life every variety of character, he lauds his gift of language (*eloquendi facultas*) quite as much as his talent for psychology; [1] and other ancient critics appear to give similar testimony. Possibly it is chiefly to the realism of their style, which is distinguished above all others by its lightness, its minuteness of detail and its delicacy of touch, that the comedies of the prince of the νέα owed that atmosphere of real life which Aristophanes of Byzantium so greatly admired and which he extolled in his well-known saying :

Ὦ Μένανδρε καὶ βίε, πότερος ἄρ' ὑμῶν πότερον ἐμιμήσατο ;

[1] Quint., X. 1, 70.

PART TWO

THE STRUCTURE OF THE PLAYS OF NEW COMEDY

CHAPTER I

THE EXTENT TO WHICH THE LATIN COMEDIES ENLIGHTEN US ABOUT THE COMPOSITION OF THEIR PROTOTYPES

WE are not in possession of nearly as many documents for the study of the composition of the comedies of the new period as for the study of their contents. Of course, recent discoveries have unearthed important parts of certain plays; still, we are not yet in a position to read the text of a complete comedy by Menander. As for the abstracts of lost comedies, they are incomplete and give few details. We must still turn to the imitations by Plautus and Terence if we wish to know how the original works looked in their complete state. But the idea that we can form from these imitations cannot possibly be exact. Some conventional touch, some particular shade of feeling, or some mannerism may, indeed, have a nationality which immediately distinguishes it; but this is not true of the plot, the treatment, and the proportions of the various parts, of qualities of logic, of probability, of truth to life nor of the corresponding defects—which appear in the economy of a dramatic work. We have positive testimony for the fact that the writers of Latin comedy did not always preserve the composition of the plays which they imitated. Let me, therefore, begin this second part of our study by endeavouring to determine how far one can rely upon them.

§ 1

CONTAMINATION

Additions, Omissions, and Substitutions

One particular liberty which the Latin comic writers often took with their models—and it is the liberty of which I propose to speak most frequently—soon came to be designated by a special term : *contaminatio*. " Contamination " consists in the fusion of two or more originals, and it is my task to point out, as far as may be, how this fusion was brought about.

As far as Terence is concerned, we get valuable information from his own statements and from the commentaries of Donatus. Three out of six plays—the *Adelphi*, the *Andria*, and the *Eunuchus*—are certainly contaminated. The chief model of each of these plays was a comedy by Menander, the Ἀδελφοὶ β', the Ἀνδρία, and the Εὐνοῦχος. But an episode in the Συναποθνῄσκοντες by Diphilus is introduced in the *Adelphi*—namely, the carrying off of the courtesan.[1] The first scene of the Περινθία was bodily transferred into the *Andria*, with the exception that in the Περινθία the father talked with his wife and not with a freed man.[2] The rôles of Byrria and of Charinus, neither of which, as we are told, occurs in the Ἀνδρία, may likewise have been taken over from the Περινθία; at any rate, we can for the present assume that this was the case. Finally, the soldier and his parasite in the *Eunuchus* [3] are borrowed from the Κόλαξ.[4] That is all we learn from the ancients on this subject, and modern scholars have made many attempts to interpret this information, but they have not always reached trustworthy and universally accepted conclusions, and will, no doubt, never succeed in doing so. Nevertheless, I do not believe that in putting forward certain facts, as I intend to do, I shall run the risk of encountering any very serious objections.

In the *Adelphi* the passage borrowed from Diphilus must extend from line 155 to line 196. Possibly it takes the place of a scene in which the young man and his companion passed quickly across the stage, leading the courtesan away. Or else, if in Menander's play the carrying off had already taken place and the ravishers had already secretly entered the house before the opening of the play, it was interpolated, just as it was, between two scenes

---

[1] *Ad.*, prol. 6 et seq.
[2] Donat., note to line 13 of the prologue to the *Andria*.
[3] *Ibid.*, note to line 301.
[4] *Eun.*, prol. 30 et seq., Donat., note to line 228.

derived from the 'Αδελφοί—the conversation between the
two old men and the soliloquy of the pander, as he follows
his slave at a distance.   It is not likely that Terence would
have made other changes—or, at least, other appreciable
changes—in the context of a play in order to introduce
this passage which did not fit into it.   Suetonius says that
Varro preferred the beginning (*principium*) of the Latin
Adelphi to that of Menander's 'Αδελφοί.[1] This does not
necessarily mean that the opening scenes differed greatly,
when regarded from the point of view of dramatic economy.
It may be that Varro was thinking merely of differences
of detail and expression.   In any case, all that we can take
for granted is that the 'Αδελφοί opened with a soliloquy
by Syrus, telling of the kidnapping as an accomplished
fact, and explaining the attendant circumstances; and
that thereupon Micio, who had been kept in ignorance of
his son's return, gave free vent to his paternal solicitude
just as he does in Terence's play.

In the first scene of the *Andria*, the dialogue, which is
borrowed from the Περινθία, was substituted for the father's
soliloquy, which served the same purpose at the beginning
of the 'Ανδρία—to explain the plot of the play.   The difference between the two was, no doubt, merely a difference
in wording.   As for Byrria and Charinus, it is clear that
their parts could be cut out of the *Andria* without depriving
that play of a complete and satisfactory plot—the plot
of the 'Ανδρία.   True, this is not the case with all the scenes
(or parts of scenes) in which these actors appear.   While
there are some scenes like Act II. scene i., Act V. scenes v.
and vi., or the first part of Act IV. scene i.—that may
have been taken from the Περινθία and simply added to
the 'Ανδρία; others—like Act II. scene ii., Act II. scene v.,
the end of scene i. Act IV., and Act IV. scene ii.—must
necessarily have had their equivalents in the 'Ανδρία.
However, the changes which the introduction of new
characters into these various passages may have called
for cannot have been very radical.   They consisted in

[1] Suet., *Vita Ter.*

simple additions, in the introduction of a few asides, of a
few replies and a few bits of dialogue. Moreover, we are
not sure that Terence took the responsibility of modifying
his principal model in all the above passages. We know
that the Ἀνδρία and the Περινθία dealt with approximately the same subject.[1] The Περινθία, from which we
have assumed that the characters of Byrria and Charinus
were borrowed, admitted of scenes analogous to those
which I am discussing, and it may very well be that several
of the above scenes were borrowed by the Latin poet.

In the *Eunuchus*, Terence did not invent the character
of Phaedria's rival; he certainly existed in the Εὐνοῦχος,
and I am inclined to believe that he was also a soldier in
that play. Nor did Terence conceive the idea of letting
this rival of Phaedria's invite the courtesan to dinner
and make her a present of a young girl; nor do I think
that the idea of an altercation arising from the recognition
of this young girl and the fact that she was entrusted to
her brother's care developed in Terence's mind. Lines
265–288; Doria's speech, Act IV. scene i.; that of Chremes,
Act IV. scene vi., excepting the allusion to the aggressor's
troops (line 755); even some portions of Act IV. scene vii.—
those in which Chremes appears as a coward, and those
in which there is reference to the gift presented to Thais
and to the freedom of Pamphila, lines 785–786, 792–795,
804–813;—all these passages may or should come from
the Εὐνοῦχος. On the other hand, the following passages
are borrowed from the Κόλαξ: without a doubt, Gnatho's
soliloquy in Act II. scene ii., lines 232–265; probably
also those portions of Act IV. scene vii. in which the
aggressor puts on the airs of a bully, while Chremes shows
himself to be a determined fellow, and in which Pamphila
might be a mistress coveted by both of them—lines 771–
783, 786–791, 796–803, 814–816. In these various scenes,
elements that are borrowed from diverse sources are simply
placed next to one another, or practically so. Of the
remaining scenes of the *Eunuchus*, in which Thraso and

---

[1] *Andr.*, prol. 10–11.

Gnatho appear, Act III. scene ii. certainly had its parallel in the Εὐνοῦχος. The introduction of the sham eunuch and Thais' advice to Pythias are, at any rate, drawn from the same source. Scene i. of Act III. is by no means necessary for the development of the plot, and it may be that this is an instance of an addition that Terence made to his chief model. The greater part of the scene, from line 395 to line 433, must have occurred in the same form in the Κόλαξ. On the other hand, the four or five lines at the beginning (lines 391-395) and the second part of the dialogue (lines 434-453) cannot have been derived from that play, for, in the Κόλαξ, the woman whom Bias and Pheidias desire to possess was the slave of a pander, and it was not her love, but her person, that was the object of contention. If scene i. of Act III. was added by Terence, these two passages very probably are the points at which he joined the new to the old. But it may also be that, in the Εὐνοῦχος, Chaerestratus' rival was impatient to know what effects his present had made, and that, like Thraso, he came to get his thanks. If this was the case, lines 391-394, and 434-453 must have been translations of a scene in the Εὐνοῦχος into the midst of which an entire episode of the Κόλαξ had been inserted; and in scene ii. Act III. Terence must have copied the Εὐνοῦχος when he allows the soldier to witness the presentation of the gift. On the other hand, we know that a detail of scene ii. Act III. was taken from the Κόλαξ (fr. 297). Still other details—as, for example, the harsh words exchanged by Parmeno and Gnatho—may come from the same source. We have still to consider the three concluding scenes, vii., viii. and ix. of Act V. Lines 1054-1060 and 1067-ad fin., in which the soldier, through the mediation of the parasite, makes a compromise with his rival, seem to me to come from the Κόλαξ. It may be that, at the close of the Εὐνοῦχος, Chaerestratus' rival made a last attempt to make friends with Chrysis, and that he was definitely rebuffed. If so, scene vii. of Act V., the remarks contained in lines 1037, 1043-1044 and 1053, as

well as the violent statements in lines 1061–1066, must
have occurred in the principal model, the part of Gnatho
being played by the buffoon's attendant. If this hypothesis is not accepted, scene vii. of Act V. and lines 1061–
1066 may be regarded as passages from the Κόλαξ which
have been slightly changed on account of Chaerea.

Terence was not the first poet to practise contamination.
He says very clearly that the earliest Roman comic poets,
and Plautus in particular, had set the example.[1] But
Plautus nowhere explains his method of procedure, and
no ancient commentator gives us the slightest information
on the subject. So we have no choice but to turn to the
comedies themselves in our effort to discover the secret
of their construction. Many scholars have done so, and
I cannot attempt to give an abstract of all their works
here. I shall merely explain how Leo, one of the scholars
who has studied this problem most methodically, regards
the construction of a few of the most suspected plays.

Miles Gloriosus. According to Leo,[2] this comedy is
made up of parts which were borrowed from two original
works—the ᾿Αλαζών and a comedy called Δίδυμαι. Lines
1–137 and the great majority of lines 813–*ad fin.*, come
from the ᾿Αλαζών, and the greater part of lines 136–812
from the Δίδυμαι. The points where the passages from
the ᾿Αλαζών were fitted into the *Miles Gloriosus* are :
lines 867–869; the allusion to the secret passage-way,
lines 1088 *et seq.*; the mention of the pretended sister,
lines 974–975, and 1102–1107. As for the portions which
are derived from the Δίδυμαι, Leo appears to consider
lines 138–155, 596–611, 765–804, and 810–811 as the
points of juncture. Granted that this was a case of contamination, it may also be that the passage 138–155 was
a fragment of a prologue, and that passages 596–611 and
765–804 were derived from the ᾿Αλαζών.

Poenulus. The *Poenulus*—according to Leo [3]—was the

---

[1] *Andr.*, prol. 18.
[2] Leo, *Plautinische Forschungen* (1895), pp. 161 et seq.
[3] *Ibid.*, pp. 153 et seq.

outgrowth of the combination of a play called Καρχηδόνιος and of a comedy by an unknown author. The Καρχηδόνιος supplied lines 1–158, 449–503; the greater part of lines 821–918; lines 920–922 and 930–1337. The anonymous comedy supplied the episode 159–189 which, by the way, occurs much earlier in Plautus' play than in the original; lines 203–409; the episode 410–448 (except lines 415–416), which, in the Greek comedy, came next to the episode 159–189; lines 504–816. The points of juncture are, in the body of the play, at lines 190–202, 415–416, 817–820, 908–909 and 919 (lines 923–929 are a mere repetition). At the close of the play the endings of the two original works must originally have been merged as we see them in lines 1338–1422, or, to be more precise—and leaving out the repetitions which extend from line 1355 to line 1397—in lines 1338–1355 and 1397–1422.

Pseudolus.[1] From the chief original work Plautus borrowed scenes ii., iii. and iv. of the first act, the second act—with the possible exception of scene i., which Leo assumes to be of his own composition—and the third and fourth acts. Scenes i. and v. of the first act and scene ii. of the fifth act (the first scene was by Plautus himself), were derived from a less important original. Points of juncture are few and imperfect. In scene i. Act I. Plautus substituted for the original text of Phoenicium's letter a text that was rather clumsily fitted into the principal original work. In scene v. Act II. he interpolated a passage of a dozen lines (524–537), in which the extortion of the twenty minae, which had just before—as in model 2—been represented as an independent undertaking, is changed into a result of the pander's discomfiture and thus takes us back to model 1. Finally, at the beginning of scene ii. Act V., and in the course of that scene, a few lines that do not fit in well with line 1314—lines 1283 and 1308 and those following it—seem to go back to an episode of model 1.

Stichus. In the *Stichus* Leo recognises three passages

---

[1] Leo, *Gött. Nachrichten*, 1903, pp. 347 et seq.

borrowed from three different plays.[1] He thinks that
scenes i. and ii. Act II. are borrowed from Menander's
'Αδελφοί α'; that scene iii. Act I. and Acts III. and IV. are
borrowed from a second play. (In this play, the scene
which served as a model for scene iii. Act I. probably
followed the scene of which Act III. is an imitation;
apparently line 459 ought to coincide with the first appearance of the parasite.)   Finally, Act V. appears to Leo to
be derived from a third play which possibly belonged to
the middle period.   In order to connect the parts that
were borrowed from these three plays, Plautus added a
few lines at the close of scene ii. Act I. in which Panegyris
declares that she intends to send the parasite to the
harbour. In scenes i. and ii. Act II. he introduces the
part of Gelasimus, and in order to explain, as well as might
be, his sudden departure, he invented the joke in line 388.
In the portion that was derived from the second play he
made occasional allusions to the wives of the two brothers
who did not have any part in that play.   In scene i.
Act III. he inserted lines 419–453 which were either
supplied by the same play as Act V. or freely invented
in order to prepare the way for Act V.; at the beginning
of scene ii. Act III. he inserted lines 454–457 in order to
connect this scene with what had gone before.

These examples show what a contaminated play must
have been—a mosaic made up of scenes, or portions of
scenes, taken from works which resembled one another in
their episodes and their situations.   Long or short passages
taken from diverse sources were placed next to one another
and joined together more or less skilfully, but they hardly
affected one another.   The habitual work of the contaminator can be summed up in two words: addition
and substitution.

Thus contamination was a procedure both clumsy and
lacking in courage, while we may assume *a priori* that
the authors who indulged in it resorted to other simple
practices as well; for example, to omissions and, in case of

[1] Leo., *Gött. Nachrichten*, 1902, pp. 375 et seq.

need, to transpositions. Indeed, we know that Plautus left
out an episode in his translation of the Συναποθνῄσκοντες [1]
and that he cut down the part of the lover as well as several
scenes at the close of the Κληρούμενοι. [2] On the other
hand, we can hardly regard it as likely that these same
authors submitted the plays which they imitated to more
serious alterations—a process which would imply a creative
activity and real originality—or, at least, that it was usual
for them to do so. To write original stories, even though
making use of borrowed elements, to change the development of a plot or to embellish it with new episodes—any
such procedure presupposes a turn of mind directly the
opposite of that of the contaminator who respects his
models even when he disfigures them. Yet the writers
of *palliatae* may sometimes have taken the risk of doing
so. According to Leo, certain scenes of the *Pseudolus*
arc entirely by Plautus; this has also been said—but
without sufficient reason, as it appears to me—of the
passage in the *Mercator* in which Demipho relates his
dream; and it seems to me that, at the close of the *Casina*,
the speech of Olympio, who suffers from the same disappointment as Lysidamus, is a repetition of his master's
speech. If Plautus really gave proof of his independence
in these various passages, these were, no doubt, exceptional
cases. I think that, as a rule, he and his rivals were
content to be mere transcribers. This is even more likely
to have been the case with writers who were more refined
and more appreciative of the merits of Attic works than
were Plautus or Naevius. When Varro says of Caecilius
that he deserves the prize for the construction of his plays
(*in argumentis poscit palmam*), I think he means to say
that this poet chose models that were especially well
constructed, and that he did not mar their composition.
Terence apologises for having practised contamination. [3]
Consequently I cannot believe that he took still greater

---

[1] *Eun.*, prol. 9–10.
[2] *Cas.*, prol. 64–66, 79 et seq. and 1012–1014.
[3] *Andr.*, 15 et seq.

liberties, and, for example, invented the entire second part of the *Heauton Timoroumenos,* or the ending of the *Adelphi,* or that the characters of Byrria and Charinus, instead of being borrowed from the Περινθία, were his own invention.

The practice of the Latin comic writers having been thus outlined, I return to the question, asked in the opening lines of this chapter—How far do their imitations allow us to form a judgment about the construction of the works of the νέα?

In Terence's plays, the alterations which he himself admits, or which ancient commentators assert that he made, are probably the only ones—or, let us say, the only important ones—which distinguish the copy from the original. We know how bitterly the poet's enemies reproached him for his contaminations, and with how much care he repeatedly explained his action in this matter. Under these circumstances the assumption that he ever " contaminated " without mentioning the fact is not admissible. Now, neither the prologue of the *Heauton Timoroumenos,* nor that of the *Phormio,* nor either of the prologues of the *Hecyra* mention two original works. Apart, then, from contamination, had Terence permitted himself to do any serious re-touching we must assume that the " malicious old poet " and the advocates of servile imitation would not have failed to reproach him for doing so, and that he would not have failed to defend himself against their charges. But we do not meet with any trace of such controversies in the prologues. On the other hand, Donatus' commentaries point out a certain number of divergences between Terence and his proto-types [1] in the matter of construction. Most of these divergences are slight enough; had there been others, and, above all, more serious ones, Donatus' list would doubtless have contained them.

The evidence of Plautus' comedies cannot be relied upon

[1] Donat., Commentary to line 14 of the *Andria,* to lines 539 and 1001 of the *Eunuchus,* and to line 825 of the *Hecyra.*

with nearly so much confidence. In the first place, his comedies are not preserved intact; their text has been altered, either through accidental omissions or by excisions made, at various periods, by rather unscrupulous theatrical managers, by arbitrary arrangement and retouching, by interpolations, or by repetitions. All this must, as far as possible, be taken into consideration before adopting the opinion—sometimes a purely subjective one—of the most authoritative Plautine scholars. Even when we think that we have before us what Plautus himself wrote, it is frequently difficult to determine where the responsibility of the imitator begins, and where that of the writers of the original works ends. At least, the incoherencies of certain comedies are such, and the faults of construction found, here and there, in several of them are so serious, that we cannot suppose the Latin poet took much personal interest in their composition. He certainly did not improve upon his models, and the only question that presents itself is to what extent he spoiled them.

In my opinion, many slips consisting of a few words or a few sentences—in other words, slips easily accounted for by the carelessness of a translator who allows his mind to wander—can be fairly charged against Plautus. But in any case these are venial errors which would not affect the reputation of a dramatist very seriously, and whether they are traced back to the original Greek writers or not, the merit of the latter would hardly be affected one way or the other.

But it is important to determine the source of serious clumsiness and of faults of construction which affect the framework of the edifice. The remarks I have made above may be of some use here. It appears to me that the activity of the Latin transcribers was almost always restricted to making omissions and to practising contamination. If, therefore, certain defects cannot be explained on the theory of omissions or of contamination, it would appear that they belong to the νέα. It is only

when the contrary is the case that Plautus can be suspected
of being the culprit.

I say that Plautus *can* be suspected, but not that his
guilt ought to be proclaimed at once. It would, indeed,
be quite arbitrary to credit the comic writers of the new
period with never-failing perfection. The νέα lived on—
or vegetated—for a long time; its authors wrote in various
surroundings that differed in point of refinement; it had
mediocre representatives whom Plautus occasionally did
not disdain to take as his models.[1] Doubtless the works,
even of its great poets, were not all masterpieces; before
becoming masters, in full possession of their powers, they
had been inexperienced and awkward beginners. The
majority of them wrote a great deal, which means that
they worked quickly, and were sometimes careless, especially when they wrote for the theatre of some small town.
I am quite willing to believe that Menander's 'Αδελφοὶ α'
was not so rude a thing as the *Stichus*; but I am less
inclined to admit that a Greek poet, living far away from
Athens and writing in a time of decadence, could have
produced a Καρχηδόνιος as good as the *Poenulus*, and
particularly as good as the *Poenulus* when improved by
the transposition of Acts III and IV.

The defects, which in a Latin play reveal divergences
from Greek originals, are not always the most serious
ones when regarded from the point of view of construction. While I am inclined to believe that the *Miles* is
contaminated, it is not because it has a double plot, nor
because there is no more talk, so to speak, in the second
part of the secret passage-way which is of such importance
in the first part, nor because the trick employed in the
second part was entirely superfluous, if Philocomasium
could have made her escape through the adjoining house.
Why should not a Greek poet have introduced such contradictions while fusing two tales into one? In my opinion,
such imperfections of detail as the inappropriateness of
lines 805 *et seq.*, and the clumsy wording of lines 1107

[1] For instance, Demophilus, whom Plautus imitated in the *Asinaria*.

et seq., betray the hand of the contaminator much more than do the serious defects of which I have just spoken. An original poet who attempted to handle, side by side, the two stories that are combined in the *Miles*, would certainly have avoided calling attention to the first story at the very moment when he was about to drop it in order to develop the second, and thus clumsily accentuating the lack of unity in his work. Lines 805 *et seq.* must come from a play in which the master, as well as the servant, is obliged to believe in the existence of two Philocomasiums—from a play of which the Latin poet has only retained the first half. On the other hand, it is rather improbable that so clumsy a dialogue as that contained in lines 1107 *et seq.* should have been composed in this form at first hand. *Ubi matrem esse aiebat soror?* asks Pyrgopolinices. This query in itself is curious; it will seem even more curious if we read the answer, in which Palaestrio says that he gets his information, not from Philocomasium's sister, but from the *nauclerus* who has brought her mother. Probably the reference to the sister does not come from the original text. It is Plautus who introduced it at this point, and he introduced it in order to connect the two portions of the play which he was the first to fuse into one comedy. Perusal of the *Pseudolus* suggests observations of the same kind. If Pseudolus promises more than he fulfils, if one of the two exploits that he boasts of having performed is simply conjured out of existence, this bit of sleight of hand may possibly be traced back to a Greek comedy; it may have served to characterise the fellow's impudent cleverness, or else it may have been a scheme or trick on the part of the author to whet the appetite of the audience by announcing a plot which was rich in matter.

Nor is the serious contradiction—or rather the premature agreement—between Phoenicium's letter and lines 342 *et seq.* necessarily explained by the merging of two plots. The lamentations of Simo in the last scene—excessive lamentations since he is to receive as much from Ballio as

he had given to Pseudolus—the promise Pseudolus gives
him to restore a part of the twenty minae—a promise
that cannot be fulfilled, since these twenty minae are
needed to reimburse Charinus and to satisfy the pander—
these things are possibly mere buffoonery. The sudden
disappearance of Callipho from the plot is more significant.
He comes upon the scene, not merely in order to receive
the confidence of Simo and serve him as a foil, but
Pseudolus asks for his friendly neutrality or even for his
help. Callipho grants this request, agrees to stay at home,
ready to come at a moment's notice, promises himself
much pleasure in watching the promised rascalities—then
quits the stage and is never seen or heard of again. This
cannot, by any possibility, have been the case in an
original play, in which lines 547–560 would necessarily
have been followed by something more. We must, therefore, assume that Plautus mutilated his model by putting
a sudden end to Callipho's part, or else that he constructed
the *Pseudolus* out of parts borrowed from several plays.

The reader has seen how carefully one must weigh
hypotheses about the changes to which the original plays
were subjected by the Roman imitator. In a word, it
does not suffice that these hypotheses explain certain
defects in the comedies of Plautus; they must explain
them in the most probable, or in the only probable way.
And this is a point which modern scholars have too often
failed to consider.

Furthermore, however carefully one may proceed, it is
unavoidable that personal views should have considerable
influence in reconstructing the plots of the νέα, and of all
my work this is, perhaps, the most delicate part and the
task in which there are most pitfalls. For my previous
observations will hardly serve as general principles of
procedure; in many cases I shall have to come to a
decision without deriving any aid from them. I shall,
therefore, point out, either in the text or in the notes,
the special reasons which have led to my decisions, and
the reader will be the judge.

§ 2

VIOLATIONS OF THE LAW OF FIVE ACTS
AND OF THE RULE OF THREE ACTORS

Hitherto I have only dealt with peculiarities of literary composition as possible indications of changes made in the original Greek works by Plautus or by Terence. Do not the details of dramatic structure afford other indications which might, in many instances, enable us to form a more trustworthy judgment?

Possibly, the violations of the well-known law of five acts will be the first thing to strike the reader, for the discoveries of recent years have made it more and more probable that this law holds good for New Comedy. Nevertheless, at the risk of appearing timid, I dare not as yet accept this assumption as a demonstrated truth. I propose to make the analyses of Latin comedies serve as a help in recognising and determining the external structure of the original Greek works, rather than in measuring the divergences between Plautus and Terence and their models. These analyses will be found in Chapter IV, § 1. The reader who is convinced in advance that the νέα observed the rule of five acts, may turn to them and read them at once in a spirit that will differ slightly from that in which they were written. He will see that they point out few violations of the rule, and that the majority of these violations simply mean the omission of pauses or breathing spells with which a vulgar audience would have little patience; but that they do not imply serious changes.

On the other hand, I think I ought to say at once what, in my opinion, is to be thought of that other supposed criterion which is afforded by the distribution of the parts.

The view is current among modern writers that the Greek comic poets had only three actors at their disposal;

U

and it must be admitted that, at first sight, this view seems
to rest on good evidence. In the *Poetics*, Aristotle does
not mention a definite number, but he appears at least
to state that the actors were limited in number.[1] According to a grammarian, this number was three, from
the time of Cratinus onwards, just as in tragedy. In
third-century inscriptions [2] from Delphi, the κωμῳδοί are
grouped in companies of three, to each of which must
have been entrusted the performance of a play.[3] In an
inscription from Ptolemaïs, six κωμῳδοί are enumerated
opposite two ποιηταὶ κωμῳδιῶν; and this indicates the
same distribution.[4] And, finally, Lucian, in one of his
comparisons, gives us to understand that, as a general
rule, the κωμῳδίαι contained three πρόσωπα.[5]

Now let us glance at the plays of Plautus and of Terence.
There is hardly a single one that could have been performed by only three actors. Many of them contain
scenes in which four or more actors appear and speak at
the same time, and though it sometimes happens that
some of them are mere supernumeraries whose part is
insignificant, quite as frequently all the speakers are
important actors. Later on I shall come back to these
scenes with many rôles, but even in the plays in which
there are not so many parts the distribution of the text
among three actors is, as a rule, impossible unless one
cuts up the parts in a ruthless fashion. Even if this
sorry expedient were adopted it would not overcome all
the difficulties. For example, in order to make it possible
for three actors to perform the *Hecyra*, one of them would
have to take off Parmeno's costume and put on that of
Laches or Phidippus (between lines 443 and 445); between

---

[1] Aristotle, *Poet.*, p. 1449 B., lines 4–5.

[2] I. Tzetzes, Περὶ Κωμῳδίας, § 16.

[3] Collitz, *Dialekt-Inschriften*, Nos. 2653 (of the year 272), 2564 (of the
year 271), 2565 (of the year 270), 2566 (of the year 269). Cf. Kelley Rees,
Rule of Three Actors, p. 69.

[4] Dittenberger, *Orientis graeci inscr.*, No. 51. The inscription from
Ptolemaïs belongs to the end of the reign of Philadelphus, or to the beginning of the reign of Euergetes.

[5] Lucian, *De Calumnia*, 6.

lines 497 and 516 Pamphilus would have to transform
himself into Myrrhina; between lines 613 and 623 Sostrata
would have to become Phidippus, thus calling for miracles
of quickness which must, of course, be regarded as impossible. But there is no need of lengthy demonstrations
to show that between the rule of " three actors " and the
Latin stage there is evident incompatibility.

Does this force us to the conclusion that, contrary to
what we said a little while ago, the writers of the *palliatae*
completely altered the plot and the structure of their
models?

Let us examine the extant Greek comedies. Kelley
Rees has recently pointed out all the details of construction in fifth-century plays that appear to him to call for
the simultaneous appearance of more than three actors.[1]
On consulting his lists, one will find that Aristophanes
alone supplies more examples than the three tragic writers
put together. If the State did not place more than three
actors at the disposal of the comic poets in this early
period, the latter must frequently have secured additional
actors in one way or another. Can one say that conditions changed, and that the regulations became more
stringent between the fifth century and the time of the
véa? Let us ask Menander himself, as we are now able
to do so. In the lengthy fragments of his works recently
published, there are never more than three persons speaking and acting on the stage at the same time. But it
does not follow that the Περικειρομένη or the ᾿Επιτρέποντες
could be performed by three actors. Up to line 201 of
the ᾿Επιτρέποντες Syriscus is constantly on the stage; up
to line 153 he is there with Smicrines and Daos; up to
line 159 with Daos only; beginning with line 165 with
Onesimus. If three actors had to perform the play, one
of them would have had to change his costume and his
rôle between line 153, or line 159, and line 165. After
line 398 Sophrona and Habrotonon go into the house,

---

[1] Kelley Rees, *The So-called Rule of the Three Actors in the Classical
Greek Drama* (Chicago, 1908).

and Onesimus rushes out into the street; at line 429
Charisius appears. If there were only three actors, Habrotonon or Sophrona must have doffed female attire and
put on the appearance of a young man—rather quickly,
I imagine—during the time that it took Onesimus to
speak about twenty lines. Such rapid transformations
are not any more probable in the Ἐπιτρέποντες than they
are in the *Hecyra*. But here is a case that leaves no
room for doubt; at line 352 of the Περικειρομένη Polemo
goes into his house; he is followed, after line 354, by
Doris; immediately afterwards, at line 355, Pataecus and
Glycera appear; at line 359 Polemo again appears. Can
one imagine that between lines 352 and 355 one actor
could transform himself from Polemo into Pataecus or
Glycera, and another change from Doris into Polemo,
between line 354 and line 359? Such an arrangement is
manifestly impossible. At line 359 the part of Polemo
must be played by the same actor as at line 352. Hence
it follows that there must have been a separate actor
for each of the parts of Doris, Glycera and Pataecus.
In other words, the Περικειρομένη cannot have been
performed by less than four actors.

The passages quoted a little while ago cannot prevail
against such evidence. Note that Aristotle does not say
anything definite, that the authority of the anonymous
grammarian is questionable from the very fact that he
pretends to know more about the matter than Aristotle
does, and that Lucian was a very late writer. The inscriptions from Delphi and from Ptolemaïs which are
contemporary with the νέα are certainly very awkward.
Still, they are later by twenty years or more than
Menander's death, and later than the period in which
the greater part of the plays imitated by Plautus and
Terence were written. It may be that, at the very time
when these inscriptions were made, the conditions which
they vouch for did not obtain universally. Tragedy began
without actors; when it began to have them, it first had
one, then two, and then three; that is to say, they went

on increasing in number. Comedy, on the contrary, appears to have begun by having an unlimited number of actors. If, at a given period, it had to be content with only three actors, this was probably the result of successive restrictions of none of which we know the date. May we not, then, assume that the first restriction was made at the instance of the companies of *technitae*,[1] and that it only became precise about the middle of the third century? Or, is it not conceivable that this restriction was never more than a nominal one, and that the inscriptions which mention three κωμῳδοί merely enumerate the chief actors of a comedy, but not all those who took part in its performance? I must say quite frankly that neither of the above hypotheses satisfies me entirely; but I would rather adopt one or the other of them than reject the testimony of Menander for the finest and most productive period of the *νέα*.

And now, what are we to think of the scenes in which more than three persons speak and act at the same time? They are not only contrary to the rule—which, as we have just seen, is quite hypothetical—which would have restricted the number of actors in a comedy to three, but also to another rule, formulated by Horace, probably on the authority of Greek theorists, or as a result of his own study of plays written in Greek: *nec quarta loqui persona laboret*.[2] Acron, Porphyrio and Diomedes define the meaning of this phrase precisely; when more than three persons are on the stage, the fourth, the fifth and all those in excess of the three, must remain silent, or merely speak a few words by way of acquiescing in a command.[3] Diomedes declares that this was the almost universal practice among the Greeks and, as we have seen, this is what takes place in the long fragments of Menander; but the Latins, Diomedes goes on to say, increased the number of speakers in order to make the play more attractive.

[1] Actor's Guilds.(—Tr.).   [2] Horace, *Ep. ad Pis.*, 192.
[3] Porphyr., *ad loc.*; Acr., *ad loc.*; Diom., *De poemat.*, IX. 2, p. 491 Keil (= Kaibel, p. 60).

As a matter of fact, several of Terence's scenes in which four persons take part appear to be the result of contamination. On the other hand, other scenes of the same nature, in Plautus and in Terence, are such that they certainly do not owe their origin to the practice of contamination nor to the mere wish to enliven the play by increasing the number of actors at every turn and without need, but are such that, if we were mentally to discard a single character, the essentials of the plot and the general plan of the play could no longer subsist. When, towards the end of the *Miles Gloriosus* ('Aλαζών), Philocomasium escapes from Pyrgopolinices' house, there are four persons on the stage : the fair lady and her lover, the soldier and Palaestrio. Now, could the play dispense with any one of these four ? Of course, there can be no question about Pleusicles and Philocomasium, who are the centre of the scene. But this scene would lose all its piquancy were not the sentimental and stupid Pyrgopolinices present to watch the escape of his mistress; and the rashness of the lovers would jeopardise the success of the trick were not Palaestrio—who could not have stayed in Pyrgopolinices' house after having derided him so maliciously— there to explain away their aberrations. Nor does the scene in the *Rudens* in which Gripus and Trachalio quarrel about the travelling bag in the presence of Daemones, whom they have chosen as arbiter, and where Palaestra describes its contents, admit of the elimination of an actor. At the close of the *Bacchides* each of the two fathers is inveigled by one of the courtesans; if one of the former or one of the latter were missing, this pretty scene would be impossible. In the *Phormio* the gentle Chremes, alone and unaided, would certainly not be the man to exhaust Phormio's patience and provoke the final outburst; and the scene with which the comedy ends, and in which Phormio struggles between the two old men, while Nausistrata appears at her door or at her window and hears the parasite's denunciation, must either be accepted or rejected in its entirety. One may say as

much about the majority of the scenes with many actors.
To admit that they were invented by the writers of the
palliata would amount to crediting them with a very
large share of initiative.

Is it proper to do so? Remember that Diomedes himself does not absolutely oblige us to do so; *in Graeco
dramate fere tres personae solae agunt.* In short, the scenes
in which more than three persons appear are few in Plautus
and in Terence, and we may also say of Latin comedies
that, *as a rule,* only three actors played simultaneously.
Diomedes' additional remark—*at Latini scriptores com-
plures personas in fabulas introduxerunt ut speciosiores
frequentia facerent*—may possibly have referred to only a
very few scenes, such as were the result of contamination.
But what we must have regard for, above all, is the spirit
rather than the letter of the rule formulated by Horace,
and also for the character of the scenes which at first
sight seem to be in conflict with that rule.

Why is it desirable that not more than three actors
should speak in the same scene? Because, if there be
more, there is danger that the dialogue will be confused
and difficult to follow. Picture to yourself four or five
actors, who wear masks that preclude facial expression,
conversing together and keeping up a running fire of
remarks in a vast ancient theatre open to the sky. Is
it not likely that, while watching such a performance,
a part, at least, of the audience would have been put
out, that many of the listeners would have become
confused and would not have rightly understood which
actor was speaking and to whom his words were addressed, and that, in the end, they would have lost
interest in the play? In contrast to this, picture to yourself, instead of from four or five persons engaged in the
same conversation, two groups, of one, two or three actors,
each soliloquising and conversing separately. The danger
I spoke of above will no longer exist except to a far
slighter degree. As long as the two groups are some distance apart, the audience will in each instance know from

which of the two groups the words they hear come; and as each group consists of only a very restricted number of actors, they will, without much effort, recognise by whom these words are spoken. In such a case as this, there will no longer be conversation between a considerable number of speakers, in the proper sense of the word; there will simply be a succession of soliloquies or of dialogues between two or, at most, three persons, and these soliloquies and dialogues will be quite as intelligible as though the other actors were not in sight while they are being pronounced. In other words, the important thing is not so much the number of actors as the manner in which their conversations are managed. It is conceivable that a scene with four or five persons may be clearer than a dialogue between three persons.

Hence it would be a mistake to say that a scene in Plautus or Terence violates the rule merely because it introduces more than three important characters. If one takes the trouble to examine passages that are suspected of doing so, it will soon be noticed that many of them consist of several parts in which, at most, three actors alternate in carrying on the conversation. This is notably the case in two of the scenes that I have quoted—the one in the *Rudens* and the one in the *Miles*. Only three persons share in the dialogue in the first part of these plays : Daemones, Trachalio and Gripus. Though Palaestra is at hand from the outset, and though she is very directly concerned in the matter that is being discussed in her presence, she does not breathe a word; indeed, her silence even surprises Gripus, and the author does not think it superfluous to let Trachalio make apologies for it.[1] On the other hand, the moment that Palaestra takes part in the conversation—that is to say, beginning with line 1127— Trachalio is silent. In the scene in the *Miles* the conversation takes place successively between : Palaestrio and Philocomasium (lines 1311–1313), Palaestrio and Pyrgopolinices (lines 1313–1314), Philocomasium and Pleusicles

---

[1] *Rud.*, 1113–1114.

(lines 1315–1319), Pyrgopolinices, Palaestrio and Philocomasium (lines 1320–1330), Palaestrio and Pyrgopolinices—with the exception of a few words spoken by Pleusicles—(lines 1330–1343), Pleusicles and Philocomasium (lines 1344–1345a), and between Pyrgopolinices and Palaestrio (from line 1346 onwards). In no part of this scene do all four actors take part at the same time. Many a scene in Latin comedy is constructed like that in the *Rudens*, or like that in the *Miles*. In fact, more than three actors rarely take an actual part in the dialogue, and, even where they do, the exchange of remarks is sometimes conducted in a manner that precludes all confusion. Confusing dialogues, which might appear to violate Horace's rule, are very few and far between. Neither in number nor in importance do they go beyond what the Greek poets—if, as I believe, they had more than three actors at their disposal—could and must have permitted themselves.

So we arrive at a negative conclusion. The number of actors who speak and act in the course of one and the same scene does not itself enable us to determine whether that scene comes from the original play.

CHAPTER II

INTERNAL STRUCTURE OF THE COMEDIES
THE PLOT OR ACTION

BROADLY speaking, a comedy of the new period represents a movement or action—that is to say, a change from one situation—usually precarious, and impatiently supported by one of the characters, to another which is stable and definite. Once the initial situation is made plain to the audience, all, or nearly all, parts of the work contribute to the realisation of this change, and once it is completed, the play is ended. This arrangement is, of course, not peculiar to the works of New Comedy; we meet with it in most dramatic works of whatever kind, ancient as well as modern. But it is worth while to point out that it seems to have been more constant and more strictly adhered to by comic writers after the time of Alexander than it was by their predecessors.

§ 1

STRUCTURE OF THE PLOT—DIGRESSIONS

It is well known how small a part the plot plays and how little it amounts to in several of Aristophanes' comedies. Let us consider the *Acharnians*. At line 720 Dicaeopolis has succeeded in passing from the tribulations of war to the blessings of peace, and the plot is at an end. For all that, the play runs on for more than five hundred lines. And of what does this entire latter part consist? Of independent scenes which have no other connecting link than the continued presence of the principal actor, and which illustrate, in so many pictures, the result of the change that has come about. The *Peace* and the latest of the poet's works, the *Plutus*, which was written in 388, are constructed on an analogous plan. So we see that to the end of his days Aristophanes wrote comedies that were not wholly given up to the development of a plot,

298

and we may assume that his contemporaries had no scruples about doing likewise. In the fourth century the generation of Antiphanes, of Anaxandrides and of Eubulus must have retained something of this loose method. One of Lucian's Dialogues, *Timon or the Misanthropist*, is supposed to be an imitation of Antiphanes' Τίμων. If this is true, the structure of that play must have been similar to that of the *Acharnians*, of the *Peace* and of the *Plutus*. The change in the hero's fortunes, which constituted the plot, was effected long before the end of the play, and just as people of all kinds—parasites, flatterers, sycophants and philosophers—passed in review before Dicaeopolis, Trygaeus or Chremylus, each of them affording occasion for a scene, so they pass before the misanthropist who has once more become wealthy. It will be remembered that many a comedy of the middle period had a proper name, the name of a politician, of a man-about-town, or of a courtesan as its title. More than one comedy may have been made up of "interludes" or episodes that were very slightly connected, and which, like the *Heracleides* or the *Theseides* at which Aristotle scoffs,[1] may have had no other unity than that afforded by the hero.

Apparently, this is no longer the case from Alexander's time onwards. Of all Plautus' or Terence's plays, only one, the *Stichus*, runs on considerably beyond the end of the plot, which, in this case, is indicated by the return of the two brothers from their journey and their restoration to the good graces of old Antipho. On the other hand, the *Casina* stops short before the expected solution of the plot. In the *Truculentus* our attention is directed, in turn, to various questions, some of which are not answered. But, in each instance, these anomalies must be laid at the door of the Latin author, who was either an unscrupulous abridger or a ruthless contaminator. So we cannot cite any one of these three plays in refutation of the testimony given by other much more numerous plays, in which the plot constitutes, as it were, the framework and the

[1] Aristotle, *Poet.*, VIII. p. 1451 A, lines 19 et seq.

scaffolding of the composition.   True, the plays imitated
by Plautus and Terence represent but a very small part of
the entire literature of the *νέα*, but the unanimous testimony of more than twenty plays by various authors and
of various dates is, for all that, important.   Moreover,
it appears to be corroborated by such knowledge as we
have or such surmises as we can make about some of the
original works : the *'Επιτρέποντες*, the *"Ηρως*, the *Σαμία*,
the *Γεωργός*, the *Περικειρομένη*, the *Φάσμα*, the *Πλόκιον*,
etc.   On the other hand, while we have so many well-
constructed plays, we cannot cite a single example of
loose construction.   Comedies having the name of an
individual as their title—and they are the ones that are
especially suspected of having been *pièces* " *à tiroirs* "[1]—
were, as we know, less frequent after the time of Alexander than they had been previously.   As for the plays
that may have been chiefly devoted to the portrayal of
a character or of a type, the *Aulularia* affords sufficient
proof that they did not necessarily lack a sustained plot.

This is not to be understood as meaning that the *νέα*
proscribed all digressions.   From time to time it admitted
them, and we must explain their nature.

In the first place, I must point out the unpopularity
of two kinds of composition which seem to have been in
high favour in the preceding period.

Many fragments of the *μέση*, and, among others, several
of the lengthiest and most refreshing of them, affect the
descriptive form.   For example, they describe the prowess
of a gourmand, the wiles of a coquette, the impertinence
of a fishmonger.   These passages suggest the idea of a
comedy in which there was more conversation than
action; their form and their tone are satirical rather than
dramatic.   In the extant works of the *νέα* such passages
as these are rare.   In Plautus I might point out, as being
of a somewhat similar style, Megadorus' diatribe against

---

[1] A piece with loosely connected episodes very much like a modern
" revue."(—Tr.).

the extravagances of women,[1] Periplecomenus' remarks
about the disadvantages of marriage and of having a
family,[2] and Lysiteles' arraignment of love;[3] and that is
about all.

Another observation which I think I ought to make
has reference to banqueting scenes. While they occur in
both periods they were not dealt with in the same way.
As far as we can see, the μέση made a point of describing
them, and it devoted itself to this task with minute care.
With the advent of the νέα this form of treatment, which
is better suited for a mime than for comedy, is no longer
so much in fashion. In the comedies of Plautus and of
Terence, with the exception of the *Persa*, which goes back
to the middle period, only two banquets take place upon
the stage or are described for their own sake : one at the
close of the *Pseudolus*, in a passage which competent
critics regard as a piece of original work by Plautus; the
other at the close of the *Stichus*—that is to say, in a contaminated play, copied from an unknown model, which
may have belonged to the μέση. Wherever else it occurs,
the banquet merely supplies a background, which serves as
a frame for something more interesting and helps to place
it in relief : in the *Mostellaria* it is the case of a dissipated
son who is disturbed by the unexpected return of his
father; in the *Asinaria* it is the infidelity of an aged
husband; in the *Eunuchus*, the brutality of a soldier; in
the *Bacchides*, the anguish of an old man who thinks
that his son is guilty of adultery and that a most humiliating punishment awaits him; and so on. In all these
instances the plot, even in the midst of orgies, moves on
towards its culmination.

What most frequently diverts the writers of New Comedy
from the plot is the desire to give a clear picture of the
character and morals of their *dramatis personae*. Apparently they did not think that the incidents of the plot in
themselves always sufficed for this purpose. They were
willing to devote one or several special scenes to it—either

[1] *Aul.*, 505 et seq.   [2] *Miles*, 685 et seq.   [3] *Trin.*, 237 et seq.

a soliloquy in which the actor describes himself and, as
it were, makes a confession of faith, or a conversation in
which he shows what kind of man he is, or else an arraignment of his misdeeds. These passages, in so far as they
are concerned with the chief characters of the play, ought
probably not to be regarded as digressions at all. Though
they do not further the plot, they at any rate secure for
it an appearance of reality by displaying before our eyes
in a separate setting and in a vivid light some of the
motives which it brings into play. Or else these scenes
dispose the audience to take a greater interest in the
play by making one or the other of its characters
sympathetic or the contrary. But it is not only of the
chief actors that the poet endeavours to give us a clear
picture; occasionally mere supernumeraries monopolise
our attention for a while. The interminable confidences
of Periplecomenus, in the *Miles*, are manifestly out of
proportion to the very insignificant part that he plays.
So is the bluster of the cook and of Antamoenides in the
Pseudolus and in the *Poenulus*, in which they are mere
episodical figures. This is also true of the gossip of
Ergasilus, in the *Captivi*, whose only business is to bring
a bit of news; of Peniculus, in the *Menaechmi*, who merely
denounces Menaechmus to his wife, and of Gelasimus, in
the *Stichus*, who does nothing at all. Of course, retouching
by Latin imitators, additions and contaminations may
occasionally have impaired the relations in which characters of this kind stood to the plot, but these digressions
must more frequently be imputed to the original Greek
poet. As far as parasites and cooks are concerned, there
is no denying the fact that the νέα took undue delight in
portraying them. Cooks can never have had more than
a slight influence on the development of the plot, while
parasites occasionally, but only in exceptional cases, had
a greater influence. Yet a glance at the collected fragments is enough to show how much space, in the plays
as a whole, is allotted to the speeches of these two classes.

Parasites and cooks are people who provoke laughter.

Hence their popularity, hence the frequent side episodes for which they provide an opportunity; and we must forgive the comic poets if they sometimes made undue sacrifices to the desire to amuse. In Menander's Ἐπι- τρέποντες, the comedy of which we have the most know- ledge, an episode which is, no doubt, in better taste than the jests of a cook, though it is of just as little use to the plot, occupies more than one hundred and fifty lines out of a total that cannot have exceeded a thousand— the great trial scene from which the play derives its title. What, as a matter of fact, is the dramatic problem which constitutes the plot of the Ἐπιτρέποντες? It hinges on the question whether the misunderstanding between Charisius and his wife is to be happily ended. For this purpose it is, of course, necessary that the ring, on which the solution depends, should be seen by Onesimus. But the question would have been exactly the same if, instead of being the subject of a quarrel, both the ring and the child had been found at once by Syriscus. By creating the part of Daos and by inventing the episode of the arbitration, Menander lost time in superfluous prelimi- naries, and thus affords another instance where the taste for ἠθοποιία[1] outweighed the author's care for the construction of the play.

Notwithstanding these shortcomings, we may say that, during the fourth century, and especially towards its close, comedy became more orderly and accepted with increasing docility the discipline exacted by the plot. We can still trace quite clearly the influences that made for this progress.

One of these acted from afar—namely, the influence of tragedy. A hundred years before Alexander and Menander the writers of Attic tragedy wrote only such plays as were a complete representation of a crisis or of a change of fortune, and contained a complication and a solution. It was natural that comedy, as the younger sister, should

---

[1] Representation of character.(—Tr.).

imitate the elder, and during the middle period its authors got into the habit of doing so through parodying a great number of tragic works; for it was, in all likelihood, not only their style and a few of their isolated episodes that were thus parodied, but some plays in their entirety must have been subjected to this treatment, their plots being followed step by step. In the course of the succeeding chapters I shall repeatedly have occasion to point out that the works of the νέα employed the same motives or adopted the same general arrangement as did the dramas of Euripides, and these similarities of detail will corroborate what I have just said in general terms about the influence of the tragic drama.

A second influence to which attention must be called— a more direct and immediate influence—is that which was doubtless exercised by the theories of Aristotle. We know how preponderating an importance the author of the *Poetics* attaches to the plot in tragedy : " The most important part of tragedy is the combination of incidents (ἡ τῶν πραγμάτων σύστασις). . . . Without a plot there could be no tragedy; without *dramatis personae* there could be one. . . . The plot is, therefore, the chief thing, and, as it were, the soul of tragedy; the *dramatis personae* occupy only a secondary place." [1] In Book I of the *Poetics*, the only book that has come down to us, these remarks apply to tragedy, but there is reason to believe that in Book II they applied to the other great order of drama as well. To the mind of the famous theorist whose doctrines were spread by Theophrastus, comedy was bound, above all, to be the *imitation of action*, and the poets of the new period did not fail to heed this advice.

§ 2

SIMPLICITY OR INTRICACY OF THE PLOT

In several of Plautus' comedies the plot is remarkably simple. A single problem is presented and clearly set

---

[1] Aristotle, *Poet.*, VI. p. 1450 A, lines 15, 23–25, 33–35, 38–39.

forth in the very first scenes, and undergoes neither change
nor complication in the course of the play. This problem
is solved at a single stroke, and if, towards the end, the
results obtained are occasionally in danger of being called
in question, the suspense is of short duration, and some
providential occurrence promptly corroborates them. Let
us examine the *Curculio*. At the very outset the embarrassing situation in which Phaedromus finds himself
is apparent; the scheme which Curculio conceives to
rescue him from it succeeds without hindrance; the
retroactive danger, if I may so call it, which appears to
be on the point of arising out of the sudden appearance
of the soldier, is promptly removed by an opportune
recognition. From beginning to end the plot moves on
continuously and in a straight line. But possibly this
is not a good example, for it has been surmised that in
the *Curculio* Plautus mutilated the original work which
had served as his model. Let us, therefore, rather
examine the *Asinaria*, the *Captivi*, the *Epidicus*, the
Pseudolus and the *Trinummus*, in which the original plot
of the plays has not undergone serious curtailment. The
simplicity of their plan is quite as great. Occasionally
the plot is made even simpler in certain points. Thus,
at the close of the *Pseudolus*, when Harpax and Ballio
discover that the slave has deceived them, neither the
slave nor his young master, Calidorus, need have any
fear of retaliation; precautions are taken to secure for
them the fruits of their success. In the *Trinummus*,
the trick which Callicles and Megaronides plan is discovered even before it is carried out, and the same occurrence that, by revealing it, precludes its being carried out—
the sudden return of Charmides—also makes it superfluous. In other words, of the three periods into which
the action is subdivided in the *Curculio*, the first is here
suppressed and the second and third are merged into one.

Such, then, are the most rudimentary plots. In order
to produce more complex and more ingenious ones the
poets make use of various methods.

x

The first of these consists in not presenting, at the outset, all the difficulties of the problem that is to be solved, but in showing, in successive scenes, how it grows more delicate and acute. In the *Eunuchus* Phaedria has at first only to fear the rivalry of Thraso; after his brother's crime he has also to fear the anger of Thais, and after Parmeno's confession, the bad humour of his father. In the Γεωργός a father's matrimonial plans form the only difficulty that at first stands in the way of the lovers getting married; subsequently the attitude of Cleaenetus seriously increases his nephew's embarrassment. Similarly, in the *Aulularia*, the attitude of Megadorus increases the perplexity of his nephew. In the Ἐπιτρέποντες the discovery of the supposed bastard furnishes Smicrines with new weapons with which to oppose his son-in-law, and to urge his daughter to leave her libertine husband. In the *Hecyra* it is only after Pamphilus appears upon the stage that we become acquainted with the complete shipwreck of his married life, and discover what are the obstacles that almost preclude the re-establishment of intimate relations between him and his wife. As these few examples show, the manner in which the problem becomes complicated is not always identical. Sometimes the new difficulties which develop in addition to those already existing have an origin of their own : for instance, the conduct of the young Cleaenetus is in no way determined by the plans of his father. Sometimes, again, the new difficulties arise from the earlier ones, or else they are due to a conflict that had already begun : in the *Eunuchus* it is the present made to Thais as an offset to Thraso's generosity that suggests to Chaerea the idea of his questionable trick, and affords him the means of carrying it out. This last kind of plot, in which the germ of some change (περιπέτεια) is contained in the opening situation, will, no doubt, be regarded as the most perfect of all. Incidentally it should be remarked that, in several instances, the episode which gives rise to a reawakening of suspense appears in the form of a fortunate occurrence.

Might it not be a piece of good fortune for penniless girls, like the daughter of Euclio or the daughter of Myrrhina, to be sought after by men in comfortable circumstances, even though the latter are no longer quite young? Do not Sostrata and Parmeno, in the *Hecyra*, does not the audience itself, hope that the arrival of Pamphilus will put an end to all disagreements? That sort of irony of fate which changes good into evil and upsets reasonable expectations, manifests itself in an especially striking manner in certain episodes in tragedy —one need only recall the unforeseen part which the messenger from Corinth plays in the *Oedipus Tyrannus*. Perhaps, therefore, the comic poets borrowed this idea from tragedy.

In the works of the νέα the solution of a problem gives occasion for a series of episodes quite as often as does the setting forth of the problem. There are cases where several attempts to solve it fail completely before one succeeds, or else where it cannot be solved at one stroke. In order to thwart her husband's intentions regarding Casina, Myrrhina first resorts to prayer, then to drawing lots, and then tries to make trouble between Lysidamus and his accomplice Alcesimus, and to scare him with the sham raving of the young girl. None of these attempts succeeds; finally, a last expedient, the dressing-up of the slave, results in her victory. Syrus, in the *Heauton Timoroumenos*, and Chrysalus, in the *Bacchides*, make use of several tricks in succession in order to obtain money. In the *Aulularia* Euclio imagines that his precious pot is the object of a series of constantly renewed attacks. In the *Menaechmi* it is only after many mistakes that the identity of each of the two brothers is established. In the Σαμία [1] Demeas' peace of mind is disturbed and the happy consummation of his son's projected marriage with his neighbour's daughter is thwarted, first by the mistake

---

[1] To be more exact, "in the extant portions of the Σαμία." There must originally have been a series of episodes which resulted in the marriage of Moschio and Plangon being decided upon.

Demeas makes regarding the parentage of the child, then by Niceratus' angry outburst, and a third time by Moschio's unexpected caprice. In the *Rudens* Palaestra escapes disaster in three stages, if I may so express it. First she is rescued from shipwreck, then from slavery, and finally she is restored to her parents. And so on.

This method of developing a plot by reiteration was sometimes practised without much skill. In the *Casina*, for example, the various episodes are merely placed next to one another. Other plays give us a more favourable idea of the comic poets' skill. Though the anger of Niceratus and the whims of Moschio, in the *Σαμία*, have nothing to do with one another, still both are called forth by Demeas' mistake and by the scandal he raised by driving away Chrysis. In the *Menaechmi* the series of adventures in which Menaechmus of Syracuse is taken for his brother have a logical connection, and each of them calls for the ensuing one; the matron's importunity is occasioned by Erotium's amiability, and it results first in the interference of the old man, and then in that of the doctor. In the *Aulularia* Megadorus asks for the hand of Phaedria, and Euclio regards this as the first menace to his treasure-trove. This offer of marriage is the occasion for the invasion of the cooks into the old man's house; and this invasion, in turn, results in the theft of the treasure. In the *Bacchides* Chrysalus is not discouraged by the failure of his first attempt on Nicobulus' purse, and makes a second and more successful assault. On the other hand, in the *Andria*, Davus' temporary success, far from removing the danger, only makes it more immediate.

The heaping-up of obstacles and of devices for overcoming them in a play does not keep our interest from being concentrated on a single problem—most frequently a kind of contest between two adversaries or between two groups of adversaries. But another method of enriching the plot is to multiply the objects of interest it contains.

The poets who adopted this method are sometimes content to show us in several scattered scenes the indirect results of the main story in the lives of some of the characters : Smicrines, in the Ἐπιτρέποντες, storming at the cook, at Sophrona, at Onesimus, at every one who comes near him; or Phidippus and Laches, in the Hecyra, quarrelling with their wives; or Lysimachus, in the Mercator, being suspected of adultery by his wife; or Gripus, in the Rudens, dreaming of a fine future, and quarrelling about his booty with Trachalio, Daemones and Labrax; and so on. These are digressions of a kind that, for a moment, divert our attention from the plot itself without, however, permitting us to lose sight of it—digressions with which no fault can be found provided they do not occur too late in the play, or awkwardly prolong it beyond its real conclusion, as is the case in the Rudens. In other plays we find a complete second plot running side by side with the main one. Many Latin plays of the class that Terence calls fabulae duplices [1] follow Greek models in bringing two love affairs upon the stage simultaneously, each of which claims its share of the spectator's interest. In the Aulularia we are not only interested to know whether Lyconides is going to marry Phaedrium, but also whether Euclio is going to keep his hoard. In the Φάσμα the honour of a married woman is at stake, quite as much as the marriage of two young people; in the Πλόκιον the domestic authority of a shrew is involved. In the Περικειρομένη the reconciliation of Polemo and Glycera, no doubt, appeared as only one of the objects aimed at in the plot; the other was the recognition of Moschio, who was in danger of involving himself and his supposed mother in a most unfortunate situation.

Such double plots as these involve a twofold danger. There is a danger that one of the two issues dealt with before the audience may appear stale and insignificant in comparison with the other, or else that both may be so slightly related as to destroy the unity of the play. This

[1] Heaut., prol. 6.

twofold difficulty is avoided in most of the plays of which we have knowledge. An examination of the Latin comedies in which two love affairs occur shows that, in almost every instance, there is an evident connection between them. It is only in the *Phormio* that the adventures of the two cousins, Antipho and Phaedria, run parallel and without influence upon one another for too long a time. Nor does it often happen that one of the two lovers becomes a matter of indifference to the spectator. This is, indeed, the case with Charinus, in the *Andria*; but perhaps Terence is to blame for it. In the *Adelphi*, the *Heauton Timoroumenos* and the *Phormio*, what follows after Aeschinus, Clinia and Antipho once get over their troubles would, no doubt, be rather dull if the outcome of the love affairs of Ctesipho, of Clitipho and of Phaedria were the only matters involved; but, as often happens when a consummate rascal fills the scene with his tricks, we become interested in them for their own sake and independently of the object they have in view. Will Syrus, in the *Adelphi*, succeed in deceiving Demea to the very end? Will Syrus, in the *Heauton Timoroumenos*, succeed in making a fool of Chremes? Will Phormio win his fight against Demipho? These questions continue to present themselves even after the young lover in each play has attained the object of his desires. I must add that two of these three plays—the *Adelphi* and the *Heauton Timoroumenos*—contain a moral problem in addition to the dramatic problem involved in the plot, and that for its solution we are obliged to wait until the very last scenes; hence there is no fear of our attention becoming slack before the end. In the *Aulularia* the story of the pot and that of the marriage of Phaedrium are interrelated as closely as possible; it was with a view to this marriage that a god had brought about the discovery of the pot; one and the same occurrence, the step taken by Megadorus, puts an end to the anxiety of Lyconides and redoubles Euclio's fears; the slave who steals the treasure is an emissary of the lover, sent by him to spy on his rival; and, finally, it is, in all likelihood, at the request of his future son-in-law, and in order to give his daughter a dowry, that Euclio parts with his money. In Plautus' play Lyconides comes upon the scene very late, and we have but slight sympathy with his anxiety because we have not been informed of it in advance, but it is not at all certain that this fault was so noticeable in the Greek poet's play; some remarks of the young man, placed at the opening of the play, may have served to take the public into his confidence and secured their sympathy. In the Περικει-ρομένη the fact that Glycera takes refuge in the house of the matron who lives next door—an episode of her quarrel with Polemo—gives rise to the twofold ἀναγνώρισις. As for the Φάσμα and the Πλόκιον, we do not know how they were constructed. But we do know that, in the Φάσμα, the very precautions which the mother takes, when visiting her daughter in her hiding-place, prepared the way for the first meeting of the lovers. From a line in fragment 403 of the Πλόκιον it appears that fear of Corbyle's anger, which is so acute in her husband's case, did not affect him alone; this fear must have explained the subterfuges of the lover, and the hesitation about making good his fault.

In short, there is abundant evidence that certain comic writers of the new period possessed a remarkable gift of combination. Is it a mere matter of chance that most of the well-constructed plays of which we know come from the pen of Menander? I may here aptly quote an anecdote that was current about the great poet in antiquity. Plutarch relates that some one once said to Menander : " How is this, Menander? The Dionysia are approaching and your comedy is not written ! " " My comedy is written," he replied. " I have settled the plan; I have only the lines to write." [1]

---

[1] Plut., De glor. Athen., III. 4.

§ 3

THE MAINSPRINGS OF THE ACTION

We have found that there was a dramatic action in all the works of New Comedy; we have studied the greater or less intricacy of this action; now we must examine the mainsprings which move it.

One of these mainsprings is chance—a clumsy device, the use of which, without very careful adjustment, shocks even the least sensitive spectator. Let us, first of all, see what use our poets made of it.

While analysing the episodes of the extant comedies one must be struck by the large number of curious coincidences that are common to all of them. In the Ἥρως it is by a mere chance that Myrrhina becomes the wife of the man who had ravished her without even knowing her. There is the same fortunate coincidence in the Cistellaria, in the Hecyra and in the Ἐπιτρέποντες; it is likewise by chance that in the last of these plays Charisius takes as his mistress the only person who can clear up the mystery which baffles him, and who can thus get him out of trouble. Again, it is by chance that Antipho, in the Phormio, had already married the very girl who had been chosen for him, and that in other plays so many young men fell in love with women who turn out to be very proper matches. A friendly chance brings Tyndarus to the house of Hegio, Palaestrio to the house of Pyrgopolinices, and Pyrgopolinices to the dwelling of Periplecomenus, the devoted friend of his rival Pleusicles, and lands Palaestra within a step of her parents' house. And so on.

A good number of happy chances, no doubt! But it should be noted that, for the most part, these coincidences are not divulged before the end of the play. In this respect the Miles, in which one may wonder at the extent to which fortune favours the interests of Pleusicles (from the prologue onwards), and the Curculio, in which Curculio would not have been able to do anything had he not met Phaedromus' rival before the opening of the play, are exceptions. As a rule, chance only intervenes to extricate the actors from situations that are sometimes desperate, after the former have throughout the play displayed qualities of real energy and intelligence. It then rewards their ingenuity, their persistence and their shrewdness, and the audience is glad to applaud.

There is another extenuating circumstance. When, in one of the last scenes of the *Andria,* Crito of Andros appears just in time to avert an impending catastrophe, his arrival, unannounced and unexpected, is a real dramatic hit; here we have chance in all its brutality, if I may so express myself. But apparently the comic poets did not often introduce such surprises. Ordinarily the happy coincidence follows upon a very natural chain of events. In the 'Ἐπιτρέποντες, for example, the truth is revealed as soon as Sophrona and Habrotonon meet; as chance has made Habrotonon the official and avowed mistress of Charisius, it is almost inevitable that some time or another she should meet Sophrona, the slave and confidante of his legitimate wife. In the *Hecyra* it is the meeting of Bacchis and Philumena that brings about the recognition; but there is nothing fortuitous about this meeting; it is arranged most judiciously by Philumena's father-in-law himself. In the Περικειρομένη it was probably while examining Glycera's gowns that Pataecus was led to suspect that she might be his daughter; we know that this examination was made at the request of Polemo, who was anxious to prove to his old friend how much he spoiled his mistress. And so on. Clearly, although the solutions of comic poets owe much to chance, they are none the less brought about by means of human intelligence. In a fragment of the Ποίησις Antiphanes ironically envies writers of tragedy for the device of the *deus ex machina*; [1] and his successors in the new period reserved the right to do the same.

Hitherto we have only seen chance behind the scenes;

_____
[1] Antiphanes, fr. 191, 13–16.

it prepared matters in advance, and then allowed the
actors to play their parts without any indiscreet interference of its own. There are other cases where chance
ventures on the stage and acts under the very eyes of
the audience; but were we to collect the known instances
of this sort of interference we should find that they are
not numerous. Only in two plays—the *Rudens* and the
Menaechmi—are the actors, almost from beginning to end,
the sport of a waggish fortune, or, what is practically the
same thing, of supernatural will; and these two cases
count for little when compared with so many other comedies in which the machinations of a crafty slave constitute
the essential part of the plot. In the Ἐπιτρέποντες the
plot would not get under way did not Onesimus—by
chance—see the ring which his master had lost, in the
hands of Syriscus, and did not Habrotonon—by chance—
overhear the conversation of the two men. Occurring, as
it does, at the opening of the play, this coincidence calls
for practically no criticism; there is no occasion to say
that without it the actors would be in a quandary, for
without it they would be doing nothing. It does not look
like an expedient, or seem improbable; it is a dramatic
starting-point for the action, and as such is quite as
acceptable as any other. There is more room for criticism
when chance plays a part after the plot is once under
way. When, in the *Pseudolus*, Harpax comes on the
scene, Pseudolus does, it is true, pretend to have worked
out a plan which he only gives up when he sees a prospect
of succeeding by other means.[1] But there is no indication
of what that plan was, and I have a strong suspicion that
the poet himself never knew anything about it; which
amounts to saying that Pseudolus would have been very
much embarrassed had not fortune at the proper moment
enabled him to make a dupe of Harpax. The case is
similar in the *Asinaria*; here Libanus and his companion
Leonidas have not yet hit upon any plan to obtain the
twenty minae which they are expected to pay, when the

[1] *Pseud.*, 601–602, 675 et seq.

donkey dealer's appearance upon the scene affords them
an unexpected windfall. In lines 249 *et seq.* Libanus
frankly admits this. A thorough examination of the
plays might add several other instances to these well-
defined ones. Would not Syrus, in the *Heauton Timoroumenos*, have been completely at a loss but for the recognition of Antiphila? Do not the soldier Cleomachus (lines
842 *et seq.* of the *Bacchides*) and Chremes (lines 732 *et seq.*
of the *Andria*) come upon the scene too much in the nick
of time? At first sight they might appear to do so, but,
as a matter of fact, the unexpected event in these scenes
only brings success nearer, and, even if it contributes to
it, it is merely because a shrewd mind knows how to
profit by it at the given moment.

Starting the action and bringing it to an end—that is
all, or about all, that the interference of chance amounts
to in the νέα. That is to say, it can easily be put up
with, and the ancient audiences must have borne with it
all the more readily because, in their day, Fortune was
commonly regarded as the supreme arbiter of human
affairs. In some of the fragments of the Ὑποβολιμαῖος
and of the Τίτθη,[1] Menander himself clearly formulates
this belief.

More objectionable than the part which Fortune takes
in the action of the play are the psychological improbabilities at the cost of which certain characters are enabled
to assist its progress.

Let me say, however, at once that of this there are
but few instances in the chief fragments of Menander.
Several actors in the Σαμία behave, no doubt, in a somewhat paradoxical manner. But although their performances are too jerky, though their changes of attitude
surprise and disconcert us, yet it cannot be said that
they are unnatural, and I have already expressed my
views on this point.[2] In the Ἐπιτρέποντες the opening
situation will hardly stand the test of analysis. Charisius

---

[1] Men., fr. 460, 482, 483.   [2] Cf. p. 242 et seq.

knows perfectly well what he did at the time of the Tauropolia; Pamphila knows perfectly well what happened to
her at the time; adventures like that which brought them
into contact with one another cannot have taken place
by the dozen at one and the same nocturnal festival.
Therefore, were Charisius to ask his wife for information—
and why should he not do so, as he still feels affection for
her?—the truth would soon be revealed. In order, however, to construct his play, Menander lets Charisius and
Pamphila hold their peace contrary to all probability.
On the other hand, the behaviour of all the other actors
throughout the play is quite natural. Can it be said that
Syriscus is unreasonably obliging when he trusts Onesimus
with the precious ring, that Onesimus is rather too ready
to tell Syriscus and Habrotonon about his master's affairs,
that Habrotonon displays excessive eagerness to interfere
in matters that do not concern her? In acting as they
do they are all swayed by their own interests or by their
personal inclination. Syriscus is a worthy man who,
being honest himself, readily believes that others are
honest; he has a keen sense of justice; Onesimus—the
slave of some one closely connected with his master—
assures him that the ring was lost by Charisius; Syriscus
does not wish to stand in the way of its being duly restored
to its rightful owner; his trust, moreover, is not blind
trust, and when the time comes for him to reclaim the
ring he does so.[1] Onesimus himself admits that his
tongue is always wagging;[2] like Parmeno, in the *Hecyra*,
he is fond of gossiping, and this fault, which may account
for his attitude in the opening dialogue, also explains his
telling Syriscus what bothers him. As for Habrotonon,
who is a sly puss, it is, above all, her hope of becoming
free that leads her to put herself forward.[3] Would any
courtesan-slave who knew what she knew, and who had
a reasonable amount of cleverness, have done less in her
place? Yet, notwithstanding her cleverness, Habrotonon

---

[1] 'Επιτρ., 226 et seq.   [2] *Ibid.*, 205–206, 357 et seq.
[3] *Ibid.*, 321 et seq., 340 et seq.

would not have been able to make Charisius speak had he wanted to keep his secret. But Charisius is drunk and has cast prudence aside; all he needs is a little urging to confess his misdeeds.[1]

In the longest original fragments the relations between actors and plot and the influence of the former on the latter are always, or almost always, quite natural, when viewed from a psychological point of view. But all the poets of the new period were, of course, not as good as Menander, and Menander himself had his faults. There are improbabilities enough in Latin comedies—in Terence's as well as in Plautus'—and the majority of them must have existed in the Greek models. I shall mention a few of these improbabilities of various kinds.

Occasionally the devices and tricks conceived by the actors have no *raison d'être*, or else there is no possibility of their resulting in any good. What purpose can Tranio's deceit serve in the *Mostellaria*? Merely to put off the discovery of his crimes and of Philolaches' misdeeds for a few moments or, at the most, for a few hours. If it be objected that during this short space of time Callidamates, the *alter ego* of Philolaches, had time to become sober, and so, together with other friends, manages to pacify Theopropides by promising that he will not have to defray his son's expenses, it must be said that this intervention to bring about peace might just as properly have taken place after an interview between father and son, and after a first outburst of anger on the part of Theopropides. There is danger that Tranio's lies, which Philolaches certainly abets in so far as he tolerates them, may increase the old man's resentment; they are, therefore, useless lies, the lies of a virtuoso, which no one in real life would permit himself to utter. In the *Andria* it is Simo who through sheer cheerfulness of heart complicates a simple situation. He has found out that his son is in love with Glycerium; instead of reproaching him for this directly, he pretends that Chremes, one of his old friends,

---

[1] Ἐπιτρ., 303–306.

whose daughter Pamphilus was at one time to have married, again agrees to let him have her, and without further ado tells the young lover that he must marry that very day. A curious expedient! In his reply to Sosia, who is surprised at this turn of events, he makes an effort to explain it—

" If," says he, " Pamphilus' passion makes him refuse to marry her, that will give me an opportunity to reprimand him, and now I am trying by means of this suggested marriage to find a legitimate cause for scolding him if he refuses his assent. At the same time, I want that scoundrel of a Davus, if he has any scheme up his sleeve, to exhaust his devilries now while they cannot harm us." [1]

But of the two reasons he alleges, the former amounts to nothing, for Simo would have quite as much right to scold if he obtained a negative response when asking his son : " Will you leave your mistress and marry? " As for the second reason, it is not worth much more than the first : Simo does Davus great honour by dreading his interference so much; he does him injustice in thinking that he would not interfere more than once. In the *Heauton Timoroumenos* it seems as though there were little left for Syrus to do after Antiphila has been recognised. It is only necessary for him to make Chremes hand out the ten minae about which he has spoken to him, under the pretext that they would serve to release his daughter, and to give this money to Bacchis and dismiss her, pretending that Clinia is leaving her with a view to getting married, and thus, with little effort, protect the interests of all his employers. But rather than follow so simple a course our man devises new schemes in which his accomplices finally get entangled. True, his discomfiture is part of the author's plan. It might, however, have been brought about in another way—namely, by an inopportune outburst of joy on the part of Clinia or by an impatient outbreak on the part of Bacchis. So, here again, it is the poet who, in the person of one of his actors, is over-elaborate in his trickery. Apparently he

[1] *Andr.*, 155 et seq.

knew that in doing so he fell in with the taste of his audience. A clever piece of trickery always had the merit of interesting the Greeks; in the days of New Comedy the spectators no doubt followed the machinations of a Davus or of a Chrysalus with quite as much pleasure as their ancestors had felt in the old days in following those of an Odysseus or of a Sinon, those heroic liars of whom one of our rascals legitimately proclaims himself the heir.[1]

At times, then, the actors in the *véa* are extravagant in their activity and cunning. At other times, on the contrary, they carry their inactivity or their stupidity to excess. The extreme credulity of Pyrgopolinices, who is blinded by self-conceit, fits into the spirit of his part. The ingenuousness of Sceledrus, in admitting the existence of the twin sisters without thinking of confronting them with one another, and the trustfulness of Harpax, in unhesitatingly and for no known reason placing the letter which establishes his credit in the hands of a stranger, are at best conceivable in inferior slaves. But there are other actors who, without having any moral or social excuse, really display a degree of credulity that is unnatural : for instance, Hegio in the *Captivi* and Nicobulus in the *Bacchides*—not to mention Dordalus, a character of the middle period. Hegio does not hesitate for a moment to believe what his two prisoners, Tyndarus and Philocrates, tell him. He takes their word for it that one of them— the one who pretends to be Philocrates and is really Tyndarus—is the son of a rich citizen of Elis. Before receiving any information about the identity of the other prisoner, who pretends to be Tyndarus and really is Philocrates, he sets him free. Similarly Nicobulus, at the critical moment of the *Bacchides*, fails to use the most ordinary precautions. That he should have believed in the story about the robbers which Chrysalus tells in the first part of the play is conceivable, but what follows is not so easy to understand. Chrysalus, whose trick has been discovered, plans another deception. He tells the

[1] *Bacch.*, 949.

old man that his son Mnesilochus has compromised himself
with a married woman, and that, in order to save himself,
he must pay damages to the soldier Cleomachus, the
supposed husband of the adulteress. Nicobulus believes
him, and hands over the money. Now, might he not
have assured himself of the social status of the young
woman with whom Mnesilochus had found favour before
he loosened his purse-strings? Is it likely that he would
again trust the artful Chrysalus immediately after having
been deceived by him? For my own part, I find it
difficult to believe.

After these instances of exaggerated credulity I shall
cite a few instances of excessive readiness to put up with
anything. In the *Heauton Timoroumenos* Clitipho lets his
friend Clinia's mistress come to his father's house without
giving the latter any intimation of his intention. Syrus
goes still further in his impudence, and dares to bring, not
a modest Antiphila, but a showy and noisy courtesan to
Chremes' house. It is a wonder that, under these circumstances, Chremes puts up with this, and that he does not
shut his door in the face of these unexpected guests. In
the *Aulularia* Megadorus very quickly falls in with the
idea of taking a wife. As a matter of fact, the prologue
suggests that his sudden change of attitude is explained by the influence of a god; but I question whether
Menander's contemporaries took a different view of this
explanation than that which we take to-day—in other
words, whether they saw anything else in it than a
failure in inventiveness, a mere *pro forma* apology. This
same play has further surprises in store for us; a stage
convention—soliloquy—of which I shall speak later on,
is carried to the very limit of psychological improbability.
I refer to lines 608 *et seq.* and 673 *et seq.* The persistence
of Euclio's efforts to betray himself is really inconceivable.
Nor is it any more natural that, in the *Curculio*, Therapontigonus, when a stranger accosts him on a public
square, should forthwith tell him what he intends to do at
Epidaurus, and about the bargain he has made with a

certain person, and about the terms of that bargain. And, finally, what shall we say of the scene in the *Cistellaria* in which Lampadio, who is neither stupid nor ill disposed, tells the first woman he meets about the youthful misfortunes of his mistress.[1] One could understand his doing so if he had had any reason to believe that Melaenis might help him in his search; but he must think that the old courtesan is questioning him from pure curiosity.

Lastly, I shall point out a few instances where the actors violate probability by omission. In the *Menaechmi*, Menaechmus Sosicles and Messenio display an incredible lack of sagacity. All the curious adventures that befall them ought to make them suspect that some mistake is being made about the identity of the people by whom they are surrounded, and as they go everywhere for the express purpose of finding Sosicles' twin brother, it would be natural that they should think of him. Hardly has Messenio's master landed at Epidaurus when he is addressed as Menaechmus, and a woman is able to tell him who he is, whence he comes and what his father's name was. And yet he never guesses for whom this woman takes him ! No Syracusan could possibly be so dull. A similar criticism might be made of a few passages in the *Mercator*. Is it conceivable that after the scene of the mock-auction Demipho should not understand who the fair Pasicompsa really is — namely, his son's mistress ? And how is it possible that Lysimachus, after having heard Pasicompsa say that she has been living with his master for two years and after having heard her call his master *adulescens*— how is it possible that he should not guess the truth ? Other old men in comedy are unduly credulous, but the old men in the *Mercator* are not willing to see what is obvious. Let us leave Plautus and take up Terence. At line 670 of the *Heauton Timoroumenos* Clinia comes out of the house of Chremes, who has just recognised Antiphila as his daughter. He is beside himself with joy. In front of the house he meets Syrus, and it is with great difficulty

---

[1] *Cist.*, 597 et seq.

Y

that the latter persuades him to contain himself and, now that his love affair is safe, not to jeopardise that of his friend Clitipho.[1] While witnessing Clinia's transports one naturally asks how it is that this youth, this impatient lover, who is so little able to control himself when Syrus is at hand to admonish him to do so, was so calm before, when he suddenly, and probably in the presence of Chremes, learned that Antiphila was a citizen and that he might therefore think of marrying her? Subsequently Bacchis, in her turn, comes out of Chremes' house. She is tired of waiting for the ten minae that Syrus has promised her, and tired of acting a part and of pretending to be Clinia's mistress. She bursts out and noisily prepares to go off to the house of another aspirant for her favour.[2] How comes it that before making all this uproar she waits until she is outside Chremes' house, and runs no risk of being heard by him? Surely this is a curious amount of consideration to show when in a temper. Or take a final instance from the *Andria*. Davus has, without at the moment believing what he was saying, informed Simo that Glycerium is about to have a new-born infant placed before Pamphilus' door, in order to compromise him. Subsequently things take such a turn that Davus is quick to resort to this device in order to cure Simo's crony, Chremes, of his wish to have his daughter marry Pamphilus. Meanwhile, however, Simo has seen Chremes. How comes it that, though he has been informed of this plan by Davus, he does not think of warning Chremes and thus ruining the success of the plot? Here, again, this discretion seems to be designed—at the cost of what is natural—in order to allow the action to run its course smoothly.

I have compiled a long list of shortcomings, and this list might be extended yet further. Still, the cases in which the *dramatis personae* act in a way that violates psychological probability constitute a very small minority

---

[1] *Heaut.*, 688 et seq.   [2] *Ibid.*, 723 et seq.

when we consider comic literature as a whole. As to the
cases where their conduct appears true to nature, there
would be no need to cite instances if this truth which is
respected were always an average and commonplace one.
But, as we have seen, the actors are not all men of one and
the same type, nor are their feelings limited to what is
conventional in human life. Each of them has a special
character of his own, which supplies him with special
motives for his acts. To construct a plot with such
characters is a more delicate task, and one that calls for
more skill than merely avoiding a formal offence against
common sense, and it will be interesting to see whether
our poets succeeded in this task.

On this point the Kôm Ishkaou fragments afford direct
and, for the most part, favourable evidence. I have said
that the successive sudden changes of fortune in the Σαμία
were due to the good-nature of Demeas, to the impetuous
and changeable disposition of Niceratus, and to the sensi-
tiveness of Moschio. We have seen that Syriscus' conciliatory spirit, Onesimus' communicativeness, and Habrotonon's cleverness and the perseverance with which she
works for her enfranchisement, were the essential features
of the plot of the 'Επιτρέποντες. As much may be said of
the characters of young Charisius and of his father-in-
law, Smicrines. If Charisius had been brutal he would
have dismissed Pamphila and would have informed her
father of the unhappy woman's misfortune. Had he been
deliberate, and had he listened to reason, he would from
the first have forgiven a supposed fault that deserved much
more pity than blame—as, indeed, he is inclined to do
when he makes his soliloquy. But Charisius is both a
man of the world and also a slave to prejudice. One of
these characteristics accounts for his saying nothing to
Smicrines, while the other accounts for his ravishing
Pamphila. The importance of the old man's harshness
and love of money in the development of the plot is manifest; a father with a different disposition would—like
Antipho, in the Stichus—no doubt have been slower

to take back his daughter against her will. In the
Περικειρομένη Polemo's impetuousness and irresolution
show their effect from beginning to end of the play. In
her account of the estrangement of the two lovers Agnoia
does, it is true, pretend that it was all her doing, and
that she drove the soldier to acts of violence that were
contrary to his nature,[1] but one must not believe her too
implicitly. Fiery and impulsive as he is, Polemo would
have been perfectly capable of treating his mistress
brutally without the aid of others. Pataecus has no
doubts about this when, in one of the closing scenes, he
advises him to drop his soldier ways and not to indulge
in any further outbursts of anger against Glycera.[2] It
may be that, in maltreating Glycera, Polemo went beyond
his natural bent, but he did not act in a way that was
absolutely foreign to his character. The same inclination
towards violence that he displays at the very beginning
of the play accounts for one of the later episodes of the
plot—the attack, or rather the preparation for an attack—
on Moschio's dwelling. On the other hand, Glycera is
entirely free to move over to her neighbour's house,
merely because of the irresoluteness of Polemo, who had
taken only half measures regarding her; and that young
woman is recognised as Pataecus' daughter merely because
Polemo, who is incapable of acting for himself when it is
necessary to take a decisive step, had conceived the idea
of asking Pataecus to convey his sentiments to her.

The more or less complete abstracts which we possess
of a few other plays and, above all, the Latin imitations,
enable us to add some further examples to those supplied
by the longer original fragments.

To begin with, the following are two instances where the
character of one of the *dramatis personae* has a decisive,
though indirect, influence on the events that take place
before the plot begins. In the *Trinummus* it is clear that
it was Charmides' distrust of his son Lesbonicus' prudence
in financial matters that led him to bury a reserve fund

---

[1] Περικ., 44 et seq.   [2] *Ibid.*, 365–366.

of three thousand sesterces in his garden before he started for Egypt. A similar course was pursued in Menander's Θησαυρός. The hero of that play, a young man who has ruined himself in riotous living, carries out one of his father's last wishes by having a commemorative banquet carried to his tomb ten years after his death. On this occasion the tomb which the father had had built during his lifetime is opened and is found to contain a hoard of money which, after various eventualities, relieves the son's financial distress. Thus the old father had foreseen his son's extravagance which, when the time came, would make this addition to his fortune necessary. He had likewise foreseen the obedience and filial devotion which would lead him to find it.

Now that I have dealt with the events that take place before the plot begins, I shall consider the plot itself. Possibly the relations between the chief actor's character and the course of events can be better and more constantly observed in the *Aulularia* than in any other Latin comedy. Were Euclio not so afraid of becoming poor, he would perhaps not be so ready to have his daughter marry the aged Megadorus—without a dowry!—a decision which, as soon as it becomes known, leads Lyconides to reveal his identity. It is because of this fear of becoming poor, which makes him suspicious of every one and of everything, that he carries his treasure-pot about with him and exposes it to the danger of being stolen, instead of leaving it securely at home. It is because of this fear of becoming poor, and because he is beset by a dread of being wronged, that he maltreats Strobilus, and through his brutal treatment inspires him with a so much greater desire to rob him of his treasure-pot. It is quite clear that the plot of the *Miles Gloriosus* hinges chiefly on the character of Pyrgopolinices. People count on his incontinency and conceit quite as correctly as they count on the cupidity and vulgarity of the pander in the *Persa* or in the *Poenulus*. In the *Eunuchus* the character of each of the two brothers in turn influences the course of events.

At the beginning of the play Phaedria is urged to allow
his rival, the soldier Thraso, to enjoy provisionally the
favour of his mistress Thais, as otherwise Thraso would
not give back the young girl Pamphila to Thais, and the
plot could not proceed. He consents because he has a
gentle and compliant nature, but I have serious doubts
whether his brother Chaerea would have consented under
similar circumstances. It is this young brother Chaerea
who subsequently carries on the plot by falling in love
with Pamphila at first sight, by gaining admission to her
home, and by taking undue advantage of a *tête-à-tête*;
all of which shows his impetuous nature. In the *Cistellaria* the eccentricity of Alcesimarchus, which is a manifestation of a passionate character, leads the servant
Halisca to drop the γνωρίσματα in the street; and this
delays the solution of the plot. In the *Bacchides* Mnesilochus' suspicion and stupidity, to which he himself pleads
guilty, account for the error into which he falls. In the
Φάσμα the romantic passion of the young hero harmonises
with the temperament revealed in fragment 530—melancholy weariness of life, love of the extraordinary. In
the *Hecyra* Philumena would not have been able to take
refuge in her parents' house were not Philippus what he
is, kind and even somewhat weak; Pamphilus would not
be beset by so much trouble did not the generosity of
Sostrata, who was ready to make any concession, deprive
him of a pretext; Bacchis would not get him out of trouble
were she not better than the average woman of her class.
In the *Andria* the easy compliance of Chremes, who is
ready to stake his daughter's happiness on the word of
a friend, and Simo's suspicious nature, of which he is himself
the victim, bring about the sudden changes of fortune
in the plot. The outcome of many a love affair depends,
in large measure, on the mood of a father. If we consider
the end of the *Mostellaria*, of the *Heauton Timoroumenos*,
of the *Adelphi* and of the *Bacchides*, we shall find that
each one is different, and that each hinges upon the decision of a father who remains true to his real nature:

Theoproprides, indifferent to everything but his purse;
Chremes, authoritative and determined; Micio, full of
gentleness; and Philoxenus, still suffering from his previous
weakness.

It is clear that it is not only chance or the author's
caprice that influences the current of events in the comedies of the new period, but also the *dramatis personae*
themselves. In many instances characters and plot are
intimately related to one another.

CHAPTER III

EXTERNAL STRUCTURE OF THE COMEDIES
STAGE CONVENTIONS

HITHERTO I have dealt with the internal structure of the comedies; now I shall deal with their external structure. I shall begin by examining the stage conventions which the writers of the νέα introduced, and the devices which the stage, as it was constituted in their day, obliged them to adopt.

§ 1

CONVENTIONS REGARDING THE OPENING OF THE PLAY
SOLILOQUIES AND ASIDES

The natural and most usual means of expression in dramatic poetry is the dialogue; several persons speak in turn, and each of them desires and intends to be heard by the others. But we need only glance at the Latin imitations, or even at what remains of the original Greek plays, to discover that this was not always the case in the comedies of the new period. Side by side with the passages in the form of dialogue there were passages—sometimes a short sentence and sometimes a long tirade—that were not meant to be heard by any of the *dramatis personae* or supernumeraries; in other words, there were soliloquies. Let us see by what conventions the comic poets were led to introduce soliloquies.

There is no room for doubt that in Plautus and Terence many soliloquies must be regarded as regular speeches that were spoken aloud. The best proof of this is to be found in the fact that a second actor, who often comes upon the scene by chance or is set there to watch, listens to the actor who delivers the soliloquy and hears what he has to say. But are so many discourses delivered in solitude psychologically probable?

Of course, we must accept the soliloquies which take the form of prayer, of invocations, or of addresses to the gods, to the native soil, or to the house to which one returns or which one is about to leave;[1] also, if need be, the tirades that contain apostrophes to the stars or to the elements,[2] notwithstanding the fact that the idea of addressing these inanimate objects savours somewhat of artificiality. On the other hand, it is quite conceivable that people who are greatly moved or preoccupied should, when they think they are alone, give audible expression to the violent emotions by which they are stirred. In the *Phormio* Demipho is furious with his son, who has married while he was away from home;[3] in the *Rudens* Palaestra and Ampelisca break forth in lamentations when each of them in turn is cast upon an unknown shore;[4] so does Euclio, after his treasure has been taken from him;[5] in the *Andria* Pamphilus expresses his indignation at his father's unceremonious methods;[6] Leonidas intones an anticipatory song of triumph;[7] Clinia and Chaerea shout their joy to the surrounding echoes.[8] The behaviour of these various actors cannot be called absolutely improbable.

I would also include here a particular class of soliloquy uttered by certain persons, always people of low station, and generally slaves, who run on to the stage—Ergasilus, Curculio, Acanthio, Davus in the *Andria*, Geta in the *Adelphi*, and Geta in the *Phormio*;[9] etc. It is natural for people whose bearing betokens exaltation to think aloud.

Notwithstanding all this, there are enough instances in which a soliloquy is hard to justify. Why does Megadorus explain his ideas about a dowry and a marriage

---

[1] e. g. *Most.*, 431 et seq.; *Merc.*, 830 et seq.

[2] Cf. *Merc.*, 3–5; Turpilius, *Leucadia*, fr. XII.; Philem., fr. 79; Men., fr. 739.

[3] *Phorm.*, 231 et seq.   [4] *Rud.*, 185 et seq., 220 et seq.

[5] *Aul.*, 713 et seq.   [6] *Andr.*, 236 et seq.   [7] *As.*, 267 et seq.

[8] *Heaut.*, 679 et seq.; *Eun.*, 1031 et seq.

[9] *Capt.*, 768 et seq.; *Curc.*, 280 et seq.; *Merc.*, 111 et seq.; *Andr.*, 338 et seq.; *Ad.*, 299 et seq.; *Phorm.*, 841 et seq.

aloud?[1]   Why does Harpax proclaim at the top of his
voice who he is and for what purpose he has come?[2]   Why
does Lysidamus, in the *Casina*, feel it incumbent upon him
to announce—within earshot of the house where he lives
with his wife—that he is in a hurry to go where he believes
that love awaits him.[3] Davus, in the *Andria*, stands in
front of his house and loudly declares his surprise at finding Simo so merciful;[4] Syrus, in the *Heauton Timoroumenos*, admonishes himself to cheat Chremes.[5] Both of
them miss a good chance to hold their tongues. I could
easily add a great many more examples of untimely
soliloquies to those already quoted. The inhabitants of
southern countries may be expansive in real life, but they
can never have been as expansive as were the actors in
the comedies of Plautus and Terence. There can be no
doubt that the writers of comedy made undue use of the
soliloquy in a loud voice.

Did the writers of ancient comedy also introduce a
soliloquy of another kind, that is found quite commonly
in modern dramatists—the "mute" or low-voiced soliloquy which conveys *to the audience only* the silent
thoughts of the actors? At first this seems probable, in
view of the passages where an actor stands close to
another whom he sees and distrusts, and says things
which are certainly not meant to be heard by the latter.
When, for example, Gnatho, in line 422 of the *Eunuchus*,
after having begged the soldier to repeat one of his clever
sayings, adds the melancholy remark: *Plus millies audivi*,
he hopes, I imagine, that it will not be heard by the
soldier. This is also true of the rather uncharitable wish
expressed in line 1028 : *Utinam tibi commitigari videam
sandalio caput!* Asides like these are frequent in all Latin
plays, and occasionally the context clearly shows that the
words are not meant to be overheard on the stage. Thus,
in line 497 of the *Andria*, Simo, who has overheard the ill-

---

[1] *Aul.*, 475 et seq.   [2] *Pseud.*, 594 et seq.
[3] *Cas.*, 563 et seq. ; cf. 217 et seq.
[4] *Andr.*, 175 et seq.   [5] *Heaut.*, 512 et seq.

timed gossip of Lesbia, gruffly asks Davus : " Do you
wish me to believe that this woman (Glycerium) has just
given birth to a child of which Pamphilus is the father? "
and in the next line he adds : " Well, you say nothing? "
In the interval the following aside is allotted to Davus :
" I understand his mistake and I see what I must do."
The inevitable conclusion seems to be that Davus has said
nothing and that the actor who played his part spoke
without speaking, and that the audience understood his
meaning. However, we must not be too confident about
adopting this conclusion, or generalising about it. Such
remarks as follow seem to me calculated to undermine it.

In comedy, actors fairly often converse in the presence
of one or more other persons without the latter hearing
what is said. It is easy to understand this when the
speakers converse together at some distance from the
other actors. But occasionally they manage to get in a
few words surreptitiously when they are in the immediate
vicinity of the others; for instance, Libanus and Leonidas,
in lines 446–447 of the *Asinaria*; Menaechmus and Messenio,
in lines 375–378, 383–386, 413–418 of the *Menaechmi*;
Palaestrio and Milphidippa, in lines 1066–1067, 1073–1074,
1088–1091 of the *Miles*; Davus speaking to Pamphilus,
in lines 416–417 of the *Andria*; Davus speaking to Mysis,
in lines 751, 752–753 of the *Hecyra*; Syrus speaking to
Clitipho, in line 829 of the *Heauton Timoroumenos*; etc.
There is no denying that these persons speak, as the person
whom they address hears what they say. But their words
are, so to say, hardly audible. The stage convention that
applies in their case is not that of a speech in place of an
unexpressed thought, but that of words in a high voice substituted for words in a low voice, clear articulation in place
of a discreet whisper. Even when reduced to these terms
the stage convention involves serious consequences. As
a matter of fact, it is a two-fold convention : in the first
place, it assumes that the supposed whispering can, at
one and the same time, be heard by the spectators who are
seated far from the actor who whispers, and that it cannot

be heard by the other actors who are quite close to him; in the second place, it assumes that the actors who hear nothing have a singularly dull sense of hearing, or else that they are strangely inattentive. It does not call for a greater, or even as great a stretch of the imagination to account for the stage asides which I mentioned above. Let us assume that they are spoken low, mumbled between the actor's teeth; the other parties to the conversation may not hear them, while conventional acoustics, the acoustics of the theatre, will accommodatingly carry them to the spectators' seats. Indeed, it is in this light that the poets themselves must have chosen to look at the matter. Witness the passages in which either an aside or a series of asides calls forth some such remark as the following from one of the actors on the stage : *Quid dixti ? Quid tute tecum ? Quid tu solus tecum loquere ? Etiam muttis ?* etc.[1] Therefore we cannot infer from the mere existence of the stage asides that the device of the " mute " soliloquy was known to the *palliata*, and we must conclude that such a device was alien to it.

In a word, some actors, when they are by themselves or believe that they are by themselves, think aloud more frequently than accords with probability; others are strangely deaf to certain things that are said in their immediate vicinity; such are the stage conventions with regard to means of expression to be met with in Plautus and in Terence. No doubt both of these abuses go back to the Greek originals. Asides are rare in the fragments of the original plays; still, they are met with occasionally.[2] As for soliloquies, there are plenty of them, and, just as in the Latin plays, attention is repeatedly and specifically called to the fact that they are spoken soliloquies; but of several of them it may be said that neither the situation nor the standing of the person who utters them nor the quality of his words justifies so much volubility.

Moreover, neither of the two devices employed by New

---

[1] e. g. *Amph.*, 381; *Aul.*, 52, 190; *Most.*, 512; 551, etc.
[2] Ἐπιτρ., 19–20; Σαμ., 168, 230–237; Περικ., 87–88.

Comedy was first introduced by it. The Homeric heroes spoke aloud to themselves—to their heart, as Homer says —and occasionally they did so at junctures when silent reflection would, I believe, have been more natural. As for the rare soliloquies in the dramatic works of the fifth century—tragedies and comedies alike—the context hardly ever shows how they are to be regarded. But most probably they are to be regarded as spoken soliloquies. The very rareness with which they occur leads one to this assumption; for the fact that the actors in Euripides and Aristophanes indulge in relatively few soliloquies is, no doubt, due to their being embarrassed by the practically constant presence of the chorus—in other words, to their fear of being overheard. If we examine the speeches pronounced by these actors when the chorus is absent and they are by themselves on the stage, or when they imagine that they are by themselves, or else when they forget that this is not the case, we shall find that more than one of them calls for the same criticism as the passages from Plautus and Terence of which I have just spoken. This is true of most, if not of all, the introductory solilo- quies in Euripides, which, it must be admitted, are of a rather special kind; and also of the slave's soliloquy, lines 747 *et seq.*, in the *Alcestis*; of that of Heracles, lines 837 *et seq.*, and of those of Menelaus, lines 368 *et seq.*, 483 *et seq.* in the *Helena*; and of many others. In Aristophanes the same criticism holds good for the soliloquy of Dicaeopolis at the beginning of the *Acharnians*, for that of Strepsiades at the beginning of the *Clouds*, for that of Blepsidemus, lines 355 *et seq.* of the *Plutus*; etc. One and the same play, the *Ecclesiazusae*, contains no less than half a dozen soliloquies which, *in so far as they are spoken soliloquies*, appear to be somewhat out of place. At the very beginning there is Praxagora's soliloquy; at lines 311 *et seq.* the soliloquy of Blepyrus; at lines 728 *et seq.*, 746 *et seq.*, the soliloquies of the good and of the bad citizen; at lines 877 *et seq.* the soliloquy of the old woman; at line 938 that of the young man.

As for stage asides, they are rather out of keeping with
the solemn style of tragedy. However, we do find a few
in Euripides; in the *Hecuba*, lines 736–738, 741–742, 745–
746, 749–751, and possibly lines 133 and 475 in the *Helena*.
In Aristophanes they are rather more frequent; lines
752–755 and 1193–1194 of the *Knights* must be spoken as
an aside by the charcoal-burner; line 992 of the *Wasps*
by Bdelycleon; the exclamations in lines 603, 604 and
609 of the *Thesmophoriazusae* by Mnesilochus; line 1202
by Euripides. New Comedy merely found justification
in its more intricate plots for a more frequent use of a
device which had been introduced a hundred years earlier.

§ 2

CONVENTIONS REGARDING LENGTH OF THE PLAYS

THE ENTR'ACTES

The plot of most Latin comedies, as well of the majority
of the original Greek plays of which we can form an idea,
is conceived as taking place within a single day, or, at
least, within twenty-four hours. The plots which begin
at night or very early in the morning—and they were
apparently quite numerous—end before the ensuing evening. The *Heauton Timoroumenos* begins towards the close
of an afternoon, when Menedemus comes home from his
work; it is interrupted during the night, begins again
at dawn of the following day, and ends in the forenoon.
Possibly the 'Επιτρέποντες likewise extended over two
days,[1] and, if so, it may have exceeded, though only
slightly, the exact limit of twenty-four hours. It is only
the plot of the *Captivi* that calls for—or seems to call for—

---

[1] At lines 197–198 Syriscus agrees to wait until the following day
before finding out what is going to become of the ring; subsequently, at
lines 226–228, after an *entr'acte*, he insists on being satisfied at once.
But we must take into consideration those words in line 228 : ἐλθεῖν δεῖ μέ
ποι, by which he apparently explains why he changes his mind.

a much longer lapse of time.[1] Indeed, in the course of this play there appears to be time for one of the actors, Philocrates, to travel from Aetolia to Elis and to return to Aetolia. And, whatever may have been said to the contrary, this would require several days. On the other hand, some things that Ergasilus, Tyndarus, and Hegio say imply that the interval between the first scenes and the last is not longer than from morning to evening. It is not impossible that Plautus omitted some details that would have explained these contradictions and would have made it possible to keep the plot within the customary limits. At any rate, if the plot of the original play extended over several days, it was certainly an exceptional case. For the most part, the plots of the νέα appear to have been short.[2]

But they were not, as a rule, as short as the performances in which they were produced. There must have been a difference between the actual duration of the latter and the supposed duration of the former, and it is worth our while to examine how this difference was adjusted.

In the first place, it was adjusted by means of *entr'actes*; between the uninterrupted series of episodes which followed upon one another as closely as possible there were more or less long intervals without any dramatic action. But there was this difference from the practice of our modern theatres, that while the spectators could no longer watch the *plot* during the *entr'actes*, the *performance* went right on. I must enlarge upon this point in order to give

---

[1] In the Περικειρομένη it is not very likely that the quarrel which arose between Glycera and Polemo, and which took place in the evening, should have been presented to the audience before Agnoia's speech; the plot opened the next morning, if not several days later.

[2] In many plots the episodes are multiplied owing to chance coincidences; it is by chance that Demipho and Chremes, in the *Phormio*, and Pamphilus and Epignomus, in the *Stichus*, return to their native land on the same day; that Philumena, in the *Hecyra*, is confined on the very day of Pamphilus' return; etc. These coincidences are certainly surprising, but they are not improbable.

the reader a correct idea of a theatrical performance at the time of the *νέα*.

Here and there in the fragments of the original plays, where there is a break in the sequence of events and the stage remains empty, the text is interrupted by the notice: *Χοροῦ*. Moreover, the anonymous author of a life of Aristophanes assures us that this was frequently the case in the manuscripts of New Comedy.[1] Now, there can be no doubt of the meaning of the word *Χοροῦ*; it means that where this word is inserted—in other words, in the *entr' actes* —there was a performance by the chorus. As a matter of fact, statements of Aeschines,[2] and of Aristotle,[3] and passages in inscriptions [4] show that the comic chorus continued to exist at least down to the middle of the second century. Of what did its performance consist? The word *Χοροῦ* is nowhere followed by the text of a passage to be sung by the members of the chorus. It might, therefore, at first sight seem as if they did not sing at all, but merely danced; but before drawing such an inference we must inquire who constituted the chorus and what were its relations to the actors in the play.

Certain details of the dialogue which in each instance are near the sign *Χοροῦ*, have led to the conjecture that, between lines 201 and 202 of the *'Επιτρέποντες*, the chorus consisted of Charisius' messmates, who are on the point of going to the banqueting hall, and that, later on in the play, after the close of the scene published by Jernstedt,[5] it was made up of these same messmates as they were leaving the hall and preparing to return to town; that in the *Σαμία*, between lines 270 and 271, it consisted of invited guests who are on their way to Demeas' house to

---

[1] Anon., XI. Dübner.

[2] *C. Tim.*, § 157. The speech against Timarchus was delivered in 345.

[3] *Polit.*, III. p. 1276 B.

[4] *Bull. de corres. hell.*, 1890, p. 396, line 85 (Delos, in the year 279); Collitz, *Dialektinschr.*, No. 2563, lines 67 et seq.; No. 2564, lines 71 et seq.; No. 2565, lines 73 et seq.; No. 2566, lines 71 et seq.; No. 2569, lines 18 et seq. (Delphi, in the years 272, 271, 270, 269, 140–100).

[5] Considered as belonging to the *'Επιτρέποντες* by van Leeuwen and Capps (*Amer. Journal of Philol.*, XXXIX. 1908, pp. 417 et seq.).

take part in his son's wedding banquet; and that, in the
Περικειρομένη, between lines 76 and 77, it consisted of a
company of young men who covered Glycera's retreat when
she moved over to Myrrhina's house, or else of a group of
Polemo's friends preceding him on his way from the house
where he had feasted—the same friends who a little later
on threatened to lay siege to the house of his rival Moschio.
It has even been conjectured that, in the Ἑαυτὸν Τιμωρούμενος of Menander, during the *entr'actes* which correspond
to those that follow lines 409 and 478 in the Latin play,
the chorus was made up of Bacchis' female servants.   But
all this is doubtful and not highly probable.   In Plautus,
the *advocati* in the *Poenulus* are no more comparable to
members of a chorus than are the three friends of Demipho
in the *Phormio*.   As for the fishermen in the *Rudens*, who,
in Plautus, come upon the stage after an *entr'acte*, one might
assume that, in Diphilus, they filled up the *entr'acte* itself
with dances and songs.   If this was the case, they would
have afforded an example of a chorus, connected with the
play—in a very desultory way it is true, for their entire
part consists in telling Trachalio that they have not seen
his master Plesidippus.   But this, too, is far from certain.
Until we have proof to the contrary we shall, therefore,
have to assume that in comedies of the new period the
chorus was, as a rule, in no way connected with the play.[1]
At most, the chorus is sometimes represented as being a
casual passer-by, an intruder, upon whose arrival the actors
leave the stage.   That is what happens in the Περικειρομένη;
an actor sees some merry-making youths coming (μεθύοντα
μειράκια σύμπολλα); and, at the approach of these gay
young sparks, he and his comrades withdraw.[2]   A similar
but even clearer instance occurs at the close of a scene which
may belong to the Ἐπιτρέποντες[3] when one of the speakers
says, " Let us go and find Charisius "; and the other
answers, " Let us go, for here comes a band of youngsters

---

[1] Note that no mention is made of a chorus in the list of the πρόσωπα
(*dramatis personae*) of the Ἥρως.

[2] Περικ., 71 et seq.   [3] In the Jernstedt fragment.

Z

who are rather tipsy (μειρακυλλίων ὄχλος ὑποβεβρεγμένων);
I think it would be better not to get in their way." Thereupon both speakers leave the stage and the chorus enters.
Before Menander's time a fragment of Alexis suggests a
similar situation.[1] The similarity between these three
passages leads one to believe that, at the time of the μέση
and of the νέα, the chorus frequently represented a κῶμος
passing through the streets. The coming of this κῶμος,
a sort of homely revival of the ancient Dionysiac procession, might, on occasion, be announced by the actors
as they left the stage, in which case it was in a sense connected, in a quite external way, if I may say so, with the
episodes of the plot. I imagine that very often there was
not even this slight connection. The members of the
chorus appeared at the end of each act and disappeared
before the actors came back, without the slightest allusion
to their presence being made in the dialogue or in the
soliloquies which preceded and came after their appearance. Their performances were interludes, in the strictest
sense of the word.

As the chorus has so little to do with the plot, we are
led to believe that its songs—if, indeed, it sang songs—had,
as a rule, no relation whatsoever to the dramatic situation.
They may have been any sort of pieces, without literary
merit, written by a different author from the rest of
the play,[2] and different ones could be employed for any
particular *entr'acte* of a particular play at the will of the
impresario; in a word, they were of such a kind as to be
naturally omitted from the manuscripts of the comedies.
Hence the fact that no lyric couplets follow the word
Χοροῦ does not prove that the χορευταὶ κωμικοί of the
new period did not sing. For my own part, I believe that
they did sing, just as the earlier chorus sang, and that
they accompanied their singing with dances or with
rhythmic evolutions. In a word, their performance was

---

[1] Alexis, fr. 107.

[2] Not a single fragment of the new period, not even fragment 312 of
Menander, can belong to a choral passage.

of the same nature as that of the ἐμβόλιμα, which Agathon introduced into tragedy,[1] and of which they kept alive the tradition.

As for the convention in virtue of which the choral parts might represent a much longer interval of time than they themselves actually occupied—this goes back to the early days of the Greek theatre. Already, in the tragedies of the fifth century, a great deal is supposed to take place, unseen by the audience, during the recital of a *stasimon* that is often of short duration. Such a fiction as this naturally became more admissible in proportion as the songs of the chorus became more and more detached from the plot.

Occasionally events followed one upon another much more rapidly behind the scenes than upon the stage, without, however, occasioning a break in the sequence of the scenes or a halt in the plot.[2] In the Περικειρομένη, Daos enters Myrrhina's house, tells her of her son's return, is snubbed by her, and comes away crestfallen, during the time that Moschio speaks the five lines 121–125. Further on, Sosia enters Polemo's house and confirms the fact that Glycera has escaped, during the time that Daos speaks the five lines 171–175. Still further on, between lines 333 and 338, Doris has time to go and find Glycera in the house where she is making her toilet, to ascertain that she is in a conciliatory mood, and to come back to Polemo.[3] In the *Andria* the midwife Lesbia, who went into Glycerium's house at line 467, has already come out at line 481, after having attended to all her professional duties. Between line 326 and line 352 of the *Hecyra*, Pamphilus is able to find out things at Myrrhina's house

---

[1] Arist., *Poet.*, XVIII. 7.

[2] Sometimes, but rarely, the opposite is the case. Thus, in the *Menaechmi*, it is hard to understand what Messenio has been doing between line 445 and line 966. In the *Adelphi*, Geta waits a long time before telling Sostrata of the carrying off of the singing girl which took place before line 81.

[3] See also Σαμία, 145–151, 203–210, 218–222, 319–324.

which it subsequently takes him more than forty lines to report. In the *Mercator*, Syra, an old " slow coach," finds Pasicompsa in Lysimachus' house and rejoins Dorippa at the door between line 677 and line 686. In the *Heauton Timoroumenos* Chremes goes to see two of his neighbours, Simus and Crito, in order to apologise for not being able to act as arbitrator between them, during the time that Menaechmus, who has remained on the stage, speaks the six lines 502–507. In the *Captivi* they go to liberate Tyndarus from jail (*latomiae*), which is *extra portam* (line 735), and bring him to Hegio, between line 950 and line 997. And so on. It is clear that these are slight liberties when compared with similar passages in Aristophanes; for example, between line 134 and line 175 of the *Acharnians* Amphitheus goes to the Peloponnesus and returns with the famous truce. Still, we must not omit to take note of these liberties, such as they are. It is to be observed that those parts of the text during which there is an accumulation of episodes behind the scene are most often soliloquies. Granting that a soliloquy is really a speech which the actor addresses to himself, yet it may be said that the *véa* did not on occasion hesitate to regard it in another light—as an abstract or epitome of a period of reflection of undetermined length.

§ 3

CONVENTIONS REGARDING STAGE-SETTING
UNITY OF PLACE

As a rule, the stage-setting of a Greek drama remained unchanged from beginning to end. It was, therefore, necessary for it to unite in a single and fixed combination all the elements which were to form the background for the successive episodes. Evidently this could not always be accomplished without violating probability. New Comedy does not introduce such highly fantastic combinations as those in which Aristophanes indulged; it no

longer displays the house of Trygaeus side by side with
that of the king of the gods, nor the temple of Heracles
next to the palace of Hades, nor the Pnyx alongside of
the farm in which Dicaeopolis celebrates the rural Dionysia;
but although it does not carry stage convention so far,
it does not renounce it entirely. As a rule, the scene of
action is a street or a square—either in a big town or
in a village—surrounded by private houses and public
buildings.[1]

Now it does, no doubt, happen more than once that,
where the episodes of the plot demand it, the houses shown
in the setting should or can be regarded as really adjoining one another; for instance, the house of Periplecomenus
and that of the soldier in the *Miles*, which have a party-
wall; the house of Euclio and that of Megadorus in the
Aulularia, whose closeness to each other influences the
latter's matrimonial plans; the houses of Myrrhina and
Polemo in the *Περικειρομένη*, those of Demeas and
Niceratus in the *Σαμία*, those of Simo and Theopropides
in the *Mostellaria*, those of Chremes and Menedemus in
the *Heauton Timoroumenos*; etc. In other plays more or
less serious objections can be raised to the close proximity
shown in the stage-setting. Is it not, for example, somewhat imprudent of Stratippocles, in the *Epidicus*, to hide
a couple of steps away from his father's house? and for
Lysidamus in the *Casina*, and Demipho in the *Mercator*,
to borrow the house of their nearest neighbour for their
merry-making? Are not Phaedria in the *Eunuchus*,
Pamphilus in the *Andria*, Aeschinus in the *Adelphi*,
Menaechmus and Argyrippus in the *Asinaria*, foolish to
carry on illicit love affairs at the very doors of their own

---

[1] Sometimes the setting was more complicated. In the *Rudens* it
included, besides the temple of Venus and the farm of Daemones, rocks
and crannies which would make it possible for Palaestra and Ampelisca
to be hidden from one another. In the *Δύσκολος* it must have shown
or suggested a mountainous region; in the *Λευκαδία* possibly the *temenos*
of Apollo Leukatas; in the *Vidularia*, and in the play to which the anonymous Latin fragment LVIII. belongs, a bit of country by the sea-side;
etc.

houses? And if Bacchis, in the *Hecyra*, lives quite near Philumena's parents and parents-in-law, must not the latter know that she has broken off relations with their son and son-in-law? In all these instances, and in many others, I imagine, the stage-setting was certainly open to criticism.

But, after all, this sort of improbability is not glaring; we may even assume that the audience often did not notice it. We meet, however, with improbabilities that are both more serious and more noticeable.

An entirely realistic representation of certain scenes in Plautus and Terence would require a good deal of space. To this class belong, in the first place, the scenes in which an actor runs on to the stage [1] and before reaching his destination indulges in occasionally lengthy tirades in full view of the audience.[2] I think there is no doubt that these scenes are imitations of Greek originals; in several of them certain details of composition indirectly prove this. When Hegio, in the *Captivi*, speaking about Ergasilus, exclaims : " *Eugepae, edictiones aedilicias hic quidem habet; mirumque adeost, ni hunc fecere sibi Aetoli agoranomum,*[3] I cannot help thinking that this sentence was translated from an original in which the word ἀγορανόμος appeared. Consequently, the parasite in the Greek comedy must have spoken much as the parasite in the Latin comedy speaks, and in all probability he ran as he spoke, just as Plautus' Ergasilus does. The list of Hellenic titles which Curculio pours forth as he comes on to the stage—*nec <homo> quisquamst tam opulentus, qui mi obsistat in via, nec strategus nec tyrannus quisquam nec agoranomus nec demarchus nec comarchus*[4]—suggests a similar inference,

---

[1] Long speeches might without too much improbability be attributed to actors who walk slowly or who may be assumed to stop every now and then in order to talk and quarrel.

[2] *Capt.*, 790 et seq.; *Curc.*, 280 et seq.; *Asin.*, 267 et seq.; *Merc.*, 111 et seq.; *Phorm.*, 179 et seq.; *Ad.*, 299 et seq.; *Stichus*, 274 et seq.; *Trin.*, 1008 et seq.

[3] *Capt.*, 823–824.   [4] *Curc.*, 284–286.

as far as the scene into which it is inserted is concerned.
In line 36 of the prologue to the *Eunuchus* Terence mentions the *servus currens* side by side with characters and
elements which were certainly borrowed from the *véa*,
and calls him one of the common types of comedy.   This
character had as ancestors on the Attic stage several of
Aristophanes' personages—Amphitheus running away from
the Acharnians, Cleisthenes running towards the *thesmophoriazusae*.   And, what is more, we are able to get a
glimpse of him in a few fragments of the new period.   "I
ran for you as no one ever ran before," says some one in
Menander; [1] much the same as Acanthio says in one of
the early scenes of the *Mercator*.   One of Philemon's actors
asks, "Do you think the king made the street for you
only?" [2] and this remark reminds one of the angry utterances of Ergasilus and Curculio.   The writers of Latin
comedy use various devices to make a limited space seem
large enough to contain such agitated scenes.   Sometimes
they represent the supposed runner as completely exhausted
and on the point of collapsing as he reaches his goal, and
being obliged to stop for breath; sometimes it is drunkenness
that slackens his pace, or else he comes to a standstill
and asks himself in what direction he is to continue; or,
on meeting the person to whom he brings news, he hesitates, half wishing to give the information, half fearing
to distress him; or else, well aware of his own importance,
he wishes to lead up to his entry and make people await
him eagerly.   If the actors played their parts in the
orchestra, which was a great deal larger than the *pulpitum*,[3]
it was possible to attain a sufficient degree of realism
without any great effort.

Occasionally, together with the running on of an actor,
there is often combined another stage device which,
broadly speaking, appears to have been quite common in
the *véa*—two actors or two groups of actors, speak and
act without seeing or hearing one another.   This happens,
naturally enough, when one actor tries to escape the notice

[1] Men., fr. 741.   [2] Philem., fr. 58.   [3] The stage.(—Tr.).

of the other. A detail of ancient stage-setting, which the Romans called *angiportus* or *angiportum*, and which, as far as we can make out, consisted of a perpendicular recess in the front of the scene and represented a narrow lane between two houses, afforded a convenient retreat for those who desired to hide themselves.[1] The embrasure of a door also served as cover for actors who were not supposed to be seen by their fellows. The miniatures in the Terence manuscripts illustrate this arrangement in several of his comedies;[2] a wall-painting at Pompeii shows a similar arrangement in an episode of a tragi-comedy.[3] Indeed, there is no doubt that it was very commonly employed. Once we admit the existence of this hiding-place, we can understand how it came about that Thraso and his companions, who are seen by Thais and Chremes as early as line 754 of the *Eunuchus*, do not discover them until thirty-four lines further on. During this interval Chremes and Thais have withdrawn a few steps behind the threshold of the house, and while they continue to be visible to the audience, who are facing or almost facing the door, they cannot be seen by a person who comes towards them from the side. A similar stage-setting may be surmised for the passage of the *Casina* in which Lysidamus comes upon the stage soliloquising and without seeing Cleostrata; for the scene in the *Aulularia* where Euclio listens to Megadorus' harangue without being seen; for the scene in the *Menaechmi* in which the matron overhears her husband's confessions; and for many other cases. Hitherto we have met with nothing which shocks our sense of probability, or for which an equivalent cannot be found in the tragic writers or in Aristophanes. I need only mention Orestes and his pedagogue spying on the proceedings of the *choephori*; the lamentations of Electra and her conversation with the women of the chorus; the Acharnians

---

[1] So in *Phorm.*, 891. For the existence of similar lanes at Delos, cf. *Bull. de corr. hellén.*, XXX. (1906), pp. 587–588.

[2] See the publication by Bethe, *Terenti codex ambrosianus, H.* 75 *inf.*, Leyden, 1903.

[3] Dieterich, *Pulcinella*, pl. II.

hiding while Dicaeopolis celebrates the rural Dionysia; the conduct of Trygaeus while Polemos prepares to pulverise the Greek cities; Dionysius and Xanthias concealing themselves while the initiated carry on their procession; Mnesilochus hiding while the slave Agatho prepares for a sacrifice. But New Comedy did not stop there. Sometimes (and for this the extant remains of earlier drama afford no analogy) it allowed an actor in perfect good faith to fail to see or hear another,[1] even when the latter made no effort to elude his attention. This is what takes place at the beginning of the *Mercator*, and in lines 768 *et seq.* of the *Captivi*, where Acanthio and Ergasilus have no idea of the presence of Charinus and Hegio until the latter addresses them; in another scene of the *Mercator*, where Charinus does not see Demipho;[2] in two scenes of the *Phormio*, where Geta hastens to go to his master without noticing that Antipho is close by, chatting with Phaedria or with Phormio;[3] in a scene of the *Adelphi*, where Geta neither sees nor hears Sostrata and Canthara, although they are on their way to meet him;[4] etc. The actors of whom I have spoken are all either under the influence of a very strong emotion, or else they are very deep in thought, and this circumstance may possibly account for their being deaf and blind. There are other cases in which this excuse can hardly be advanced. In lines 566 *et seq.* and 682 *et seq.* of the *Mostellaria* Theopropides is perfectly calm and ought to know what is going on about him, and yet he does not hear a word of what Tranio and his neighbour Simo are talking about, although they are not speaking in a low tone. Nay, more, he only hears a part of what the usurer says, although the latter is shouting at the top of his voice. Whatever precautions Plautus may have taken to disarm criticism,[5] on the Roman stage the performance of such a passage as this must have

---

[1] Of course, I do not refer to the scenes in which an actor pretends not to see or not to hear what he actually sees or hears perfectly well.
[2] *Merc.*, 335 et seq. [3] *Phorm.*, 179 et seq., 841 et seq.
[4] *Ad.*, 301 et seq. [5] *Most.*, 575–576, 609a.

appeared somewhat forced; in Greece, in the orchestra, it may have seemed more admissible.

We now come to other instances of improbability which are much more disconcerting. Several scenes in Plautus' comedies ought really to take place indoors.[1] Possibly it is consistent with the habits of a southern country that slaves should choose a spot in front of their master's house in which to carouse, but Greek ladies surely did not sit in the street to chat and work. Nor did they make their toilet there, or rest there on a sofa after their confinements. And a married man in comfortable circumstances who had taken the precaution of going to his mistress' house by a devious route would not come out of her house to sup with her in full view of all who passed by. And yet there is no doubt that Plautus placed some of the scenes to which I refer out of doors. When, in the *Mostellaria*, the father of the family is about to arrive, Tranio hurriedly has the paraphernalia of a banquet and the besotted guests removed from the very spot where a few moments ago Philematium was engaged in making her toilet.[2] Apparently, then, all this took place in front of the house, for otherwise it would only have been necessary to shut the door on all these proceedings in order to prevent a new-comer from seeing them. Moreover, the remarks of Tranio and of Philolaches are very significant—

Abi tu hinc intro atque ornamenta haec aufer.[3]
Abripite hunc intro actutum inter manus.[4]
. . . non modo ne intro eat, verum etiam ut fugiat longe ab aedibus.[5]
Omnium primum, Philematium, intro abi, et tu, Delphium.[6]

Evidently the opposite of *intro* is out of doors. Nor is

[1] This is also true of the scenes to which certain original fragments belong, banqueting scenes or scenes of some other kind : Diph., fr. 20, 50, 58; Men., fr. 71, 151, 273–274, 292, 311, 377, 437, 451; etc.
[2] *Most.*, 371 et seq.   [3] *Ibid.*, 294.   [4] *Ibid.*, 385.
[5] *Ibid.*, 390.   [6] *Ibid.*, 397.

the situation less clear in the *Truculentus*. After having received Stratophancs, Phronesium, who pretends to have been confined, declares that the air is giving her a headache. She goes *indoors* (*me intro acturum ducite*) and shuts in the soldier's face a door—which is no other than the door of her house.[1] The episodes in the *Asinaria* and the *Stichus* seem, at first sight, to call for a different stage-setting. In the latter play the aged Antipho, who is on his way to the house of his daughter Panegyris, notices, as he approaches it, that the door is wide open.[2] Whereupon the two young women, who have heard him coming, go out to meet him and ask him to be seated.[3] In the *Asinaria* Artemona spies on her husband for quite a long time, without being seen by him, before she attacks him.[4] In the *Stichus*, therefore, we must, perhaps, assume that a wall with a door in it stood between Antipho and his two daughters while he was on his way to the house in which they were.[5] In the *Asinaria* the banquet must have been held indoors and the matron must have looked on through a partially opened door, just as Nicobulus does in the *Bacchides*. I find it difficult to conceive how such an arrangement could have been carried out on a Greek stage. Nowadays we should erect a perpendicular partition at the back of the stage in a way that would allow the audience to see the street on one side of it and the interior of the house on the other. It is very improbable that the ancients ever made use of such an arrangement.[6] Can

---

[1] *Truc.*, 634 et seq. Cf. 480 and 583.   [2] *Stich.*, 87.
[3] *Ibid.*, 88 et seq.   [4] *As.*, 880 et seq.
[5] The fact that this door was open would explain how the two young women could hear their father coming.

[6] The only documents which might lead us to think that they did so are certain illustrations in manuscripts of Terence in which a door is shown between two groups of actors. But these illustrations contain elements which in themselves make their testimony untrustworthy. In one of them—the one which in the *Parisinus* illustrates scene 1, Act III. of the *Andria* (Bethe, pl. XII. 1), we see Simo and Davus, Lesbia and Mysis to the right of the door, that is to say, out of doors; to the left of the door, that is to say, within the house, we see Glycerium and a woman who is helping her. Now, it is clearly established that the audience was not allowed to see the scene in which the confinement took place. This detail,

we assume that a part of the background could be opened
at will, to display the interior of a house? As a matter of
fact it seems not unlikely that the προσκήνιον—in front of
which Dörpfeld thinks the actors performed in the time
of the νέα—consisted of movable πίνακες, which were set up
for each play, between columns or pillars,[1] one or several
of which might, on occasion, be left out. On the other
hand, on the Naples bas-relief, representing a scene from
comedy, we see a curtain which adjoins the façade of a
house in a curious fashion.[2] In itself, therefore, the suggestion made above would not be inadmissible, but in
each of the passages in question a detail occurs which puts
it out of question. In the *Stichus* Panegyris says to her
sister, after Antipho has left them : *nunc, soror, abeamus
intro.*[3] At the very end of the *Asinaria* Philaenium
ironically invites Demaenetus to follow her, and she does
so with these words : *Immo intro potius.*[4] Just as Philolaches and his guests, and Phronesium and her maid-
servants, were really out of doors, so were Antipho's
daughters during the time they were chatting together
and receiving their father, and Philaenium and her two
lovers while they were carousing.

Of late, attempts have been made to minimise the rigour
of this conclusion, not only in so far as it affects the scenes
in the *Stichus* and in the *Asinaria*, but in all analogous
scenes as well. It is claimed that the scenes which ought
to take place indoors but which are performed out of doors,
did not, as a matter of fact, take place in the street, but
were acted in the πρόθυρον or *vestibulum*,[5] a structure

---

among others, proves that the illustrations in the manuscripts of Terence
do not give an exact picture of the actual stage-setting used in the
performances.

[1] Dörpfeld-Reisch, *Das griech. Theater*, p. 380 (cf. pp. 103, 148, 150,
etc.); *Bull. de corr. hellén.*, XX. (1896), pp. 566–567; Wiegand and
Schrader, *Priene*, p. 247; Hiller von Gärtringen, *Thera*, vol. iii. p. 254.

[2] Dörpfeld-Reisch, *Op. cit.*, p. 328 and fig. 81. This bas-relief possibly
dates from the third century.

[3] *Stichus*, 147.   [4] *As.*, 941 (Fleckeisen's text).

[5] Vitruvius (VI. 7, 5) vouches for the fact that these two words are
synonymous.

attached to the house. To have placed these scenes in such a spot, which is neither public nor private, would, of course, also have been a mere stage device, but it is a sort of compromise which would decrease the inherent improbability and make it more admissible. This theory is certainly alluring, but on what is it based, and what should we gain by accepting it?

In the first place, it is well to remember that the πρόθυρον or *vestibulum* is rarely mentioned in extant Greek comedies, either in their original form or in imitations. Some scholars think there is a very decided difference in Plautus and Terence between the meaning of the words *in via* and *ante aedes, ante ianuam, ante ostium*, and that only the first of these expressions means " in the street," while the others refer to things that take place in the *vestibulum*, or πρόθυρον. This seems to me an arbitrary distinction. In lines 894–895 of the *Eunuchus* Thais asks Chaerea, who is still dressed in his motley clothes : *Vin interea, dum venit, domi opperiamur potius quam hic ante ostium?* Before going indoors they exchange a few more words. Whereupon Chremes' coming is announced, and Chaerea says to Thais : *Obsecro, abeamus intro, Thais; nolo me in via cum hac veste videat.*[1] There is no indication that the actors moved from the spot between line 895 and line 905. Hence *in via* and *ante ostium* are synonymous. This passage in itself would suffice to overthrow the hypothesis to which I referred above, and several other passages appear to be decidedly against it. For example, when, in the *Menaechmi*, Menaechmus Sosicles, who has not the slightest acquaintance with Erotium, walks up and down before her house—*ante ostium*[2]—how can this be taken to mean that he is in the πρόθυρον? When, at line 727 of the *Aulularia*, Lyconides hears Euclio's lamentations and comes out of Megadorus' house, asking : *Quisnam homo hic ante aedes nostras conqueritur moerens?* are we to imagine that Euclio pours forth his lamentations in Megadorus' πρόθυρον? Certainly not. But if we do not attribute a more or less

---

[1] *Eun.*, 905–907.   [2] *Menaech.*, 276. Cf. 357 : *ante aedis.*

technical meaning to the words *ante aedes, ante ostium* in these and similar passages, why should we do so elsewhere? This remark also applies to the Greek expressions πρόσθε τῶν θυρῶν, πρὸς ταῖς θύραις, ἐπὶ ταῖς θύραις. In half a dozen passages in Menander [1] and in fragment 3 of Ephippus, they may simply mean before the door, at the door, *on the door-step.*[2] The only passages in comedy in which we are obliged to assume that an episode takes place in a πρόθυρον or *vestibulum* are those in which these terms actually appear, that is to say, in the following:

— Aristophanes, *Wasps*, 800–804. A comparison of this passage with lines 871 and 875 seems to show that Labes' burlesque lawsuit is tried in Philocleon's πρόθυρον.

— Theopompus, fr. 63: "This πρόθυρον seems to me like a chamber of torture, and this house like a dungeon."

— Plautus, *Most.*, 817. Tranio asks Theopropides to admire the *vestibulum* of Simo's house: *Viden vestibulum ante aedes hoc et ambulacrum cuius modi?*

— Plautus, fr. inc. fab. **XXVII.**: *Exi tu, Dave, age, sparge; mundum esse hoc vestibulum volo. Venus ventura est nostra, nolo hoc pulveret.*

To the above I may add a note of Varro's (*De lingua latina*, VII. 81) commenting on line 955 of the *Pseudolus* (*ut tranversus, non proversus, cedit, quasi cancer solet*): *Dicitur de eo qui in id quo it est versus et ideo qui exit in vestibulum, quod est ante domum, prodire et procedere. Quod cum leno non faceret, sed secundum parietem transversus iret, dixit.* . . . .

As we see, the list is not long.

But even if we concede that all the indoor scenes were placed in the πρόθυρον, how would this affect their performance on the stage? As a matter of fact, a πρόθυρον or *vestibulum* may simply have been an uncovered area in front of the house enclosed by nothing more than a palisade, and containing various accessories—household

---

[1] Περικ., 34 and 109; Σαμία, 142 and 190, 420 and 830.
[2] Similarly in Aristophanes, *Ach.*, 989; *Eccles.*, 865; *Wasps*, 273; etc.

altars, hermae, etc.—in short, a sort of front yard, or small entrance-way.[1] It is certainly not in this sort of a πρόθυρον that a banquet or a toilet scene could be placed—they might as well be in the street itself. The πρόθυρον that we are asked to picture to ourselves is a sort of portico or antechamber forming a structural adjunct of the house itself. That such structures did exist in Greece during the period in which the νέα flourished I am not proposing to deny. As a matter of fact, πρόθυρα which extended beyond the alignment of the façade of a house must have been the exception, if, indeed, any such ever existed. As far as I know, the ruins of houses of the classical period and of the centuries which immediately followed it do not afford an example of such a structure, and no writer makes any clear allusion to such a thing. But at Priene—and the same thing also occurs elsewhere—it is common to find the θύρα αὔλειος set very much back in comparison with the wall of the façade, and preceded by a vestibule which is wide open to the street.[2] In a building at the Piraeus, dating from the third century, probably a luxurious dwelling-place, the opening of this vestibule, which is much wider than it is deep, is adorned by a colonnade.[3] Hence contemporary architecture did provide stage decorators with actual models for πρόθυρα forming part of a building; but it remains to be seen whether they copied these models; and on this point I am extremely doubtful.

Neither the passage from Aristophanes, nor the fragment of Theopompus, nor the two passages from Plautus, nor Varro's note suggest anything else than an open space lying in front of the façade and the main entrance.[3] And

---

[1] Cf. Aulus Gellius, XVI. 53.

[2] Wiegand and Schrader, *Priene*, p. 285.

[3] Cf. *Athen. Mitteilungen*, IX. (1884), Plate XIII.

[4] The *postes* mentioned in the *Mostellaria*, immediately after the *vestibulum-ambulacrum* (818 et seq.), are the door-posts of the entrance doorway. The painting which Tranio describes (832 et seq.), if it was there at all, may have adorned a part of the front wall of the house (cf. Ussing, *ad loc.*) Theopropides' answer to Tranio's question—*Luculentum edepol profecto* (818)—does not prove that there was anything structural. A *vestibulum luculentum* might simply be a very spacious *vestibulum*.

what do we learn from works of art containing figures? We have a few marble or terra-cotta bas-reliefs representing scenes from comedies [1] in which the arrangement is probably that of the Hellenistic stage. To these may be added some other bas-reliefs which contain no figures,[2] as well as a few vase-paintings depicting scenes from the φλύακες (farces).[3] In several of these works of art we see either colonnades or doors between columns, but the actors move about in front of the columns; and where the back wall is shown the columns are apparently engaged columns. On the other hand, on certain vases dating from the end of the fourth century which are ornamented with tragic episodes, the actors are seen in little buildings that have the shape of porticoes and show on their façade two or three columns surmounted by a pediment.[4] Some of the scenes represented under these porticoes are, no doubt, indoor scenes. It should be added, however, that some of these were in all probability never performed on the stage; like the slaughter of the children of Heracles painted by Assteas, they were, it is true, episodes of tragedy, but episodes which took place, or were supposed to take place, behind the scenes. The little building is, therefore, not a πρόθυρον, but a miniature of the palace in which the chief actors dwelt. The works of art in which the hypothesis of the walled πρόθυρον seems to find its strongest support are the wall-paintings at Pompeii.[5] In many of the architectural decorations we find here, details—such as masks, curtains and small stairways—recall the stage.

---

[1] Dörpfeld-Reisch, *Das griechische Theater*, pp. 327–323; Rizzo, *Wiener Jahreshefte*, 1905, p. 214 et seq. and Plate V.

[2] Dörpfeld-Reisch, *op. cit.*, pp. 332–334. (the Sant-Angelo terra-cotta is published in the *Jahrb. des arch. Inst.*, XV. (1900), p. 61).

[3] Dörpfeld-Reisch, *op. cit.*, pp. 311 et seq.; Rizzo, *Röm. Mitteilungen*, 1900, Plate VI.

[4] Dörpfeld-Reisch, *op. cit.*, pp. 307 et seq.

[5] As the miniatures in the manuscripts of Terence have no precise documentary worth as far as the stage-setting is concerned, it would be a mistake to look to them for proof of the existence of the πρόθυρον, as Bethe has done. Moreover, such doors as appear in these miniatures seem always to be the doors of houses.

Moreover, Vitruvius tells us that, from the beginning of the first century B.C. onwards, the paintings which ornamented the walls of houses were frequently inspired by *scenae tragicae, comicae* or *satyricae*.[1] Now, at Pompeii, doors are frequently represented as having a colonnade in front of them, and figures of men and women are painted *inside* the porticoes, galleries and various small buildings.[2] Do, then, these wall-paintings supply us with a picture, or at least with reminiscences, of Hellenistic stage-setting? It is a curious fact that, in the very paintings which are claimed to resemble a stage-setting most closely, the figures which lend life to the composition are not theatrical figures, but a herald blowing a trumpet, a victor escorted by a Nike, an " apoxyomenus,"—obviously athletic figures in statuesque poses. Moreover, even granting that the architecture in these paintings reproduces stage decorations, it does not seem to me that the disposition of the human figures gives us a sure clue about the *mise-en-scène*. The actors may have behaved quite differently from these purely decorative figures.

Furthermore, it is not always easy to imagine to what use the interpreters of what I have called " indoor scenes " put Pompeian architecture. Let us return to the scene in the *Stichus*. Assuming that the women are seated in a πρόθυρον, *the door of which is open*, this πρόθυρον is necessarily something different from a portico; it must be an enclosed space, and so enclosed that it afforded shelter from the eyes of outsiders, for otherwise Antipho would at once see his daughters. But the paintings do not in any way suggest an arrangement of this sort; and it is, moreover, hard to understand how, under these circumstances, the two women could at one and the same time be visible to the audience and invisible to Antipho, unless, indeed, Panegyris and her sister are seated in the embrasure of

---

[1] Vitr., VII. 5.
[2] Puchstein, *Archaeol. Anzeiger*, XI. (1896), pp. 29 et seq.; Bethe, *Prolegomena zur Geschichte des Theaters im Altertum*, pp. 261 et seq.; *Jahrb. des arch. Instituts*, XV. (1900), p. 77, XVIII. (1903), p. 107.

A A

the door itself; and of this the text gives no indication.[1]
What difference is there, as far as the stage-setting is
concerned, between a πρόθυρον into which one cannot
look from out-of-doors and a room in the house itself?

In a word, it remains very doubtful whether comic
scenes were acted in πρόθυρα of any kind. Moreover, I
fail to see what would have been gained thereby. It is
urged that such a compromise lessened the improbability
of the situation. In my opinion it would rather have
emphasised it. We must not forget that the composition
of the Naples bas-relief, of the Campana plaques and of
other similar works of art is to a great extent fanciful.
In the age of New Comedy the façades of houses very
rarely carried columns. Played before such a background
the performance of " indoor scenes " took place, in fact,
nowhere; and so their representation disturbed nobody.
But had they been set in an actual architectural frame that
was familiar to every one, but unsuitable to them, the contrast between their character and the frame in which they
were set would immediately have struck the spectators.
Possibly, curtains or movable screens shut in some of
the scenes on the sides, and made it possible for one actor
to escape the notice of another—for example, affording
Philolaches a coign of vantage, or Artemona a cover for
her ambush; but this arrangement had nothing in common with the πρόθυρα of real life. At the beginning of the
Stichus I imagine the women are installed in front of
Panegyris' house, on the side of the entrance doorway
furthest from Antipho's house, from which they are hidden
by a screen. Hence Antipho does not see them as he comes
from his house. He comes to the open door, makes the
remark I have quoted, and at that moment his daughters
come out to meet him. In the Asinaria, a scene which
has been lost and of which lines 828–829 are a part, may
have showed the audience (at the very beginning, I think,
of the last act) Demaenetus, Argyrippus and Philaenium

---

[1] When Antipho speaks of the door being open (line 87) he does not
see his daughters.

preparing to sit down to a banquet in front of the background.   Diabolus and his parasite approach, and are
supposed not to see the diners; they enter Philaenium's
house, where *they are represented as being shocked at sight
of the feast*, and come out again immediately.   Thereupon
the parasite goes to fetch Artemona, who, *without going
inside*, spies upon her husband in the manner previously
explained.   Here we have stage convention pure and
unadulterated, and it is quite as good as an unsuccessful
attempt at realism.

Moreover, the liberties which the writers of the *véa* took
were not without precedent.   In Aristophanes, Dicaeopolis
cooks and lounges about out of doors; Strepsiades drags
the truckle-bed on which he means to lie and indulge in
meditation, in front of Socrates' house; Philocleon makes
his toilet in the street, in full view of the passers-by, just
as Philematium does.   In Euripides, too, there is more
than one " indoor scene " that takes place *sub divo*.   It
must be admitted that, as a rule, this poet finds a pretext
for placing out of doors actions that ought really to be
performed indoors.   If Alcestis is represented as coming
out of her palace to die, it is, says the poet, because she
wishes for the last time to look upon the light of the sun.
Phaedra has her sick-bed brought outside the palace
because she longs for fresh air.   But sometimes there is
no pretext : thus no explanation is given why Orestes—
Orestes who is in need of rest and quiet, Orestes who
shuns the eye of man—sleeps, groans, and falls into a
frenzy outside the door, instead of remaining in the
innermost chamber of his palace.

Since scenes that have all the characteristics of indoor
scenes are nevertheless placed out of doors by the comic
poets, we need not be surprised at sometimes hearing
actors discuss confidential matters out of doors, or even
at seeing them come out of their houses in order to
converse in the street.   Doubtless there are cases in
which such behaviour may find its justification either
in the customs of the period, in social usage, or in the

whim of a particular actor. The disinclination of the Greeks to receive strangers in their houses is sufficient explanation for the curious fact that, in the *Epidicus*, Periphanes prefers to send for the sham Acropolistis and to introduce the soldier to her in the street, rather than to take him to her house.[1] But is it conceivable that he should proceed in the same fashion when it is a question of bringing together Philippa,[2] whom he means to marry, and the young woman whom he believes to be his daughter? Similarly, one can understand that Laches, in the *Hecyra*, does not care to enter the house of Bacchis—a courtesan! —nor to let her come into his house;[3] and that Erotium and the Athenian Bacchis come down to the threshold of their house to chat with the men whom they wish to entice.[4] It is less easy to understand that Glycera, in the Περικειρομένη, should send Doris to fetch the box containing the γνωρίσματα in order to show it to Pataecus out of doors,[5] or that, towards the end of the play, Pataecus should betroth his daughter to Polemo in the street.[6] That a tyrannical and hypochondriacal old man like Euclio should not bother to go into his house, but have his house-keeper come out of doors where he happens to be and give her his orders there,[7] is conceivable. But when Erotium, who is about to go indoors, makes her cook Cylindrus come out in order to send him to market, we have reason to be surprised.[8] Nor is it probable that Ballio would hold a review of his retinue on the public highway,[9] nor that Cleostrata and Lysidamus, in the *Casina*, would betake themselves thither for the drawing of lots.[10] In the *Aulularia* Eunomia drags Megadorus out of his house in order to speak to him of marriage;[11] in the *Cistellaria* Selenium, who has just had Gymnasium and her mother to lunch, waits until she has left the table, the dining-room—nay, the house—before pouring out her

[1] *Epid.*, 472 et seq.　　[2] *Ibid.*, 507 et seq.　　[3] *Hec.*, 719–720.
[4] *Bacch.*, 35 et seq.; *Menaech.*, 179 et seq.　　[5] Περικ., 301 et seq.
[6] *Ibid.*, 361 et seq.　　[7] *Aul.*, 268 et seq.　　[8] *Menaech.*, 218.
[9] *Pseud.*, 133 et seq.　　[10] *Cas.*, 295–296, 350 et seq.
[11] *Aul.*, 133–134.

heart to these two women and asking for their help;[1] in the *Truculentus* Phronesium goes out of doors with Diniarchus and carefully gets out of earshot of the servants in order to tell him of the fraud she is practising on Stratophanes.[2] However small the Greek house may frequently have been, surely it would have been just as easy to find a quiet corner in it as to seek seclusion in the street? In the *Bacchides* Chrysalus, who might quite easily have gone into the Athenian Bacchis' house and written his lying letter there in peace, has all the writing utensils brought out of doors, a stone's throw from Nicobulus' door,[3] thus foolishly exposing himself to discovery. In the *Miles* Palaestrio and his friends, who might so easily have held their council within the shelter of Periplecomenes' four walls, hold their consultation out of doors, and run the risk of being seen by Pyrgopolinices or some of his people.[4] And so on. These are all improbabilities whose only justification lies in the poet's desire not to allow the audience to miss anything they ought to hear.

Broadly speaking, it may be said that in the νέα the actors use the public highway as a sitting-room; they appear to be unaware that it is public property and that they run the risk of meeting inconvenient people there. It is true that occasionally one of the actors [5] suggests going indoors in order to converse at leisure. Others take precautions; before they begin to speak they make sure that no indiscreet person is near to overhear what they are about to say.[6] But by far the greater number have no such scruples and speak freely on all subjects out of doors.

Is it necessary once more to remind the reader that such practices were known on the stage long before the time of the νέα? Sophocles' Antigone, and Agamemnon

---

[1] *Cist.*, 1 et seq. [2] *Truc.*, 352 et seq., 386.
[3] *Bacch.*, 714 et seq. [4] *Miles*, 596 et seq., 1137 et seq.

[5] 'Επιτρ., 397–398; *Merc.*, 1005–1006; *Trin.*, 710–711, 1101–1102; *Phorm.*, 818.

[6] *Trin.*, 69, 146–147, 151; *Most.*, 472; *Miles*, 596 et seq., 915, 944 et seq., 1137; etc.

in the *Iphigenia in Aulis*, prefer to hold their confidential
conversations out of doors rather than indoors, just as
Phronesium and Eunomia do.[1] Oedipus in the *Oedipus
Tyrannus*, Creon and Euridyce in the *Antigone*, Iocasta
in the *Phoenician Women*, and Medea in the tragedy that
bears her name, come out to meet visitors or messengers
instead of receiving them in their palace, just as the false
Telestis does.[2] Like Palaestrio and his accomplices,
Orestes and Electra in Sophocles, Helen and Menelaus
in Euripides, and the *ecclesiazusae* in Aristophanes con-
spire out of doors, in the vicinity of the very persons
whom they mean to deceive, and in a place where any
one may surprise them at any moment.[3] Possibly the
older writers were more careful than were their successors
to invent pretexts for such imprudent and inconsequen-
tial conduct. In the long run, the reiteration of pretexts that were often weak must have been regarded as
useless and tedious, and by a tacit understanding between
the poets and the public they were taken for granted
without being expressed.

Finally, let me draw this discussion to a close by calling
attention to various devices which appear to have been
very generally employed by the comic writers of the
new period in order to make more direct communication
between indoors and out of doors.

The first of these devices consists in letting the actors
who come out of the house stand at the door and give
injunctions or address threats or words of advice to those
who are supposed to remain within. This method, of
which there is barely any trace in the drama of the fifth
century, is often entirely, or very nearly, free from convention. When, for example, Sosius, in the *Περικειρομένη*,
after having at a glance discovered Glycera's escape,
hastily comes out of Polemo's house and curses the

---

[1] *Antig.*, 1 et seq.; *Iphig. in Aul.*, 1 et seq.
[2] *Oed. Tyr.*, 945 et seq.; *Antig.*, 387 et seq., 1183 et seq.; *Phoen.*, 1072
et seq.; *Med.*, 214 et seq.
[3] *El.*, 1288 et seq.; *Hel.*, 1032 et seq.; *Eccles.*, 30 et seq.

servants who have allowed the young woman to get away,[1]
or when Hegio, in the *Adelphi*, who has been accompanied
to his door by Sostrata, takes leave of her and comforts
her,[2] the stage action is in perfect conformity with what
one may see any day. But it also happens that speeches
addressed to actors off the stage do sometimes, for one
reason or another, overstep the limits of dramatic probability. Witness the passage in the *Andria*, where Simo
by chance overhears the injunctions of the midwife Lesbia.
She is already outside Glycerium's house, but continues to
address the serving maids. "What curious behaviour,"
says Simo. "While she was with the patient this woman
ordered none of the things a woman requires for a confinement. But as soon as she gets out of the house she
calls out aloud to those who are within!" It must be
admitted that Simo's distrust is not entirely unreasonable; Lesbia waits too long before she speaks. Now let
us look at lines 243 *et seq.* of the *Hecyra*. Phidippus
comes out of his house and chides his daughter. Now,
Philumena is ill, and about to be confined in a few minutes.
Can we imagine that when Phidippus addresses her she
would be near enough to the door to hear his harangue?
Even if we assume that Phidippus' house is extremely
small, this would be difficult.

The same sort of improbability as I have just pointed
out in the *Hecyra* occurs frequently; occasionally it is
even more serious—as, for instance, when an actor who
is outside a house is nevertheless supposed to hear what is
being said indoors, or else to be himself heard by those
within. That Euclio's prolonged and vehement lamentations should penetrate Megadorus' house and reach the
ears of Lyconides, who was probably on the point of
coming out, or that Periplecomenes' little servant should,
while out of doors, hear the shouts of Pyrgopolinices,[3]
who must have been arrested as soon as he entered his
neighbour's house, is natural enough. But is it not strange

---

[1] Περικ., 176 et seq.   [2] *Ad.*, 511 et seq., also 635–636,
[3] *Miles*, 1393,

that Nausistrata, in the *Phormio*, should, while at home, hear the parasite calling,[1] or that Philocomasium should hear Periplecomenes' advice while she is in the soldier's house,[2] or that the groans of women in confinement and the comforting words of those who are helping them should be heard in the street?[3] True, Plutarch tells us that a visitor might find the owners of a house and their slaves engaged in all kind of domestic occupations immediately behind the doors of the αὔλειος θύρα.[4] But that was not the usual place for a dignified and self-respecting matron to take up her position, nor for the most intimate occurrences in a woman's life to occur, especially when everybody about her was trying to keep them secret. Such passages as have just occupied our attention occasionally force us to surmise that the actors communicated with one another through a window. But in most of these cases the wisest course will be frankly to recognise the existence of a stage convention.

I may at once add that this same convention already existed in tragedy. In Euripides' *Orestes* the groans of Helen are heard from without, as she is being murdered; the same is true of the heroine's lamentations in the *Medea*; of Hippolytus' quarrel with the aged nurse in the *Hippolytus*; and so on. Conversely, quite a number of personages, instead of being fetched from inside their palaces, answer calls made to them from without. For instance, in the *Phoenissae* alone, Iocasta does so twice, and subsequently Antigone and Oedipus do the like.[5] In the case of princes, towards whom one would expect to see a certain degree of decorum observed, and who, presumably, dwelt in spacious houses, both the informality and the success of these summonses are improbable. When transferred to the commonplace surroundings of comedy, there is less improbability in such situations.

[1] *Phorm.*, 985 et seq.   [2] *Miles*, 522 et seq.
[3] *Aul.*, 691–692; *Andr.*, 473; *Ad.*, 486–487; *Hec.*, 315 et seq.; etc.
[4] Plut., *De curios.*, 3.
[5] *Phoen.*, 296 et seq., 1069 et seq., 1264 et seq., 1530 et seq.

After studying the stage setting it will be interesting to examine the movements of the actors. The meeting of actors behind the scenes, out of sight of the audience, does not always strictly follow the rules of probability. Sometimes an actor leaves the stage in search of another, as when Plesidippus goes in search of the shipwrecked Labrax,[1] and, contrary to all probability, misses him; sometimes one of two actors who, it would seem, ought to go away together — for instance, Lysimachus and Demipho, in the *Mercator*, after they have done their marketing for an entertainment—stops longer than the other without having any good reason for doing so; and sometimes an actor—for example, Messenio in the *Menaechmi* [2]—disappears from the scene for a while, though no explanation of his long absence is vouchsafed us. But here we may invert Horace's remark—

> *Segnius irritant animos demissa per aures*
> *quam quae sunt oculis subiecta fidelibus . . .*

As these faults in construction were not displayed on the stage, they may very well have passed unobserved. We may, therefore, disregard them, and limit ourselves to an examination of those movements which were seen.

Our poets were obliged to observe the unity of place, just as all the writers of classical drama were, and consequently they had to bring the actors of their plays together at the same spot in turn, and to make them meet one another, and depart in order to avoid meeting one another, as the case demanded. However ingeniously they may have arranged the setting, the fact that they had to do this complicated their task vastly. As long as they were content to introduce natural combinations in which each actor had a good reason for being where he was, and for coming whence he came, no objections can be raised. Megadorus goes to Euclio's house to ask for his daughter's hand, and meets that worthy as he is returning home

---

[1] *Rud.*, 157–158.

[2] He disappears at line 445, and does not reappear before line 966.

from a distribution of public money.[1] In the *Andria*,
Chremes reaches Simo's door at the very moment when
the latter is preparing to go to see him;[2] and so on. Such
coincidences as these, which the actors hail with delight
as being favours bestowed by fortune, are, of course, rarer
in real life than on the stage. They may, however, occur
in real life, and that is quite sufficient defence as far as
the author is concerned. But it is reprehensible for the
actors to appear upon the scene, stay there or leave it,
for no other discoverable reason than the exigency of the
dramatic situation.

I have already mentioned cases in which actors, as soon
as their presence becomes necessary, come out somewhat
too opportunely from one of the houses on the stage.
It would be easy to cite additional instances.[3] Sometimes actors emerge from the *parodoi* suddenly and for
no particular reason.[4] Sometimes they go into their
houses, or more usually disappear under some futile
pretext, for the sole purpose of leaving the field free for
their partners or for actors who have just come upon the
stage,[5] so that some interesting scene may take place before
the audience.[6] And frequently actors remain on the
stage an unjustifiably long time before entering the house
in which they have something to do, or before setting out
for some given point.[7]

Such imperfections as these are the almost unavoidable
consequence of observing the rule of the unity of place.
They were not unknown to the stage before the *véa*,[8]
and they could only be made a special ground of reproach

[1] *Aul.*, 177.   [2] *Andr.*, 532.
[3] 'Επιτρ., 166; *Asin.*, 504; *Bacch.*, 178; *Cas.*, 531; *Cist.*, 639; etc.
[4] *Curc.*, 533; *Merc.*, 335; *Menaech.*, 1050; etc.
[5] *Bacch.*, 924; *Capt.*, 192; *Menaech.*, 213; etc.
[6] *Miles*, 1280; *Poen.*, 197; *Andr.*, 171; *Eun.*, 225, etc.
[7] *Ad.*, 540 et seq.; *Eun.*, 615 et seq.; *Phorm.*, 231 et seq., 784 et seq.;
Hec., 281 et seq.; *Amph.*, 551 et seq.; *Aul.*, 475 et seq.; *Bacch.*, 109
et seq., 385 et seq., 405 et seq.; etc.
[8] As far as tragedy is concerned, see W. Felsch's dissertation, *Quibus
artificiis adhibitis poetae tragici Graeci unitates illas et temporis et loci observa-
verint*, in the *Breslauer philologische Abhandlungen*, Vol. IX. fasc. 4 (1907).

to our poets if they permitted these imperfections to occur too often. Consequently, it is not out of place to put readers on their guard against being too severe. Every movement of an actor for which he himself gives no explanation is not necessarily unjustifiable. In many instances it was plainly the privilege and the duty of the audience to supply an explanation which the text failed to give. Stage-play helped them in doing so, or else other more explicit passages showed them by analogy what was to be understood, though it was not expressed.

I shall cite a few examples. It may seem strange that, at line 198 of the *Hecyra*, Sostrata and Laches should come out into the street in order to quarrel. But if we think of other scenes, such as scene ii, Act I of the *Menaechmi*, or scene ii, Act III of the *Mostellaria*, in which a husband leaves his house in order to escape the society of a disagreeable wife, all is plain. Laches is worn out by his wife's protestations; he leaves the house in order to escape them, and his wife follows him in order to win him over. In the *Heauton Timoroumenos*, line 614, Sostrata rushes out of doors after discovering the identity of Antiphila; is that a mistake? No. Sostrata is impatiently awaiting some one—her husband, to whom she is anxious to tell the news. She goes out into the street in order to watch for him and see him the sooner.[1] As a matter of fact, she runs against Chremes and loses no time in telling him what she has just found out, which is quite natural. Thereupon husband and wife go into their house in order to see Antiphila. Syrus remains on the stage and is promptly joined by Clinia. Here again there is no room for criticism. Syrus does not share Sostrata's happiness nor the soberer satisfaction of Chremes, for the discovery of Antiphila's identity upsets his plans. He has no desire whatever to be a witness to it, and prefers to think over the situation in solitude. As for Clinia,

---

[1] Cf. *Stichus*, 641 et seq. : *More hoc fit, atque stulte mea sententia ; si quem hominem exspectant, eum solent provisere, qui hercle illa causa ocius nihilo venit.*

he is so extremely happy that he cannot stay quiet in one spot. Towards the close of the *Phormio* Sophrona comes out of Demipho's house just in time to meet Chremes. Is her remark in line 738 to be taken literally, and are we to believe that she is hoping to find Phanium's father? Certainly not. Sophrona is beside herself and does not know which way to turn; she bustles about in order to dispel her anxiety. At line 288 of the *Adelphi* Sostrata leaves her daughter just as the latter is about to be confined. Though it seems absurd that she should do so, it is, nevertheless, not unjustifiable. The poor woman dreads being alone with her suffering daughter; she cannot make up her mind to let Canthara, whose kind words comfort her, depart. Further on in the same play Demea rushes out of doors to express his grief over the discovery of Clitipho's dissoluteness. He has been terrified by an unexpected spectacle, and the horror he feels is stronger than his anger. When taken to task by Micio, he resigns himself willy nilly, and makes up his mind to spend a day in merry-making himself. But he does not go back into the house with his brother, for he wishes to examine his conscience, far away from everybody. In the *Eunuchus* Thais comes out of her house to question Pythias about the things that have taken place during her absence,[1] for Pythias was trying to get out of the way because she felt that the time for unpleasant explanations was at hand. Thais stays close by her and follows her out of doors. Cleareta appears at line 153 of the *Asinaria* because she is attracted by the noise in front of her house. At line 701 of the *Aulularia* Strobilus, with the stolen pot in his hands, walks across the stage, that is to say, past Euclio's house. Can this be called imprudent? No. Because Strobilus knows better than any one that Euclio has not yet returned and, as his master has made an appointment with him, he must be anxious to know what has become of Lyconides. Moreover, when he leaves the stage at line 681 he is about to leave town; when he

---

[1] *Eun.*, 817.

returns at line 808 he comes from town. Now it seems that, in order to leave town, the actors went out through one of the *parodoi*, and that they came in through the other when they returned from town.[1] If, then, Strobilus leaves the stage, through the right *parodos*, at line 681, and is to reappear, through the left *parodos*, at line 808, it is well that the audience should see him crossing the stage from right to left during the interval. Indeed, it was an almost universal rule in the days of New Comedy that an actor should, in each case, come back upon the stage through the same door, or the same *parodos*, through which he had made his last exit. The fact that there was an *entr'acte* between his exit and return, just as there probably was between line 681 and line 808 of the *Aulularia*, does not alter the case.

If the reader will examine the entrances and the exits of comic actors with even the slightest degree of good-will and impartiality, he will find sufficient motive for many of them. Moreover, it must be admitted that on the stage, as in real life, people may occasionally come and go with no precise aim, with no definite intention, and simply because they have nothing else to do and because they are fond of walking. "To go for a walk round the square" is a commonplace pretext that repeatedly serves to account for the exit of an actor. I admit that occasionally this pretext is not very plausible. Menaechmus and Lysidamus, who are intent on a "good time," and Apoecides, who has to accompany Epidicus to the slave-dealer's house, choose their time so badly that they run the risk of an embarrassing encounter.[2] As a rule, however, such a pretext must have seemed entirely natural to a Greek audience. For at Athens and elsewhere honest citizens were in the habit of strolling about continually in the agora and gossiping all day in the shops or at the banker's offices. As for the slaves, it is hardly

---

[1] Cf. Alb. Müller, *Griech. Bühnenalt.* (1886), pp. 158–159 and notes; Kretschmar, *De Menandri reliquiis nuper repertis*, pp. 21–22.

[2] *Menaech.*, 213–214; *Cas.*, 526; *Epid.*, 303–304.

necessary to say that to stroll about far from the eye of
their master, nose in air and swinging their arms, was a
great delight. And, finally, we must not forget, particularly as regards the length of time spent by actors at the
door of this or that house, that very often their staying
there is perhaps only apparent. I have already shown
that, in virtue of a stage convention, the area in which the
actors move about is an epitome, so to speak, of a much
larger space. Consequently the spectator is free to
imagine that the actors who appear to be walking about
aimlessly or to tarry in one spot, are on their way to the
scene of action or to some distant place.

This last remark must be borne in mind in order to get
a just appreciation of certain details of construction which,
at first sight, offend us, and which may as well be pointed
out here. Regarded from a dramatic point of view, it
does not always suffice to bring the actor whom one needs
upon the stage at the right moment. It often happens
in New Comedy—incomparably more often than in fifth-
century tragedy and in Aristophanes—that two actors
come upon the stage at the same moment, and are engaged
in conversation as they appear. In such cases we have a
right to expect that their conversation should not begin
too obviously at the very moment of their appearance
upon the scene. Above all, the actors ought not to
appear to have kept things for the ears of the audience
that they should have told one another before they came
upon the stage. There are many passages both Greek
and Latin whose composition is, in this regard, above all
criticism.[1] Elsewhere, the holding back of certain explanations, of certain questions and certain answers, is
more or less justified. In the *Rudens* Plesidippus never
tires of hearing the joyful news that Trachalio gives him;[2]
in the *Hecyra* Pamphilus dares not believe Parmeno's

---

[1] Ἐπιτρ., 1, 464; Γεωργ., 22; Περικ., 77; Σαμ., 68; *Aul.*, 682; *Epid.*,
166, 320; *Andr.*, 820; *Ad.*, 447, 592; etc. Note abrupt beginnings as
in line 957 of the *Mercator*, line 242 of the *Heauton Timoroumenos*, line 415
of the *Hecyra*; etc.
[2] *Rud.*, 1265.

story, and makes him repeat it in order to persuade himself of its correctness.[1] Similarly, although for another reason, Amphitryon cannot make up his mind to trust Sosia's statements.[2] In the *Phormio* Phaedria can never make up his mind to regard the pander's refusal as final, and constantly repeats his request.[3] But, in the *Asinaria*, it is hardly likely that Diabolus should put off having the draft of the contract which the parasite has made read to him until the very moment in which he is about to enter Cleareta's house.[4] Nor is it more probable that Palaestrio should wait, not until after he is in his house—which we could understand—but until he reaches the door, before speaking to Pyrgopolinices about the advances the lady next door is supposed to have made.[5] When, in the *Phormio*, Chremes appears with his brother, we learn from their conversation that he has not yet given an account of his journey to Lemnos, and that he has not yet spoken about Antipho's marriage;[6] what, then, was the subject of the conversation of the two brothers up to that point? In such passages as these we may perhaps put forward the stage fiction of which I spoke above as an excuse or an extenuating circumstance. If we assume that Demipho and Chremes, Palaestrio and Pyrgopolinices, begin to be heard, not when they reach their door, but somewhat earlier, while they are on their way home, the tenor of their conversation becomes less open to criticism.

* * *

The adventures which New Comedy had to depict were at once more realistic and more complex than those which constituted the plot of tragedy and of earlier comedy. But it succeeded in doing so without resorting to devices that were unknown to the stage in earlier times. It was not New Comedy that first employed more than three actors upon the stage simultaneously. Soliloquies, stage asides, *entr'actes*, discrepancy between the time

---

[1] *Hec.*, 845. [2] *Amph.*, 576, 619. [3] *Phorm.*, 485 et seq.
[4] *As.*, 746 et seq. [5] *Miles*, 951 et seq. [6] *Phorm.*, 567 et seq.

required for what the audience saw and for what they did not see, the juxtaposition of buildings and of places that ought really to be far apart, animated scenes crowded into a contracted space, indoor scenes that are placed out of doors, the exchange of confidences on the public highway, too easy communication between indoors and out of doors, the arbitrary moving about of actors—these are all so many conventions, so many improbabilities, of which examples, or at least the germs, are already found in Euripides and Aristophanes. If the task of the authors of the *véa* was, in certain respects, easier than that of their predecessors, this was not due to the fact that they invented new devices, but to the fact that they omitted a troublesome element—the chorus. In a realistic drama the chorus, as it existed in earlier times, would have been an anomaly. In most cases it would have been difficult to know of whom it should consist or on what pretext to keep it on the stage from almost the beginning to the end of the play. Above all, the continuous presence of such an onlooker would have put a restraint on the intimate conversations, the confidences, the plotting, and the effusions and meditations in which these plays abound. Unencumbered by the chorus during the entire course of the play, the stage remained, in fact, a street, an open place where any one might be expected to appear at any moment. For the most part one may suppose that this street or open place was deserted, and the comic poets were entirely free to depict their actors coming and going, hiding themselves or springing on each other, conversing or thinking aloud. This detail of dramatic technique which differentiates the *véa* from tragedy and from earlier comedy—as well as the much freer use of soliloquy [1]—is a natural outcome of the virtual disappearance of the chorus. I do not think it is far wide of the mark to regard this practical disappearance as the most determining factor in giving New Comedy its special character. The chorus must have disappeared in the time

[1] Cf. Chap. IV, § 2 and 3.

of Philemon, Menander and Diphilus, as there is no certainty, nor even probability, that a single fragment of these authors' writings belongs to a choral passage. It did not disappear earlier, because various fragments by such authors of the μέση as Antiphanes, Anaxilas and others were, in all probability, either spoken by members of the chorus [1] or represent the latter as interested in the plot.[2] But it is not likely that so far-reaching a change should have been made all at once. The comic writers of the middle period, no doubt, accustomed themselves to it gradually, and got their audiences used to seeing the chorus eliminated from the plot; and I presume that these authors already began to gather the fruits of this decisive reform.

But the phrase " disappearance of the chorus " does not necessarily imply the total elimination of lyrical passages and songs. As a matter of fact, the *palliata*, in which there is no chorus, contains *cantica*, or monodies, that were recited to musical accompaniment. This is not the place to study the origin of the *cantica*, nor to discuss whether they were suggested to the Roman poets by Aristophanic comedy, by tragedy, or by Alexandrian mimes. What we are concerned in establishing is the fact that Naevius and his successors did not find an equivalent for them in the works of the νέα. According to the statement of the ancient grammarians,[3] the νέα employed only two kinds of metre—iambic trimetre and trochaic tetrametre, and, as a matter of fact, these two are the only metres met with in the lengthy fragments of the original plays that have been published in recent years, and notably in the Kôm Ishkaou fragments. True, some other fragments which have been known for a long time afford examples of more varied metres that are better adapted for singing,[4]

---

[1] Meineke, *Historia Comicorum*, pp. 301–302; Leo, *Der Monolog im Drama*, p. 41.

[2] Antiphanes, fr. 91; Alexis, fr. 237; Heniochus, fr. 5; Timocles, fr. 25.

[3] Hephaist., Περὶ ποιήμ., p. 64, 12 Consbr.; Mar. Victor., p. 57, 14.

[4] Cf. Meineke, *Hist. Comic.*, pp. 441 et seq.; Leo, *Rhein. Mus.*, X. (1885), p. 163.

B B

but their number is very small. As a general rule, the choral interludes appear to have been the only part of a comedy that was sung in the time of the *νέα*. In adopting ordinary spoken language as its usual and practically constant medium, New Comedy remained true to its principles. Occasionally, indeed, it could, without overstepping the bounds of realism, introduce actors who sang a love song or a drinking song, or chanted a prayer or an invocation, and the fragments written in lyric measure are probably parts of passages of this kind. But in real life men do not converse, or argue, or inveigh against one another, or lament their fate, in music. If comic actors were not to sing more than their living prototypes do, song would have had to be practically excluded from comedy. And, as a matter of fact, together with the elimination of the chorus the exclusion of song was the feature which most markedly differentiated New Comedy from the earlier styles of drama, when regarded from the point of view of form; and it is this more than anything else which establishes a close kinship between the *νέα* and modern drama, though they are separated by so many centuries. An Attic tragedy or comedy of the earlier period, if revived before a modern audience, would appear a strange, naïve and artificial production. A comedy by Menander—if we took from it the masks, the costumes, and certain peculiarities of stage-setting [1]— would not surprise a modern audience more than a great many of Molière's plays do.

[1] The chief peculiarity is, of course, the unchanging out-of-door scene. From the point of view of stage-setting, the greatest difference between modern and ancient plays consists in the practice in the former of showing the audience the interior of a house. This detail of stage-setting is, in many regards, a determining factor in the construction of plays, and even in the choice of their subjects.

CHAPTER IV

EXTERNAL STRUCTURE OF THE COMEDIES
PECULIARITIES OF DRAMATIC TECHNIQUE

THE composition of a literary work is not always governed solely by the laws of logic and art. On these necessary and salutary laws caprice and routine sometimes impose other rules, that are not calculated to increase the beauty or the clearness of the work, while they complicate the author's labour to no purpose; and without being confined by such a rigid setting as some modern scholars have maintained, Attic comedy of the fifth century was not, apparently, entirely free from such trammels. We may, therefore, properly ask ourselves— and this is what I mean to do now—whether the comic writers of the new period as well had to submit to some such tyranny.

§ 1

DIVISION INTO FIVE ACTS

In modern editions of Latin comedies the plays are uniformly divided into five acts. True, for Plautus' plays this division only dates from the sixteenth century, but for Terence's plays it appears to be of much earlier date— as early as the time of Varro.[1] Varro, whose example scholars in the Renaissance rightly or wrongly followed, was in a position to know many a thing about the νέα that we no longer know. He read Menander and Philemon, Diphilus and Apollodorus, in the original. He had access to the treatises Περὶ κωμῳδίας which formulated rules for this style of composition. We may assume a priori that when he applied the division into five acts to Latin imitations, he intended to record their resemblance to the models imitated, and that he remained true to the original intention of the Greek poets. We are, therefore,

---

[1] Donatus, praef. *Hec.*, III. 6 (Vol. II. p. 192 Wessner); cf. praef. *Andr.*, III. 6 (Vol. I. p. 40); praef. *Ad.*, I. 4 (Vol. II. p. 4).

led to ask : Did the rule of five acts, that famous law
promulgated by Horace in his *Epistle to the Pisos* —

> *Neve minor neu sit quinto productior actu*
> *fabula* . . . .[1]

govern the works of New Comedy from the beginning?

We have but meagre information about the origin of
this law which was destined to survive so long.[2] At the
same time it is curious that the only drama of Hellenistic
times of whose structure we now have reliable information—a play for marionettes, the *Nauplios*, which was
performed during the lifetime of Philo of Byzantium—
had exactly five μέρη.[3] This fact gives some reason for
assuming that the rule of five acts was already in effect at
the time of Philo. Hence it would have become established between the time of Aristotle, who makes no mention
of it whatsoever, and the second half of the third century.
If it originated nearer the earlier date, it may very well
have been observed during the time at which the νέα was
at its height. Strictly speaking, the subject matter of
the *Nauplios* belongs to tragedy, and it is in a passage
concerning tragedy that we find Horace's well-known
lines. But we know that New Comedy copied the technique
of tragedy in more than one respect, and probably the
new parts of that technique were not the last to be adopted.

[1] Hor., *Ep. ad Pis.*, 189–190.

[2] There is nothing to be got out of Chapter XVI of the *Florida*, in
which Apuleius, in the course of his account of Philemon's death, says
that the comic writers of that period were in the habit of calling forth
the most agreeable emotions (*iucundiores affectus*) in the course of the
third act; for this may refer either to the last act or to the middle act.
Moreover, it is not impossible that Apuleius was guilty of an anachronism.
Nor is anything to be got out of Cicero, *Ad Quintum fratrem*, I. 1, or out
of Varro, *De re rustica*, III. 16. It is not the word *fabulae*, nor anything
similar, that must be supplied after *tertius actus*, in the former of these two
passages, but *imperii*. And though, according to the second passage,
Merula's account must be complete in three parts or acts, it does not
follow that this was true of contemporary drama.

[3] The plot of the *Nauplios* and its division into acts are described by
Hero of Alexandria, based on Philo of Byzantium, in Book II of the
Αὐτοματοποιητικά. Philo of Byzantium lived and wrote in the second
half of the third century B.C.

We have other evidence that bears directly upon the *véa*. For instance, Donatus' statement : *Hoc etiam ut caetera eiusmodi poemata quinque actus habeat necesse est choris divisos a graecis poetis ;* [1] and this amplification by Evanthius : *Comoedia vetus ab initio chorus fuit paulatimque personarum numero in quinque actus processit. . . . Nam postquam otioso tempore fastidiosior spectator effectus est . . ., res admonuit poetas ut primo quidem choros tollerent locum eis relinquentes, ut Menander fecit . . . ; postremo ne locum quidem reliquerunt, quod latini fecerunt comici, unde apud illos dirimere actus quinquepartitos difficile est.* [2] Up to quite recent times passages of this sort were not very convincing. Even the existence of a chorus in Menander's comedies seemed to be very doubtful; indeed, there was some cause to fear that the grammarians had invented an entire system in order to vindicate Varro's scheme. But we now know that plays of the new period were really divided into parts by choral interludes (*choris divisos*), and that their authors set aside spaces for these interludes (*locum eis relinquentes*) in various parts of the plot. The grammarians told the truth when they declared that *entr'actes* existed, and this leads us to believe that they also told the truth when they claimed that there was a definite number of acts, and that this number was five.

So we have serious theoretical reasons for assuming that New Comedy was subject to the rule of five acts. Nevertheless, a verification of this assumption by experiment would be welcome. But the original fragments, even the lengthiest of them, do not supply us with matter for such a verification; for though we find the term Χοροῦ in them, we can never know how often the same term recurred in the course of the same play. We are no better off now than we were before the recent discoveries, and our only means of investigation is to study the Latin imitations.

[1] Praef. *Ad.*, I. 4 (Vol. II. p. 4 Wessner).
[2] *De com.*, III. 1 (pp. 64–65 Kaibel).

The very least that the rule with which we are concerned can apparently signify, is that the plot of every drama in which it is followed should be interrupted four times.[1] We must, therefore, first of all, see whether Plautus' and Terence's plays uniformly admitted of four pauses—a much mooted question, which has given rise to a number of conflicting treatises from the time of the Renaissance onwards. Without stopping to criticise the combinations proposed by others, I shall indicate, play by play, the subdivisions which seem to me to be most plausible [2]—

ADELPHI: Act I. 1–154 (154 lines); Act II. 155–354 (200 lines); Act III. 355–516 (162 lines); Act IV. 517–712 (196 lines); Act V. 713–997 (285 lines).

AMPHITRYON: Act I. 1–550 (550 lines); Act II. 551–860 (310 lines); Act III. 861–1034 and beyond (there are about 180 more lines of this act); Act IV. began before line 1035 and ended at 1052 (it is almost entirely lost); Act V. 1053–1146 (94 lines).

ASINARIA: Act I. 1–126 (126 lines); Act II. 127–248 (122 lines); Act III. 249–503 (255 lines); Act IV. 504–745 (242 lines); Act V. 746–941 (196 lines).

AULULARIA: Act I. 1–119 (119 lines); Act II. 120–279 (160 lines); Act III. 280–586 (307 lines); Act IV. 587–681 (95 lines); Act V. 682–833 and beyond (more than 150 lines).

BACCHIDES: Act I. up to line 108 (at least 104 lines); Act II. 109–384 (276 lines); Act III. 385–525 (141 lines); Act IV. 526–1075 (550 lines); Act V. 1076–1206 (131 lines).

CAPTIVI: Act I. 1–194 (194 lines); Act II. 195–460 (266 lines); Act III. 461–767 (307 lines); Act IV. 768–908 (141 lines); Act V. 909–1028 (120 lines).

---

[1] Whatever Donatus may say in his commentary on the *Andria* (Vol. I. p. 38 Wessner), there was certainly not an *entr'acte* each time the stage was empty, if it was only empty for a few moments.

[2] For the justification of the subdivision here proposed, cf. *Daos* (French Edition), pp. 468 et seq. Briefly, but convincingly, the author there analyses each plot with a view to discovering the points at which an act would most naturally end.(—Tr.).

CASINA : Act I. 1–143 (143 lines); Act II. 144–530 (387 lines); Act III. 531–758 (228 lines); Act IV. 759–854 (96 lines); Act V. 855–1011 (157 lines).

CURCULIO : Act I. 1–215 (215 lines); Act II. 216–370 (155 lines); Act III. 371–532 (162 lines); Act IV. 533–590 (58 lines); Act V. 591–729 (139 lines).

EPIDICUS : Act I. 1–165 (165 lines); Act II. 166–319 (154 lines); Act III. 320–381 (62 lines); Act IV. 382–606 (225 lines); Act V. 607–731 (125 lines).

EUNUCHUS : Act I. 1–206 (206 lines); Act II. 207–390 (184 lines); Act III. 391–538 (148 lines); Act IV. 539–816 (278 lines); Act V. 817–1094 (278 lines).

HEAUTON TIMOROUMENOS : Act I. 1–229 (229 lines); Act II. 230–409 (180 lines); Act III. 410–748 (339 lines); Act IV. 749–873 (125 lines); Act V. 874–1067 (194 lines).

HECYRA : Act I. 1–197 (197 lines); Act II. 198–280 (83 lines); Act III. 281–576 (296 lines); Act IV. 577–798 (222 lines); Act V. 799–880 (82 lines).

MENAECHMI : Act I. 1–225 (225 lines); Act II. 226–445 (220 lines); Act III. 446–700 (255 lines); Act IV. 701–881 (181 lines); Act V. 882–1162 (281 lines).

MERCATOR : Act I. 1–224 (224 lines); Act II. 225–498 (274 lines); Act III. 299–666 (168 lines); Act IV. 667–802 (136 lines); Act V. 803–1026 (224 lines).

PHORMIO : Act I. 1–152 (152 lines); Act II. 153–314 (162 lines); Act III. 315–566 (252 lines); Act IV. 567–765 (199 lines); Act V. 766–1055 (290 lines).

PSEUDOLUS : Act I. 1–573a (574 lines); Act II. 574–766 (193 lines); Act III. 767–1051 (285 lines); Act IV. 1052–1245 (194 lines); Act V. 1246–1335 (90 lines).

TRINUMMUS : Act I. 1–222 (222 lines); Act II. 223–601 (379 lines); Act III. 602–819 (218 lines); Act IV. 820–1114 (295 lines); Act V. 1115–1189 (75 lines).

Here we have more than fifteen plays which allow—if, indeed, they do not demand—the division into five acts. To tell the truth, we know that in some of them the Latin imitator modified his model. But what we know of the modifications introduced by him does not by any means lead to the assumption that the Greek original contained either more or fewer pauses. Let us consider these plays in their order :

— We know that Terence inserted a passage that is an imitation of Diphilus at the beginning of Act II. of the *Adelphi*. But if we omit this passage, that is to say the first forty lines, the pause which precedes, far from being less acceptable, would be rather more so; for Sannio would no longer have to defend himself against the violence of Aeschinus, as the time for that is past. Having got on the track of the young man, he could still recriminate and claim his due—a thing which it is never too late to do.

— It is possible, and even probable, that, in the Ὀναγός, Argyrippus appeared on the scene sooner than in the *Asinaria*—that is, before he leaves Philaenium (line 591)— for I believe that the scenes of Act II. are played by Diabolus. But this hypothesis does not necessarily call for an additional pause. The Greek lover may very well have appeared immediately after the conversation between Libanus and Demaenetus in a scene which the Latin imitator omitted. On the other hand, in Act IV. I imagine that he came out of his father's house after the courtesan and the old woman had gone home (line 544), gave vent to his grief in a soliloquy, and betook himself to the neighbour- ing house, out of which he was driven a few moments later.

— The *Aulularia* is incomplete, but the contents of the part that is lost have been reconstructed in a very probable manner. Euclio came out of his house; Lyconides told him that he had found the pot again and declared that he proposed to keep it as Phaedrium's dowry; Euclio pro- tested, and they made Megadorus arbiter; finally, Euclio was defeated and resigned himself to bear his loss manfully. There was no need of a pause. Moreover, an additional pause in the last part would not prevent our dividing the *Aulularia* into five acts; we need only omit the *entr'acte* between line 586 and line 587—a course that is quite admissible.

— The *Casina* is a mutilated play. In the *Κληρούμενοι* the recognition of the young girl takes place before the eyes of the audience. Elsewhere, I have shown that this episode may have been inserted into the last scene of the Latin comedy;[1] but, in order to make room for it, it is not at all necessary to assume that there was an additional *entr'acte*.

— Apparently the *Curculio* is not a complete reproduction of the Greek play from which it is copied. Nevertheless, it does not seem likely that the acts in the latter play were divided in a different manner from those of Plautus' comedy. If, between the line that corresponds to 454 and the line that corresponds to 455, the banker took the sham soldier home with him in order to receive the thirty minae, the pander, who had returned from the temple of Asclepios, may have occupied the stage with a soliloquy up to the time of his return. At least, others besides myself, who were not looking for traces of a division into five acts, have been led to this hypothesis by an examination of the context.[2]

— The *Eunuchus* contains scenes borrowed from the *Κόλαξ*. But, of the four pauses which I have recognised in it, three seem to me to be necessary for reasons especially connected with Chaerea's adventure. They must, therefore, have existed in Menander's *Εὐνοῦχος*. As for the fourth pause—the one which comes first in the play—it is followed by a scene, the entire burden of which is, as a matter of fact, borne by the parasite, a character taken from the *Κόλαξ*; so that, at all events, it was not in order to give Gnatho time to appear that we accepted it.

— A note by Donatus on line 825 of the *Hecyra*, which ought, in all probability, to refer to line 830 *et seq.*, makes it appear probable that, in the Greek *Ἑκυρά*, the recognition between Myrrhina and Bacchis was witnessed by

---

[1] In the *Rev. Ét. Gr.*, XV. (1902), pp. 376 et seq.

[2] Cf. Bosscher, *De Plauti Curculione disputatio* (Diss. Leyden, 1903), p. 65.

the audience.   I imagine that Myrrhina had been informed by her husband of Bacchis' coming, and that she went to meet her, possibly intending to forbid her entering the house, that she saw the ring and made her explain whence it came.   Thus, the last of the *entr'actes* which I have adopted was less indispensable in Apollodorus than in his Latin imitator; and yet it may have been convenient if, after learning what she desired to know, the matron took the courtesan into her house in order to question her at greater leisure,[1] and make her repeat, in the actual presence of the woman who had been confined, the story that filled her with delight.

— The *Pseudolus* is very probably a " contaminated " play or an incomplete one.   Supposing we admit, with Leo, that it is contaminated?   The structure of the chief original appears to be reproduced exactly, and if the triumph of Pseudolus, with which Act V. deals, is drawn from a secondary original, the chief original must have contained something equivalent.   Supposing, on the other hand, we assume that the *Pseudolus* is a mutilated reproduction of a single original, and that, in this model, Pseudolus' first victory was followed by a second triumph over Simo, the latter did not necessarily fill more than one act, and Act V. might very well have sufficed for its portrayal.

— As for the *Amphitryon*, the question is more embarrassing.   There can be no doubt the play would be more agreeable if no allusion were made to the advanced state of Alcmena's pregnancy or to her confinement, and if, after the thunderclap which alarms Amphitryon, Jupiter were to reveal his presence to him and cheer him up with a few kind words—in other words, if Act V. were left out.   Nevertheless, one must not look for more improbabilities in the Latin play than it really contains.   It is not true that in this play Heracles is supposed to be born a few hours after he is conceived; line 482 expressly declares that Jupiter's relations with Alcmena began seven months

[1] Cf. 'Επιτρ., 397–398; *Phorm.*, 765.

before. It is arbitrary to interpret the words *in tempore*, in line 877, as implying a distant future, and it is equally arbitrary to infer from Alcmena's silence about her pregnancy that she does not know that her confinement is so near at hand. Until I get further light on the subject I shall continue to doubt that the *Amphitryon* is a contaminated play, and that Act V. constitutes an addition to the main original play. My doubts are the greater because it would be impossible to understand why such an addition should have been made, as Act V. is far from comic.

In a word, what has been said about the number and distribution of the pauses in the Latin comedies hitherto examined must hold good for the lost Greek works on which they were modelled.

Let us examine the remaining plays [1]—

ANDRIA : The only passage in this comedy where the link between two succeeding scenes is not indicated is between line 819 and line 820.

MILES GLORIOSUS : There must be a pause after line 946; and a pause between line 595 and line 596 would be acceptable. That is all.

MOSTELLARIA : There must be a pause between line 529 and line 530,[2] and another would fit in between line 857 and line 858; a third pause would be equally appropriate between line 1040 and line 1041. Apart from these three passages, the close succession of one scene upon another is nowhere broken.

POENULUS : [3] A pause between line 488 and line 489; one between line 929 and line 504; and a third pause

---

[1] Cf. note 2, p. 374, and *Daos* (French Edition), pp. 482 et seq.

[2] The fact that Tranio remains on the stage is of no consequence. It occasionally happens in tragedy (for example, in the *Medea* and in the *Trojan Women*) that an actor remains on the stage, during an entire act, without moving or speaking. This may also have been the case in New Comedy.

[3] I think the various parts of the *Poenulus* ought to follow one another in this order : 1–503, 817–929, 504–816, 930 to the end.

between line 816 and line 930. Everywhere else the scenes follow closely upon one another.

RUDENS : A pause between line 289 and line 290 would be welcome; a second appears necessary between line 891 and line 892; and a third is convenient between line 1190 and line 1191. That is all.

STICHUS : There must be a pause between line 401 and line 402; a second between line 504 and line 505, and a third is probable between line 640 and line 641. Although the stage is empty after line 672 and after line 682, the play must go on without interruption to the end.

TRUCULENTUS : There must be a pause between line 447 and line 448; between line 644 and line 645, one would be acceptable; and a third may seem convenient between line 698 and line 699. Everywhere else there are actors on the stage.

We need not consider the *Cistellaria*, which is so mutilated that we cannot reach any trustworthy conclusion as to the point under consideration; but there remain at least seven plays for which I do not think a division into five acts is practicable. This division was, therefore, not especially dear to the hearts of writers of Latin comedy, for there is no indication that traces of such a division were obliterated by later modifications in the case of these seven plays. Hence we may, with all the more confidence, assert our belief that, as far as the comedies are concerned in which we have established its existence, its origin was really Greek.

But let us return to the seven comedies that do not conform to rule.

— Two of them, the *Stichus* and the *Truculentus*, are the products of contamination or of abbreviation; and we need not, I think, concern ourselves with them.

— Two others, the *Miles* and the *Poenulus*, are likewise regarded by very many critics as contaminated plays. As far as the *Poenulus* is concerned, I think this is a mistake; and even for the *Miles* I am not quite sure that it is right. I must add that in both plays it is not impossible to discern traces of an original division into five acts which has been obliterated by the Latin imitator. At line 259 *et seq.* Palaestrio declares that he is going into Pyrgopolinices' house; he does no such thing in Plautus, and the scene which begins at line 272 follows directly on the one that precedes it. But in the original play it is possible that the case was different, and that there was a pause here, in addition to the two pauses indicated above. Similarly, at line 1278, Pyrgopolinices announces his intention of rejoining Acroteleutium; he does not accompany her at once. In Plautus' play this delay, which is unjustifiable, serves to allow of Pyrgopolinices meeting Pleusicles; in the Greek play it may have prepared the way for another pause—the fourth in the play.[1] In the *Poenulus* lines 1162 and 1173, which belong to a version which is perhaps closer to the original text than other parts of the play, appear to indicate a halt, a breathing spell. Subsequently, we see that Hanno is in no hurry to be recognised, and we must concede that as Adelphasium and Anterastilis had gone to the temple in order to see and be seen, they would prolong their stay there. It is, therefore, possible that in the Καρχηδόνιος there may have been a pause—the fourth—between the recognition of Agorastocles and that of the two young girls.[2]

In the *Andria*, we know that certain parts—the rôles of Charinus and of Byrria—were added to Menander's Ἀνδρία by Terence. The addition of these few passages cannot have seriously altered the economy of the play. As in the *Poenulus* and the *Miles*, but more distinctly, I seem to see room for four pauses in the *Andria*. A pause would certainly be suitable between scene ii. of Act I.

[1] Proposed division (with all reservations): Act I. 1–[259] (259 lines); Act II. [260]–595 (336 lines); Act III. 596–946 (351 lines); Act IV. 947–[1280] (334 lines); Act V. [1281]–1437 (157 lines).

[2] Proposed division: Act I. 1–448 (448 lines); Act II. 449–503 (and 817–929) (168 lines); Act III. 504–816 (313 lines); Act IV. 930–[1173] (244 lines); Act V. [1174]–1422 (249 lines).

and scene v. of Act I., in order that in the interval Simo
may be able to join Pamphilus at the market-place and
inform him of his wishes; similarly, between scene iii.
of Act I. and scene ii. of Act II., in order that Davus may
have time to devote himself to the little investigation
whose outcome he explains in lines 355–365; and this
pause would most naturally occur between scenes iii. and
iv. of Act I. In Terence's version the two scenes follow
upon one another without any interruption; but is it
not singular that Davus should go off without giving a
reason for doing so, after he has seen Mysis come out of
the Andrian woman's house? Farther on, at line 598,
it is rather surprising that Simo should ask where his son
is, as, at line 424, he had himself enjoined upon him to
stay at home. It would be much easier to understand
his question if, after line 424, there had been an *entr'acte*
during which Pamphilus might have gone out; and we
are in a position to indicate the point in the plot at which
such a pause would be most appropriate. It is after the
conversation between Simo and Davus, which, in Terence,
ends at line 523. And finally, a pause would be welcome
between scene iv. of Act III. and scene iv. of Act IV.,
as it would give Chremes a chance to make his arrange-
ments for the impending marriage of his daughter. I
should like to place this pause at that point in the plot
to which scene v. of Act III. in Terence's play brings us.
In the Latin poet the first scene of Act IV. follows this
scene without interruption, but the former is one of the
scenes in which Charinus appears, and it may well be that
Terence, at this point, altered the context of his model.
Thus, in Menander's 'Ανδρία, three pauses would have
preceded the only one that I have indicated for the *Andria*.[1]

The two remaining plays, the *Mostellaria* and the
Rudens, are neither of them seriously suspected of being
contaminated. In the *Mostellaria*, in addition to the

---

[1] Proposed division : Act I. 1–[227] (227 lines); Act II. [228]–[523]
(296 lines); Act III. [524]–[624] (101 lines); Act IV. [625]–819 (195 lines);
Act V. 820–981 (162 lines).

three pauses which I have already pointed out, a fourth would be very appropriate between Tranio's departure for the harbour (line 75) and his reappearance (line 348). Possibly, on the Athenian stage the banqueting scene was embellished with songs and dances and so prolonged as to serve as an *entr'acte*, in which case the original play from which the *Mostellaria* was copied would likewise have been divided into five μέρη.[1] In the *Rudens* there is a contradiction between lines 162 *et seq.*, in which Sceparnio describes the shipwreck of the two women which he is supposed to have seen from a distance, and lines 559 *et seq.*, according to which he has just heard from them of their misadventure of the night before. An attempt has been made to explain this inconsistency by assuming that the two first scenes of the comedy (lines 83–184) were added to the beginning of Diphilus' play. I am more inclined to think that only the latter part of the second scene, beginning at line 162, was added by Plautus. Apart from this, a pause might occur between the exit of Daemones and his slave and the appearance of Palaestra.[2]

The conclusion to be drawn from all the foregoing analyses is that the rule of five acts was generally, though not always, observed by the comic writers of the new period. If one recalls the conditions that existed on the Greek stage in Menander's day, this conclusion will not seem surprising. I have said that, after the exclusion of the comic chorus from the plot itself, the part that fell to it was to fill up the *entr'acte*. As a matter of fact, according to Agathon's tradition, the tragic chorus served no other purpose than this. The songs which took the place of the *stasima* of earlier times had been relegated to a purely secondary place. As Weil says, they were merely " a luxury, a digression that was retained out of regard for

---

[1] Proposed division : Act I. 1–[347] (347 lines); Act II. [348]–529 (182 lines); Act III. 530–857 (328 lines); Act IV. 858–1040 (183 lines); Act V. 1041–1181 (141 lines).

[2] Proposed division : Act I. 1–[184] (184 lines); Act II. [185]–289 (105 lines); Act III. 290–891 (602 lines); Act IV. 892–1190 (299 lines); Act V. 1191–1423 (233 lines).

the old masters." Such being the case, the idea of re-
stricting their number may well have arisen. If we only
take into consideration the fortuitous causes that led to
its coming into being, the rule of five acts might, I believe,
quite properly be called the " rule of four *entr'actes*."
By this I do not mean to imply that the exigencies of stage
management alone suffice to explain this rule. It was the
number of *entr'actes* that had to be decided upon, and this
at once determined the number of acts; but if the number
of *entr'actes* was fixed at four—and consequently that of
the acts at five—this was, as I believe, dictated by literary
experience. As will readily be seen, the acts or μέρη
indicated in my analyses, besides in each case consisting
of a series of connected incidents, represent so many
chapters of the plot. The pauses are not placed haphazard;
the first pause most often follows the exposition of the
initial situation, and the others mark the principal stages
by which the story moves on to its conclusion, whether
in a straight line or in a devious course. Now, a dramatic
plot which rises to a culminating point, and then descends,
resolves itself quite naturally into an uneven number
of parts. Exposition, plot, solution—πρότασις, ἐπίτασις,
καταστροφή—to use the terms of an ancient classification [1]—these are its primordial elements. If we take
this division as a basis, a symmetrical subdivision of its
constituent parts would result in a separation into five,
seven or more parts. But it would be irksome to go to
extremes in dividing up a drama. Hence the division
into five parts is, *a priori*, likely to be put into practice.
Let us consider the tragedies of Euripides. If, in dividing
these plays, we allow ourselves to be guided blindly and
exclusively by the distribution of the long choral passages—
parodoi sung by the entire chorus, *stasima* sung in dialogue
form by the members of the chorus—we shall often find
either more or fewer than five μέρη. But occasionally a
passage of one or the other of these categories occurs at a

---

[1] Evanthius, *De com.*, IV. 5, p. 22 Wessner; Donatus, *Exc. de com.*,
VII. 1, 4, pp. 27–28.

place where there is no break in the continuity of the plot; and sometimes, but only exceptionally, there is a break in the continuity without the interposition of a choral song. If we investigate how often the sequence of events is interrupted, we shall find that it is frequently four times.[1] This is the case in the *Rhesus*,[2] and also in the *Persa*.[3] Consequently, when the rule of five acts came into existence, it was very probably merely a sanctioning of an established practice.

Even if such was its origin, this rule, which made obligatory what had been optional, must, in certain cases, have been embarrassing. However, it does not appear to have bound the poets to anything beyond a fixed number of pauses and of dramatic divisions. It certainly did not prescribe an equal or an approximately equal length for the acts; like the μέρη in Euripides' plays, the five acts in Plautus and in Terence vary greatly in length. As I have pointed out, the dramatists of the new period rarely took the trouble to give a reason for the appearance of the chorus during each *entr'acte*; and when they did so it was very often in a trivial and conventional way. An effort has been made to find in the Latin plays a more or less strict correlation between the acts or phases of the plot, on the one hand, and the lyric parts or *cantica*, on the other. Spengel, whose method, by the way, frequently leads him to subdivide the comedies of Plautus in a manner different from that which I have adopted, thought that

---

[1] In the *Hecuba*, after lines 443, 628, 904, 1022. In the *Medea*, after lines 409, 626, 823, 975. In the *Hippolytus*, after lines 120, 524, 731, 1101. In the *Alcestis*, after lines 212, 434, 567, 961. In the *Andromache*, after lines 116, 463, 765, 1008. In the *Suppliants*, after lines 364, 597, 777, 954. In the *Iphigeneia in Aulis*, after lines 163, 750, 1035, 1510. In the *Iphigeneia in Tauris*, after lines 122, 391, 1088, 1233. In the *Bacchae*, after lines 369, 861, 976, 1152. In the *Children of Heracles*, after lines 352, 607, 747, 891. In the *Helena*, between line 163 and line 179, after lines 1106, 1300, 1450. In the *Ion*, after lines 451, 675, 1047, 1228. In the *Mad Heracles*, after line 347, 636, 874, 1015.

[2] After lines 223, 341, 526, between line 664 and line 674.

[3] In the *Persa*, a pause fits well before line 53, another after line 328; between line 448 and line 449, and between line 752 and line 753. Cf. *Daos* (French edition), p. 488, note 5.

C C

a well-constructed act must, at its beginning and at its
end, have two passages in six-foot iambics, a passage in
lyric metre in the middle, and two passages in seven-foot
trochaics in the intervals.[1] Much more recently Leo has
called attention to the fact that quite a number of *cantica*
are placed immediately after the end of an act, and that
others either accompany the appearance of an actor who
is essential to the *dénouement* of the plot, or announce the
approach of the catastrophe.[2] Whatever one may think
of these observations and of these combinations in their
relation to Latin comedy, they cannot hold good for the
works of the *νέα*, because, in the latter, there was practically no equivalent for the *cantica*. The lyrical elements
in Greek comedies of the new period were never so plentiful
that rules for their distribution became a burden on the
poets.

Nor had the comic poets to put any strain upon
themselves in order to place — as they often did — a
monologue at the beginning and at the end of their
plays. There is hardly an instance in comedy of an act
beginning with the presentation of several actors on the
stage engaged in a conversation. At the beginning of an
act, as throughout the play, the actors had to come upon
the stage. Occasionally several of them come on the scene
together while conversing; but more often they come on
the stage one by one. Now it is the usual thing in the *νέα*—
and I shall prove this at greater length further on—for
an actor to introduce himself by a soliloquy in which he
explains why and whence he comes, and what he has done
since his last appearance on the scene. Consequently,
the soliloquies which very frequently constitute the
beginning of an act have nothing peculiar about them.
Nor is it more difficult to account for those which constitute the close of an act. Just as the actors come upon
the stage one by one, so, in most cases, they leave it one

---

[1] Spengel, *Die Akteinteilung der Komödien des Plautus* (Munich, 1877).
[2] Leo, *Die plautinischen Cantica und die hellenistische Lyrik* (*Göttingen Abhandlungen*, N.F., I. 1896–1897), pp. 113–114.

by one. Unless, therefore, he is to make his exit in silence, the last actor to leave the stage has no choice but to take leave of the audience in a soliloquy.

§ 2

PROLOGUE AND EXPOSITION

When limited to the part which it played in the *νέα*— if, indeed, it was ever recognised by the *νέα*—the necessity of having five acts in each play did not greatly complicate the task of the comic poets. Their chief struggle must have been with the difficulties inherent in their art itself, and it is face to face with these that we must now place them, and ourselves as well. As far as composition is concerned, the special task of the dramatist may be defined as follows: to enable the spectators to under-stand, step by step, what is taking place, without how-ever, thrusting his own personality into the exposition of the plot, and without too evidently disregarding the naturalness of the rôles and situations. I shall endeavour to show how far the writers of the new period took their share in this task and with what success they fulfilled it.

It was the opening up of the theme that called for the greatest skill. The author had to introduce actors whose outward appearance—mask and dress—revealed nothing but their sex, their age, and occasionally their social rank, and whose name—pronounced, wherever possible in the very first lines of the play—did not suffice, as it does in the case of tragic heroes, to explain their story. He had to say where the action was about to take place, to map out a situation for the beginning of the play, to acquaint the audience with what had gone before, with facts which, notwithstanding the repetition of similar themes in comic literature, could not be guessed at. Anti-phanes, a poet of the middle period, tells us, in humorous accents of despair, how ticklish the undertaking appeared to him.[1] Long after Antiphanes' day the same difficulties must still have existed.

[1] Antiphanes, fr. 191.

In Plautus' plays, as we know them, it would, at first sight, appear that these difficulties are frequently shirked. At the beginning of fully half of his plays the preliminary exposition is found in a passage *ad hoc*, frankly addressed to the spectators—a sort of announcement, or preface, which Donatus calls *prologus argumentativus*.[1]

Occasionally this prologue is spoken by an actor in the play who, for the time being, forgets more or less completely what befits his part (*Mercator, Amphitryon, Miles Gloriosus, Cistellaria*). Elsewhere, a god, or at least an allegorical being, who has no part in the play itself, pronounces the prologue : the *Lar familiaris* of Euclio's house (*Aulularia*), Arcturus (*Rudens*), Fides (*Casina*), Auxilium (*Cistellaria*). The first two are supposed to be interested in one of the *dramatis personae*. Fides and Auxilium have not even this warrant for appearing; as their names show, it is only out of consideration for the audience that they intervene, to help them to understand and to give them information that is absolutely trustworthy. And finally, at the beginning of the *Captivi*, of the *Menaechmi*, of the *Poenulus* and of the *Truculentus*, an impersonal speaker is entrusted with the task of " posting up " the audience—*Prologus*, the prologue in human form. Convenient expedients indeed ! and they will claim our attention for the present.

There can be no doubt that these expedients were used by the authors of the new period, and fragments of Greek plays supply us with exact analogies of several of the varieties of prologue that I have pointed out.

The extant part of the Περικειρομένη begins with the latter part of a soliloquy, spoken by Ignorance, in the shape of the goddess Agnoia. From her the audience not only learn who Glycera, the heroine of the play, is, but they also hear the story of her life up to the time when the play begins, and how Polemo had quarrelled with her. In another fragment of a prologue which was deciphered in a Strassburg papyrus, and which appears to date back

---

[1] Donatus (*Excerpta de comoedia*, VII. 2, p. 27 Wessner).

to the νέα, we find a god — possibly Dionysus, Hermes, or Apollo, giving the audience an account of the previous history of the characters that were about to appear before them.[1] At any rate, we learn from the first lines that have survived that, at this period, it was quite commonly a " garrulous god " (μακρολόγος θεός) who was entrusted with the task of introducing comic plots. From line 14 we gather that this god was often an imaginary god of the type of Auxilium. It is, no doubt, at the beginning of one of Philemon's plays that Aër, the personification of air, spoke fragment 91—

" I am he from whom no one, man or god, can hide any of his acts, present, future or past. Being a god, I am everywhere, here at Athens, at Patras, in Sicily. And he who is everywhere must necessarily know everything."

At the beginning of Menander's Δύσκολος the god Pan gave the audience some needful information.[2] In the second scene of the "Ηρως " the Hero, a divinity " ("Ηρως, θεός)—probably the eponymous hero of some Athenian deme, or else the heroic ancestor of some family—appeared upon the scene to enlighten the audience.[3] Lucian tells us that in another play by Menander, Elenchos, the god of proof, appeared and told the audience σύμπαντα τοῦ δράματος τὸν λόγον—that is to say, as Lucian explains a little further on, everything that went before and prepared the way for the plot. But let us return to the prologues of the Casina and the Cistellaria. Practically

---

[1] Lines 12–15—

Ὑμᾶς δ' ἐξ ἀνάγκης βούλομαι
[πᾶν καταν]οῆσαι, καὶ θεοῦ τι, νὴ Δία,
[ἄξιον ἐνε]γκεῖν αὐτός, ἀλλ' ὄντως θεοῦ·
[πρέπει Διο]νύσῳ γάρ τι πιστεύειν ἐμοί.

These lines have been variously interpreted by the first editor (Gött. Nachrichten, 1899, p. 549), by Reitzenstein (Hermes, 1900, p. 6239) and by Weil (Rev. Ét. Gr., 1900, p. 429).

[2] Men., fr. 127.

[3] His name appears third in the list of actors (τὰ τοῦ δράματος πρόσωπα), after those of Geta and Daos. He must, therefore, have appeared immediately after the dialogue of the two slaves with which the play opens.

no explanation is given for the intervention of Fides and
Auxilium, and this must be taken as evidence that it was
not conceived by Plautus. In all probability the Latin
poet substituted these two · characters for their Hellenic
equivalents, Pistis and Boetheia, who were introduced
more skilfully. Arcturus, the father of the Attic Erigone,
was, no doubt, more familiar to the Athenians of the
fourth and third centuries than to Plautus' Roman contemporaries. As for the *Lar familiaris*, he may have
been substituted for some domestic hero, or for a θεὸς
πατρῷος, or for Hermes, the god of lucky finds. In a word,
we have a superabundance of evidence to warrant us in
making the νέα responsible for the speeches of obliging
gods.[1]

The fragments of the original plays do not afford such
clear instances of an actor who sets himself unblushingly
to instruct the audience. But in Aristophanes, in the work
of his contemporaries of the fifth century and of his
successors in the fourth, actors repeatedly behave in
just the same way as Palaestrio, Charinus or the aged
courtesan. In one of the first scenes of the *Knights*,
Demosthenes suddenly asks Nicias : " Do you wish me
to explain matters to the audience?—That's not a bad
idea; and we shall ask them one favour : to show us by
their faces whether our acting and gestures suit their
taste.—Well, I'll begin. We have a very brutal master,[2]
etc." We find the same sort of thing at the beginning
of the *Wasps*, of the *Peace* and of the *Birds* ; [3] also in a
fragment of the ῾Υπέρβολος by Plato, the comic writer,
and in another fragment of his Συμμαχία ; [4] in fragment
613 of uncertain date ; and in the time of the μέση, in
fragment 12 of Theophilus and fragment 108 of Alexis.
There is every reason to believe that the comic writers of

---

[1] Cf. Evanthius (*De com.*, III. 2, p. 65 Kaibel) : *Deinde θεοὺς ἀπὸ μηχανῆς,*
id est deos argumentis narrandis machinatos, ceteri Latini instar Graecorum
habent, Terentius non habet.
[2] Aristoph., *Knights*, 36 et seq.
[3] Aristoph., *Wasps*, 54 et seq. ; *Peace*, 50 et seq. ; *Birds*, 30 et seq.
[4] Plato, fr. 167, 152.

the new period imitated their predecessors in this matter. They found a convenient tradition ready at hand, and they cannot have failed to take advantage of it.

As regards the explanations given by Prologus and the person of Prologus himself, their origin, in spite of the most recent investigations into these matters, remains extremely uncertain. A sentence of Evanthius has been adduced as proof of their being Latin inventions : *Tum etiam Graeci prologos non habent more nostrorum, quos Latini habent.*[1] In two other parallel phrases the author speaks of θεοὶ ἀπὸ μηχανῆς and of πρόσωπα προτατικά, and this might make one think that, like θεοί and like πρόσωπα, *prologos* signifies a class of persons. But if it were a question of a personified Prologue, should we not have the singular *Prologum*? I must add that the end of the sentence—*more nostrorum, quos Latini habent*— has evidently been altered; he may have referred to the Terentian prologue devoted to literary polemics. Against Evanthius a passage from Demetrius has been cited. In paragraph 123 of the treatise Περὶ Ἑρμηνείας, he contrasts a character in Sophron's mimes with one whom he calls ὁ πρόλογος τῆς Μεσσηνίας (the Μεσσηνία is a play by Menander). From this it has been inferred that this πρόλογος must have been a personified Prologue like the Prologus of the Romans. But this is by no means certain. Some statements of Lucian's[2] do, indeed, show that the word may very well designate any person to whom the task of making the exposition is entrusted. Yet, in the end, there is no evidence either to prove or to confute, in a decisive and direct manner, the Hellenic origin of " Prologus." On the other hand, I regard it as highly probable that the prologue of Greek plays was sometimes spoken by an anonymous actor, in the name of the author. A fragment of the prologue of the Θαΐς, handed down by Plutarch, seems to me to be of the greatest importance in this connection—

[1] Evanthius, *De comoedia*, III. 2, p. 65 Kaibel.
[2] Lucian, *Pseudolog.*, § 4,

'Εμοὶ μὲν οὖν ἄειδε τοιαύτην, θεά,
θρασεῖαν, ὡραίαν δὲ καὶ πιθανὴν ἅμα, κτλ.

Who else could have pronounced this invocation to the
Muse but one who spoke for the poet? It is certainly
but a short step from an interpreter of this sort to the
" Prologus " of the Romans, and it is not at all impossible
that at one time or another this step was taken.

But, after all, this is of little consequence. Even though
we are told that he is friendly to one of the actors in the
play, a θεὸς προλογίζων, like Arcturus or Lar, is not less
foreign to the plot than the impersonal Prologus; and a
θεὸς προλογίζων such as Fides or Auxilium is evidently
quite as foreign to it. The prologue of the *Poenulus*
might be allotted to Eros, that of the *Captivi* to Elenchos,
that of the *Menaechmi* to Aër, without there being between
these deities and the comedies they introduce any closer
or more real relation, and without giving the author a
claim to greater praise for his composition. The essential
point that must be established—and I am in a position
to do this—is that, whether or not they introduced a
Prologus, the greatest writers of the νέα, in order to
explain the subject of their comedies, occasionally introduced passages that were independent of the play and
were spoken by special actors. When regarded from
our modern point of view, accustomed as we are to a
more stringent technique, this method of procedure constitutes a serious weakness. Before, therefore, proceeding
any further, let me point out the considerations which
excuse or even justify it.

In the first place, it must be borne in mind that, in
taking this easy way out of the difficulty, our poets
followed a course that was sanctioned by custom. I have
already pointed this out in regard to actors who step
out of their regular rôles in order to enlighten the
audience. Nor were the θεοὶ προλογίζοντες an invention of New Comedy. They appear in the works of the
earlier comic writers at the end of the fifth and during
the fourth century. Thus, in the second Θεσμοφοριάζουσαι,

Calligeneia, a personification of one of the days of the Thesmophoria, explains the subject of the play; [1] in the ʿΗρακλῆς by Philyllius, Dorpia, the first day of the Apaturia, does so; [2] in a play—or several plays—of uncertain date, possibly in Plato's Νὺξ μακρά, it is Night that does so. [3] It was especially in the exposition of tragedies that the θεοὶ προλογίζοντες had their allotted place ever since the time of Euripides. At the beginning of the *Alcestis*, of the *Ion*, of the *Hippolytus* and of the *Trojan Women*, divinities such as Apollo, Hermes, Aphrodite and Poseidon explain what has preceded the play, as well as the situation at the beginning of the plot. At the beginning of the *Hecuba* this part is performed, if not by a god, at least by a supernatural being—the shade of Polydorus. It is true that all these personages avoid speaking directly to the audience, as Agnoia, Aër and Arcturus do. But the difference is slight; even though they pretend to be ignorant of the fact that the spectators can hear them, it is evidently none the less in order to be heard by these spectators that the gods of Euripides speak.

Such being their antecedents, we must in all fairness allow the dramatists of the νέα the benefit of extenuating circumstances. A careful examination of the *prologi argumentativi*, of their subdivisions, of their contents, and of their relation to the plays themselves, will show that we must go even further in making just allowances.

If we look at the comedies of Plautus, at the beginning of which either a god or a Prologus communicates the contents of the plot, we shall see that nearly all of them contain a scene of recognition; this is true of the *Captivi*, of the *Casina*, of the *Cistellaria*, of the *Menaechmi*, of the *Poenulus*, the *Rudens* and the *Truculentus*; the *Aulularia* alone is an exception. Similarly there is a scene of recognition in the Περικειρομένη, and there was also one in the ῞Ηρως. In none of these cases could the true qualities of the persons who, towards the end of the play, are the

---

[1] Schol., *Thesmoph.*, 298 (Aristoph., fr. 335).
[2] Phylillius, fr. 8.   [3] Fr. adesp. 819.

objects of the ἀναγνώρισις, be pointed out by an actor in
the play. In a few simple and straightforward sentences
Auxilium, Arcturus and Prologus set forth the social
position of Selenium, Palaestra, Adelphasium and Anterastilis, of the two brothers Menaechmi, and of Tyndarus.[1]
There is no reason to doubt that Agnoia did as much for
Glycera and for Moschio in the first part of her speech,
and Hero for Plangon and Gorgias, nor that the prologue
of the *Truculentus*, of which the complete text no longer
exists, performed a similar service for Phronesium's
supposed child.

We are now in a position to discern a *raison d'être*, an
excuse, for the *prologus argumentativus* : it served to inform the audience, even before the play began, of things
that the actors were not to know before the end. This
precaution may appear superfluous to our modern eyes;
though no doubt to-day, as in earlier times, the finest
scenes of the *Captivi* would not have their full effect did
we not know in advance that the slave who is left in
Hegio's keeping as a hostage, and is ill-treated by Hegio,
is, in reality, Hegio's son; Palaestra's despair, and the
sad memories which recur to Daemones when he sees her,
would seem less touching did we not know that, at the
very moment when they think they are separated for
ever, the father and daughter are close to one another,
were we not afraid that they might pass one another
without meeting, that they might see one another without
recognising each other. But what should we lose if we
remained ignorant of the origin of Glycera and Pataecus,
Selenium and Phanostrata, Adelphasium and Agorastocles,
until the close of the Περικειρομένη, the *Cistellaria* and
the *Poenulus* respectively? Nothing at all, one would
say. This was also Terence's opinion, who consistently
disdained to use the *prologus argumentativus*. But the

[1] In the prologue to the *Casina*, Fides simply says that Casina is a young
Athenian girl born in freedom (line 82); she does not say whose daughter
she is. I think that Pistis, in Diphilus' play, was more explicit. As
Plautus omitted the final recognition (cf. 1012–1014) he shortened that
part of the prologue which announced it.

ancient Greeks thought otherwise. Long before the time
of the νέα, some of Euripides' prologues, in which a
summary of the plot is given in advance of the play,
prove that they did not care for the pleasure of being
surprised. The prologues of the *Ion* and of the *Bacchae*,
in particular, give the audience the fullest particulars
about the identity of the *dramatis personae*. The people
who went to see the plays of Menander, of Philemon and
of Diphilus were apparently in the same frame of mind
as those who had gone to see Euripides' plays. Owing
to a taste which this is not the place to criticise, they
wished, at the very start, to know things which audiences
in our day would be content to learn little by little.

The remarks which I have just made regarding certain
extant comedies would, I think, apply to a great many
others. Aër and Elenchos in Philemon's and Menander's
plays were omniscient beings, and they, no doubt, came
upon the scene, just as Pistis and Boetheia did, in order
to give explanations which none of the actors in the
plays would have been in a position to proffer. Broadly
speaking, the prologue spoken by a god or by the Greek
prototype of Prologus, was probably introduced almost
exclusively in works of a special character, in which the
poet could not, by means of the usual methods of exposition, give the audience as much enlightenment as they
desired to have. Hence the use of the prologue should
not be regarded as evidence of an author's incapacity or
indolence; in the majority of cases it was a necessity of
his profession. As for the prologue of the *Aulularia*,
which is the only one of its kind that cannot be explained
on the grounds indicated, the poet was, no doubt, led
to introduce it by the fact that he had a quite special
object in view. Megadorus is at first opposed to the
marriage, and then suddenly becomes resigned to it; but
the poet had to make this change of attitude appear
natural by making it depend upon the influence of a god.

The above remarks do not afford a complete excuse for
the *prologi argumentativi*. On the one hand, they do not

apply to the prologues spoken by one of the actors in the play who steps out of his rôle for that purpose. On the other hand, neither the θεοὶ προλογίζοντες nor Prologus limit themselves as a rule to making the revelation for which their appearance is indispensable. Much of the information that they give might, at the proper moment, be supplied by actors of the play. Can the writers of comedy, then, be accused of making undue use of the convenient prologue? In this connection two remarks may be made.

In the first place, it should be noted that certain things in the passages which I am criticising are expressed with a precision and an emphasis which are contrary to the laws governing dramatic composition. In the prologue of the *Aulularia* the god Lar formally points out what things are known or unknown to the various actors: " She (Phaedrium) was ravished by a young man of very good family; he knows her, but she does not know him; and the father knows nothing of her misfortune." [1] Before the opening of the *Menaechmi* Prologus warns the audience of the fact that both twins have the same name: " So that you may make no mistake, I tell you about it now: both brothers have the same name." [2] Similar warnings, meant to forestall misapprehension, are found in the speeches of Mercury and of Palaestrio.[3] An author who had regard for dramatic propriety would certainly not have been so explicit. Those who considered it proper to explain matters so circumstantially would necessarily—either by means of a god, or Prologus, or personage of some kind—have addressed the spectators themselves.

Let us now glance at the scenes in the works of Plautus which follow—or precede—the *prologus argumentativus*. We shall soon discover that many of the details supplied by the prologue have either already been made known in advance, in the course of the play, or else are repeated

---

[1] *Aul.*, 27, 30; cf. *Cist.*, 145–146; *Capt.*, 21, 29, 50.
[2] *Menaech.*, 47–48.   [3] *Miles*, 150–152; *Amph.*, 140–147.

in it. The love affair of Alcesimarchus and Selenium,
the plans of Alcesimarchus' father, the hostility of Selenium's mother, the quarrel of the two lovers—all of which
the god Auxilium mentions in lines 190–196 of the *Cistellaria*—had already been confided to her companions by
Selenium in the first scene of the play. At the beginning
of the *Captivi* the parasite Ergasilus deplores his wretched
state, and repeats what Prologus had said about the capture
of Philopolemus by the Eleans, and about Hegio's attempt
to free him by purchasing prisoners from Elis.[1] Further
on in the play, Philocrates and Tyndarus converse together
at a distance from their guards, speak quite frankly of the
comedy they are playing, and tell the audience how each
of them has assumed the rôle of the other, in order to get
the better of Hegio.[2] Through lines 61 *et seq.*, 67 *et seq.*,
and 113 *et seq.* of the *Aulularia*, it is at once made clear that
a short time previously Euclio had become the owner of
a treasure, and that he is full of anxiety about its preserva-
tion. From lines 74 *et seq.* it appears that his daughter
has had an adventure, that she is pregnant and is about
to be confined. Strobilus' soliloquy (lines 603 *et seq.*)
reveals the fact that Megadorus has a rival of whose
existence he knows nothing. Lines 682 *et seq.* show that
this rival is his own nephew, young Lyconides, the very
youth who has ravished the young girl. Thus one can
understand the *Aulularia* from beginning to end without
having recourse to the prologue. A perusal of the *Rudens*
and of the *Poenulus* suffices to show that this is true
of these plays as well. In the *Menaechmi* a few words
added to the first reply made by Menaechmus of Syracuse
would suffice to make the play perfectly clear and enable
us to dispense with the prologue. The *Epidicus* and the
Curculio, both of which plays contained a scene of recognition, probably had a *prologus argumentativus* which has
not been preserved. The disappearance of this prologue
has not resulted in any obscurity, as far as the *Curculio*
is concerned. In the *Epidicus*, on the other hand, the

[1] *Capt.*, 29–101.   [2] *Ibid.*, 224–241.

absence of the prologue does make it hard to understand why Periphanes, on the mere word of a slave, was so ready to accept Acropoliscis as his daughter; but a sentence added to Epidicus' first soliloquy would have sufficed to give us light on this point. As for the very long prologue of the *Mercator*, fully three-quarters of it contributes absolutely nothing to our understanding of the plot, and the rest might just as well have been allotted, as it stands, to Charinus, in his rôle of an anxious lover, as to the same Charinus in his capacity as prologue. The only comedies in which, as far as I know, the prologue appreciably helps in the exposition of the plot, are the *Amphitryon*, the *Miles*, the *Casina*, the *Cistellaria*, and, I think, the *Truculentus*. But it must be remarked that one of the last three plays is incomplete, and that the two others are, in all likelihood, imperfect reproductions of the original Greek comedies. Possibly the actors in the Greek works did more than they do in Plautus to explain the situations as they followed one upon another. In a word, the *prologus argumentativus* frequently merely performs the work of the exposition twice over. It supplies more details and gives more past history; but these added details and these references to the past have only a secondary interest.

Let me recapitulate. The prologue may be superfluous; it delights in details; it takes special care to point out whatever is complicated in the plot. These qualities go well together and they suggest one and the same conclusion : an author was often led to write a prologue by his desire to make things perfectly clear, and owing to a certain lack of confidence in the audience, or at least in some of the audience, rather than by his wish to avoid a difficult task. Attention and acumen are needed, especially in animated scenes, in order promptly to grasp those occasional elements which enable us to know what has happened before the opening of the plot, and to understand what is but half expressed. The writers of comedy well knew that the members of the mixed public which listened to their plays did not all possess these qualities in equal measure. There were dull and inattentive people among the spectators, and possibly they were in the majority. If the author desired to keep such people well informed he must not hesitate to insist and to repeat; even when the actors were in a position to explain everything, and even when they did explain everything, a preface that was at once didactic, very clear and full of detail, and that commanded attention by its very bulk, if I may so express myself, was useful, if not even imperative.

Let no one object that in arguing thus I confound the Greeks and the Romans, nor that I wrong the former. No doubt, many of Menander's Athenian contemporaries were more cultured and more refined than any of Plautus' Roman contemporaries. But side by side with them at the dramatic performances, which were at that time popular festivals, there were seated dullards like those ἄγροικοι with whom the comic writers themselves make us acquainted. Rustics from Attica and rustics from Latium were, no doubt, equally dull, and they obliged the poet to take the same precautions. Indeed, I can quote explanatory phrases from Greek texts which are entirely similar to those I have cited above. " The priestess," says Hermes, in the prologue of the *Ion*, " took the child and brought it up. *She does not know that Apollo is its father nor what mother gave it birth ; the child itself does not know who its parents are.*" [1] One might think that the god Lar was speaking. " I was the stake in the fight against the Phrygians," says Helen, also in Euripides,[2] and she at once prudently adds, " not my person, but only my name " (that is, the phantom which Hera had formed in her image and of which she had spoken before). This is quite on a par with some of Palaestrio's statements. Such analogies are instructive. They warrant the belief that, in his *prologi argumentativi*, the Roman writer hardly outdid the meticulous precision

---

[1] *Ion*, 49–51.   [2] *Hel.*, 42–43.

of the original works—in other words, that the comic
writers of the new period had quite as little confidence
in the intelligence of their audiences as Plautus had.
Unless I am mistaken, we have a very good instance of
this lack of confidence in a fragment in which Philemon
complains of the "unintelligent listeners whose stupidity
keeps them from laying blame on themselves" (χαλεπόν
γ᾽ ἀκροατὴς ἀσύνετος καθήμενος· ὑπὸ γὰρ ἀνοίας οὐχ ἑαυτὸν
μέμφεται)[2]: I imagine it was in the theatre itself that
Philemon used to see these ἀσύνετοι ἀκροαταί.

Hence we can, with a perfectly good conscience, make
the observations suggested by a perusal of Plautus apply
to the dramatic works of the νέα. Should we desire to
prove the correctness of these observations, we have the
means of doing so at hand. If the desire to inform the
audience promptly of the real nature of all the actors
in a play, and the fear of not being understood while
developing a complicated plot—if these considerations
account for the use of the prologue, we might expect
that comedies whose plot is simple, and in which there
are no scenes of recognition, would not be preceded by
such an introduction. Leaving aside the *Mercator*, whose
prologue gives but very slight indications of the plot, and
the *Aulularia*, about which I have already expressed my
views—this is just what we find to be the case. Plautus
refrains from explaining the plot of the *Asinaria* before
the play itself begins.[2] Before the beginning of the
Trinummus he merely tells us that a youth who has
been ruined by his foolish extravagance lives in one of
the houses shown on the stage: "as for the subject-
matter of the play," he adds, "do not expect to hear
about it for the present: the old men who are about to
come on the stage will tell you the story."[3] We know,
however, that Plautus was not, like Terence, a confirmed
enemy of the *prologi argumentativi*. The fact that the
Trinummus and the *Asinaria* are not preceded by pro-

---

[1] Philemon, fr. 143.   Weil's text is here adopted.(—Tr.).
[2] *Asin.*, 8.   [3] *Trin.*, 12–13.

logues must be due to the circumstance that there were
no prologues to the originals of these plays, the Θησαυρός
and the 'Ονάγός. Similarly, the originals of the *Persa,*
of the *Stichus* and of the *Mostellaria* very probably resembled the Latin plays in that they had no prologues;
possibly this was also true of one or the other of the
plays imitated by Terence—for instance of the 'Αδελφοὶ β',
for which the ancients would have considered a preface
unnecessary.

In a word, the comic writers were relatively discreet in
their use of the *prologus argumentativus*; and in many
cases its use does not affect the problem of the exposition
of the plot to any extent.

Before proceeding to examine the various solutions that
have been suggested for this problem, I think I ought to
make a digression; for a number of interesting questions
present themselves regarding the prologues of New Comedy,
their contents, and the spirit in which they are conceived.
To defer a study of these questions would render frag-
mentary the description of these curious introductions;
so that it would be better to give an exhaustive description
of them at once.

The Latin prologues do not, by any means, exclusively
serve to announce and prepare the way for the plot.
Indeed, in Terence's prologues, and in some of Plautus',
there is no *argumentum*. Other methods of making the
exposition either take its place or are adopted side by
side with it, and we must now seek to trace their origin.

We may begin by excluding information such as is ordinarily given in the *didascaliae*. They sometimes contain the
name of the poet and the title of the play, the name of
the Greek author who supplied the model, and the title
of this model. Of these data the two latter certainly
had no parallel among the Greeks, because the works of a
Menander, of a Philemon, or of a Diphilus were original
plays. As for the former—the name of the poet and the
title of the play—we do not find them in any fragment of

D D

the middle period or of the new period, nor I may say,
broadly speaking, in any Greek prologue. The Athenian
audience got this information before the performance,
either through an announcement made during the προάγων [1]
or in some other way.

In addition to such information, the prologue of the
Trinummus contains an episode of a special kind, which
is unique as far as prologues to comedy are concerned.
It consists in a dialogue between two allegorical persons—
Prodigality (*Luxuria*) and her daughter, Poverty (*Inopia*).
The former brings the latter to the house of Lesbonicus;
then she tells the audience who she is and, briefly, why
they have come. And yet it is clearly not the object of
the prologue to make known the subject-matter of the
play. It is a " curtain-raiser " and is meant to arouse
curiosity, to heighten expectation, and must have been
an idea of Philemon's, as *Luxuria* and *Inopia* are Latin
translations of Τρυφή and Ἀπορία. The author of the
Θησαυρός may have got his inspiration from some of Euripides' plays, from the dialogues between divinities which
we find at the beginning of the *Alcestis* and of the *Trojan
Women*, or rather from the scene which serves as an introduction to the second part of the *Mad Heracles*—that
scene in which we see Iris leading Lyssa into the interior
of the hero's palace. Plautus has spoiled his model by
rather clumsily adding didascalic matters. He may have
shortened it, but he did not alter its general character.

But there are very frequently to be found in Latin
prologues elements which, by borrowing from the termin-
ology of rhetoric, we may put together under the heading *captatio benevolentiae*; that is, greetings and wishes
addressed to the spectators, appeals to their friendly
attention, requests for silence, praise of the play which
is about to be performed, bits of literary criticism, vin-
dication of the poet by the poet himself, and attacks on
his enemies. Doubtless all these elements are not taken
over from the Greek prologues. Some of them, like those

[1] The rehearsal.(—Tr.).

in which Terence's prologues abound, have a very immediate interest, and sound a frankly personal note. But it is an open question whether Greek works did not afford precedents for all of them, even though they may not have furnished their actual models.

In a passage of his prologue to the Ποίησις Antiphanes pokes fun at the writers of tragedy.[1] So does Diphilus in fragment 30, which must also be part of a prologue, as it speaks of the place in which the play is acted. The Strassburg prologue finds fault with the unsatisfactory and interminable explanations which certain θεοὶ προλογί-ζοντες delight in giving. In point of literary criticism [2] these are the formal documents. To them must be added several passages from Plautus, about the Greek origin of which I think there can be no question; for instance, the first lines of the *Mercator*, which find fault with the stage lovers who proclaim their troubles to the day and to the night, to the sun and to the moon; lines 53 *et seq.* of the *Captivi*, in which the novelty of the subject and the worthiness of the play are extolled. The remarks about tragi-comedy in the prologue of the *Amphitryon*, and the protest against the mania for placing all comic plots at Athens, may also date from the third century. The former passage calls to mind the peripatetic definitions handed down by Diomedes and by Evanthius, in which tragedy is restricted to noble characters and comedy to vulgar ones. The latter passage may be compared with some original fragments which make fun of the claim that Athens is " Greece *par excellence*," for example, with fragment 28 of Poscidippus. I admit that none of these passages contains a polemic, strictly speaking, nor a plea *pro domo* on the part of the poet, such as are found in Terence's prologues. But possibly such things were to be found elsewhere. When Lucian bids Elenchos

---

[1] Antiph., fr. 191.
[2] Are not fragment 268 of Antiphanes (an apology for the long explanations), fragment 97 of Philemon (same subject) and fragment 130 (professed enthusiasm for Euripides) parts of prologues?

explain to his readers the origin of his quarrel with the
" pseudologist," he adds this advice : " Do not, my
dearest Elenchos, sing my praises to them, and do not
inconsiderately in advance display before their eyes all
this person's disgraceful qualities. For it would be unworthy of you, who are a god, to discuss such abomin-
able subjects with your lips." [1] From this passage it
would appear that, had Elenchos sung the praises of the
author and railed at his enemy, he would have kept quite
within the customary rôle of prologues. Several fifth-
century parabases—those of the *Acharnians*, the *Knights*,
the *Wasps*, the *Clouds* and the *Peace*—contain passages
of this kind, and it is not at all impossible that, in the
period that followed, the prologue took over the functions
of the lost parabasis.[2]

The original fragments contain but few compliments,
reproaches or recommendations, addressed to the public.
The only instances that I can cite are the last words
of Agnoia's speech : Ἔρρωσθ᾽, εὐμενεῖς τε γενόμενοι ἡμῖν,
θεαταί, καὶ τὰ λοιπὰ σώζετε, and the remarks of Philemon
about unintelligent listeners which I have already quoted.
But besides this direct evidence we have some indirect
testimony. In the first place, let me call attention to
the fact that requests for silence, for attention, as well
as more or less clever allusions to the alleged good taste
of the audience are found in various passages in Aristophanes—in the parabases or in the preliminary blandish-
ments which have a resemblance to our prologues.[3] In
the beginning of the prologue to the *Amphitryon* Mercury
promises the audience that he will help them in their
business and in their undertakings if they receive the
play well. The same idea is conveyed in a passage in

---

[1] Lucian, *Pseudolog.*, § 4.

[2] As the Greek word shows, the parabasis was a *digression* from the
plot. In the parabasis of old comedy the chorus addressed the audience
in the poet's name. The parabasis was in no way connected with the
plot itself.(—Tr.).

[3] *Knights*, 503 et seq.; *Clouds*, 521 et seq., 561–562, 575; *Wasps*, 64–65,
86, 1015.

the *Birds*.[1] Note that Mercury mentions good news among the favours which he can grant; but in Plautus' time the Roman Mercury was not generally regarded—as he came to be later by analogy with Hermes—as the typical messenger of his gods. In the *Casina* Fides, the goddess of credit, bids the audience forget their business and their financial worries in order that they may be all attention : " We are having a holiday," she says, " and it is also a holiday for the bankers; everything is calm; halcyon days hover over the forum (*Alcedonia sunt circa forum*)." What is said here about the forum may have been said by Diphilus about the agora of Athens, where the τραπεζῖται had their shops; the mention of halcyon days, during which the sea is perfectly calm, was of a kind that would have greater interest for Attic sailors than for the farmers of Latium. These days coincided with the time of the rural Dionysia, and I can easily imagine Diphilus writing, for a performance at the Piraeus, the passage which we find in the Latin comedy.

Several passages in Plautus' prologues which describe and find fault with the confusion prevailing in the audience have been regarded as interpolations; and they certainly contain traces of Roman customs. However, some of these passages may, as far as their essential points are concerned, possibly date back to the age of New Comedy. Turn, for example, to lines 16–45 of the *Poenulus*. The audience are supposed to be seated, but this does not prove, as Ritschl claims, that the passage was written after Plautus' time.[2] Courtesans are forbidden to sit *in proscaenio*; and the *designator* is not allowed to conduct late comers to their seats while the actors are on the stage. These are, of course, Roman expressions, but would not *proscaenium* be the Latin word for προεδρία?[3] And is it not well to recall that in Greece certain persons were, as a special privilege, solemnly escorted to the

---

[1] *Birds*, 1101 et seq.

[2] Cf. Fabia, *Revue de Philologie*, XXI. (1897), pp. 11 et seq.

[3] Front seat.(—Tr.).

theatre?[1] The *matronae* are requested not to make too much noise, and as there seems to be no doubt that women went to see comedies in Greece,[2] this request may have appeared in the original play. I think this also applies to what is said about nurses and slaves,[3] and to the remarks addressed to those who presided over the games.[4] As for the general form of the passage—that of an *edictum* —it conforms with the taste of Greek comedy, which loved to parody official texts, decrees and laws, proclamations and oaths. It is, therefore, not improbable that, but for a few details, lines 16–45 of the *Poenulus* were imitations of a similar passage in the Καρχηδόνιος. I think this is even more probable in the case of line 6 *et seq.* Here fault is found with people who are so imprudent as to come to the theatre with empty stomachs. In the last couplet of the parabasis of the *Birds*, Aristophanes alludes to spectators who are tormented either by hunger or some other physical distress during the performance.[5] Evidently the two passages are related to one another.

It is the form of the prologues to Plautus' comedies that has chiefly stood in the way of their being regarded as imitations of Greek works, or even as authentic productions of the Latin poet. Even if we cut out the repetitions and the parts that are probably interpolations, the prologues are still verbose. They also abound in jokes—" Dull jests and useless loquacity," as Ussing puts it. Can we make Menander's compatriots responsible for these failings? It would seem so. We have already seen that " loquacity " is not always " useless," and that it may be occasioned by a desire to be clear. The Strassburg prologue speaks of it as being quite customary, and certain peculiarities of style which help to increase the length of Plautus' prologues can certainly

---

[1] Cf. Dittenberger, *Sylloge* 2, 430, lines 22 et seq.
[2] Cf. Navarre, *Utrum mulieres Athenienses scaenicos ludos spectaverint necne* (Thesis, Paris, 1900).
[3] Cf. Plato, *Gorgias*, p. 502 D; Theophrastus, *Char.*, II. 11.
[4] Cf. Aristoph., *Peace*, 734–735.
[5] *Birds*, 787, 799.

be traced back to Greek comedy; for instance, the wealth
of moral reflections which interrupt the statement of facts.[1]
When the rhetorician Theon seeks for an instance of this
sort of *epiphonema* he quotes the beginning of one of
Menander's plays, either the *Δάρδανος* or the *Ξενόλογος*.[2]
Sometimes Plautus invites the audience to express their
views,[3] or else he pretends to forestall criticism.[4] Here
again we have Attic devices. Witness lines 37 *et seq.*
of the *Knights*, 53 *et seq.* of the *Peace*, fragments 307 of
Cratinus, 154 of Pherecrates, 5 of Heniochus, the last
lines of the Strassburg fragments, lines 18–19 of the
Φάσμα, etc. At the beginning of the prologue to the
Captivi the author assumes that a stupid spectator refuses to understand, and advises him to go away; towards
the end of the prologue to the *Casina* he offers to make a
bet with the audience. These passages are similar in
tone to lines 71 *et seq.* of the *Wasps*, in which the audience
is asked to guess what ails Philocleon. It would certainly
seem as if the poets of the *νέα* had, in their prologues,
preserved something of the burlesque style in which
ancient comedy delighted. Demetrius asserts that the
prologue of Menander's *Μεσσηνία* contained samples of a
somewhat unrefined humour—humour consisting of in-
coherence.[5] The play on words contained in lines 37–38
of the prologue to the *Casina* (*est ei quidam servos qui in
morbo cubat—immo hercle vero in lecto, ne quid mentiar*)
is forced in Latin, but it appears to be a translation of
Diphilus' text in which it would have been more natural
(*ἐν νόσῳ κεῖται*).[6] Line 59 of the prologue to the *Menaechmi—ei liberorum, nisi divitiae, nil erat—*is probably a
translation of a Greek phrase in which the writer played
on the various meanings of the word *τόκος*.[7]

---

[1] *Captivi*, 22, 44–45, 51; *Amph.*, 493; *Cist.*, 191; *Miles*, 100; *Truc.*,
15; etc.
[2] Theon, *Soph. progymn.*, IV. p. 91, 11 Spengel.
[3] *Cas.*, 3–4. [4] *Ibid.*, 67 et seq.
[5] Demetr., Περὶ ἑρμην., § 153.
[6] Cf. *Deutsch. Rhein. Mus.* LV (1900), p. 272 ff.
[7] Birth, child, interest (on money), produce of land.(—Tr.).

In a word, in substance as well as in form, Plautus'
prologues must be fairly accurate copies of Greek models,
and when read in connection with the original fragments
they give us a fairly good idea of the prologues of New
Comedy. Still we are left in the dark regarding a very
important question : did the *νέα* contain any prologues
that were entirely given over to *captatio benevolentiae*,
such as we find in Terence? Neither the prologue of the
Trinummus nor that of the *Asinaria* need be considered
here. The former is of Attic origin and, as I have already
pointed out, is a curtain-raiser rather than a prologue;
the latter is probably of Latin origin, and contains only
the usual information given in *didascaliae*. In view of the
character of the play I do not think that the prologue
to the *Pseudolus* was a *prologus argumentativus ;* but very
little of it has survived—only two lines, and possibly they
were not written by Plautus. As for the prologue to the
Vidularia, one can see that it consisted entirely of polemics
and literary criticism. Unfortunately, it is too mutilated
to allow of our forming a trustworthy judgment about its
age and origin. As we do not possess the text of the
Greek prologues, two passages claim our attention. In
the first place, there is the statement of Evanthius, which
I have already quoted, and for which the following reading
has been suggested : *tum etiam Graeci prologos non habent
more nostrorum* (*scil. Terentianorum*), *quos < etiam alii >
Latini habent*. Secondly, there is the classification of
prologues, in which prologues that explain the subject-
matter of the play (*prologi argumentativi*) are contrasted
with prologues called *συστατικοί* in Greek (in Latin :
commendaticius, quo poeta vel fabula commendatur), or
ἐπιτιμητικοί (in Latin : *relativus, quo aut adversario
maledictum aut populo gratiae referuntur*).[1] These two
passages contradict one another, as the one tends to
exclude prologues without *argumentum* from the *νέα*, and
the other to admit them. Neither passage is very trustworthy. The sentence from Evanthius may have read as

[1] Donatus, *Exc. de comoedia*, VII. 2, p. 27 Wessner (= Kaibel, p. 69).

I have suggested, but of this we have no certainty; moreover, Evanthius' authority is not unimpeachable. As for Donatus' classification, I seriously doubt whether it is of Greek origin. If it were, the *prologus argumentativus* would not also be called δραματικός, for this epithet, when used by the theoretical writers of antiquity, has by no means the signification which Donatus gives it; it applies to everything that is spoken by one of the *dramatis personae*, as distinguished from the statements made by the author in his own name. If anything can lead one to suppose that the Greek had prologues that were purely συστατικοί or ἐπιτιμητικοί, such as we find in Terence, it would, in my opinion, rather be the analogy offered by the parabasis to which I have already adverted. In ancient comedy the parabasis afforded the poet an opportunity to address the audience without the pretext or even the desire of explaining the subject-matter of the play. One can readily understand that, when later comedy lost the parabasis, it was not willing to lose this privilege also.

But enough of conjecture ! If I am to limit my observations to what is certain or very probable, I may say that there was a great diversity in prologues. They differed in content, in style and in the person who spoke them. The majority of them were placed at the very beginning of a comedy; but some of them came after a scene in dialogue, just as Aristophanes' addresses to the public do. The latter was the case in the Ἥρως, in the Περικειρομένη, in the *Cistellaria* and in the *Miles* (Ἀλαζών). Occasionally the prologue constituted an entirely independent part, that had no connection with the scene which preceded and followed it. In other cases the actor who spoke it made some allusion to the persons who had been on the stage before him, or else announced the coming of those who were to follow him. One may ask whether this diversity was governed by laws, whether these various types of prologue existed at one and the same time or whether they succeeded one another, and whether one poet preferred one type and another poet some other

type. In the present state of our knowledge of the subject
it is not easy to answer these questions. We possess too
few texts, especially too few texts that can be assigned
to a given author or fixed at a definite date. The Strassburg prologue condemns the speeches of the μακρολόγοι
θεοί; are we to infer from this that the prologues were
not spoken by gods subsequently, or that they no longer
sinned in the matter of verbosity? Certainly not. Nor,
indeed, are we warranted in thinking that, after this
manifesto, more space was given to literary criticism in the
prologues. Several prologues written by the three great
authors of the νέα—Menander, Philemon and Diphilus—
are known to us through fragments, through allusions
or through imitations. Those written by Diphilus—in
other words, the prologues to the *Casina* and to the
Rudens—have certain similarities : both of them are
spoken by supernatural beings, and both of them are
slow and monotonous. But how great is the difference
between the prologue to the *Trinummus* and the prologue
to the *Mercator*, both plays by Philemon ! And how
very different from these must have been the prologue to
which fragment 91, spoken by Aër, belongs ! And finally,
in Menander, we see the prologue assigned to gods (Hero,
the god Pan), to allegorical beings (Agnoia, Boetheia,
Elenchos), to actors in the play (the aged courtesan in the
Cistellaria, possibly the youth in the ʿΥδρία),[1] or to a spokesman of the poet's (in the Θαΐς). I imagine that, far from
limiting himself to the same style of prologue throughout
his career, or even a part of it, each author must have
passed from one style to another, thus varying the effect
produced. For there was one fault above all that had to
be feared in exposition by narrative—dullness. Some of
Euripides' prologues are distinctly tiresome, while, if we are
to believe a malicious remark of Gnathaena's, Diphilus'
prologues were chilling.[2] In order to avoid boring his
audience and with the object of " warming them up," the
comic writer, as we have seen, did not disdain occasionally

---

[1] Quintilian, XI. 3, 91.   [2] Machon in Athenaeus, p. 580 A.

to resort occasionally to somewhat gross jests. This was an extreme measure, and by diversifying the substance, the form and the treatment of the prologue, it was possible to devise others that were in better taste. For instance, the appearance of the person who was to enlighten the audience might in itself be interesting and claim attention. Without being as fantastic as the costumes of the chorus in the fifth century, the " get-up " of one of these superhuman beings might give rise to curious combinations. How, we may ask, were Arcturus and Aër dressed? What were the characteristic attributes of Agnoia, of Elenchos, of Boetheia and of Pistis? Even in the choice of the speakers of the prologue, in the way in which their appearance was accounted for, and in the invention of the allegorical beings, there was room for more or less ingenuity. Were not the spectators perplexed at seeing the star-god Arcturus come upon the stage in order to explain a comedy, and at hearing him open with a couplet about divine justice? Did they not think it paradoxical and curious that Ignorance personified should appear to give them information? But, above all, the character of the incidents that were contained in the setting forth of the subject, the arrangement of its various parts, the relative importance attributed to each of them, the note sounded by the poet, according as it was humorous or grave, personal or impersonal, might vary from prologue to prologue. Herein lay the poets' opportunity to display their originality, their imagination and their humour, and they did not let the opportunity slip.

Let us now close this digression and proceed to the study of the dramatic exposition. After what has been said in the section devoted to the prologue, it will not surprise the reader if, for the purpose of this study, I rely, not only upon fragments of the original plays and upon the opening scenes of Plautus' comedies, but also upon those of Terence's plays. It is quite possible that the majority of the plays imitated by Terence had a

prologus argumentativus, but the analyses which I have
made above have taught us that a regular exposition may
be found side by side with such a preface. Therefore I
do not think that we need imagine that the opening scenes
of Terence's plays differed materially from the opening
scenes of the plays which served as his models, save where
trustworthy evidence affords special reasons for recognising
such differences.

The best form of exposition consists in a dialogue
between two actors, neither of whom is too expressly or
too noticeably bent on putting the other in touch with
the situation. This finer style of exposition was already
known in the fifth century, and New Comedy was not
unacquainted with it. In the *Mostellaria* the altercation between the two slaves, the toilet scene, and the
scene of the interrupted banquet, all of them full of life,
grace and truth, quite suffice to acquaint us with everything we need know in order to understand what follows.
Elsewhere, animated dialogues have a large share in
setting forth the story, though they do not in themselves
constitute a complete exposition; for instance, the threats
which Euclio addresses to Staphyla in the *Aulularia*;
the dispute between Chalinus and Olympio in the *Casina*;
the questioning of Thesprio in the *Epidicus*; the story
of Aeschinus' misdeeds which Demea serves up hot to his
brother in the *Adelphi*; and so on.

The last scenes mentioned are in a way a transition
to another kind of exposition, by means of dialogue, that
is less perfect than the above. In it one of the actors
tells the other—as though in confidence—the things
which the audience are to know. There are different
ways of doing this. In the first place, there are unsolicited
confidences which support and pave the way to a request
for help. In the *Eunuchus*, for example, Thais, in order
to persuade her lover to give her up for a few days, tells
him the complete story of her young companion's life.
The expositions in the *Asinaria*, the *Poenulus* and the
Andria (Περινθία) are of the same kind, as well as that in

the *Persa*, the only known comedy of the middle period. Of the dramatic works of the fifth century, the *Antigone*, the *Philoctetes*, the *Lysistrata* and the *Frogs* begin in a similar manner. Elsewhere, these confidences are invited instead of being spontaneous, and in most cases it is a friend or a devoted servant who calls them forth, when he sees his master or his friend in distress and is anxious to afford assistance. In the *Cistellaria*, for instance, Gymnasium is anxious to know what makes her friend Selenium weep; in the *Heauton Timoroumenos* Chremes is touched by the great distress of Menedemus, and rather hesitatingly decides to ask him what occasions it. Ancient, as well as modern comedy, and also tragedy, afforded precedents for this method of introducing the exposition. It will suffice to mention the beginning of the *Iphigeneia in Aulis*, which was probably written by the younger Euripides; lines 71 *et seq.* of Aristophanes' *Thesmophoriazusae*; fragment 235 of Antiphanes, among the fragments of the μέση. Elsewhere again—as, for instance, in the *Trinummus* or in the *Curculio*—confidences are called forth, not by a manifestation of sympathy, but by a charge which the incriminated person refutes by explaining his behaviour. This device, like the foregoing ones, is of ancient origin, and we find instances of it in Aristophanes—at the beginning of the *Plutus*, of the *Peace*, and in the very first lines of the *Thesmophoriazusae*. Finally, confidences are sometimes elicited by pure curiosity. This is the case at the beginning of the *Ἥρως*, of the *Phormio*, and of the *Hecyra*, and I think it was the case in the opening scenes of the *Ἐπιτρέποντες*, to which fragments 600, 849 and 850 of Menander must belong.

When the exposition is made in any of the above ways there are two serious faults to be feared. The first consists in allowing confidences to be addressed to a person whom we believe to be already acquainted with the facts, thus making them manifestly superfluous. Phaedria may, of course, know nothing of the past life, nor of the family affairs, of Thais, the foreign courtesan, nor need

Chremes know anything of the misfortunes of Menedemus,
who has recently become his neighbour. But let us go
back to the *Curculio*. Phaedromus has already for a long
time been paying court to the girl who boards at the house
of the pander Cappadox, and the conversation he has with
her at the beginning of the play is certainly not the first
he has had. How, then, can it be that Palinurus, who is
that youth's regular, accredited attendant, knows nothing
of this love affair? In Menander's Περινθία it was to
his wife that the father gave a long account of the beginnings of Pamphilus' love affair and of its consequences.
But, whatever one may think of an Athenian family, the
young man's mother must have known all this, and it
was a good idea of Terence's to let Sosia receive the confidences instead of the mother. Thus it appears that
even the greatest of the comic writers of the new period
sometimes ran upon the rocks. More than one of the
actors who, in their plays, is the recipient of confidences,
might with perfect propriety declare with Milphio in the
Poenulus : Iam pridem quidem istuc ex te audivi.[1] But
I may remind the reader that similar imperfections were
already to be met with in earlier dramatic works. In
Sophocles' *Electra*, the account which Orestes gives his
pedagogue—his guide and mentor—of his visits to the
oracle at Delphi is out of place, and it is perfectly clear
that it is given for the benefit of the audience. Nor is
it conceivable that, at the beginning of the *Plutus*,
Chremylus' slave should not know a good deal of what
Chremylus tells him.

The desire to keep these confidences from being regarded
as superfluous led to an increase in the number of *protatic*
persons. This term was applied to the actors who appeared
in the very first scenes of a play but did not come upon
the stage again, nor play any further part.[2] We already
find them in fifth-century plays—in Aristophanes, at the
beginning of the *Knights*, of the *Frogs* and of the *Peace*;
but the use made of them there is not the same as was to

---

[1] *Poen.*, 156.   [2] Donatus, praef. *Andria*, I. 8.

prevail in later times. Having no relation to the plot and
not belonging to the ordinary *entourage* of the chief actors,
the protatic actors of New Comedy may, without violating
the laws of probability, know nothing of the situation
at the beginning of the play or of the events that led
up to it. Hence there is less risk that the detailed explanation which is vouchsafed them will appear superfluous. Here, however, we come to another danger. In
order that these confidences may be above criticism they
must not only avoid the charge of superfluity, but they
must also be prudent and justifiable. But as soon as they
are addressed to a protatic actor—that is, to a person who
is either indifferent or a casual passer-by—there is little
probability of their being so. The cook in the *'Επιτρέποντες*,[1]
Geta in the *"Ηρως*, Philotis in the *Hecyra*, and Davus in
the *Phormio*—what claim have they to the confidences
of Onesimus, of Daos, of Parmeno and of Geta? And
why should they be given them? The writers of comedy
tried, by hook or crook, to get over this danger. One
way of doing this was to let the person who asks for the
information appear to be exceedingly inquisitive, while
the person who gives it is longing to speak. This frequently led to using slaves, or persons of inferior rank,
who are by nature indiscreet and garrulous, for the purpose of the exposition. " You are inquisitive," says
Onesimus to the cook at the beginning of the *'Επιτρέποντες*,[2]
and the cook replies, " Yes, because nothing is more
agreeable than to know all about everything." [3] The
reader will recall the beginning of the *Hecyra*, which is a
model of its kind. Here, Parmeno does not start blabbing
before he has taken certain precautions, nor before he
has secured a promise of secrecy. Geta acts similarly
at the beginning of the *Phormio*, and it is probably to
some opening scene of the same kind that fragment 1 of
Phocnicides belongs : " Can you keep quiet? " — " So

---

[1] I think Leo has proved that it was a hired cook to whom Onesimus
spoke in the opening scene of the Ἐπιτρέποντες.

[2] Men., fr. 849.   [3] *Ibid.*, fr. 850.

quiet, that, compared with me, the men who are making
the treaty would appear to be shouting." [1]

Like many of the methods of exposition to which I
have hitherto referred, these appeals to the love of gossip,
this amusing mixture of indiscretion and prudence, had
their prototypes in earlier days. " I shall not be able to
keep silent," declares one of Trygaeus' slaves, " unless
you tell me whither you intend to fly." [2]   And in almost
the same words Cario says to Chremylus, "I shall not
be able to keep silent, my master, unless you explain to
me why we are following that man." [3]   " What is the
matter, aged sir ? " Medea's nurse asks the children's
pedagogue; " Do not refuse to tell me. I shall be able to
keep silence, if need be." [4]   With the help of these devices
the comic writers succeeded in making acceptable, expositions that were, at best, rather artificial. In the first
scene of the *Hecyra*, for instance, there is hardly anything
to which one can raise objection. The indiscretions of
the slave are cleverly called forth, and there is the less
fault to be found with them as they are in accord with
Parmeno's behaviour during the rest of the play. The
beginning of the *Phormio*, on the contrary, although it
is constructed in the same way, is too short and has no
connection with what follows; its artificiality is apparent,
and there is something conventional about it.

In whatever way it is managed, exposition by means of
dialogue is a difficult thing to handle. So we need not
be surprised to find that the comic writers of the new
period frequently preferred to adopt another form of
exposition, in which they had to deal with less complex
dramatic conventions—namely, soliloquy. The prototypes of this form are well known; Euripides, above all,
made it popular. Aristophanes, who had used it in two
of his earliest comedies—the *Acharnians* and the *Clouds*—

---

[1] The reference is to a treaty mysteriously concluded between Pyrrhus
and Demetrius Poliorcetes, or else between Pyrrhus and Antigonus
Gonatas.

[2] *Peace*, 102 et seq.   [3] *Plutus*, 18–19.   [4] *Medea*, 63–66.

parodies the method of the tragic writers in the opening scene of the *Ecclesiazusae*. Still, this method appears to have been in favour with his successors of the μέση, for fragment 168 of Antiphanes is, no doubt, part of an explanatory soliloquy; in all probability this is also true of fragment 88 of Eubulus, of fragments 89 and 148 of Alexis, both of which were spoken by night, and of fragment 12 of Theophilus. The νέα followed suit. In several of the plays with which I have dealt, soliloquy, coupled with dialogue, helped to explain the plot; in the *Aulularia* we have Euclio's soliloquy; in the *Casina* Lysidamus' soliloquy; in the *Epidicus* that of the slave; and above all, in the *Adelphi* that of Micio. Elsewhere soliloquy plays an even more important part in the exposition. In the *Captivi* the soliloquy of the parasite Ergasilus makes us acquainted with Hegio's troubles— his son's captivity, the traffic in prisoners which his fatherly affection leads him to undertake. We know that it was a soliloquy by the father that explained the plot at the beginning of the 'Ανδρία. And particularly frequent—if we can believe Charinus (in the *Mercator*)—are explanatory soliloquies spoken by lovers.

I have already said that a false and conventional note is struck in most soliloquies when they are supposed to be audible. But, at present, we are only concerned with them as a means of expression. Regarded from this point of view, a soliloquy must be considered justifiable if it conveys what an actor might have uttered or said to himself at a given moment—in other words, if it gives us a correct idea of interests, thoughts and sentiments that are appropriate to the occasion. Particularly in the case of explanatory soliloquies the author was confronted with this problem—to let it appear that the speaker is in a state of mind that makes his reviewing past events appear as a natural thing for him to do. This problem is happily solved at the beginning of the *Adelphi* : Micio is worried because his adopted son Aeschinus does not come home, and there is nothing improbable about his reference

E E

to the method by which he is educating him, and to the
heated discussions which he is obliged to have with
the strict Demea on this subject. In the first scene of
the Γεωργός the lover recapitulates the various phases of
the situation in order to see how he is to manage matters;
so does Epidicus after Thesprio's departure. In the
Captivi Ergasilus bewails the captivity of Philopolemus
which obliges him to go hungry. In the *Truculentus*
Diniarchus criticises his faithless mistress in a melancholy
vein. Each of these persons instructs the audience
without abandoning his true rôle. Elsewhere—as, for
example, in Menander's Ἐπίκληρος, in his Μισούμενος,
and in the anonymous play of which fragment 739 is a
part—it was in order to while away the long hours of
a sleepless night that anxious or discontented persons
mentally rehearsed their troubles. This was not a new
idea. The reader will remember the nocturnal soliloquies
of Strepsiades, of Euripides' Electra, and of the watcher
in the *Agamemnon*. In itself it is not a bad idea, but
the comic writers apparently made singularly bad use of
it. What such texts as we possess allow us really to see
is not any feverish and irresistible anxiety, but, at best,
a vague desire to unburden one's self, with which custom
has a good deal to do; to tell one's troubles to the night,
or to the moon, seems simply to be a variant of the
γῇ κ' οὐρανῷ λέγειν of tragedy—a worthless pretext. Similarly, in the second scene of the *Cistellaria*, the soliloquy
of the old courtesan is weak : " Because I have duly
lined my paunch, and filled myself with the flower of
Bacchus, I am overcome with the desire to let my tongue
wag, and I haven't got the strength to keep quiet about
what ought to be kept quiet." [1] It is perfectly clear that
such reasons as these are nothing more than pretexts.
Moreover, the poets themselves did not take them seriously,
and this is proved by the fact that, side by side with them,
we occasionally find a formal abandonment of dramatic
probability. After having attempted to find an excuse

[1] *Cist.*, 120 et seq.

for her garrulousness, the old courtesan quite frankly addresses her remarks to the audience, and inversely, Charinus, in the *Mercator*, who at the outset addresses the audience, says, later on, that his love is responsible for the length and incoherency of his explanations.

Thus, at the close of my discussion, I come back to a kind of exposition which claimed my attention at its beginning—namely, the soliloquising prologues. The difference between them and dramatic soliloquies is not always very clear. We have just seen that, although Charinus and the aged courtesan speak to the audience, they make a point of remaining true to their rôles and to their character; and in what they say features of both kinds of soliloquy are to be found. But do we meet with soliloquies that lack the characteristics of either variety, in which the actor pretends to ignore the presence of the audience and makes no effort whatsoever to show that his speeches are opportune? Such soliloquies, addressed to no one in particular, are not rare at the beginning of tragedies, while the extant remains of comedy do not afford any examples of them. But occasionally a sentence that savours of being didactic does find its way, as it were parenthetically, into an animated soliloquy. The young hero of the Γεωργός is engaged in picturing to himself the moment of his home-coming; he says that he has found his father's house full of preparations for his wedding, and that his father wishes him to marry a daughter of his. Then he adds dryly : " For I have a half-sister of marriageable age whom the present wife of my father is bringing up at home." [1] In like manner Micio, in the *Adelphi*, allows some historical details, as it were, to find their way into remarks which are quite consistent with his state of mind. Ergasilus, in the *Captivi*, in the midst of his complaints about the hardness of the times, does the like.[2] Although the poet does not address the audience directly, the remarks made by his actors in such cases as these are certainly meant for them.

[1] Γεωργ., 10-11.   [2] *Ad.*, 40 et seq. ; *Capt.*, 94 et seq.

It is quite probable that the tone and style of some of the numerous soliloquies which explained the subject-matter of comedies made them nothing more than a means of communication between author and audience.

No study of the methods of exposition can be complete that ends with a description of the various forms it took in the *νέα*. Attention must be called to another point— the very considerable length to which it sometimes attained. It is at the very beginning of their comedies, before the plot gets under way, that our poets prefer to introduce convenient character sketches and character scenes, of whose popularity we have found evidence; they made a point, it seems, of seeing that the audience was well acquainted with the actors before presenting them in the grip of the plot. Moreover, the writers of comedy loved to emphasise the initial situation—not only to outline it, but to draw a detailed picture and as lively a one as possible. In the *Mostellaria* the dialogue of the two slaves gives us quite enough information about how matters stand. But this dialogue is followed by a long soliloquy by Philolaches which gives us a picture of his unsettled frame of mind. An even lengthier scene depicts his passion for Philematium, and another the dissolute life he leads with her and some merry companions. It is only at line 348 that the exposition really ends. In the *Curculio* the plot does not get under way until after the return of the parasite—that is to say, after more than two hundred lines. There is the same slowness about getting started in the first part of the *Pseudolus,* of the *Asinaria,* of the *Poenulus,* and of the *Bacchides.* In the *Menaechmi* the first mistaking of one twin for the other does not occur until after line 275. In the *Adelphi* the moral issue of the play is formulated early, but the real dramatic problem is not indicated until much later— until after Geta has denounced Aeschinus (299 *et seq.*) and Demea has grown suspicious about Ctesipho's behaviour (355 *et seq.*). In the *Trinummus* all that precedes

Philto's proposal to Lesbonicus is of interest, merely because it paves the way for what is to follow, and it takes up fully one third of the play. The comedies whose plot begins almost at the outset, like the *Andria*, the *Heauton Timoroumenos*, the *Mercator*, the *Epidicus*, the *Phormio* and the Γεωργός, are, as far as our knowledge goes, in the minority—and they probably were so in the sum total of comic plays.

It is worth noting that, in this slowness in coming to the point, the authors of the νέα merely followed the example of the tragedians. It was usual in Sophocles, and the rule in Euripides, and doubtless, too, in the works of his imitators in the fourth century, for the scenes which preceded the appearance of the chorus to serve merely as expositions. Aristotle confirms this in his definition of the πρόλογος · μέρος ὅλον τραγῳδίας τὸ πρὸ χοροῦ παρόδου.[1] Now, the scenes in question, to say nothing of the prologue itself, might be rather lengthy. At the beginning of the *Phoenician Women* the τειχοσκοπία[2] covers 200 lines; in the *Helena* the interview between Helen and Teucer occupies 177 lines, and in the *Electra* the conversation between Electra and the labourer, Orestes' soliloquy and the lamentations of Electra extend over 166 lines. Moreover, it is not uncommon in tragedy to find that the exposition includes the parodos itself and one or several of the scenes that follow it, in addition to the scenes that precede it. This is the case, for example, in Sophocles' *Electra* and in the *Trachinians*, the *Ion*, the *Orestes*, the *Helen*, the *Medea*, the *Bacchantes* and the *Hippolytus*.

§ 3

SOME METHODS USED TO MAKE THE PLOT INTELLIGIBLE

Once the audience has learned from the opening scenes what the starting-point of the plot is, it is a much less delicate task to make them understand its development

[1] Arist., *Poet.*, XII. 2.
[2] Review from the wall; a part of the third book of the *Iliad* was known by this name.(—Tr.).

as it proceeds. Nevertheless, there are cases where the difficulties which beset the proper opening of the play recur to a certain degree. This happens, in the first place, when new characters appear upon the stage for the first time; and, in the second place, when the audience is to be promptly informed of what is supposed to have taken place behind the scenes. Let us see how the comic writers get over these difficulties.

In the whole of Latin comedy [1] we hardly find a case in which the appearance upon the scene of an actor can have disconcerted the audience or confused it to any extent. This does not, of course, mean that it was always apparent from the first words spoken by the new-comers how their parts and their concerns were connected with those of the actors who had appeared before them. Any one who does not know the prologue of the *Aulularia* would not at once see what Megadorus and Eunomia have to do with Euclio, and would have to wait until nearly the conclusion of the scene before grasping it. In the *Adelphi* the relations of Sostrata and Canthara to Aeschinus do not become apparent until several sentences have been spoken. But as soon as the conversation begins one does at least understand in what relations the persons concerned stand, and how they are disposed towards one another; and that is the essential thing. Only in two or three scenes of such parts of Latin comedy as have survived is there danger—or, rather, but for the *prologus argumentativus* there would be danger—that uncertainty or misapprehension about the identity of new-comers on the stage may last too long. This occurs in the *Cistellaria*, when Lampadio gives Phanostrata an account of his interview with the aged courtesan; in the scene of the *Asinaria* in which the impecunious lover, whom one naturally takes for Argyrippus, whereas he must really be Diabolus, is driven out of Cleareta's

---

[1] The extant fragments of the original Greek plays are not trustworthy material in this connection.

house; in the scene of the *Aulularia* in which Strobilus, when taking up his post of observation in front of Megadorus' house, does not tell us who he is until he reaches the end of a rather long soliloquy. But, as we know, the text of the *Cistellaria* is very much mutilated. In the 'Οναγός, the Greek original of the *Asinaria*, the driving out of Diabolus was perhaps preceded by some complaints uttered by Argyrippus, who made himself known to the audience and told them about his rival. Possibly, also, Lyconides came upon the stage in the first part of the Greek original of the *Aulularia*, and even if Strobilus did not then accompany him, his words sufficed to allow one subsequently to guess who the young lover was who had sent Strobylus as his emissary.

Frequently the natural development of the plot, unaided by any device, and without any special precaution being taken, made it possible to identify new arrivals. Many of these persons when they came upon the scene were expected both by the other actors and by the audience; as for example, Theopropides in the *Mostellaria*, Demipho in the *Mercator*, and Cappadox in the *Curculio*; and so on. When the coming of a certain number of other actors was not expected, the way was so clearly paved for it in the earlier scenes that the audience knew who they were as soon as they began to speak; witness Laches and Sostrata in the *Hecyra*, Philippa in the *Epidicus*, Sostrata in the *Heauton Timoroumenos*, Lyco and Therapontigonus [1] in the *Curculio*; and so on. But in addition to this paving of the way, and sometimes concurrently with it, the comic writers had special methods for introducing new characters which I ought to point out.

The following, a heritage of fifth-century drama, was one of the commonest and simplest. As a new actor came upon the scene, the actors who were already on

---

[1] The identification of certain characters was made easier by their costume (soldiers, panders, slaves), that of others through their relation to the stage-setting. (Thus when, in the *Heauton Timoroumenos*, Sostrata comes out of Chremes' house, she can hardly be any one but his wife.)

the stage mentioned his name and introduced him to the
audience. This is the case, for example, in a fragment
of the *Γεωργός*. Just as Daos, the trusted slave of the
young hero's parents, is about to appear, Myrrhina points
him out to Philinna in these words : " A truce to talk !
Here comes Daos, their body-servant, from the country ! "
There is hardly a play by Plautus or by Terence in which
this device is not used repeatedly; in some of their plays,
as in the *Andria* (excepting in the parts of Charinus and
of Byrria) or in the *Mostellaria*, we meet with it almost
constantly. Elsewhere, when specific introductions are
lacking, announcements of some ingenuity are made.
It appears that writers of New Comedy made a special
point of making some reference to a new-comer as shortly
as possible before he came upon the stage. " O, how much
cause have I to wish for my son's return ! " says Sostrata,
somewhere in the *Hecyra*; thereupon she goes off the stage
and the next actor to come on is none other than this son
whose presence is so much desired. " What's this ? "
asks Daemones, in the *Rudens*; " what has become of our
slave, Gripus, who went fishing before daybreak ? . . ."
He devotes a few sentences to finding fault with such
untimely zeal, and then goes back into his house—whereupon Gripus appears.

Coincidences of this sort certainly savour of conventionality; and broadly speaking, one may say that actors
in the *νέα* display an excess of zeal about introducing
themselves and about announcing one another's coming.
Nevertheless, this does not, as a rule, diminish the naturalness of the dramatic situations. There is more danger of
this happening in some of the passages in which the actors
who have just come upon the scene make an effort themselves to acquaint the audience with their identity. These
passages are frequently soliloquies, and it cannot be denied
that for many of them there seems to be a justification,
if we judge them by the rule which I have set up elsewhere.[1] For example, Chrysalus, in the *Bacchides*, tells

1 Cf. p. 417.

us who he is while he thanks the gods for having brought him back to Athens safe and sound, and asks them to let him meet Pistoclerus, his young master's friend, as soon as possible; Nicobulus proclaims his identity by saying that he is going down to the Piraeus to see whether Mnesilochus has arrived there; Mnesilochus tells us who he is while congratulating himself on having so devoted a friend as Pistoclerus, and while he is bracing himself for the impending recognition; Cleomachus does as much while uttering threats against his rival. In all these and other similar cases, the persons who make their first appearance upon the stage introduce themselves to the audience merely by pursuing the course of their own thoughts. But when the parasite Cleomachus declares point blank : " I am the parasite of a coxcomb, of a good-for-nothing, of this soldier who has brought his mistress here from Samos," [1] we have to deal with a soliloquy which is as undramatic as the worst explanatory soliloquies. However, such passages are very infrequent in extant comedies.

It is by means, too, of soliloquies that comic writers frequently acquaint the audience with everything that takes place behind the scenes. Again and again an actor in Plautus' or Terence's plays tells us where he is going and what he means to do, as he is about to go off the stage; on returning, he tells us whence he comes and what he has seen and done. As long as he does this while under the influence of a strong emotion or of some natural preoccupation, and as long as he expresses himself in pathetic words that fit his state of mind, there is no fault to find. Soliloquies such as those of Onesimus, in lines 202 *et seq.*, 399 *et seq.* of the Ἐπιτρέποντες; of Charisius, in lines 429 *et seq.*; of Lydus, in lines 308 *et seq.* of the *Bacchides*; of Aeschinus, in lines 610 *et seq.* of the *Adelphi*; of Pamphilus, in lines 252 *et seq.* of the *Andria*, are as natural as any soliloquies can be. The actors do not review the past nor anticipate the future beyond a point that is warranted by their momentary emotions, by their

[1] *Bacch.*, 573–574.

perplexity, their remorse, their indignation, their anxiety, or their spite. If they give a detailed account of certain occurrences they have just witnessed, and even if they repeat certain words they have just heard, it is because the circumstances connected with those occurrences have made a deep impression on them, and because the echo of those words still sounds, as it were, in their ears. The general character of their speeches is not narrative; it is deliberative or impassioned.

Unfortunately, besides such soliloquies as these, there are others which, in a more or less serious way, overstep the limits of dramatic probability. In the Σαμία Demeas explains in a lengthy soliloquy how he was led to suspect that his concubine's child is the offspring of his son. Of course, one can understand that before regarding this as a certainty he should wish to rehearse the incidents that had aroused his suspicion, in order to see whether his interpretation of them was correct. But what need is there of his going back so far, and giving so many details? Some of his remarks—the parenthesis in lines 19–21, which describes the respective positions of cellar and staircase, and lines 21–23, which serve to introduce Moschio's nurse—are certainly addressed to the audience. They are characteristic of the passage, and when compared with the soliloquies of which I approved above, the first part of Demeas' soliloquy affects the narrative style too much. The same defect is noticeable in more than one passage in Latin comedy and in the fragments. After Pamphilus, in the *Hecyra*, has by chance learned of Philumena's suspected confinement, he gives a well-connected and detailed account of his discovery—a performance requiring considerable *sang-froid* on the part of the one who says that he is so distressed. A similar misuse of the narrative form is found in Dorias' account of the beginning of the quarrel between Thais and Thraso,[1] and when Hegio tells how he had spent his time from the moment when he left the stage up to his return with Aristophontes,[2] or when

---

[1] *Eun.*, 615 et seq.   [2] *Capt.*, 498 et seq.

Euclio comes back from market,[1] and in many other instances.

But even if the soliloquies of these various persons have rather too much of the narrative form about them, it is not at all improbable that the occurrences to which they refer do, for the moment, occupy the thoughts of the soliloquisers. Occasionally, however, even this sort of verisimilitude is lacking, in substance as well as in form, and the soliloquy which enlightens us about the progress of the plot has no dramatic fitness. This is the case in lines 1041 *et seq.* of the *Mostellaria*, when Tranio relates how he effected the escape of Philolaches and his crew from Theopropides' house; in the *Eunuchus*, in lines 840 *et seq.*, when Chaerea explains why he had not been able to change his clothes at his friend's house; in the *Mercator*, in lines 499–500, when Lysimachus declares that he has just bought Pasicompsa for Demipho. The fragments of Greek originals supply several examples of equally improbable soliloquies—for instance, the remarks which Polemo's body-servant Sosias makes in two passages of the Περικειρομένη. In the first passage, it is for the audience's sake that he says his master has consumption and has sent him to get news.[2] In the second passage, he says that he has been sent again, on some pretext, in order to watch Glycera.[3] It must be admitted that many of the statements which I am criticising are very short. Moreover, a speech conceived in a more natural spirit is often closely and immediately connected with them. " My master has sent me back with his cloak and sword, in order that I may see what Glycera is doing, and go and tell him about it," explains Sosias in lines 164–166. The only reason for making this remark is a desire to enlighten the audience; but Sosias goes on, " I would gladly tell him that I caught her lover in her house, so as to make him jump up and run, were it not that I am heartily sorry for him, poor chap ! " That is entirely in keeping with his rôle. " I have done my friend and neighbour a good

---

[1] *Aul.*, 371 et seq. [2] Περικ., 52 et seq. [3] *Ibid.*, 164 et seq.

turn; I have purchased these goods for him, as he asked me to," says Lysimachus, rather inopportunely, and thereupon immediately addresses these words to Pasicompsa : " As you belong to me, follow me; do not weep; it is foolish to spoil such pretty eyes, etc." These animated words efface and conceal whatever clumsiness there was in his earlier statement. Owing to their brevity and their close proximity to elements of better alloy, many of these " notices to the public " are not very conspicuous, and consequently do not give offence. Nevertheless, considered by themselves, they are stamped with the mark of convention.

In a word, it must be admitted that the authors of the *véa* made excessive use of narrative soliloquy in the plays themselves, as well as in the introductions. Furthermore, it is not only in the scenes which serve as expositions that they violate dramatic fiction and frankly address the audience. Evanthius praises Terence because his actors " never speak for the benefit of the audience, as though they had nothing to do with the plot." [1] Plautus' actors, on the contrary, take this liberty often, and at any point in the play. We now know which of the two poets carried on the Attic tradition, for here and there, in the newly discovered fragments of Menander, we find the vocative ἄνδρες, which no doubt indicates an apostrophe to the audience.[2] This vocative does not, of course, prove that the author had no regard for psychological truth, as one can see by reading the context; but it does prove that, at the height of the new period, the greatest poets never completely gave up the unconventionality and easy freedom of manner that were found in early comedy.

Nevertheless, it was not in the school of ancient comedy nor, speaking more broadly, in the school of the authors of the fifth century, that they learned to use narrative soliloquy in the way in which we have seen them use it.

---

[1] Evanthius, *De com.*, III. 8 (p. 66 Kaibel).
[2] Ἐπιτρ., 392; Σαμ., 114, 338.   Cf. Men., fr. 24, 461, 536; fr. adesp. 104.

True, in Aristophanes, hardly any part of the plot is supposed to take place behind the scenes. On the other hand, in the tragic writers, the combats, the murders, and the suicides, which so frequently form a part of the story, regularly take place behind the scenes; but they are all described by one actor to another on the stage. Are, then, the dramatists of the *véa* from this point of view inferior to the tragedians? Is it fair to reproach them with lack of skill and with carelessness when we compare them with their predecessors? We must remember that, in tragedy, the account of the occurrences which the audience does not see is generally given by characters introduced *ad hoc*, by messengers (ἄγγελοι), who do not always have very valid reasons for coming to tell their story. Furthermore, we must remember that this story is not always told to persons who are entitled to hear it— especially when it is told to the chorus—and that, after having done away with the chorus, who, in many cases, would have been embarrassing both as listeners and witnesses, New Comedy found that, in other cases, it had deprived its actors of a kindly disposed listener. These considerations ought to make us somewhat indulgent in dealing with narrative soliloquies. Taken all in all, the story of more than one ἄγγελος oversteps the bounds of probability quite as much as these soliloquies do.

Moreover, it would be unfair to attribute more importance to these soliloquies than they actually possessed in the economy of the works of the *véa*. But less objectionable methods are employed in comedy as well. In the first place, it goes without saying that occasionally one person tells another what he has just seen or heard, and there is no denying that, as a rule, there is good reason for his doing so. Or else, a parting exhortation made by an actor, as he comes upon the stage, to persons whom the audience do not see, or a few sentences of conversation of which they hear only the conclusion, suffice to inform them about what has happened behind the scenes. I have discussed these devices, which are quite as old as

narrative soliloquy itself, in the course of Chapter III.
I merely refer to them here.

Just as it is necessary to acquaint the audience with
things that take place, unseen by them, in the course of
the play, so it seems to me desirable to spare them a too
lengthy description of incidents that have taken place
before their eyes, and also a too detailed announcement of
the incidents they are about to witness.

As regards the first point, the practice of the *véa* seems
in conformity with our tastes. I find only one or two
scenes in Plautus and in Terence in which one actor tells
another about things of which the audience is sufficiently
informed : a scene in the *Eunuchus* in which Chaerea
explains to Antipho how he got the idea of disguising
himself,[1] and a scene in the *Trinummus* in which Callicles
explains to Charmides the trick of the false messenger.[2]
The first of these repetitions cannot have occurred in the
Greek play,[3] and it was so easy to avoid the second
that the poet must have had some special reason for
introducing it. Further on, I shall try to show what that
reason was. Other scenes, like that between Trachalio
and Plesidippus, in lines 1265 *et seq.* of the *Rudens*, and
that between Amphitryon and Sosia, in lines 551 *et seq.*
of the *Amphitryon*, where an actor, in the course of a
dialogue, reviews things that have taken place before the
play begins, are not entirely unimpeachable, but at least
their faults do not consist in slowness or dullness. The
retrospective explanations for which one actor asks, or
might reasonably ask, another, but which might risk
appearing tedious, are occasionally left out of a scene
owing to stage conventions, the street not being a place
in which those concerned could undisturbedly give them
or hear them.[4] Or else they are systematically avoided :
for instance, in the Phormio, line 861 (*omitto proloqui ;*

---

[1] *Eun.*, 562–575.   [2] *Trin.*, 1137 et seq.
[3] Because in it the sham eunuch was not speaking to any one.
[4] 'Επιτρ., 397–398; *Merc.*, 1005–1006; *Phorm.*, 765; *Trin.*, 1101–1102.

nam nil ad hanc rem'st, Antipho); in the *Mercator*, line 904 (*ut inique rogas*); in the *Heauton Timoroumenos*, line 824 (*ipsa re experibere*); in the *Epidicus*, line 656 (*cetera haec posterius faxo scibis, ubi erit otium*); in the *Pseudolus*, lines 720–721 (*horum causa haec agitur spectatorum fabula ; hi sciunt, qui hic adfuerunt; vobis post narravero*). Pseudolus' sally humorously expresses the real purpose of all these evasions. We must, nevertheless, admit that, from a dramatic point of view, they are quite permissible; when it is time to act, words are out of season. With equal fitness certain actors in Latin comedy refuse to divulge their plans. " What will you do? " Pamphilus asks Davus, in the *Andria*. Davus replies, " I am afraid the day will not be long enough for my plans and, believe me, I haven't got time to tell you of them." [1]

The opposite course, pursued by certain persons who announce and explain in advance all that is about to happen, deserves our attention much more. In lines 466 *et seq.* of the *Amphitryon*, Mercury, after having got rid of Sosia, gives an outline in advance of the impending imbroglio. Further on, in lines 873 *et seq.*, even Jupiter himself deigns to resume and complete this information, and when he bids Sosia go to invite Blepharo, he adds, for the benefit of the audience : " Blepharo will have to go without his dinner, and will be in a ridiculous fix when I take Amphitryon by the neck and drag him away from here." [2] Elsewhere, tricks that are to be played before the eyes of the spectators are emphatically and minutely explained in advance. In the first part of the *Miles* (*Δίδυμαι*) Philocomasium is alternately taken for her twin sister and for herself; Palaestrio, who plays the part of the prologue, informs the audience of this double rôle.[3] Subsequently, while conversing with Periplecomenus, he explains the fraud they are planning,[4] and it seems as though it might be perpetrated without any further notice to the public; and yet, before the sham Dicea

---

[1] *Andr.*, 705–706; Cf. *Heaut.*, 335–336; *Phorm.*, 566; *Pseud.*, 387–388.
[2] *Amph.*, 952–953.   [3] *Miles*, prol. 150 et seq.   [4] *Ibid.*, 237 et seq.

appears, Philocomasium once more explains point by point what is about to happen.[1] Were Sceledrus not so stupid, this extraordinary coincidence would arouse his suspicions. In the second part of the same play (᾽Αλαζών) Pyrgopolinices is to be made to believe that Acroteleutium is his neighbour's wife, and that she is enamoured of him. The purpose of this mystification is to persuade the soldier to dismiss his mistress, who is to make room for his new favourite. Pleusicles, disguised as a sailor, is to appear in the nick of time to reinstate the young woman. This plan, which can be stated in a few words, is not at all complicated, but the author develops it little by little, as though he did not wish to subject the audience to too much of a mental strain. It is at the eleventh hour, when the time for action has almost come, that Pleusicles receives his instructions, hears what costume he is to wear, what gestures he is to make, and what he is to say.[2] It is only after Pyrgopolinices has begun to nibble at the bait that the first reference is made to the dismissal of Philocomasium.[3] In short, Palaestrio's accomplices follow him without apparently knowing where they are going; and this is certainly surprising. On the other hand, before the first move is made—that is, before the amorous advances, which Acroteleutium is to feign, take place, and in order to ensure their success, these accomplices are given most detailed instructions, only not once, but again and again, without any apparent fear of repetition. To begin with, Palaestrio explains his plan to Periplecomenus when he asks him for his ring and comes to him in search of helpmates.[4] A little later on, Periplecomenus brings in the two women whom he has already instructed. For all that, Palaestrio begins to coach Acroteleutium,[5] and, on taking leave of the conspirators and going to his master, he repeats the essential features of the plot, though there is little need of his doing so.[6] But this is not all; just before he sets Milphidippa at

---

[1] *Miles*, 380 et seq. [2] *Ibid.*, 1175 et seq. [3] *Ibid.*, 974 et seq.
[4] *Ibid.*, 770 et seq. [5] *Ibid.*, 904 et seq. [6] *Ibid.*, 930 et seq.

loggerheads with Pyrgopolinices, Palaestrio repeats in a few words what the soldier is to be made to believe;[1] and he returns to the subject in greater detail when Acroteleutium is preparing to come upon the scene.[2] Now, Acroteleutium and her attendant are not stupid women who need to have the same thing told them so often. From a dramatic point of view, all these repetitions are useless, if not unnatural. The poet felt this—so much so, that he apologises for it [3]—but he wished, above all, to be understood—understood by the masses, by the ἀσύνετοι ἀκροαταί, as well as by the intelligent part of the audience, and he used such means as he could. A similar desire probably inspired a passage in the *Trinummus*, of which I have spoken above—the scene in which Callicles explains to Charmides who the sham messenger is, and why he was set to work. Here we have a supplementary retrospective explanation of a trick that has already been explained.

This same desire for clearness, which in certain lengthy passages appears in a particularly clumsy form, often leads comic writers to assign explanatory asides to their actors, of a kind that serve to make clear the meaning of an episode and to forestall embarrassing mistakes. *Palaestrionis somnium narratur*, says Palaestrio in line 386 of the *Miles*, while Philocomasium, who has been coached by him, relates the dream she pretends to have had. Several times this shrewd person and his accomplice Milphidippa declare, *ut ludo, ut sublecto*, while they are maliciously giving Pyrgopolinices extravagant praise and holding out alluring promises to him.[4] Similarly, Pardalisca says, in lines 683 *et seq.* of the *Casina*, in the scene where she tells Lysidamus that the young girl suffers from acute attacks of insanity: *Ludo ego hunc facete; nam quae facta dixi, omnia huic falsa dixi; hera atque haec dolum ex proxumo hunc protulerunt, ego hunc missa*

---

[1] *Miles*, 1026 et seq.   [2] *Ibid.*, 1159 et seq.
[3] *Ibid.*, 355, 881, 904, 914 et seq.   [4] *Ibid.*, 1066, 1072.

F F

sum ludere. In lines 831–832 of the *Menaechmi* Menaechmus Sosicles informs the audience that he is about to feign insanity. In lines 662 *et seq.* of the *Mostellaria* Tranio informs them that he is preparing to tell a lie.

Possibly, other details ought to be added to those just mentioned. In Latin comedy, sentences inserted without any special intention by one of the *dramatis personae* occasionally give notice of what is about to occur. Certain remarks made by Hegio in the *Captivi*,[1] by Daemones in the *Rudens*,[2] by Myrrhina in the *Hecyra*,[3] and by Davus in the *Andria*,[4] pave the way for the ἀναγνωρίσεις which are to take place towards the close of those plays. In such cases as these the forestalling of dramatic incidents does not overstep the limits of naturalness, and deserves nothing but praise. Elsewhere it is not free from conventionality. Some of the comedies of the new period contain prophetic dreams. As we know, this is an old device; but our poets occasionally made rather peculiar use of it. Contrary to the practice of tragedy, the account of Daemones' dream (in the *Rudens*) is given when the play is well advanced;[5] it comes as a surprise after what has been said of a terrible night, during which the dwellers on the shore are supposed not to have closed an eye. Demipho's dream is related in great detail in the *Mercator*, and the allusions found in it are so forced that doubts have arisen as to whether Philemon can have been the author of the passage.[6] In my opinion, one and the same reason accounts for these two anomalies. Both Philemon and Diphilus wished to make the dream serve more effectively as notice of what is to follow; and that is why the former placed the dream as close as possible to the occurrences to which it refers, and the latter unduly emphasised the similarity between the vision and reality.

Thus that anxious sort of condescension which implies considerable contempt for the audience, and which led the comic poets to write their prologues, manifests itself

---

[1] *Capt.*, 759–761.   [2] *Rud.*, 742–744.   [3] *Hec.*, 572–574.
[4] *Andr.*, 220–224.   [5] *Rud.*, 106, 593 et seq.   [6] *Merc.*, 225 et seq.

throughout their plots. Even at the close of their plays we find traces of it; witness lines 365 *et seq.* in the last scene of the *Hecyra*, in which the situation at the end of the play is explained as clearly and as explicitly as was the situation at the beginning by many a *prologus argumentativus.*

* * *

The analysis I have made shows that the technique used by writers of New Comedy was not very strict or always satisfactory from the point of view of modern taste. In more than one respect they went on repeating the defects of tragedy and of earlier comedy. From the latter they took over the privilege of conversing with the audience, and from the former the introduction of pro-logues spoken by gods, while they occasionally substi-tuted narrative soliloquies for the stories told by ἄγγελοι. Were I asked to point out what more particularly dis-tinguished New Comedy from the earlier dramatic styles, as far as details of composition are concerned, I should mention, in the first place, the speeches that are addressed to actors who are off the stage, the conversations that are supposed to have been begun behind the scenes and which get into full swing as soon as the actors are on the stage, and, above all, the frequent asides, and the very great number of soliloquies. Mention of the great frequency of soliloquies in the works of the νέα was incidentally made at the close of the preceding chapter, and it was accounted for by the practical disappearance of the chorus; but I think it will serve a good purpose to call special attention to it once more. Whether properly or im-properly introduced, whether emotional or narrative, soliloquies, both in Plautus and Terence, play a consider-able part. Leo has made a list of them in his interesting monograph, *Der Monolog im Drama.* Reference to this work will show that a single comedy ordinarily contains more than ten soliloquies, and sometimes twenty, or even more. In such a play as the *Aulularia*, long passages

consist almost exclusively of successive soliloquies. A
series of these soliloquies is not a rare thing, and two
successive soliloquies frequently come before a dialogue,
each actor talking to himself before discovering the presence
of the other actor, or before making up his mind to address
him.   Like the disappearance of the chorus with which
it is connected, this frequent use of soliloquy must date
from the middle period.   The *Persa* contains no less than
twelve soliloquies, and in two passages we find two
soliloquies following immediately upon one another.

PART III

PURPOSE OF NEW COMEDY
AND THE CAUSES OF ITS SUCCESS

CHAPTER I

DIDACTIC PURPOSE AND MORAL VALUE OF NEW COMEDY

I HAVE analysed the contents of the works of the *νέα*, and I have given an idea of their dramatic structure. My work would be incomplete were I not, in the third place, to inquire into the aims of the chief representatives of this style, and to find out what led them to write, and to what they owed their success; in other words, did I not endeavour to make the reader acquainted with the spirit of New Comedy, as well as with its subject-matter and its form.

§ 1

PLAYS WITH A THESIS AND MORAL PRECEPTS

In the fifth century Aristophanes did not think that his mission was fulfilled the moment he had amused his audience. Each of his plays sought to influence either their conduct or their opinions, and to inspire love for one thing or dislike for another; in a word, each of his plays contained a political, social, or literary thesis. Is this also the case at the time of the *νέα*? Or rather—for everybody knows in advance that this is no longer the case—to what extent does the early spirit survive? To what extent does New Comedy still seek to instruct?

It takes little interest in political questions. As I have said in a previous chapter, comic writers still occasionally attack statesmen, princes and important people, but they do so solely for the pleasure of abusing them or, at most, in a passing burst of anger or of patriotism, but not with the intention of recommending or discouraging a certain line of conduct. Fragments that go beyond personal satire are extremely rare. The most interesting of them are fragment 71 of Philemon's *Πύρρος* and fragment 5 of Apollodorus of Carystus. In the former a peasant lauds

439

the benefits of peace, which, he says " gives us weddings, feasts, parents, children, friends, wealth, health, bread, wine and pleasure." The second fragment deals with the same theme, but treats it more fancifully. But these statements, in which a rather insipid Utopia is suggested, are only faint echoes of Aristophanes' glowing pleas in favour of peace. I may add that the title of the play to which they belong, Γραμματειδιαποιός, or *The Manufacturer of Writing Tablets*, in no way suggests politics. More suggestive titles are occasionally met with in the comedies of the μέση; for instance, there is Antiphanes' Φιλοθήβαιος. At the time of the νέα such titles had almost entirely disappeared.[1]

As far as social problems are concerned, there is one to which Menander, at least, appears to have paid attention— the problem of education. Two of the plays which Terence imitated, the *Adelphi* and the *Heauton Timoroumenos*, may be regarded as " Schools for Fathers," and in one respect they well deserve this name, on account of the abundance of judicious precepts which they contain. Nevertheless, considered as a whole, they are not didactic works, for neither of them clearly and unreservedly proposes a fixed system that is to serve as a model to the audience. In the greater part of these two plays Micio and Chremes are represented as wise men. But, for all that, the former is deceived by his pupil, no less than Demea is deceived by his. As for the latter, although he is a learned theoretician and a glib counsellor, he is, in point of fact, no cleverer than Menedemus. The fact that his son Clitipho does not turn his back upon him, as Clinia does upon his father, is not due to a better use of parental authority, but much more to the circumstance that that young man is less determined and less high minded. Indeed, Micio and Chremes misjudge the situation, and end by appearing

---

[1] The Φιλολάκων by Stephanus—the date of which is, by the way, uncertain — probably ridiculed the Laconomania of certain Athenians, which had no more political significance than the Anglomania of many a Frenchman.

ridiculous; so that, did we seek for the moral of a play only at its conclusion, we should have to infer that it was Menander's intention to scoff at the new methods of education. Or else, if we include all the episodes of the plot in our survey, without, however, looking into the matter more deeply, we should have to say that the author professes complete scepticism regarding pedagogy. As a matter of fact, this is not the case. I am convinced that the ideas which Micio and Chremes express were approved by Menander. But by attributing them to persons who are not able to make good practical use of them, the poet made his own views less manifest. He played the part of a comic writer and not that of a moralist. The moral that is to be found in his writing has no conspicuous place in the plot; he hid it intentionally.

As regards morality in the individual, comedy would have had definitely to make a point of not driving home its lessons as sharply as real life does, if it was to avoid occasionally showing how sin, as the saying is, brings its own punishment, and makes people the victims of their own transgressions. In one of the closing scenes of the Ἐπιτρέποντες Onesimus informs Smicrines that the gods are not responsible for the happiness or for the unhappiness of mankind. " To each of us they have given a character that fits him to be master of his fate. One man makes bad use of it : his character is his undoing. For another it is his salvation; " and so on. The truth of this remark, which is repeated several times in the writings of the comic poets, is shown again and again in their plays, but, as a rule, they leave it to the audience to discover it, or, if they point it out themselves, they do so in a cursory and general way. But to make a didactic purpose evident more than a casual word is required. For example, in the course of a single play we ought to see how a person suffers as a consequence of some sin, and then, after being reformed, is made happy by a corresponding virtue; or else how one of two persons whose conduct is directly the opposite of that of the other

is punished, while the other person is rewarded. Did the
νέα exhibit this moral process at work? The almost complete disappearance of " character plays " precludes our
giving a decisive answer. At any rate, what remains shows
us nothing of the kind. We have already seen that
Demea's *ἀγροικία* and Micio's urbanity are qualities each
counterbalanced by their corresponding defects. Towards
the close of the *Adelphi* Demea examines his conscience, and
seems to be on the point of changing his attitude.[1] But I
cannot think he is sincere about his conversion when I
see how he makes fun of Micio and pays him with his
own coin,[2] and, above all, when I hear him end the
comedy with the following words : " But if you choose
rather, in points where your youthful eyes cannot see far,
where your desires are stronger and your consideration
inadequate, to have one to reprove and correct you and
to indulge you when it is right, here am I to do it for you." [3]
Demea, swayed by a lively scene of discomfiture, is beginning to be assailed by doubt, or rather, he suffers from a
momentary weariness. He bitterly points out what seems
to him to be an injustice and a folly, but this does not
mean that he condemns his past conduct, nor that he
becomes a convert to other principles, nor, above all, that
his supposed conversion is set up as an example. In the
last part of the *Aulularia* Euclio likewise reviews his past
troubles, and congratulates himself on the change that
has taken place.[4] This change, however, is by no means
a permanent reform. In the first place, Euclio does not
willingly give up his treasure; it is taken from him. And
then, even when he bears his misfortune courageously
and congratulates himself on being rid of a source of
worry, he does not necessarily renounce the faults of
his character; he may continue to be suspicious, grumb-
ling and avaricious, but merely has one reason less to
be stingy, to grumble and to be suspicious.

Thus we see there were very few, or no plays with a

---

[1] *Ad.*, 859 et seq.   [2] *Ibid.*, 958.
[3] *Ibid.*, 992 et seq.   [4] *Aul.*, fr. III. and IV.

thesis, and very few, or no plays which, as a whole, aimed at proving anything. But though such an aim did not pervade entire plays, certain details may have been introduced with a view to instruct the public, and certain episodes may have been invented for the same purpose. Thus, besides examining the plots, we must consider the dissertations, the moral, social, or philosophical maxims which are uttered by the characters.

A glance at Kock's collection of *Fragmenta* will promptly show that there is a great abundance of passages of this sort. As a matter of fact, there is a special reason for this : many of these passages have been preserved by Stobaeus in a collection of excerpts which he intended to use in educating his son. Stobaeus, however, did not think of attributing these maxims to any special authors of the *νέα*, and, at all events, it is only as regards the proportion of moralising contained in the works of the comic poets that he can mislead us. Latin imitators and the long passages from the original plays that have been published recently, supply fuller evidence and give us more trustworthy information.

Here, we fairly often find an actor giving himself or others advice either seriously or by way of a joke. Let us look more particularly at the passages in which the means of getting into a certain social position, or into some other specified situation, are stated at length. Scapha, Astaphium, Cleareta, the mother of Gymnasium— all make love and being loved their special business. At the beginning of the *Eunuchus*, Gnatho, like Struthias in the *Κόλαξ*, expounds the theory of the flatterer's profession. In the *Aulularia*, the *Mostellaria*, and the *Menaechmi* slaves explain their duties and how to arrange matters in order to live in bondage without suffering too much. These various passages are more didactic in form than in purpose. There were very few people in the audience at a Greek theatre who could profit by the wisdom of a Strobilus, a Phaniscus, a Messenio, or of any

other teachers of how slaves should behave. As for the
speeches of Gnatho and of Scapha, the poets certainly
did not intend that they should call into life a new crop
of clever exploiters or of wheedling women. If these
speeches were meant to point any moral, it was to urge
the eventual victims of those unscrupulous persons to be
more wide-awake and distrustful.

More frequent than these theories, and also more calculated to edify the public, were moral maxims. Some of
them are found in the extant parts of Greek plays. In
the *Κόλαξ*, lines 54 *et seq.*, Pheidias' slave warns him
against the pernicious brood of flatterers. Here the
speaker is a pedagogue and his remarks are addressed
to his *τρόφιμος*.[1] Hence his didactic tone is peculiarly
appropriate. But when Daos, in the *Γεωργός*, speaks to
the matron Myrrhina, he is hardly less sententious : " You
will give up struggling against poverty, that odious
monster who is deaf to your words. For one must either
be rich like our neighbour, or else live where one has
not so many witnesses of one's wretchedness; for this the
country and solitude are desirable." [2] At the beginning
of the *Ἐπιτρέποντες* Syriscus preaches human solidarity
to Smicrines, and reminds him that, whenever they get
a chance to do so, it is the duty of all good people to see
that justice triumphs.[3] Towards the end of this comedy
Onesimus gives this crabbed person a lecture on the
conduct of terrestrial affairs, on the indifference of the
gods, and on man's responsibility.[4] In the play of which
Jouguet has edited the fragments, the young man who
thinks he has been betrayed also takes occasion to philosophise about the shamelessness of false friends. One can
easily find similar tirades and remarks in Plautus and in
Terence. Such of Plautus' plays as are imitations of
Philemon's comedies contain the greatest number. At the
beginning of the *Mostellaria* Philolaches gives himself up
to a lengthy scrutiny of his conscience, in the course of

---

[1] Pupil.(—Tr.).   [2] Γεωργ., 77 et seq.
[3] Ἐπιτρ., 15 et seq.   [4] *Ibid.*, 486 et seq.

which he depicts the demoralising influence of laziness and of pleasure. In the *Mercator*, lines 18 *et seq.*, we find a dissertation about the effects of love; in lines 547 *et seq.* reflections about the use one should make of the various periods of life; in lines 649 *et seq.* an excursus on the idea that it is useless for a man to seek escape from his sorrow by changing his abode, for " his sorrow mounts the crupper and gallops along with him; " in lines 817 *et seq.* remarks about the injustice of the laws to women, and a programme of reform such as is frequently found in Euripides; and finally, in the last scene, lines 969–970, 984, etc., Eutychus deluges the unfortunate Demipho with a flood of maxims. What shall we say of the *Trinummus*, the third play that Plautus borrowed from Philemon? Almost from beginning to end it is a veritable collection of homilies and meditations. In lines 23 *et seq.* the aged Megaronides holds forth on reprehensible weakness towards one's friends; in lines 199 *et seq.* he speaks of malicious gossips; in lines 223–275 young Lysiteles inveighs against the dangers of love, which, by the way, that precocious preacher knows only by hearsay; in lines 280 *et seq.* the aged Philto speaks of the corruption of the age; in lines 667 *et seq.* young Lysiteles, whom I have already mentioned, still virtuous and still incompetent, speaks about love; and in one of the last scenes the slave Stasimus attacks the perverseness of modern habits. In this list I have included only soliloquies and uninterrupted tirades. But even the dialogues are not secure against maxims. Witness the conversation between Philto and Lysiteles, in lines 324 *et seq.* I like to think that Philemon rarely indulged his taste for philosophising so much as in the *Trinummus*, and that this predilection was less exaggerated in the other poets of the νέα. But traces of it are found nearly everywhere. In the second part of the *Miles Gloriosus*, lines 627 *et seq.*, Periplecomenus praises, at considerable length, the life he has chosen—the life of a careless, cheerful, accommodating and companionable bachelor. It was probably in Menander's works that

Plautus found the model for Megadorus' speech about
women's extravagance and the disadvantages of a dowry
in lines 478 *et seq.* of the *Aulularia*. Menander was also
the model for Mnesilochus' remarks about friendship and
gratitude, in lines 385 *et seq.* of the *Bacchides*; for the
pedagogue Lydus, who, after a lapse of a hundred years,
takes up anew a theme of Aristophanes' *Clouds*, and
replies to a panegyric on the old style of education with
a satire on modern education; for Pistoclerus and Mnesilochus, when between them they draw a picture of the
false friend who is officious in his protestations but
unable to render any service; and so forth. In Terence's
adaptations the Greek authors appear to be less prone
to the habit of philosophising; but this may be due to
Terence himself. A comparison of the Latin comedies
with the fragments of the original plays shows, in certain
cases, clear traces of the simplification and abridgment
to which Terence subjected them. For instance, among
the fragments of the Ἀδελφοί there are two sententious
bits, Nos. 4 and 5, to which nothing in the *Adelphi*
corresponds.

Thus we see that New Comedy was, in a general way,
quite disposed to be didactic and sententious, and herein
we again find a confirmation of its kinship with the
tragedies of Euripides.

We must not, however, expect that the lessons conveyed
in it should be, as a rule, conspicuously dignified or novel.
We do, of course, find some characters who were above
the ordinary in point of intellect and morals, such as the
philosophers, the disciples of philosophers, the pedagogues
who had a smattering of philosophy and were eager to
display their knowledge; or else certain eccentric characters, fault-finding and fantastic spirits. But such persons
were the exception. The majority of the characters were
quite simple and respectable people, good citizens, common
men of the people, to whom, in most cases, other than
commonplace views could not be attributed without
violating dramatic probability. As a matter of fact, the

fragments and the Latin imitations generally contain adages that are as old as Greek thought, and precepts whose wisdom is utterly commonplace. To be prepared for all the pranks of fortune, to bear them with courage and resignation; not to take things too much to heart; to avoid tears, which have never cured anything; not to ask more of life than it can offer; to be satisfied if one's life contains more good than evil; to find consolation for distress in observing the distress of one's neighbour; to consider a true friend as one of the rarest possessions; to be prepared for man's ingratitude; to recognise the supreme power of money; not to disparage one's self; to be temperate in all things; not to act under the influence of anger; to distrust flatterers; to avoid bad counsellors and bad company; to fear calumny; to be on one's guard against flatterers and slanderers; not to be deceived by assumed modesty; to have the courage to reprimand one's friends when occasion offers; not to imagine that anything can be done without an effort, nor that a thing begun is a thing done; to help fortune; never to put off things which have been entrusted to one; to foresee the probable consequences of one's acts and to prepare for them in advance; not to condemn one's neighbour before examining one's self; to know that a loan to a friend is a gift, and that, as a rule, he who borrowed yesterday is an enemy to-morrow; not to associate with people of higher station than one's own; if one is poor, to live away from the wealthy, and preferably in the country, in order to avoid suffering by comparing one's lot with theirs; to prefer to call forth envy rather than pity; not to become too much attached to earthly goods, and to remember that they are transient; to prefer a tranquil competence to anxious opulence; to respect one's parents, to fear opposing them and, in case of need, to disarm them through gentleness and persuasion; when one desires to marry, to consider the beauty and the character of the girl rather than her dowry; not to become engaged or married to a girl against one's wish; to live according to one's age, not to play the young man when one's hair is white; for the father of a family, not to give his children the whip-hand by telling them of his former foibles, nor to let them discover that, in order to forestall a rash deed on their part, he will put up with all their whims; for a woman under the control of a husband, to bear with the pranks of her lord and master, to be satisfied if she receives enough from him to live at ease in her household, to remain at home, not to give occasion for gossip; for one who has many servants, to hope that they may fall out, so that it will be all the easier to keep them under control; and so on. Such precepts as these certainly did not teach the spectators much; many of them did not even aim at making them either better or wiser. They were merely statements of experience—every one's experience—rather than precepts.

But occasionally it does happen that comic writers, influenced by the great thinkers of their age, or as a result of their own genius, rise to conceptions that are less commonplace. We know how many schools of philosophy flourished at the end of the fourth century and the beginning of the third. With the probable exception of Menander, the representatives of the νέα were apparently not men of very great culture, nor fully acquainted with the various systems, nor disciples of any one of them, any more than their predecessors of the early and middle period had been. What they sought for in the lives of philosophers and in their ideas was, above all, a chance for raising a laugh, and not material that would serve as instruction; and what they say about a doctrine is often not more than the majority of their contemporaries must have known. Every now and then, however, they do seem consciously and intentionally to have acted the part of popular instructor. This is, for example, the case at the end of the Ἐπιτρέποντες, when Onesimus says to Smicrines that the gods have no care for men. Here, there can hardly be a doubt that Menander constituted himself the interpreter of Epicurus. Such cases are rare.[1] But, even when it did not so evidently reproduce the doctrines of a particular school, comedy was able to do its share in making current a new frame of mind, new theories and new views; and I believe that it did so.

One of these frames of mind is somewhat sombre. It consists in a form of melancholy, born of the feeling that man is frail and the morrow uncertain. The life of man is ephemeral; at any moment something—a chance meeting, a glance at the tombs that line the road—gives him a foretaste, as it were, of death.[2] And then, what unavoidable evils, what disasters within the limits of this brief existence ! Man must submit to the law of labour.[3] If, at least, man's efforts and good qualities were sure of a reward ! But no, fortune is capricious and unjust. " You are a man," says Menander; " which amounts to saying that there is no creature that can by more rapid changes of fortune be exalted in order to be subsequently abased " ;[4] and elsewhere : " If one of the gods came to look for me, and said : ' Crito, after your death, you will begin a new life; you shall be whatever you choose—a dog, a sheep, a goat, a man or a horse; for you must live twice, that is the order of destiny; but choose as you like '—I think I should hasten to reply, ' Rather anything—make anything of me rather than a man. For he is the only creature who is unjustly happy or unhappy. A good horse is the object of more care than the inferior one; if you are a good dog you are respected much more highly than a bad dog; a lusty cock is fed quite differently from a weak one, and the latter fears his prowess. But with man, whatever his virtue, his nobility, his generosity of character, they serve him naught in the times in which we live.' "[5]

---

[1] Many of the maxims which are common to the writers of comedy and to the philosophers were already found in other writers of drama, especially in Euripides, or else they were proverbial. Comedies more frequently prove that certain philosophical ideas had already permeated the masses, or that, in formulating them, the theorists were in accord with popular opinion, than give us the opportunity of witnessing the propagation of such ideas.

[2] Philem., fr. 116; [Men.], fr. 538.   [3] *Ibid.*, fr. 88; cf. fr. 89, 93.
[4] Men., fr. 531, 10–12.   [5] *Ibid.*, fr. 223.

G G

These are very discouraging reflections. Fortunately, the comic writers did not cling to them. In many other passages they have shown us by what means we can fight against misfortune and lighten its burdens, instead of groaning over it. Sometimes they advise men mutually to help one another, so as to give Fortune less chance to thwart them,[1] or counsel honest men to unite in stopping injustice.[2] Sometimes they inveigh against social prejudice in a manner that recalls some of Euripides' diatribes. In fragment 533 of Menander a character of a lost comedy raises his voice against prejudice of birth. In fragment 532 it is fashionable marriages that are hotly criticised. Megadorus, in the *Aulularia*, is not content merely to find fault with such marriages; half seriously, half playfully, he suggests a reform, the effect of which would, according to him, be most fortunate for society : the wealthy are to marry the daughters of poor citizens without a dowry, and the world will be much better off.[3] Elsewhere, the position of women—those cursed women whom comedy is so quick to vilify—is the subject of judicious remarks. Syra, in the *Mercator*, says that the law is much more severe on them than on men, and is indignant at such unfairness.[4] It is true Syra is a woman, and it may seem that her objections are prompted by *esprit de corps*. But in the Ἐπιτρέποντες it is Charisius, a man without sin, who admits that before the moral law both sexes are equal. Nay, we know that he goes still further; after some reflection, the misadventure of Pamphila, who had been ravished before her marriage, appears to him in its true light—as a misfortune, and not as a sin—and renouncing traditional Pharisaism, he is perfectly satisfied to keep her as his wife. Even the slave, the scum of ancient society, comes in for a share in the sympathy of the poets, who make generous appeals in his favour. They urge men to treat them gently,[5] and above all, they proclaim

---

[1] Men., fr. 679.   [2] Ἐπιτρ., 15 et seq.; Men., fr. 542.
[3] *Aul.*, 478 et seq.   [4] *Merc.*, 817 et seq.
[5] Men., fr. 370.

that the slave, too, is a man.¹ In a word, the remains of
comedy contain a large number of precepts that display
a remarkable disposition towards universal goodwill, and
a striking tendency to treat all men as equals. The words
charity and fraternity are not yet used; but, in matters
of this kind, the substance may exist without the words,
just as words often exist while their substance is lacking.
The reader will recall the famous lines in which, at the
beginning of the *Heauton Timoroumenos*, Chremes explains
his sympathy for his neighbour Menedemus, who is as yet
a stranger to him : *Homo sum ; humani nil a me alienum
puto.*² By frequently expressing the belief that, notwithstanding accidental differences, all human beings have the
same nature and a common destiny, and by making it
familiar to every one, the comic authors prepared their
audiences—to the great benefit of mankind—to think and
act as Chremes does.

Another quality, closely related to the moral views of
Epicurus, which their works were calculated to develop
both by example and by precept, was forbearance towards
the sins of others. *Humanum ignoscere 'st*, proclaims
Demipho, in the *Mercator*, under conditions which—it is
true—deprive this maxim of much of its value.³ Pataccus
congratulates his daughter on the patience she shows
Polemon, and says that it is the act of a truly Greek soul.⁴
Forbearance and readiness to forgive are the regular thing
in Menander's comedies, and they constitute the chief
charm of his most lovable characters—Glycera in the
Περικειρομένη, and Pamphila in the *Ἐπιτρέποντες*. These
qualities win our sympathies for other characters in
whom they are found side by side with certain weaknesses : Micio in the *Adelphi*, and Demeas in the *Σαμία*.
And what is the real meaning of this forbearance ? Another
comic writer, Philemon, supplies the answer to this question
in the words of Philto in the *Trinummus* : " He who is
satisfied with himself is neither an honest nor a virtuous

---

¹ Philem., fr. 95.   Cf. fr. 22, 31.   ² *Heaut.*, 77.   Cf. Men., fr. 602.
³ *Merc.*, 320.   ⁴ Περικ, 355–357.

man. He who judges himself with severity is the true
man of worth." [1] Forbearance is the natural result of
humility. How can one be exacting towards others if
one has recognised how little one is worth one's self?
Charisius in the 'Επιτρέποντες, brought up, as we must
assume, in the haughty school of Stoicism, thought himself infallible, and, standing on the lofty pedestal of his
supposed infallibility, pitilessly condemns the errors of
others. But one fine day he is obliged to recognise that
he himself has gravely erred. Then his eyes are opened,
and by comparison with Pamphila, who had at once forgiven him for everything, he finds out how small, ridiculous
and odious he is. He now understands the beauty, the
need, of forbearance, and is converted. Let the haughty
apostles of virtue meditate upon his experience! Let
them also meditate upon the discomfiture of certain
educators, like Demea and Menedemus! They will see
how severity calls forth lies and how self-sufficiency begets
disaffection. Taken as a whole, neither the *Heauton
Timoroumenos* nor the *Adelphi* is, as I have already pointed
out, a didactic comedy. For all that, there is a great
deal in what Micio and Chremes say that is worth remembering. Both of them, when they express the wish that
sons, instead of acting clandestinely, would unbosom themselves to their fathers without fear and ask their advice,
give expression to aspirations which, though easy to ridicule, are yet dignified, If the father of a family, instead of
playing the part of a stern master, would only show himself to his children as he is—full of affection for them—
if he would only win their friendship and their gratitude,
and by his kind treatment kindle in their souls the desire
not to displease him, then young people would behave
much better than when restrained by severe measures.

" Respect man's dignity; show more gentleness and
more tolerance in your relations to your fellow men,"
these are two pieces of advice which the comic writers,
or at least some of the greatest of them, wished, I believe,

[1] *Trin.*, 318 et seq.

to give to their contemporaries. Had they given no other it would suffice to keep their works from appearing to lack serious purpose and moral significance.

§ 2

EDIFYING AND OFFENSIVE SUBJECTS

When dramatists use their art for the purpose of educating the public, they display a noble ambition for which we must be grateful. But while they have an eye to virtue, there is another, more modest, task which should be the object of their constant care : namely, to avoid all cause of offence and not to destroy laudable beliefs and inclinations in the souls of their audience. The charge has been brought against New Comedy of being a school of perversity. I would like to examine whether this charge is well founded.

As regards religion, our comic writers were certainly not always orthodox. A fair number of passages in their works are opposed to traditional views about the divinity, its nature, its power, and its relation to the order of the universe. But such passages are not so numerous, nor are they, as a rule, so elaborate, that they could have contributed in any appreciable manner to the overthrow of the ancient faith, which had long since been shaken and battered down on all sides. Besides, to counterbalance these, comic literature contains more than one passage that is capable of edifying devout souls. I need only remind the reader of the prologues to the *Rudens* and the *Aulularia*, which contradict the Epicurean doctrine by showing us gods intervening in our mundane affairs, and playing the part of Providence. But, on the other hand, what about passages in which an actor—like Strobilus in the act of stealing the treasure-pot [1]—asks the aid of the gods in a dishonest undertaking, or else boasts of having had them as his accomplices, or—like Chaerea in

[1] *Aul.*, 621–622.

the *Eunuchus* [1]—finds a justification for his evil deed in the example set by the gods? It is only too probable that such ideas seemed perfectly natural, and scandalised hardly any one, in the days of the *véa*. As for the irreverent tirades of a Libanus or of an Ergasilus, who demand divine honours for themselves,[2] or of a Leonidas, who declares that he would not listen to the prayers of the king of the gods himself,[3] or of Pistoclerus when he makes a god of a sweet kiss (*Suavisaviatio*),[4] they are quite harmless and quite discreet when compared with the outrageous parodies and the biting ridicule with which the stage of the fifth and fourth century had riddled the dwellers in Olympus. I think there is no need of insisting any further on this point. Taken as a whole, the *véa* was not irreligious; it did not spread ungodliness.

Was it harmful to morals?

It is soothing for the public conscience for vice to be punished and virtue rewarded. Now, a glance at the known endings of the *véa* will show that this occurs often. In some of these endings, as, for example, in the Ἐπιτρέποντες, the *Rudens* or the *Captivi*, there is hardly any fault to be found as far as retributive justice is concerned. Whole classes of actors may be said to get their due. If, for example, we consider the female characters, who are more or less completely sympathetic—the faithful wives like the two sisters in the *Stichus*, young girls who have been violated, the women whose love is sincere and unselfish, the good courtesan like Thais in the *Eunuchus* and Bacchis in the *Hecyra*—we shall find that, as a rule, and especially in Menander, these lovable persons have reason to rejoice at the turn things take in the end. Two women in Philemon's comedies, Pasicompsa in the *Mercator* and Philematium in the *Mostellaria*, are, it is true, treated much less fairly. The love and faithfulness of both is touching. Yet Pasicompsa remains a slave, an instru-

---

[1] *Eun.*, 584 et seq.   [2] *Asin.*, 711 et seq.; *Capt.*, 863–865.
[2] *Ibid.* 414–415.   [4] *Bacch.*, 116.

ment of pleasure, while Philematium, who has already
been freed before the opening of the plot, remains a
courtesan whom Philolaches will perhaps desert when, to
use Scapha's words, age has changed the colour of her
hair.   What occurs at the end of these two of Philemon's
plays may have occurred at the end of others.   Indeed,
we know that gratitude played a relatively small part in
the works of this poet.   Was this due to his contempt for
women and their qualities, or to a conscious desire to
copy real life, in which the best people do not always
enjoy the greatest happiness?   We have no way of
deciding.

From rewards we come to punishments.   Certain classes
of people, who certainly deserve it to the full, are not
spared; for instance, panders, who are cheated, robbed,
thrashed and derided; swaggering soldiers, who are regularly humiliated and exploited; dissolute husbands, who
are always caught *in delicto*, and whose shrewish wives
make them pay dearly for their escapades.   But other
classes of people enjoy a curious immunity.

First of all, the slaves.   In comedy a *servus callidus* may
be guilty of all sorts of mischief, of every imaginable
rascality, without being punished.   In most cases some
one intercedes for him and secures his pardon; or else,
when it comes to settling accounts, he is either forgotten,
or unforeseen events make it impossible for his master
to chastise him.   Such general immunity from punishment
is contrary to justice.   Occasionally a scamp of a slave,
who ought to be whipped and put in chains, not only
escapes well-deserved punishment, but even has benefits
showered upon him, and is finally given his freedom.   Take
the case of Epidicus; twice in succession he has impudently
deceived Periphanes; he has stolen from him and made
fun of him.   Surely such misdeeds call for punishment!
But at the last moment Epidicus discovers that a captive
girl who has been brought home by Stratippocles, who
wishes her to be his mistress, is the lost daughter of
Periphanes.   Beside himself with joy, Periphanes forgives

Epidicus, sets him free, and promises to support him; and
the play ends with this moral saw: *Hic is homo est qui
libertatem malitia invenit sua!   Malitia sua*—these are
words to be remembered.   What stood the *servi callidi* in
good stead—if, indeed, they were regarded as responsible
agents, and not merely as part of the machinery of the plot
—was their cleverness.   In the eyes of the Greeks, cleverness always placed those who possessed it above the rules
of ordinary morality.   In the days of the *Odyssey* a man
merely required to be skilful at deceiving his fellows to
become a favourite of Athena's; in the days of New
Comedy this quality gave him a claim to the favour of
the queen of the world—omnipotent Tyche.

Next to slaves, in point of getting better treatment
than they deserve, rank the sons who are engaged in some
amorous adventure without the knowledge and consent of
their fathers.   In the end, they are rarely separated from
the girl they love.   Whatever the wrongdoings and lies of
which they have been guilty, fortune generally favours
them, and their wishes either coincide with their father's
in some unforeseen manner, or else the father stops thwart-
ing them.   But what entitles all these youths to so much
happiness?   It is not their cleverness, for almost all of
them are awkward and unable to get out of a scrape
without the aid of a slave.   Nor is it the generosity of
their feelings, for some of them have been led to their
acts by caprice, or by sensuous impulses, or have been
caught in the snare of an intriguing woman.   But they
are all in love, and that suffices as a claim to forbearance.
In comedy a sort of religion or superstition of love was
apparently developed, which flourished later on in Alexandrian poetry, and pervades Latin poetry to the point
of satiety.   The comic writers had not as yet set up the
principle which was formulated after their day, that love
has an absolute claim to be requited, but they had already
accepted another axiom : that love may do whatever it
likes, and that the end of love justifies the means—in the
case of young men, at all events.   For when an old man,

even though he be a bachelor, ventures to fall in love, he lays claim to a right that is no longer his; and comic writers are not slow to point this out to him, as, for instance, at the end of the *Mercator*, where young Eutychus passes a mock edict against love-sick greybeards. One would almost think that the young men, the only legitimate dwellers in the realm of affection, have a mission to drive off intruders. All the more reason why they should have a right not to be disturbed in that realm! Even regard for a father's authority cannot always prevail against this right.

Glory for cleverness! Freedom for love! That seems to be the moral of many a comedy. Doubtless the first of these commandments shocked only a small part of the spectators—the philosophers. As for the second, it is hard for me to believe that it ever conformed to the views of the masses. But, to judge from a passage in the *Symposium*, it appears that as early as the time of Plato there were some who were inclined to recognise it, and when clothed in humorous form, two or three centuries later, it cannot have scandalised many.

Hitherto I have spoken only of the endings of plays. But, notwithstanding their importance, they are not the only thing to be considered in the *véa*. The rewards which they bring come late, and they do not always remove the impression of what has gone before. Even when wickedness is formally reproved at the end of a play, if it has previously been depicted in alluring colours, and if virtue, on the other hand, has been ridiculed, the play may exert a demoralising influence. Is this true of our comedies?

Many of the people whom it brings upon the stage are a mixture of good and evil. A man who is a booby has a kind heart and a righteous soul; another who is despotic errs by excess of laudable solicitude; and so on. Where such complexity of characters exists, it is not surprising that our sympathies should go out to persons who are not above criticism, or that they should be withheld

from others who may have some claim on them. Of
course this is unfair, but do we not daily make like mistakes in our judgment of men in real life? Fault might
justly be found with writers of comedy if they had set
themselves to give credit to new ones and to mislead the
judgment of their contemporaries on some fresh points.
But it does not appear that they laid themselves open to
any such charge.

They made light of marriage and caricatured family life;
but I do not believe that their sarcastic remarks ever
spoiled any one's taste for the one or the other. Moreover,
everybody knew that in depicting married life as almost
always unhappy, and parents and children almost invari-
ably at loggerheads, the poets merely followed the require-
ments of a given style of composition, and were influenced by a recognised preference for what was grotesque
and ugly. People were not so simple as to imagine that
these portrayals represented—or even pretended to represent—things as they actually were in family life as a
rule.

But it may be alleged that comedy invited the audience
to sympathise with a number of wicked people—such as
Thais in the *Eunuchus*, or Bacchis in the *Hecyra*, or
Habrotonon in the 'Επιτρέποντες. There is no denying
this. But we must not lose sight of the fact that such
characters are few and far between in comedy. It would,
I think, be a mistake to regard them as the creations
of a perverse taste for paradox. Courtesans may be good
women, and if the comic writers occasionally credited
representatives of this ill-reputed class with some virtue,
there was nothing more paradoxical in their doing so
than in depicting certain poor devils, or even slaves, as
being moved by noble sentiments. Characters like Habrotonon and Thais are not the products of a diseased imagination that desires at all costs to run counter to accepted
views, but of a sincere observation which does not permit
itself to be influenced by social conditions, and which is
able to see people as they are. As for the rôle of Bacchis,

it was, in my opinion, lack of skill, rather than intention, that led Apollodorus to go to such extremes in creating it. With the exception of the courtesans, no class of ill-reputed persons is painted in bright colours in the *νέα*; panders, male and female, sycophants, parasites and bullies always repel us. Similarly, in the family circle, the poet never encourages the audience to sympathise with unfaithful husbands nor excuses their misconduct. Disobedient sons certainly fare better, and very often we are led to feel kindly disposed towards them. But this does not imply that the comic writers have a word to say against paternal authority. As I have already pointed out, even the characters who oppose it admit that they are in the wrong and blush for it. It must also be pointed out that there is no trace of the Don Juan about even the most dissipated of the young heroes. Their blood is hot, their heads are weak, but their hearts are not corrupted. For all of them we can cherish the hope that after a few years of folly they will become respectable men.

In short, one cannot charge the *νέα* with having sought to make vice attractive, nor with having attacked the morals of ordinary society. It remains to be considered whether, without malice prepense, it was not, by its very choice of subjects, capable of corrupting the audience.

It is true that Athenian men and women who had just been to a comedy could not, as a rule, have had their minds filled with noble images or chaste thoughts. Now and again, of course, they had occasion to watch some edifying character or some scene calculated to create a taste for proper conduct. But more frequently misconduct and bad morals supplied material for the play. A work like the *Captivi*—*ad pudicos mores facta fabula, comoedia ubi boni meliores fiant*—was certainly a rare thing. New Comedy may accordingly appear to have disposed people towards vice by making them familiar with it. But, in order to get a just appreciation of the harm it may have done, we must consider it in relation to the times and in comparison with the other literary productions that flourished at the same period. As the contemporaries of Philemon, Menander and Posidippus were, broadly speaking, very indulgent towards sins of the flesh, they ran no risk in witnessing the performance of so many erotic episodes on the stage. In their place, we should have found no cause for offence in the fact that amorous adventures form the framework of most of the plays. Rather than take umbrage at this, or reproach the νέα too severely for occasionally introducing dangerous episodes, we ought, to its honour, to credit it with a certain amount of restraint.

Thus, the bestial tyranny of certain characters in Herondas or in Alciphron, who impose on their slaves, and the shamelessness of the 'Ιδιάζουσαι, are, as far as we know, without a parallel in comedy. Above all, unnatural love does not seem to have been dealt with, and though the νέα makes occasional allusions to paederasty, we have no reason to believe that it brought ἐρασταί or ἐρώμενοι upon the stage. At most, Παιδερασταί, the title of one of Diphilus' works—a new version, by the way, of a play of the middle period—and a fragment of Damoxenus give cause for anxiety in this respect. Plutarch declares that paederasty was excluded from all the numerous plays that Menander wrote.[1] Now, we know from other documents what the habits of the period were; accordingly New Comedy displayed laudable reserve in regard to at least one important point. But this is not all. Conjugal infidelity, which, moreover, it depicts in such ugly colours, was by no means one of its favourite themes. There are but few adulterous husbands in extant comic literature; there is not a single untrue wife. Young girls who had been seduced must also have been a type practically unknown. A young girl of good family, as portrayed in comedy, does not listen to the proposals of a gay young spark; she does not give way to sensuous passion; if she succumbs her fall is always due to violence.

[1] Plut., *Quaest. conviv.*, VII. 8, 3, 8.

Thus, one of the most shocking features found in comic plots may have owed its vogue to a curious regard for propriety; by aspersing the character of the young men of their day and representing them as gross fellows, the poets avoided setting their women readers and listeners a pernicious example. Scruples of the same sort were probably responsible for more than one romantic episode. A considerable number of the explanatory narrations in which comedy abounded were, I imagine, invented in order to introduce an Antiphila or a Selenium—that is to say, a girl who is sincerely in love. This would have been a roundabout method had the comic writers been willing to place the language of love on the lips of young women of good family. But, out of respect for the women of their times, they refused to have recourse to this. In their comedies affectionate wives and young women of gentle birth who are in love either remain invisible, or are very reserved in their language. The privilege of speaking and acting like one who is in love is only extended to women who are *déclassées*, or placed by chance in an unusual position. This is due to the fact that the latter are exceptional beings, and a woman who lives peacefully under her father's or husband's roof must regard herself as very far removed from them. Hence there is less fear of their exerting a bad influence, and one may cherish the hope that their transports, their effusions and their immorality will not be contagious.

Here again we find, in the domain of morals, in the strict sense of the word, that same fear of giving offence, that same *respectability* which, in the case of a lie or a piece of rascality, places the shame upon a slave. In its own way New Comedy was prudish. Vice has fewer forms, it is less refined and, if I may so express myself, is at the disposal of fewer people than in elegy or tragedy. In the latter we have adultery, incest, wanton virgins, and men and women who indulge in unnatural passions. In the former we have almost exclusively young men who sow their wild oats, but who, foolish as they are,

follow Palinurus' wise counsel : " to keep away from
married women, widows, girls, boys, and children of free
men " ;[1] stories of *liaisons* with courtesans, whose business
it is to sell themselves, and with unfortunate women of
low birth whose disgrace is of little account—in a word,
nothing that could have disturbed the average conscience
of the period. If, judging by the works of our poets, the
modern student comes to the conclusion that society was
in their day particularly corrupt, and on the road to
decadence, this verdict, although, no doubt, somewhat
exaggerated, may possibly be accepted as correct. But
it is one thing to reflect the corruption of one's environ-
ment, and quite another thing to encourage it. Taking
everything into account, the *νέα* must have been inoffensive
as far as morals were concerned.

[1] *Curc.*, 37–38.

CHAPTER II

COMIC ELEMENTS

POETS, says Horace in the *Epistle to the Pisos*, desire
either to be useful or to give pleasure : *aut prodesse
aut delectare*. The last chapter has clearly shown that the
comic writers of the new period cared little about being
useful. First and foremost, they wished to give pleasure.
Any description of their work necessitates an account of
how they set about this.

The characteristically comic way to " give pleasure "
is to amuse people, to make them laugh. This was just
as true in the days of the *νέα* as it had been in earlier
days. But from one period to another the quantity and,
to a certain extent, the quality of subjects for laughter
varied. By what means, then, and with how much persistence did New Comedy strive to provoke laughter?
These are two problems which I must now investigate.

§ 1

GROSS FUN AND REFINED FUN

The comic poets of the fifth century, especially Aristophanes, were rather unscrupulous in the choice of their
methods. They introduced indiscriminately the grossest
burlesques, the sharpest satire and the most disgusting
obscenity. Even the fragments of the middle period
contain many things which offend a delicate taste. Moreover, in the *Coislin Treatise*, in which there seems to be a
survival of classifications taken from the second book of the
Poetics, the *ἤθη κωμικά* are divided into three categories,
one of which especially includes buffoonery (*τὰ βωμολόχα*);
among the resources of the *γελοῖον ἐκ τῶν πραγμάτων*
devices suited to farce are mentioned, such as the use of
ugly masks and unseemly gestures, and the author makes
a special point of the comic vocabulary, its divisions and
subdivisions. All this gives us a rather unfavourable idea

of comedy in Aristotle's day. In short, buffoonery and triviality were traditional in Greek comedy. To what extent are these characteristics found in the νέα?

I have already said that the νέα almost completely abandoned personal attacks, and that it no longer gave grotesque travesties of mythological tales and heroes. These two statements are encouraging. But travesty and personal abuse are only two resources of low comedy. I shall therefore approach the question without allowing myself to be affected by any preconceived views.

In the fragments of the original plays we find both ῥήσεις and passages of dialogue to which the epithet βωμολοχικά seems to be well suited; for in them the actors indulge in absurd exaggerations, more or less smart paradoxes and whimsical conceits. In Diphilus' Παράσιτος the person after whom the play is named utters the following complaint—

"Euripides, whose words are golden, has rightly said : ' I am conquered by necessity and my wretched stomach.' Truly nothing is more wretched than the stomach. Everything can be crammed into it at once, which is impossible in the case of any other receptacle. For instance, in a sack you can carry bread, but not soup without danger of losing it; in a basket you can carry cakes, but not a purée; in a bottle you can carry wine, but not a lobster. But into this cursed stomach which the gods hate, it is possible to stuff things which are entirely different from one another. . . ." [1]

Fragment 61, which is spoken by the same actor, is a sort of profession of faith, and its cynicism is amusing—

"When I am invited by a rich man who gives an entertainment, I pay no attention to the triglyphs nor to the ceilings, I do not examine the Corinthian vases, but keep my eyes fixed on the smoke from the kitchen. If it comes out strong and mounts straight up, then I am happy and

[1] Diph., fr. 60.

flap my wings. But if it goes up slanting and in a thin cloud, I know at once that it is a case of a bloodless feast."

In another passage, fragment 62, he pretends to be irritated by one of his companions, who was apparently planning to celebrate a wedding without inserting in the programme the customary mention of culinary rejoicings. Fragment 73, which belongs to the Συνωρίς, also brings a facetious parasite upon the stage who plays dice with a courtesan and makes sham quotations from Euripides. So much for Diphilus' comedies. In Apollodorus of Carystus, who imitated Menander, an actor delights in drawing the picture of an age of gold which shall, above all, be an age of feasting,[1] In Baton, a gay young dog gives lively expression to the idea that, by enjoying himself, he does homage to the gods and plays the part of a good citizen by making business brisk.[2] In another play by the same poet, a pedagogue is seriously accused of having debauched his pupil, and impudently makes Epicurus responsible for his strange educational methods.[3] But, above all, cooks are repeatedly heard holding forth with burlesque solemnity, and telling stories that send people to sleep. In Hegesippus one of them claims that if he were to serve a meal to people who come from a funeral, he would only need to raise the corner of the cover from his dishes to change their tears into smiles; more than that, he can repeat the seductive arts of the Sirens, and by the mere smoke that escapes from his kitchen hold persons spellbound.[4] In Philemon another culinary artist ends a tirade of self-glorification by saying : " I have discovered the secret of immortality. To those who are already dead I give back life when they smell my dishes.[5] It appears that one of his fellows in a comedy by Baton said something similar.[6] One of Euphron's cooks gravely enumerates the seven wise men of the kitchen.[7] Another relates how Soterides, whose pupil he was, made king Nicomedes

[1] Apoll. Car., fr. 5. [2] Baton, fr. 2. [3] *Ibid.*, fr. 5. [4] Heges., fr. 1.
[5] Phil., fr. 79. [6] Baton, fr. 4. [7] Euphron, fr. 1, 1–12.

H H

take a piece of horse-radish which he had disguised,
tricked out and cleverly seasoned, for a sardine;[1] " for,"
he adds, " there is no difference whatever between a cook
and a poet." Other cooks go still further and say that
the masters of their art possess the most unexpected attainments—knowledge of natural science, of architecture, of
astronomy, of strategy.[2] A perusal of passages such as
these inclines one to the belief that many of the scenes
and burlesque tirades which abound in Plautus' plays
were supplied by the Greek plays which he imitated. The
cook in the *Pseudolus*, who claims that he can prolong the
life of his customers to two hundred years and nourish
Jupiter with the perfume of his pots,[3] is probably closely
related to all the other boasters whom I have just mentioned. As a matter of fact, it is not often that we can
verify the jests of the Latin poet by such exact analogies;
though many passages contain internal evidence of their
Hellenic origin.

The absurd and exaggerated rodomontades of certain
boasters do, no doubt, exceed anything similar found in
fragments of the original plays, in Terence's *Eunuchus*,
in the *Epistles* of Alciphron or in the *Dialogues* of Lucian.
Does it follow that the author of the *Miles Gloriosus*, of
the *Poenulus*, and of the *Curculio* was alone responsible
for this? I do not think so. The countries which our
mighty warriors are supposed to have subjugated, the
races which they have laid low, Persians, Paphlagonians,
people of Sinope, Carians, etc.—to these we may add the
Centaurs and the Amazons—are races and countries whose
names must have occurred more readily to a Greek of the
fourth or third century than to a Roman contemporary
of Hannibal. The improbable exploit of Pyrgopolinices,
who broke the thigh-bone of an elephant with a blow of
his fist, has its precedent in the doughty deeds with which
famous athletes were credited in Greece (they were said
to have felled an ox in the same way), or in those with
which Aristobulus, Alexander's flattering biographer,

---

[1] Euphron, fr. 11.   [2] Sosipatros, fr. 1.   [3] *Pseud.*, 829–830, 844.

credited his king.[1] The battle in which Pyrgopolinices
says he rescued Mars and served under the command of
Neptune's son, is like a parody of the Homeric battles in
which gods and the sons of gods mingled with ordinary
mortals. The victory of Antamoenides over the winged
men recalls other episodes in the old epic poems—Heracles'
combat with the Stymphalian birds, the fight of the sons
of Boreas with the Harpies; and above all, the battle of
Apollonius' Argonauts with the birds of Aretias. If, as
I believe, the word used of this victory is *ptenanthropica*,[2]
it proves the nationality of the writer who invented it.

The stinginess displayed by Euclio in the *Aulularia* is
not less exaggerated than the bragging indulged in by
soldiers. But we have positive evidence that the Greek
Smicrines was likewise something of a caricature. Pythodicus says that Euclio is sorry to see the smoke that issues
from his house disappear;[3] Smicrines is afraid that it
might rob him of something as it passes out.[4] Another
detail in the *Aulularia* has its parallel in Aristophanes.
Euclio suspects Staphyla's rooster of having allowed itself
to be bought by the cooks in order to show them where
the treasure lay hid;[5] Philocleon suspected his rooster,
who crowed late, of having been bribed by the defendants
so that he should not wake him in time.[6]

The unnatural gluttony of the parasites in Latin comedy
was certainly equalled by that of the parasites of the μέση.
Several of the extant fragments prove this.[7] We may
assume that some of the parasites of the νέα were quite
the equals of their ancestors; one of the lists of dishes with
which Ergasilus regales us consists in part of Greek names.[8]
As for the amusing soliloquies found in various parts of
the *Captivi*, at the beginning of the *Menaechmi*, and in the

---

[1] Lucian, *Quomodo historia conscribenda*, § 12.
[2] *Poen.*, 471.   [3] *Aul.*, 300–301.
[4] This is quoted by Choricius in the *Apology for Actors* (*Rev. de Philol.*
I. p. 228).
[5] *Aul.*, 465 et seq.   [6] Aristoph., *Wasps*, 100–102.
[7] Alexis, fr. 178, 231, 261; Timocles, fr. 29; Epigones, fr. 1; etc.
[8] *Capt.*, 850–851.

first part of the *Stichus*—if we exclude a few repetitions, a few amplifications and a few Roman elements which were no doubt added—they may, in my opinion, come from the original plays. Nothing was more common at Athens than such expressive surnames as *Peniculus* for gourmets and spungers. Actual parasites were called *Lagunion* or *Pternokopis*; one of Philemon's parasites was called. *Zomion.* The beginning of Ergasilus' first soliloquy— *Iuventus nomen indidit Scorto mihi, eo quia invocatus soleo esse in conviviis*—is very similar in form to one of Antiphanes' sentences : καλοῦσί μ' οἱ νεώτεροι διὰ ταῦτα πάντα σκηπτόν.[1] A play on words similar to the one indulged in by the Latin actor which is based on the double meaning of *vocare* (call, invoke) is found in Apollodorus.[2] Fragment 367 of Menander contains a fairly close parallel to the lamentations of a poor devil over the meagre success with which his broad hints meet.[3] The mocking invitation which Gelasimus, in the *Stichus*, gives Epignomus[4] also reminds one of a characteristic which Menander attributes to the well-known Chaerephon in one of the fragments (fr. 320) of the *Μέθη.* When Ergasilus speaks of the famished parasites of the *Lacones*, when he deplores the fact that gilded youths now go in person to drive their bargains in the market or at the pander's,[5] he talks Greek in Latin words.[6] This is probably also the case when he compares his fellow parasites to mice who gnaw at other people's belongings,[7] or when he proposes to give up being a parasite and become a porter.[8] The plan proposed by Peniculus—no longer to keep prisoners in jail by means of chains which they may break, but by the safer bond of good food [9]—is one of those schemes of reform for which the Greek stage always had a taste. The very words that Plautus uses in line 89 (*apud mensam plenam homini rostrum deliges*) reminds one of a saying of

---

[1] Antiph., fr. 195.   [2] Apoll. Car., fr. 26.   [3] *Capt.*, 478 et seq.
[4] *Stichus*, 471 et seq.   [5] *Capt.*, 471, 474 et seq.
[6] Cf. Theoph., *Char.*, XI.   [7] *Capt.*, 77.   Cf. Diog. Laert., VI. 40.
[8] *Capt.*, 90 et seq.   Cf. Alciphron, III. 4.
[9] *Menaech.*, 79 et seq.

one of Menander's parasites : ἀνθρώπους φάτνην ἔχειν.[1] And
finally, as for the idea of the auction sale that Gelasimus
means to hold of his person [2] and of all his belongings,
I am very much inclined to believe that it goes back to a
Greek original. The names or the nature of some of the
objects which are put up for sale—the strigil and the
ampulla, the *logi ridiculi* and the *unctiones*—have an
obviously Hellenic stamp; and finally, the description
Gelasimus gives of himself—*parasitum inanem quo recondas
reliquias*—bears some resemblance to an expression used
by the poet Phoenicides regarding the glutton Chaerippus :
τοιοῦτ᾽ ἔχει ταμιεῖον ὥσπερ οἰκίας (or ἐν τῇ κοιλίᾳ?).[3]

But enough of parasites and their tricks. Chrysalus'
triumphant soliloquy, in lines 925 *et seq.* of the *Bacchides*,
affords us an example of a passage replete with Attic
fancies of another kind. No comic author of the sixth
century after the foundation of Rome would of his own
accord have conceived the idea of giving a detailed comparison between the Trojan war and the rascality of a
slave; for the greater part of his audience would not have
been able to see the point. But such playfulness is natural
on the part of a poet of the new period; it has a family
resemblance to the parallels—and they are without a
doubt Greek—drawn between a wicked scamp and some
great person, like Agathocles or Alexander.[4] Broadly
speaking, it may be said that the irreverential comparison
of people famous in history or in legend with people or
things of low estate is a favourite device of the *véa*. I
have already mentioned the seven sages of the kitchen.
In one of Diphilus' plays an actor complains about having
been obliged to purchase a conger-eel for its weight in gold,
just as Priam purchased the body of his son.[5] Another
groans over the poverty of the market, and declares that
he has to fight for a sprig of parsley, just as people struggle

[1] Men., fr. 937. Φάτνη is a feeding-trough.(—Tr.).
[2] *Stichus*, 171 et seq.
[3] Phoenicides, fr. 3. Ταμιεῖον is a storehouse.(—Tr.).
[4] Men., fr. 924; *Most.*, 775 et seq.; *Pseud.*, 532.
[5] Diph., fr. 33.

for a prize at the Isthmian Games.[1]   In Diodorus, a parasite claims that his profession is an invention of Zeus Philios, and likens himself and his fellow-parasites to the liturgical "parasites of Heracles."[2]   In the Σαμία the adventure of Plangon, who has been seduced by Moschio, is compared to that of Danae;[3] and so on.[4] One of the things that contributes to the fun in the scene of the *Menaechmi* in which Menaechmus pretends to be crazy, is the fact that it reproduces episodes of well-known tragedies in a travestied form.   Menaechmus apostrophises Bacchus and Apollo, and pretends to be obeying their commands, just as Orestes or a Bacchante would.   Greeks would have been able to grasp the intended parody, but the majority of Plautus' audience certainly could have not seen it, nor would the allusions to Cycnus and to Tithonus have been very clear to them.

With this scene of madness let us compare another scene which is supposed to be one of the most burlesque in Plautus — the scene in the *Mercator* in which Charinus remains on the stage while he imagines that he is making a long journey.   It, too, abounds in features that prove its origin; for instance, the description of the travelling costumes which the lover takes off or puts on piece by piece, according as he is hopeful or despondent—*chlamys, machaera, ampulla*;[5] the enumeration of the countries which says he is visiting : Cyprus and Chalcis—though it is a curious idea to go to Cyprus in a carriage—; and Eutychus' remark : *Calchas iste quidem Zacynthiust.*

Drunkenness, which supplied Plautus with comic effects of a somewhat vulgar nature, was not unknown in New Comedy.   Several passages warrant the belief that the νέα occasionally introduced actors whose heads and feet were a bit shaky. Witness fragments **67** and **229** of

---

[1] Diph., fr. 32.
[2] Diodorus, fr. 2. Cf. Nicolaus, fr. 1. The παράσιτοι in Greek ritual assisted the priest at the sacrifice and banquet.
[3] Σαμ., 244–246.
[4] *Pseud.*, 192–193, 199–200; *Bacch.*, 111, 155, 156, 242, 810.
[5] Cf. Σαμ., 314 et seq.

Menander, fragment 84 of Philemon, and the reference to
Daos in a hilarious state in Dio Chrysostom.[1] The scenes
in the *Mostellaria* in which Callidamates is under the
influence of wine and indulges in all sorts of eccentricities,
are doubtless entirely the invention of Philemon, and the
most trivial detail of all—*Iam hercle ego vos pro matula
habebo, nisi mihi matulam datis*—must not be thought too
gross for Greek ears. In Attic comedy the utensil referred
to was always to be found at a drinking-bout.[2]

It has been surmised that the scenes in the *Casina* which
turn upon Chalinus' disguises were added by the Latin
poet, but I do not think there is any convincing reason
for this assumption. The scene in which we witness the
marriage procession and see Lysidamus making his first
familiar advances to the delicate person—*corpusculum
malaculum*—of the supposed bride, conforms entirely to
the taste of early Attic comedy. The two other scenes in
which we see Olympio and his master, each in turn, coming
back crestfallen,[3] are, to a certain extent, repetitions;
and I am inclined to believe that the first and more obscene
one was added by Plautus. In the second scene, on the
other hand, several details enable us to trace the hand of
the translator at work : the word *dismarite*, which occurs
nowhere else and which seems to me to be an adaptation
of δυσάνερ; the construction of *moechissat*, used, like
μοιχᾶν or μοιχεύειν, with a direct object; the mention
of the cane, the usual complement of a man's attire at
Athens, in connection with the *pallium* which Lysidamus
has lost; the allusion to the immorality of the Massaliotes,
which was proverbial among the Greeks, and the reference
to the Bacchantes, for which the scandals connected with
the Roman Bacchanalia would not be sufficient explanation.

The buffoonery of which I have been speaking has not
always much relation to the plot. However, this does

---

[1] Dio Chrys., XXXII. p. 699 R. (fr. adesp. 306).

[2] Cf. Aristoph., *Thesm.*, 633; *Frogs*, 544; Eupolis, fr. 341; Epicrates,
fr. 5; Diphilus, fr. 43, lines 34–35; *Berliner Klassikertexte*, V. 2, p. 114
(line 32), fr. adesp. 375; etc. Also Aeschylus, fr. 180 Nauck ('Οστολόγοι).

[3] See the end of Aristophanes' *Peace*.

not, as a rule, delay the progress of events in an entirely
improbable way. But there are other instances where
the fun is not only vulgar but also out of place. This
is especially the case when a character who has to com-
municate, to announce or to request something important,
stops to make endless preambles, and indulges in all sorts
of circumlocutions. In real life it would certainly not
occur to a slave who brings good news (as Pinacium does in
lines 274 *et seq.* of the *Stichus*) to ask the questions which
Pinacium asks : " Shall I go and inform my mistress ? Or
would it not be better to wait for her to send me an embassy to find out what I know ? " And so on. Nor would
a messenger, when he has found the person for whom he
has been searching, lose time in quarrelling with a third
person, as Pinacium, to whom I have already referred,
does, and as Acanthio does in one of the early scenes of
the *Mercator*. Nor would he expect the person whom he
is addressing, before he has been told anything, to give
expression to feelings or to make declarations and preparations for which the information he is about to give is the
only justification. But Pinacium (in lines 347 *et seq.* of
the *Stichus*) and Ergasilus (in lines 838 *et seq.* of the
Captivi) do demand this with unreasonable persistence.
It is also absurd that when Trachalio implores Daemones
to interfere and save Palaestra, he should introduce the
pleasantries into his request which are found in lines 629
et seq. of Plautus' *Rudens ;* or that Calidorus, when meditat-
ing hanging himself in despair, should begin by asking his
slave to lend him the money to buy a rope.[1] In this case
and elsewhere Plautus' characters indulge in fun at the
wrong moment. However, it seems that herein they
frequently imitated the original Greek works. Let us go
back to the examples which I have just cited. In the
passage from the *Pseudolus* the word *drachuma*, in that
from the *Rudens* the word *exagoga* and the definite allusion
to a common infirmity of the Cyreneans seem to me to be
straws worth noting. The soliloquy pronounced by the

[1] *Pseud.*, 85 et seq.

waggish Pinacium begins with a statement which better
suits the Greek Hermes than the Roman Mercury (*Mer-
curius Iovis qui nuntius perhibetur*, etc.). This soliloquy
ends in lines that were, no doubt, translated word for word
(*Contundam facta Talthubi contemnamque omnis nuntios :
simulque cursuram meditabor ad ludos Olympios*) and the
honours asked for in the most important passage—*oratores,
dona ex auro, quadrigas*—bear a strong resemblance to those
which the flattering adulation of the Athenians invented
for some of Menander's contemporaries. The passage in
the *Captivi* in which Ergasilus orders a huge banquet
without saying why or in honour of what he does so, is
very much like its prototype in a scene from Greek comedy
which affords a good basis for comparison, notwithstanding
the fact that it does not belong to the new period—namely,
the scene in Aristophanes' *Plutus*, in which Cario approaches
his mistress after the blind man has been cured.[1]

The foregoing observations all relate to scenes or to
parts of scenes which are fairly lengthy. As soon as we
attempt to get an idea of the comic elements found in
mere details, we shall discover that the choice of words
must have played an appreciable part in them. Certain
passages which contain a conceit often owe much of their
humorous effect to mere combinations of words. Take,
for example, fragment 7 of Apollodorus—

" We fathers are at a great disadvantage. If your
father does not do everything you wish, you reproach him
by saying, ' Weren't you young once yourself? ' (*Οὐ
γέγονας αὐτὸς νέος;*); but if his son behaves badly, a father
cannot say to him, ' Weren't you old once yourself? ' "
(*Οὐ γέγονας αὐτὸς γέρων;*).

Οὐ γέγονας αὐτὸς γέρων; this curious question, which
sounds like nonsense, and which corresponds word for
word with the refrain of the young men, is as amusing in
its form as in its meaning. This is true also of Lysidamus'

---

[1] *Plutus*, 644 et seq.

sally in lines 263–264 of the *Casina*, which is a version
of Philocleon's words : [1] *At quamquam unicust, nihilo
magis ille unicust mihi filius quam ego illi pater*. When,
in the Γεωργός, Daos ironically sings the praises of his
master's property, the juxtaposition of the two first words
—ἀγρὸν εὐσεβέστερον—is sure to puzzle the spectators;
they might almost be a riddle set to the audience, of
which what follows gives the explanation—

" A more pious property no one cultivates, I do believe.
Ours produces myrtle, ivy, laurel, every flower; moreover,
if you put anything into it, it gives it back honestly and
fairly, not a whit more, but exactly the same quantity." [2]

The same artifice is found in a passage by Philemon :
" I did not know that in my field I had a physician "
(Ἐγὼ τὸν ἀγρὸν ἰατρὸν ἐλελήθειν ἔχων); and by way of
justifying this curious statement he goes on—
" For it feeds me like a patient, and gives me a few
grains of corn, a mere whiff of wine, a leaf of salad, and,
by Zeus ! those wee products of the rocks, capers, thyme
and asparagus, and nothing more.   I am really afraid that
it will make me so thin that I shall become a corpse." [3]

Though the fragments of the νέα do not afford equivalents
for some of Plautus' sentences, the ending of which is
amusing because it is unexpected, such as Lycus' statement: *Nunc ibo, amicos consulam, quo me modo suspendere
aequo censeant potissimum*,[4] Aristophanes' plays do. Take,
for example, this sentence in the *Acharnians* : Ἄνδρες
πρόβουλοι τοῦτ᾽ ἔπραττον τᾷ πόλει, ὅπως τάχιστα καὶ κάκιστ᾽
ἀπολοίμεθα.[5] We have every reason to believe that such
sentences are translated from the Greek.

However, these are not, strictly speaking, plays on
words. But we have proof that similar devices—puns,
alliterations, etymological pleasantries—did not disappear entirely, though Menander [6] disdained to use

---

[1] *Wasps*, 1359.   [2] Γεωργ., 35–39.   [3] Philemon, fr. 98.
[4] *Poen.*, 794–795.   Cf. *Stichus*, 503–504.   [5] *Acharn.*, 755–756.
[6] Plut., *Compar. Aristoph. and Men.*, I. 2.

them, and they occurred, as a rule, much less frequently
in the νέα than in the comic writers of the fifth century.
A number of them are found in the fragments. When
making fun of Magas, Philemon plays on the double meaning of the word γράμματα—letters that are sent, and
written characters.[1] Elsewhere, he plays on the name of
the parasite Carabus.[2] Euphranor plays on the name of
the cook Lycus,[3] and Archedicus on that of the courtesan
Scotodine.[4] In two consecutive lines by Archedicus the
word τράχηλος designates a highly prized part of certain
shell-fish as well as the neck of the person who is speaking.[5]
In a fragment of Posidippus the word στόμα must be taken
to mean both the mouth of the gourmets and the narrow
entrance to a harbour.[6] In a fragment of Baton τόπος
and κεφαλή have both their usual meaning and that of
rhetorical terms.[7] The word χορδή at the end of one of
Euphron's tirades signifies both blood-pudding, chitter-
lings, and the string of a lyre.[8] In another fragment of
Euphron a slave who has an empty stomach is given the
name of a fish, κεστρεύς,[9] because the word νῆστις, which
is used of a man who has not yet broken his fast, designates
a variety of that species of fish. The same joke is found
in Diphilus.[10] An actor in one of Alexis' comedies implores
a cook to chop the meat up fine (κόπτειν), but not to chop
him up—that is to say, not to kill him (μὴ κόπτε μ᾽, ἀλλὰ τὰ
κρέα).[11] This joke, which must have been a traditional
one, is also found in lines 70 and 77 of Menander's Σαμία.
In Apollodorus of Carystus a wag uses the word καλεῖν in
two senses in quick succession—to *invoke* and to *invite* :
" I invoke Ares and Nike for the success of my expedition,
and I also invoke Chaerephon; for if I do not invoke him
(*i. e.* if I do not invite him) he'll come without being invited (κ᾽ ἂν γὰρ μὴ καλῶ, ἄκλητος ἥξει)." [12] In a fragment
of Phoenicides a courtesan tells of her misfortune. She

[1] Philem., fr. 144.	[2] *Ibid.*, fr. 42.	[3] Euphron, fr. 1, lines 30–31.
[4] Archedicus, fr. 1.	[5] *Ibid.*, fr. 3.	[6] Posid., fr. 26.
[7] Baton, fr. 5.	[8] Euphron, fr. 1.	[9] *Ibid.*, fr. 2.
[10] Diph., fr. 54.	[11] Alexis, fr. 175.	[12] Apoll. Car., fr. 26.

has been the victim of a soldier who, according to his own account, was waiting to receive a gratuity from the king (δωρεάν), " and," she says, " while waiting for this *gratuity*, the wretch had me *gratis* for a whole year (διὰ ταύτην ἣν λέγω τὴν δωρεὰν ἐνιαυτὸν ἔσχε μ᾽ ὁ κακοδαίμων δωρεάν).[1] In Menander, the mother of another courtesan boasts of her daughter's *philanthropic* disposition (πάνυ γὰρ ἐστι τῇ φύσει . . . φιλάνθρωπον τὸ παιδάριον σφόδρα).[2] In an anonymous fragment an actor declares that for every twenty bushels (μέδιμνοι) that he sows, his field yields him thirteen, and he humorously adds : οἱ δ᾽ ἔπτ᾽ ἐπὶ Θήβας ἐστράτευσάν μοι δοκῶ. And, not content with this joke, he declares that his field gratifies the oft-expressed wish : ὀνησιφόρα γένοιτο. And why? ῞Ο γὰρ φέρει νῦν οὗτος, εἷς ὄνος φέρει.[3] The attentive reader will discover further examples of this sort in Plautus, besides those which have come down to us in the original Greek fragments. It is perfectly clear that many of the plays on words that abound in the Latin poet are entirely his own. But underlying some of them we can see the signs of a similar joke on the part of the Greek author. Furthermore, if we translate some of these Latin sentences, in which there is no trace of a play on words, into Greek, we are occasionally led to suspect that there was one in the original version. I have already shown that this was so in a sentence in the prologue to the *Casina* and in a line in the prologue to the *Menaechmi*,[4] and it can be shown that it was also the case in passages that do not occur in prologues. For instance, in lines 241, 703–704 of the *Bacchides*, 630 of the *Stichus*, 187, 648, 775 of the *Poenulus*, 229, 653–654, 712 and 736 of the *Pseudolus*, 437–438 of the *Miles*, 517 of the *Mercator*, 331–332 of the *Amphitryon*, 826–827 of the *Rudens*, and 25 of the *Epidicus*, the jokes or apparent jokes on the names Chrysalus, Gelasimus, Lycus,

---

[1] Phoenicides, fr. 4, lines 9–10.   [2] Men., fr. 428.

[3] Fr. adesp. 109. A single donkey can carry what this field now bears.(—Tr.).

[4] See p. 407.

Phoenicium, Harpax and Charinus, Dicea, Pasicompsa, Sosia, Palaestra, and Epidicus are manifestly of Greek origin. Line 721 of the *Stichus* (*Satin ut facete,* <*aeque*> *atque ex pictura, adstitit*), is in all probability a translation of a line that contained a play on the words πίναξ and Πινάκιον; and line 886 of the *Poenulus* (*Continuo is me ex Syncerasto Crurifragium fecerit*) is probably a translation of a line in which Συγκεραστός was contrasted with some compound of κρεμαστός. Line 585 of the *Pseudolus* (*Ballionem exballistabo lepide*) is possibly a Latin rendering of a phrase in which the name Ballio was brought into connection with a compound of βάλλειν. In the following passage from the *Casina :* Quasi venator tu quidem es ; dies atque noctes cum cane aetatem exigis,[1] a scholar has discovered an etymological joke, suggested by the word κυνηγέτης. In the *Aulularia* Pythodicus and the cooks play on the verbs *disperti* and *dividere*,[2] and I suspect that their Greek prototypes played in the same way on διαμερίζειν and διαμηρίζειν. The jokes suggested by the false name Summanus, in the *Curculio*,[3] could be made in Greek about the name Οὔριος. Like *Summanus, Οὔριος* is a name appropriate for the most powerful of the gods, and its resemblance to the verb οὐρεῖν strikes one immediately. When, in line 375 of the *Mostellaria,* Philolaches says to Callidamates : *Valet ille quidem* (*sc. pater*), *atque* <*ego*> *disperii,* and the latter replies : *Bis periisti ? qui potest ?* the quid pro quo is not apparent in the Latin text. I imagine that in Philemon the confusion arose from the two prefixes δυς- and δις-, which must have been pronounced practically in the same way. Further on, in line 892, Pinacium says to Phaniscus, whom he charges with being his master's favourite : *Tace sis, faber qui cudere soles plumbeos nummos.* In order to understand the malice of these words one should, I think, bear in mind that false coins are called κίβδηλα in Greek, and that κύβδα denotes a stoop-

---

[1] *Casina*, 319–320. [2] *Aul.*, 280 et seq.
[3] *Curc.*, 414–416. See Ussing's commentary.

ing attitude with which Phaniscus was presumably familiar.[1] In line 822 of the *Truculentus* the maid-servant of Callicles addresses Diniarchus in the following terms : *Video ego te, propter male facta qui es patronus parieti.* If we imagine the expression translated into the Greek, and the word *patronus* replaced by προστάτης (literally : *the man who stands in front*), the joke will become much clearer. After Mercury has declared, in lines 325–326 of the *Amphitryon : Vox mi ad aures advolavit,* Sosia sadly replies : *Ne ego homo infelix fui, qui non alas intervelli; volucrem vocem gestito.* Further on, in line 333, Mercury says that a voice strikes his ears (*aures verberat*), and Sosia remarks in a stage aside : *Metuo vocis ne vicem hodie hic vapulem, quae hunc verberat.* Both of these jokes could be made in Greek, as προσπέτεσθαι and ὦτα βάλλειν were both commonly used in connection with the voice. The same remark applies to the joke in lines 367 *et seq.* : Merc. *Advenisti consutis dolis.* Sos. *Immo quidem tunicis consutis huc advenio, non dolis,* because ῥάπτειν is used in a metaphorical sense, just as *consuere* is; and to the play on words in line 1001 : *Faciam ut sit madidus sobrius,* because a man who was drunk was called a *moistened* or *damp* man (βεβρεγμένος) in Greece as well as in Rome. Patient researches made by one who is thoroughly versed in Latin and Greek would, I am sure, make it possible to extend this list considerably.

Here is a list chosen at random from among the comic metaphors and jokes which cannot have been invented by Plautus—

— *Trin.*, 1011 : *Cave sis tibi, ne bubuli in te cottabi crebri crepent ; Epid.*, 125 : *Sine meo sumptu paratae iam sunt scapulis symbolae ;* 311 : *ne ulmos parasitos faciat, quae usque attondeant :* 625–626 : *Ex tuis verbis meum futurum corium pulchrum praedicas, quem Apella atque Zeuxis duo pingent pigmentis ulmeis.* The use of

---

[1] Cf. Aristoph., *Thesm.*, 489; Machon ap. Ath., p. 580 D.

the words *cottabi, symbolae, parasiti*, which recall local
customs, and that of the names Apelles and Zeuxis,
sufficiently indicate the origin of these passages.

— *Pseud.*, 229 : *Cras Phoenicium poeniceo corio invises
pergulam.* There is a similar passage in lines 111–112
of the *Acharnians* : "Αγε δὴ σὺ φράσον ἐμοὶ σαφῶς πρὸς
τουτονί, ἵνα μέ σε βάψω βάμμα Σαρδιανικόν, and in lines
319–320 : 'Ειπέ μοι, τὶ φειδόμεσθα τῶν λίθων, ὦ δημόται, μὴ
οὐ καταξαίνειν τὸν ἄνδρα τοῦτον ἐς φοινικίδα.

— *Epid.*, 16–17 : Th. *Perpetuen valuisti ?* Ep. *Varie.*
Th. *Qui varie valent, capreaginum hominum non placet
mihi neque pantherinum genus.* Compare line 89 of
Herondas' third mimiamb : 'Αλλ' ἐστὶν ὕδρης ποικιλώτερον
πολλῷ.

— *Poen.*, 398 : *Itaque iam quasi ostrealum tergum
ulceribus gestito.* This reminds one of Xanthias' exclamation, in lines 1292 *et seq.* of Aristophanes' *Wasps* :
'Ιὼ χελῶναι μακαρίαι τοῦ δέρματος . . . ὡς εὖ κατηρέψασθε
καὶ νουβυστικῶς κεράμῳ τὸ νῶτον ὥστε τὰς πληγὰς στέγειν.

— *Poen.*, 700 : *Ubi tu. . . . vetustate vino edentulo
aetatem inriges.* The same expression is found in fragment 167 of Alexis : ἔσται (οἶνος) καὶ μάλα ἡδύς γ', ὀδόντας
οὐκ ἔχων.

— *Poen.*, 759–760 : Lyc. *Calidum prandisti prandium
hodie ? Dic mihi.* Agor. *Quid iam ?* Lyc. *Quia os
nunc frigefactas, quom rogas.* We know that the adjective
ψυχρός is used figuratively, just as *frigidus* is in Latin.
The following passage from fragment 4 of Theophilus may
be compared with the above lines of the *Poenulus* : " Πῶς
ἔχεις πρὸς κάραβον; " " Ψυχρός ἐστιν, ἄπαγε," φησί · " ῥητόρων
οὐ γεύομαι; " and also Gnathaena's *bon mot* about the
prologues of Diphilus which, according to her, are capable.
of chilling water.

— *Cas.*, 356 (After Chalinus has told Cleostrata that
her husband would be glad to see her dead) : Lys. *Plus
artificum est mihi quam rebar ; hariolum hunc habeo domi.*
There is the same turn in the Περικειρομένη, 181–182 :
Μάντιν ὁ στρατιώτης [ἔλαθ' ἔχων] τοῦτον · ἐπιτυγχάνει τι. The

jokes made on this subject in several passages of Plautus
are, like the subject itself, probably of Greek origin.

— *Rud.*, 586 *et seq.* : *Quasi vinis graecis Neptunus
nobis suffudit mare, itaque alvom prodi speravit nobis salsis
poculis.* Plautus himself admits that he is following his
Greek model by speaking of *Greek wines ;* he refers to
what was known as οἶνος τεθαλαττωμένος.

It would be easy to add a number of further examples.

Two practices in which the authors of the middle period
had delighted — parodying lofty style and the πνῖγος
(an accumulation of words that had to be pronounced
in one breath)—do not seem to have enjoyed as much
popularity in the days of the νέα. In the original fragments, as well as in Plautus' plays, we do, it is true, find
enumerations, and especially enumerations of utensils
or of eatables ; but hardly one of them is long enough to
provoke laughter.[1] The only one that can be compared
to the litanies of the μέση in point of length is the list of
purveyors whom Megadorus enumerates in his satirical
comments on the extravagance of women. Considering
the names of many of these purveyors and the luxurious
nature of their trades, I think it extremely likely that
this passage is a translation. But it must be pointed out
that this enumeration is not conceived in the same taste
as in the works of the earlier authors, and that its comic
effect is based on other motives. When, for example,
Anaxandrides, in fragment 41, enumerates, in a single
breath, nearly a hundred dishes, this tirade derives its
humour from the mere juxtaposition of words, and the
laughter it finally provokes is due to the fact that it tickles
the ears. In Megadorus' catalogue each word appeals
directly to the imagination ; the listener imagines that
he sees the luckless husband bombarded by the endless
crowd of creditors who present their claims, and it is this
picture that makes him laugh. There is something more
frankly burlesque about those passages in which an actor

---

[1] *Aul.*, 508 et seq.

calls to witness a host of gods in order to lend weight to
his words; [1] in these passages, however—and there are not
many of them—the enumerations are short.

Parodies of lofty style are still to be found here and
there, but we must not imagine we see them where they
do not exist. In many cases the fact that the words of
comic characters affect a certain dignity, which reminds
one of the lofty style of tragedy, of didactic poetry or of
an epic, is due to the situation or to the nature of the
actor—or else it is due to lack of skill on the part of the
poet, who was unable to give his lines the informality of
familiar talk. But there are passages in which the discrepancy between subject-matter and style is certainly
intentional, and where it is designed to provoke laughter.
This is the case in fragment 79 of Philemon, a cook's
soliloquy, the first two lines of which (ὡς ἱμερός μ᾿ὑπῆλθε
γῇ τε κοὐρανῷ λέξαι μολόντι τοὔψον ὡς ἐσκεύασα) are a
parody on lines 57–58 of Euripides' *Medea* (ὥσθ᾿ ἱμερός μ᾿
ὑπῆλθε γῇ τε κοὐρανῷ λέξαι μολούσῃ δεῦρο Μηδείας τύχας); in
fragment 348, in which the safe arrival of a captain of
a merchant vessel is announced in the same terms which
Poseidon uses to introduce himself to the public at the
beginning of the *Trojan Women*; in the lamentations of
Demeas, lines 110–111 of the Σαμία (ὦ πόλισμα Κεκροπίας
χθονός, ὦ ταναὸς αἰθήρ); in fragment 126 of Diphilus, a
burlesque incantation in hexameters; in fragment 8 of
Euphron, in which the grandiloquent circumlocution Νηρεῖα
τέκνα is used of fish that are being cooked, and a parasite
is called Νεῖλον βία; in fragment 1 of Strato, in which
a learned cook, "a male Sphinx," insists on using only
Homeric words that are incomprehensible for any one
who does not happen to have at hand the learned commentary by Philitas; in Chrysalus' laughably pathetic
invocation, line 932 of the *Bacchides* (*O Troia, O patria,
O Pergamum, O Priame, periisti, senex*); in Pseudolus'
exclamations, line 703 of the play that bears his name
(*Io te te, turanne, te te ego, qui imperitas Pseudolo*, etc.);

[1] Σαμ., 94–95; *Bacch.*, 892 et seq.

in the question which Ptolemocratia asks (lines 268–269 of
the *Rudens*) in oracular style of the two suppliant women
who are drenched with sea-water (*Nempe equo ligneo per
vias caerulas estis vectae?*); and so on. In other cases some
passage of a tragedy is merely cited, indicated or adapted
in a more or less humorous way without much insistence,
and the authority of a tragic writer—usually Euripides—
is invoked in an absurd manner. In the 'Επιτρέποντες
Sophrona uses a sentence from the *Auge* to excuse herself and her ward : ἡ φύσις ἐβούλεθ' ᾗ νόμων οὐδὲν μέλει.
Fragment 263 of Menander is very much like fragments
666 and 709 of Euripides, and fragment 366 greatly
resembles fragment 1016 of the same poet, while fragment
(doubtful) 1112 is much like line 930 of the *Andromache*.
We have already seen that some of Diphilus' parasites
quote their favourite poets, word for word. Indeed, the
second line of fragment 60 is a very close copy of a sentence
found in Nauck's collection, No. 907. The sham quotation in fragment 73 comprises, as its first element, a line
from Nauck's fragment 187, and as its third element
line 535 of the *Iphigeneia in Tauris*, both transcribed as
they stand in the original.

A comic style of expression has its foundation in words
that are themselves droll. Aristophanes abounds in
them; in the poets of the new period they were much
rarer. In the first place, it seems that the later poets
did not coin many words. The only words of this kind,
found in the fragments, are ψωμοκόλαφος, invented by
Diphilus after the model of ψωμοκόλαξ,[1] and possibly
λῃστοσαλπιγκτής, which is used by Menander.[2] As for the
comical proper names in which early comedy delighted,
there is only one instance of the sort in the fragments—
the title of a play by Diphilus, Αἱρησιτείχης. Those
which occur in Plautus—Artotrogus and Miccotrogus,
Thensaurochrysonicochrysides, Pyrgopolinices and Poly-
machaeroplagides, Therapontigonus Platagidorus and
Bumbomachides, Clutomistaridysarchides—are of uncer-

---

[1] Diph., fr. 49.   [2] Men., fr. 1030.

tain origin. I ought, however, to say that, as far as the
latter are concerned, I do not think it unreasonable to
suppose that they come from the *véa*. Plautus was quite
able when he chose to make up comic names from elements
that were exclusively Latin. Take, for example, the
assumed names of the sham Persian—Vaniloquidorus,
Virginisvendonides, Nugiepiloquides, Argentumextere-
bronides, Quodsemelarripides Nunquameripides; or the
names of countries, like Peredia and Perbibesia; or of
people, like the Panicei, the Pistorienses and the Ficedu-
lenses. If he also introduces names which are entirely
Greek and are formed in the regular way, surely it must
have been because he found them in the plays which he
imitated.

As I have already said in my remarks about foreigners
and rustics, the *véa* did not entirely eschew the comic effects
to be obtained from clumsy or peculiar elocution. When
Hanno jabbers stage-Carthaginian which Milphio interprets, God knows how, and then suddenly stops to use
the same language which the others speak, he reminds
one of Pseudartabas, the Persian ambassador in the
Acharnians. When the *truculentus* speaks of *rabo* (instead
of *arrabo*) and of *conia* (instead of *ciconia*), he indulges
in one of the forms of humour that are enumerated in the
Coislin Treatise—the corruption of words κατ' ἀφαίρεσιν.
In addition to the instances of this sort found in Plautus'
comedies, a few passages from the fragments are entitled
to special mention. Athenaeus says explicitly that Philemon delighted in the exotic appellations βατιάκια and
σαννάκια, which were given to certain kinds of drinking
cups.[1] An actor in one of Euphron's comedies is annoyed
at hearing people use the words ψυγεύς, σεῦτλον and φακέα
to designate things that were called ψυκτήρια, τευτλίον
and φακῆ at Athens.[2] Menander, Diphilus, Posidippus
and Philidippus brought purists upon the scene who pre-
sumed to correct the language used by their fellows.[3]

---

[1] Ath., p. 497 F.; Philem., fr. 87.   [2] Euphron, fr. 3.
[3] Men., fr. 300; Diph., fr. 47; Posid., fr. 38; Philipp., fr. 30.

One of the characters in the Θαΐς, by Hipparchus, takes a
λαβρώνιος for an animal.[1] In Diphilus an actor makes
the same mistake when he hears of πρίστις and τραγέλαφος,
λαβρώνιος and βατιάκη.[2] In a fragment of Epinicus
some one takes, or pretends to take, a *rhython* of the
ἐλέφας type for an elephant. Subsequently, when the
speaker prides himself on being able to drain this huge
vessel, which, as he declares, an elephant could not drain,
our friend pays him the following pretty compliment :
Οὐδὲν ἐλέφαντος γὰρ διαφέρεις οὐδὲ σύ;[3] ἐλέφας was a term
applied to imbeciles.

Occasionally, the most familiar terms, slang and crude
expressions are used. In Menander we meet with ξενύδρια[4]
and in Diphilus with μναδαρία[5] by way of comical diminutives. Menander does not hesitate to use the word
σκατοφάγος of a skinflint or of a brutal fellow.[6] He calls
a stupid old man " dung of a rat " (μνόχοδος);[7] a booby
who has been duped, " poor sniveller " (ἄθλιος λέμφος);[8]
a eunuch with a wrinkled skin, " old lizard " (γαλεώτης
γέρων).[9] Such amenities as Pseudolus and his master
lavish on the pander Ballio have well-known equivalents
in Greek : in line 368 (*verberasti patrem atque matrem*) it is
easy to discern a translation of πατραλοίας, μητραλοίας;
and possibly *bustirape*, in line 361, stands for τυμβωρύχος.
The words *perfossor parietum*, in line 980, are an exact
translation of τοιχωρύχος. In line 41 of the *Mostellaria*
the word κοπρών, which is a counterpart of the Latin
insulting term *caenum, sterculinum*, appears in its original
form. In line 149 of the Ἐπιτρέποντες Syriscus calls Daos
ἐργαστήριον, meaning *lupanar*;[10] and so on. And not
only were isolated opprobious terms taken over from the
original Greek plays, but they must have constituted an
inexhaustible fund of words which certain people used

---

[1] Hipparchus, fr. 3.   Λαβρώνιος is a large cup with handles.(—Tr.).
[2] Diph., fr. 80.   [3] Epinicus, fr. 2.   [4] Men., fr. 462.
[5] Diph., fr. 21.   [6] Men., fr. 825; Περικ., 204; Σαμ., 205.
[7] *Ibid.*, fr. 430.   [8] *Ibid.*, fr. 493. Cf. Ἐπιτρ., 344.
[0] *Ibid.*, fr. 188.   [10] Brothel.(—Tr.).

as invectives against their fellows. Among the exclamations used by Ballio, in the scene of the *Pseudolus*, which punctuate, as it were, the litany of abuse, we find several, like *babai* and *bombax*, that could not claim a birthright in Rome. On the other hand, the ironical approbation which the sad father bestows upon those who insult him reminds one of the approbation bestowed on the λόγος δίκαιος by the ἄδικος λογος in the *Clouds*.[1]

The νέα does not even hesitate to introduce indecent words. There is no doubt that in this respect it was much less audacious than earlier comedy had been. In an account that Philemon gives of a visit to a place of ill-fame he manages to avoid saying anything too gross.[2] In another passage he stops short just as he is about to use an indecent word.[3] It is the same with Menander at the end of the Ἐπιτρέποντες.[4] In a tirade against lewd people Apollodorus is almost equally careful to observe the proprieties.[5] But it was not usual to practise such reserve. In his play Θησεύς Diphilus lets three young girls from Samos discuss curious subjects and call a spade a spade.[6] In Poseidippus two cooks exchange insults that are worthy of Cleon and Agoracritus.[7] In Archedicus, Democharus is charged with the same debauched practices as was the lewd Ariphrades in earlier days.[8] Certain expressions that were dear to the writers of early comedy—προσπέρδειν, μινθοῦν, σποδεῖν, βινεῖν—reappear in Sosipatrus, in Damoxenus, in Apollodorus of Carystus, and in an anonymous fragment. Even Menander occasionally used indecent expressions. In the fragments of his works one finds words like χαμαιτύπη, βάκηλος, πόσθων, καπρᾶν, ὑπο-βινητιᾶν. In lines 220–221 of the Περικειρομένη a soldier, talking to a courtesan, indulges in indecent plays on the words ἀναβαίνειν and περικαθῆσθαι. In a scene which

---

[1] *Clouds*, 910 et seq.; cf. 1328–1330.
[2] Philem., fr. 4.   [3] *Ibid.*, fr. 126.
[4] Ἐπιτρ., 520 et seq. ON. . . . ταύτην λαβὼν χορῶν ἀποσπασθεῖσαν—Αἰσθάνει γε; ΣΜ. Ναί.
[5] Apollod., fr. 13.   [6] Ath., p. 451 B.
[7] Posid., fr. 1.   [8] Archedicus, fr. 4.

appears to belong to the Περινθία a frightened slave is—
by implication, it is true—said to meet with a " sudden
call." [1]

Hitherto I have only spoken of the fun that appeared
in the texts. In order to get a correct idea of the νέα
one must draw upon one's imagination for the fun conveyed
by the costumes or by the acting of the players.

In the fifth century, as well as in the first half of the
fourth, comic writers relied largely on the strange appearance of the masks and on the grotesqueness of the costumes
to provoke laughter. Their successors in the new period
made more limited use of these minor devices. The almost
complete disappearance (excepting in the prologues) of
supernatural beings greatly restricted the range of the
costumer's fancy. Furthermore, the absurd accoutrements which, as we learn through the texts and from a few
works of art, were worn by ordinary human folk—the
exaggerated phallus, the excessive padding of the stomach
and of the buttocks—fell into disuse. Most of the actors
of the νέα wore the costume of the common people, and
their masks often bore normal faces, and occasionally made
some claim to beauty. But the grotesque still held its
own. In Plautus we meet with portraits of certain people
that are certainly not flattering. Leonidas, in the
Asinaria, has a thin face, his hair is rather red, he has a
paunch, a fierce look and a rough appearance. [2] Pseudolus
is a red-haired fellow with a paunch and fat legs; his
skin is brown, his head big, his eye vivacious, his complexion red, and his feet enormous. [3] Labrax, in the
Rudens, displays a bald head, a flat nose, a big paunch,
slanting eyebrows and a wrinkled forehead. [4] Cappadox,
in the Curculio, has an enormous paunch, grass-coloured
eyes and an extraordinary complexion. [5] Lysimachus, in
the Mercator, is crooked, fat, bloated and thickset, lantern-

---

[1] Oxyrh. Pap., Vol. VI. No. 855; cf. Hermes, 1909, p. 311.
[2] Asin., 400–401.   [3] Pseud., 1218–1220.
[4] Rud., 317–318.   [5] Curc., 230 et seq.

jawed and a little bandy-legged.[1] In these portraits one
immediately recognises certain details which, ever since
the fifth century, succeeded in amusing the Athenian
public—paunch bellies, bald heads and scrubby red hair.
As a whole, therefore, these descriptions must date back
to the original Greek plays. Moreover, other documents
corroborate and complete these descriptions. In the first
place, we have the chapter in Pollux in which he gives a
description of the costumes of a Hellenistic theatrical
troupe.[2] And then we have various works of art. In
the illustrated manuscripts of Terence's comedies we see
masks that are simply hideous, alongside of others that are
normal or pretty. The same differences may be observed
in paintings, whether frescoes or vase paintings, mosaics
or pieces of sculpture that either illustrate scenes from
the νέα or give a symbolical version of its subject-matter.[3]
Among the grotesque figures that survived in the νέα the
first and foremost place was held by the slaves. In his
descriptions of their masks Pollux mentions complete or
partial baldness, the fiery colour of the hair and the lack
of symmetry in the face, as usual characteristics. Many
of the grotesque terra-cotta figures which date from the
fourth and subsequent centuries represent slaves whom
one can recognise by their dress.[4] Although there is, as a
rule, no indication of a mask on their faces, these grotesque
figures are probably reminiscences of the various types
of slaves that appeared on the stage in those days, and
especially of the slaves of the νέα. Many of them would
not be out of place in a chamber of horrors. Old men and
old women must often have been caricatured, just as slaves,
parasites and panders were. In the tabulae larvarum of

[1] Merc., 639–640.
[2] Pollux, Onom., IV. 143 et seq. Cf. Lucian, De Saltat., § 29; Platonius,
Περὶ διαφορᾶς κωμφδιῶν, p. 13.
[3] See, for example, Schreiber, Hellen. Reliefbilder, plates 82, 84, 88;
Arch. Zeit., 1878, plates 3–5; Dieterich, Pulcinella, pl. III.; Alb. Müller,
Griech. Bühnenalt., pp. 274–275.
[4] Cf. Otto, Die Terracotten von Sicilien, plates LI., LII.; Winter, Typen der
figürlichen Terrakotten, II. pp. 402 et seq., 414 et seq., 432 et seq., passim.

the MS. *Vaticanus* and MS. *Parisinus*, Phormio, the accomplished parasite, is represented by a grotesque mask; so are Dorio, Chremes, Demipho and one of the *advocati*. Pollux says of the πορνοβοσκός (pander) that he knits his eyebrows when he opens his mouth, and that he has a bald head; of the parasite, that he has a hooked nose, his ears in shreds, and a crafty or else a beaming face. Besides being ugly, certain old men, no doubt, provoked laughter by their peevish looks. As for old women, Pollux's words summon up a picture of dirty, fat, flat-nosed, grimacing creatures, and his description is corroborated by certain terra-cotta figurines.[1]

Grotesqueness in costumes was displayed by foreigners, rustics and soldiers. Various passages in the *Poenulus* show how people made sport of outlandish costumes.[2] From other sources we know that the ἄγροικοι appeared on the stage in the costume of their class, dressed in the skins of animals, carrying sacks, sticks and shepherds' crooks.[3] It is also probable that they wore the large shoes of which Theophrastus speaks,[4] and that their entire "get-up" fitted their faces and was ridiculously vulgar. Swaggering soldiers must still have worn some of the accoutrements of the Aristophanic Lamachus. Even their flowing hair, about which they were so vain,[5] and their gorgeous sweeping cloaks[6] sufficed to make them a laughing-stock. In order to look formidable they donned plumed helmets[7] and girded themselves with scaly breastplates[8] and wore dragons as insignia.[9] Cooks, who occasionally ventured to cross swords with military men, were decked out with a whole array of knives.[10] Philosophers probably wore exaggerated beards and pretentious

---

[1] Cf. Winter, *Typen der figürlichen Terrakotten*, II. p. 456 et seq. (especially p. 468).

[2] *Poen.*, 975 et seq., 1298 et seq.

[3] Varro, *De re rustica*, II. 11, 11; Poll., IV. 119, 120; 'Επιτρ., 12–13.

[4] Theoph., *Char.*, IV. 4.

[5] Pollux, IV. 147. Cf. *Miles*, 64, 768, 923.

[6] Donatus, *Exc. de com.*, VIII. 6; Pollux, VII. 46; Plut., *Mor.*, p. 615 D.; *Epid.*, 436.

[7] Περικ., 104.   [8] Posid., fr. 26, 7–8.   [9] *Ibid.*   [10] Σαμ., 69.

τρίβωνες (shabby cloaks).[1] Other characters, besides those already mentioned, may have provoked laughter by the way in which they chanced to be dressed : take, for example, Menaechmus when he appeared enveloped in his wife's cloak; or Olympio and Chalinus in the guise of country bride and bridegroom; or the sham eunuch dressed up in a showy, many-coloured gown; or the soldier mentioned in fragment 55 of Diphilus, who carried about so many things that he might have been taken for a wandering bazaar.

What is to be said about the actors' gestures? If we are to judge by the indications found in the texts of the comedies themselves, by the commentaries, and by works of art, they must, as a rule, have been very lively—often too lively to suit modern taste. But this liveliness of gesture was excusable. As Greek actors wore masks, they were, of course, obliged to substitute gestures for facial expression, which was practically precluded. Besides, their audiences consisted of Southerners, who were accustomed to gesticulate much more freely than we do. We know how important Demosthenes thought gesticulation, and how many of Quintilian's precepts deal with it. Many a gesture which that teacher of eloquence describes and recommends to his pupils has a great resemblance to those shown in the illustrated manuscripts of Terence and those of which Donatus' commentaries convey an idea. Nevertheless, Quintilian makes a clear distinction between the gesticulation of an actor and that which befits an orator,[2] and there is reason to believe that even in the days of the νέα the gesticulation of comic actors, which was anticipated and prescribed by the poets, was frequently characterised as φορτική (vulgar) by members of polite society. In one of the recently recovered comedies, the Σαμία, the chief actors fling themselves about as though they were possessed. Demeas precipitates himself headlong into his house in order to drive out Chrysis, and

---

[1] Cf. Phoenicides, fr. 4, line 17; fr. adesp. 796.
[2] Quint., XI. 3, 89 et seq.; 181 et seq.

terrifies the cowardly cook; Niceratus rushes in and out
of the house like a whirlwind and raises his stick against
his companion. In the Περικειρομένη a violent altercation takes place at Myrrhina's door. I have already
called attention to fragment 741 of Menander, in which
we get a glimpse of a breathless runner. I may also call
attention to a line by Philemon, in which one actor reminds
another that he does not " own the whole street "; [1] to
a fragment of Menander spoken by a person who seeks to
separate two people who are fighting; [2] to other fragments in which a slave, who is no doubt hard pressed,
hastily finds a place of refuge, [3] or a drunkard threatens
to force a woman to drink, [4] or some one complains that he
has been thrashed. [5] In a passage of a comedy by Diphilus
a cook is informed that, unless he keeps still, blows will
put an end to his tiresome talk; [6] in a play by Poseidippus
another cook informs us that members of his profession
are sometimes maltreated. [7]

Latin comedies complete our information on this subject.
Even in Terence, though he knows what constitutes " the
gentleman," comic effects are occasionally accompanied
by exaggerated gestures, brawls, grimaces and contortions.
The audience must have laughed when they saw the eunuch
trembling before Phaedria's bad temper, Thraso and his
attendants attacking Thais' house, Sannio counting his
wounds and ready to take to flight at the smallest movement on the part of Aeschinus, Chremes and Demipho
trying to drag away the parasite, who gets rid of them by
a home thrust. But it is the plays of Plautus that are,
above all, replete with burlesque stage business, some of
which was not of Roman origin. In line 458 et seq. of
the Pseudolus the actor who plays the part of the hero
is supposed to affect an attitude of comic solemnity. Very
likely the Greek original called for something similar, as
is shown by the use of the word basilicum in the very
sentence in which Simo refers to this attitude, and a little

¹ Philem., fr. 58.   ² Men., fr. 457.   ³ Ibid., fr. 748.   ⁴ Ibid., fr. 15.
⁵ Ibid., fr. 33.   ⁶ Diph.. fr. 43, 32 et seq.   ⁷ Posid., fr. 26, 14.

further on by the comparison made between Pseudolus and
Socrates. Similarly, line 213 of the *Miles*, which consists
entirely of foreign words, leads one to think that the foregoing description, which it sums up, as well as the mute
stage business to which that description refers, are taken
over from the *νέα*. In several passages whose text I have
examined, the humour of the words involves the humour
of the gestures. If the former can be traced back to the
Greek original, the latter must likewise have originated
there. Here are some other examples which I intentionally choose from among the most burlesque scenes. The
very title of the *Κληρούμενοι*, of which the *Casina* is an
imitation, proves that the Greek playwright made a good
deal of the episode of the drawing of lots; the exchange
of blows between the two slaves had, I believe, some
relation to this episode. Some of the expressions which
accompany it—line 406 : *Quia Juppiter jussit meus ;*
line 408 : *Quia jussit haec Juno mea*—are, indeed, inspired
by the same spirit as lines 333 *et seq.* in which Diphilus
probably alludes to the recent death of Alexander. In the
Rudens the two *lorarii*, Turbalio and Sparax, have expressive names which must have come down to them from the
original play, in which they no doubt took pains to earn
these names by thrashing the luckless pander, just as
they do in Plautus. The mention of Zeuxis and Apelles,
in line 1271 of the *Poenulus*, shows who was the originator
of the picture of ridiculous embraces to which that line
refers. The scene in the *Asinaria* in which Argyrippus
is obliged to carry his slave Libanus about on his back is
a masterpiece of burlesque writing. The occurrence of a
Greek word barely latinised—*badissas*—in line 699, at the
crisis of this scene, proves beyond a doubt that here,
too, Plautus meekly followed the play that served as his
model.

These examples suffice to show that New Comedy was
not always " refined " comedy. It was not always averse
to farce and noisy fun. To use an expression of Aeschylus,

in the *Frogs*, its wine was not always perfumed. Still, none of Plautus' comedies contains such an accumulation of horseplay and nonsense as is found in any one of Aristophanes' comedies. The *Persa*, one of the plays in which we find most of that sort of thing, is based on a comedy of the middle period. So we may say that comedy went through a process of refinement between the fifth and the third century—a process, by the way, whose effect on the various authors and their works was far from uniform. In some poets, like Diphilus, Poseidippus, Euphron and others, we still find more of the antique spirit of primitive grossness. In Menander, on the other hand, these unpleasant features seem hardly to have survived. The Σαμία, which must be one of his early plays, contains some; a few apparently occurred in the Περινθία, the plot of which he again took up and treated in a different way in the Ἀνδρία; in the Ἐπιτρέποντες and in the Περικειρομένη, products of his mature years, there is hardly any trace of them. The plays that Plautus copied from Menander— especially the *Aulularia* and the *Bacchides*—are among those in which there is the least buffoonery. It is well known that Menander was the favourite model for the fastidious Terence, and when this poet chose to introduce a relatively brutal episode into the *Adelphi*, in order to enliven the play, he did not borrow it from that writer, but from Diphilus, the originator of the *Casina* and the *Rudens*. Thus, both Roman comic authors bear witness to the same fact : they lead us, just as the *Fragmenta* and certain scattered indications found in ancient critics do, to regard Menander as a writer who was neither prudish nor conventional, but whose taste was more austere than that of the majority of his contemporaries and of those who came after him.

Possibly it was owing to this austerity that the greatest poet of the νέα had but little success in the competitions. At any rate, I cannot believe that the public demanded that raising of comedy to a nobler plane of which he set an example. In the fourth and third century the majority of the audience were plebeians, just as they had been in the fifth century, and it was not the plebs whom lapse of time had made more refined. The precepts of Isocrates regarding good breeding had doubtless not reached their ears. They took a sort of habitual, untiring and endless pleasure in listening to a repetition of the same nonsense and of the same jests. Captains, cooks, gormandisers and others were dear to them, as old friends, whose ways one knows and whose witty sayings one can foresee before they are uttered. They would have welcomed a revival of the burlesque; a restriction of it was not at all to their taste. On the other hand, nothing that we know about Menander's personality precludes our giving him the credit of having initiated this improvement in tone; indeed, we have every reason to do so. In Athens many comic authors were poor devils or Bohemians who led ill-regulated lives. An Athenian by birth and apparently reared in wealth, Menander was a man of good breeding; several written documents and portraits give evidence of the elegance of his manners and of the care he took of his dress and of his person.[1] He indulged freely in the pleasures of life, but always kept within the bounds of decency. His *liaison* with Glycera, to judge from the accounts we have of it, gave no offence to the prevailing ideas of propriety, and was not devoid of refinement. In a word, both in point of birth and of morals, Menander compares favourably with the majority of his fellows. Hence it is not at all surprising that it was repugnant to him to become, like them, a mere entertainer of the crowd.

Moreover, Menander had in his youth been a pupil of Theophrastus, and must have been well acquainted with Aristotle's theories about laughter and about the use of

---

[1] Anon. Περὶ κωμῳδίας, III. Dühn (= II. Kaib.), § 17 : λαμπρὸς καὶ βίῳ καὶ γένει. Cf. Phaedr., V. 1, 12 et seq. According to Studniczka, Menander's portrait is preserved in several copies or imitations of a work of the school of Lysippus, especially in a head in the Jacobsen collection (No. 1082). The seated statue in the Vatican which was long regarded as a statue of Menander is really that of a Roman of the last years of the Republic.

the various forms of the ridiculous. Now, what was
Aristotle's theory? A few words in the *Rhetoric* prove
that in the second part of the *Poetics*, devoted to comedy,
he distinguishes several kinds of γελοῖον, some proper for
a free man, others for a slave.[1] A passage in the *Ethica
Nicomachea* completes this discussion. It shows that
Aristotle, who condemned every kind of excess, also condemned the constant effort to amuse, the desire to provoke laughter at any cost. He thought horseplay (τὰ
βωμολοχικά) unworthy of a free man.[2] There is reason
to believe that in the *Poetics* he applied the same rules
to the stage as to life, and placed a ban upon horseplay,
at least as far as certain rôles were concerned. But
Aristotle went even further; he not only forbade a free
man, a man of gentle breeding, to utter vulgar jokes, but
also to listen to them or to take pleasure in them. Hence
he must have regarded a comedy in which such jokes
abounded as an entertainment fit for the rabble, and I
believe he more or less openly urged the poets to cultivate
a more elevated type of comedy. A sentence in the
Coislin Treatise (§ 6) apparently preserves his views on
this point : συμμετρία τοῦ φόβου θέλει εἶναι ἐν ταῖς τραγῳδίαις
καὶ τοῦ γελοίου ἐν ταῖς κωμῳδίαις. No doubt this means
that the hilarity occasioned by comedy should keep within
proper bounds and not degenerate into sarcastic sneers
or into unbridled vulgar gaiety. Just as good tragedy
accustoms us to feel a proper degree of pity and fear in
the presence of an object worthy of it, so comedy ought
to accustom us to laugh where it is seemly to do so. In
other words, it ought to educate us in laughter. Hence
it may be that by showing that he was more scrupulous
than his predecessors in the choice of laughter-provoking
episodes, Menander consciously and purposely put into
practice the teachings of the Lyceum. Indeed, this is
not the first time that we discover the potent influence
of Aristotle in the early stages of the νέα.

---

[1] *Rhetor.*, III. 18, 7 P., 1419.
[2] *Eth. Nic.*, p. 1127 B, 1, 33–1128 B, 4.

§ 2

COMIC CHARACTERS AND SITUATIONS

I have thought it necessary to insist at some length on
the vulgar elements of the νέα because we are sometimes
too much inclined to ignore them.   The contrast between
the new style and that which preceded it, and the sustained
elegance of Terence help to mislead us.   At the same
time, I must not neglect to add that the νέα abounds
in comic effects that are more justifiable and of better
alloy.

In the lengthy fragments that have been recently
discovered, comic effects are most frequently produced in
a spontaneous way, and without violating good taste, by
the natural development of characters and situations.
While watching a performance of the ᾿Επιτρέποντες the
spectators must have laughed at the sallies of Smicrines,
in which he assures Daos and Syriscus that he has not
the slightest interest in their affairs; at the impatience of
Syriscus, who has to be called to order and menaced with a
stick; at the plight of Daos and the mechanical stubbornness with which he goes on repeating the same lamentations; at the fresh trouble that comes to Syriscus as soon
as he gets possession of the γνωρίσματα; at the ingenuous
manner in which Habrotonon gives voice to the views of
a courtesan, and at the way in which she parodies the talk
current among women of her class, without seeing any harm
in doing so.   No doubt they smiled when Onesimus exposes
the scheme of that sly little person, and were amused at
the mighty wrath of the terrible grumbler when he rubs
up against the innocent Sophrone, at his fright while
Onesimus derides him, and at his consternation when,
without beating about the bush, the roguish fellow tells
him the whole story.   In the Σαμία Demeas provokes
laughter when he puts himself on a wrong scent in
order to exculpate Moschio, or when, in the presence of
the Samian woman, he unsuccessfully exerts himself to

act like a brutal person; further on, it is Moschio's turn
to provoke laughter when he plans pretending to join the
army in order to scare his father, but is horribly afraid
that he will not be prevented. In the Περικειρομένη it is
amusing to see Daos coming crestfallen out of Myrrhina's
house, after having boasted that he had gained the lady's
favour for his master. Towards the end of the play
Polemo quite unconsciously amuses us when he shows
how uncertain and full of contradictions is love. In the
Γεωργός Daos entertains us by his impudence, his burgher
pride, and the turn he gives his story; after having
promised to give good tidings he relates a chapter of
disasters. The women to whom he speaks are quite overcome, but the sly fellow enjoys their disappointment and
goes on imperturbably.

While we wait for new discoveries to increase our store
of Greek comedies, the Roman comic writers prove that
the art of provoking laughter had no secrets for their
predecessors. We need not hesitate to credit the latter,
who invented the plots and created the characters, with
the comic effects arising from the action or the vagaries
of the players.

In Plautus, as well as in Terence, such effects are numerous. We laugh at an unexpected turn, at the brusque
right-about-face on the part of one of the characters, the
unexpected change of attitude which he affects or which
is forced upon him; at Chremes (in the *Heauton Timoroumenos*) forgetting all about his system and his forbearance
as soon as he has troubles of his own; at Ballio smitten
in the midst of his triumph and cast down in the twinkling
of an eye from the lofty pedestal of his arrogance; at
Antipho (in the *Phormio*) taking to his heels as soon as
he hears his scolding father approach. Sometimes, on
the other hand, laughter is provoked by constant repetition of the same thing; for instance, in the *Adelphi*, when
the marplot Demeas constantly returns to the charge; in
the *Pseudolus*, where the arrival of the real Harpax, after
that of the false one, gives rise to an amusing repetition;

in the *Aulularia*, when Euclio immediately regards everything that he sees or hears as an additional menace to his beloved treasure. Some characters provoke laughter because they choke with rage : for instance, Aristophontes in the *Captivi*, where he is described to his face as a crazy epileptic; or Artemona in the *Asinaria*, who is obliged to listen, in the presence of witnesses, to a recital of her shortcomings. In the case of other characters the comic element consists in their clumsy inability to disguise their feelings; thus Chremes, in the *Eunuchus*, displays his lack of courage in whatever he does, and Lysidamus, in the *Casina*, continually and unwittingly divulges his plans to people who are likely to compromise him. Perplexity is also a theme that supplies amusing scenes. It is entertaining to see Epidicus, Davus (in the *Andria*), Syrus (in the *Heauton Timoroumenos*), or some other such rogue, temporarily worsted. The situation is even more comic when the hero is stupid, has no ideas, or only such as cannot be realised, and flounders about in pitiable impotence. This is what happens to many a young lover, as well as to many a greybeard, even when they ask advice of others. An instance is supplied by the passage of the *Phormio* in which Demipho consults his friends and finds himself more at a loss than ever.

I cannot pretend to enumerate here all the means to which New Comedy resorted in order to provoke laughter. Such an enumeration would necessarily be incomplete and, to a certain extent, useless, for among these means many belong to the stock-in-trade of comedy of all times. But there is one kind of comic effect that does demand our attention on account of the special favour with which our poets regarded it—I mean the comic effect arising from misunderstanding, or, as the *Coislin Treatise* puts it, based upon ἀπατή.

There are plays—the *Menaechmi*, for instance—which consist almost from beginning to end in a series of entertaining blunders. In the majority of the other plays one

K K

or more scenes show us a man who allows himself to be
deceived by false appearances, who follows a false trail,
who gets excited and acts in a manner out of keeping with
the actual state of affairs and contrary to his own wishes.
We see Demea trying to remember the fantastic itinerary
which Syrus prescribes for him, and declaring, after a long
goose-chase, that he is tired out; [1] or Theopropides, whom
Tranio terrifies with the adventure of the ghost, and
who, placing faith in the lying slave, believes that he is
in a house of his own while he is really in one belonging
the neighbour Simo, examines the house which he thinks
he has purchased and sympathises with the regrets of the
self-styled seller. Elsewhere, Periphanes enthusiastically
adopts the splendid plan conceived by Epidicus.[2] Hegio
(in the *Captivi*) thinks that he sees the symptoms of
acute madness in Aristophontes' face.[3] Parmeno (in the
Eunuchus) is terrified by the consequences which, according to the mischievous Pythias, followed on the disguising
of Chaerea as a eunuch, which he himself had planned.
Other instances are legion.

Often the comic element inherent in a blunder is increased
by some accidental circumstance, by the manœuvres which
lead up to it, or by the attitude of the mystifier or of the
person mystified.

In order better to deceive their dupe, thoroughgoing
knaves allow him to overhear feigned stage asides, in
which, of course, they are careful to say only what they
wish to make him believe. This is the method pursued by
the malicious Milphidippa, the maid in the *Miles* : " Are
there not people about here who are more interested in
the affairs of others than in their own, who might spy
upon me ? I dread such people, who might annoy me and
block the way, if my mistress were to pass by here in
going from her house to him whom she desires to possess—
the soldier whom she loves—that charming, handsome
Pyrgopolinices " (lines 994 *et seq.*). As was to be expected,

---

[1] *Ad.*, 572 et seq., 713 et seq.   [2] *Ep.*, 280 et seq.
[3] *Capt.*, 559, 599, 603.

the " handsome Pyrgopolinices " does not fail to take the bait. Sometimes the deception is carried on by two actors. In the *Asinaria* Leonidas, in the presence of the donkey-seller, but without appearing to see him, makes believe that he is a tyrannical master to Libanus, and Libanus, his accomplice, pretends to fear him; [1] in the *Phormio* Geta, aware that Demipho is listening to him, heaps insults on the parasite, under the pretext that he is defending his master's reputation against his slanders. Elsewhere, the cheat makes some third party who is not in the secret take a hand, without knowing it, in his plot : for example, the servant Mysis in the *Andria*, whose amazement is so comic. [2]

But it does not suffice to know how to lie with assurance, and to have a fertile imagination, in order to fool people. A bit of sentimental comedy is occasionally helpful. The stage profligates do not fail to make use of it, and they discover new means of provoking laughter through such hypocritical displays. We may, for example, call to mind how Chrysalus and Davus (in the *Andria*) parade their fine sentiments. The former pretends to be deeply moved by the paternal troubles of Nicobolus; in tones of sincere attachment, if not of politeness, he deplores his losing his faculties and " failing " from old age. [3] The latter, on the other hand, pretends to admire Simo's schemes, which he has seen through, [4] and while both of them are the objects of very well-founded suspicion, they put on great airs of injured innocence.

On the other hand, those who are cheated or make mistakes may become particularly ridiculous if, following their natural disposition, misled by their whims and blinded by their conceit, they blunder with zest and satisfaction. Pyrgopolinices is delighted by the lies with which he is bombarded and which, for the time, gratify the old braggart's vanity. [5] Theopropides is beside himself with

---

[1] *As.*, 407 et seq.   [2] *Andr.*, 745 et seq.
[3] *Bacch.*, 816 et seq.   [4] *Andr.*, 588–589.
[5] *Miles*, 985, 999 et seq., 1038 et seq., 1224, 1269 et seq.

joy when Tranio tells him that his son has begun to speculate.[1]   Demea is proud to see, in the behaviour with which Syrus credits Ctesiphon, the natural result of his own excellent instruction.[2]   Ballio receives Harpax, who is responsible for his discomfiture, haughtily, and loftily disdains the machinations of the enemy at the very moment when we discover that he has already fallen a victim to them.[3]

Foolish suspicion can be just as laughable as too ready credulity.   Simo, in the *Andria*, is a case in point.   When Pamphilus is ready, or pretends to be ready, to yield to his authority, and declares that he is willing to marry, Simo at first manifests a disappointment that is comic; [4] he ought to be delighted, as everything is shaping itself in accordance with his wishes; but, on the contrary, he is a little bit disappointed, and seems sorry that all his preparations for a struggle have been entirely wasted. Later on, when the midwife inconsiderately speaks of the new-born child, it is Simo's suspicious mood that saves the compromising situation at his own expense; by too quickly coming to the conclusion that he is being cheated he suggests to his antagonist the idea and the means of cheating him.[5]

Another amusing character is the cheat caught in his own trap.   Davus (in the *Andria*) succeeds all too well in making the aged Simo believe that Pamphilus would, if need be, marry Chremes' daughter.   He is taken at his word, and his successful lie is his ruin.   Towards the end of the *Miles* Palaestrio has a narrow escape from a similar experience; he makes such a masterly pretence of being brokenhearted at leaving Pyrgopolinices that the good-natured fellow is on the point of changing his mind and keeping so devoted a servant.[6]

The special humour of certain expressions adds to the fun of the situation in many scenes that are concerned

---

[1] *Most.*, 638–639.   [2] *Ad.*, 564 et seq.   [3] *Pseud.*, 1162 et seq.
[4] *Andr.*, 434 et seq.   [5] *Ibid.*, 492 et seq.
[6] *Miles*, 1358 et seq., 1368 et seq.

with a blunder. At least this is often the case in Plautus
and Terence, and I imagine that it was also the case in the
Greek poets whom they imitated.

Some of these expressions are amusing simply because
they emphasise the error into which one or the other of
the actors has fallen, and because they enable us at once
to gauge its extent. This is the case when, after the
comedy has been played at his expense, Chremes (in the
Andria) maintains that he has discovered the real truth:
" I saw with my own eyes the serving-maid quarrelling
with Davus." In vain does Simo, who likewise stubbornly
persists in his error, declare that one of the actors—
according to him it was Mysis—was merely trying to
frighten him. Chremes, unwilling to retract, replies:
" they were quarrelling for all they were worth; neither
of them knew I was present." [1]

We must give special attention to the humour of
ambiguous expressions. As a rule, such ambiguity is a
subtlety on the part of the cheat—an additional score off
his dupe. When they are face to face with Hegio, who
mistakes the one for the other,[2] the two "captives" make
endless allusions to their true personalities. In the *Mostellaria* Tranio compares his master Theopropides and his
neighbour Simo in ambiguous terms to two buzzards who
are made fun of by a crow.[3] Nor is Chrysalus, in the
Bacchides, less impudent. In his presence Nicobolus
complains that the treacherous message of Mnesilochus
is written in such small characters that he cannot read it.
" Yes," says Chrysalus, who had dictated the letter,
" the writing is small for one who does not see well, but
it is big enough for one who has good eyes." [4] Elsewhere
an actor unwittingly makes use of expressions in which
the audience, who are acquainted with the secrets of the
plot, are delighted to discover a double meaning. The
blustering soldier [5] has just dismissed his mistress, and tells
us how touching the leave-taking was: " Never," says

---

[1] *Andr.*, 838 et seq.   [2] *Capt.*, 417–418, 426–427.
[3] *Most.*, 832 et seq.   [4] *Bacch.*, 991–992.   [5] *Miles*, 1202

he, " was I loved so much by that woman as to-day ";
the poor fellow is far from suspecting that the reason for
such a display of affection was delight at the separation.
Simo, in the *Andria*, is unconsciously ironical when he
thanks Davus and confides in him after having come to
terms with Chremes : " Now, Davus, since it is to you only
that I owe this marriage, I beg you to make every effort
to reform my son." I may also call attention to the
famous scene between Lyconides and Euclio, in the
Aulularia, in which each of the speakers mistakes the meaning of the other's words, the old man thinking only of his
pot and the youth of his lady-love, the latter accusing
himself of having ravished the girl, the former complaining of robbery. The ambiguity continues as long as the
utmost limits of probability allow, thus adding vastly to
our entertainment.

We have seen how many changes can be rung on the
motif of misunderstandings. The way in which the comic
poets constantly like to return to it seems to me to be
quite characteristic, and the diversity of effects they
derived from it is an interesting proof of their imaginative
resources.

CHAPTER III

PATHETIC ELEMENTS IN NEW COMEDY
EXTENT AND DIVERSITY OF THEIR DOMAIN

HOWEVER frequent the occasions for laughter may have been in the νέα, they were not continuous. But for a few lyrical passages, there are hardly five or six successive lines in Aristophanes that do not contain something calculated to make people split their sides with laughter. Everything is steeped in comedy. Things that are in themselves most serious, things by which the poet places the greatest store, present a humorous side in his plays. This, however, was no longer the case in the age of New Comedy. Scenes like the scene of insanity in the *Mercator*, in which an actor makes it his business to be droll in a situation which does not lend itself to that sort of thing, were, as I believe, the exception. The νέα does, indeed, still keep rude jesters whose sorrow and wrath, and even despair, provoke laughter—figures, that is, who more than the rest preserved the element of the grotesque in their appearance, such as slaves and parasites. But side by side with them, the other actors may, if the situation calls for it, speak the language of reason or express the most serious sentiments. In the lengthy fragments of the original plays, especially in those of the Γεωργός, the Κόλαξ, the Ἐπιτρέποντες, and the Περικειρομένη, and in the fragments of the anonymous plays published by M. Jouguet, the author by no means gives us occasion for uninterrupted hilarity. If we examine the Roman imitators, Terence moves us more than he amuses us. Even Plautus, the cheerful Plautus, is occasionally serious or pathetic. In the plays of both of these poets we sometimes find specialists, if I may use the term, who represent the comic element, associated with persons who would not by themselves provoke laughter, as, for instance, Parmeno as a third party between Phaedria and Thais,[1] or Stasimus

---

[1] *Eun.*, 98 et seq.

(in the *Trinummus*) between Lesbonicus and Philto,[1] or the two slaves in the *Asinaria* whose horseplay affords such a glaring contrast to the lamentations of the lovers.[2] But occasionally these specialists also withdraw, and the fun is simply interrupted.

Moreover, the proportion of elements that do not provoke laughter varies very much to suit various cases. The *Trinummus*, in which, throughout long scenes, there is not even the ghost of a joke, and the *Hecyra*, the prototype of pathetic comedy, are probably, in so far as they are " mixed " plays, the limit of what the public tolerated. It is worth noting that one of these dramas is by Apollodorus of Carystos, who belongs to the second generation of New Comedy, and that the other is an imitation of a work by Philemon, the oldest representative of this style, and is not apparently a product of the last years of his career. On the other hand, the original of the *Menaechmi*, one of the merriest of all the plays, was written after the accession of Hiero, that is to say, after 275 or 270. This statement suffices to keep us from thinking that the tone of the comic writers grew less and less hilarious. There was no sustained evolution of this sort, and if in successive periods there was a general preference for more or less fun, we are not able to distinguish these periods. From the point of view I am now taking it is even difficult to classify the chief representatives of the νέα. Among the plays of Menander there is at least one, the Σαμία, in which everything that has survived is amusing. Plautus has preserved for us two of Philemon's plays : the *Trinummus*, which is in part so serious, and the *Mostellaria*, which is amusing almost from beginning to end. In the *Phormio* and in the *Hecyra* Terence has preserved for us two examples of Apollodorus' plays which, though they vary in point of sprightliness, we may regard as equally representative of his style. Hence we have good reason to be cautious about drawing conclusions.

---

[1] *Trin.*, 454 et seq.   [2] *As.*, 591 et seq.

Let us now consider the nature of the incidents that interrupt the laughter-provoking elements, and what effects they may be expected to produce.

To our taste, the least interesting, or, at all events, the least dramatic of them, are the moral discourses of which I have spoken in a former chapter. If they are at all lengthy we are apt to think them tedious, and I am inclined to believe that, in too large doses, they also bored a Greek audience. In this respect, however, the Greeks appear to have been particularly patient. Reasoners and pedants as they were, the Greeks of every epoch lent a willing ear to sententious utterances.[1] These are to be found as early as the Homeric epics; they abound in Hesiod and Pindar, they are the basic element of elegiac poetry, and, above all, after the time of Euripides invaded the domain of tragedy. Hence the people who went to see New Comedy were prepared long beforehand to hear and relish them.

The purpose of many passages is to call forth pity or emotion, though I am not sure that the distress of Ballio's little servant,[2] or even the timid complaints of Philaenium,[3] in spite of their poetic qualities, stirred the mass of the ancient spectators very deeply; in the former case it is a question of a slave; in the latter of a poor girl of uncertain birth, both creatures hardly worthy of much interest. But at all events Palaestra's [4] lamentations, Sostrata's complaints in the *Adelphi*,[5] the account of Chrysis' last moments or of her funeral in the *Andria*,[6] or the portrayal of Phanium's distress at the beginning of the *Phormio*,[7] cannot have failed, then as now, to move sensitive souls. A pathetic theme that was very often introduced by the poets of the new period is the grief for a person who is absent or has disappeared. Very frequently they disdained to introduce it on account of its triteness, just as they avoided the effusions of the ἀναγνωρίσεις, or else

---

[1] Cf. Stickney, *Les Sentences dans la poésie grecque* (Paris, 1903).
[2] *Pseud.*, 767 et seq.   [3] *As.*, 515 et seq.   [4] *Rud.*, 185 et seq.
[5] *Ad.*, 288 et seq.   [6] *Andr.*, 127 et seq., 282 et seq.   [7] *Phorm.*, 91 et seq.

condensed them into a few words. But this was not
always the case. In the *Rudens* a few words suffice to
indicate Daemones' grief.[1] In the *Captivi* Hegio's wound
is still fresh, and we cannot but pity the poor father,
although the violence of his pain leads him to indulge
in unwarranted harshness. And finally, in the *Heauton
Timoroumenos*, Menedemus, tormented by remorse, is a
truly touching figure, and excites unbounded compassion.
One of the original comedies, the Ἐπιτρέποντες, presents,
in the person of Charisius, another actor who gives vent
to his remorse in very strong terms. Who would not be
moved when the unhappy man, having been forgiven by
Pamphila and disowned by Smicrines after the discovery
of his transgression, admits, in words that betray a wild
despair, the downfall of his pride and the failure of his
life?

But it is chiefly the emotion of lovers, their griefs, and
sometimes their joys that make appeal to our sympathy.
Emotional scenes abound in Terence, and we find similar
scenes in the original in the fragments of the Γεωργός, the
Ἥρως, the Σαμία and the Περικειρομένη. There are several in
Plautus, and there are signs indicating that he suppressed
others in order not to fatigue a vulgar audience. True, not
all the passages on which we can pass judgment rise to
great heights of pathos. The lamentations of the lover in
the Γεωργός must have left the audience somewhat cold.
Their interest lay rather in their contents than in their
tone, more in the information they gave about the trend
of the plot than in the portrayal of a state of mind.
Doubtless this was true of many similar soliloquies that
occur at the beginning of a comedy. Elsewhere the impression is spoiled by pompousness or by affectation. The
appeals to the gods, to the stars, the imprecations, the
proposed suicides, certainly soon came to be considered
as mere conventions, if, indeed, they had not always been
so considered. When he is not making jests, Charinus,
in the *Mercator*, indulges in puerile reflections.[2] With

---

[1] *Rud.*, 106, 742 et seq.   [2] *Merc.*, 590, 591.

the exception of that thoroughly delightful scene of
the *Asinaria* in which Argyrippus and Philaenium take
leave of one another, there is none that is not marred by
some pretentiousness, which can, I believe, be traced to
Demophilus—

A.: "Farewell, Philaenium; I shall see you in Pluto's
realm, for I have fully decided to end my life."
Ph.: "Why, I beg you, do you desire to bring about my
death, which I have not deserved?" A.: "Bring about
your death? I, who, if I saw that life were deserting you,
would give you mine and would add my days to yours?"
Ph.: "Wherefore, then, your threats to put an end to
your life? For what, think you, shall I do, if you do
what you say? I am resolved; I shall do to myself what
you do to yourself." [1]

Other passages, on the other hand, are conceived in a
spirit of delightful candour. Witness Phaedria's farewell
to his beloved Thais, in the *Eunuchus*—

"You ask what I desire? That, though you are with
this soldier, you should be far away from him; that, day
and night, you should love me, long for me, dream of me,
wait for me, think of me, wish for me; that I should be
your joy, that you should belong entirely to me—in a
word, that your heart should be mine, since I am yours." [2]

Fénelon relished this passage. He writes: "Can one
ask for anything more frankly and truly dramatic?"
His praise is well deserved, and I think the greater part
of it ought to be awarded to Menander. Other passages
that go straight to the heart are: Aeschinus' soliloquy in
the *Adelphi*,[3] certain parts of the rôle of Pamphilus in
the *Hecyra*,[4] and the mournful confession of Selenium at
the beginning of the *Cistellaria*; for in them we feel that
hearts have really been moved. Sometimes a few words
underscored by a bit of stage play suffice to produce exceedingly pathetic effects. This is the case in the *Heauton*

[1] *Asin.*, 606 et seq.   [2] *Eun.*, 190 et seq.
[3] *Ad.*, 610 et seq.   [4] *Hec.*, 281 et seq., 402 et seq., 485 et seq.

Timoroumenos when Antiphila suddenly meets Clinia.[1]
In the Περικειρομένη the impetuous Polemo, after getting
over an attack of anger, can do nothing but repeat, like
a weeping child : " Glycera has left me, she has left
me—Glycera, O, Pataecus ! " [2] His stammering and his
sobs of grief are more eloquent of the poor man's state of
mind than any long speeches could be.

The passages of which I have just spoken correspond,
in the comedies of the *νέα*, to the scenes in tragedy which
make appeal to our pity. Other passages correspond to
the tragic scenes of terror, due allowance being made for
the difference of spirit. To this class belongs the scene
in the *Rudens* in which Labrax, who was supposed to have
been drowned, unexpectedly appears and again jeopardises
the freedom of two unfortunate women who have barely
escaped shipwreck,[3] and also the passage in the *Captivi*
in which Tyndarus, frightened at the discovery of his
rascality, takes flight at the approach of Aristophontes,[4]
as well as the subsequent passage in which he finds himself the defenceless victim of cruel retaliation. As a rule
we do not take the apprehensions of slaves very seriously,
nor worry about the punishment that awaits them, as
even they themselves refer to it in a jocose vein. But the
calamities and the squaring of accounts which we should
view with composure, or even with amusement, if they
were about to befall a mere Scapin, appear in a different
light when they suddenly menace the honour, the love,
or the dearest interests of persons who are sympathetic
to us. When, in lines 231 of the *Phormio*, Demipho,
announced by the trembling Geta, comes raging on to the
stage, and in a loud voice declaims against the disregard
of paternal authority, we experience something like the
fear that drove Antipho to flight. While watching
Pamphilus and Simo face to face with one another at the
close of the *Andria*, the spectators must have started and
felt their hearts beat if the scene were well performed.

---

[1] *Heaut.*, 405 et seq.　　　　[2] Περικ., 243–244.
[3] *Rud.*, 442 et seq.　　　　　[4] *Capt.*, 516 et seq.

In reading the *Hecyra* curiosity and even compassion yield to anxiety as soon as we find out what is going on at Myrrhina's house; we dread lest the secret be discovered, and Philumena be doomed to dishonour. On the other hand, in the *Rudens* and in the *Cistellaria* we are stirred by the delay that occurs in the recognition of the heroines, and by the sudden changes of fortune through which they risk losing their σημεῖα.

Besides fear and pity, tragedy sometimes calls forth admiration and transmits to the souls of the audience a thrill of noble enthusiasm and of lofty sentiment. Effects similar to these occur in the νέα, though they are, of course, on a more humble and everyday scale. Certain characters in the plays please us on account of their uprightness, because they portray mankind in a favourable light, and because they gratify the philanthropic optimism that lies dormant in many of us. To this class belong Syriscus, in the Ἐπιτρέποντες, who so eagerly looks after the interests of a poor foundling; Hegio and Geta, in the *Adelphi*, both so concerned about protecting Sostrata; the gentle and modest Eunomia, entirely absorbed in the happiness of her brother; Philematium, that model of gratitude; Chremes, in the *Heauton Timoroumenos*, who inquires with solicitude after the troubles of a stranger, his neighbour of a few weeks; the compassionate Ptolemocratia, in the *Rudens*, and the hospitable Daemones; the good, but peevish, Cleaenetus, in the Γεωργός; unselfish Crito, in the *Andria*; Bacchis, in the *Hecyra*, who rejoices that she has been able to re-establish peace in the household of her former lover; the two sisters, in the *Stichus*, who are devotedly attached to their husbands. All these personages, and many others, I imagine, formed in the theatre a sort of band of honest folk in whose company honest folk among the audience felt themselves at home, while even the less virtuous spectators doubtless condescended to show a moment's sympathy. Occasionally one of the *dramatis personae* rises beyond the level of ordinary virtue and reaches the heights of sacrifice. In the *Cistellaria* Selenium subordinates herself, disappears without a murmur, and does not wish to have the faithless Alcesimarchus saddened by reproaches about his betrayal after he has deserted her—or at least when she thinks that he has deserted her. In the *Hecyra* Sostrata, fearing to stand in the way of the conjugal happiness of her son, humbles herself, renounces all the comforts of her ordinary existence, and condemns herself to exile in the country. In the *Andria* Pamphilus is willing to sacrifice his wealth and his social standing to his love, and later on, when confronted with Simo's suspicions, he is prepared to sacrifice even his love to his honour. And finally, in the *Captivi*, pathos rises to a height worthy, as one would have said in former times, of the *cothurnus*. It is very difficult not to share Hegio's admiration while listening to the pseudo-Philocrates' farewell to the sham Tyndarus, even though one does not share his mistake.[1] And further on, when the bold lie has been discovered, how striking is the tone in which Tyndarus answers threats and reproaches !

" Little do I care for death as long as I have not deserved it through evil deeds of my own. Should I die here, and should he not return as he has promised to, I should, after my death, have the honour of having rescued my captive master from slavery and out of the hands of the enemy, and of having enabled him to return as a free man to his country and to his father, and of having preferred to expose myself to danger in order that he should not perish.—Hegio : Go, then, and rejoice in your glory on the shores of the Acheron.—Tyndarus : He who dies by a courageous act perishes, but does not lose his life." [2]

Never has the satisfaction that comes of duty performed at whatever cost found nobler expression, and this passage deserves to be compared to certain scenes in tragedy; for instance, to the scene in which Antigone, after her heroic act of disobedience, defies the wrath of Creon.

[1] *Capt.*, 432 et seq.   [2] *Ibid.*, 682 et seq.

These examples suffice to give an idea of the scope of the *νέα*; as a matter of fact, it contains the whole gamut of human passions. Though limited in its subject matter —more limited than that of ancient comedy—its wider range gave it the advantage over its elder sister. Plutarch openly says as much when he admires in the comic writers of the new period, in comparison with their predecessors, "the mixture of gaiety with seriousness." [1] Quintilian alludes to this when he praises the sustained dignity of speech with which Menander endows all his actors—fathers and sons, soldiers and rustics, rich and poor, *angry people and suppliants, gentle as well as surly characters.*[2] Towards the end of the fourth and during the third century the performance of a comedy offered an entertainment of a very varied character. The vulgar part of the audience was treated to the traditional horse-play, much of which constituted a sort of interlude or side dish in the course of the performance. Tender-hearted people and young folk had a chance of experiencing pleasant sensations; they were glad to discover in the play a portrayal of their joys and of their troubles. Mature and experienced people liked to listen to the voice of reason, and applauded the judicious utterances, the concise formulae in which their own views about life, the world and mankind shone forth with the brilliancy of thoughts well expressed. Thinkers and liberal and courageous minds were now and then led to meditate, to examine society with a critical eye, and to abandon errors and prejudices; sensitive spirits and learned people enjoyed the truthful psychology, the correctness and grace of style, the discreet humour and the fine irony. Thus men of quite divergent temperaments found something to satisfy them, as they sat side by side watching the same play.

It goes without saying that not all the poets of the *νέα* were able to make equally felicitous use of the resources at their command. Diphilus, as far as we can judge his

[1] Plut., *Quaest. Sympos.*, VII. 8, 3, 7.   [2] Quint., X. 1.

writings by the fragments and by two of Plautus' plays
(the *Rudens* and the *Casina*), appears to have clung to
the earlier tradition, and to have attached scant importance to incidents that were not amusing.   When Philemon
ceases to provoke laughter by means that often lacked
refinement, he readily goes to an opposite extreme, and
runs the risk of making us yawn. A critic has rightly
said that his moral discourses, which, as I have already
pointed out, are very frequent, easily become pedantic.
Even the most attractive of the serious passages that
Plautus copied from him — the conversation between
Philematium and Scapha — is open to this reproach.
Apollodorus, if the *Phormio* and the *Hecyra* afford a fair
basis on which to form an opinion of his talent, sinned
in the way of monotony and affectation. He was more
sentimental than impassioned, more mournful than
pathetic. Probably some of the points in which Menander
showed great superiority were the versatility and diversity
of his style, and his ability to set all the chords of the
soul vibrating without shock or jar. He was certainly
something very different—and much greater—than a mere
fashionable writer and maker of fine speeches. His art
was not an art of semi-tones, as one might be led to suppose by some of the Latin imitations. Owing to recent
discoveries we are now able to recognise that forcefulness
which good judges in ancient times found and admired in
him, and we have proof that in his plays graceful sentiments and restrained emotions alternated with the most
fierce and violent transports, all portrayed in a manner
true to nature.

The variety of dramatic effects which a single play of
the new period was capable of producing explains why
this style of composition met with widespread success in
its day, and also why this success was lasting. If we
read the comedies of Plautus and Terence in quick succession it is hard to avoid a feeling of satiety, and we should
be likely to declare that " it is always the same thing."

Such a summary judgment—as little flattering for the audiences of early days as for the playwrights—would be unjust, and I think that it will not be amiss to revise it, now that my review of the νέα is drawing to a close.

We have seen that the conditions surrounding dramatic poetry in the fourth and third centuries made it excusable for authors to take up themes that had already been dealt with. Similarly, we might allege that, as the public went to the theatre only at great intervals, they meanwhile forgot what they had heard, and were not bored by repetition. But such an excuse would be weak and hardly fair. There are other more valid ones to bring forward.

What are the chief grounds for this charge of monotony that is raised against the νέα? There can be no doubt that certain episodes and certain situations reappear in several comedies; indeed, I have shown this at some length myself, and there is no reason to deny it. Nevertheless, it is the material and the ending of the plot that are repeated most persistently, and this repetition is chiefly responsible for the general similarity existing between many of the plays. Before the regular plot begins we hear a story of seduction or of rape, of children exposed by their parents and brought up by strangers; at the close of the play we witness a recognition, often brought about by material things (rings, jewellery, garments, etc.), a reconciliation, or a marriage. But between the beginning and the end the field is open for countless variants and for countless new incidents. The frame remains the same, but the pictures which appear in it may vary. Hence we must avoid a hasty judgment which might include a host of playwrights of all ages, as well as the comic writers of the new period. How many plays in our own day begin with adultery or divorce, and end, according to the character of the author or the fashion of the day, with a final separation of two people who had thought they were in love, or else with forgiveness—forgiveness on one side, or both sides, and more or less steeped in

L L

tears ?   Yet the authors would protest were we to insinuate that they say the same thing over and over again—and they would be quite right.   Such and such a repetition, at which a modern reader of Menander, of Terence or of Plautus takes umbrage, because he discovers it four or five times, would, I believe, appear less serious to him were he able to go through the entire répertoire of the νέα, and thus to find that it recurs incessantly.   By the force of facts the optical illusion, the lack of perspective that caused his strictures, would then disappear; he would learn no longer to confound the essential with the non-essential, and that to understand an ancient work of art he must acquire the taste of the ancients.

We must not lose sight of the fact that when the writers of New Comedy dealt with the same subjects several times, they, after all, only followed a course that was taken by all the artists of Greece.   The Greeks never demanded that works of art should be highly original.   As has been correctly observed, their architects during many centuries always built one temple just like another; [1] several of their sculptors, even some of the greatest, limited them-selves to reproducing a few types, a few attitudes; their story-writers, long before they wrote purely imaginative tales or romances, repeated, without becoming bored themselves or boring anybody else, old legends, famous adventures, which in their original version were not even always of Hellenic origin; [2] their tragic writers, instead of entering on the path opened up by Agathon, who wrote a tragedy in which everything—including the facts and the characters—was free invention, dealt more and more with the misfortunes of a few heroes, like Oedipus, Telephus and Orestes, with which the audience was already familiar. What the artists were concerned with and what pleased the public was not a complete novelty, but subtle variants, clever retouches, and in certain cases the plot may have appeared to have the greater merit the more the subjects

[1] Lechat, Le Temple grec., p. 89.
[2] Cf. Bérard, Les Phéniciens et l'Odyssée, V., II. p. 584.

with which it dealt had been used, and the narrower
the limits in which it moved. Rightly considered, Greek
comedy was neither more nor less monotonous than
tragedy, narrative poetry, sculpture or architecture, and
it must be judged according to the same principles and
with due regard to the same state of mind.

Besides, Greek comedy was not so monotonous as the
palliata would lead us to suppose. We must not forget
what I have said of the diversity of personages who,
though they lacked very striking characteristics, often
possessed an individual disposition and way of thinking.
In order to get an idea of how large and how varied the
domain of the *véa* was, we ought somehow to multiply
this diversity by that of the sentiments, the emotions and
the passions which the *dramatis personae* felt. Neither
Plautus nor Terence allows us to see the product of this
multiplication. Plautus had a contempt for psychological
subtleties, and gives undue importance to certain traits
while he suppresses others; he spoils the light and shade
and omits entire portions of the picture in order to make
room for grimaces and quibbles. Terence is much more
careful and well-meaning, but he lacks the vigour necessary
to reproduce the outlines and the vividness of his models;
he blurs the contours, weakens the tones, and envelops
the whole plot in a rather dull, grey atmosphere; in a
word, his plays reproduce only "a half of Menander."[1]
Hence the style of which Menander was a representative
cannot have lacked diversity. It must certainly be admitted that this diversity did not so much concern the
more immediately apparent elements of comedy, such as
its incidents or the social standing of the *dramatis personae*,
as it concerned details of character, of pathos and expression. In the field of literature it was analogous to that
diversity which, at about the same period, distinguished
those most attractive of all works of art—the terra-cotta
statuettes from Tanagra. Like the characters in comedy,
the pretty figurines of these clay-modellers are not engaged

---

[1] O dimidiate Menander ! (Caesar).

in very diverse occupations, nor do their poses differ very
much from one another. But who would dare to say
that they are all alike, or who would be bored by looking
at them? Even when the pose remains the same, some
detail in the figure or in the costume—a more slender or
more supple waist, a loftier brow or one that is bent in
meditation, a firmer or more languishing bearing, a more
nervous or spiritless gesture, a flowing cloak, or one that
clings to the body—suffices to ensure endless variations.
A faithful portrayal of the countless peculiarities in which
human souls differ when brought face to face with the
identical occurrences must have done as much for the
characters of the νέα.

Of course, one must have a keen mind, a delicate sensibility, in order to discover this kind of diversity. But
these qualities were certainly not lacking in the Athens of
Hypereides and Epicurus, nor, as I believe, in many other
parts of the Hellenic world of that period. It is clear
that what I have said in various parts of this book about
ἀσύνετοι ἀκροαταί, the vulgar and unintelligent crowd with
which our poets had to reckon, because they filled the
seats in the theatre, does not apply to the entire audience.
As I neither failed to recognise nor tried to disguise the
fact that not every Athenian was Attic, I shall certainly
not be suspected of entertaining too much admiration for
ancient Greece when I say that, of the audiences that
went to the plays of a Philemon, a Menander or an
Apollodorus, a goodly number were worthy of these
authors. At the close of the classical period the refinement
and subtilty—in the best sense of the word—that were
at all times innate in almost every Greek had, by more
than a century and a half of remarkable intellectual
training, grown to a very high degree of perfection.
Great-grandsons of Socrates' companions, or of the sophists
and the admirers of Euripides, grandsons of the disciples
of Plato and of the readers of Isocrates, sons of those who
had heard, or who themselves had heard, powerful orators
and gifted speech-writers and philosophers, expert in

psychological and ethical analyses, the cultivated Athenians during the last third of the fourth century and the greater part of the third must have constituted a picked audience which did not allow an iota of the most subtle variants or of the most unobtrusive innovations to escape their attention. With such an audience the *νέα* could well have a fairly long career before it exhausted itself.

CONCLUSION

SUCH was New Comedy. Now that I am about to bid it farewell it seems useless to repeat, in a general conclusion, what has already been said in the special conclusions of the various chapters. I shall rather indicate, in a few words, the place New Comedy held in the whole history and evolution of Greek letters.

A short time ago Maurice Croiset wrote an essay entitled *Menander, the Last of the Attic Writers*,[1] and what Croiset says of Menander can be said of that style of composition in which Menander excelled; the νέα was the last form of literature that can be called Attic.

By this I mean, in the first place, that it was the last that had its centre at Athens. Beginning with the third century, poems of another kind—elegies, epigrams, idylls, didactic poems—flourished in the Peloponnesus and on the shores of Asia, in the islands and in Egypt, as well as elsewhere. For those who cultivated these classes of poetry Athens was no longer a fatherland nor a place of meeting; for those of our own day who write their history the name of the city of Euripides, of Plato and of Demosthenes makes room for that of Alexandria, Cos, Pydna, Antioch and Pergamum. But New Comedy had for its most illustrious representative an Athenian of the Athenians, whose entire life was passed in sight of the Acropolis and the shores of Salamis, who, when invited to seek gain and glory at the court of King Ptolemy, refused; whose devotion to Attic soil Alciphron [1]— doubtlessly according to a reliable tradition—has pictured in graceful and forceful words. Many of his rivals and successors were foreigners, natives of the most diverse parts of the Hellenic world. Philemon was born at Syracuse or at Soloi, Diphilus at Sinope, Lynceus at Samos, one Apollodorus at Carystus and another at Gela,

[1] *Ménandre le dernier des Attiques. Revue des Deux Mondes*, April 15, 1909.
[2] Alc., IV. 18.

518

Phoenicides at Megara, Poseidippus at Cassandria; and so on. But almost all of them spent a considerable part of their life at Athens, and although all their works were not written for Attic theatres, the best of them were destined for that stage. To secure the votes of the people of Cecrops, to be included in the ἀναγραφαί of the poets who won prizes at the Lenaea or the Dionysia ἐν ἄστει, was, in their eyes, a consecration which very few of them failed to seek. When Athenaeus says of Macho of Sicyon (or of Corinth), a contemporary of Apollodorus of Carystus, Οὐκ ἐδίδαξε δ' Ἀθήνησι τὰς κωμῳδίας τὰς ἑαυτοῦ, ἀλλ' ἐν Ἀλεξανδρείᾳ, he evidently intends to call attention to something exceptional.[1]

By remaining true to the Athenian public and to the stage that had been glorified by Aeschylus, Sophocles and Euripides, by Cratinus, Eupolis and Aristophanes, by Plato the comic writer, by Antiphanes and Eubulus, the poets of the new period no doubt enjoyed the advantage of having to deal with a public that was more cultivated and more capable of enjoying their works, but they lost the opportunity of finding richer material for their plays. The Athens in which they lived had sunk to the rank of a small town. I am far from believing that its inhabitants, regarded as men, were not the equals of their ancestors, but they no longer had great questions to discuss or great interests to defend. Though they were affected by the turmoil of the age, their country was no longer an important factor in the world's history; it was no longer the heart or the brain of Hellenism. The life that people led at Athens when they were not blockaded and starved by hostile armies or oppressed by a tyrant must have been somewhat drowsy, monotonous and narrow. This accounts for that poverty of ideas in the works of the νέα which could not be disguised by skilful treatment. The comic writers of this period were excellent painters, but they had mediocre models. This fact does not detract from their merit, but it detracts from the interest of their

[1] Ath., p. 664 A.

works. We cannot but regret that the greatest of them were not able to behold the ever fresh, infinitely diverse and vivid spectacle of the great Hellenistic centres, instead of living and writing in the midst of a super-annuated society and of having their vision limited by a narrow horizon to traditional characters and petty occur-rences which afforded no variety. When we read in Quintilian that Menander gave "a complete picture of life," [1] and that, in watching the poet's plays, or, more generally speaking, the plays of the *véa*, we can resuscitate the memory of the time in which they appeared, we must recognise that Quintilian's words require some correction and reservation. A "complete picture," perhaps, of "life" as far as character is concerned; but of the life of society what a small, insignificant part! And how strange it is that the comedy of a period like that of the Diadochi and of the first Epigoni, full of effervescence, of innovations and upheavals, of a period that looked so exclusively towards the future, should have subsisted on worn-out incidents and elements that had been inherited from the past!

Not only is New Comedy the last great form of literary production, in point of time, that flourished at Athens, but it is the culmination of much progress of which Attica had been the scene and Attic writers the chief promoters, and in it are concentrated for a supreme outburst of glory some of the most precious qualities of Athenian genius. On this point I need not waste many words, as I need only confirm observations previously made. The clever-ness and subtlety of observation that make the works of the *véa* attractive had manifested themselves much earlier, in older comedy and in the tragedies of Euripides, in some Socratic writings and in the orations of the speech-writers. Whenever I re-read the soliloquy of Demeas in the *Σαμία* I involuntarily think of the account of the murder of Eratosthenes in Lysias' oration, and certainly it is not merely the similarity—which, as a matter of

[1] Quint., X. 1, 70.

fact, is far from complete—between the misfortunes of the comic character and those of Lysias' client which calls forth this reminiscence. Works like the orations *On the murder of Eratosthenes, Against Simo, For the Invalid, On the inheritance of Philoctemon, Against Neaera, Against Eubulides, Against Evergos and Mnesibulos, Against Conon, Against Callicles, Against Athenogenes, For Lycophron*—I quote almost at random—contain many qualities that reveal the same quickness of vision, the same sense of picturesque and vivid detail, the same " skill in playing new parts," that we admire in our poets, and which, in spite of the difference in their style of writing, create a kinship between men like Lysias, Hypereides, Apollodorus, and even Demosthenes, on the one hand, and Philemon and Menander on the other. The art of dialogue which was brought to so high a degree of perfection by certain drama-tists of the new period had developed in the drama and in philosophical literature since the fifth century. Tragedy alone had supplied abundant examples of the portrayal of love. Tragedy had also served as a guide in the con-struction of plays, and especially in the art of leading up to the plot, while the older comedy taught its younger sister convenient and amusing devices. In a word, not-withstanding the disappearance of so many works of the fifth and fourth centuries, and notwithstanding the loss of the μέση, we are in a position to determine with cer-tainty the antecedents for almost everything that charac-terises New Comedy in point of ideas, as well as of form; and it appears to us to be the universal heir, as it were, of all that went before.

This, however, does not mean that, in the history of literature, New Comedy is interesting merely as a re-capitulation and a last phase. Granted that it received much and from all possible sources, it also gave much, and many later works, besides those to which I have resorted in reconstructing it, owe something to it—some portion of their substance, some turn of thought, some

settings, some forms of expression. The literary posterity
of the *véa* is long and very ramified. But it is not within
the scope of my plan to give an account, however
succinct, of them, and it must, therefore, suffice, in conclusion, to point out its descendants, so to speak, in the
first degree.

In the Hellenistic period mimes of various kinds
flourished or had their revival. But was the grand
dramatic mime known as early as this—that mingling of
prose and verse, of declamation and song, accompanied
by dancing and music, which was later on to be the
delight of Rome and Byzantium for many hundred years?
Notwithstanding the researches of Reich,[1] this is an open
question. The only remnants of a composition of this
order, some fragments found at Oxyrhynchus,[2] are of
uncertain date; perhaps they are not older than the
papyrus itself which has preserved them, which dates
from the second century after Christ. On the other
hand, passages from Aristocles and Aristoxenus of
Tarentum, handed down by Athenaeus,[3] conclusively
prove the existence among the Alexandrians of chanted
mimes, of which the " Grenfell fragment," [4] a papyrus
from Tebtunis,[5] a potsherd from Thebes [6] and possibly
also the Λοκρικὸν ᾆσμα, classified by Bergk as a popular
song,[7] still give us some idea. The urban idylls of
Theocritus, the mimiambs of Herondas (a theme from one
of them reappears in the Oxyrhynchus Μοιχευτρία),[8] are
typical, from the beginning of the third century onwards,
of another variety of mimes which were meant to be read
or recited. And finally, a terra-cotta lamp, found at

---

[1] Reich, *Der Mimus*, I. (Berlin, 1903, Chap. VI. § 6, p. 475–562).

[2] Oxyrh., Chap. VIII. p. 41 et seq. *Herondae Mimiambi,* fourth edition,
by Crusius (1905), p. 102 et seq.

[3] Ath., p. 620 D et seq., 621 B et seq.

[4] Grenfell, *An Alexandrian Erotic Fragment* (Oxford, 1896), *Herondae
Mim.*[4], p. 117 et seq.

[5] *Tebtunis papyri*, Vol. I. p. 8 et seq. *Herondae Mim.*[4], p. 124–125.

[6] *Melanges Perrot* (1902), p. 291. *Herondae Mim.*[4], p. 126–127.

[7] Ath., p. 697 B. See Crusius' note, *Herondae Mim.*[4], p. 120.

[8] *Oxyrh. pap.*, Vol. III. p. 47 et seq. *Herondae Mim.*[4], p. 111 et seq.

Athens, but probably made in Egypt, represents three persons without masks (whom a description designates as μιμολόγοι), engaged in an animated conversation.[1] This proves that very shortly after the best period of the νέα, if not during that period, short plays with several actors, which were perhaps to a large extent improvisations, were regularly played outside the theatre, and that they enjoyed popular favour. Naturally, the question arises what these various mimes—all of which are more or less closely related to the dramatic style—may have owed to New Comedy.

There certainly was a kinship between them. Aristoxenus of Tarentum said of one class of chanted mimes, which were performed by λυσιῳδοί or μαγῳδοί, that they were παρὰ τὴν κωμῳδίαν. Among the characters portrayed by these μαγῳδοί, Athenaeus, probably quoting Aristocles, mentions procuresses, gay lovers who visit their mistresses—two types that were not ignored in comedy—and he adds that the μαγῳδοί frequently chose comic subjects (κωμικὰς ὑποθέσεις λαβόντες) and performed them after their own fashion (ὑπεκρίθησαν κατὰ τὴν ἰδίαν ἀγωγὴν καὶ διάθεσιν). The title of the dramatic performance, a scene of which is represented on a terra-cotta lamp (the title appears near the actors), belongs to the comic repertoire : Ἑκυρά. More than one incident in Herondas reminds us of comedy. In the first mimiamb the situation of the young wife whose husband has been abroad for a long time resembles the situation of the two sisters in the *Stichus*; her virtue is assaulted by a faithless counsellor, just as the virtue of Philematium was by Scapha in the *Mostellaria*. In the second mimiamb the pander Baltarus had the same mishaps as Sannio in the *Adelphi*. By bringing the man who had insulted him to justice, he carries out a threat of Sannio's, and when he cynically admits his own infamy, and recalls with satisfaction that of his father and grandfather, he likewise resembles Sannio, or the stage parasites

[1] *Ath. Mitth.*, 1901, p. 1 et seq. and Plato, I.; cf. *Philologus*, 1903, p. 35 et seq.

whose degradation has been handed down from father to son.

Of course, I cannot pretend to point out in a few words all the analogies that can be found between the mime and New Comedy. But how many differences and contrasts exist, side by side with these analogies! Many of the subjects which were, as far as we know, dealt with in these " mimes " are entirely foreign to high comedy.[1] For example, the school scene in the third mimiamb, the outburst of fierce jealousy on the part of Bitinna in Herondas and that of the Oxyrhynchus μοιχευτρία, the obscene conversation in the sixth mimiamb, and the tales about adultery committed by women which, according to Aristocles, formed the chief subject of the poems recited by the λυσιῳδοί. Even the scene of the temptation in the first mimiamb, in which we have just recognised elements that are familiar to the νέα, when taken in its entirety, is not an episode of comedy, for in comedy the folk like Gyllis do not direct their attacks against respectable married women. Nor is the *paraklausithyron* of the " Grenfell fragment " like a scene in comedy, for on the stage it is not the woman who sighs at the door of the man she loves, but the man who tries to move the hard-hearted beauty. If other subjects which occur in the mimes are also found in the comic poets, they are not, at any rate, a part of the special répertoire of the new period, but belong rather to that of earlier comedy. To this order belong the scenes taken from the life of craftsmen, like that which is the subject of the seventh mimiamb, or like those which are apparently indicated by the titles Συνεργαζόμενοι and Ἰσχαδοπώλης, or the visit to the temple of Asclepius in the fourth mimiamb, and—though Menander himself wrote a Συναριστῶσαι—the banquet by which the Ἀπονηστίζουσαι broke their liturgical fast.

---

[1] Incidentally I may observe that in the mimiambs of Herondas the scene is almost always indoors—the interior of a shop, of a school, of a law-court, a temple or a private house. As we know, nothing is more foreign to comedy.

Even in instances where there is a real or an apparent coincidence between the νέα and the mime it does not necessarily follow that the latter was inspired by the former. The mime did not originate in the third century; it is as old as—nay, older than comedy, and at a very early period it favoured certain types that were also used by the comic writers. If the μιμολόγοι of the third century performed a play called ʽΕκυρά, it does not by any means follow that their poet got his inspiration from a play by Apollodorus which had the same title, or from some play of the νέα in which a mother-in-law appeared. The ʽΕκυρά of the μιμολόγοι may well have originated in the domain of the mime without being under any obligation to comedy, and the same may be said of Herondas' Μαστροπός and Πορνοβοσκός. Moreover, in addition to the choice of subjects, the tone of the mime distinguishes it in an unmistakable manner from New Comedy. In the mimes it is, as a rule, more coarsely realistic and vulgar. In order to provoke laughter the jester in the " Oxyrhynchus mime " uses and misuses a broad joke of which there can hardly be any question in the plays of the fifth century: πορδή. In Herondas the *dramatis personae* are anything but prudes; they call everything they speak of by its true name, and they speak of everything; the archaic dialect of their speech does not disguise its popular tone. In the fragments of the chanted mimes the style is less homogeneous, and occasionally it admits of pompousness and of a certain pretence of poetry. Elsewhere the words are no less bold than the thoughts. Hence, as a whole, there is something sensual and dissolute in the mimes that must have accorded well with the female attire of the λυσιῳδοί and their indecent gestures, and we might search in vain for anything like it in the extant works of our comic writers.

In short, the development of the mimes on Greek soil during the last centuries before the Christian era appears to have been coincident with, rather than subordinate to, that of comedy. If, after the time in which the νέα

flourished, this style of play attracted more talented men
and created more stir, it is not, as I believe, because they
found models and encouragement in the works of authors
like Philemon, Menander or Apollodorus. This recrudes-
cence of activity—which, by the way, is perhaps more
apparent than real—is sufficiently explained by the growing taste for realism and by the relaxation of the literary
tyranny of Athens, owing to which styles of writing that
had hitherto been spurned and despised by Athenian
pride ventured to claim attention. Far from giving
encouragement to the mimes, New Comedy injured it by
keeping it in the background; subsequently the mime
was to have a signal revenge, and from the beginning of
our era to supplant comedy for centuries.

Let us pursue our inquiry in another direction.

Among the epigrams of the third and second centuries
which have been preserved, more than one reminds us
strongly of a situation, a character or a sentimental
incident met with in the comic writers. " Take a dozen
shrimps—but you must select them—and five wreaths,
wreaths of roses. What's that? You say you have no
money? We have been robbed ! Will no one go and
beat that Lapith? He is a pirate, and not a servant.
Aren't you robbing us? Eh? Bring your account.
Phryne, come here with the counters. Oh, the sly fox !
Wine, five drachmae; sausage, two drachmae; eggs, hare,
mackerel, oil-cakes, honey-cakes. . . . To-morrow we'll
reckon it all up. Now go to Aischra the perfumer . . ."
(*Anth. Pal.*, V. 181). " Go to market, Demetrius, ask
Amyntas for three blue fish, ten small seaweed fish and
crook-backed shrimps—he is to count them himself—two
dozen. Get these things and come back. Also fetch six
wreaths of roses at Thauborius'. Make haste, and, as you
pass, just tell Tryphera to come " (*Anth. Pal.*, V. 185).
These two epigrams by Asclepiades might have been
uttered by Philolaches when he sends Tranio to market,
or by Lesbonicus when he makes up accounts with
Stasimus. " One day I was dallying with the enchanting

Hermione; she wore a belt embroidered with flowers, and, O Goddess of Paphos! on it one read these words in letters of gold : Love me always and do not grieve if I give myself to another " (*Anth. Pal.*, V. 158). " Do not imagine, Philaenis, that you deceive me with your eloquent tears. Yes, I know you love no one more dearly than me, as long as you lie by my side. But if some one else embraced you, you would say that you loved him more dearly than you do me " (*Anth. Pal.*, V. 186). The first of these passages is by Asclepiades, the second by Poseidippus. Philaenis and Hermione are of the same school as Menander's Phronesium or Thais. " Euphro, Thais, Boïdion, old hags who would be worthy daughters of Diomedes, forty-oared galleys for the use of privateer captains, have thrown over Agis, Cleophon and Antagoras respectively, stark naked, and poorer than if they had been shipwrecked. Wherefore flee with your ships from the pirates of Aphrodite! They are worse than the Sirens " (*Anth. Pal.*, V. 161). This epigram is attributed to Asclepiades or to Hedylus. It transports us to a world with which we are well acquainted—the world of the mariners, with their coarse pleasures, and of the low women who "pluck" them. The likening of the ruined ναύκληρος to a shipwrecked man who is cast naked upon the shore recalls the passage containing the lamentations of Diabolus; [1] the likening of the rapacious courtesan to a pirate recalls an expression of Messenio's; [2] the comparison with the Sirens is identical with those which occur in Anaxilas [3] and in several of Alciphron's epistles, [4] and like those which Plautus, in various passages, implies rather than freely expresses. [5] " If Pythias has company, I'm off; but if she is sleeping alone, by Zeus! Nico, let me in. And say to her, so that she may know who I am : He came drunk, through the midst of the robbers (?), with saucy Eros as his guide." [6] Such are the words

---

[1] *Asin.*, 134–135.
[2] *Menaech.*, 344.
[3] Anaxilas, fr. 22.
[4] *Alc.*, I. 6, 2; 21, 3.
[5] *Bacch.*, 471; *Truc.*, 350, 568; etc.
[6] *Anth. Pal.*, V. 213.

of Poseidippus (or possibly of Asclepiades). Diniarchus
might have said as much to Astaphium. Now let us
listen to Callimachus : " Conopion, may you sleep as you
make me pass the night here on the icy threshold of your
house; may you sleep as you make your lover rest. And
you felt no pity, not even in your dreams ! The neighbours take pity, but you, not even in your dreams ! But
ere long your white hair will make you remember all
this." [1] The lover forced to remain at the door is, as we
know, a figure belonging to the comic répertoire. The
last thrust recalls Epicrates' spiteful words to Lais, who
has grown old,[2] or the pessimistic predictions of Scapha.[3]
" Callignotus has sworn to Ionis that no man or woman
friend would ever be dearer to him than she is. He has
sworn, but there is good reason for saying that a lover's
oaths do not enter the ears of the Immortals. Now he
glows with a fire lighted by a man, and as for the poor
woman, there is as little talk or concern about her as
about the Megarians" (*Anth. Pal.*, V. 6). The misfortune
that befell Ionis is the same that Selenium dreaded, and
Callignotus' oath is on a par with that of Alcesimarchus.[4]
The poet's remark about the treachery of love is like that
of the aged courtesan : *Nil amori injurium'st*.[5] " Zeus, my
friend, say nothing" (Asclepiades exclaims, after having
told of one of his amorous exploits); "thou, too, hast
known love " (*Anth. Pal.*, V. 767). And elsewhere : " I
am impelled by the god who is thine own master, O Zeus,
by the god whom thou didst obey when thou didst penetrate a brazen chamber " (*Anth. Pal.*, V. 64). The omnipotence of Eros is often proclaimed in comedy, and comic
heroes are quick to excuse their failings by invoking the
example set by the gods. Now let us turn to Meleager.
" Timarion, your kiss is birdlime, your glance is fire. If
you look at me you burn; if you touch me, I am caught "
(*Anth. Pal.*, V. 96). *Viscus merus vostra'st blanditia,*

---

[1] *Anth. Pal.*, V. 23.   [2] Epicrates, fr. 3.
[3] *Most.*, 201–202.   [4] *Cist.*, 99–103.
[5] *Ibid.*, 103. Cf. Men., fr. 449.

says Pistoclerus to Bacchis;[1] and Cleareta compares the profession of a courtesan to the occupation of a fowler.[2] " My soul counsels me to flee the love of Heliodora, knowing by experience what tears and torments it costs. Thus speaks my soul; but I have not the courage to fly, for my imprudent soul itself that counsels me, while counselling, loves Heliodora " (*Anth. Pal.*, V. 24). Here we have the state of mind of Diniarchus,[3] or rather that of Phaedria,[4] expressed in subtle terms. " Tell her this, Dorcas; listen, repeat it all to her two or three times, Dorcas. Run; do not tarry, fly. One moment, I beg you, one moment, Dorcas; wait a bit. Dorcas, whither are you running before you know it all? To what I told you long ago add this. . . . But why should I rave any more? Say nothing at all . . . unless . . . Say everything, do not spare yourself about saying everything. Really, Dorcas, what is the use of sending you? See, I will go with you myself—and ahead of you " (*Anth. Pal.*, V. 182). This pretty passage recalls a passage in the Περικειρομένη, in which Polemo sends Doris to Glycera, and follows her to the door and overwhelms her with advice.

These comparisons, to which I could easily add many more, are interesting in themselves, but the main point is that they lead to another more important and more far-reaching comparison. In the course of this book I have, on several occasions, though only incidentally, called attention to the striking resemblance between comedy and Latin elegy. A careful comparison of these two kinds of poetry warrants the assertion that they have many points of contact, and a great number of common elements. In the elegiac poets, as in the comic writers, the god of love is regarded as the most powerful of the gods, and as lord of the universe; they speculate as to why sculptors and painters should have given him a pair of wings; recommend a life of pleasure

---

[1] *Bacch.*, 50.   [2] *Asin.*, 215.
[3] *Truc.*, 766 et seq.   [4] *Eun.*, 70 et seq.

M M

in view of the dreariness of old age and the approach
of death; pity and rebuke old men who meddle with
love; they declare, now, that beauty needs no elegance
of dress in order to please, and again, that careful
attire increases beauty, or makes up for the lack of
it. In both kinds of poetry we find the same types
of character and the same kind of people: the lover
deeply, and sometimes charmingly, in love, who sees a
richer rival given preference; the woman who is greedy
for money and for presents, quick to ask and quick to
refuse, wheedling and mendacious; the serving-maid who
is the accomplice of her mistress's deceit; the duenna who
corrupts young girls and suppresses their inclination
towards unselfishness, honesty and fidelity, and teaches
them how to make their fortunes. We have the same
cult of amorous exploits: passion suddenly awakens and
promptly invades the heart of the lover; at sight of his
beloved he becomes rigid, mute and stupid; he declares
that the pangs of love are the most cruel in the world, and
describes them with the help of metaphors consecrated
by custom, and compares them to the worst tortures in
mythology; they cannot be hidden, and make him who
endures them look pale and thin; nothing can make him
forget them; they grant him no repose, and force the
lover constantly to besiege the door of his fair one, drive
him to violence, to house-breaking, to nocturnal excesses
which the Roman police would, I believe, have regarded
with an unfriendly eye. I am not attempting to do more
than give a few general and superficial hints; for a more
precise statement and for further details I refer the reader
to the commentaries on the Latin elegiac poets—particularly on Propertius and Ovid—to Leo's *Plautinische
Forschungen* and to Hölzer's dissertation *De poesi amatoria
a comicis atticis exculta, ab elegiacis imitatione expressa*
(Marburg, 1899).

How can we explain so many similarities between the
comic writers and the elegiac poets? Doubtless Propertius
and Ovid may have imitated Menander directly, for his

name occurs several times in their works, as does that of
one of his heroines—the celebrated Thais. But the fact
that these similarities also occur in Greek authors of a late
period, who cannot have imitated either the comic writers
or the Roman elegiacs—in authors like Musaeus and
Nonnus, the writers of epistles, Philostratus and Aristaenetus, and in the writers of romances—makes another
explanation more plausible. The common source of all
these writers and of the poets of the Augustan age was
probably, in the majority of cases, a style of composition
which had itself been derived from New Comedy: Hellenistic love poetry. What was this poetry? This question
has given rise to much controversy. According to one
view, the only love-poems known to the Alexandrians in
which the poet spoke in his own name and described his
own feelings, were the epigrams, and the great elegies of
Philetas and Callimachus always retained a narrative
character. According to another view, the third century
already witnessed the production of lengthy subjective
compositions which were in every way analogous to the
works of Propertius, Tibullus and Ovid.[1] We need not
take sides in this discussion. Epigram or elegy, it matters
little. Besides, the difference between the two is not
always clear, and certain poems, considered by themselves, may just as correctly be called short elegies as long
epigrams. The main thing for us is the recognition of
the fact that, beginning with the third century, a whole
series of themes found in the νέα spread beyond the
stage and furnished regular material to a new order of
poetry. Moreover, though they do not entirely agree, all
modern investigations into the sources of Roman elegiac
poetry, as well as those into the sources of the erotic
letters or tales of the later period, agree in warranting

---

[1] See the contemporaneous and conflicting works of Jacoby (*Zur
Entstehung der römischen Elegie*, in the *Rheinisches Museum*, 1905, p. 38
et seq.), and of Gollnisch (*Quaestiones elegiacae*, Diss. Breslau, 1905), which
refer to the works of their predecessors. For a full discussion of this
question consult Auguste Couat, *La poésie alexandrine sous les trois
premiers Ptolémées*, passim.(—Tr.).

this conclusion. Hence the relation existing between New Comedy and that poetry which so soon afterwards shone forth in the brightest light—erotic poetry—is not one of mere succession, but of true kinship. The latter descended from the former, and it was from the former that it received the lighted torch.

INDEX

Action. *See* Plot.

Actors, Rule of Three, **289-297**; rarely applicable to Plautus and Terence, **290**; nor to Menander, **290**; examples of more than three speakers at once, **293**; meaning and purpose of rule, **295**; the law does not aid in determining the origin of scenes in question, **297**.

Actors, their movements, **361-367**.

Acts, Law of Five, **289**; ancient testimony, **371-373**; origin of rule, **383-385**; usually observed, **383**; antiquity of the division, **371-372**; acts divided by chorus, **373**; original fragments give no decisive evidence, **373**; division of the several plays into acts, **374-383**.

Adventures, character of, in N. C., **184-205**. Of war, politics, civic life, **184-185**; business life, **185-187**; legal affairs, **185-187**; travel, **185**; pleasure, **187-188**. Love affairs, **188-197**: inception, **189-190**; obstacles, **190-197**; competition between rivals, **192**; quarrels, **192-193**; ways of raising money, **193-194**; cheating of the pander, **195**; father's opposition, **195-197**. Accouchements, **197**. Exposure of infants, **198, 199, 210-211**; practised even by respectable families, **211**. Substitution of children, **199, 211**; as a protection against divorce, **211**. Kidnapping, **199, 207-208**. Παρακλαυσίθυρα, **191**. Abductions, **192**. Divorce, **198-199**. Recognitions, **200-201**; commonly of exposed children, **200**; resulting in marriage, **201**. Pirates, **207**. Rape and assault, **208-210**. Wearing of disguises, **195**. Other occurrences, **201-205**. Most are not inventions of N. C., **231-232**.

Aelian, *Epist. Rust.* 13-16, **166**.

Afranius, imitated Menander's Θαΐς, **29**.

Alciphron, relation to N. C., **3, 17-18, 51**; his value in determining the nature of Comedy, **50-51**. *Epist. Parasit.* relate to M. C. as well as to N. C., **18**; parasites, **74, 76-77**;

courtesans, **79-80, 88**, some are really in love, **91**; banquets, **187**. References to the *Epist.* : II 2. **70**; II 8. **59**; II 11. **60, 101**; II 13. **60**; II 17. **59**; II 26. **61**; II 28. **59**; II 37. **59**; II 38. **60, 101**. III 2. **75**; III 3. **74**; III 4. **74, 468**; III 5. **75**; III 7. **74, 76**; III 8. **76**; III 9. **74**; III 10. **78**; III 11. **78**; III 12. **74**; III 13. **74, 76**; III 14. **76, 86**; III 15. **54, 74**; III 17. **78**; III 24. **54**; III 25. **74**; III 26. **74, 123**; III 27. **74**; III 28. **76, 101**; III 32. **74**; III 33. **74, 123**; III 34. **59, 61, 63, 74**; III 35. **74**; III 37. **78**. IV 1. **18**; IV 2. **18**; IV 3. **18**; IV 4. **18**; IV 5. **18**; IV 9. **80**; IV 10. **18**; IV 11. **91**; IV 12. **88**; IV 13. **89**; IV 14. **89**; IV 15. **80**; IV 18. **18**; IV 19. **18, 163**.

Alexandria as a literary centre, **518-519**.

Alexis, belongs partly to N. C., **10**; relation to Lucian, **17**; treatment of parasites, **26**, of philosophers, **101**; frg. 2, **165**; Ἀπεγλαυκωμένος, probably the original of Naevius' *Glaucoma*, **16, 202**; Δημήτριος, probably the original of Turpilius' *Demetrius*, **16**; Δωρίδης, **29**; Εἰσοικιζόμενος, **201**; frg. 89, **417**; Καρχηδόνιος, possibly the original of Plautus' *Poenulus*, **14, 280-281**, its date, **14**, its division into acts, **381**; frg. 107, **338**; Μανδραγοριζομένη, **202**; frg. 148, **417**; frg. 156, **231**.

Amphis, belongs to M. C., **10**.

Amusements, **46**; life of pleasure, **187-188**; banquets, **187-188**; games and festivals, **188**.

Anaxilas, treatment of panders, **228**; Ἄγροικος, **253**.

Anaxandrides, frg. 41, **480**.

Anaxippus, treatment of parasites, **26**; Ἐγκαλυπτόμενος, **191**; Κεραυνός, **29**.

Angiportus, stage devices, **344**.

Antiphanes, two comic poets of this name, **10**; attacks on parasites, **26**; the cook one of his favourite char-

533

THE END

PRINTED IN GREAT BRITAIN BY
RICHARD CLAY & SONS, LIMITED,
BRUNSWICK ST., STAMFORD ST., S.E.,
AND BUNGAY SUFFOLK.